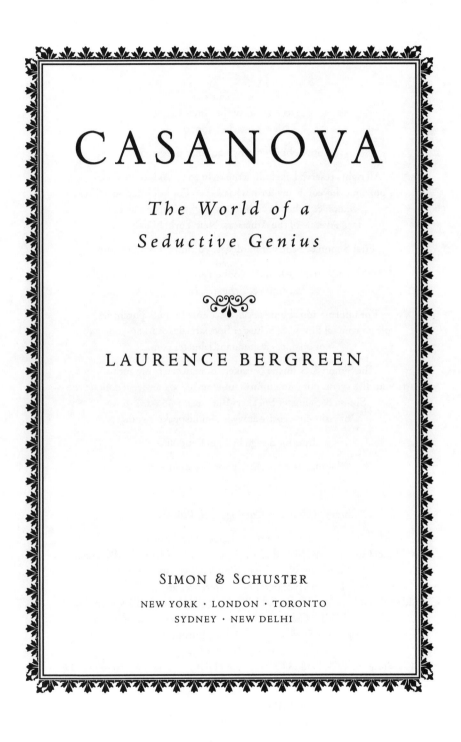

CASANOVA

*The World of a
Seductive Genius*

LAURENCE BERGREEN

SIMON & SCHUSTER

NEW YORK · LONDON · TORONTO
SYDNEY · NEW DELHI

Simon & Schuster
1230 Avenue of the Americas
New York, NY 10020

First Simon & Schuster hardcover edition November 2016

SIMON & SCHUSTER and colophon are registered trademarks of
Simon & Schuster, Inc.

For information about special discounts for bulk purchases,
please contact Simon & Schuster Special Sales at 1-866-506-1949
or business@simonandschuster.com.

The Simon & Schuster Speakers Bureau can bring authors
to your live event. For more information or to book an event contact the
Simon & Schuster Speakers Bureau at 1-866-248-3049
or visit our website at www.simonspeakers.com.

Interior design by Paul Dippolito

Manufactured in the United States of America

1   3   5   7   9   10   8   6   4   2

Library of Congress Cataloging-in-Publication Data
Names: Bergreen, Laurence, author.
Title: Casanova : the world of a seductive genius / Laurence Bergreen.
Description: New York : Simon & Schuster, [2016] |
Includes bibliographical references and index.
Identifiers: LCCN 2016019500| ISBN 9781476716497 | ISBN 1476716498
Subjects: LCSH: Casanova, Giacomo, 1725-1798. | Adventure and
adventurers—Europe—Biography. | Europe—History—18th
century–Biography.
Classification: LCC D285.8.C4 B47 2016 | DDC 940.2/53092 [B] —dc22 LC
record available at https://lccn.loc.gov/2016019500

ISBN 978-1-4767-1649-7
ISBN 978-1-4767-1652-7 (ebook)

To Zata, Jacqueline, and the memory of my mother

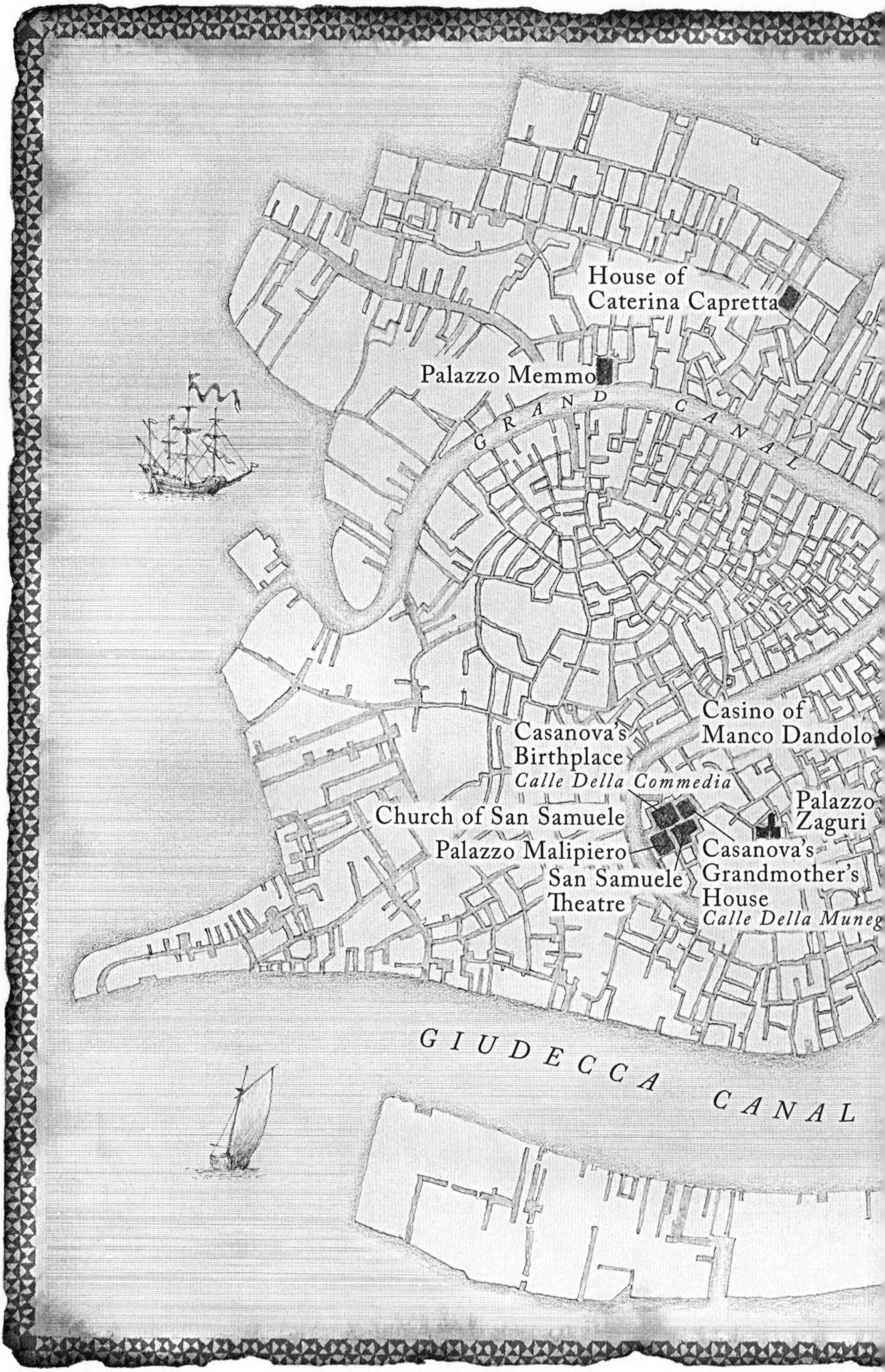

House of
Caterina Capretta

Palazzo Memmo

GRAND CANAL

Casanova's
Birthplace
Calle Della Commedia

Casino of
Manco Dandolo

Palazzo
Zaguri

Church of San Samuele

Palazzo Malipiero

San Samuele
Theatre

Casanova's
Grandmother's
House
Calle Della Muneg

GIUDECCA CANAL

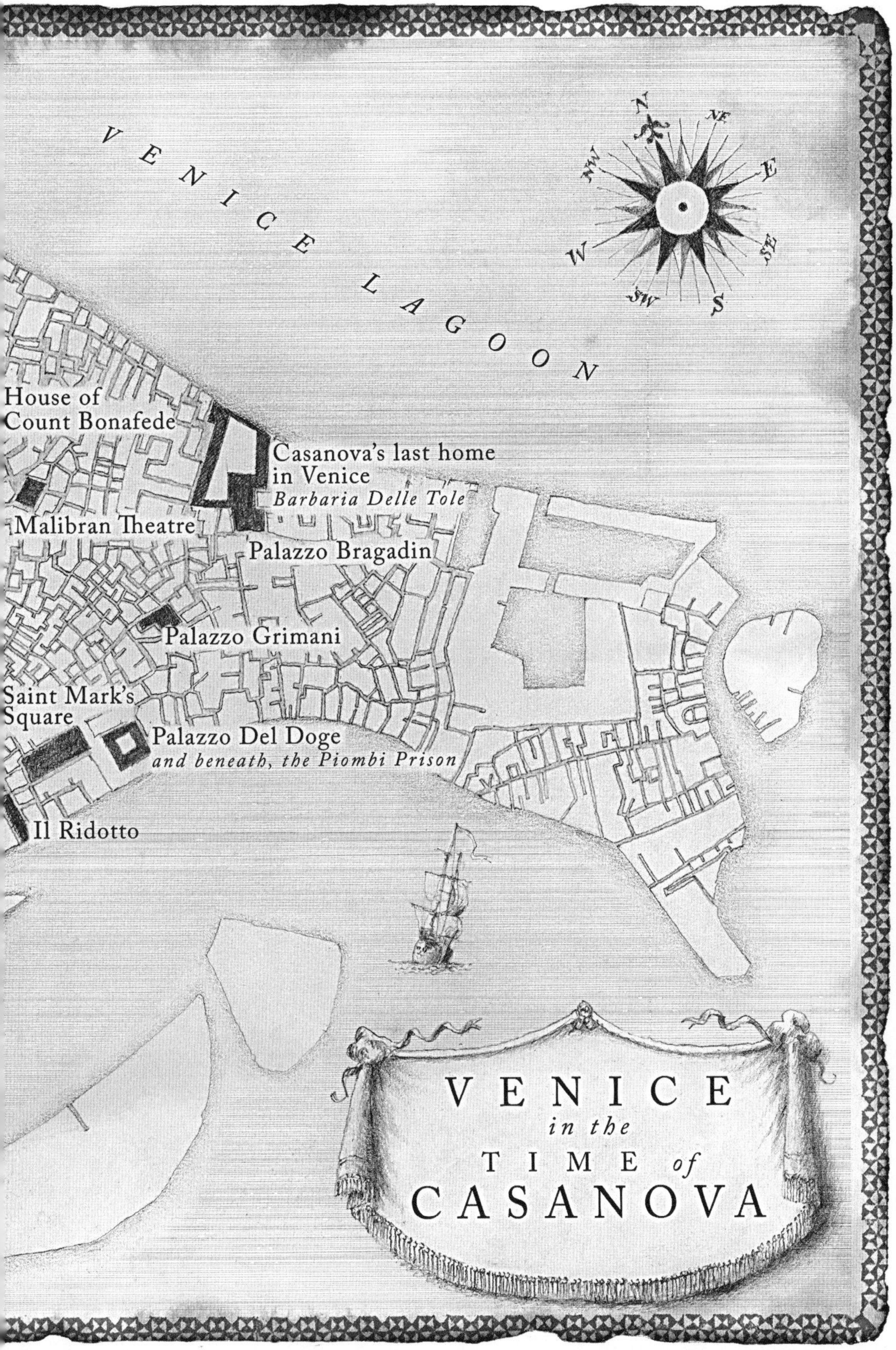

VENICE LAGOON

N
NW · NE
W · E
SW · SE
S

House of
Count Bonafede

Casanova's last home
in Venice
Barbaria Delle Tole

Malibran Theatre

Palazzo Bragadin

Palazzo Grimani

Saint Mark's
Square

Palazzo Del Doge
and beneath, the Piombi Prison

Il Ridotto

VENICE
in the
TIME *of*
CASANOVA

Love is three quarters curiosity.

—GIACOMO CASANOVA

CONTENTS

PREFACE

Nowadays, Giacomo Casanova signifies the archetypical Latin lover, and there's a bit of Casanova in nearly everyone. But to his eighteenth-century contemporaries, the name Casanova meant something else—the Venetian adventurer, spy, duelist, gambler, escape artist, and author of nearly one hundred novels, poems, and treatises. Jean-Jacques Rousseau, Voltaire, Catherine the Great of Russia, Benjamin Franklin, Mozart, and Lorenzo Da Ponte—the librettist for Mozart's *Don Giovanni* and a flamboyant figure in his own right—all were friends and correspondents. To them, Giacomo Casanova personified the spirit of liberation and, more than that, libertinism—unrestrained sexual pleasure. We think of Europe in the eighteenth century as the Age of Revolution or the Age of Enlightenment, but it was also the Age of Casanova, the Venetian arriviste who incarnated its passions and pleasures. And we think of Casanova as a great narcissist, yet he played many other roles in society as he sought to find a place to match his exalted yet fragile self-image. He was a genuinely outrageous figure who also happened to be a literary, psychological, and mathematical genius; a master of self-invention and self-promotion; a dedicated cardsharp, con artist, and escape artist who devised the French lottery (still in use today); and made himself into one of the first celebrities of the modern era.

Why are we still fascinated by this upstart more than two hundred years after his death? He was neither handsome, nor well-educated, nor well-born. He lacked position and power. Somehow, this impoverished son of an actress made himself into the most celebrated libertine of all time and a major literary figure of his era. His was a life lived in letters no less than in the boudoir. Casanova is legendary for personifying an archetype of the endlessly romantic, promiscuous, seductive male, yet his lesser known but equally remarkable accomplishments in mathematics and literature have received belated and only partial recognition. He broke hearts from Venice to Paris to Prague. Casanova exalted women even as he exploited them. He preferred to make love (the more romantic the better), not war, as he lived out his sexual and romantic fantasies. His desire knew no bounds; this was a man who claimed to seduce his own daughter and lured her into watching him make love to her mother. How did this reckless nobody wind up consorting with the most beautiful women and the greatest minds of his day? How did he come to write the consummate erotic memoir? How did this least-loved, cast-off child become the most celebrated lover in history?

The real-life Casanova (in a portrait by his brother Francesco) bore scant resemblance to the popular image of the fabled seducer. He was tall, at least six feet two inches, swarthy, angular, with a large forehead and prominent nose that caused him to resemble a giant goose. He generally wore a powdered wig in the fashion of the time, tight silk breeches, tricorn black hat, and a *tabarro*, or cloak, generally black, cascading over the shoulders, and decorated with frills. Most strikingly of all, true Venetians, and only Venetians, wore the *bauta*, or rigid white mask, at all times, or close to it. The nobility, men and women alike, wore masks in public and often in private. In theaters, ushers made sure that masks were in place, although

Giacomo Casanova in profile, c. 1750,
by his brother Francesco Giuseppe

patricians could remove them once the play had begun. Patricians meeting with ambassadors for official reasons had to wear the *bauta*, as did the envoys. The entire costume was the face that Venice presented to the world, and to itself.

Women of the Republic hid behind the eerie black *moretta*, a velvet mask held in place with a button in the front teeth, preventing the wearer from talking. (The named derived from the word *moro*, Venetian for the color black.) It was also known as the *servetta muta*, or "silent mask," and it was, if anything, even more stylized and sinister than the *bauta*. These costumes were not just for Carnival or for balls. With few exceptions, Venetians wore them year-round, and Venetian laws specified severe punishments for those who violated the code.

Men often found Casanova off-putting and pompous. "I thought him a blockhead," wrote the biographer James Boswell after they met. "He is a dandy, full of himself, blown up with vanity like a balloon and fussing about like a watermill," said the Venetian playwright Pietro Chiari, a bitter rival. But women responded to his charm, attentiveness, and agile cunning. Although he was reluctant to admit it, Casanova was not completely heterosexual; he was attracted to men disguised as women, and women disguised as men. Everything about him was ambiguous, both disconcerting and alluring.

He slept with one hundred and twenty-two women, by his count, and perhaps with a few men. In a society devoted to excess and indulgence, many Venetians boasted of more conquests, but unlike those other libertines, he recorded every last detail of his exploits in vivid, at times pornographic, detail. In this *Kama Sutra* of Venice, he revealed, with surprising accuracy and meticulousness, the exploits of a lifetime, relishing his peccadilloes, his conquests, reversals, and carnal indulgences. Seeking revenge for his lack of status at birth, he embarked on a lifelong quest to right this wrong by putting himself out to stud. He would use sex as a weapon of class destruction, siring eight children out of wedlock, each with a different woman whom he refused to marry. At times he behaved like a cad, at other times like a genius. He was the archetypal bad boyfriend: irresistible, dangerous, amoral. Casanova wasn't the only dedicated hedonist of his day nor the most brilliant literary figure, and certainly not the only rogue, but he was unique in playing all three roles to the hilt.

Although Casanova's place in the history of sensuality and the lore of love is secure, it comes as a surprise to many that he was a flesh-and-blood person, an outstanding figure of the Englightenment. His twelve-volume *Histoire de ma vie*, written in French, represents the most important source of information about his life and loves and a kaleidoscopic view of his times. Its three thousand seven hundred pages, in Casanova's beautiful, steady hand, repose at the Bibliothèque national de France in Paris. They are a recent addition. After a French commission declared the work a national treasure, the BnF paid nine million dollars to acquire the manuscript: the most expensive acquisition in the library's history. Casanova, nothing if not vain, would have been extremely proud of this confirmation of his central place in French letters and the intellectual life of his era.

If his epic of seduction, espionage, and social climbing had been published during his lifetime, it would have shocked his contemporaries and compromised the lives and reputations of the prominent Venetians and other important persons whose foibles and escapades make for such enjoyable reading. Sexual transgressions, even the seduction of his illegitimate daughter, who might have become pregnant with Casanova's child—his son and grandson—were revealed here in a world as regimented as it was amoral.

Casanova did publish extensively in his lifetime. He completed a multi-volume science-fiction novel; a history of Poland, also in several volumes; translated the *Iliad* into French; composed four hundred poems; devised a polemic refuting Voltaire; penned nearly two thousand letters on any idea that came into his head; and left another three thousand pages of unfinished literary projects, all the while pursuing ardent love affairs and elaborate intrigues. He was hyper-sexed and hyper-literary.

Superstition ruled Casanova's Venice. It was believed that magic and the devil caused people to lose their way in the city's labyrinthine streets or even to go mad. Venetians routinely acknowledged the existence of ghosts. To this day some Venetians swear that when they place their fingertips on the wall of a house, they can feel the presence of the departed and hear their voices.

The Republic straddled one hundred and eighteen small islands in a lagoon, or marsh, settled by desperate refugees from Rome, Padua, and other cities ransacked by invaders in the early centuries of Rome's Christian era.

Rebelling against prelates and generals, they established the first Doge—a title derived from *dux*, Latin for leader—in AD 726, and appropriated the trappings of empire. Venetian merchants spirited away relics of Mark the Evangelist, one of the Disciples, from Alexandria in 828 and brought them to Venice, where they remain today in St. Mark's Basilica, the city spiritual center.

Beyond the confines of the lagoon, the Englightenment—dedicated to social reform, the advancement of knowledge, and sexual freedom—circulated invigorating new ideas across Western Europe, but Venetians stubbornly rejected external influences. The educated, multilingual Casanova roundly criticized Voltaire and Rousseau, two of the Enlightenment's leading figures. Yet it might have been Casanova whom Voltaire had in mind when, in 1770, he proclaimed that the perfect is the enemy of the good. Casanova was as far from perfect as could be; his message is one of rejoicing in sexual exploration as the path to fulfillment and englightenment. Nevertheless, he kept his allegiance to the old, familiar, corrupt order; he preferred the thrill of escape to the responsibility of freedom. He believed devoutly in God, and pitied those who did not. But as a libertine, Freemason, epicurean, and devotee of the Kabbalah, he was always trying to burst the bounds of Venetian institutions to exalt the self—and one's sexuality. He believed in everything that came his way: religion, philosophy, magic, science, and especially love. He spiked the Age of Enlightenment with sex, and more sex. He exploited women shamelessly. At the same time, he gave himself to the women he possessed. "I don't conquer, I submit," he explained. He exalted women beyond reason. Each love affair was, for him, a meeting of the mind and spirit, a glimpse of eternity and ecstasy.

Book One

VENICE

Chapter 1

Zanetta

Of all the women in Giacomo Casanova's life, his flamboyant, elusive mother, Zanetta Farussi, came first. She was known to the public by her stage name, La Buranella, a tribute to her ancestral home in the Venetian lagoon's cheerful miniature island of Burano, dotted with houses daubed with fuchsia, teal, yellow, green, lime, olive, and other whimsical hues. From her, Casanova imbibed a beguiling blend of artifice, whimsy, and deception.

The daughter of a cobbler, Zanetta transformed herself into a fêted actress and courtesan, the heroine of a fairy tale for adults. She came into the world on August 27, 1707, the illegitimate daughter of Girolamo Farussi and the widowed Marzia Baldissara, and was baptized on September 4 at the ancient Church of San Giacomo dell'Orio, in the center of Venice. Within months, the little family settled in the Parish of San Simeone Grande, and on January 31, 1709, her father and mother married, and moved again, this time to the Calle delle Muneghe, a crowded, boisterous conduit in the Parish of San Samuele.

That winter was reportedly the coldest in five hundred years. The Venetian lagoon became a block of ice. Livestock perished, combs of chickens froze and fell off, burst in the frigid air, and travelers perished. Famine was ubiquitous. Venetians endured, as always. Much of the stage-struck Venetian populace found employment as hairdressers, ticket takers, singing and acting coaches, stagehands, and lighting specialists. Their ranks swelled with the stage-door Johnnies, hangers-on, and would-be performers. Playwrights yearning for attention read their scripts to indifferent listeners, and secret admirers of actresses maneuvered to peek at their idols. Carlo Goldoni, a Venetian student studying for the priesthood, tried his hand at adapting Greek and Roman comedies for the stage, and he transformed the

3

improvised knockabout comedy known as *commedia dell'arte*. Audiences felt thoroughly at home with the genre's stock figures—Pantalone, Pulcinella, Columbina—and their madcap routines. Everyone knew what Harlequin would say before the words were out of his mouth, so Goldoni gave characters new words. Actors came to rely on his dialogue and stage directions. To feed the hunger for novelty, he cobbled together his scripts in a matter of days. Copyrights and royalties were unknown. When Goldoni delivered *sixteen* full-length plays to his manager in one season, he collected no bonus for his efforts—"Not a penny over the year's salary, nothing at all." He did receive plenty of praise, but, he observed, "one needs more than glory to live on."

Amid the ferment, a young actor named Gaetano Casanova became enamored of an actress known as La Fragoletta—a diminutive of "strawberry." In reality, this voluptuous creature was Giovanna Benozzi. In about 1713, Gaetano abandoned his native Parma to join her in Venice, where she managed two theaters, San Luca and San Samuele, on behalf of the powerful Grimani dynasty. Much later, Giacomo claimed that he'd heard that Gaetano, his father, had begun his career as a dancer, and later turned to acting, "becoming even more highly regarded for his probity than for his talent"—a tactful way of saying that he lacked aptitude.

Something went awry with Gaetano's pursuit of La Fragoletta, and she fled to Paris with another theater troupe. Remaining behind in Venice, Gaetano became a fixture at the Theatre San Samuele, performing in farces and pantomimes and lodging at the Calle degli Orbi in a house owned by shoemakers who rented rooms to actors. In Giacomo's telling, the little household included Girolamo Farussi, his wife, Marzia, and their sixteen-year-old daughter, Zanetta.

Gaetano fell in love with Zanetta in 1723, and immediately met resistance. "Being an actor," Giacomo explained in his memoirs, "[Gaetano] could not hope to obtain her by gaining the consent of Marzia her mother, still less that of Girolamo her father," who "thought an actor an abomination." When Girolamo died the following year, Marzia salvaged the right to live out her life in the Calle delle Muneghe in a house owned by a charity, and the chief obstacle to the union of Zanetta and Gaetano was removed. On February 27, 1724, they wed in the Church of San Samuele.

In Casanova's heightened rendition, the lovers eloped, with Marzia "protesting loudly," and her father "dying of grief" shortly after the marriage, not before. In less operatic reality, the newlyweds moved in with Marzia, Gaetano's widowed mother-in-law, who welcomed their companionship and honorable arrangement. For a time, life was as normal as could be for a couple of struggling young actors in Venice. Gaetano kept his job at the theater and Zanetta occasionally took on small roles, despite her vow to renounce the theater after her marriage. The lively young soubrette caught the eye of the theater's owner, Michele Grimani, who belonged to one of the ruling families of Venice, a tightly knit caste of about four hundred families. This was an august personage indeed. Gossip about their carrying on never ceased, especially when Zanetta became pregnant—in all likelihood by Gaetano.

Casanova writes that he was "born of this marriage nine months later, on April 2, 1725," and was baptized three days later. So ran his official account of his origins. In his declining years, he revisited the subject of his paternity by writing and publishing a long satirical account, *Nè amore, nè donne*, claiming that Michele Grimani, not the beleaguered Gaetano Casanova, was his true father. So much of Casanova's identity and legacy as the gallant, seductive, learned seducer, is bound up in the enigma of his paternity. If his father was indeed the humble, good-natured actor from Parma, the flamboyant persona his son fashioned for himself was one of the most successful and sustained acts of self-invention of the era, a lifelong performance that outdid anything either of his parents could have imagined. But if his father was the aristocratic Grimani, his parents could never wed. Venetian nobility frequently had children out of wedlock even as the rules of their society barred marriage to outsiders. If Giacomo Casanova was actually Grimani's illegitimate son, he joined a large but unacknowledged class of children, and Zanetta's marriage served to cover her indiscretion. Either way, the child would always be an outcast, denied access to the rigid, privileged world of Venetian nobility. So long as he stayed in Venice, he would be reminded of his lack of status on a daily basis. Was he an illegitimate prince or a pauper? This identity crisis animated, teased, and tormented him throughout the years. He would spend his life trying to cajole and on occasion force his way into the circle from which he believed he'd been excluded.

Restless and ambitious, Zanetta brought herself to the attention of Goldoni, who modeled himself on the great French comic voice of the previous century, Molière. But this was Italy. "In France," a theater director once advised him, "you can try to please the public, but here in Italy it is the actors and actresses whom you must consult." That was as true in life as it was onstage; in Venice, personalities prevailed over customs, and among the most alluring whom Goldoni encountered was Zanetta. She struck him as "beautiful and very talented," and won a singing part in his musical interludes, charming audiences with her "taste, perfect ear, and execution."

While on tour in London, Zanetta gave birth to her second child, Francesco, in 1727. Giacomo was the child she left behind in Venice; Francesco the infant she kept at her side in London. He became her favorite, the one most likely to succeed in life. And what of Giacomo? He slipped into the role of the forgotten, inconvenient offspring. Yet this least-loved, cast-off child became the most famous lover in modern times, as well as a mathematical and literary genius. And Francesco? He became an esteemed artist in his day; his fame far surpassed that of his scapegrace older brother.

As he grew into adulthood, Giacomo became familiar with the outlines of his mother's theatrical career, and her attempt to forge her own identity; she bequeathed to her son the drive to create his own. Years later, he traveled to London and Dresden and Prague, the cities where she had lived and loved and performed, as if trying to capture her faded glory. Wherever he went, he sought his young mother's face, arms, lips, eyes, and scent in every lover he encountered. In his mind, they were all manifestations of Zanetta, so he seduced them into seducing him.

The story of how this disadvantaged ugly duckling metamorphosed into the sleek Venetian swan known as Casanova is remarkable. As a child he never spoke, and was considered something of an imbecile, destined for anonymity. Giacomo, who eventually wrote twelve volumes of memoirs recalling people and events of his life in exquisite and engaging detail, maintained he had no memories of the first eight years of his life.

———•———

In August 1733, everything changed as his "organ of memory developed." And behold: "I was standing in the corner of a room, leaning against the wall, holding my head, and staring at the blood that was streaming to the floor from my nose. My grandmother Marzia, whose pet I was, came to me, washed my face with cold water, and, unknown to anyone in the house, boarded a gondola and took me to Murano. This is a densely populated island about half an hour from Venice. Leaving the gondola, we enter a hovel, where we find an old woman sitting on a pallet, with a black cat in her arms and five or six others around her. She was a witch."

Marzia conversed with the witch in the Friulian dialect, incomprehensible to Giacomo, and gave her a silver ducat, whereupon "she opened a chest, took me up in her arms, put me into it, shut it, and locked the lid on me, telling me not to be afraid." As he lay in the darkness, holding a handkerchief to his bloody nose, he listened to "alternate laughter and weeping, cries, singing, and sundry thumps on the chest." The witch rescued him, and subjected him to "numberless caresses." She then wrapped him in a sheet, recited incantations, released him, and finally gave him food, then resumed caressing him with a soothing unguent, and dressed him as she cautioned that his bleeding would diminish so long as he told no one about this treatment. Otherwise, he would bleed to death. Ultimately, a "charming lady" would visit him, and his "happiness would depend upon her."

He went home with his grandmother, and at that point, "I saw, or thought I saw"—he added carefully—"a dazzlingly beautiful woman come down by the chimney . . . with a crown on her head with a profusion of stones that seemed to be sparkling with fire." She sat on his bed, and opened several small boxes. "After delivering a long discourse, of which I understood nothing, and kissing me, she left as she had entered."

At the time Giacomo never spoke to anyone of this mystical incident. He kept it sealed "in the most secret corner of my budding memory," to be opened years later, when he wrote his memoirs. It was his first and most powerful recollection, his origin myth, telling of the frail, suffering Giacomo brought back to health by a benign, ravishing woman. "The remedies for the worst diseases are not always found in pharmacy," he advised; they might be found in the furthest reaches of the cosmos, or the heart. Despite this manifestation of a feminine sensuality that both saved his life and revived his hibernating intellect, he remained more of a skeptic than a mystic. "There have never been wizards on this earth," he explained, only those "able to cajole [others] into believing them as such."

After the treatment Giacomo appeared as hopeless as before, "very poor company," in his words. "People felt sorry for me and left me alone; everyone supposed I would not live long. My mother and father never spoke to me." Nevertheless, he miraculously came to life. The bleeding subsided. His mind began to churn, and "in less than a month I learned to read."

With intellect came deception. Three months later, Giacomo remembered with a shudder, he and his younger brother Francesco were observing their father, having given up acting, at work in his optician's studio. "On the table I noticed a large round crystal cut in facets." How enchanting to hold it to his eyes and behold "everything multiplied." The next moment, "seeing that no one was watching me, I seized the opportunity to slip it into my pocket." As his father searched for the valuable object, Francesco truthfully claimed he knew nothing about it, and Giacomo falsely claimed the same thing.

Gaetano threatened to beat the culprit. Young Giacomo made a show of searching for the crystal before transferring it to the pocket of his unsuspecting brother. "I was instantly sorry," he admitted, "but the crime was already committed. My father, exasperated by our fruitless efforts, searches us, finds the crystal in my innocent brother's pocket, and inflicts the promised punishment." Giacomo couldn't hold his tongue: "Three or four years later I was stupid enough to boast to my brother that I had played this trick on him. He has never forgiven me and has taken every opportunity to avenge himself." Francesco would be the first of many men to take Giacomo to task.

Six weeks later, a far greater disaster occurred. In Giacomo's telling, "My father was attacked by an abscess inside his head at the level of the ear, which brought him to the grave in a week." The remedies applied by a physician only made matters worse.

Two days before he died, Gaetano summoned his family and closest friends; their ranks included Signor Grimani, the Venetian nobleman reported to be Zanetta's lover. Gaetano made them vow to protect his children, and as tears flowed, asked for more. "He made our mother, who dissolved in tears, swear that she would bring none of his children up for the stage, on which he would never have appeared if he had not been driven to it by an unfortunate passion. . . . She took the oath."

Zanetta, who needed the income from her stage career to feed her children, was six months pregnant. She never remarried—"beautiful and young as she was, she refused her hand to all who sued for it." As for Giacomo, "I was extremely weak, had no appetite, was unable to apply myself to anything, and looked like an idiot."

He was still losing copious amounts of blood, more, it seemed to his family, than his small body could produce. Doctors arrived, grim-faced; one advised him to breathe with an open mouth to keep his lungs full. A friend of his father, a poet and aristocrat by the name of Signor Baffo, determined that the boy should be sent to Padua for treatment "and to whom, in consequence, I owe my life."

A priest known to the family located a boardinghouse in Padua for the boy. "On April 2, 1734, the day on which I completed my ninth year, I was taken to Padua in a *burchiello*," which, he explained, "may be considered a small floating house. It has a saloon with a cabin at either end, and quarters for servants at the bow and stern." They served as floating parties, and inspired an outpouring of literary appreciation. Goldoni, Byron, Goethe, Montaigne, and eventually Casanova all wrote in praise of the vessels.

The journey over water lasted through the night. At dawn, his mother "opened a window that was across from the bed, so that the rays of the rising sun falling on my face made me open my eyes." And when he did, he glimpsed a parade of trees slowly moving past. "'Oh! My dear mother!' I cried, 'what does this mean? The trees are walking.'" As bystanders laughed at the poor child, she explained, "It is the boat that is moving, and not the trees. Get dressed."

Beginning to exercise his reason, he decided that it was possible "the sun does not move, and that it is we who turn from West to East." Zanetta, impatient, "cries out at such stupidity, Signor Grimani pities my lack of intelligence, and I am completely taken aback and on the verge of tears."

Venetian post barge, or *burchiello*, by Giandomenico Tiepolo

In contrast, Signor Baffo assures him, "You are right my child. The sun does not move, take courage, always reason logically, and let people laugh." Deeply suspicious of such radical advice, Zanetta asked the aristocrat if he was "out of his mind," to which he replied with a "theory adapted to my simple, unspoiled reason." The affirmation of the power of reason meant a great deal to the afflicted child: "This was the first real pleasure I enjoyed in my life."

At last they came to Padua, less than thirty miles from Venice. Padua maintained close ties to Venice but at the same time, it was a world away. Those who desired to escape the confines and perpetual penumbra of Venice sought the sun-splashed open spaces of Padua. Venice was a stronghold of commerce, combat, and mysticism; Padua a center of faith and learning. Its massive Basilica Pontificia di Sant'Antonio di Padova drew pilgrims from across Europe who came to worship at the burial site of Anthony of Padua, "il Santo," venerated as a teacher, and canonized just a year after his death in 1231, at the age of thirty-five.

Founded in 1222 as a school of law, the University of Padua had enjoyed a reputation as one of the most influential and largest institutions of its kind in Europe. Any Venetian seeking an education went there because Venice itself, for all its palaces, churches, theaters, and workshops, had no university. Over time, the university's school of law expanded, and a school of medicine opened. The anatomical theater attracted both physicians and artists to study dissections. The university's botanical garden claimed to be the oldest academic facility of its kind. Nicolaus Copernicus studied medicine at the university. Galileo Galilei held the chair of mathematics from 1592 until 1610.

The place hummed with students, their debates, intellectual ferment, and protests. Slowly, young Giacomo began to flourish. After his mother left, he stayed briefly at the home of a family friend named Ottaviani, "whose wife gave me many caresses." The five or six Ottaviani children promised to end his years of isolation.

Regrettably, his stay there was brief. He was soon assigned to the home of an "old Slavonian woman" who lived fifty paces away and viewed her young lodger as a convenient source of income. The pain of that moment still fresh in his mind seven decades later, he recalled his arrival at her boardinghouse: "My little trunk was opened in her presence and she was given an inventory of all that it contained." She demanded and received payment in advance for six months. "For just six zecchini she was to feed me, keep me clean and neat, and send me to school." She protested that the amount wasn't enough to care for him, but none of his relatives heeded her. "I was kissed, told always to obey her in everything, and left standing where I was. So they got rid of me."

———•———

The Slavonian landlady escorted him to his assigned bed in the attic, "the last in a row with four others, three of which belonged to boys of my own age, who were then at school, and the fourth to the maidservant, who was charged with making us say our prayers and keeping an eye on us to prevent us from indulging in the mischief and lewdness usual among schoolboys." Amid these stark new surroundings, the innocent boy felt numb, "neither happy nor unhappy; I said nothing; I experienced neither hope nor despair nor even curiosity." His landlady repelled him. "Her masculine features unnerved me every time I raised my eyes to her face to listen to what she was saying to me." Her black hair, sallow complexion, bushy eyebrows turned his heart to ice; he could not avert his gaze from the horrid little hairs springing from her chin. Her breasts were "hideous, half-exposed" and "hung, with a great cleft between them, halfway down her tall body."

At the midday meal, "I sat down at the table and, seeing a wooden spoon before me, I push it away and demand my silver service, which I cherished as a present from grandmother," but it was denied him. He had to conform to the other boys while under the landlady's roof. Equality was her watchword, so he ate his soup as the others did, straight from the tureen, as if they were scarcely better than hogs at a feeding trough. The revolting soup was replaced by tough dried cod and an apple—nothing more. It was the season of Lent, they were reminded, and that meant they were denied even cups. Everyone drank from the same clay jug containing *grappa*, the residue of boiled grape stems—not even the grapes themselves.

And then it was time to meet his teacher, a priest by the name of Antonio Maria Gozzi, destined to spend the entirety of his career in posts near Padua. Giacomo's landlady paid the priest a pittance to instruct the new arrival. Dr. Gozzi was all of twenty-six, in Giacomo's estimation, "plump, modest, and ceremoniously polite." At nine, Giacomo appeared decidedly slow, so Dr. Gozzi placed him with five-year-olds learning to write. The children "at once fell to jeering me."

Supper proved even more disgusting and meager than the midday meal, and then it was time for bed, and fresh horrors: "Three notorious insects would not let me shut my eyes." Rats scampered across the floor and jumped onto his bed, "filling me with fear that froze my blood." From his suffering, Giacomo drew a moral: "Thus did I begin to learn what it is to be unhappy and to bear misfortune patiently. Meanwhile, the insects that were devouring me lessened the terror that the rats inspired, and my terror in turn made me less conscious of the insect bites. My soul profited from the competition between my afflictions."

When a few rays of morning sunshine pierced the gloom of the attic, Giacomo rose from his "nest of vermin." The maid appeared, the boy complained of his agonies, and requested a fresh shirt, "since the one I wore was hideous with the stains from the lice." There would be no fresh linen for him, not this morning, only on Sundays. He threatened to protest to the slovenly, callous landlady, and the maid responded with peals of laughter at his predicament. "I heard my companions mocking me. They were in the same state I was; but they were accustomed to it."

Giacomo dozed during the morning lessons until Dr. Gozzi took it upon himself to see what was wrong. In private, the boy told him of his miseries, and examined the angry welts on his young flesh. With that he marched the boy to the boardinghouse, confronted the landlady, who blamed the maid, who in turned blamed the infestation on the landlady. Gozzi discovered that the beds were all just as vile. The landlady responded by slapping the maid; then the maid slapped the landlady and stormed off, as the priest sternly lectured the Slavonian landlady that Giacomo could not return to class until she saw to it that he was "as clean as the other pupils." When the priest departed, Giacomo received a "violent scolding." If he ever made a fuss over nothing again, she warned, she would throw him out of the boardinghouse.

"I felt completely bewildered," he said. But he got a fresh shirt—flung in his face—and shortly after that the maid—a new one—changed his grimy sheets.

His living situation settled for the moment, Giacomo applied himself to his studies. A congenial instructor, Dr. Gozzi "had me sit at his own table, where, to convince him that I deserved the distinction, I applied myself to studying with all my power." By month's end, "I was writing so well that he set me to grammar."

He rapidly matured physically no less than intellectually, and began to thrive. "The new life I was leading, the hunger I was forced to endure, and above all, the air of Padua brought me such health as I had never conceived of before." No longer sickly, he embarked on a growth spurt. His rude health was accompanied by a new torment: "I was as ravenous as a dog." When he finally ate, he slept—"nine hours of the deepest sleep untroubled by any dreams"—except for one, in which he was "satisfying my cruel appetite." To supplement the food he received at the lodging house, Giacomo resolved to "steal and swallow anything edible I could lay my hands on when I was sure I was not being observed." He devoured fifty smoked herring; quantities of raw sausage; freshly laid eggs, still warm—all "exquisite food." He even stole from Dr. Gozzi's pantry. Nevertheless, he remained as "thin as a skeleton, mere skin and bones."

He made rapid intellectual progress, filling his mind no less than his belly. Within six months, Dr. Gozzi appointed him as proctor, or monitor, of the other students. He tried to be strict, but, he admitted, his charges learned to win his favor and soften his judgment with little bribes of "roast chickens and cutlets and often gave me money," all of which had the effect of turning him, in his own description, into a tyrant who withheld approval unless he received the appropriate inducement. The students whom he had extorted banded together to denounce him to the very same Dr. Gozzi who had recently come to his rescue. The priest relieved Giacomo of his duties as proctor, but, continuing to see the possibility of good in him, proposed a scheme to free the lad from the horrid Slavonian landlady and board instead with him. All he had to do was write to Signor Baffo and his mother to petition them to make the change. But his mercurial mother was busy pursuing her acting and love life, and so he substituted his "good grandmother." He described "all my sufferings" for her, "and prophesied my death if I were not rescued from the clutches of the Slavonian woman and put to board with my schoolmaster, who was willing to take me but who asked two *zecchini* a month."

Grimani rebuffed the boy, but his beloved, illiterate grandmother, hear-

ing about the contents of the letter, tracked him down in his wretched Slavonian lair. "As soon as I saw her I flung myself on her neck, unable to hold
back my tears, which she instantly joined." He showed her his paltry meal
and detestable bed. He had suffered here for six months! The Slavonian
landlady bluntly informed Marzia that, given the small amount of money
his family paid, this was the best she could do. "It was true," Casanova recalled, but "who obliged her to keep a boardinghouse and so become the
murderess of boys whom avarice put in her care?"

Giacomo's grandmother instructed the boy to pack his things because
they were going away. He brought his silver service with him as evidence of
his neglected worth. She took him to an inn, where he amazed her with his
ravenous appetite. Dr. Gozzi materialized, and they entered brief negotiations concerning the boy's future. Terms: twenty-four zecchini for a year's
lodging, for which she received a receipt. She wasn't done with her grandson
just yet. She spent the next three days obtaining clothes for him to wear as an
abate, or priest, in training. Abates generally wore black, they were forbidden
dancing and dueling, but otherwise they lived as everyone else. She had his
hair, hopelessly matted and fouled, shorn, and outfitted him with a wig.

Strange as the family's choice of career for the boy seemed, he faced
limited options. The child of two actors, he had no place in society. There
would be no fortune to inherit, no estate to manage, no heiress to wed. Venetian law and custom forbade his marrying an aristocrat. He could become a tradesman, a cobbler, for instance, like his grandfather. As a priest,
in contrast, he would avoid penury, and, if he became intellectually accomplished, he might make a name for himself. There would be honor in the
family's giving a child to the church. Zanetta wrote from Warsaw to encourage the plan: "Can you imagine my comfort if twenty or thirty years
from now I know you will be a bishop?"

In preparation for this new stage in his life, Giacomo joined Dr. Gozzi's
little family: his mother, "ugly, old, and ill-tempered"; his father, who
"worked all day and never spoke to anyone" except for his occasional out-
ings to a tavern from which he invariably returned "wild and drunk"; and
the priest's younger sister, Bettina, thirteen, "pretty, lighthearted, and a
reader of romances." She became Giacomo's first love: "It was she who little
by little kindled in my heart the first sparks of a feeling which later became
my ruling passion."

For the moment, Giacomo admired Bettina from a distance as he studied under Dr. Gozzi, whose other pupils drifted off. "They all left because I was the sole object of his attentions." To make up for the lost income, the priest decided to start a small boarding school, but it would take two years to put that plan into action. "During those two years he taught me all that he knew, which, to tell the truth, was very little," wrote his student, "but enough to initiate me into all branches of learning." At the same time, the good priest instructed the lad in the intricacies of the violin, another facility that would prove intermittently valuable. Casanova had little love or aptitude for music, strangely enough, but in Venice, a flair for music making counted as a survival skill no less than a weapon.

The two engaged in philosophical debates spurred by their lessons. When the priest attempted to drill into Giacomo's thick head the idea that God had created the universe out of nothing, the boy claimed he "proved" that the notion was absurd. Dr. Gozzi retorted that the boy was a "fool," and the debate resumed. Through all the quarreling, the boy retained his personal regard for his tutor, noting that the priest "laughed at the stupidity of people who spent time over newspapers, which, according to him, never told the truth and always said the same thing."

On Sundays he gave sermons, bloated with Latin and Greek passages asserting that the "sin of the flesh was the greatest of all sins," filled the pews of his church with women. The sight impressed Giacomo, who was awakening to feminine allure. He took issue with his texts, asserting that the sin of the flesh was the *least* of all sins, infuriating his mentor.

———•———

Early in 1736, as Giacomo was about to turn eleven, his mother, impulsive as always, invited Dr. Gozzi to bring her son to Venice, to which she had returned for a brief time from a theatrical engagement in St. Petersburg. Dr. Gozzi, a simple priest from Padua, had "never seen Venice nor good society, and he did not want to appear a novice in any respect." Soon he and Giacomo boarded a stylish *burchiello* bound for Venice. Zanetta, practiced in the art of appearances, received her son and Dr. Gozzi "with perfect good breeding," but the priest "found himself in the uncomfortable situation of having to converse with her, yet not daring to look her in the face." She in turn couldn't resist flirting with him.

After two years' absence, the awkward, slow-witted child had become a self-possessed boy in a blond wig, which, as he recalled, "stood out against my dark complexion and made the most crying contrast to my eyebrows and my back eyes." Zanetta placed Bettina, of whom Giacomo was so fond, in charge of the boy's appearance, and ordered a new, more stylish wig to match his dark complexion. He took the measure of his siblings: Francesco and his drawings, "which I pretended to consider passable"; and Giovanni, who struck Giacomo as "stupid." The others were too young to matter.

At dinner that evening, Dr. Gozzi thoroughly embarrassed himself when an Englishman eating with the family addressed him in Latin, expecting that the priest would reply in kind, and he awkwardly replied that he didn't understand English. Moving along, the Englishman proposed to test precocious Giacomo's mettle with a bawdy Latin riddle: why was the Latin word for vagina—*cunnus*—masculine and the Latin word for penis—*mentula*—feminine? Where was the logic in that?

Giacomo claimed to have replied, in Latin pentameter, "Because the slave takes his name from his master." (*Disce quod a domino nomina servus habet*.) Pleased with himself, and what he called his first literary exploit, "the seeds of my desire for the fame which comes from literature were sown in my soul." And so the most celebrated lover in history took his first steps toward immortality, at least in his own mind.

"The astonished Englishman, after remarking that no boy of eleven had ever done as much, first embraced me several times and then made me a present of his watch." Delighted with her precocious son, Zanetta produced another watch, this one meant for Dr. Gozzi, "whose inability to express the extremity of his gratitude to her turned the scene into high comedy." Zanetta kissed the priest on both cheeks, and then offered hers in return for his kisses, "but the poor man was so embarrassed that he would rather have died than give them to her." Four days later, when the visit ended, "My mother gave me a present for Bettina, and the Abate Grimani gave me four zecchini to buy books. A week after that, my mother left for Petersburg."

At Padua once more, Dr. Gozzi, smitten with the coquettish Zanetta, spent the next four months talking of her. Bettina grew still fonder of Giacomo when she opened her present, a generous length of silky fabric and a dozen pairs of gloves. She groomed the lad with increasing intimacy: "She took care of my hair so well that in less than six months I was able to leave off wearing my wig. She came to comb my hair every day, and when I was still in bed, saying that she did not have time to wait for me to dress. She washed my face and neck and chest, and gave me childish caresses which, since I was bound to consider them innocent, made me chide myself for letting them trouble me," but trouble him they did. Still, she was older, "and she could not love me with any evil intent, and this made me angry at the evil that I felt in myself." When she grasped his flesh to show that he was putting on weight, "she roused the most intense emotions in me." And when "she told me that I had a soft skin, the tickling made me draw away, and I was put out with myself for not daring to do as much to her." When she washed him, she covered him with "the sweetest kisses" and called him her "dear child," but still he restrained himself as she taunted him for his "timidity." When she finally left, apparently unruffled by their encounters, he plunged into despair "over not having followed my natural inclination."

To make matters worse, a fifteen-year-old by the name of Candiani appeared, and there was no mistaking Bettina's attraction to him. Giacomo claims he felt "neither jealousy nor indignation" for this new rival, "for as the coarse, ignorant, stupid, ill-mannered son of a farmer," Candiani couldn't compete with Giacomo, except that the older boy had reached puberty.

Bettina accused Giacomo of envy, the perfect provocation. Soon after, she came to his bed to give him a present of white stockings she had knitted for him. She dressed his hair, and instructed him to try them on for her, so she could see how they looked. (Dr. Gozzi was out of the house, at mass, and so, presumably, was the boorish Candiani.) She sat on his bed, and as she put the stockings on him, she told Giacomo his thighs were dirty and "at once began washing them without asking my leave"—as if he would have withheld it! He succumbed to a "voluptuous feeling" that she aroused until it finally ran its course, much to his chagrin. He apologized to her, as he had "committed a crime," but Bettina told him "the fault was entirely hers." She would make sure it never happened again, and so left him in a thoroughly befuddled state.

He would atone for his sin by marrying Bettina, if she would have him, but he never got the chance to ask her. Day after day passed without her visiting his bed, and he was plunged into the "blackest melancholy." Her calculating behavior could only mean that she loved him. He called on his pen to rise to his defense. "I thought my letter a masterpiece, and more than enough to make her adore me and give me preference over Candiani, whom I considered a brute beast." In reply, she said she would come to his bed, but she stayed away. "I was furious," Giacomo noted. At dinner she asked Giacomo if he would like her to dress him "as a girl and go with her to a ball" given by a neighbor, Dr. Olivo. "The entire table applauded the idea, and I consented." But the ball never took place; instead, a "veritable tragicomedy" ensued.

Hearing that Dr. Gozzi would be away, Giacomo informed Bettina that he would leave his door open in expectation of a late-night visit from her. He retreated to his room, snuffed the candle, and waited. By midnight she had not appeared, and snow was falling. Finally at dawn, having waited for her in vain for the entire night, he tiptoed downstairs and approached the room where he thought Bettina was sleeping, but the door was locked. When the door eventually opened, Giacomo beheld Candiani, "who gives me such a kick in the belly that I find myself stretched out, half buried in the snow." Regaining his footing, Giacomo threatened to strangle Bettina, but she had hidden herself behind another locked door. He gave it a mighty kick, and a dog, startled, began to bark. Humiliated, Casanova ran to his room, threw himself on his bed, and tried to recover from his humiliation. He'd get his revenge . . . he'd poison the two of them . . . he'd tell the Doctor about Bettina's misdeeds. But he was much too young for such "heroic plans of vengeance." The next thing he knew, Bettina's mother was wailing that her daughter was dying.

"Aggrieved that she should die before I killed her, I rise, go downstairs, and find her in her father's bed in frightful convulsions." The sight was terrifying. "She twisted, she writhed, hitting out at random with fists and feet, and escaping by violent jerks" from family members "trying to hold her still." Dr. Olivo, a physician, arrived on the scene, as did a midwife, only to discover that Bettina wasn't in labor, she was having seizures. Giacomo, looking on in astonishment, marveled that she could "possess so much strength" and blamed her wild paroxysms on her tryst with Candiani. After rifling through the pockets of her clothing, and discovering a letter from Candiani planning their latest romp, Giacomo realized with a painful laugh he had been made a "perfect dupe," and, as a result, "I believed I was cured of my love." He would scorn Bettina and forgive Candiani—until Giacomo remembered the nasty kick the older boy had given him.

Bettina's convulsions returned the next day and lasted through the night. In the morning, the girl's mother declared that her family's elderly servant was actually a witch, and responsible for the girl's affliction. As proof, Bettina's mother said the servant made a habit of barricading the door to her room with crossed broomsticks. She demanded to know where the servant had been the previous Thursday evening, and accused her of attending a witches' Sabbath, "for you are a witch, and you have bewitched my daughter." She spat in the servant's face, and "raised her cane to thrash the old woman," who fled the house.

Dr. Gozzi chased after the maid and gave her a few coins to hold her tongue. He returned to the house, knowing what he must do: Bettina was possessed by the devil, and he would have to perform an exorcism.

A hush fell over the Gozzi family, and the rite began. Giacomo remained skeptical of the whole business. "I thought all these people either insane or idiots," he declared in his memoir. "I could not picture devils in Bettina's body without laughing." It wasn't that Giacomo lacked faith—on the contrary, he remained devout throughout his life—but this behavior in the name of religion struck him as folly.

The priest and Dr. Gozzi mumbled between themselves about faith, and Giacomo, believing himself unobserved, bent over and whispered in her ear: "Take courage, get well, and count on my silence." The day passed quietly; perhaps the exorcism had worked; perhaps his own reassuring words had cured her. Yet the following day she became delirious, babbling in Latin and Greek. It was time for stronger measures.

Bettina's mother sought the "most celebrated exorcist in Padua," who happened to be an "extremely ugly Capuchin monk named Fra Prospero da Bovolenta." (Capuchins belong to a branch of the austere Franciscan order; they generally wear beards and take their name from the hood, or *cappuccio*, of their habit.) Catching sight of the monk, Bettina laughed, calling him an "ignorant, stinking impostor," among other insults. The Capuchin "fell to hitting Bettina with a great crucifix, saying that he was beating the devil," as Giacomo watched in atonishment. The monk withdrew "only when he saw her ready to throw a chamber pot at his head."

The Capuchin demanded to speak with the devil, and Bettina replied that if he cut off his beard, the devil, speaking through Bettina, would depart. Giacomo laughed so hard that the Capuchin ordered the boy out of the room. At the door, he caught sight of Bettina spitting on the exorcist's hand when he instructed her to kiss it. "Here was this incredibly talented girl, confounding the Capuchin, yet no one was surprised because all her words were ascribed to the devil!" Later, she flung some sort of foul black

liquid in his face, splattering Candiani in the process, much to Casanova's
delight. At last, the Capuchin gave up in frustration, telling Dr. Gozzi to
find himself another exorcist.

———————

The Gozzi household resumed its peaceful ways. Bettina slept contentedly
and appeared at the dinner table to join her family. As if nothing had happened, she talked animatedly of attending the ball the following day, and
she expected Giacomo to keep his word and go with her dressed as a girl;
she was planning to dress his hair in the morning, ignoring his advice to rest
and remain calm after the ordeal she had endured. Alone in his room that
night, he found the following note concealed in his nightcap: "Either come
to the ball with me dressed as a girl, or I will show you something that will
make you cry." But he replied that he would not attend.

In the morning, she resumed her demonic ranting, and Dr. Gozzi prepared to consult another exorcist, the eminent Father Mancia, who made
a striking impression, "tall and majestic, his age about thirty years," with
blond hair and blue eyes. They spent hours together, praying and meditating, and by the end she appeared to be cured. Even better, she wrote Giacomo a note claiming that she stopped speaking to Candiani "since the fatal
night that made me wretched," and "It is to you alone that I owe my life and
honor."

Giacomo detected "unparalleled effrontery" in an effort to "bind me in
her chains again." Where had she learned her wiles? In the pages of the romances she read, he supposed. Later, when she came to his bed, where he
was recovering from painful chilblains brought on by the incessant cold, he
calmly rebuffed her: she had "stifled the seed of a beautiful passion in an instant," meaning the humiliating, infuriating kick he'd received from Candiani. Since then he'd "despised" her. Finally, he forgave her, and even gained
an appreciation of her intelligence. "I was its dupe, but no matter: it exists,
it is amazing, divine, I admire it, I love it." He requested that she treat him
the same way, with respect and friendship, "for I can love only if I am sure
of being loved without a rival." Bettina insisted she'd never loved Candiani,
and convulsed with tears.

"What she had just told me was plausible," Giacomo decided, "and flattering: but I had seen too much." The specter of Candiani still hung over them
both. Bettina wove an elaborate tale of half truths about how she planned

to set matters right with Candiani and her family. "They say that I am bewitched and that demons have taken control of me. I know nothing about such things; but if it is true, I am the most wretched girl alive." Or the most deceitful, Giacomo thought. And he was troubled by the handsome Father Mancia. "I will tell you that the way your devils prefer the handsome monk's exorcisms to those of the ugly Capuchin do you no honor," he warned.

Her ordeal resumed. She suffered delirium and fevers, and spots— smallpox—appeared on her skin. "Poor Bettina was so covered with the pestilential spots that by the sixth day it was impossible to see her skin anywhere on her body. Her eyes closed and all her hair had to be cut off." Worse, "her mouth and throat were found to be so full of spots that nothing but a few drops of honey could be introduced into her esophagus." Her head swelled "until it was bigger by a third." Her nose disappeared into her face, and it was feared that she would go blind. And then there was her "stinking sweat" that he forced himself to endure.

After eleven days, Bettina hovered near death. "Her pustules had turned black and were discharging with a stench that made the air unbreathable." On the thirteenth day, she flailed around in her bed, suffering from "intolerable itching, which no medicine could have soothed more than the potent words I repeated to her: 'Remember, Bettina, that you are going to get well; but if you dare to scratch yourself, you will be so ugly that no one will ever love you again.'"

As the weeks dragged on, an abscess in her neck confined her to bed, and she infected him with eight or ten pustules, "which left an indelible mark on my face." His wounds endeared him to Bettina, "who now realized that only I deserved her affection."

She recovered slowly, those angry red spots marring her skin for a full year. This once beautiful girl married a humble shoemaker, Pigozzo, "a base scoundrel who brought her to poverty and misery." Giacomo met her again forty years later, in 1776. "I found Bettina old, ill, and dying," he wrote, and she perished the following day, remembered mostly by Casanova, who had loved her, and scorned her.

So began his education in love and women. They were his shadow self, his "ruling passion." He would dedicate his life to trying to understand everything about women. He would become a libertine. He would give free rein to his senses, suspend moral judgment, and indulge his appetites. To be a libertine was to stand apart from society, to refuse to accept definitions and restrictions. The child of two actors, two outcasts, he would spend his life as a performer on the world's stage, trying on an endlessly changing array of roles and costumes, playing all the parts, villain and hero. His imagination would attempt to vanquish them all.

Giacomo resumed his life to find that his mother, the mercurial Zanetta, had unexpectedly arrived in Padua. Six months later, Giacomo visited his mother again, this time in Venice, just before she departed for Dresden, where she had accepted an appointment "in the service of the Elector of Saxony August III, King of Poland," just right for an actress in her declining years.

Zanetta did not bring Giacomo with her to Dresden; he remained in Padua to complete his studies, but she did take his young sister Maria Maddalena and his brother Giovanni, then eight years old. Giacomo remarked that the boy "wept desperately when they left, which led me to suspect that he was not especially intelligent, for there was nothing tragic about the departure."

After Zanetta's departure, Giacomo rarely saw her again. She remained in Dresden for the rest of her days, except for a sojourn in Prague. She had abandoned him, and so with every woman Giacomo Casanova pursued as an adult, he sought to re-create the intimacy he had once experienced with his mother until she had left to pursue her career and various lovers—how very Casanova-like of her. Indeed, she was the original.

Giacomo enrolled as a student at the University of Padua on November 28, 1737, at the age of twelve, to pursue a curriculum combining secondary and university courses. (His name doesn't appear on law exam lists, so we must rely on his word for this phase of his academic career. And there are certificates of attendance for him for the following year, 1739.) The Padovan educational system was well known. "The principle of the Venetian government"—which administered Padua—"was to pay very high stipends to professors of great renown and to let those who came to hear their lectures live in the utmost freedom." The students were responsible only to a head of the student body, the "Syndic," who acted as a go-between between them and the powers that be. His means of discipline ranged from nonexistent to mild, but his presence was enough to keep the local law enforcement officers at bay. "The ordinary *sbirri*"—or officers—"would never have dared to arrest a student," Giacomo noted. Amid the merriment he endured a clash between the *sbirri* and students, which left two scholars dead. "Armed with pistols and a carbine I went out with my fellow students every day, searching for the enemy," but they failed to encounter a single *sbirro*. He wrote to his grandmother for help, and she responded by coming to Padua and plucking him out of Dr. Gozzi's home. The two of them reached Venice on October 1, 1739, and Giacomo returned to the same apartment where he had lived on the Calle degli Orbi, still leased by his absent mother.

No longer a withdrawn, sickly child, Giacomo was now tall and self-possessed. "'He has just come from Padua, where he has been studying at the University,' was the phrase used to introduce me everywhere," he boasted. He received the "compliments of fathers, and the caresses of old women," including "some who were not really old but were willing to pass as such so that they could embrace me without impropriety." And those caresses were forbidden because he was training for the priesthood. He was assigned to the parish church, San Samuele, and applied himself to advanced classes in the Italian language and in poetry taught by the Abate (or Abbot) Schiavo. On February 14, 1740, as he approached his fifteenth birthday, he was tonsured by the Patriarch of Venice, Antonio Francesco Correr, as a sign of humility. His new way would be better and purer, but how long would it last?

Chapter 2

Angela

Just when it seemed the priesthood beckoned, Casanova became the protégé of Alvise Gasparo Malipiero, a Venetian senator. "Not wishing to occupy himself with affairs of state at his age, which was seventy"—actually, Malipiero was even older—"[he] led a pleasant life in his palazzo, eating well and every evening entertaining a most select company made up of ladies who had all gone the pace and men of wit and intelligence who were sure to know of the latest happenings in the city."

Casanova remembered the senator, whom he always addressed as "Your Excellency," as a wealthy old bachelor who suffered from severe gout "so that his entire body was crippled. Only his head, his lungs, and his stomach had been spared." Yet the venerable statesman remained mentally alert, handsome, eloquent, and the lover of twenty mistresses, only to realize that "he must give up all hope of pleasing even one."

By ingratiating himself with the senator, Casanova gained access to one of the most celebrated homes in Venice. The Palazzo Malipiero, while close to San Samuele, commanded a view of the Grand Canal. Of Byzantine design, the palazzo had been frequently renovated but retained its essential aristocratic character as it loomed above the gondolas and other watercraft gliding past its shuttered windows. During their prolonged meals together, the younger man learned that Malipiero, despite his crippling infirmities, "still nurtured an amorous inclination" for Teresa Imer, the daughter of a powerful Venetian theatrical impresario, Giuseppe Imer, who lived so close to the senator's palazzo that the impresario's windows opened onto the senator's bedchamber.

Teresa Imer was a prize, only seventeen (two years older than Casanova, and countless years younger than the toothless old senator who fancied her); and "pretty, willful, and a flirt." She filled her days studying music for her contemplated stage career, and displaying herself in the window, tantalizing Malipiero to the point of intoxication. Casanova believed that the girl tormented the lovelorn senator with a shrewd and calculating cruelty. "She came almost every day to pay him a visit, but she was always accompanied by her mother, an old actress who had retired from the stage to pursue the salvation of her soul."

Their routine consisted of mass every day, confession on Sunday, and afternoons visiting the libidinous old senator. When Teresa refused him a kiss, even with her mother present, he would fly into a terrifying rage. Casanova said the old man permitted him to observe these humiliating incidents, including those in which Teresa's "scoundrel of a mother applauded her daughter's resistance" and scolded the paralyzed senator.

After witnessing several bizarre visits, Casanova suggested that the senator marry the young temptress to bring her into his grasp, only to learn that she'd already refused his proposal.

"Offer her a large sum of money, a position," he advised.

"She says she would not commit a mortal sin to become queen of the world."

The young man proposed more extreme strategies. "You must violate her," or, failing that, "banish her."

His Excellency replied, reasonably enough, that he was incapable of carrying out the former, and unwilling to resort to the latter. This being Venice, where women enjoyed few rights, Casanova insisted: "*Kill her!*"

The enfeebled senator admitted that he just might, if he didn't die first.

Why, Casanova wanted to know, did the senator always receive Teresa; why not *visit* her? No, the older man mysteriously replied, he might then fall in love with her. There was nothing to be done, *niente*.

———•———

Secure in the senator's favor, Casanova moved into the splendid Palazzo Malipiero, among the grandest Venetian residences. He maintained his academic and ecclesiastical studies, although the profane world held a greater fascination for him than obdurate Latin texts or theological conundrums. During his time at the Palazzo Malipiero, Casanova learned to follow the house rules as laid down by the senator. He would not speak unless spoken to, "and above all never to express my opinion on any subject, for at the age of fifteen I was not entitled to have one." And he was strongly cautioned not to gossip about the society figures he met; otherwise he'd earn a reputation as a scoundrel. "Thus he inculcated the sound precept of discretion in me." He won the senator's trust "and within a few days I was the pet of all the ladies who visited." Considering him a young man of no importance, they invited him on their visits to their daughters and nieces in the convents where they'd been sent to be educated and to avoid romantic entanglements. When the novitiates realized a man was approaching they scurried away, until he turned out nothing more than a harmless boy. "I was delighted by their trustfulness," Casanova remarked with a conspiratorial wink to the reader.

His priest refused to be corrupted by this distracting world of artifice and hypocrisy, and warned Casanova to please God with his "state of mind" and "condemned my elaborate curls and the delicate perfume of my pomade; he told me the devil had me by the hair." A thick thatch of hair or wig now obscured Casanova's priestly tonsure. If he continued on this course, he ran the risk of excommunication. Even his benign grandmother lent her voice to the criticism. Stung, he reeled off the names of a "hundred abati" who wore twice, no, three times as much powder, or who applied a pomade "scented with ambergris that would make a woman in childbirth faint," whereas he, Casanova, went about with only a faint scent of jasmine that elicited compliments far and wide. If he'd wanted to stink, he sharply lectured the priest, he would have made himself into a bearded Capuchin monk. So, he was very sorry, but he refused to submit to the priest's absurd instructions.

Early one morning, when he was fast asleep at home, the same priest came calling, and prevailed on Casanova's grandmother to admit him. "The presumptuous priest, who loved me, softly approached and, with a pair of good scissors, cut off all my front hair from ear to ear." When Casanova awoke, he felt his head, and ran to the mirror, erupting with indignation when he observed "the state to which the audacious priest had reduced me!" He would see the advocate Carrara, whom he had met at the Palazzo Malipiero, to file suit against the offending priest. Carrara egged him on, discussing a Slavonian merchant whose mustache had been shorn away, and in revenge he had brought an entire family to ruin, and that was just over a mustache, whereas Casanova had suffered a much greater indignity!

On the way to Carrara's office the next day, he was waylaid by a hairdresser provided by the senator himself, who inspected the damage and burst out laughing, telling the youth to leave it to him, "he would make it possible for me to go out even more elegantly curled than before." The hairdresser deftly trimmed the hair in front to a uniform length and neatly brushed it "to such effect that I found myself pleased, satisfied, and avenged." Indeed, his hair was so elegantly curled that he really did "deserve excommunication."

He assumed the matter had come to an end, but then the senator, invoking his position as "President of the Confraternity of the Blessed Sacrament," invited his prodigal charge to "deliver a panegyric," or speech of praise, on the day after Christmas. Casanova thought the elderly senator might be joking, "for it had never entered my head to become a preacher, still less that I had the ability to compose a sermon and deliver it," but he insisted "I was born to be the most famous preacher of the century as soon as I had put on flesh, for in those days I was extremely thin." The only condition, to which Casanova agreed, was to submit the speech to a priest to make certain it contained nothing heretical.

When his grandmother learned of this remarkable turnabout in Casanova's fortunes, she "could do nothing but weep for joy." And he appeared destined for ecclesiastical glory until he read his panegyric for the priest, who strenuously disapproved. The text under examination had come not from the Bible but from Horace: "They lamented that their merits did not meet with the gratitude for which they had hoped." It would not suffice. Dismayed, Casanova stumbled to the priest's house to seek reassurance, but the priest could not be found.

Fate intervened. Her name was Angela. She was the priest's niece, about his age, and she was toiling fetchingly at her embroidery frame. She was lively and flirtatious. She'd heard about the head-shaving incident, and she encouraged Casanova to tell her all about it. As he did, he fell in love with Angela—not puppy love, but a love that determined his fate, so he claimed, because it led to still more loves, and those led to still others, all of these cascades of passion eventually "obliging me to renounce being a churchman." But first he had to deliver his panegyric.

He hoped to keep his original text, until he showed it to Dr. Gozzi "out of vanity," who condemned it and asked Giacomo if he'd "gone mad."

No matter, Casanova delivered the sermon at the Church of San Samuele to "a most select audience," who showered the young preacher with "great praise" and predicted he would "become the greatest preacher of the century," or so he recalled. Afterward, he tallied the offerings from the mass: "nearly fifty *zecchini*, together with love letters that scandalized the bigots" and tantalized their recipient. Public moralizing and private transgression went hand in hand. He saw no reason to choose between the love of God and the love of women.

Daily he went to the priest's house for his help in attaining his ecclesiastical goal, each time encountering his niece Angela, "who was willing to let me love her but who, showing herself to be a perfect dragon of virtue, obstinately refused to grant me the slightest favor"—unless he renounced the priesthood and married her. Naturally, "I could not bring myself to do this."

On March 19, 1741, he planned to deliver another panegyric, anticipating even greater rewards this time, yet "it was fated that I should not preach more than once on this earth." He'd written the sermon himself and committed it to memory. He might trip over a sentence now and then, but he could ad-lib "just as I never found myself at a loss when discoursing with other people." Confident, he ate and drank his fill in the company of aristocrats. When he was summoned to the church, his stomach full and his head clouded with wine, he launched into his sermon, but after making a brave start, he lost his way. As he feebly improvised, the worshippers grew restless and uneasy. Laughter escaped the lips of an irreverent few. He became dizzy, and, intentionally or not, "dropped to the floor of the pulpit, at the same time hitting the wall with my head and wishing that I had split my skull." Two clergyman carried him away.

He fled home in disgrace, hurriedly packed his belongings, and made for Padua, where he reinserted himself into the household of Dr. Gozzi, keeping the triumph and disgrace he'd experienced in Venice to himself. He diligently pursued his studies, received his next degree, and when he returned to Venice after Easter, found that all had been forgotten. He received half-hearted encouragement to resume his preaching, but he'd "renounced the profession." Instead, he followed Angela to her embroidery school, only to realize that "her parsimony in granting me favors irritated me, and I already found my love a torment." With his passionate temperament, he "needed a girl of Bettina's type, one who enjoyed appeasing the flame of love"— apparently with her lovely hands on his inflamed manhood—"without quenching it." But his affair with the "recalcitrant Angela" was going nowhere. "She was drying me up; I was growing thin." When he tracked her down at school, his "pathetic and plaintive speeches" impressed the other girls, but left Angela unmoved. If only he'd looked around, he would have noticed two sisters who signaled their availability, but Angela had made him "obstinate" with her tales. She said she was prepared to marry him if only he would formally propose. "She exasperated me beyond measure when, as a mark of extreme favor, she told me that abstinence made her suffer as much as it did me," he wrote with clenched teeth. *Magansesa!* Treacherous!

———•———

Distraction arrived late that summer in the form of an unexpected invitation from the Countess of Montereale—a title always caught Casanova's attention—to her estate, Pasiano, in Friuli, in the northeastern region of Italy. Although under the sway of Venice, Friuli had a character all its own, hilly and verdant, and known for its tangy white wine. There he anticipated "brilliant company," including the Countess's daughter. She was intelligent and beautiful, and, he magnanimously added, "had one eye so lovely that it made up for the other, rendered hideous" by a white scar on the cornea.

As soon as he arrived and was shown his room on the ground floor with a view of the garden, he forgot all about the torments of Angela. He slept blissfully on the bed, and in the morning a serving girl perhaps seventeen years of age, with white skin, black eyes, fetchingly loose hair, and a petticoat "exposing half her bare leg to view," came with breakfast, regarding him "as frankly and calmly as if I had been an old acquaintance." The conversation turned to the comfort of his bed, and she introduced herself as Lucia, the caretaker's daughter, and said she was just fourteen. She promised to wait on him herself, inflaming his imagination. She sat on his bed as he sipped his coffee and chatted until her parents walked in, apologized for her behavior, and she left. In her absence, her parents extolled her virtues, but cautioned that she had a single fault: her extreme youth. Later she returned, curtsied, kissed her mother repeatedly, and sat on her father's lap, declining Casanova's offer to return to the bed.

Lucia repeated the performance the next morning. Surely she realized that she ran the risk of setting Casanova on fire, as he put it. He decided to test her. "I extend the libertine hand toward her, and by what appears an involuntary movement she draws back." After a few moments of confusion, the two resumed talking as before, this time for hours, until he invited her to fend off the Friulian chill by joining him under the covers, but he asked, what if her mother appeared? "She won't think it any harm," Lucia responded.

"Come here, but you know the risk we're running."

"Of course," Lucia said. "I'm no fool; but you are good, and, what's more, a priest."

"Then come, but first shut the door."

Leaving it open, she slunk into bed with him, as he forced himself to remain still, "not wishing to surrender to the movements of nature." Finally, when the clock struck a late hour, she made her excuses. With that, she left him in bed "in a state of violent excitement."

And when Lucia returned the next morning, the conversation convinced him that she really was as naive as her parents insisted. She was innocent, guileless, an angel, all of which saddened Casanova, who guessed that she would "fall victim to the first libertine who should take her in hand." It would not be Giacomo Casanova, whoever it was. He couldn't despoil her for his own pleasure and so betray the confidence of her "respectable parents" who entrusted her to him each morning. "So I chose the course of suffering." The visits persisted, two or three hours of stimulating conversation every morning, during which "the company of this angel made me suffer the pangs of hell." She'd bring her face inches away from his, and just when he wanted to cover it with kisses, she would say she wanted to be his sister. All the while, "I felt I had become as flammable as straw." He confessed how she made him feel, and because he was an abate, a priest in training, she listened in silence. "At the conclusion of my sermon"—a telling choice of word—"she wiped away my tears with the front of her shift, never dreaming that by this charitable act she exposed to my view two rocks eminently adapted to make the most skillful of pilots suffer shipwreck."

He claimed his love for her was harming him, and he feared bringing her to ruin. These arguments struck the girl as senseless. "My dear Abate," she said, "if love is a torture for you, I am sorry. Could it be that you were born not to love?" She assured him she could never stop loving him, no matter what he did or said or thought. Carried away, he clasped her in his arms, and they held each other in stunned silence for an hour, until her mother complimented Casanova on his "fine color," and instructed Lucia to prepare for mass. She returned to confide in him: "If your perfect happiness depends only on me, be happy! I can refuse you nothing."

He felt himself hovering on "the very edge of the abyss"—a delicious

predicament. Naturally, he fell into it without further delay. "After spending the whole month of September there in the country, I found myself in
possession of Lucia for eleven successive nights, which knowing that her
mother was a sound sleeper, she came and spent in my arms." She "did everything in her power" to force Casanova to renounce his "abstinence," because
"she could not taste the sweetness of the forbidden fruit except by letting me
eat it. She tried a hundred times to deceive me by saying that I already gathered it, but Bettina had taught me too much for me to be taken in."

Casanova's description of his sexual initiation became a tour de force
of titillation coupled with obfuscation. One could surmise from whispered
hints that they enjoyed fellatio and manual stimulation and endless kissing,
but it's not certain they had intercourse during their eleven-day idyll. At the
end of their time together, he promised to return to Pasiano in the spring,
yet events in his life outran him and his desires.

In Venice again, Casanova pushed Lucia to the back of his mind and sought
out Angela, the embroidery student, "hoping to achieve at least what I had
achieved with Lucia," yet a certain "terror of consequences fatal to my future
career held me back from full enjoyment." He spoke without restraint of his
affection for Angela, alarming the embroidery school's head, "a sanctimo-
nious old woman," who went right to Angela's uncle the priest. Casanova
related the outcome with witty understatement: "He one day gently warned
me that I should not frequent the house so much, since my assiduity might
be wrongly interpreted and in a manner prejudicial to his niece's honor."

Suffering pangs of conscience, he unburdened himself to Signor Malipiero, who admitted that he "was in the same situation with respect to Teresa." Teresa? He remembered the way she enticed and taunted the old man
to the brink of insanity. Meanwhile, the old senator ordered his servants to
feed Casanova, and when he saw the lad "eat with the appetite of a dog," he
started to laugh, and Casanova laughed along with him. Life was absurd,
and so were women.

He returned to his studies in Padua. In this arena, he displayed confidence
and skill as he defended his thesis on metaphysics, and he received his doc-
torate in civil and canon law at the age of sixteen, having written his thesis

in civil law on wills ("De testamentis") and in canon law on the question of whether Jews could build new synagogues. He approved. Yet he wasn't preparing a career in either the law or in the Church, but in medicine, for which he felt "a strong inclination." But it wasn't to be; he was told to study law, "for which I felt an unconquerable aversion." If only he could have been a physician, "in which profession quackery is even more effective than it is in legal practice," he commented. "Legal squabbling ruins more families than it supports; and those who are killed by physicians are far more numerous than those who are cured. It follows that mankind would be far less wretched without these two breeds."

No matter. He rejoiced in the student's life in Padua. The word "free" kept occurring to him; he was a free man, free to enjoy himself, free to associate with whom he wanted, especially "the greatest libertines, gamblers, frequenters of places of ill repute, drunkards, debauchees, seducers of decent girls." The students were blissfully free of stifling morality, and the university officials looked the other way, "for the interest of the State could not allow such severity to diminish the number of students who flocked to this famous University from every part of Europe."

———•———

And then it was back to Venice, and Angela's web of romantic intrigue. She wished to know from his own lips if he still loved her. Off he went to the assignation with two bottles of wine and "a smoked tongue in my pocket." But Angela had been detained until suppertime, so he heard. This turn of events emboldened Casanova to declare that he would spend the night instead with two sisters, Nanetta and Marta. It was a startling turn of events, to be scorned by one and tempted by two.

"You shall go to bed here," Nanetta declared, "and we will go and sleep on the couch in the other room."

Before the sisters did, they set three places for dinner. The more they ate and drank, the more pleasing the two young women became in his eyes, and their mutual seduction became his revenge on the deceitful Angela. He asked if they disapproved of the "contemptible way" that Angela had treated him. Of course! In that case, they should exchange pledges of eternal faithfulness to one another with kisses "in the innocence of our hearts." In that spirit, they traded "harmless kisses," yet after a while these same kisses "began to kindle a fire in the three of us which must have taken us aback."

They broke apart, looked at each other in shock and embarrassment, and Casanova felt himself falling in love with both Nanetta *and* Marta. Weren't they prettier than the absent Angela? And more intelligent?

Although he had moved beyond Angela, the conversation turned to her, and they revealed that when Angela slept with them, as she did on occasion, she covered Marta with kisses, and called her "My dear Abate," meaning Casanova. As her sister tried to stop her, Marta said that their guest "could not fail to know what two girls who were good friends did when they were in bed together."

"Everyone knows about these little games," he declared. Who played the part of husband, he wanted to know, and who played the wife? Casanova proposed that all three of them should undress and sleep together. "Count on my word of honor, that I now give you, that I will not touch you." They could simply leave the bed if he didn't behave, and with that he turned his back to them and pretended to fall asleep.

In the darkness, he carefully moved toward one of the girls, not knowing whether she was Nanetta or Marta: a delightful predicament. "I found her curled up and covered by her shift, but by doing nothing to startle her and proceeding step by step as gradually as possible, I soon convinced her that her best course was to feign sleep and let me go on. Little by little I straightened her out, little by little she uncurled, and little by little, with slow, successive, but wonderfully natural movements she put herself in a position which was the most favorable she could offer without betraying herself. I set to work, but to crown my labors it was necessary that she should join them openly and undeniably, and nature finally forced her to do so. I found this first sister beyond suspicion, and suspecting the pain she must have endured I was surprised." He was deflowering her, no less than she was deflowering him, enabling him to experience "a pleasure the sweetness of which I was tasting for the first time in my life." It was as though he were plucking a rosebud of endless satiny petals. After he recovered from the ordeal of pleasure, "I let the victim alone and turned the other way to do the same thing with her sister."

She lay still on her back "in a deep, untroubled sleep," but Casanova did trouble himself to identify the sister he was about to ravish. Instead, "with the greatest of precautions, and every appearance of fearing to waken her, I began by delighting her soul," apparently massaging her vulva with his finger, or his tongue, or both, as he assured himself "that she was as untouched as her sister; and I continued the same treatment until, affecting a most natural movement without which I could not have crowned my labors"— ejaculating—"she helped me to triumph; but at that moment of crisis she no longer had the strength to maintain her pretense. Throwing off the mask, she clasped me in her arms and pressed her mouth on mine."

When they had recovered enough strength to speak, he ventured to guess that he held Nanetta in his arms. He had first deflowered Marta, then moved on to Nanetta. Euphoric, he exclaimed, "All that we have done was the work of love."

The giddy trio rose from the bed, and "made an improvised toilet in a bucket of water." In the "costume of the Golden Age," that is, naked, or nearly so, they wolfed down the tongue and bottle of water, and, refreshed, returned to their bed where they "spent the rest of the night in ever varied skirmishes."

At dawn, he quietly bid adieu and went home, where he slept until midday. When he awoke, Signor Malipiero noticed his "happy look and the dark circles" under his eyes. "I let him imagine whatever he pleased but told him nothing."

⸺•⸺

He had his delayed revenge on Angela soon after, when she happened to spend the night with Nanetta and Marta, who confessed the entire delectable business with Casanova to her, and even blamed her for setting events in motion that led to their behavior. "She treated them to the coarsest insults," Casanova revealed, and "swore never to set foot in the house again, but they did not care." Angela moved to neighboring Vicenza to live with her father, a minor painter named Iseppo Tosello, and spent years thereafter adorning houses with frescoes, while Casanova passed "at least two nights a week" with his affectionate playmates, who had presented him with an impression of their bedroom key in dough, from which he had a copy produced.

His experiences with the two sisters emboldened him to venture deeper into Venetian society. In April 1742, with Carnival just ended, he encountered Giulietta Preato, a notorious courtesan known as La Caramacchie— dialect for "the spot cleaner," after her father's line of work, according to Casanova. Like all Venetian courtesans, she harbored a plan. She wanted to borrow the drawing room in Signor Malipiero's house to host a ball. She would pay for everything, including the chandeliers, and her servants would make the arrangements; there would be a reward of twenty-four zecchini for him. A ball in Venice at that time was like no other; they were elaborate, masked affairs. Guests came costumed as seductive sylphs; aristocrats turned themselves into human furniture for others to use as they wished; faux nuns were actually women of easy virtue. Dances provided opportunities to fondle and grope. The guests indulged their fantasies in spectacles that were renowned across Europe for their debauchery and blasphemy.

After supper, as the guests danced a Venetian variation of the minuet, Giulietta took him to a room, locked the door, and instructed him to dress her as an abate, and dressed him in her clothes. Cross-dressed, they would make a fitting couple for the event. "I quickly coil up her long hair and let them make me a chignon that she arranges very neatly under her own bonnet," he noted. She applied rouge to his face, "frankly letting her see that I am enjoying it," and she kissed him just once on condition that he not ask for more. Even a courtesan had to be careful. "Meanwhile I warn her that I adore her."

Deftly she disrobed in his presence and put on his drawers; the garment fit, but his breeches were "too tight in the waist . . . and thighs." He attempted to loosen the breeches, but she ripped them apart. She donned his stockings, shoes, and shirt, but as he "arranged the ruffle and the neckband she finds my hands too curious, for her bosom was bare." He shrugged off the "vile names" she called him and reminded himself that he was dealing with a "woman for whom a hundred thousand *scudi* had been paid"— almost a million dollars, but in Venice, women were prized above all else. She put her shift on Casanova, her skirt, and then turned away and scolded him for exposing the "too visible effect of her charms on me," in the form of a quivering erection. Worse, she "refuses me the relief that would have calmed me in an instant." He tried to kiss her again, she resisted, and in the midst of their tussle, "the result of my incontinence visibly stains the shift." This was not the shy youth she'd expected. "My readiness seemed to her a lack of respect." As they bickered, she finished dressing him in her clothes, their erotic spell broken.

They returned to the ball, and the applause their appearance elicited from the guests restored their good humor. "Everyone supposed I had made the conquest that [in reality] escaped me," and to sustain the illusion Giulietta behaved toward him as a lover would. Later that evening, "all the men felt entitled to take liberties with Giulietta in her role as an abate," while

Casanova, cavorting in Giulietta's snug clothing, imbued with the pungent scent of her flesh, "did not restrain myself with the girls." Everyone reveled in the licentious charade, with the exception of Marta and Nanetta. Those generous vestals had believed that Casanova belonged to them alone. Now they understood how naive they had been.

As the ball drew to a conclusion, he removed Giulietta's clothes and attempted to kiss the courtesan, this time more aggressively, while promising to give her "all the satisfaction she deserved." In return for his presumptuous gallantry, "she gave me such a violent box on the ear that I very nearly returned the compliment." It might be slapstick, but it lacked comedy when it was performed on him. He washed his face to rid himself of all traces of Giulietta's makeup and tried to compose himself, but her palm print proved stubborn. When the quarreling couple rejoined the party, the guests saw her angry mark on his cheek, yet she still wasn't done with this infuriating upstart. "Before she left, she took me aside and told me emphatically that if I had any wish to get myself thrown out of a window I had only to come to her house, and that she would have me assassinated if what happened between us became known."

Casanova relented. "I gave her no cause to do either."

Marta and Nanetta were willing to forgive Casanova for abandoning them, and took him back into their hearts and their busy bed, and he resumed his ecclesiastical studies as if nothing had happened.

————•————

After Easter, he returned to Pasiano, where he had again been invited by the Countess of Montereale. There he sampled the Friulian wine and sought out Lucia, but she was nowhere to be found. Intead, he encountered her father, "looking woebegone." Casanova anxiously questioned the old man about his daughter. Was she dead? No, he explained, it was worse than that: Lucia had run off with a courier in the service of Count Daniele and a "famous scoundrel." Casanova was filled with self-reproach. "I had been virtuous enough to leave her a virgin," he reasoned, yet his "foolish restraint" had led to folly and disgrace.

The next time he found himself attracted to a woman, he resolved to behave more boldly. The opportunity arrived when he embarked on a seemingly pointless flirtation with a married woman. She was young, about eighteen or twenty, he judged, and he dismissed her young husband as a complete idiot. On Ascension Day, in late May, he joined a party on a journey by carriage to visit a local society figure. Four of the guests, including the nameless young woman, occupied one carriage, leaving Casanova in the remaining carriage, a two-seater, by himself. To show that she trusted Casanova, one of the young women sat with him, and off they went to the forest of Cecchini.

Half an hour later, the clear skies had become obscured by a violent thunderstorm. Their carriage was covered, but, he warned his companion, the rain would soak her dress. "What do I care about my dress?" she said. "It's the thunder I'm afraid of." The storm gained in fury, and lightning flashed, accompanied by an ear-splitting snarl. A bolt touched down a hundred paces away. As the horses reared up in terror, she threw herself on Casanova, who clutched her tightly, raising her skirt in the process. Another bolt caused her to pitch forward onto him. "Wanting to put the cloak over her again, I draw her toward me; she literally falls on me, and I quickly put her astride me. Since her position could not be more propitious, I lose no time, I adjust myself to it in an instant by pretending to settle my watch in the belt of my breeches." He maneuvered her into position and instructed her to pretend she'd fainted. She fought back and called him "impious monster." No matter. "I clasp her by the buttocks, and carry off the most complete victory that ever a skillful swordsman won." He was completely untroubled by his conquest or its consequences.

The moment they arrived at the Countess's house, she darted from the carriage to her room and bolted the door.

That night at supper, the wife's husband naively remarked that he was certain Casanova would never travel with her again. "Nor I with him," she hissed. "He is an unbeliever who conjured up the lightning with his jokes." Her postcoital aversion to him was palpable, and so, he sighed, "I never found myself alone with her again."

Each of his romances so far had taken a surprising turn. But none can compare in intimacy and mystery to his next love.

———•———

Celebrated, notorious, renowned as the most beautiful in Europe, the women of Venice flaunted the powers granted to them by men and held in reserve additional powers all their own. Venetian women had a style all their own. Outsiders were irresistibly drawn to their seductive, playful, fiery style. One never knew where one stood with a Venetian woman, even a courtesan, and the uncertainty formed part of their allure. They dyed their hair many subtle shades of blond, they wore elaborate makeup, and they regarded their admirers with a provocative expression, the *smorfia*, daring them to try their luck.

Tourists from across the continent came to Venice, considered the most depraved city in Europe, to seduce and be seduced. "These girls of Venice are lighter than a feather," wrote Philippe Monnier, a visitor in search of love. "The Inquisitor cannot sleep a wink on their account. In vain does the Inquisitor search their paper, confiscate their books, shut up their country houses, confine them to their palazzo, command them through their grown-up sons to keep the peace. They muzzle the Inquisitor; they mock his terrors." They seemed capable of *everything*; they could be "dainty, delicate, unabashed, graceful, ravishingly sweet." And still they were mysterious. For this scandalous state of affairs, the Republic's governing body, the secretive Council of Ten, blamed the women, readily identified by their provocative, high-heeled, jewel-studded wooden clogs, called *zoccoli*. A Venetian woman tottering about in *zoccoli* needed the help of her servants just to maintain her balance; for assignations, she exchanged the shoes for slippers adorned with shimmering brocade. "Much, much too convenient," scowled the Doge.

For all their sensuality, Venetian women remained in the thrall of Parisian fashions. At Ascension Day, in May, mannequins displayed the latest French couture and French fabrics. Goldoni satirized this fawning admiration in his farce *Le femmine puntigliose* ("The Fussy Woman"), in which a lady rejects a dress made of *Venetian* fabric. Unlike their French counterparts, Venetian women maintained high standards for personal hygiene, softening their skin to buttery texture with creams and ointments, scenting their bathwater with mint, musk, or myrrh, or hiding beneath a facial mask fashioned from strips of milk-drenched veal.

The pursuit of beauty occupied Venetian women around the clock. By one estimate, they spent seven hours per day at their toilette, much of it with their hairdressers, who applied a rainbow of dyes to make their hair shimmer like spun gold. Venetian women yearned to be blond, and spent hours lightening their hair. Rouge and strong perfume were forbidden, but no beauty in Venice would be considered complete without the *sfrontata* on her nose; the *civetta* or coquette, on a dimple; the *passionata*, a patch at the corner of her eye; and devastating *assassina* in the corner of her mouth.

Venetian woman with a beauty mark, by Pietro Longhi

The hairdressers became confidants, confessors, and at times lovers of the ladies they attended. Despite their finery and allure, married women led cloistered existences; a visiting Frenchman described them as "hidden away from every living soul." Occasionally a Venetian lady would show herself on a balcony, briefly, and that was all. One of the few escapes from this cloistered existence was the gondola, in which she might spend the hours between dusk and dawn floating along the canals. No one knew where she went during these excursions—meeting a lover? attending a séance? gambling in one of the casinos?—not even her husband knew, and the gondoliers were sworn to secrecy. If one gave out details, he risked expulsion from the guild, or drowning. In Venice, with its masks, secrecy, and hidden alleyways, casual murder was a fact of life. In a society consisting of arranged marriages based on lineage and wealth, husbands and wives went their separate ways after fulfilling their duty to produce heirs. Married couples were careful to present themselves at public events such as weddings and funerals, but otherwise they lived separate lives, socially, romantically, and sexually.

When not accompanied by their hairdressers in private, every Venetian woman of fashion went out with a *cavaliere servente*, or *cicisbeo*, an effeminate but not necessarily homosexual companion, who acted as a constant companion in a close-knit yet ambiguous relationship. The *cicisbeo* devoted his time and attention to accommodating his lady's whims. He tended to her hair, her makeup, her wardrobe; he complimented her, he shielded her skin from bright sun, he warned away unpleasant intruders. He accompanied her to public events, clutching her arm, clasping her hand, whispering in her ear. "He is like a shadow at her side," said one observer.

He rode with her in a gondola, shut within the cabin behind Venetian blinds. At day's end, he helped her undress, untying her ribbons, removing her garters, selecting a change of clothing, and accompanying her until she slept. Perhaps he did more than accompany her; no one could say; a *cicisbeo* acted with discretion. If a Venetian husband and wife—he with his young mistress, and she with her young *cicisbeo*—recognized one another at a casino or ball, they took no notice. A French visitor declared that such women were "ten times more married to them than to their husbands."

Unconcerned, the husbands—old, wealthy, and powerful—pursued their commercial interests and visited their mistresses as the mood suited them. Marital annulments in Venice were common, and many members of the nobility, including most of the Doges, or supreme rulers, never bothered to marry. Venetians who did generally stood to inherit dynastic wealth. In a family with three or four sons, the designated heir married, while the others enjoyed a prolonged bachelorhood enlivened by Venice's courtesans, a varied, accomplished, and mercenary lot—as Casanova discovered in his dealings with Giulietta—who aimed to make the most of their informal but widely recognized status. They dressed stylishly and provocatively, and their speech suggested refinement and education. The best of them became celebrities who charged an outrageous fee for their company. "They give the whole of their hearts away," chirped a popular refrain, "and nothing but silver and gold to pay."

The prostitutes of Venice, numerous, anonymous, and generally tolerated, ranked below the courtesans. They gathered after dark beneath church doorways, holding candles, transforming houses of worship into whore-houses. Occasionally a city ordinance banished them; no one paid attention. Inquisition spies, with nothing better to do, obsessively tracked their movements. "Prostitutes are there in plenty," wrote one agent in his official report on coffeehouses. "They are going in all the time, coming out with one man or another, and off to a nearby courtyard or into the alleyways."

In crowded Venice, a narrow passageway illuminated by a guttering candle before an image of the Virgin provided all the shelter a masked couple needed to satisfy their urges. Their pimps, *mangiamarroni*, or "chestnut eaters," argued that they provided a necessary service.

Jean-Jacques Rousseau, the Genevan philosopher of the Enlightenment and revolution, came to Venice in 1743, at the time Casanova was learning his early lessons in love. With prostitutes everywhere, he decided that Venice was "no place to keep away from loose women," and became a regular client of two girls.

Parents hired servants to raise their children and saw the little strangers only at formal occasions such as christenings and funerals. Custom decreed that children wear ostentatious lace coats, sparkling with gold filigree as they made the rounds of tutors and prepared to take their place in Venetian society. Male students without academic aptitude acquired a mistress by the age of sixteen. Girls went directly to the convent, where they remained until they wed, *if* they wed. Since marriages were arranged, they were introduced to their future husbands when they signed the nuptial contracts, briefly luring their new husbands away from their mistresses. Officially, marriage was a sacrament, and unofficially, a punishment. Benedict XIV, whose papacy extended from 1740 to 1758, advised, "You have to marry, so you can enjoy the blessings of widowhood some day."

Couples frequently petitioned the Council of Ten for divorce. For form's sake, there had to be grounds, and the most common was impotence, even if the couple already had children. Once the divorce was granted, the man often escaped to the arms of his mistresses, and the woman took refuge in a convent, seeing only her parents, her lawyer, and her admirers.

Posing as spiritual retreats, the convents of Venice often functioned as genteel brothels attracting pleasure-seeking tourists from across Europe. "The convents . . . had the reputation of favouring assignations," wrote a French visitor. "Indeed, these nuns are the most attractive among all the women in Venice, and if I had to remain a long while here it is to them that I would pay my attentions. All those that I have seen at the celebration of the Mass behind the grating, talking and laughing among themselves all the time, seemed extremely attractive; and their costume enhanced their good looks."

Under these circumstances, two thirds of Venetian aristocrats remained unwed. Several Venetian dynasties became extinct, and by Casanova's day, only forty-two families ruled the Republic, many of them financially over-extended. To replenish the ranks of leadership, the Great Council resorted to selling seats to non-Venetians for one hundred thousand ducats, and even that desperate strategy often failed. When a wealthy merchant reached this apex, he generally retired to his country estates, especially during the languorous summer months. Greek and Jewish merchants took over many of the neglected commercial enterprises. Although the Venetian economy stagnated and its society became even more licentious, the Republic's future still seemed assured. The city-state had endured for a millennium, outlasting dynasties across Europe, but its security, undermined from within, had become an illusion.

———

When Casanova returned to Venice from Padua, he expected to resume his life with his family, but his grandmother's illness prompted him to stay by her side until she died, on March 18, 1743.

The death of Marzia Farussi meant the end of Casanova's youth. "She could leave me nothing, for she had given me all she possessed during her lifetime." As a result, "this death had consequences that obliged me to adopt a new way of life." His mother wrote that she wouldn't be able to return to Venice now, or ever. She would quit the lease on the house in which he lived. Once again, she had abandoned him at the moment he needed support. From then he would have to obey the Abate Grimani, who acted as his guardian. He would sell the furnishings, install Giacomo and his brothers and sister in a respectable boardinghouse, and they would have to fend for themselves. "I called on Signor Grimani to assure him that he would always find me obedient to his commands. The rent for the house was paid until the end of the year." That declaration marked the end of his formal allegiance. He was virtually orphaned. His father was dead, his mother in a foreign country, never to return, and the one person on whom he could rely, his unlettered but loving and protective grandmother, was gone. He was only eighteen years old.

Desperate for funds, he rashly sold all the linen, tapestries, and porcelain in the house, and then disposed of the mirrors and beds. "I knew that I should be taken to task; but it was my father's inheritance, upon which my mother had no claim; I considered myself within my rights. As for my brothers, there would always be time to discuss it." This sale would return to haunt him, but for now the Casanovas fended for themselves as best they could. Fortunately, Grimani placed Maddalena Casanova with an associate, and Francesco Casanova started as an apprentice to Antonio Joli, a stage painter for opera productions at the theaters owned by the Grimanis, San Samuele and San Giovanni Grisostomo. Casanova moved to a house near the latter to see what the future held for him.

Weeks later, at the end of May, Zanetta wrote from Warsaw to say that she had been active on his behalf, lobbying with all her powers of persuasion. "I have made the acquaintance here, my dear son, of a learned Minimite"— this was Bernardino de Bernardis, who belonged to a strict mendicant order of Franciscan monks—"whose great qualities made me think of you every time he honored me with a visit." Not for nothing was his mother an actress. Now she played the part of impresario, arranging a choice role for her son the priest, demonstrating her affection, at a distance. The two arrived at an arrangement. Bernardino would assume responsibility for Casanova if she could persuade the Queen of Poland, a great personage to whom she had access at court, to appoint him to a bishopric. "I flung myself at Her Majesty's feet," Zanetta told her son, "and I found favor."

The Pope appointed Bernardino de Bernardis the Bishop of Martirano in Calabria on May 16, and in preparation for his new life, Casanova moved out of his boardinghouse and into the Seminary of Saint Cipriano on the island of Murano, where as a child he'd visited the witch who'd cured him of his mysterious afflictions. It was only a short distance from the Grimani theaters, but Murano and its seminary were a world away from the life Casanova had come to know.

"Good-bye, Venice!" Casanova exclaimed. "Absolutely certain that the highest fortune would be mine at the end of the course, I could not wait to enter upon it." He told himself that he was done with childish things, and "in the future I shall concern myself with all that is great and substantial." Signor Malipiero, who had come to know Casanova, foibles and all, expressed delight "when he saw me on the verge of setting out to fulfill my destiny elsewhere." Once again, he was bound to serve God as a priest, without the women who ruled his passions.

———•———

Signor Malipiero looked after two other protégées in addition to Casanova, both women. One was Teresa Imer, the other a gondolier's daughter, Gardela by name, three years younger than Casanova. Accordingly, he called her the Gardela girl. She was taking dancing lessons to improve her chances in life. "The ball cannot go into the pocket unless someone gives it a push," Malipiero quipped, and she would enjoy a brilliant career as an actress and mistress to a wealthy patron. One day, Malipiero invited all three to dine with him, then excused himself to take a siesta. Next, Gardela excused herself to take a lesson, leaving Casanova alone with Teresa Imer. He found her attractive, but never dared to flirt with the creature, who had been protected by her mother. On this occasion, the two "in our innocent gaiety" decided "to compare the differences between our shapes," one of his favorite gambits. "We were at a most interesting point in the examination when a violent blow from a cane descended on my neck, followed by another, which would have been followed by yet more, if I had not escaped from the hailstorm at top speed by running out of the room." Recovering from the shock at his temporary lodgings, he received a messenger bearing the hat and cloak he had left behind together with a note from Malipiero's housekeeper warning him "never again to dare to set foot in His Excellency's palace."

His irate retort—"You struck me in anger, hence, you cannot boast of having given me a lesson. By the same token I have learned nothing"—had no effect. Malipiero had banished Giacomo Casanova, as "the whole town laughed at the story" and Teresa refused to utter a word in his defense.

Casanova endured these wrenching dislocations with equanimity and even excitement. Routine dulled his appetite for life; change, voluntary or not, whetted it. He was much happier improvising as he went. A new challenge confronted him: a messenger with a sinister appearance—black wig, tan visage, and scarlet cloak—gave him a missive from Signor Grimani "directing me to put all the furniture in the house at his disposition." Reviewing the items with the messenger, Casanova admitted that he had sold the furniture to avoid debt.

Grimani denounced Casanova and ordered him out of the house. "Beside myself with rage, I start off to find a Jew to whom I can sell whatever is left," Casanova reported. At the time, the Jews of Venice inhabited the original Ghetto. (In Venetian dialect, the word *ghèto* refers to the molten metal pouring from local foundries.) Many ran pawnshops and gave out loans to bankrupt noblemen, luckless gamblers, and anyone else who could offer security.

Along the way, he was served with a summons from Antonio Razzetta, the man who'd worn the black wig and scarlet cloak. When Casanova tried to enter the family house, he discovered it had been sealed, and even his bedroom was off limits, for now. Keeping his wits about him, Casanova arranged for the house to be opened the following day and for a lawyer to summon Razzetta, but he needed a place to spend the night, and so he lodged with his "angels," whoever the women were.

After another day or two of legal maneuvering, Casanova received an invitation to visit Grimani, who demanded that the young man explain his defiance. The confrontation ended in a truce: Grimani supplied Casanova with a room on the ground floor of a home that he owned in San Giovanni Grisostomo. "Have your clothes and books taken there and come to dine with me every day," he instructed. "I put your brother in a good house and your sister in a good house, so everything is settled." He discovered that the second floor of this house was occupied by a young dancer known as La Tintoretta, the stage name of Margherita Giovanna Grisellini. He would remain for six months until he resumed his studies for the priesthood, and take his initial steps along what he now called "the road to the Papacy." He immediately punctured his own delusions of grandeur. "Such were my castles in Spain."

He naturally studied La Tintoretta, judging her a "mediocre dancer but an intelligent girl who was neither pretty nor ugly." She occasionally alternated her current lover, Prince Waldeck, with her prior protector, Girolamo Lin, older but a patrician. One day she invited Casanova to a reception in her second-floor apartment, "taking off her glove to give me her hand to kiss." Although a Venetian, she insisted on speaking French. "I begged her to speak the language of our country," he recalled, because he didn't know French. They exchanged gifts, a "very bad" sonnet he had arranged to be printed for her, and a gold snuffbox for him. If he weren't planning on becoming a bishop and perhaps Pope, he would have fallen in love with her. The mere fact of his proximity to her caused his mother to write to Grimani to find Casanova a more "decent and dignified dwelling." She wanted him out of Venice and arranged for him to follow the newly appointed Bishop of Martorano to his new post within several months. Meanwhile, the priests supervising his education transferred him to a seminary, before he fell prey to the snares of the world. "Their idea was sheer madness," Casanova snorted, but in the end, he agreed.

Attired as a seminarian, Casanova traveled to the monasteries of Murano and San Cipriano, where stillness, silence, and piety reigned, and where it seemed that legions of Romans, Etruscans, and other invaders had departed only the other day. In these surroundings, he would lead an elemental yet refined existence.

"I was shown three rooms in which there were at least a hundred and fifty seminarians, ten or twelve classrooms, the refectory, the dormitory, the gardens for walks during the hours of recreation, and I was given to expect that my life here would be the happiest a young man could desire." All of it, burnished by the monks' eloquence, "made me laugh." Only the night before he had slept with two women he jokingly called his "wives." They had "sprinkled the bed with their tears mingled with mine." Two angels!

The girls occupied his thoughts during the gondola ride to Murano when he was seized with a fit of vomiting. Bewildered, the priests plied him with remedies, wholly unaware that "the attack was the effect of the amorous efforts I had made all night with my two angels, whom I feared I was holding in my arms for the last time." He stumbled off in the direction of his dormitory, where his trunk, cloak, and hat awaited him. He expected to be put into a class with adults because of his height, but he wasn't old enough. He told the rector he wished to join the school of doctrinal theology, to learn the history of the Church, yet when the time came to take a simple exam, he sabotaged himself, and was placed in a class consisting of nine- and ten-year-old boys, to whom he grandly explained that he was actually a doctor. Later that day, the rector confronted him: "Why did you pretend ignorance at your examination?" to which Casanova retorted, "Why were you so unjust as to make me take it?" He later forged a bond with a fifteen-year-old seminarian. "Within four days we became such fond friends that we were jealous of each other. We sulked when one of us left to walk with anyone else."

Sleeping in the dormitory proved more difficult. A prefect, "whose principal duty was to make very sure that no seminarian got into bed with another," presided. Masturbation was strictly forbidden. Such restrictions outraged Casanova. "Ignorant fools," he protested, and cited the example of schoolboys in Germany who responded to similar rules by masturbating even more. "The healthy man" needs release, yet the "prohibition stimulates him," he declared. Schoolboys masturbated "in order to have the pleasure of disobeying, a pleasure natural to all men since the time of Eve and Adam." In this regard, he preferred to side with the mother superiors of convents, who "know from experience that there is not a girl who does not begin masturbating at the age of seven, and they never think of forbidding them this childish practice, although it can produce unfortunate results in girls, too, though less extensive because the excretion is slight."

Nine days after arriving at the seminary, Casanova was startled to find his young friend crawling into bed with him, but the prank alarmed him; they risked committing "the oldest of crimes." At that moment, the prefect caught the two together. Casanova's friend, fleeing the dormitory, knocked the prefect flat, and ran into the darkness.

The next day, the rector promised to protect the anonymity of the two offenders so long as they came to him to confess. The matter would have ended there if Casanova hadn't decided to visit the same boy in his dormitory a few nights later. This time, they bungled their escape, and their lies only made matters worse. Even Casanova couldn't talk his way out of a severe punishment: "Four menservants seized us, tied our arms together behind our backs, brought us back inside, and made us kneel down before the great crucifix." With the boys thus terrorized, the rector preached a sermon, and servants went to work. "I then felt seven or eight strokes from the rope or stick rain down on my shoulders, all of which, like my stupid companion, I took without uttering a single word of complaint." The pain was excruciating; his body soon recovered, but his mind would take much longer than that.

The moment he was freed, he asked for permission to write a few lines to place "at the foot of the crucifix." In them, he protested his innocence. The letter spurred protests among the seminarians, who drove away the rector "amid a storm of whistles and catcalls"—to no avail. The rector ordered all the offenders confined to a prison on the sixth floor of the monastery. Merely climbing the steps was a form of penance. Casanova fretted in a cell with only his bed for company, and two meals a day. On the fourth day, a priest he knew, Tosello, arrived to commiserate. "The rector refuses to admit he is wrong." In that case, Casanova would flee with Tosello's help. They made for a Jesuit monastery, where Tosello abandoned him "without a *soldo* and possessed of nothing but what I had."

He refreshed himself at the home of some acquaintances, and sought out his two female angels for some sport, but soon he was on his way to have supper with his brother Francesco, now living in a boardinghouse where "tyranny was as heavy on him as it was on me." Casanova promised to free his brother. First, he visited the pair of girls he'd taken calling his "little wives, but, I confess to my shame, worry disabled love, despite the two weeks I had spent in abstinence." He vowed that the following night when they met he would be in an altogether different state. After spending a morning in the elegant Marciana Library in the Piazza San Marco, he was approached by a soldier who informed him that a gondola awaited Casanova; the announcement made him cringe. "I loathed scandal and the disgrace of publicity." Not exactly: he thrived on it.

The gondola, as he expected, belonged to Grimani. He entered into the dark cabin, the curtain drew back, and the craft silently slid toward the Lido, the long sandbar on the outskirts of Venice, known at this time for the fortress of Sant'Andrea. Casanova still had no idea what would befall him at this semi-remote location. He found himself confined to a guardhouse. Another soldier explained that he would remain there, receiving a soldier's meager pay, ten soldi a day. Exhausted, he "spent a sleepless night in the company of some Slavonian soldiers who did nothing but sing, eat garlic, smoke tobacco that poisoned the air, and drink Slavonian wine. It is like ink, and only a Slavonian can drink it."

He supped with the major, his wife, and several officers, whom he diverted with his "natural gaiety" and a three-hour narrative of his adventures and difficulties since the death of his grandmother. They all tried to turn his struggle into a joke, and they went to bed in good humor. Whenever people stopped to listen to his misfortune, he reflected, "I inspired in them friendliness enough to take my part and be useful to me." The trick, he explained, was to reveal even the most embarrassing parts and blameworthy deeds. "I believe that a guilty man who dares to admit his guilt to a just judge is more likely to be absolved than an innocent man who equivocates." Casanova was just such a man.

He had stumbled across his métier. Recounting his various escapades, defying authorities, seducing and being seduced by women and then telling stories about it served as entertainment, confession, penance, and validation. He had discovered his favorite subject: himself.

———•———

On the morning of April 2, 1743, his eighteenth birthday, or as an irritable Giacomo Casanova put it, "the fatal day of my entrance into this world," he encountered a "beautiful Greek woman" who beseeched him for help. She claimed her husband hadn't been promoted because she wouldn't sleep with his commanding officer. If only Casanova could write a petition on behalf of her poor husband, she would thank him with all her heart. He wrote the letter, but she resisted his advances "as a matter of form" until she yielded to him. The encounter was so enjoyable that he returned for more, and "she comes and rewards me yet again."

Two days later, he discovered she'd given him a case of venereal disease. He castigated the beautiful Greek woman for her "base conduct," but she replied that it was *his* responsibility to take precautions. "Burning with fury, she treated me to every insult that an outraged woman could hurl at a man who had presumed to forget himself." He bowed deeply and excused himself from her presence as she denounced him as a "conceited ass."

He was reminded of his shame weeks later, on Ascension Day in May, when his two angels—still nameless—visited him at his fortress on the Lido to view the annual ceremony of the marriage of Venice and sea, highlighted by the tossing of the wedding ring into the waves. When they were alone, he recalled, the girls "flung themselves on my neck, thinking I would quickly give them good proof of my constancy." But not while he suffered from his venereal inflammation. "Alas! I gave them only a profusion of kisses, pretending to be afraid that someone would come in," and the reunion sputtered to a conclusion.

As the days and weeks in the fortress dragged on, he fell victim to melancholy. In the oppressive June heat, as he watched sunlight sift aimlessly through the gloom, he became bored, unhappy, and angry. In the midst of the doldrums, he was visited accompanied by one of his tormentors, Razzetta, the emissary from Grimani with the tan complexion, black wig, and scarlet cloak. The hatred between the two men became so intense that Razzetta prepared to strike his enemy with a cane, but was restrained.

Casanova lusted for escape. He speculated that "a boat under my window into which I could drop, could put me in Venice for the night and bring me back to the fortress before dawn, after I had accomplished my purpose." A few zecchini purchased the services of a boatman named Biago who agreed to approach Casanova's window at nightfall. When the boatman maneuvered into position, Casanova lowered himself into the craft, and the two vigorously rowed to Venice, disembarking at the Riva degli Schiavoni, the broad waterfront promenade beside Saint Mark's Square.

Disguised in a sailor's cloak, Casanova found his way to Razzetta's house, waiting until he saw his prey approaching from the Campo San Polo. That was all he needed to know, and he swiftly returned to the fortress, with none the wiser for his brief absence.

A few days later, Casanova pretended to sprain his ankle badly enough to be confined to bed in his room, where he encouraged his attendants to drink themselves senseless. As they lay in a stupor, he returned to Venice in the boat with Biago, and went straight to a narrow canal beside the Campo San Polo. It seemed "made on purpose for me to throw my enemy into." When Razzetta approached, Casanova raised his cudgel and smacked him on the head, on the arm, and with still more blows pushed him into the fetid canal. He fled across the square "like a bird," traversed the canal, and climbed aboard the boat in which he'd arrived. Returning to his room at Sant'Andrea by midnight, he feigned convulsions to awaken his sleeping caretakers, surreptitiously tossed out the potions they administered to treat it, and fell asleep. He awoke to the "great news" that Razzetta had been beaten and tossed into the canal, yet survived. "All the better for you, for your case would be much worse. Everyone is convinced that it was you who committed the crime."

Suffering a broken nose, missing teeth, and painful bruises, Razzetta yearned to punish his attacker, but a formal investigation cleared Casanova, who had been the suspect, but was believed to have an alibi, and Razzetta, the victim, had to pay court costs. What a crazy affair! With a combination of guile and luck, Casanova had gotten away with attempted murder and made a reputation as a young man not to be trifled with.

Shortly afterward, he petitioned for his release from Sant'Andrea, and to his surprise, he received it. In jest, he told the major in charge that "I preferred his house to the city of Venice," and the major responded by confining him to the fortress for an extra week. During that time, he was joined by an illustrious cell mate, Count Giuseppe Bonafede, a Florentine who'd settled in Venice and occasionally spied for the Republic. Of greater interest was the Count's visiting fifteen-year-old daughter, "who struck me as a beauty of a new kind. She was light blonde, with large blue eyes, an aquiline nose, and a fine mouth." Furthermore, "her figure was so slight that it seemed artificial, and her bosom, which was broad above, revealed itself as a splendid tablet unbroken save by two little rosebuds, rather far apart."

As they strolled around the fortress, the Signorina boasted of her sketches of Adam and Eve. He assumed her Eve would be lifelike and Adam idealized, but she corrected him: Adam displayed every single muscle. The innuendo became so intense that he "became indecent and quite unable to hide the fact, for, the heat being intense, I was wearing linen breeches." The situation became even more dire when she lost one of her shoes; as he knelt to replace it on her foot, he looked up and realized she wore nothing under her skirt. The glimpse "very nearly made me drop dead." The awkward flirtation "made me feel so ashamed that I hated myself and did not doubt that she not only hated me in return but despised me."

On the eighth day of his additional confinement, Casanova obtained his formal release from the fortress. He spent his first night of liberty with his two angels. In the morning, he went to see Grimani in the company of the major. Surprised by Grimani's advice to "forgive Razzetta," Casanova confessed that he had cudgeled the brute. The admission was met with disbelief. How could Casanova have done this while confined in the fortress with a sprained ankle? Perhaps he'd devised the perfect alibi, after all.

He called on the young Contessa whom he'd met at the fortress. "Going to see an angel, I believed that I should enter a corner of Paradise." Instead, "I find myself in a drawing room in which was nothing but three or four rotting wooden chairs and an old, dirty table." This was not the splendid nobility he had imagined when he first encountered the Count and his daughter; they were *barnabotti*, the destitute nobility who subsisted on meager charity, centered around the parish of San Barnaba, from which they took their name. Even in reduced circumstances, they kept their seats in the Great Council, but, uneducated and undesirable, the *barnabotti* toiled as shopkeepers or lived on public charity. Free housing was available for this privileged but disenfranchised caste so long as they refrained from marriage and children. They were so poor that they pawned their good clothing, went without eating for days to collect a few coins, and attended mass regularly so that their names remained on the church's charity rolls.

Casanova uttered a few words of consolation to the girl, who was ready to display her drawings of Adam and Eve. Explaining "I have long been accustomed to poverty," she showed him her spare room containing a table, chair, a small mirror, and "a bed turned up so that only the bottom of the mattress was visible. The spectator was thus left free to imagine that there were sheets." But there were none. A "stench of no recent date" overwhelmed him. "Never was a lover more quickly cured." He wanted to fling a handful of zecchini at this pitiable family and flee. Instead, he forced himself to view the girl's drawings. They showed talent, and he asked why she didn't learn to paint, in the hope of selling her wares. She explained that a box of colors cost two zecchini, more than she could afford. He offered her six, and she tearfully accepted. "I placed a kiss on her lips that she was free to believe came from tenderness." He promised to return, but ten years would pass before he saw the young Contessa again.

"What a lesson!" he reflected after his departure, as he pondered the ways women inflame and deceive men by appealing to the imagination. And most men were only too willing to be deceived in the name of love.

When the time came to leave Venice for the South of Italy to join the Bishop of Martorano, Casanova accompanied the Venetian Ambassador to Ancona, a seaport located on the Adriatic about two hundred and fifty miles south of Venice. Neither as grand nor as debauched as Venice, Ancona boasted a large cathedral dating to the thirteenth century, and hosted an expanding Jewish population that invigorated the city's economy. Casanova couldn't wait to go, but first he visited his two angels, "who were certain that they would never see me again," which meant that they "spent the night between joy and sorrow, between laughter and tears."

There remained the necessity of packing his belongings, his papers, and, he added, "all the forbidden books I owned," without specifying what they might be. The Venetian Inquisition considered books about mysticism and the Kabbalah blasphemous, and in all likelihood these were books on those subjects. Casanova had no idea how long he would be gone from Venice; perhaps he never would return. His landlady of the moment predicted his absence would last no more than a year; with her extensive knowledge of the world she'd never been wrong, or so she said.

One last thing: Grimani, relieved to see the reckless boy depart, gave him ten zecchini, sufficient to sustain him. En route he lost the ten zecchini, and thirty more of his own, playing faro, an addictive card game involving a single deck, a banker, and several punters, or gamblers, who won or lost according to whether or not exposed cards matched. When the game was played strictly according to the rules, the house, or bank, had practically no advantage, so in time gambling establishments everywhere devised subtle ways to dupe the punters. This was precisely what happened to Casanova. To raise funds for another round of gambling, he pawned the contents of his trunk, bet the proceeds, and lost it all again.

As he prepared for bed, he saw "the loathsome signs of the same malady of which I had been cured less than two months before. I went to sleep stupefied. I woke eleven hours later, but I was so utterly dejected that I continued to drowse." He couldn't bear bringing his condition to the attention of a doctor, or to return to Venice. "My life had become a burden to me," he lamented. Instead, he continued the journey, refusing to eat, "in a state of complete apathy," finding relief only when he bedded a flirtatious housekeeper. For a while he forgot "all the causes of gloom that could not but overwhelm any reasonable man," hesitating at the point of committing what he called an "unforgivable sin," that is, transmitting his stubborn venereal disease. But she was alluring; there was no turning back, and so he possessed her, enjoying his sweet release as he managed to conceal his condition from her.

———•———

At last he arrived by boat in Ancona. A loyal Venetian, he considered the port inferior, "except for a dike built at great expense." He disembarked, prepared to endure twenty-eight days of quarantine in a *lazaretto* on suspicion of harboring plague. Wearily accustomed to this form of confinement, "I rented from the Jews a bed, table, some chairs, the hire for which I was to pay at the end of the quarantine." A monk, Frate Steffano, kept him company, slept on straw, and won his trust. Before long Casanova was telling him of his "sad situation," which, to his surprise, delighted the monk, who proposed an arrangement. He would take care of the young man if he in turn would write letters for the monk, who could scrawl his name (with either hand, he boasted), but that was all. Casanova naturally agreed, adding passages in Latin as the monk directed ("even the ones addressed to women"). Occasionally he corrected the monk's shaky grasp of ecclesiastical history, only to be rebuffed, and when he refused to write any more, the monk threatened to stop feeding him.

Casanova planned to journey on foot to Loreto, in the province of Ancona, the seat of the Basilica della Santa Casa, a sacred destination popular with pilgrims. "I reached that holy city tired to death. It was the first time in my life that I had done fifteen miles on foot, drinking nothing but water." At a comfortable inn he slept for ten hours. Refreshed, he hiked inland for hours to the town of Muccia, where he tried jumping over a ditch and sprained his ankle "so painfully I could not walk another step." He had no recourse except to pray for help. Deliverance arrived an hour later in the form of a peasant, who transported him to Serravale, where he passed writhing in agony on a bed of straw in a peasant's house.

At last a surgeon came to examine Casanova's ankle, prescribed three days' rest, and arranged to have his patient transported to an inn. On the fourth day, he was ready to be on his way, but there remained the awkward necessity of settling the bill. Casanova had only his riding coat to offer; it was raining, and he dreaded giving it away, but he had no choice. Frate Steffano, making the same journey, but at a slower pace, appeared, "laughing like a madman." The coincidence astonished the young man, who wondered about the role Providence played in his life, "yet I felt comforted when I saw this fool, this rascal, this ignorant scoundrel appear, because I did not doubt for a moment that he would rescue me from my difficulties."

When the mismatched pair of pilgrims finally reached Rome, the Bishop was no longer there, having left instructions for Casanova to meet him in Naples. Casanova finally caught up with his elusive quarry in the remote village of Martorano, Calabria. It was quickly apparent to both that this grim setting would never do. The Bishop sent Casanova back to Rome bearing letters of introduction to Cardinal Acquaviva and a priest, Father Georgi, reputed to be on good terms with the Pope. "Don't make any acquaintances without consulting me," Father Georgi advised Casanova. And avoid the coffeehouses. "If you must go, listen and do not talk." And when Casanova presented his credentials to the Cardinal, he must dress as a "modest abate."

Armed with this advice, Casanova ambled about Rome. In the coffeehouses, he listened to "harsh criticism" of the Pope and various ministers without interjecting his opinion. After a week, he concluded that "there is not a Catholic Christian city in the world where people were less strict in matters of religion than they are in Rome." In the laissez-faire Eternal City, they ate meat on Saturdays: the transgression gave him pause. "The Romans are like the employees at the tobacco monopoly, who are allowed to take away as much as they pleased for nothing."

Despite the permissive climate, he wrote, that "I finally made up my mind to be tonsured," as if for the first time. Perhaps the act signified a fresh start. The Cardinal finally received him, and admonished the neophyte to start learning French, the language of diplomacy.

Even at this sensitive time, he began a flirtation with two sisters, Angelica and Lucrezia. But before he went any further with them, he slipped into a coffeehouse, where he encountered a "pretty-faced abate. His hips and thighs make me think him a girl in disguise." The abate in question was Beppino della Mammana, the stage name of Giuseppe Ricciarelli, a well-known castrato. "He gives me a bold look and says that he will serve me as a boy or girl, whichever I choose." Casanova took the offer in stride, preferring the company of Lucrezia. She was married, but her situation heightened the excitement of conquest. His opportunity arrived as they sauntered through the lush garden of a villa, where he asked her, as his opening gambit, to explain, "out of the metaphysics of your love, how it can be that at this moment I feel as if I were about to plunge into the delights of love with you for the first time." She glanced in his direction, but said nothing. Encouraged, he searched for an "altar to Venus," where they could "sacrifice until we perish." Even if the Pope surprised them *in flagrante*, they wouldn't cease; indeed, he'd bless them, wouldn't he? They found a suitable spot in an arbor where turf has been molded into the shape of a bed. "We looked at it and laughed. It was an eloquent bed," and their moment arrived. "Intensely serious, looking only into each other's eyes, we unlaced, we unbuttoned, our hearts throbbed, our hands hurried to calm their impatience."

They spent two hours engaged in bursts of "combat," at the end of which they looked into one another's eyes, saying, "Love, I thank thee." They kissed again, but when Lucrezia saw that "she was restoring me to life," she broke off and suggested they dress. Even then, they settled into a "long, narrow seat without a back, which could be straddled like a riding mule," where the "combat began and was proceeding vigorously," but this time their climax proved difficult to achieve, and so "we put it off until we should be face to face in the darkness of night to the music of four trotting horse."

In the carriage they laughed their way to the lush gardens of Tivoli, with its pools, cascades, water jets, and fountains, where they would spend the night at her brother-in-law's house. "We passed two hours face to face in the carriage playing a comedy that we could not finish. Arriving at their house, we had to ring down the curtain." The acts of love concluded, and time resumed. "I went to bed rather tired; but a good sleep restored me completely." The next morning, only the memory of the "pretty-faced" castrato who offered to serve him either as a man or as a woman disturbed his thoughts.

———•———

Attending receptions at the palace of "my master the Cardinal," he attracted the attention of a certain Marchesa G. who spoke a few words to him in French, but he always responded in Italian to avoid appearing foolish. He was afraid of falling for the Marchesa, or encouraging her interest in him, because he already loved Lucrezia. Yet others noticed, including the Portuguese Abate Gama, who asked Casanova if he occasionally visited her home. "You need not have yourself announced," the abate explained. "Simply go to see her when the double doors of the room are open. You will find it full of people paying her court." And so he did.

Casanova first encountered the urbane Benedict XIV, who had given such memorable advice about marriage. With the Reformation easing, the mood in Rome relaxed and the papacy with it. Like many others, Casanova found Pope Benedict "learned," and "a man who liked his joke, and extremely agreeable." His witticisms had gained currency in Rome and beyond. In France, Voltaire, notorious for his relentless attacks on the Church, saw fit to dedicate one of his works to this Pope. About the worst that others had to say about him was that he wrote too much and governed too little. The Pope supported libraries, especially ecclesiastical ones, and founded academies to promote the study of law, church history, and antiquity. It was now known to all that the youthful Venetian abate had met the Holy Father.

And then he paid court to the Marchesa, as she had "more or less commanded" him to do. Moving without hesitation from the sacred to the profane, he entered her reception room. She smiled. He bowed. Something else was expected of him, some token of his fealty to her. Instead, he went to dinner. "She was pretty, and a power in Rome; but I could not bring myself to crawl. Roman manners exasperated me." So he did nothing.

———•———

In November he reasserted himself with Lucrezia in Tivoli, sixteen miles from Rome. Sharing a phaeton with Lucrezia's family, he found himself drawn to another sister, Cecilia. He interpreted her remarks as a "very clear declaration of love. I was almost paralyzed"—especially when Lucrezia reached over and shook him, demanding to know what Cecilia had said. Casanova told her the truth, and she promised to "take her sister in hand."

After a day touring the sights of Tivoli, they returned home, "exhausted and dying of hunger," indulged in a supper of "exquisite dishes and the excellent wine of Tivoli," and went to bed. But matters were not quite that simple. Casanova was separated from a third sister, Angelica, by means of a locked door, for which he had the key. "I put my eye to the keyhole," he recalled, and watched Lucrezia and Angelica enter. They sat on the couch, and seventeen-year-old Angelica, "the virgin, unaware that she was observed, takes off even her shift and in this striking array crosses to the other side of the room. Lucrezia extinguishes the night light, blows out the candles, and lies down, too."

In the dark, Casanova slowly opened the door with his key, and approached Lucrezia. And then, "I never undressed more quickly. I opened the door and fell into the arms of Lucrezia," who told Angelica to hold her tongue. In less than a minute, they became a "single being" as "the raging fire scorch[ed] us; it would have burned us had we tried to restrain it." They commenced a prolonged "combat, which, enchanting all our senses, could have no fault but that of ending too soon; but I excelled at the art of prolonging it."

The entwined couple slept until dawn. "Beware your sister," Casanova whispered to Lucrezia, "she might turn and see us."

Seizing on the idea, Lucrezia commanded her virgin sister, "Turn and see what awaits you when love makes you his slave."

Lucrezia beseeched her little sister to forgive them, and invoked "the power of Love" to excuse her behavior. Then she went a step further: "Telling me to kiss her, Lucrezia gets on the other side of me and enjoys the spectacle of her sister in my arms, languishing and showing no signs of resistance." Casanova "clasped her frenziedly, at the same time reveling in the ecstasy I saw on the face of Angelica, who was witnessing so splendid a combat for the first time." Then Lucrezia pushed him on top of Angelica, who "clasps me to her bosom so strongly that she achieves happiness"—her orgasm—"almost without my participation." Lucrezia was thrilled to see her sister succumb to passion. She mopped Casanova's brow, and then "perished for the third time."

When Casanova entered the drawing room an hour later, he was "delighted to see that my fair conquests look fresh and rosy. Donna Lucrezia was perfectly relaxed, Angelica gayer than usual and radiant." The idyll wouldn't last for much longer. Lucrezia's husband was about to return after an extended absence.

After the family departed, Casanova, abruptly isolated, "was left in the state of lassitude to which a young man succumbs when his heart is empty." He passed his days in his room, summarizing and cataloguing the Cardinal's correspondence. It was meticulous, dreary labor.

The Marchesa G. fluttered across the periphery of his consciousness, but "her manner to me was cool." Perhaps word of his exploits in Tivoli had reached her, for she told the Cardinal that his young secretary was working hard to cure his grief. All the while, Casanova maintained that his love for Lucrezia, though real, was entirely innocent. The fiction proved sufficient for the Marchesa to declare her deep personal interest in him "under cover of her grandeur." No one, he explained, would have seen anything inappropriate in her interest in him. "A young abate like myself of no importance could only aspire to her protection." Peering into the near future, he judged her worthy of "succeeding Donna Lucrezia," for she was "beautiful, young, intelligent, witty, highly cultivated, well-read, and a power in Rome." He would naturally feign obliviousness to her designs on him, and even to hint that he "loved her without daring to hope."

After days of intricate maneuvering and writing sonnets in the hope of winning her admiration, he came face-to-face with her one evening on a balustrade; they stood so close to one another that her knee pressed against the pocket containing his watch. "I adore you, Signora," he blurted out, but "if you do not permit me hope, I will never to see you again. Pronounce sentence on me."

And so she did. "I believe you are a libertine and inconstant."

"I am neither," he insisted, and "saluted her lips with an amorous kiss."

He tried to tear off her clothes. *Not now!* she said. She tried to convince him that she and the Cardinal were merely good friends as Casanova claimed to be with Lucrezia, and so he decided to "wait for another day to obtain a greater favor." Without warning, His Eminence appeared, offering copious, if suspect, apologies for keeping them waiting.

As word of the understanding between Casanova and the Marchesa spread, Father Georgi warned him not to give her up for someone else. Those in Rome preferred to think of matters as they should be rather than as they were. And in Casanova's case, Rome, in the person of Cardinal Aquaviva, was changing its mind about him. What would it mean to his future?

Chapter 3

Bellino

During the season of Lent, Cardinal Acquaviva summoned Giacomo Casanova on the pretext that the young man had been tangentially involved in a scandal concerning an elopement. "I find myself obliged to ask you to leave not only my service but Rome as well," he told the young man. To save face, he would be permitted to "announce to the world" that he was carrying out the Cardinal's business. "You must be ready to leave in a week," he advised. "Believe me, I am really sorry to lose you," he added, as the young man yielded to tears.

Seeking solace in the gardens at the Villa Borghese, "I walked for two hours in desperation, for I loved Rome and, having started on the high road to fortune, I saw myself as an outcast not knowing which way to turn and with all my hopes blighted." If only he'd paid attention to subtle signs, and listened more attentively to Father Georgi's advice. The Cardinal summoned him once again. "I described the grief I felt at leaving him," Casanova said, "painting it in the liveliest colors." His tearful pleas lasted a full hour, but the Cardinal would not be moved, asking Casanova where he wished to go next.

"The word which despair and resentment"—combined with calculation—"brought to my lips was 'Constantinople,'" the ancient capital of the Ottoman Empire, where the Venetian Ambassador's office was undergoing a reorganization. Casanova wiped away his tears, considering his choice the result of "the mysterious power of my Genius, summoning there in concert with my destiny," as the Cardinal realized the advantages of transferring the young abate to a posting nearly a thousand miles from Rome. At length he said, "You can tell everyone that I am sending you to Constantinople, for nobody will believe you" and extended his hand for Casanova to kiss.

He hadn't the slightest idea what to do in Constantinople or whom to see? The Cardinal, who'd boasted of friends everywhere, remained silent on the subject. Although the prospect of adventure cheered Casanova, he was devastated by "having to leave the Marchesa G., with whom I was in love, and from whom I had obtained nothing of consequence."

Before leaving Rome, he visited his friends and lovers and would-be lovers, including Angelica, now married. He hadn't been invited to her wedding. But he did receive the Pope's blessing. "I was not surprised to hear him tell me of his acquaintances in Constantinople." In addition, the Holy Father bestowed "a rosary of agates connected by a thin gold chain," adding with a note of deflation, "which might be worth twelve *zecchini*." The Cardinal, in contrast, showered him with coins "worth seven hundred *zecchini*" to add to the three hundred he had managed to save.

Adequately funded for once, he took his leave of Rome in a compact, elegant coach known as a berlin. Beside him sat a mother accompanying her daughter to Loreto to fulfill a religious vow, but "the girl was ugly. I was bored during the whole journey."

———————

In Ancona once again, Casanova lodged at the city's most comfortable inn on the night of February 25, 1744. He ordered meat for dinner, but the innkeeper reminded him that it was Lent. Casanova impudently responded that he'd received special dispensation from the Pope to eat meat. He'd just come from Rome where different rules applied, or no rules at all! He was on his way to Constantinople on a confidential mission, for God's sake, and he wanted meat! "I swear, I curse; whereupon a solemn-looking individual comes out of a room and proceeds to tell me that I was *wrong* to want to eat meat, since fish was better in Ancona." Momentarily humbled, the impatient Venetian compared the lodger's "cool common sense with my hasty petulance," acknowledging that "he is worthy of teaching me a thing or two." With that, Casanova devoured his supper.

The man, a Spaniard in the service of the army, gave his name as Sancho Pico, invited Giacomo to listen to some music, and offered to introduce him to an actress lodging at the inn. "The word 'actress' roused my curiosity," Casanova confessed. Instead of an actress, he noticed a "youth" of indeterminate gender who struck him as "ravishingly handsome" and "not more than sixteen or seventeen years old" who was dining with his family: his mother, brother, and a sister or two. "The family came from Bologna and made a living by its talents. Affability and lightheartedness made up for their poverty." The child of actors, Casanova found himself among the sort of people he knew, itinerant merchants of art and seduction, gypsies of the soul and thieves of the heart. They all played their parts until fantasy overwhelmed reality.

It was a well-known castrato called Bellino who had caught his eye. Castrati had been a fixture in Italian music ever since the mid-sixteenth century. The castration itself consisted of removing the testicles or cutting the ducts that carried blood to them, usually with the patient insensate from opium. The practice received religious blessing when, in 1588, Pope Sixtus V took a verse from Corinthians—"Let your women keep silence in church; it is not permitted unto them to speak"—to ban women from choirs and stages. Their roles went instead to castrati. In time, some composers came to prefer the voices of castrati. Monteverdi's opera *L'Orfeo*

Farinelli, the famous castrato, in costume

(1607) featured their sweet, poignant, spine-tingling voices, and by the seventeenth century, Christoph Willibald Gluck and George Frideric Handel were casting castrati in leading operatic roles. Farinelli, Scalzi, Senesio were all celebrated castrati, in demand and wealthy, with an appeal to women, especially. In years to come, even Napoleon would become a connoisseur of castrati, known by genteel euphemism of *musico* or occasionally *evirato*. According to one estimate, no fewer than four thousand boys were castrated each year at about the time Casanova encountered Bellino. They performed throughout Europe, but they were particularly popular in Italy. Although some people reviled castrati as homosexuals, many if not most castrati identified as heterosexuals, to the point of boasting of their exploits with women, but with their immature genitalia combined with a prohibition on their marrying, such escapades probably owe more to legend than to reality. Casanova once described a favorite castrato of Cardinal Borghese this way: "It was obvious that he hoped to inspire the love of those who liked him as a man, and probably would not have done so as a woman."

Casanova watched with rapt attention as the youth sat down at a harpsichord and "accompanied himself in an air which he sang with the voice of an angel." Even the stolid Don Pico "seemed to be in ecstasy." The Venetian studied Bellino's dark eyes, "which sparkled with a fire which burned my soul." At times this creature reminded him of his Roman loves, Lucrezia and Marchesa G., so feminine did his face seem, and even though Bellino dressed as a young boy, Casanova detected a "certain fullness of bosom, which put it into my head that despite the billing, this must be a girl." He found himself falling in love with Bellino. Having decided this must be a girl, "I made no resistance to the desires that he aroused in me." Or did Casanova mean "she"?

In the morning, Bellino appeared at the door to his room, and Casanova made him sit on the bed, "intending to treat him as a girl," until they were interrupted by two of Bellino's sisters. A little later, after asking the two sisters to leave him alone with their "brother," he got right to the point.

CASANOVA: My dear Bellino, I am sure that you are not of my sex.
BELLINO: I am of your sex, but a castrato; I have been examined.
CASANOVA: Let me examine you . . .
BELLINO: No, for it is clear that you are in love with me, and religion forbids me to let you.

> CASANOVA: You were not so scrupulous with the Bishop's
> confessor.
> BELLINO: He was old, and all he did was take a hasty look at my
> unfortunate condition.

(Casanova put out his hand to feel Bellino, who pushed it away and stood up. The stubborn resistance angered him, and he ostentatiously sulked. He soon recovered, and they joined Bellino's sisters eating chestnuts by the fire. Casanova kissed the others, all of whom accepted his gesture, including Bellino, at which point he deftly slid his hand behind the ruffle of Bellino's shirt, grasping a warm and pliable mound that could only be a breast.)

> CASANOVA: This breast proclaims you a girl, and you cannot
> deny it.
> BELLINO: All of us castrati have the same deformity.
> CASANOVA: So I am aware. But I know enough about it to tell the
> one kind from the other. This alabaster breast, my dear Bellino,
> is the charming breast of a girl of seventeen.

"Completely on fire," as he put it, Casanova tried to kiss Bellino's breast with "panting lips," but "the imposter," sensing his suitor's "forbidden pleasure," gets up and walks away. "I am left raging, yet unable to blame him."

Frustrated and embarrassed, he prepared to resume his journey to Constantinople. Just before leaving, he heard from one of the sisters that Bellino wished to accompany him as far as Rimini, where the castrato was to perform in an opera after Easter. "Go and tell him," Casanova responded, "that I am ready to do him the favor if he will first do me that of showing me, in your presence, whether he is a girl or a boy."

At the same time, Casanova invited Bellino's sister Cecilia to spend the night with him. He loved her, he said. He would be kind to her. "I love you, too," the girl said. "I'll go and let my mother know." She soon returned "in high spirits," locked the door, and fell into his arms "with the abandon of love." She might even have been a virgin, he wasn't sure. Afterward, she told him he'd made her happy. Casanova took a dispassionate view of their lovemaking: "She was tender, I was tender." He fell asleep in her arms, and in the morning, gave her coins, which, he claimed, pleased her more than "vows of eternal constancy." How ridiculous those vows of love and matrimony were, he ruminated as the girl brought the coins to her delighted mother. Sex served as the true coin of the realm.

Repercussions immediately followed. Bellino's other sister, Marina, complained to Casanova, "Cecilia spent the night with you, you go off tomorrow with Bellino, and I am the only unlucky one."

To which he could only think of one reply, "Do you want money?"

No! She loved him.

But she was too young, he countered.

"Age has nothing to do with it. I am better developed than my sister." In that case, she might already have a lover, or so he suggested, but she denied it.

"So much the better. We'll find out this evening."

Marina declared that she would tell her mother to have extra sheets ready for the event, "otherwise the maid would guess what happened."

Casanova chuckled at the prospect of deflowering Marina. "I found these comedies in the highest degree entertaining," he remarked.

———— ✦ ————

Before Casanova could continue his journey, Bellino's sister Marina "happily locked my door," and proceeded to review her sexual knowledge for his benefit, trying to convince him that, young as she was, she was a "past mistress in the mysteries of love," her roundabout way of explaining that she was no virgin. Amused, he opined that "virginity in girls seemed to me only childish imagination." When the two made love after this elaborate prelude, he had the pleasure of finding her "superior to her sister in every way" both that night and again in the morning. By way of discharging his obligation, he gave her three coins, snapped up by her mother. Now he knew Bellino's price based on the transactions with his sister, if it came to that.

At supper, Bellino, "whether from whim or ruse," appeared "dressed as a girl, followed by his two very pretty sisters, whom he totally eclipsed." If Casanova had any doubts left about Bellino's real gender, they had vanished. "It was impossible to imagine a prettier girl." During the meal— white truffles, shellfish, sherry, and champagne, and Spanish wines—he couldn't take his eyes from "this being whom my depraved nature impelled me to love." They dined, Bellino sang, and Casanova at length escorted his quarry to his room. If Bellino was a young man, he would leave. If a young woman, she would spend the night with Casanova, who would give her a hundred zecchini in the morning for her trouble. Bellino rejected the offer. "I am a castrato," Bellino repeated as if by rote. "I cannot satisfy your curiosity."

Casanova shifted his hand "to the place where I should find out if I was right or wrong," but Bellino blocked the maneuver, and when he ordered Bellino to remove his hand, Bellino refused, "for I see you are in a state that horrifies me." Casanova collected himself, and tried to thrust his hand down Bellino's back, only to be blocked again. But he felt . . . *something*. "It was at this moment I saw he was a man." The shock was overwhelming. Casanova described himself as "astonished, angered, mortified, disgusted." Bellino calmly departed, having made his case.

His sisters obligingly arrived to join Casanova, but he dismissed them and fastened his door. In the morning, he traveled with Bellino, as agreed, but he couldn't look at his companion without starting to "burn with love."

Casanova blurted out that he needed to fondle Bellino's member to convince himself that whatever he'd seen in private wasn't a "monstrous clitoris." And so he reached again for Bellino, and whatever it was that Casanova grasped persuaded him that Bellino was, in fact, a man. Casanova could never love him! "That is an abomination for which—God be praised!—I feel no inclination." Furthermore, he now had cause for grievance, because, as he accused Bellino, "You hatched the cruel scheme of making me fall in love and then driving me mad by refusing me the proof that alone can restore me to sanity." Bellino "melted into tears" at the accusation, and Casanova "withdrew into the bleakest possible silence" until their coach drew near to Sinigaglia (now called Senigallia), a small port about fifteen miles north of Ancona, where he planned to spend the night.

At this point, Bellino announced flatly, "You are in love with me whether I am a girl or a boy." The two of them continued their quarrel with mounting fury.

"All I ask of you is to let me touch an object that cannot but fill me with disgust!" Casanova cried.

To which Bellino replied that if by chance he were a girl, matters would be far worse, for Casanova would lose control over himself and produce a "torrent that no dam could hold back." If Bellino withheld his feminine charms, for the sake of argument, "You would finally threaten me with death." He'd rather die than yield his essence to Casanova on the altar of lust.

"You exaggerate," Casanova replied, gaining control over himself as they arrived at their inn at Sinigaglia, where only one bed was available. Should they make other arrangements? Casanova reported, "He surprised me by gently answering that he had no objection to sleeping in my bed."

They sat down to supper in a subdued mood. "After sending for a night lamp, Bellino fastened the door, undressed, and got into bed. I had done the same without uttering a word. And so we were in bed together." He was alone with the personification of unruly Eros.

"I was overcome to see him moving toward me. I clasp him to me, I see that he is fired by the same transport. The exordium of our dialogue was a deluge of mingling kisses. His arms were the first to slip down my back to my loins. I stretch mine, still lower, it is revelation enough that I am happy, I sense it, I feel it, I am convinced of it." He silently exulted, for "I fear that if I speak I shall no longer be happy or be happy as I would not wish to be, and I give myself, body and soul, to the joy that flooded my entire being, and which I saw was shared." As he approached his climax, "The excess of my bliss seizes all my senses with such force that it reaches the degree at which nature, drowning in the highest of all pleasures, is exhausted." For a minute or two he languished in a postcoital haze, "motionless in the act of contemplating and worshiping my own apotheosis." He had experienced supreme sensuality with Bellino.

In fact, Casanova suspected this well in advance. She wasn't the only castrato impersonator attempting this masquerade. In a culture of deception, people were quite willing to be fooled for the sake of entertainment.

The question of Bellino's true nature was settled at last, but the question of Casanova's identity proved more stubborn to resolve. Was he a priest or a libertine? Aristocrat or plebeian? Nor did he know where he belonged—in Venice, Padua, or some other location, or perhaps nowhere at all? For now, the only place where he felt he belonged was entwined with his beloved in bed.

After a brief respite, the lovers resumed their amorous experiment, "Bellino by assuring me of it every quarter of an hour by the sweetest moans; I by refusing to reach the end of my course again," the better for Bellino to enjoy herself.

He immediately wondered, "What has become of the monstrous clitoris I saw yesterday?"

Finally, Bellino let the whole truth tumble out. Her real name was Te-

resa. She was the nearly destitute daughter of someone she would only describe as an "employee" of a distinguished educational facility, the Institute
of Bologna.

When she was twelve, Salimbeni, a well-known castrato, lodged at her
house, and taught her to sing and play the harpsichord. As her musical
abilities increased, she and Salimbeni became intimate; castrato or not, he
claimed her virginity: "I did not feel ashamed to grant it to him." Indeed,
she worshiped him. It was a strange, ambiguous introduction to sex, to be
the mistress of a man who was old enough to be her father, yet whose mas-
culinity was compromised. "Men like yourself are certainly to be preferred
to men like my first lover," she explained, "but Salimbeni was an exception."
He was attractive, talented, sensitive, generous, and discreet. Women threw
themselves at him, yet he never boasted of his conquests. And still, he was
a castrato. "His mutilation made him a monster," she admitted, "but a monster of adorable qualities."

This particular monster had a young protégé, a man who had been cas-

Teresa Lanti, known as Bellino,
Casanova's mistress

trated at a young age and went by the name Bellino. He was the son of Casanova's new lover's mother. In short order, Teresa's father died, as did the
original Bellino. Salimbeni proposed training Teresa to pose as Bellino and
to board with the deceased boy's mother "who, being poor, would find it to
her advantage to keep the secret."

Salimbeni bequeathed one other item to complete Bellino's transition
to a new identity, a "little apparatus" that he would teach her to wear under
her clothing at all times. So that was the origin of the "monstrous clitoris!"

To mislead prying admirers, the apparatus would be so effective at
showing "the difference of sex that the deceit will pass unnoticed" if she ever
had to undergo a physical examination. The object in question, Casanova
saw, was a "long, soft gut, as thick as one's thumb, white and with a very
smooth surface."

She boasted, "I had to laugh when you called it a clitoris."

Proving her status as a castrato whenever she performed meant that she
had to submit to the same degrading examination, "for wherever I go people
think I look so much like a girl that they will not believe I am a man until
they have been convinced." (No wonder Bellino was so adept at confounding
Casanova.) Her official examiners, by the way, were priests, who "were innocently satisfied with having seen, and then certified me to the bishop." She
found it more difficult to reveal the truth of her sex to potential lovers, for
fear that, "becoming curious, they will want to use the apparatus to satisfy
monstrous desires." Even worse, she said, were those "wretches who perse-
cute me beyond endurance" in the misguided belief that they loved Bellino,
"the castrato I pretend to be." She feared she might even "stab one of them."

To keep her safe from this hellish predicament, she pleaded with Casanova as her lover and protector to take her with him as his "loving mistress." She insisted she would be faithful to him. "I believe I did not become
truly a woman until I tasted the perfect pleasure of love in your arms," she
declared.

Hearing this story, Casanova concluded they were "very nearly kindred
spirits," an observation often taken to refer to his ambiguous or homosexual
feelings, but which actually meant they were both carrying on masquerades,
she as a castrato, he as a gentleman. Their concealed identities united them
as impostors and soul mates.

He remained unconvinced that she loved him with the same ardor that
he felt for her, to which she replied, reasonably enough, "When I saw you

change so readily from Cecilia to Marina, I thought that you would treat me the same way as soon as you had satisfied your desires." But he had a plan. He would take Bellino to Venice, dressed as a woman under an assumed name, and they would live out their days together. Bellino agreed to do his bidding; with Salimbeni dead, she could act as a free agent. Now that he was beginning to get his way, he asked to see her "with the strange device that Salimbeni gave you." He described the transformation of his treasured love with mingled wonder, arousal, and anxiety: "She gets out of bed, pours water into a glass, opens her trunk, takes out her apparatus and her gums, dissolves them, and fits on the mask. I see something unbelievable. A charming girl, who looked it in every part of her body, and who, with this extraordinary attachment, seemed to me even more interesting, for the white pendant offered no obstruction to the well of her sex. I told her she had been wise not to let me touch it, for it would have intoxicated me and made me become what I was not, unless she had calmed me by revealing the truth. . . . Our skirmish was comical. We fell asleep afterward and did not wake until very late."

In the morning, Casanova returned to the idea of marriage. "You perhaps suppose that I am a man of high birth, but I am of a rank lower than your own," with no place in society, "neither relatives nor friends nor rightful claims to any settled plan." He had only a "modicum of intelligence" and the "bare beginnings of a career in literature." And, she should know, "My nature tends toward extravagance"—to put it mildly. Now she saw him as he really was: a nobody, the least-born, least-loved offspring of outsiders.

Bellino, whom he began to call by her real name, Teresa, claimed to be surprised by his candor. "Let us go to Venice," she said, "and my talent will earn our living." She demanded only that he must love her "and no one else." Casanova reminded Teresa, and perhaps himself, that he was en route to Constantinople in fulfillment of an ecclesiastical mission. Undeterred, she proposed that he marry her, "and then your right over me will be legal." He promised to wed his beloved in Bologna "the day after tomorrow at the latest." In preparation, they spent the rest of the day and night in bed, making love.

—•—

One day early in March 1744 they set out. They stumbled into a skirmish between Austrian and Spanish troops during the War of the Austrian Succession, already in progress for four years. In Pesaro, less than a hundred miles from Bologna, military officers demanded their passports. Teresa presented hers, but Casanova had lost his passport.

"No one loses a passport," the commandant said.

"Indeed they do, and the proof is that I have lost mine."

He was arrested. He explained that he was en route from Rome with a letter from Cardinal Acquaviva, bound for Constantinople. He presented the letter, sealed with the Cardinal's emblem. He repeated his story to a general, who replied, "Only a fool loses a passport, and the Cardinal will learn not to entrust his errands to fools." Casanova received permission to write to the Cardinal for a replacement passport, and then he was jailed in a ruined cathedral. He bid farewell to Teresa, "whom this untimely mishap had plunged into gloom." He gave her a hundred zecchini and reminded her to wait for him in Rimini, thirty miles to the north.

Confined to the guardhouse of Santa Maria, as the prison was known, he sat on his trunk and barked orders at his guard. He desired a servant, food, drink, and he had the means to pay for them, but the guard ignored Casanova's pleas. Exhausted and famished, he spent the night sleeping fitfully on a pile of straw amid Catalan soldiers. He tried to become philosophical about his misery, ruminating about classical thinkers and consoling himself that he'd reunite with Teresa within days.

In the morning, his guard yielded his post to a French officer who addressed Casanova as "abate," immediately establishing a cordial tone. Charmed by Casanova, the guard ordered a soldier to tend to their guest, and transported Casanova's jailhouse bed to the guard's quarters, invited him to dine, and after a spirited card game known as Piquet, advised him not to play against the other officers, who would take all his money. The guard even permitted Casanova to stroll out of the guardhouse, trusting him to return of his own free will.

On one of these rambles, he observed an officer dismount a horse, drop the reins, and disappear on an errand. "For no particular reason, I pick up the reins, put my foot in the stirrup, and mount. It was the first time in my life I had ever been on the back of a horse." Before he knew it, "the horse starts off like a thunderbolt," his right foot flailing, unable to find the stirrup. Seeing the horse approaching at a gallop, a sentry ordered Casanova to halt, but "I was incapable of obeying." Even when he heard musket fire, he couldn't control the runaway steed until two guards stopped his horse, and hauled him to the guardhouse at Rimini, where he encountered Prince Georg Christian Lobkowitz, to whom he related the improbable tale. Taking a liking to Casanova, the Prince ordered an adjutant to escort him to the outskirts of the town, and warned the young wanderer "to take good care not to come back into his army again without passport." Casanova learned that he could obtain a replacement passport in Bologna; with it, he would return to Pesaro to collect his trunk and reunite with Teresa.

He reached the outskirts of Rimini in a downpour. His silk stockings were absolutely ruined! He needed a proper carriage, but none was to be found. Instead he reversed his elegant redingote—a long, double-breasted riding coat—"so as not to be recognized as an abate," and then he waited. Rain-spattered mules trudged past him in the mud, forty in all, on their way to Rimini, his immediate destination. "I approach one of the mules, put my hand on its neck, really with no particular intention, and slowly keeping pace with the mule, I reenter the city of Rimini, and since I appear to be a muleteer no one says a word to me."

Soaked with rain, his hair tucked under a cap, his fine cane concealed beneath his clothing, he found his way to Teresa, who was "dressed as a girl" and accompanied by members of her family, but their reunion disappointed him. He spoke of his troubles, but Teresa faulted his rash behavior. She had news of her own: in Rimini, unlike Ancona, women were allowed to appear onstage, and so she need not disguise her sex. She had committed to twenty performances after Easter, after which she would join Casanova at the place of his choosing. Her mother pointed out that Teresa had passed up a thousand zecchini in fees by not performing in Rome during Carnival, to which he responded, "She would have been unmasked at Rome and put in some wretched convent for the rest of her life."

The lovers went their separate ways a little while longer, Teresa to perform at Rimini, and Casanova to obtain his passport in Bologna, seventy-five miles distant, where he exchanged an abate's plain cassock for a splendid officer's uniform in white and blue, accented with silver and gold braids. The charade emboldened him, "for I knew that Bologna was a city in which people lived in perfect freedom." Here he played the part of an insolent, strutting military man until a Pesaro gazette published an article informing readers that "Signior Casanova, an officer in the Queen's Regiment, has deserted after killing his captain in a duel," thereafter running off with the dead officer's horse. Yes, he had borrowed the horse, but there had been no duel, no killing! Nor was he an officer, appearances to the contrary. To avoid suspicion, he insisted to anyone who happened to inquire that the scurrilous article referred to another man by the same name.

As he languished in Bologna, plotting his return to Venice—his mission to Constantinople apparently postponed again—Teresa, guided by her mother, wrote that she had been offered a thousand *zecchini* plus expenses to perform for a year at the new Teatro San Carlo in Naples. She included a copy of the contract, which she was about to sign, together with a second document in which "she undertook to serve me as long as she lived." Pondering these two developments, he confessed, "I was in a state of the greatest irresolution." He hated the idea of causing Teresa to give up the rich contract; on the other hand, how could he appear in Naples "without any position in the world but that of a dastard living at the expense of his wife or mistress?" He advised her by letter to sign the contract, go to Naples, and take a respectable-looking maid to discourage scandal.

———•———

On his return to Venice he endured yet another quarantine, "for Venice was particularly strict in matters of health." What to do? He posed as an inhabitant of the State of Mantua, which did not require a quarantine, and bribed clerks to let him pass with a health certificate. Having negotiated all hurdles, he arrived in Venice on April 2, 1744, his nineteenth birthday, as he recalled. (He might have been off by a year, and returned in 1745, when he was twenty. Casanova was generally on firmer ground with names, places, and dialogue than he was with dates.)

He immediately arranged for passage to Constantinople, his long-neglected goal, but no ships would be sailing to that distant port for two or three months. Instead, he boarded *Our Lady of the Rosary* (a name he adored), bound for Corfu, eight hundred miles to the south; she would depart in several weeks, calling first at Orsara, a small fishing village on the Istrian coast, in Croatia. Until then, he determined to make the most of his time in Venice. After his sojourn in Rome, it no longer seemed the center of the world, as Venetians assumed, but it was home. The slurred Venetian language, Vèneto, was as familiar as his skin. And the flirtatious women of Venice, the *civette*, were still unsurpassed as they tottered about on their *zoccoli*, pausing occasionally to toss a *smorfia* his way.

In the Piazza San Marco, he encountered the Abate Grimani, who greeted him with boisterous good humor, surprised only by the military uniform Casanova affected. The younger man explained that he had abandoned the Church to become an adventurer.

In his new guise, he sought out Nanetta and Marta, whom he entertained for "three delicious hours" with tales of his travels. "I saw the joy on the faces of my two little wives, who regained their empire over my heart despite the image of Teresa that was before the eyes of my soul at every moment." The next day, he moved into their home, adapting swiftly to his new surroundings. "The first night they both slept with me, and on the following nights they took turns." It was to be a brief interlude. On May 5, "very well off in clothing, jewels, and cash," he set sail for Corfu.

Chapter 4

Zelmi

After four days at sea, he nearly drowned in a tempest. The chaplain, a Slavonian priest to whom Casanova had taken an instant dislike, propped himself on deck to exorcise the devils that he alone discerned in the storm clouds. The terrified sailors wept uncontrollably and allowed the ship to drift perilously close to rocks. "I very imprudently considered it my duty to intervene," Casanova observed, so he climbed the rigging, and exhorted the sailors to put their backs into it. There were no devils in the clouds, he shouted, and the "priest who was pointing them out was a madman," whereupon the priest denounced Casanova as an atheist and turned the crew against him.

The storms convinced them all that he was a Jonah, a bad luck omen, and would have to be sacrificed. By pre-arranged signal, one of them pushed Casanova overboard "by hitting me such a blow with a rope as could not but knock me down." Tumbling into the waves, he clenched an anchor, and was rescued by a crew member. When he climbed back on the deck, he seized his attacker's stick and beat him with it, as the other sailors and the priest came to the sailor's defense. A few days after the crisis, the passengers and crew disembarked on the island of Corfu in the Ionian Sea. Casanova presented his bona fides as soon as he went ashore. Imbued with Greek heritage reaching back to antiquity, Corfu had been part of the Venetian sphere of influence since the thirteenth century, reinforced by a succession of naval sieges. Venetians brought their culture, cuisine, music, and language with them. When Casanova landed there, he could be forgiven for believing that he was still in Venice.

In mid-July, he arrived at the house of Osman, Pasha of Karamania, in reality a French officer, the Count de Bonneval, who had converted to Islam. There he was, a "stout elderly gentleman in complete French apparel" asking what he could do for the protégé of the esteemed Cardinal Acquaviva. Although Casanova had exchanged his clerical garb for a soldier's uniform, his dress made scant impression on his host, who professed to envy the young man who, "without either cares or plans or any fixed abode, abandoned himself to Fortune, fearing nothing and expecting nothing."

Hearing of his guest's literary inclinations, the Pasha escorted him to a room equipped with cupboards and wire grilles, which Casanova assumed contained books, but instead concealed bottles of fine wine. Alcohol was forbidden by the faith to which he had converted, but, as he reckoned, "that is no bar to anyone's being free to damn himself if he pleases." There was no Inquisition here in Constantinople. The two of them savored an "excellent white Burgundy" as they chatted pleasantly about Venice, Rome, and religion. The Pasha confided that he'd received dispensation from the rite of circumcision: "At my age it would have been dangerous." As a concession to his adopted land he wore a turban, of which he seemed quite proud. In all, he claimed to be well rid of Venice, where, as he put it, "the soup had eaten up the china." Despite these protestations, Casanova sensed his host's longing for friends he'd left behind in *La Serenissima*.

⸺•⸺

At that moment he made the acquaintance of Yusef Ali, who offered his guest a pipe, which he "politely refused," preferring to puff on his own. The two smoking companions established a rapport based on mutual intellectual respect, and when Yusef Ali invited the young Venetian to his home, Casanova accepted, on the grounds that "boredom is more of a threat to foreigners than the plague."

At the house, he was greeted by Yusef's servant, an illiterate Neapolitan who had begun life as a sailor, been captured, enslaved, and for the past thirty years had labored for his master as a gardener, saying that he was so happy with his lot that if Yusef ever gave him his freedom, he would consider it punishment. Yusef himself drew up on horseback, and the two of them passed the hours speculating on the pleasures of a "perfect tobacco" and debating the concept of pleasure. Even discussions about their differing views of God and faith drew them closer. Yusef revealed that he had three wives, two of whom were deceased, two sons, both launched and prosperous, as well as a daughter, Zelmi, who was destined to inherit her father's property. She was then fifteen years old, beautiful—and unmarried.

Casanova blurted out that he had no intention of ever marrying. If so, Yusef replied, his young Venetian friend couldn't call himself a Christian or a "complete man."

"I am a complete man, and I am a Christian," he insisted. "I will further tell you that I love the fair sex and that I hope to enjoy many conquests among them."

"Your religion says you will be damned," Yusef retorted.

Absolutely not, Casanova replied. Once he confessed to a priest, he would be forgiven. "They are obliged to absolve us," he assured Yusef, who insisted that only God could forgive a crime. And then he went to another, perhaps related subject, masturbation. Was that a crime among Christians? Yes, indeed, Casanova assured him, "an even greater crime than unlawful copulation," a decree that struck Yusef as absurd, unenforceable, and in the case of a single man, extremely dangerous because, in his desire to avoid masturbation, he could contract a "mortal disease." At the end of their debate, Yusef stunned Casanova with a proposal:

"When I die, Zelmi"—Yusef's fifteen-year-old daughter—"will have all I possess, and I am in a position to make a rich man of anyone who marries her while I am alive." He painted a picture of her loveliness, her dark eyes and hair, her good figure and "gentle nature," not omitting to mention that she was well-educated, fluent in Greek and Italian, accomplished in music and embroidering, and so carefully sheltered that no man "can boast of having seen her face." This pristine specimen could be Casanova's—after he spent a year living with Yusef's relative in Adrianople (now Edirne), a battle-scarred town in northern Turkey, to learn the language, customs, and religion of his people. As soon as he became a Muslim—and he could see for himself how easily the French count had accomplished the transition— Zelmi would become his wife, and "you shall have a house, slaves of your own, and an income that will permit you to live in luxury."

There was a catch. Until he declared himself, Casanova couldn't see or even converse with Zelmi, whom her father kept hidden, and even if he had caught a glimpse of the girl, she would be veiled. To decide how to respond, Casanova need only obey the will of God "according to the inevitable decree of your destiny," and with Zelmi by his side, "You will become—I foresee it—a pillar of the Ottoman Empire." Yusef embraced Casanova, who stumbled back to his quarters, too dazed to think.

He kept his own counsel for four days before going to see Yusef again, and when he did, he asked: What if Zelmi, with all her gifts and beauty, simply didn't like him?

"My daughter loves you," Yusuf proclaimed. She had seen him surreptitiously as he talked with her father, and fervently hoped that he would become a believer so that they could share their destiny.

But Casanova had yet to catch a glimpse of her! "I am very glad that you are forbidden to let me see her, for she might dazzle me, and then it would be passion that would tip the scales, and then I could not have the satisfaction of having decided in all the purity of my soul," he replied, half believing his answer. If she actually was beautiful, she would be that much more difficult to resist, and the thought of changing his religion, even for the prospect of great wealth, meant that he had to abandon his goal of attaining fame in "the fine arts or in literature" in the "polished nations" of Europe. Only sincere believers would "assume the turban," as he put it, "and I did not count myself among them." And what if the charming Zelmi turned out not to be so charming, after all? That was cause enough for misery, especially if Yusef, who no doubt would supervise every aspect of the marriage from finances to child-rearing, lived for another twenty years, or still longer.

Days later, at a party featuring "handsome Neapolitan slaves of both sexes" dancing and performing farces, Casanova wished to demonstrate the *furlana,* a popular Friulian folk dance, for the guests. Within minutes, a violinist materialized, as did a "beautiful woman" wearing a black velvet *moretta.* "The goddess strikes the opening pose, I join her, and we dance six *furlane* one after the other. I am now out of breath, for there is no national dance more violent; but the beauty still stands there, motionless and without the least sign of fatigue, as if to defy me. During the whirl, which is the most tiring part of the dance, she seemed to float; I was beside myself with amazement. I did not remember having seen the dance performed so well in Venice itself." He caught his breath, embarrassed by his lack of stamina, and gasped to his masked partner, "*Ancora sei, e poi basta, se non volete vedermia morire,*" that is, "Six more, and an end, if you do not want to see me dying." Clenching the *moretta*'s button between her teeth, she found it "impossible to utter a word; but a squeeze of her hand that no one could see told me a great deal." She vanished as abruptly as she had arrived, leaving her grateful partner to marvel at her agility, and savoring "the only real pleasure" he had experienced in this distant land.

Afterward, he went around asking if the lady in the *moretta* was Venetian; how could she be anything *but* Venetian? No one answered his question.

The former Count de Bonneval explained that the female slave's flirtatiousness had harmed her owner's reputation, and Casanova would be wise to avoid her. "Be prudent," he advised, "for considering the stringency of Turkish customs, all intrigues are dangerous." Casanova promised to avoid intrigue, but, he confessed, or boasted, "I did not keep my word."

Days later, he received a mysterious invitation written by an unknown hand to a rendezvous with the woman, informing him that she was indeed Venetian. Just then, an old woman approached to tell him that Zelmi was observing him at that very moment. The girl was very attractive, she assured him. He had only to agree to become her husband. By now, he confessed, "I was even more afraid of entering a labyrinth in which I could have only too easily lost my way." The mere sight of a turban filled him with anxiety.

Yusef tempted Casanova by inviting him to his house, where a woman, her identity concealed behind a veil, spoke seductively. This must be Zelmi, he thought, but she identified herself as Yusef's wife, just eighteen years old. "A beautiful clothed body," he observed, "can only arouse desires that are easily satisfied; the fire it kindles is like burning straw." He saw naked arms, and hands, her full bosom, "two small globes," he urgently noted, "separated by a hollow, which seemed to me a rivulet of milk created to quench my thirst and for my lips to devour."

He reached out to lift her veil, to behold her eyes and therefore her soul, but, she warned, "Do you deserve Yusef's friendship when you violate hospitality by insulting his wife?"

He begged her forgiveness, fearing that Yusef might do him great harm, and threw himself at her feet. She ordered him to be seated, "crossing her legs in such a way that the disarrangement of her skirt gave me a moment's glimpse of the charms which would have intoxicated me completely if they had been visible a moment longer."

"You are on fire," she said . . .

. . . at which point Yusef entered the room, murmuring, "Peace be with you."

"I thought that I was with Zelmi," Casanova said.

"I cannot imagine a decent man thrusting his own daughter into the company of a stranger."

Casanova ran to a rowboat, made for a fishing vessel, and escaped. At midnight, he was put ashore, he had no idea where. Perhaps twenty miles from Corfu "in a place where no one could suppose me to be." It was the beginning of December, the nights were cold, he had no cloak, and only a light uniform, and so, "I was chilled to the bone."

In the morning, he stumbled across an elderly man at the helm of a lateen-rigged ship known as a tartan. The skipper offered to sell Casanova a pistol for ten zecchini, whereas anyone on Corfu would pay twelve for the firearm. There was nothing to do but "abandon myself to the demands of the moment," which meant employing his new weapon to obtain food by firing at a sheep.

———•———

Casanova made his way back to Corfu, where he again contracted venereal disease. During his final weeks in Corfu, "No one listened when I talked, or, if anyone did, it was only to find me dull instead of the wit" he'd once been taken for. It seemed that "people shunned me as if my bad luck was infectious; and perhaps they were right."

By September he could report that he'd returned to "excellent health" as a result of his doctor's treatment, or despite it. From the details that he related, he likely suffered from a less severe version of sexually transmitted disease, which is often self-healing. In that case, his arduous treatments and social isolation were unnecessary.

He sailed from Corfu at month's end in a fleet of five galleys. The ships dropped anchor in the port of Venice on October 14, 1745; then came a month in quarantine, and finally, on November 25, he was at large in Venice again.

———•———

He resumed wearing his *bauta* and sought out his former bed companions with whom he had shared so many nights. They had not been idle during his absence. Nanetta had married; she was now a Countess, hopelessly out of reach. And Marta had become a nun on the island of Murano. He received a letter from her to warn him "in the name of Jesus Christ and the Holy Virgin" never to see her again. She forgave him the "crime" of seducing her, but she would spend the rest of her life repenting of it and praying for his conversion.

He called on other acquaintances, but he met with indifference. His brother Francesco, the painter, lived in the fortress of Sant'Andrea, where Giacomo had spent time. He discovered that Francesco's confinement had been arranged by the family nemesis Antonio Razzetta, whom Giacomo had beaten and tossed into a canal one night. Giacomo used his limited influence to free Francesco from these embarrassing circumstances. By this time their sister, Maria Maddalena, about whom he generally has little to say, had joined their elusive mother in Dresden.

Casanova faced limited prospects even if he were to marry. In Venice, nobles of undisputed lineage formally joined the influential Great Council when they turned twenty-five. A patrician who married beneath his station was automatically excluded from the Great Council, deprived of noble rank, including the ultimate privilege of serving as Doge, the military and spiritual ruler of Venice. As a result, patricians married into families from the same caste, and the women of the ruling class needed husbands of their circumstances to continue the line, recorded in the *Libro d'Oro*, or Golden Book, the official directory of nobles in the Republic of Venice. No Venetian dynasty would jeopardize its status for Casanova's sake.

For lack of anything better, he gambled until bankrupt as if to punish himself for his licentiousness in Corfu. He'd given up his ambitions in the Church ("forced to become an ecclesiastic, and unable to succeed by any other course than that of hypocrisy, I should have been disgusted with myself"), and in the military ("I should have had to practice a patience of which I had no reason to believe myself capable"), or a celebrated writer and wit, because he needed money. And so he became a fiddler, despite his indifference to music. "Dr. Gozzi had taught me enough so that I could scrape away in the theater orchestra." After performances, he followed his musical colleagues to a tavern, "which we left only in a state of intoxication to spend the night in a house of ill fame." If the brothel happened to be full, he and his companions tossed the other patrons onto the street, and when Casanova and his rowdy crew of seven or eight, often with his brother Francesco, had finished their orgy, they left "without paying the unhappy women who submitted to our brutality."

On other nights, they roamed the streets of Venice playing malicious practical jokes; they untied gondolas from their moorings in front of palazzos and watched the current carry them away, stranding their owners. They sent midwives to attend to women who had no need for their services. They dispatched credulous physicians to noblemen's homes on the pretext

that were suffering from "apoplexy." Nor did they spare priests, whom they
roused from their beds, "and packed them off to pray for the souls of people in perfect health who, we said, were at death's door." They severed bells
from their bell cords, overturned venerable landmarks; they climbed towers
and rang tocsins to announce nonexistent fires, they ran away from gondoliers to escape paying for their rides . . . until one night during Carnival
when their carousing turned ugly.

At midnight, eight of them were "roving through the city," trying to
think of some new mischief to impress their companions. Their masks
gave them license to do as they pleased. In Santa Croce, one of seventy-
two parishes in Venice, they came across a tavern where a "rather pretty
woman" was drinking peacefully with three male companions. Wouldn't
it be amusing to kidnap the woman and "use her afterward for our good
pleasure"? Their leader, whom Casanova described as a nobleman, coor-
dinated the assault, which they carried out in their Carnival masks. One
part of the crew seized the three men and led them to a boat, where Casanova and the woman joined them. As the men feared for their lives, the
boat took them to the island of San Giorgio Maggiore, known for its huge
church, and left them there, relieved, but the woman was spirited away to
another district, San Marcuolo, where Francesco and other members of
the crew awaited them. Their leader, the young nobleman, attempted to
calm the frightened lady. "We will go and drink a glass in the Rialto and
then we will take you home," he murmured, but she wanted her husband,
and no one else. The nobleman promised that she'd see her spouse the first
thing in the morning.

Relieved, she accompanied her masked escorts to a tavern, the Two
Swords, near the Rialto. They made a fire to ward off the nighttime chill,
ordered food and drink, dispatched the waiter, and removed their masks, at
which point the woman "became all amiability at the sight of our faces and
the way in which we behaved." Soon after, "there befell her what she could
not have expected," beginning with the crew's aristocratic leader, who became the "first to pay her his amorous duty, after most politely overcoming
her resistance to yield to him in the presence of us all." She allowed him to
do what he pleased, but her compliant smile vanished when young Casanova stepped forward, and it was obvious that he would take her again, and
after he was through with her, another member of the group would have his
way with her, until "she no longer doubted her happy fate," as Casanova de-

scribed it. Francesco hesitated to join the rape, until he realized "he had no other choice, for the law among us irrevocably demanded that each of us do what the other did." Ultimately, he went along with the others. When the crew finished their "fine exploit," they put their masks back in place and escorted their victim home as if concluding an evening's festivities. "None of us could keep from laughing when she thanked us sincerely and in the most perfect good faith."

The victim's husband, a weaver, presented a complaint to the three judges of the Council of Ten, accurate in most details, with one critical exception: the document stated that the eight masked men "had subjected the woman to no ill treatment." It only described the crew carrying her off as a Carnival prank. Perhaps the awful reality of the violation was too much for the weaver, his wife, and their reputation to bear.

Casanova recorded the complaint's consequences: "The first was to set the whole city laughing. The second was to send every idler to San Giobbe"—where the weaver and his wife lived—"to hear the heroine herself tell the story. The third was to make the tribunal issue a decree promising five hundred *ducati* to anyone who should reveal the guilty parties, even if it were one of themselves, except only their leader." The size of the reward would have struck fear into the perpetrators if their leader hadn't been a Venetian nobleman. And even if he had turned informer, as Casanova thought possible, the tribunal "would have done nothing, since it would have had to punish a patrician." If any good came of the affair, Casanova and his crew became "so frightened that we all mended our ways, and our nocturnal expeditions came to an end."

But he was mistaken if he thought he'd gotten away with rape. Several months later, a State Inquisitor, or judge, drawing on a network of spies, "astonished me by telling me the whole story of the escapade, and naming all my companions in it." From then on the Inquisition would be watching him.

———•———

By this time, Casanova despaired of his prospects in Venice. He had lost his way, or, as he put it, "I let my ambition sleep." After his hard-won education, his "grounding in letters," not to mention his "accidental personal advantages" such as his charm and his height, now over six feet, "here I am, at the age of twenty, become a menial journeyman of a sublime art"—music—"in which if he who excels is admired, the mediocrity is rightly despised." Instrumentalists were in demand in Venice, with its vibrant theatrical culture, and he found work in this "sorry profession" as a violinist in the orchestra of Grimani's Teatro San Samuele, where he earned a paltry salary, "stayed away from all fashionable gatherings," and suffered the indignity of overhearing others disparage him. "Seeing myself reduced to this condition after having enjoyed such splendid opportunities, I felt ashamed, but I kept it to myself." He'd known adversity, and he trusted that Fortune helped the young, "and I was young."

——————◆——————

On April 20, 1746, a patrician named Girolamo Cornaro married the daughter of another prominent Venetian family. Casanova recalled, "I was one of the fiddlers making up one of the several orchestras for the balls" that lasted for three days to celebrate the occasion. "On the third day, when the festivities were nearly over, I leave the orchestra an hour before dawn to go home, and as I go down the stairs, I notice a Senator in his red robe about to get into his gondola." At that instant, the senator drops a letter as he takes his handkerchief from his pocket, and Casanova stoops to retrieve it, "catching up with the imposing Signore just as he is going down the steps," and hands it to him. The senator courteously thanks Casanova, asks his name, and offers to take him home.

Three minutes after they are seated in the gondola, the senator announces, "I feel such a numbness that I seem not to have this arm at all." He asked Casanova to shake the affected arm, which he does vigorously.

Just then, "I hear him tell me, in ill-articulated words, that he felt as if he were losing his whole leg too and that he thought he was dying." The symptoms Casanova reports strongly suggest that the senator had just suffered a stroke. "Greatly alarmed, I open the curtain, take the lantern, look at his face, and am terrified to see that his mouth was drawn up to the left ear and his eyes were losing their luster. I call to the Gondoliers to stop and let me get out to find a surgeon who will come at once and bleed His Excellency, who had certainly been struck by apoplexy." They drew up to a bridge beside the Calle Bernardo, where, three years earlier, he'd beaten Razzetta with a cudgel. He ran to a coffeehouse, shouting for a surgeon. He dragged one from bed, and led him to the gondola, where he bled the nobleman, the accepted medical practice of the day.

The gondola made its way to the Palazzo Bragadin, a fifteenth-century behemoth. They roused the servants, who carried their afflicted master from the gondola into his second-floor apartment. By the time they undressed him and stretched him out in bed, he seemed dead, or nearly so. On instinct, Casanova stayed by the aristocrat's bedside, considering it his duty not to leave, until another patrician arrives, and the aristocrat questioned the gondoliers, who directed them to the young fiddler in their midst. By then a priest had been summoned to administer last rites. The hours passed, and Casanova in the company of two patricians remained with the sick man. They told him he could leave, if he wished; they would keep their vigil the following night on mattresses beside their friend. In that case, the young fiddler said he would spend the night. If he left, he was afraid the patient would die, "just as I felt certain that he could not die so long as I remained there." The other patricians, astonished, exchanged looks but allowed the young man to stay.

Over supper, Casanova learned that the afflicted patrician was none other than Signor Matteo Giovanni Bragadin. Now it was the young man's turn to be astonished. "This Signor Bragadin was celebrated in Venice not only because of his eloquence and his talents as a statesman but also because of his love affairs." In that regard, he was a man after Casanova's heart. His brother, Daniele Bragadin, had served for the past eleven years as the Procurature—or attorney—di San Marco, officially charged with administration of Saint Mark's Basilica, the cathedral church of the Roman Catholic Archdiocese of Venice, and thus the second most influential person in Venice after the Doge. Yet beneath their red patrician robes, the Bragadin brothers were vicious enemies. Ten years earlier, Daniele had fallen ill and suspected that his brother had tried to poison him. There had a been a great scandal, investigation, and trial before the Council of Ten. Matteo Bragadin was acquitted, but the rancor between the brothers persisted.

For the moment, however, Matteo Bragadin was being treated by a physician named Ferro, whose counterfeit remedies alarmed Casanova, especially a pernicious mercury ointment applied to the chest. "In less than twenty-four hours the patient was troubled by a violent brain fever." Ferro explained in medical doubletalk that the effect was to be expected. Casanova wondered if the physician was planning to kill the patient in order to cure him.

By midnight Bragadin could scarcely breathe, and Casanova roused the other two patricians from their slumber. He then washed away the offending mercury ointment, and within a matter of minutes, the patient was resting comfortably. Dr. Ferro returned in the morning to find Bragadin much improved, at which point Dandolo, one of the friends, explained that Casanova had removed the poisonous mercury. "I maintained a modest silence," he recalled, "though finding it difficult to stifle my laughter." Ferro, glaring at him, "rightly concluded that I was a brazen charlatan who had dared to supplant him," whereupon he announced that he was withdrawing immediately from the case. All at once, Giacomo Casanova, obscure musician and notorious scoundrel, became "physician to one of the most illustrious members of the Venetian Senate. All in all, I was delighted." He'd always been an outsider, and his erratic efforts to penetrate Venice's aristocratic circle had come to nothing—until now.

As Dr. Ferro disparaged Casanova throughout Venice, the patient recovered his health. When one of his relatives expressed astonishment that he'd made a mere "fiddler from a theater orchestra his physician," Bragadin responded with a laugh that the fiddler in question knew more than all the physicians in Venice combined.

Casanova played his new part to the fullest. He became Bragadin's alter ego, his oracle. "I spoke as a physician," Casanova recalled. "I dogmatized, and I cited authors whom I had never read."

Impressed by Casanova's display of erudition, Bragadin, who was inclined toward mysticism, confided that he believed the young man possessed a "supernatural gift" for healing. It was true, wasn't it? He had to know.

Casanova agreed that it was, and bluffed his way through the inquiry by claiming that he possessed a "numerical calculus" that imparted knowledge to him and him alone.

Ah! exclaimed Bragadin. He knew—or thought he knew—exactly what Casanova meant: the *Key of Solomon,* written in Hebrew, translated into Latin, explaining how to gain power over the spirits of hell and other esoteric matters—the ancient Kabbalah. This school of religious and mystical thought went back for centuries, and was originally the province of Jews. More recently the Kabbalah had been adopted by some Christians and gained a wider audience, and in Venice it became something of a theological fad.

Yes, Casanova nodded, maintaining the farce, it was indeed the Kabbalah, with its ancient mysteries and wisdom.

Where, Bragadin asked, had he learned of the mysteries of the Kaballah?

Why, from a hermit living in a remote region of the Apennine mountains.

Bragadin drew back in amazement. "You are in possession of a treasure, and it rests with you to derive the greatest advantage from it."

Casanova protested that the answers his calculus had been generating of late had disappointed him, and he had ceased to use it, although if he hadn't constructed his kabbalistic "pyramid" only three weeks earlier, he would never had met Bragadin. (Kabbalists expressed letters with numbers and vice versa. They employed the twenty-two letters of the Hebrew alphabet to express both modes, and to construct different versions of their *arcana*, their secrets, in the form of pyramids.)

He explained that his oracle had admonished him to leave the festivities at precisely four o'clock in the morning, the moment when he encountered Signor Bragadin and his two friends. To test Casanova, one of Bragadin's friends, Signor Dandolo, wrote out a question. Casanova understood nothing of it, but made up an intricate numerical reply that seemed to satisfy Dandolo, who declared it the product of an "immortal intelligence."

The three of them showered Casanova with questions, finding his answers "divine"—what luck!—and prompting their young friend to thank them for causing him to appreciate the value of something that he had taken for granted.

They asked if he would teach them the rules of the calculus.

Happily, he replied, "even though the hermit had told me that if I taught it to anyone before I reached the age of fifty I would drop dead three days afterward." But, he assured them, he didn't believe the hermit's threat, only to be told by Signor Bragadin that the warning should be taken seriously, "and from then on not one of the three again asked me to teach them the art of the Kabbalah."

Casanova came to understand how credulous and eccentric these three patricians were behind their red robes and formidable palaces. He considered them all highly intelligent, "but a prejudiced intelligence reasons badly." For instance they considered the Resurrection "so trifling a matter that they could not think it a miracle," and he found himself laughing silently as they derided others whom they considered less intelligent.

Stranger still, "All three of them were unmarried, and all three had become irreconcilable enemies of women, after renouncing them," in marked contrast to Casanova, who was enthralled by women. The men would only traffic with those who had committed to the same renunciation, so Casanova, in the days and weeks that followed, told them the story of his life, excluding his complex relationships with women.

"I know I deceived them," he admitted, "but if my reader is a man of the world, I ask him to think a little before considering me unworthy of his indulgence." Otherwise, he would have had to return to sawing away on his violin in a little theater orchestra, earning a pittance. On reflection, "should I have had the barbarity to leave these worthy men open to the deceits of some dishonest scoundrel who might have contrived to make their acquaintance and ruined them?" Of course not! Instead, "I took the most creditable, the noblest, the only natural course. I decided to put myself in a position where I need no longer go without the necessities of life," and who knew better than he what those necessities were? Not just fine clothes and furnishings, jewelry, and perhaps a servant or two, but, more important, entrée into the Republic's most exclusive conclaves. "With the friendship of these three eminent persons, I became a man who would enjoy consideration and prestige in his own country." His name would constantly be on others' lips. "No one in Venice could understand how an intimacy could exist between myself and three men of their character, they all heaven and I all earth; they most severe in their morals, and I addicted to every kind of dissolute living."

By June 1746, Bragadin had recovered from his crisis sufficiently to return to the Senate. Before resuming his duties, he addressed Casanova: "Whoever you are, I owe you my life. Your patrons who wanted to make you a priest, a scholar, an advocate, a soldier, and then a violinist were fools who did not know you. God commanded your angel to bring you to me." He offered to treat Casanova as a son, readied an apartment in the palazzo for the young man, along with a servant, a gondola, and a stipend of ten zecchini a month, advising, "At your age my father did not give me a larger allowance."

Casanova flung himself at his patron's feet, addressed him as "father," and swore to obey him as a son.

No sooner had he reached this apotheosis than he set about destroying it. Here he was, "At no loss for money, endowed by nature with a striking exterior, a resolute gambler, a spendthrift, a great talker with a sharp tongue, completely without modesty, fearless, running after pretty women, supplanting rivals, and thinking no company good except such as amused me." No wonder he "could not but be hated."

Bragadin tolerated Casanova's follies, and laughingly told him that he was living "the wild life he had led at my age," but he warned the young man "to be prepared to pay the price for it, and to find myself punished as he had when I reached his age." Casanova couldn't imagine any punishment dampening his enjoyment. "I made a joke of his dire prophecies and went on my way." He gave no thought to the consequences of his behavior, only to his insatiable appetite for the next triumph at the gambling tables and the next conquest in the bedroom.

———•———

"At the beginning of October [1746], the theaters being open, I came out of the posthouse for Rome masked and was proceeding on my way when I saw the figure of a girl, with her head wrapped in the hood of her cloak," Casanova wrote. She had just disembarked from a mail boat, or *corriere*, from Ferrara, seventy miles south of Venice. "Seeing that she was alone, and noticing her uncertainty, I feel impelled by an occult force to approach her and offer my services if she needed them."

She replied that she needed directions. Instead, Casanova invited her to a wine bar where she could talk freely. How long until he slipped into her bed, and between her legs, to drink a deeper and sweeter nectar?

At a little wine bar steps from the quay, they arranged themselves face-to-face. He removed his *bauta* to reveal his glistening eyes, protruding lips, and beaklike nose. She undid her hood, although coils of her hair obscured most of her face, revealing only her eyes, nose, mouth, and chin. *Che bella!* The things he saw in her face: youth, beauty, sadness, nobility, candor: a sonnet without words. She revealed that she was of noble birth. She had come to Venice to find a certain Venetian man who had seduced her, abandoned her, and "destroyed her happiness."

"I suppose he promised to marry you."

"He gave me his promise in writing. The favor I ask of you is to take me to his house, to leave me there, and to be discreet."

"You may count, Signora, on the sentiments of a man of honor. I am such, and I already take a deep interest in all that concerns you. Who is this man?" She withdrew a letter from her breast and handed it to Casanova, who recognized the handwriting, which was that of Zanetto (Giovanni) Steffani, promising to marry the Contessina in Venice within a week.

Casanova returned the letter to her, and revealed that he knew the man in question. He was a highly placed government clerk—and in Venice, nothing went forward without their seals and stamps and ribbons and signatures—and it should come as no surprise to her that her suitor was a libertine. Someday, when his mother died, he would be wealthy, but for the moment, he was burdened with debt. Not a wise choice for a husband, Casanova advised.

"Take me to his house," she commanded.

Casanova warned her about this hasty plan. Since Steffani had abandoned her, he certainly would not be pleased to see her show up unexpectedly at his doorstep. Instead, she should keep her own counsel. In the meantime, Casanova offered to find out what Steffani "means to do about you, and what he can be made to do."

But where should she go for the night? She was willing to lodge with Casanova so long as he was married, but he admitted he was a bachelor, so he took her to a respectable widow's home. They boarded a gondola, and slid through the black water. During the ride, she divulged the details of her romance with Steffani, how they'd met a month earlier when his carriage broke down in her city, and they fell in love. Steffani remained nearby for four weeks to court her, lingering under her window. He said he loved her, of course, and that his intentions were honorable, of course, and so she directed him to her parents to ask for her hand in marriage. Instead, he encouraged her to have confidence in him, spend three days alone with him, after which her entire city would regard her as his wife, and when they returned, he would own up to their situation. "Love blinded me," she told Casanova, who had no need of being told. "I believed him, I consented."

The following night, she "consented to the crime." Afterward, Steffani promised to return. She waited in vain, and eventually learned that the "monster" had left. If she couldn't find him and put matters right, she resolved to die. She walked the streets of her city all night, refusing to eat until shortly before boarding the *corriere* bound for Venice. She prayed throughout the entire journey, until she encountered Giacomo Casanova. Now that she had confessed everything, she beseeched him not to "let my pliancy incline you to think ill of my intelligence." Until a month ago, she had been rational, educated, prudent, and now she said amid her tears, "Love made me succumb, together with lack of experience."

Casanova bluntly told her that Steffani had seduced and deceived her solely for his own gratification, and if she thought of him at all, it should be to seek revenge. Far from motivating her, his words caused her to bury her face in her hands. With that, he committed her to the care of the widow for the night, and, echoing Steffani, promised to return to her in the morning.

———•———

Alone, Casanova hurried to Steffani's dwelling. No one knew where he was, not even his mother. She told him to wait, Steffani would eventually turn up.

That evening, Casanova returned to the Contessina bearing gifts: a clavichord and music—she had told him that she was a musician—and "slippers of different sizes." He supposed that her nocturnal walk had worn holes in her shoes. He had no intention of inspiring her to love him, and no desire to fall in love with her. In any case, she wouldn't have been "open to a new love in her terrible condition."

He had assumed what he considered a "delicate obligation" toward the wronged Contessina. He persuaded himself that he was playing his part in a "heroic intrigue" that doubled as an "experiment on myself." He improvised, telling her that she hadn't fallen in love with Steffani, that unworthy cur, she had fallen in love with love itself and temporarily lost her reason. She rushed to agree with him. "I hate the monster!" she declared. Her brother would challenge Steffani to a duel and no doubt kill him.

No, Casanova countered, a coward such as Steffani would never die an honorable death.

At that moment, the Contessina extracted a ten-inch-long stiletto from her pocket and placed it on the table before them. She explained that she had planned to plunge the stiletto into her own breast, but after Casanova's ministrations, she had experienced the will to live again. Greatly agitated, Casanova took the stiletto and left, overwhelmed by his thoughts.

The following day he visited her after the midday meal, determined to coax her into playing the clavichord. He came upon her "combing out a head of very long pale blond hair of a fineness that words are powerless to describe." The sight of her face, neck, shoulders, and arms inflamed him. He babbled about her perfume until his eyes fell on a portrait that resembled her in all respects, except the figure it portrayed had jet-black hair. Her

brother, she explained, a military officer, two years older than she. Emboldened, he offered to place her ring on her finger. She extended her hand, and,
in a gallant gesture, he bowed to kiss it, but she retracted it. He apologized,
and she replied that she must think first of protecting herself from herself rather than from *him*, a remark that he took to be a subtle and telling
compliment.

Then, to his delight, she sat down at the clavichord—at last!—and
played one piece after another, "in the most accomplished manner," and
when she sang an air as she played, Casanova swooned. "Love instantly
bore me to heaven." Again he asked for her hand to kiss. She permitted
him to take it, which he did, fighting to restrain himself from "devouring
it." He knew he was in love, and he must declare himself to her. But what of
Steffani?

He should have told her who he was when they first met, but it was
too late now. That same evening, he treated the Contessina to a carefully
edited tale of his favorite subject, himself, "better than anyone else could
have done it." Before their love affair could proceed, they had to locate Steffani, who might be in the next city, or the next room, no one knew exactly
where he was. His long absence was incomprehensible. She spoke of him
with "hatred" and threatened to seek refuge in a convent.

Casanova learned from Signor Barbaro, one of his trio of patrons, that
the scandal involving Steffani and the Contessina had percolated through
the aristocracy and might soon come before the formidable Council of
Ten. She pleaded with Casanova to intercede "for she would choose death
rather than become the wife of a monster." To demonstrate the perfidy to
which Steffani had subjected her, she produced his written proposal of
marriage.

Later that night, he consulted an oracle and heard that Steffani had
been condemned to death. He professed to be amazed, but at the same time
he'd had the feeling that "Steffani was destined to die at someone's hands."
Signor Bragadin himself had declared that the wretch was already dead,
and all that remained was to persuade the Contessina's family to forgive her
rash actions, for she had been duped and was blameless.

These developments, both occult and obvious, conspired to bring Casanova closer to his love. The "direct intervention of eternal Providence,
of the divine power of our guardian angels," no mere figure of speech, had
been responsible, "and so we fell in love with each other." Caressing her sub-

lime hands with his lips, he asked if she would "fear" him, to which she replied, "The only thing I fear is that I shall lose you." With that admission, he "abandoned" himself to his feelings, and embraced the Contessina, who lowered her eyes and sighed. All around them clocks struck midnight, and the necessity of preserving her honor compelled him to leave. He affixed his mask to his face, clamped his three-cornered hat on his head, and abruptly departed.

On waking in the morning, he brooded over Steffani's death sentence. How could he hate the man responsible for bringing him so much happiness? If only there was some way to revoke the verdict.

At dinner with Signor Bragadin that day, the conversation inevitably turned to Steffani's whereabouts and the Contessina's subsequent behavior. Signor Bragadin had heard from the captain of the *corriere* transporting her to Venice that a masked man met her at the quay, and they left together. Was it Steffani? No, not him. Steffani was short, the masked man tall, like Casanova, but no one made the connection. Instead, they assumed that he must have been a friend of Steffani's. Whoever he was he would have to answer to the Council of Ten. A guessing game as to the identity of the masked man ensued, and Bragadin produced a written list of suspects. Signor Barbaro read the list aloud, and the last name on it belonged to Giacomo Casanova. "When I heard my name I gave a start that set my three friends laughing hilariously." They fell silent when the patrician rushed to his defense, saying that the Contessina would be safe with him "even though he does not have the look of a man to whom one would entrust girls."

Apprehensive, Casanova changed gondolas three times on his way to the Contessina. "In the vast city of Venice this is the best way to foil the efforts of spies who follow a person to learn where he is going." His mask was tightly affixed to his face, his head down, his *tabarro*, or cloak, drawn about him, his whole body in a crouch as he tried to appear just another figure stirring in the foggy atmosphere of Venice, where midnight secrets had a way of becoming midday business, and unseen eyes observed from darkened windows soaring above the canals.

Arriving at his destination, he related the extraordinary dinner conversation to the Contessina, who began crying and laughing, and best of all, embracing Casanova for bringing her this news. Afterward, "We ate supper gaily, without mentioning either Steffani or revenge." And then, "Love had his way with us," he recalled. "I left her at midnight, assuring her that she would see me again seven or eight hours later."

———•———

Casanova refrained from staying with his inamorata because, he explained, "I wanted the hostess to be able to swear that I had never spent even one night there." Despite this sweetest of conquests, he remained vigilant.

When he returned to the Bragadin palazzo, he found his three patrons awaiting him to impart the news that Steffani had "taken the habit of a Capuchin"—the austere religious order—"and the whole Senate knows the fact." This resolution meant additional complications for Casanova, because his three patrons insisted on finding the woman whom Steffani had wronged, and they remained unaware that she had any relationship with their young protégé. They began to pray in unison to the mystical angel they shared, Paralis, who would reveal the answer.

The turn of events roused Casanova to action. He informed his patrons about the Contessina. Signor Dandolo and Signor Barbaro were dumbfounded to learn that Casanova and the girl had been together for nearly two weeks, but Signor Bragadin ascribed these unfathomable events to the workings of the Kabbalah. Casanova had deftly contrived to bring his patrons around to his side.

It was time for him to visit his beloved once more. "I enter, I see her in bed, and I am delighted to observe a smiling cheerfulness in a face in which for ten whole days I had seen nothing but sadness." Only after "long encounters" with her did he reveal what he had learned from his three patrician guardians. True, "the news of Steffani, who, instead of killing himself, had become a Capuchin, took her completely aback," but only for a moment. On reflection, she pitied him. Even Steffani's mother agreed that her son had only two choices, to become a Capuchin monk or to kill himself. Casanova begged to differ. "The world is full of such vindictive mothers," he snorted. "They think they are righteous only when they are trampling on nature. They are evil women." Could it be that he felt a measure of sympathy for Steffani's plight?

In short order, he arranged a reconciliation between the Contessina and her grateful family, pausing briefly to admire his achievement. "What a scene for the stage! The love of a brother and sister expressed in two angelic faces cast in the same mold. A pure shining joy from the most tender em-

braces," and, of course, "Myself, the chief architect of this noble edifice, left
to be a silent spectator, completely forgotten," but only until she placed her
hand in his, and declared Giacomo Casanova "who guarded me from a hundred shames of which I had no conception, and who, you see, is now kissing this hand for the first time" her savior. No sooner had she uttered those
words than she began to cry in a most decorous manner. It was her pure
and virtuous soul speaking, not his own base desires, which he satisfied the
following morning when both lovers thought they might be spending their
last hours together. "She saw my soul sweating blood." After she dressed,
she kissed the slippers he'd given her, and said she was determined to keep
them for the rest of her life, and Casanova requested a length of hair "so that
I could have it made into a braid."

With that tribute accomplished, all that remained was to wish her a safe
journey aboard the same *corriere* that brought her to Venice. He had no intention of spending another minute with her.

———◆———

The summer season in Padua was well under way, the city packed with Venetians on holiday, Casanova among them. He and his three patrician patrons had arrived in the middle of June to attend the fair of Sant'Antonio in
the center of Padua. Returning to the city after a long absence, he discovered that his former teacher Dr. Gozzi had settled in another town, along
with his sister Bettina. As Casanova had predicted, she'd abandoned her
loutish husband, "who had only married her to strip her of her . . . dowry."

Restless in Padua, he "fell in love with one of the most celebrated Venetian courtesans of the time." Her name was Ancilla, Latin for "assistant," and
he met her through a "a young man as harebrained as myself," also given to
living as an adventurer, with a literary streak, named Count Tommaso Medina, who enjoyed pride of place as first among Ancilla's lovers, but Casanova hoped there would be room for one more. Her beauty was legendary,
her reputation immense. Ancilla ran a gambling establishment, and Count
Medina "introduced me to her only in order to make me his dupe at cards."
Casanova naively cooperated until the "fatal moment" when he caught his
glamorous companions cheating him, and put a pistol to Count Medina's
chest.

Ancilla fainted, as the Count slowly repaid Casanova, and ended by
challenging the reckless young Venetian to a duel. The combatants pro-

ceeded to the great square beside the Basilica of Saint Anthony to carry out their folly. Dueling was common, but Casanova, an inexperienced swordsman, was at a disadvantage.

Swords drawn, their blades clashing by moonlight, Casanova "had the good fortune to wound him in the shoulder"—it could have been more serious for them both—and the Count, clutching his arm, surrendered. Casanova went directly home, thinking the dispute resolved, but Signor Bragadin, better schooled in these matters, warned him to leave Padua immediately and return to Venice. The problem was *not* resolved; far from it. "This Count Medina was my enemy all the rest of my life." Nor was he done with the courtesan Ancilla.

Chapter 5

Henriette

C asanova gambled obsessively, but his luck ran out and he lost everything. He found himself in desperate need of two hundred *zecchini*.
To pay the debt, he borrowed an expensive diamond ring, which
he planned to pawn in Treviso, about fifteen miles away. "This admirable
institution is not to be found in Venice," he observed, "because the Jews are
powerful enough to prevent its establishment," although they did maintain
a similar facility in Venice for the poor. He would travel by gondola and
carriage to Treviso, obtain his *zecchini*, and return to Venice the same day
to settle his debt. One thing led to another, and he remained in Treviso for
most of the year.

In the autumn of 1747, a friend of Casanova's introduced him to a zany
family living in the town of Zero Blanco, near Treviso. "There was gaming,
lovemaking, and much amusing practical joking," he noted. "Taking offense
at anything was not allowed. You had to see the joke or be written off as
a fool." This seemed a world made for Casanova, with his love of make-
believe, disguise, and sleight of hand.

One day, in the company of several women, he took a shortcut across
a farm; they came to a plank crossing a ditch. They refused to cross it, so
he went first to encourage them, "and when I was halfway across, the piece
of plank on which I had set my foot suddenly gives and drops me into the
ditch, which was full not of water but of dirty, stinking mud. I was buried in filth up to my neck." He was obliged to join in the general hilarity at
his plight, as peasants dragged him from the foul muck. "My new fall suit
embroidered with sequins was ruined, as well as my stockings and shoes."
More serious was the injury to his vanity. As he laughed, "I was determined
to take cruel revenge, for the joke was cruel," he told himself. What had
begun as a prank quickly became a blood feud.

Noticing that the plank had been sawn in advance, he bribed a peasant woman to tell him the name of the perpetrator, who turned out to be a young man hired by the actual malefactor, Signor Demetrio, a middle-aged Greek spice merchant. As it happened, Casanova liked Signor Demetrio. True, he had played a practical joke on the Greek by seducing his girlfriend, a simple chambermaid, but what harm could there be in that little piece of mischief? The question now was how to have his revenge on the "malicious Greek." Nothing came to mind until he encountered the burial of a corpse. Late that night, he wrote, "I went to the graveyard alone with my hunting knife, I uncovered the dead man, I cut off his arm at the shoulder, not without great difficulty." He reinterred the disfigured corpse and carried the severed arm to his room.

The next day, Casanova concealed himself beneath the Greek's bed, holding the arm of the corpse and waiting for his victim to return to his room. "When I think he is asleep I pull down the covers at the foot until he is bare to the hips. I hear him laugh and say: 'Whoever you are, go away and let me sleep. I don't believe in ghosts.'" He pulled the covers up and tried to go back to sleep. A few minutes later, Casanova repeated the trick, this time grasping the sheets, so that the Greek reached to tug them back. "Instead of letting him find my hand I make him find the dead man's." The Greek pulled harder and harder until Casanova finally released the severed arm. He expected to hear the Greek cry out in horror. Instead, there was only silence. "My play"—note Casanova's theatrical context—"being over, I go to my room, sure that I had given him a great fright but had done no other harm."

In the morning, the mistress of the house informed him: "Signor Demetrio is dying."

Did I kill him? Casanova asked himself.

He went to the room where he'd left the Greek; it was now occupied by the entire household, a priest, and a beadle, who was refusing to rebury the severed arm. When Casanova entered, "they all look at me with horror, and only laugh when I insist that I know nothing about the matter." How could they find him guilty? To which they answer collectively that he's the only one they knew who was capable of such a deed. In the hours that followed, the Greek merchant, having been bled (or despite having been bled), regained the ability to move his eyes, but he still couldn't speak or move his arms and legs; the following day, he regained the power of speech, but remained spasmodic. It seemed he'd suffered a stroke, and, Casanova says, "He passed the rest of his life in the same condition."

Casanova received a summons to appear before a special court on charges of blasphemy. Demanding to know the reason for the indictment, he declared himself "astonished" to learn that he'd been accused of cutting off the dead man's arm. He thought his exploits a practical joke, not criminal behavior. Soon after, he was charged with having disinterred and disfigured a corpse. Even Casanova recognized that his behavior amounted to a "crime of the utmost gravity."

Signor Bragadin advised him to "bow before the storm." Assured by his three sponsors that within a year he would be free and clear of these charges, Casanova became a fugitive.

———•———

He wandered from city to city in the north of Italy. In Mantua, a policeman arrested Casanova for failing to carry a lantern one evening. The supervising captain ordered him freed, and within a couple of hours, two officers joined them, as well as "two disgusting prostitutes." The four of them drank and gambled. When Casanova lurched outside to catch his breath and clear his head, one of the prostitutes followed, attempting to grope her way to his affection; she succeeded and as a result he suffered his fourth outbreak of venereal disease.

"I cured myself completely in six weeks simply by drinking a decoction of saltpeter, but at the same time observing a diet that I found extremely monotonous," he explained.

Easter 1748 arrived on April 14. On the festive day Casanova found himself chatting amiably with an elderly woman, an actress who'd retired from the stage twenty years before.

Casanova was impressed by the effort she made to maintain her appearance, covering herself with powder, heightening her features with rouge, dying her eyebrows black, and wearing false teeth top and bottom. "She displayed one half of her flaccid bosom, which aroused disgust because it showed what it might have been." She reeked of ambergris, a popular perfume of the era, and as he approached to shake her trembling hand, he saw that "her hair was nothing but a wig that adhered very imperfectly to her forehead and temples." He winced, and suppressed a laugh to see that her sense of fashion was at least twenty years out of date. Finally, "I saw with terror the marks of hideous old age on a face, which, before time had ruined it, must have made many a man a lover." Despite everything, she carried herself as if she were one of the most attractive women in the world. At that moment, he noticed something about her that had resisted time: "the bright strawberry mark on her chest" that gave her the name she would always have: La Fragoletta, the little strawberry. He trembled because, as he put it, "the phantom before me was the cause of my existence." This was the actress "whose magic had seduced my father thirty years earlier." If not for her, his father "would never have begotten me on a Venetian woman." Now here before him was his father's first love, Zanetta's predecessor, La Fragoletta, Giovanna Benozzi, a fading theatrical legend with whom he had a secret connection. It was as though he were simultaneously hurtled back to a time before his life began and forward to the fragile future of the most important women in his life.

La Fragoletta asked his name. "Casanova," he informed her. She stirred.

"Yes, Signora, and my father, whose name was Gaetano, was from Parma."

The elderly actress came to life. "I adored your father."

Giacomo had always heard that La Fragoletta had tired of Gaetano and moved on, but at this moment she added a twist to the ancient story. His father, she said, had been "unjustly jealous," and so, "he abandoned me. But for that, you would have been my son." The circumstances of his father's abandonment of her no longer mattered. "Let me embrace you like a mother," she proposed.

Casanova let her hold him, caress him, and soothe him with tender sentiments of what might have been but never was. This decorous intimacy was more than he could bear. She wiped away her tears, "always the actress," he observed, as she begged him not to doubt her sincerity, although she didn't appear distraught. The vanity of the creature! She'd loved his father, she said, his only fault being his "ingratitude." Casanova explained in his memoir that "she was to find the same fault in his son, for despite all the obliging offers she made me, I did not set foot in her house again."

———•———

By 1749, Casanova was less impressionable than his younger self, and as outrageous as ever as he waited out his exile from Venice. In the summer of that year, he took an interest in a woman he described as an officer's mistress. He'd peeked at her when she was hiding in bed at the same inn in which he was staying, and later, when talking over the midday meal, "she displayed the kind of wit which I greatly admired, which is seldom found in Italy and often found in France." He decided she would be an easy conquest, and her male companion realistic and accommodating. All he had to do was offer them seats in his carriage, and travel with them. He learned they were going to Parma; therefore, *he* was going to Parma. The officer, as expected, immediately accepted Casanova's offer, and directed him to his desirable companion, on whom he bestowed the revealing yet concealing pseudonym of Henriette.

Her true identity has long intrigued Casanova scholars. Some have proposed Jeanne Marie d'Albert de Saint-Hippolyte, thirty-one years of age, and freshly separated from her husband to whom she had been married for five years. Another candidate is Anne-Henriette de Bourbon, one of Louis XV's eight daughters. The third, and perhaps most likely candidate, is her sister, Adélaïde de Gueidan. In *Casanova's Women*, Judith Summers mounts a convincing case on behalf of Adélaïde, who was born on December 14, 1725, educated in a convent, became a marquise through marriage, and the mother of three children. More sophisticated and gracious than the courtesans, harridans, and rough-hewn country girls whom he was accustomed to seducing or being seduced by, she was touched with magnificence. In Casanova's memoirs, she always remained, simply, Henriette: "Will you, Madame Henriette, grant me the honor of conducting you to Parma."

"I would be delighted."

So began the most obsessive love affair of his life. First, he had to obtain a carriage. He'd been bluffing when he made his generous offer. Now he went to a local café, found an appropriate carriage, asking price two hundred zecchini, obtained a pair of horses, and in and around making arrangements, amused himself by talking with Henriette. "I admired a wit in her which was entirely new to me, for I had never conversed with a Frenchwoman." At first, he assumed she was an "adventuress" seeking the next swindle, a pretender like all the rest—himself included—yet he was "surprised to find her entertaining sentiments that I thought could only be the fruit of a most refined education." And she was maddeningly discreet, refusing to divulge the slightest crumb about her companion and lover, the officer, yet maintaining an effortless charm. He was confident that he could please her "since I had plenty of money and was completely my own master," and within two or three days, at most, they would consummate their relationship. In his imagination, even her companion the officer, who spoke Hungarian, willed it. "Aside from the fact that on the physical side I had all that an acceptable lover could have in order to hope to please, I also appeared to be very rich, even though I had no servant." He talked his way around that omission that having no servant meant no spy, no thief in his house. "Henriette understood me perfectly; and in short my future happiness intoxicated me."

When the time came to depart, a "contest of politeness" took place between Casanova and the compliant officer over who would sit beside Henriette. Casanova found himself directly across from her so that he could look her in the eye without turning his head. The three of them made halting, mostly unintelligible conversation in Hungarian (the officer), French (Henriette), and Latin (Casanova). It was impossible to engage in flirtatious repartee amid the babel: "In all the languages of the world what one learns last is their wit; and it is very often the idiom that makes the joke."

Yet his suit progressed quickly because by the end of the day, when they stopped at an inn between Bologna and Rimini, "the girl had struck me as so unpredictable I was afraid she would leave her lover's bed and get into mine." If that happened, Casanova, who spoke not a word of Hungarian, would be unable to negotiate with her companion. "I wished to obtain possession of Henriette in peace and quiet, as the result of an amicable and honorable arrangement." What did Henriette see in him? She never mentioned her family, and Casanova never revealed his disreputable recent history: the severed arm, the dabbling in magic, or his dubious status in Venice.

To add to the mystery, Henriette possessed "nothing but the male attire she was wearing, not a scrap of woman's clothing, not even a shirt. When she changed hers, she put on a fresh shirt belonging to her lover. This was as new to me as it was puzzling." The outfit's hermaphrodism transfixed Casanova as Bellino's convincing transvestism once had. He questioned Henriette about her origins, her motives, but she deferred to her companion, whose account, when translated from Hungarian to Latin, proved equally baffling. "I can tell you nothing about her situation. All I know is that she wishes to be called Henriette, that she must be French, that she is as gentle as a lamb, that she seems to have had an excellent education, that she is in perfect health, and that she must be both intelligent and courageous." Perhaps she would relate her story to Casanova; if so, the Hungarian would be pleased to hear it. Despite their closeness, and even their presumed physical intimacy, they weren't in love; the Hungarian considered Henriette a dear friend.

When both men turned to Henriette for an explanation, she responded, "The same principle that forbids me to lie does not allow me to tell the truth." Approaching Parma, she expressed the wish that her older traveling companion would forget her, and if they met again by chance, would "pretend not to know me." With those words, she embraced the Hungarian with "far more compassion than love." Casanova translated her parting words for the old man, and observed their mortifying effect. A melancholy mood settled over the three of them, as Casanova studied Henriette's "fiery red" face.

"Who can this girl be, who combines the finest feelings with an appearance of the greatest libertinism?" he wondered as he readied himself for bed. He would most likely lose her the moment they reached Parma, when she flitted to her next assignation, but what if, "in a spirit of unbridled libertinism, she means to defy fortune to plunge into the most terrible abyss?" That would be the "project of a madwoman or a woman in despair." The officer had tried to give her zecchini, and she had refused even that modest amount despite "the risk of finding herself on the street of Parma." What calculations had led to that decision? And why had she made him fall in love with her? She must have known that he would seduce her sooner rather than later. "If she thought she could play the prude with me and make me her dupe, I ought to show her that she was mistaken," he decided. Before falling asleep, he vowed to ask her "to grant the same favors that she has granted the officer," and if she refused, he'd obtain his revenge "by showing her the most humiliating contempt." He expected no trouble from the Hungarian, "sensible man" that he was.

Henriette appeared to him that night in a dream, telling him that she loved him, that she knew not a soul in Parma, that she was "neither mad nor desperate," and, most important, "I want only to be yours." In the dream, she yielded to his "amorous transports," as he claimed the phantom for his own throughout the night. "What a long dream!" He'd dreamed of women before, but nothing like this, never for the entire night, until the reverie rivaled reality. When he finally roused himself from sleep, and realized the perplexing truth of his "blissful dream," he acknowledged that even awake he was "helplessly in love."

In this altered state, he dressed and went to the room Henriette shared with the Hungarian. "I inform the officer that I have fallen in love with Henriette." Would he mind if Casanova "tried to persuade her" to become his mistress? He desired half an hour to discuss the matter with her, and if she refused, he would remain here, at this way station, while the two of them traveled onward to their destination. Why, no, the Hungarian would not mind; Casanova could have two hours with her to "persuade her to do what you wish." In fact, he confided, "I should be infinitely happy to leave her in your custody."

Once again, Casanova took to referring to the goings-on as a "play." He invited Henriette to tour Bologna with him; she agreed so long as she was dressed as a woman. The last thing she wanted was to "go about showing herself to the whole city in men's clothes." As soon as the Hungarian left them alone, Casanova interrogated her with lovelorn desperation. Was he merely part of an endless series of mysterious affairs? Not precisely. She feared the harm caused by the Hungarian's inquiries. Casanova had shown himself to be her friend, and she would not make the same demand of him.

"I cannot possibly leave you alone," he burst out, "with no money and nothing you can sell, in the middle of the street in a city in which you cannot converse." And besides, anyone who complied with her request was not truly her friend. But she remained convinced the Hungarian would forget her.

In that case, said Casanova, "the friendship he feels for you is of an entirely different nature from mine," because—and here he finally declared himself—"I love you." Summoning melodrama appropriate to the occasion, he concluded, "Know, Madame, that a Frenchman"—or, for that matter, a Hungarian—"may be able to forget, but an Italian, to judge by myself, has no such strange power." Should he accompany her to Parma, or go his separate way? "Choose, before that worthy and only too desperate man returns."

Henriette laughed. "I have never in my life conceived of a declaration of love being made in anger." When he should have been tender, he was demanding.

He understood, but they weren't characters in a novel; this was real life, "history," as he put it, and less tidy than fiction. "Do you realize the excruciating condition of a man in love at the moment when he must choose a course that can determine his very life?" he asked, choking on his inquiry.

"Still the same tone?" Henriette complained. "Do you know that you appear to be in a rage?"

No! he countered, he was not in a rage, he was in the grip of a "violent paroxysm." Only her decision could relieve him of this exquisite agony. He dared her to invite—no, not to invite, as if to a garden party—to *tell* him to come to Parma with her.

Yes, she finally replied, *venez à Parme.*

"I fell at her feet, I clasped her knees, kissing them a hundred times; no more anger, no more harsh tones, tender, submissive, grateful, ardent, I swear I will never even ask to kiss her hands until I have deserved her heart." She instructed her supplicant to rise and whispered that she was sure that he loved her, and that she would do everything in her power to keep him faithful. "I had my lips pressed to her beautiful hands when the Captain came in. He congratulated us. I told him happily that I would go and order the horses, and left him with her. We set off together, all three of us well satisfied."

By nightfall, the Hungarian, his mission complete, left Casanova and Henriette at an inn while he went on to Parma alone. At dinner, they groped for a suitable topic of discussion. "We knew we were going to sleep together; but we would have thought it indiscreet to say so to each other. What a night! What a woman she was, this Henriette whom I loved so greatly, who made me so happy!"

They arrived in Parma, Casanova going by his mother's name, Farussi, and Henriette calling herself Anne d'Arci. A young Frenchman directed them to an inn, D'Andremont's, with French food, wine, and furnishings. Casanova engaged the young man as their lackey.

The recent conclusion of the War of the Austrian Succession brought a new order to Parma. On March 7, 1749, Prince Philip of Spain had entered the city to take possession. To Casanova, this abrupt political transition meant that "spies must be everywhere." As if to confirm his misgivings, "I heard passers-by speaking together in French or in Spanish." When he tried to purchase petticoats and corsets for Henriette, he found the shopkeeper in a state of panic over the political situation. Instead, he arranged for a seamstress to come to their inn to fashion "dresses, hats, mantles, everything, for as a woman you can imagine her stark naked." So long as he could pay, the excited seamstress told him, the lady would lack for nothing. He would reconstruct her, in the manner of Pygmalion. "I told the seamstress, who was with her daughter, to follow me, carrying my linen. I stop only to buy both silk and cotton stockings, and as I enter my apartment, I bring in my shoe-maker, who was at the door. That was the moment of true pleasure! Henri-ette, to whom I had said nothing, watches everything being laid out on the table with a look of the most complete contentment." They hired a reti-nue of servants to complement their shoemaker and seamstresses, a varied group conversing in French, Flemish, Italian, and, when the captain joined them, Hungarian. Henriette called the captain "Papa," and Casanova took to calling Henriette "my dear wife."

Late that night, Henriette, turning melancholy, said that if Casanova was spending his money to make her love him, he was "throwing it away, for I love you more than I did yesterday." Casanova, for his part, beseeched her never to abandon him. "Who can be certain of the future?" she rejoined. Was he at liberty? Of course he was. But she could not match his claim. "I am certain I am being sought; and I know that if they catch up with me they can easily find means to gain possession of me." If they did, she vowed to kill herself. She stepped back a bit, explaining that she did not think she was in imminent peril, merely relieved to have been done with her previous companion, on whom she lavished her favors only because he protected her, not because of any true affection between the two of them. She resorted to this expedient to prevent her father-in-law from placing her in a con-vent, tantamount to a prison sentence. More than that, she refused to di-vulge. And so, "We went to bed in love, only to rise in the morning even more in love. I spent three months with her, always as much in love and constantly congratulating myself that I was so." What had started as infat-uation ripened into delirium. He felt launched into the empyrean, gulping great drafts of immortality with her. In addition to all her sensual charms, the divine Henriette appealed to his snobbery, his wish to participate vicar-iously in the nobility and thus raise himself to a higher level of existence than was possible in stratified Venice. Perhaps she knew she was slumming, but with a genius eager to satisfy her whims, who had willingly abandoned everything for her. He was both her servant and her incubus.

In the morning, Valentin de la Haye, a language teacher and professor of mathematics, arrived to instruct Henriette in Italian; she paid him six lire for a two-hour lesson. (Those were Parmesan lire, Casanova noted, equiva-lent to thirty French sous, or a twentieth of a franc.) In addition, she tipped him two zecchini after the lesson to buy the latest novels.

With de la Haye, "learnèd in an old-fashioned way," Casanova engaged in a spirited debate concerning Copernicus' discovery, in 1543, that the earth revolved around the sun. A Christian, the teacher said, could accept the Copernican revolution only as an "ingenious hypothesis" not to be found in Scripture, a pronouncement that gave Casanova the ammunition he needed to affirm "that Scripture was not the book from which a Christian could learn physics." Nevertheless, if this veritable "Tartuffe"—by this Casanova meant Molière's pious hypocrite—"could amuse Henriette and teach her Italian, it was all I wanted."

Casanova exulted in one of the happiest phases of his life, as far removed from the deprivations of his schoolboy days and its vermin-infested beds as he could imagine. He was constantly united with the object of his affections, and protected from the vicissitudes of reality, at least for the time being. He'd never known such love, so generous, so intense, so constant. "They who do not believe that a woman is capable of making a man equally happy all the twenty-four hours of a day have never known a Henriette," he wrote in a celebrated passage. "The joy that flooded my soul was far greater when I conversed with her during the day than when I held her in my arms during the night. Having read a great deal and having natural taste, Henriette judged rightly of everything and, though not learned, she reasoned like a geometrician. Since she did not pretend to intellect, she never said anything important except with a laugh which, by giving it the color of frivolity, put it within the capacity of the entire company." At times she was like a wife to him, at other times, a mistress. "When we went to bed together, it seemed as if it were for the first time."

Although Casanova experienced bliss with Henriette, he echoed the era's condescending assessment of female intellect. "In a woman, learning is out of place; it compromises the essential qualities of her sex; then, too, it never goes beyond the limits of what is already known. No scientific discoveries have been made by women. To go beyond required a vigor that the female sex cannot have. But in simple reasoning and in delicacy of feeling we must yield to women."

As the idyll with Henriette in Parma ran on, small fissures appeared. After dressing her in the finest raiment obtainable, he naturally wanted to parade her about the city, but she was deathly afraid of being discovered, captured, and spirited away. To allay her anxiety, he obtained for her a list of visiting foreigners; she inspected it, and none of the names raised a red flag. Hearing that the wife of the Prince of France had arrived in Parma, Casanova, still flush, engaged a box at the opera, where she was sure to be found—not once a month or once a week, but once a day. "*You mean you want us to go to the opera every day?*" asked Henriette, appalled. She was no lover of opera, and she was fearful of showing herself in public, but Casanova was becoming more Venetian all the time. The opera, the theater, and melody were all in his blood.

"I am mad about music, my dear; I cannot help trembling at the very thought of going out."

"If you tremble, I shudder."

To respect Henriette's need for privacy, Casanova took a box in the second tier. The theater was so small "a pretty woman could not fail to be noticed in it." They arrived, Henriette cowering in the dark without a candle, without rouge, trying to pass as another face in the crowd. She hid behind her opera glasses, never examining the occupants of the boxes. "No one seemed curious about us, so we went home well satisfied, in the bosom of peace and love." To recapture the moment, he tried to obtain the score of the finale of the second act, as well as a harpsichord, but "she had never learned to play the instrument."

Life went on for about a month in this artificial mode; Henriette learned to speak Italian, pleasing Casanova; they went to the opera "a score of times without making any acquaintances." Other than that, they never went out, and they refused to receive callers, of which there were none. "I knew no one and no one knew me." The Hungarian admirer departed. "Living together in this fashion, and tasting the delights of true happiness, we scoffed at the philosophy that denies that happiness can be perfect, because, it maintains, it is not enduring."

Henriette begged to differ. "Lifelong happiness could be compared to a bouquet composed of various flowers that would make a combination so beautiful and so harmonious that one would take it for a single flower." It would crown their happiness, she said, for the two of them to die together after a lifetime of bliss. "I was very happy with Henriette," Casanova affirmed, "and she was no less happy with me."

They did, in time, allow themselves to be lured to a supper party with visiting musicians in attendance. This wasn't Venice, no one wore masks, but they might as well have, for overly informative introductions and prying questions had no part in the proceedings. Henriette forced herself to endure the scrutiny of the other guests. If something went awry, if she were recognized, Casanova was prepared to flee with her to England, so he said. Everyone, it seemed, paid compliments to the beautiful Henriette, "which she received with an ease unknown anywhere but in France, and indeed only in the most exalted circles."

The evening became a revelation when the musicians gathered to perform a composition for a small orchestra. At the conclusion, Henriette rose without warning and asked one of the musicians to give her his cello. "She sits down in his place, takes the instrument between her knees, and asks the orchestra to begin the concerto over again." Silence descended; Casanova was aghast; Henriette couldn't play the harpsichord, let alone a cello, he recalled, as she readied herself to perform. "I thought it was only a joke that would end with this really charming tableau; but when I saw her make the first stroke of the bow, I thought the excessive palpitation of my heart would strike me dead." As Casanova held his breath, she played, and the audience applauded, rattling him to the marrow of his bones, but seeming to have no effect on Henriette, "at least visibly." She played her solo through not once but six times, refused to acknowledge the applause she'd elicited, and said only that she'd never played on a better instrument, as if to transfer responsibility for her virtuosity. She ended by apologizing for lengthening the concert by half an hour.

Casanova excused himself and daubed at his tears, and when he returned to the guests, only Henriette knew what the red tinge in the whites of his eyes meant. At supper, she continued her triumph, conquering with wit, as the host looked on as if he were a proud impresario. At first, he "pretended submission and the most profound respect for the goddess" seated before him, until he came to realize that "she wanted everyone to understand that I was her oracle." Him! Giacomo Casanova. Perhaps they assumed she was his wife. The host tried tripping her up by asking whether she preferred France or Spain, in front of guests of both nations. Casanova squirmed, but he needn't have: "She talked so well that the Spaniards wished they were French and the Frenchmen wished they were Spanish." The host even queried her about the Italians, at which point Casanova longed to disappear through a hole in the floor. Henriette explained that since she knew just one Italian, she couldn't draw any hard and fast conclusions. Her modesty had won the day. "I should have been the stupidest of men if I had shown the least sign that I had heard Henriette's magnificent answer," he recalled. She then explained that she'd learned the cello in a convent and would have continued her musical training "in the hope of pleasing my mother," but the abbess wouldn't allow it because "she insisted that I could not hold the instrument except by assuming an indecent posture." The severe Spaniards, Casanova reported, bit their lips on hearing this account, "but the Frenchmen roared with laughter." Soon after, Henriette rose, and, accompanied by Casanova, steeped in the delight of love, departed.

"At this moment, I must be mortally hated," he boasted to her. "You are my universe. Cruel Henriette! You very nearly killed me with your cello! As I could not believe that you would have kept it a secret, I thought you had gone mad, and as soon as I heard you, I had to go out to dry the tears that you forced from my heart." What other hidden skills did she possess? She must confess so that he wouldn't "die of terror or surprise." When she played, the cello's almost human voice went straight to his heart. At length she assured him that she had "emptied my sack, and now you know your Henriette completely." Or did he? Despite his unbounded admiration for her, Casanova conceded that she had a way of saying one thing and doing another. She was even more adept at disguise than he.

———•———

In pursuit of a milieu commensurate with his new love, Casanova had recklessly exposed Henriette to spies and scouts. Now her task was to keep him well disposed to her, especially after he had tended to her needs and vanity, and protected her from unnamed predators. For a time, she succeeded; Casanova recalled that they "spent three or four weeks lost in happiness. In the sweet union of our hearts and our souls not one empty moment ever came to show us that dreary specimen of misery known as a yawn." Occasionally they went for a drive in a carriage, which they never left, and never met anyone, despite inquiries from those—especially men—who had encountered Henriette at the party. No one recognized her!

They attended a lavish party at the Ducal Palace in Colorno, near Parma, where the French court was receiving guests. For Casanova, strolling through the gardens was a delight, but for the reclusive Henriette it meant risking discovery. Soon enough a Chevalier, or member of an order of merit or chivalry, began following them. He was an older gentleman, and when he caught up with them, he introduced himself as D'Antoine, or to give his full name and title, Count François d'Antoine-Placas, Gentleman of the Bedchamber to the Duke of Parma and Chief Equerry—stable manager—to the Duchess Louise Elisabeth. Henriette fixed him with a frosty gaze.

"I do not remember, Monsieur, that I have ever had the honor of seeing you."

"That is enough, Madame. I beg you to forgive me."

Later that night, she admitted that she was aware of d'Antoine, or at least his family, "well known in Provence." Her discomfort worried Casanova, who proposed that they move on to Venice. The idea of Henriette in Venice! Yet when they returned to Parma, they realized they were not yet rid of d'Antoine, who'd requested a meeting. At Henriette's urging, Casanova agreed to appear in the ducal garden at half past eleven, where he met the gentleman, who vouchsafed him a sealed letter intended for the lady, who, if she chose, could allow him to read it. After that encounter, matters deteriorated quickly. Henriette opened the four-page document, read it carefully, but on a point of honor would not permit Casanova to do the same. Worse, she'd have to receive Monsieur d'Antoine because they were related.

"Miserable wretch that I am!" he exclaimed with all the conviction he could muster, and castigated himself for his stupidity in remaining with her in Parma, where the likelihood of her being discovered was nearly as great as it would have been in France. "Could I have made more stupid mistake?" he cried. Now it was too late to correct it, and he was filled with gloom concerning the "most painful outcome that I can imagine."

Henriette tried to assuage his concerns. Yes, she would meet d'Antoine, but no, she would not agree to his promptings. She would not return to France; instead, "We will go and spend the rest of our days together wherever you choose." And yet . . . that might not be the best course for them. They would have to consider the alternatives, and to think of ways to live and be happy in the future without one another, if it came to that. "Trust in me," she implored. They had not made a mistake by negotiating with Monsieur d'Antoine; otherwise, he might have decided to make his own investigation and report the scandalous findings to her family, "which would have exposed me to violent proceedings which your love could not have tolerated."

"From that moment," he wrote, "our love began to grow sad, and sadness is a disease that in the end kills love." They stared at one another for an hour without speaking. The light that was Henriette dimmed. Their idyll was coming to its inevitable end. Both lovers were fugitives in the chaos of Parma, Henriette fleeing her family, Casanova escaping the Venetian authorities.

The next day, Monsieur d'Antoine came, and spent most of the day with Henriette. "I spent six very boring hours alone, pretending I was writing," Casanova recalled with anguish, as he glanced them in his mirror. "I could see nothing but the saddest of outcomes."

When her visitor had departed, Henriette came to him, her eyes swollen with tears. They would go away together, but only for two weeks, during which time she would fear no violence. "I can no longer bear this city!" she said of Parma.

"I loathe it," Casanova agreed. "Shall we go to Milan!"

"Excellent! To Milan."

———•———

After two weeks of melancholy indulgence in a love grown old, they returned to Parma, and d'Antoine showed up for dinner, uninvited, imposing his unwelcome self. When he left, she came to Casanova, grief-stricken, and said the time had come to depart. They would travel to Geneva together, and go their separate ways. Several days later, at nightfall, they set out, pausing at Turin to engage a servant for the rest of the journey to Geneva. It was winter, and the track took them over a frozen Alpine pass in sedan chairs and, later, in a sleigh.

Five days later, they arrived in Geneva, where they stayed at the city's best hotel, Á la Balance, a name appropriate to their tottering life. There Henriette made financial arrangement with her banker, and they "remained together, gloomy and pensive, as one is when the most profound sorrow weighs on the mind." Parma, and all the rest of it, the precious, irretrievable moments, the joys and sorrows, vanished like tendrils of smoke in the cold Geneva gusts. They tried to comfort one another by exchanging gifts, each one of which only emphasized the reality of their farewell. Casanova, who'd been paying their extravagant expenses since they'd been together, accepted five rolls of a hundred louis each, roughly ten thousand francs in gold coins, "a poor consolation for my heart, only too oppressed by so cruel a parting." And then, sighs, tears, embraces, but no hope of a reunion. In fact, Henriette specifically asked him never to inquire about her, and if their paths should ever cross again by accident, he must pretend not to know her. At least he would have no false hope: cold comfort.

Henriette's expert stage-managing of their parting continued the next day when she instructed Casanova to remain in Geneva until he received a letter that she would send to him from the first place she changed horses on her voyage home. "She left at daybreak, with her lady-in-waiting beside her and a footman on the coachman's seat and another ahead on horseback. I did not go back upstairs to our room until after I had followed the carriage with my eyes and long after lost it from sight. After ordering the waiter not to enter my room until the horses with which Henriette was traveling should have returned, I went to bed, hoping that sleep would come to the aid of my grief-stricken soul."

Casanova didn't hear from Henriette until the next day, when the coach from Châtillon, the first stop on the highway to France, returned to Geneva, bearing a letter from her. Mad with expectation, he tore it open, and read its single, unarguable word: "Farewell." Not "I love you," nor "I will always keep you in my heart." Her decision to return to her family plunged him into despondency; he compared love to an incurable illness and a divine monster. "I spent two of the saddest days of my life alone in my room," he recalled. "On one of its two windows I saw written: 'You will forget Henriette too.'" *Tu oublieras aussi Henriette.* "She had written the words with the point of a small diamond, set in a ring, which I had given her." It seemed a heartless command, but it was designed to free him from enslavement to her memory. She was wrong. He never did forget her, "and it is a balm to my soul every time I remember her."

In the morning, he commenced the arduous journey from Geneva to Venice. Who could tell what adventures awaited him when he arrived?

Chapter 6

Mimi

t first, he felt a "kind of despair that also has a certain sweetness" as he traversed the Alps over the Great St. Bernard Pass. At an altitude of eight thousand feet, the route was as still, cold, and otherworldly as death. Descending the slippery, icy path, he returned to Parma in January 1750, where he lodged at a dreary hovel, as if to scourge himself after his months of indulgence in this city with Henriette. Once there, he carried out her last request, to deliver a letter to d'Antoine, but when the recipient opened it, he handed it back to Casanova, for it contained a letter meant for *him*.

"Let us not complain of our destiny," she beseeched him, comparing their time together to an agreeable dream. She would take care of herself for the rest of her life, and be as happy as she could without him. Even now she admitted that she still didn't know who he really was, yet "no one in the world knows you better than I do." She assured him that she would have no more lovers in her entire life—how could he tell?—but she hoped, that is, acknowledged, that he wouldn't even think of emulating her in that regard, and in closing, she wrote, "I wish you to love again, and even to find another Henriette."

He went to bed for days, neither eating nor drinking. "Such is the effect of a great sorrow." In time Valentin de la Haye, the language teacher and Jesuit, rescued him, coaxed him into taking broth, and later a light meal, and preached a sermon on "the vanity of this mortal life." The longer de la Haye stayed, the more Casanova came to like him. Meanwhile, another encounter, this time with an "actress"—a synonym for prostitute—which he hoped would help banish thoughts of Henriette, left him with his third or fourth, no, his *fifth* case of venereal disease, and each time he should have known better than to have relations with a whore—but he kept his misery to himself because he considered it just punishment "for having so basely abandoned myself after having belonged to a Henriette."

He confessed his plight to his apparently impoverished dining companion and spiritual advisor de la Haye, who located the surgeon, Jacques Frémont (who doubled as a dentist), to treat his friend's condition with the regimen Casanova called "the great cure," which involved mercury, erroneously thought to heal veneral disease, and isolation of six tedious weeks in his little room, where his only visitor was, inevitably, de la Haye, who preached that Casanova should consider himself lucky to have acquired this disease, which gave him an opportunity to seek salvation in God. He wept with contrition, and de la Haye sobbed along with him, talking about Paradise "as if he had been there in person." By this time Casanova was so addled that, as he recalled, "I did not laugh at him." The two men embraced, as de la Haye assured his protégé that he was "following the one sure road to Heaven." Casanova was too befuddled to disagree.

By April, with the weather improving, his venereal disease apparently resolved, and his isolation ended, Casanova learned that the charges against him in Venice for exhuming a corpse and using the severed arm to harm an old man had been dropped. Feeling lighter of heart than he had for months, he arranged to return to Venice with de la Haye, who'd taken to calling Casanova his son, and prattling about the "divine mark of predestination" stamped on the young man's visage.

———•———

"After a year's absence my friends received me as if I were an angel come from Heaven," Casanova boasted. Bragadin and the others happily made the acquaintance of de la Haye. How splendid it was to be back among familiar sights and sounds after his turbulent year of exile, to see familiar faces, and listen to the shouts of children and merchants ricocheting off the walls, and to watch the gondolas silently ply their trade and the masked denizens of Venice glide past in their *tabarri* like swarms of black jellyfish.

He came to realize that de la Haye, though he played the role of "thorough Christian to perfection," was in fact a "thorough hypocrite . . . who at bottom cared for nothing but his own well-being" and with "no inclination for sex." He spoke incessantly of "God, angels, and eternal glory, always going to one church after another" with the three patricians, who fancied him a holy hermit, a member of a secret order, or Casanova's mysterious instructor in Kabbalah. His playacting succeeded. "In the short space of three weeks I saw him obtain such an ascendancy over their minds that he was foolish enough to think that he had no further need of me to maintain his standing and even had enough standing to knock me head over heels if he felt so inclined."

De la Haye and the three patricians communicated in a private language, pointedly excluding Casanova. To poison the patricians' mind against their protégé, de la Haye began "complaining, though in honeyed words, when I spent the night no one knew where," and to imply that Casanova was leading him astray. At the same time, Casanova tried to reestablish the Kabbalistic bond with his three protectors. He told them that the oracle they unhesitatingly obeyed had warned them to do nothing concerning any suggestions that de la Haye might make without first consulting him. "I had no doubt they would obey the order." Seeing a change in the three patricians' attitude toward him, de la Haye "began to behave more sensibly."

———•———

Carnival arrived, and with it endless celebration and gambling and whoring. He'd been playing cards every day, and losing. His chosen place of humiliation was, as he described it, "a small casino for members to which no Venetian nobleman dared to come" because one of the members was an officer of the Spanish embassy. The complicated rules of diplomacy in Venice prohibited patricians from mixing with foreigners except in official situations. Without explaining how, he received a quarter share of a patrician's bet, "and on the first day of Lent we found ourselves the winners by a sufficient sum." Yes! He'd won the Venetian lottery: three thousand ducats. He'd accomplished this trick simply by hitting the winning combination, known as a *terno*, consisting of three numbers.

He had his windfall, and he had his freedom, and an impulsive new friend, Antonio Balletti, a dancer and would-be ballet impresario, who planned to reunite with his theatrical family in Paris and to perform with them. Casanova felt he couldn't "choose company more agreeable and more apt to procure me countless advantages in Paris and a quantity of brilliant acquaintances." He took his leave of Signor Bragadin and pledged to return in two years time, in the spring of 1752, and he assured his brother Francesco, the painter, "that I would think of him when I was in Paris, where in those days genius was certain to make its way to fortune."

On June 1, 1750, he set out with high expectations, well-dressed, well-equipped, thanks to his lottery winnings, "with plenty of money, and certain not to be in want if I behaved properly." He embarked on a *peota*, a pilot ship, whose oarsmen conducted him overnight to a port near the city of Ferrara, about seventy miles south of Venice. He disembarked, hired a *calèche*, and arrived in time for the midday meal and a rendezvous with Balletti.

The next day he arrived at the fair at Reggio, which ranked as a disappointment, but at least he rejoined Balletti there, and the two proceeded to Turin, where he took in the sights, its "streets full of beggars," the opulent Teatro Regio, and even the King of Sardinia, Carlo Emmanuel I. Casanova had never seen a king, and strained for a closer look. "A spurious idea made me believe that a king should have something rarely beautiful or majestic in his physiognomy, not shared by the rest of mankind. As a young, thinking republican, my idea was not entirely stupid," yet he was dismayed by the sight of this monarch: "ugly, hunchbacked, morose, and common even in his manners." By comparison, Giacomo Casanova, well-dressed and well-educated, saw himself as a prince.

------◆------

"No amorous incline disturbed the peace of my soul in Turin, except for the daughter of a washerwoman." With her he endured an accident that he set down "only because it taught me a lesson in physiology." He devoted considerable effort to, as he carefully put it, "arrange an interview in my lodging or in hers or anywhere at all and not succeeding." What the situation called for, he decided, was "a little violence at the foot of the concealed staircase" she climbed to his lodgings in the course of her work. He concealed himself at the foot of the stairs, "and when I saw that she was within reach I sprang on her, and, partly by persuasion and partly by swift action, I subjugated her on the last steps." All was going as planned, "but at the first thrust of our union a most extraordinary sound, proceeding from the place next to the one I was occupying, stayed my fury." *Ffft!* "The victim," as he candidly called the washerwoman's daughter, clapped her hand across her face "to hide the shame she felt at her indiscretions." Ignoring these distractions, he endeavored to "reassure" her with a kiss, "but lo! a second sound, louder than the first" came forth, followed by a third, "and so regularly that it was like the bass of an orchestra giving the time for a piece of music." *Bfft!* In the end, "this aural phenomenon, together with the embarrassment and confusion that I saw in my victim, suddenly took possession of my soul; all together they presented so comical an idea to my mind that, laughter having overpowered all my faculties, I had to let go."

The moment he released his grip, she fled, leaving him sitting on the stairs for fifteen minutes, convulsed with laughter. Conceivably, an anomaly in the "configuration of her organ" had caused the response, thereby helping her preserve her virtue. "I believe that three out of four loose women would cease to be if they were subject to this phenomenon," he speculated. But if their lovers had the same peculiarity, the "strange symphony might become one more charm of a happy union."

Quitting Turin for Lyon in the company of his friend Balletti, Casanova found his way to secret societies and fraternities, orders claiming ancient pedigree and mystical powers. This aficionado of the Kabbalah joined the most controversial alliance of them all, the Freemasons. The relationship came about through Balletti, who, like many French actors, was already a member of this influential and deeply suspect organization, whose ranks included George Washington, Benjamin Franklin, Paul Revere, Leopold Mozart, and Wolfgang Amadeus Mozart, whose opera *The Magic Flute*, composed in 1791, is a delirious Masonic allegory.

So pervasive is this organization that a version of its primary symbol, the Eye of Providence, occasionally referred to as the All-Seeing Eye of God Watching over Humanity, appears prominently on the reverse side of the Great Seal of the United States, and on the United States one-dollar bill.

Freemasons trace their roots to the construction of King Solomon's Temple in Jerusalem in the tenth century BC. In this allegory, the builders of the temple were stonemasons and forefathers of modern Freemasons. At times Freemasons have been connected with another mystical order, the Knights Templar, monks said to have discovered immense treasure amid the ruins of King Solomon's Temple until King Philip IV of France claimed it in the fourteenth century. After that episode, the Knights Templar had all but disappeared, only to reemerge in Casanova's day. So ran the legend. A more pragmatic explanation of the origin of Freemasonry involved workers who built churches and castles in France, England, and Scotland. Those who carved designs into soft stone, or freestone, were known as "freestone masons," and later, "free masons." To preserve their trade monopoly, they formed guilds, and founded lodges to dine and store their working tools, relying on secret handshakes and code words to recognize one another. By Casanova's day, Freemasonry had evolved from a trade guild—although it retained some of the masons' tools for their symbolic value—into a fellowship promoting intellectual exchanges and religious tolerance. As aristocrats and artists crowded out the craftsmen originally associated with the organization, it became fashionable and exclusive. In 1717, four Freemason lodges in London formed the first Grand Lodge, with authority over other lodges throughout England.

As Freemasonry flourished, governments and the Church became suspicious of the organization's penchant for secrecy, idiosyncratic rites, and broad-minded religious beliefs. King Louis XV of France banned Freemasonry in 1737, and the following year Pope Clement XII barred Catholics from becoming Freemasons on pain of excommunication. Portugal declared Freemasonry punishable by death.

For Casanova, a forbidden society of powerful individuals and lofty ideals held boundless appeal.

Balletti introduced him to François de la Rochefoucauld, Marquis de Rochebaron, who "procured me the privilege of being admitted into the company of those who see the light," Casanova wrote, adopting Freemason imagery. "I became an apprentice *Freemason*." Within months, he reached the second degree, and then the third, "which is the mastership. It is the highest." At that time, French Masonic lodges offered three degrees, just as he stated, later extending to thirty-three.

Freemasonry granted him access to a hallowed set of social and mystical coordinates. Its tenets conferred an obligation to pursue the sacred truths of Nature hidden in ancient Masonic rituals that derived from King Solomon's Temple. Nothing could be calculated to appeal to Casanova's intellect and vanity more than a mystical quest in the company of intellectuals and aristocrats. If Freemasonry hadn't already existed, he might have invented it. He recommended that "every young man who travels, who wishes to know society, who does not wish to be inferior to another and excluded from the company of his equals in the age in which we live, should be initiated into what is called Freemasonry," but, he warned, he must "make the right choice of the lodge of which he wishes to become a member, for though evil company cannot act in the lodge, it may be present in it, and the candidate must be aware of dangerous connections."

He touched on the core of Freemasonry, the "secret of the brotherhood," without revealing its meaning. "The secret of Masonry is inviolable by its own nature," he observed in his *Memoirs*, "since the Mason who knows it, knows it only because he has divined it. He has learned it from no one. He has discovered it by virtue of going to the lodge, observing, reasoning, and deducing. When he has arrived at it, he takes great care not to share his discovery with anyone, were it his best friend and a Mason, because if he has not had the ability to find it out, he will by the same token not have the ability to profit by it if he learns it by words of mouth. The secret, then, will always be a secret."

His journey with Balletti from Lyon to Paris, about three hundred miles, meant enduring five days of jostling in a stagecoach. On arrival at the palace of Fontainebleau, south of Paris, the coach was met by Balletti's mother. One again he was at home among actors. Unlike their Italian counterparts, the French called one another exclusively by their stage names, so it was "Bonjour, Monsieur Arlequin; bonjour, Monsieur Pantalon," both onstage and off. Even Balletti's aunt, Elena Virginia Balletti, went by her stage name, Flaminia, at dinner.

Casanova came to Flaminia's attention "as a candidate in the Republic of Letters," that is, an aspiring writer, and "she saw fit to honor me with her conversation" even though he found her "repulsive in her face, her tone, her style, and even her voice." He turned his attention to Balletti's mother, Silvia, "easy, affable, pleasant, well-spoken, obliging to everyone, full of wit, yet completely unpretentious." He couldn't decide whether she was beautiful or homely, a bit of both perhaps, endowed with an "occult power" drawing her admirers to her. He was well aware of her importance in French theatrical life, "the idol of all France," in his words, and her talent was the "mainstay of all the comedies that the greatest authors wrote for her." Even more surprisingly, "her life was pure. She was ready to make friends of men, but never lovers—scorning a privilege that she could have enjoyed but that would have made her base in her own estimation. For this reason she gained a reputation for respectability at an age when it would seem absurd and almost insulting to all women of her profession." No one spoke ill of her when she was offstage, nor did anyone hiss her when she appeared onstage. "By general and unanimous consent, Silvia was a woman above her profession"—a profession that was still held in disrepute, despite the popularity of actresses such as she. The Church denied them marital rites and burial in consecrated ground. When Silvia died ten years later, the clergy made an exception; she was buried in the graveyard of a parish church, as a priest intoned that her being an actress "had never prevented her from being a Christian," as if hers was an exceptional case.

———

Paris glittered at the height of *la Lumière*, the Enlightenment, a movement of intellectuals devoted to reason, individuality, freethinking, and libertinism, including sexual exploration and excess. The French *philosophes* of the Enlightenment—public intellectuals, writers, scientists, and philosophers, who examined subjects of concern to all, seeking reforms—included René Descartes, the mathematician; Bernard Le Bovier de Fontenelle, perhaps the most admired man of letters of the era; the social critics Voltaire and Montesquieu; and Denis Diderot, the reclusive yet intellectually adventurous joint editor (with Jean d'Alembert) of the revolutionary *Encyclopédie, the chef d'oeuvre* of the French Enlightenment. This work, in its various editions, sold a quarter of a million copies to a public starved for equality of information. Along with these torchbearers came Jean-Jacques Rousseau; Georges-Louis Leclerc, Comte de Buffon, mathematician, cosmologist, and naturalist; Étienne Bonnot de Condillac, philosopher and epistomologist; Anne-Robert-Jacques Turgot, economist and statesman; and Nicolas de Condorcet, the mathematician, philosopher, and political scientist who advocated equality for men and women of all races. These figures and others like them embodied the era's craving for knowledge, no matter where it led. It was as though Casanova had traveled from the Venetian medieval mind-set with its curses and superstitions all the way to the Enlightenment. "If there is something you know, communicate it," the *Encyclopédie* exhorted. "If there is something you don't know, search for it." It was a message that Casanova took to heart as he patrolled the streets of Paris, queried its inhabitants, savored its ladies of the evening, and marveled at the wealth of knowledge to be found in its libraries and in the minds of its *philosophes*.

The tumult of Paris overwhelmed him. He went about gawking, as any tourist would. Even the Parisians gawked at their own city, beholding the marvel they inhabited "from morning to night, being amused by everything and admiring everything." There was so much at which to marvel: "the beauty of the high road, the immortal work of Louis XV, the cleanliness of the inns, the fare which they supplied, the promptness with which we were served, the excellence of the beds, the modest manner of the person who served us at table, who was usually the most accomplished daughter of the house and whose bearing, cleanliness, and manner were enough to check any licentiousness." It was all so different from Venice.

If there was a single location that embodied the Enlightenment for Casanova, it was the sprawling Palais-Royale, the former residence of Cardinal Richelieu. The public gardens attracted sightseers and those in search of assignations with ladies of the evening. Seating himself in a rented chair, he ordered a hot chocolate that he found disappointing, and fell to quarreling with the waiter. Asked for gossip, the waiter proved happy to oblige: the Dauphine had just given birth to a prince. But he was zealously corrected by an abbé, who informed him it was a *princess*, triggering a vigorous debate. Soon Casanova was jesting with the abbé, who introduced him to a gentleman of the robe, that is, an advocate, Patu, who claimed to be knowledgeable in Italian literature. Casanova spoke to the gentleman in Italian, and he replied "exactly in the style of Boccaccio," prompting the Venetian to remark that although the advocate's Italian was technically correct, one no longer spoke in the manner of the fourteenth-century and *The Decameron*. The two became friends, discussing literature, exchanging addresses, and promising to visit one another.

"You cannot imagine what good souls the Parisians are," his friend enthused. "You are in the only country in the world in which intelligence can make its way to fortune either if it displays itself in genuine contribution, in which case it is welcomed by intelligence, or if it imposes what is specious, in which case it is rewarded by stupidity." As for Louis XV matters were a bit more complicated. "Everything that happens in France makes foreigners believe that the nation admires its King; but those among us who think see that this is only tinsel," his friend explained. When the King visits Paris, he explained, "Everyone cries, 'Long Live the King' because some idler has begun shouting it. It is a cry that comes from high spirits, or perhaps from fear, and which the King himself, believe me, does not take seriously. He cannot wait to get back to Versailles, where there are twenty-five thousand men to protect him from the fury of the same populace that, grown wise, might take it into their heads to cry: 'Death to the King.'"

Patu explained that, with a few sentimental exceptions, "France has never loved her Kings." After surviving an illness, Louis XV commented, "I am amazed at these rejoicings because I have recovered my health, for I cannot see any reason why I should be so much loved." That lack of loyalty and respect appeared even in casual conversation. Louis never warmed to the role he was born to play, and struck many as cold and aloof. In fact, he was so shy that when faced with the task of delivering a speech, he gave it to a minister to read it aloud for him.

The King's principal mistress at the time was the celebrated, influential Madame de Pompadour, born Jeanne-Antoinette Poisson. The daughter of a scandal-ridden financier, she insinuated herself into the French court, where she charmed the King, who proclaimed her the best lover in the world, only to be reminded by a courtier that if His Majesty had vis-

Louis XV, King of France, 1715–1774,
by Maurice Quentin de la Tour

ited a bordello to compare her with other courtesans, he might not be so quick to extol her amorous gifts. The courtier was soon banished for his flippancy, but Madame de Pompadour stayed on. To hold the King's interest, she organized orgies and other forms of debauchery, appreciated by the King, who called her the "Immaculate Wonder."

In Paris, Casanova applied himself to the study of French language and literature. In conversation with the octogenarian writer Prosper Jolyot de Crébillon (father of the better-known Claude, the novelist), Casanova characterized himself as an "intolerable pupil, always questioning, curious, demanding, insatiable." Furthermore, he said, he wasn't rich enough to pay for a competent French teacher, assuming that he could find one. The come-on proved irresistible to the old *littérateur*, who claimed he'd been looking for just such a pupil for fifty years and offered to pay *him* to come to his apartment in the Marais on the Right Bank of the Seine, in the rue des Douze Portes, for lessons.

In that era, the Marais was considered an aristocratic quarter of Paris, and Casanova was charmed by the grand old man himself, six feet tall, with the visage of a lion, simultaneously eating and dispensing witticisms, a homebody with a pipe in his mouth, presiding over a harem of twenty cats, with which he played constantly. His housekeeper managed his life, as he discharged his responsibilities in the antiquated role of "royal censor," commenting on works that his housekeeper read aloud. "I visited Crébillon three times a week for a year, and I learned from him all the French I know, but I have never been able to rid myself of Italianisms," Casanova admitted. "I recognize them when I find them in others; but when they come from my pen I do not recognize them."

During the next few weeks, he visited the opera, the theater, and various gatherings in the company of his friend Patu, familiarizing himself with French society despite making many "awkward blunders." He committed an egregious lapse while visiting a ballet school, where a young student—she couldn't have been more than thirteen or fourteen—complained of a headache. Casanova offered her a concoction, and she replied, "It is not that. I think I am pregnant."

"Like a fool," he replied that he "should never have thought that Madame was married," at which point she turned scarlet, glanced at her friend, and the two of them guffawed "with all their hearts." Shocked and amused, Casanova departed "covered with shame and determined that in the future I would never impute virtue to young women of the theater." As the son of an actress who'd abandoned him, he had more to say on the subject of virtue: "They pride themselves on not having it, and they laugh at the stupidity of those who impute it to them."

As Casanova discovered, many of the young women performers wanted nothing so much as to trade their grueling profession for the life of a kept woman of a wealthy sponsor; whether he was married or not scarcely mattered. For them, the stage was a means to an end, and they perpetually auditioned for the role of mistress. In this louche milieu, women of easy virtue, or no virtue at all, became his preferred companions. The dependably licentious Patu introduced him to "all the women of pleasure who enjoyed some reputation in Paris." Finally, the women of Paris! It seemed as if Casanova was about to recount his experiences with them, for Patu "loved the fair sex as much as I did, but unfortunately for him he did not have as strong a constitution as mine, and he paid for it with his life": an incalculable loss, in Casanova's opinion. He died at thirty, and "If he'd lived he would have taken Voltaire's place." Patu's poignant memory remained strong enough to steer Casanova away from women toward his other grand pursuit, the study of language and literature. Patu had taught him a secret that "French writers use poetry to make sure their prose is perfect." They wrote their important prose documents, such as eulogies or letters of dedication, in unrhymed verse, alexandrines, specifically, "that is, a line of twelve syllables with a caesura, or break, in the middle, at the sixth syllable."

Casanova remained unconvinced by the exercise, a "great deal of trouble for nothing," he declared. When he asked Crébillon, his tutor, about this technique, the old man confirmed its existence, but denied that he ever employed it himself.

———•———

On December 10, 1751, Patu accompanied Casanova to the celebrated Opéra in the Palais-Royal for a revival of a showpiece called *Les Fêtes vénitiennes*. The production commenced with a shimmering overture, but when the curtain went up, "I see a set representing the Piazzetta seen from the little island of San Giorgio Maggiore; but I am surprised to see the Doge's Palace on my left and the Procuratie"—buildings in St. Mark's Square—

"and the great campanile on my right. This ridiculous mistake—a disgrace to my century—makes me laugh, and Patu, whom I enlighten, had to laugh, as well." He attributed this gross error "to the crass ignorance of the painter, who had botched copying a print." As the opera unfolded, the music began to bore him, and the recitative absolutely distressed him "because of its monotony and senseless shrieks." The setting, Carnival, and the costumes struck him as "false but amusing. But what really made me laugh was seeing the Doge and twelve Councilors come out of the wings in bizarre robes and start dancing a passacaglia," a slow *Spanish* formula. Later, he observed the aging dancer known as Camargo, "the first woman dancer who dared to leap," Patu boasted, "and the wonderful thing is that she does not wear drawers."

"I saw," Casanova interjected.

"What did you see? It was only her skin, which, to tell the truth, is not white."

He preferred the pleasures afforded by the *Comédie Française*, founded by Louis XIV in 1680 by merging the city's two acting troupes. In time it became known as the house of Molière, the stage name of Jean-Baptiste Poquelin, playwright and actor. At the time of Casanova's visits, the theater was located in a tennis court in the rue des Fossés-Saint-German. He attended performances of Molière's *The Miser* and *The Misanthrope* amid an audience of less than two hundred. The experience of watching Molière's tragicomic figures—a category to which Molière himself belonged, collapsing during a performance of his late masterpiece, *The Imaginary Invalid*, in 1673 and dying of tuberculosis hours later—was more than diversion for Casanova; it amounted to an education in the possibilities of theater beyond the rude pleasures of *commedia dell'arte*. After the performances, he engaged the actors in conversation. When he mentioned the beauty of a particular actress, an older woman agreed that she was "delicious," adding that she was "very agreeable in company and shows a great deal of promise." He expressed a desire to meet her, which he heard would be easy to accomplish. "Her father and mother are civility itself, and I am sure they will be delighted if you ask them to invite you to supper. They will not be in your way; they will go off to bed and leave you at the table with the girl for as long as you please. You are in France, Monsieur, where people know what life is worth and try to make the most of it." All that remained was to be introduced to the girl.

More social climbing brought him before the man he believed to be the wealthiest of the Italian expatriate actors in Paris, Carlo Veronese. Casanova began courting the actor's two daughters, Coralline and Camilla. That experience led to his meeting the well-connected Catherine Charlotte Thérèse, the Duchess of Ruffec. But when he was introduced to the great lady, he was aghast to see "a woman of sixty"—actually, she was closer to forty—"with a face covered with rouge, a blotchy complexion, thin, ugly, and faded, sitting immodestly on a sofa."

"Oh, what a handsome young man!" she cried on seeing him, as she invited him to sit beside her. He complied, but was "immediately repelled by an unbearable stench of musk." Forcing himself to look in her direction, "I see a hideous bosom, which the virago displayed in its entirety, and pimples, not visible because they were covered with patches, but palpable." The moment they were left alone, "the harpy surprises me with two drooling lips that offer me a kiss I should perhaps have put up with, but at the same time she extends a gaunt arm."

"Let's see if you have a fine . . ." she cooed as she reached for his shrunken manhood.

"Oh my God! Madame la Duchesse!"

"You draw back? You are acting like a child. What is the matter with you?"

He whispered that he suffered from a nasty case of *la chaudepisse,* or gonorrhea: a useful fiction.

"Filthy creature!"

He raced out of the house, and later, in the company of Patu, consoled himself at the Hôtel de Roule, a notorious Parisian brothel efficiently operated by Justine Paris, real name Bienfait, who might have served as the model for the character of Juliette, the amoral nymphomaniac portrayed in the licentious 1797 novel by the Marquis de Sade. She wasn't the best-known madam in Paris at the time—that accolade belonged to Marquerite Gourdan, who later became her business partner—but a visit to her place of business was de rigueur for an adventurer with time and money.

When he visited, Casanova recalled with wonder the "twelve to fourteen choice girls" employed there, in addition to a "good cook, good wines, excellent beds." Because her establishment was on the outskirts of Paris, in the village of Chaillot (now a suburb), she could be "certain that those who came to her place were people of means, for it was too far to go on

foot." Her clients knew the price list by heart. "One paid six francs to breakfast with a girl, twelve francs to dine there, and a louis"—a gold coin worth
about twenty francs—"to sup and spend the night."

Casanova and Patu dismissed their coach, and entered the Hôtel de
Roule, where a "well-dressed, polite woman, with one eye missing, who
seemed to be about fifty, asks us if we have come to dine there and to see
the young ladies of her household. We answer yes, and she conducts us to
a drawing room where we see fourteen girls wearing identical dresses of
white muslin, with their sewing in their hands, sitting in a semicircle; when
we appear they all rise and simultaneously make us a deep curtsy. They all
had their hair nicely dressed, were all about the same age, and all pretty—
some tall, others of middle height, and others short, some were brunettes,
some blondes, some auburn-haired. We pass them all in review, saying a few
words to each, and just as Patu was choosing his, I take hold of mine. Our
two choices cry out joyously, throw themselves on our necks, hurry us out
of the room to show us the garden while we wait to be called for dinner." In
the back, Madame Paris encouraged the two visitors to "enjoy the good air
and the peace and the silence" that reigned in her house, assuring them, by
the way, "I answer to you for the good health of the girls you have chosen."

Paris brothel, c. 1795

No sooner had they dined with their companions than "the one-eyed dame appears, watch in hand, to tell us that our turn was over." If they paid another six francs, they could continue to amuse themselves. They decided to stay until their time was up again. The two of them concluded that pleasures "measured out by the hour fall short of perfection." They decide to return for a *third* session, but this time pay enough in advance to assure themselves that the women they choose "will be in our power until tomorrow." The madam praised them for showing themselves to be "men of discernment."

Casanova selected his third girl of the evening, whose charms he paid to enjoy for the next fourteen hours. "A beauty," he notes, named Gabrielle Siberre, who went by the name of "Saint-Hilaire." "She looked at me with an air of pride and scorn. It took me more than an hour's walk with her to calm her. She considered me unworthy to sleep with her because I had presumed not to take her either the first or the second time." (Patu later complimented Casanova on his choice by availing himself of her services the following week.) The night went well, according to Casanova, who was pleased to hear that La Saint-Hilaire was "very well satisfied" with him, and even "boasted of it to her companions." And he was so well satisfied with her that he returned to the Hôtel de Roule "more than ten times." "I did not have the heart to take another girl," he explained. "Saint-Hilaire was proud of having been able to hold me."

———•———

Come summer Casanova availed himself of more refined pleasures. "In August I saw at the Louvre the new paintings that the members of the Royal Academy of Painting were exhibiting to the public." None offered a military theme, but he knew someone who could remedy the omission. "I formed a plan to bring my brother Francesco to Paris; he was in Venice and was talented in the genre." If all went well, "I thought my brother could make his fortune." He wrote Signor Grimani and to Francesco, and they agreed to the plan, but it would be months until Francesco finally arrived.

Until that time, Casanova distracted himself with an extended visit to Fontainebleau, the royal residence. The Ballettis, including Silvia and her husband, invited him to join them in their rented lodging house. He accepted with alacrity, for "I could not have enjoyed a better opportunity to become acquainted with all the court of Louis XV and all the foreign envoys." And what a court he observed, perpetually at play. The King was entering his forties, having ruled France since the age of five; he was popularly known as *Louis le bien aimé*, Louis the Beloved, despite a multitude of ill-conceived deeds that would prove to be highly deleterious to the monarchy. He was, as Casanova explained, "passionately fond of hunting, [and] in the habit of spending six weeks of the autumn of every year at Fontainebleau. He always returned to Versailles by the middle of November. The journey cost him five millions; he took with him everything that could contribute to the enjoyment of all the foreign envoys of the whole court. The French and Italian comedians and his actors and actresses of the Opéra were commanded to follow him. During these six weeks Fontainebleau was far more brilliant than Versailles."

He accompanied the Venetian Ambassador to France to the first of these bucolic opera performances, a work by Jean-Baptiste Lully, an Italian who renounced his citizenship for France, and composed operas of elaborate artifice. When a well-known diva, Lemaure, opened her mouth, Casanova heard a "shriek so loud and unexpected that I thought she had gone mad. I gave a little laugh, in all innocence, never imagining that anyone would think it out of place." But a dignitary took exception to the outburst, and haughtily asked the offender where he was from. "I answer curtly that I am from Venice."

"When I was in Venice, I often laughed at the recitatives in your opera, too."

Casanova countered, "I am equally certain that no one there ever thought of preventing you from laughing." He was one riposte away from a duel; instead, a laugh from Madame de Pompadour, the king's longtime mistress, interrupted, and she inquired if the young Venetian was really from "down there."

He informed Madame that Venice was not "down," but "up."

"This answer of mine was thought even odder than my first, and the whole box falls to deciding whether Venice was down or up. Apparently it was concluded that I was right, and I was not attacked again."

He resumed listening to Lully's opera, struggling to repress his laughter and ostentatiously blowing his nose. His attention-getting behavior provoked a scolding from Madame de Pompadour, who ventured to ask him which of the two actresses they'd seen pleased him more. "In assessing the beauty of a woman, the first thing I consider is her legs," Casanova brazenly replied, employing the French term *écarter*, meaning both to "spread apart" and to "put aside." The bawdy pun, of which he claimed to be unaware, "gave me standing and made the company in the box curious about me." (Then again, much of what the hypersexual Casanova said could be construed as a double entendre.)

---·---

Soon after he glimpsed—so he said—the King on the way to mass, followed by the royal family, and the ladies of the court, "who surprised me by their ugliness as those of the court of Turin had surprised me by their beauty." They came, he was told, from the Queen's apartment, "and they walk so awkwardly because their slippers have heels half a foot high, which makes them walk with their knees bent."

And there, all at once, was the King himself, an arm flung around one of his minister's shoulders. "Louis XV's head was ravishingly beautiful and set on his neck to perfection. Not even a most skillful painter could draw the attitude the monarch gave it when he turned to look at someone. One felt instantly forced to love him." That exceedingly vain monarch could hardly have put it better himself. No wonder Madame de Pompadour had fallen in love with him. Now that the King supped with her, his Polish queen, Marie Leszczyńska, to whom he'd been married for a quarter of a century, and with whom he'd had ten children, seven of whom survived to adulthood, dined alone, "without rouge, wearing a large bonnet, looking old and pious, thanking two nuns who set on the table a plate containing fresh butter." The royal pantomime continued, closely observed by Casanova. "The Queen begins to eat, looking at no one, and keeping her eyes fixed on her plate. She had eaten some of a dish and, finding it to her taste, she returned to it, but as she returned to it she cast her eyes over the company, apparently to see if she recognized anyone to whom she could justify her epicureanism"—her pleasure in food. Her gaze alighted on a man even taller than Casanova, a Russian Count, who bowed and took three steps in her direction. And then at last she spoke: "I believe that the best ragout of all is a fricassee of chicken."

"I am of that opinion, Madame," he responded "in the same tone in which a death sentence is pronounced at a court-martial." The French—he could only marvel at their *hauteur*. So long as he remained calm, he enjoyed matching wits with the French, alternately mocking them and learning from them, even as they mocked him and succumbed to his Venetian charm and ineradicable accent. A quick study and skilled mimic, he managed to blend in with the aristocracy. What was life at the court but a new play—or was it the same play performed day after day?—with the actors doubling as the audience?

———•———

Returning to his halcyon days in Paris, Casanova reflected on his first brush with French law, when he was accused of seducing his landlady's daughter, which was likely the case, but he put his own spin on the matter: Madame Quinson's youngest daughter, Mimi, "often came to my room unsummoned." He decided somehow that she loved him, and would have considered it strange if he'd been cold to her, especially because she "had a pretty voice, she read all the new publications, and rattled away about everything with a vivacity that was charming. Her age was an ambrosial fifteen or sixteen."

For months, he said, nothing between the two of them occurred, "but happening one night to come in very late I found her asleep in my bed. Curious to see if she would awake, I undressed by myself, I got in, and the rest goes without saying." He might have been caught, had not a milliner and her daughter come to his room to sell him a chapeau or two, and as they left, "in comes Madame Quinson and Mimi to make my bed."

Working at his desk, he heard Madame Quinson mutter, "Oh! The sluts!" To whom did she refer? "These sheets are ruined," she explained, implying that the milliner and daughter were actually a madam and her young prostitute, whose virginity he had just stolen, staining the sheets.

Casanova asked Madame Quinson to carry on as if nothing had happened.

"Just let the sluts come back?" Madame Quinson asked.

When she excused herself to fetch fresh sheets, said Casanova, "Mimi remains, I reproach her for her imprudence, she laughs and says that Heaven has protected the innocence of our doings." In other words, the blood on the sheets was Mimi's, not the milliner's daughter's. "From that day on," Casanova maintained, "Mimi came to sleep with me when she felt the need, and I, no less unceremoniously, sent her away when I did not want her, and our little household was as harmonious as possible"—until Mimi became pregnant.

Stunned, Casanova dismissed Mimi's plea that they marry. "What will happen, will happen," he said. "As for me, I will not give it another thought." That, of course, proved impossible. "By the fifth or sixth month Mimi's belly leaves her mother in no doubt of the state of things," and her mother, previously mild and polite, reacted savagely, grasping Mimi by the hair, beating her, and forcing her to admit the truth, or, as Casanova expressed it, "who is responsible for her girth." Inevitably, "Mimi tells her—and perhaps truthfully—that it is I."

Casanova faced her maternal fury. "Madame Quinson comes upstairs and enters my room, raging. She flings herself into an armchair, recovers her breath, relieves her anger by insulting me, and ends by saying I must prepare to marry her daughter." Receiving the ultimatum, he informed her that he was already married—in Italy.

"Then why did you go and give my daughter a baby?"

"I assure you I had no such intention, and besides, who told you that it is I?"

"She did, Monsieur. She is certain of it."

"I congratulate her," but he was not so certain.

"Then what?"

"Then . . . nothing. If she is pregnant, she will bear a child."

She left, muttering imprecations. The next day, at the local police station, where he'd been summoned to appear, he confronted both a police investigator and his nemesis, Madame Quinson, "in battle array." The investigator subjected him to a list of blunt questions, and to confess that he'd mistreated Madame's daughter. After asking the functionary to write down his answer verbatim, Casanova replied, "I have done no wrong to Mimi, daughter of Madame Quinson here present, and I refer you to Mimi herself, who has always shown me the same friendship that I have shown her"—as proper a reply as a libertine could give.

The two of them bickered.

"What did you give her to seduce her?" asked the investigator.

"Nothing, for it was she who seduced me, and we were of one mind in an instant."

"Was she a virgin?" Casanova had no idea.

When her mother demanded "reparations," as if this private matter were an international incident, he refused, despite the police investigator's belief that Casanova had transgressed "the laws of society." *Au contraire*, he insisted, the mother sent the daughter to his room, so it was a case of entrapment, and they must be prepared to suffer the consequences of their behavior. Everything they'd done together had been mutual, "nothing by force, or outside my room, for which I have always punctually paid the rent." So he would not pay the penalty, and if judged guilty, he would appeal "to the last jurisdiction." A principle was at stake: "I shall never have the ill grace to refuse my caresses to a girl who attracts me and who comes to my room to submit to them, especially when I am certain that she has come with her mother's consent." When he finished, he read and signed his statement.

The lieutenant-general of police, after hearing the testimony, acquitted the Venetian and ordered the "imprudent mother to pay the costs." Casanova yielded to Mimi's tearful pleas to pay for bearing the child, a boy, who was born at a foundling hospital, but his financial support ended there.

———— • ————

For two years Giacomo Casanova lived the fashionable, profligate life to which he had aspired, as if he were playing out a farce by Goldoni in which the Venetian upstart tried to emulate the French. Patu functioned as his partner in seduction and transgression. All that was missing was a suitable object of conquest. In time he found himself in the home of an actress of Irish descent, Victoire Morphy, but no matter, he didn't want to sleep with her, even at her bargain rate, so he settled for the solitude of a couch, only to be distracted by "La Morphy's younger sister, a pretty, ragged, dirty little creature," also available at a cut-rate price, makeshift bed included. Casanova agreed, on condition that she remain naked. "All right," she said, "but you mustn't do anything to me."

He embarked on parallel negotiations, one financial, the other erotic, with the girl, Marie-Louise O'Murphy. As he watched, "She undressed, lies down, and covers herself with an old curtain. She was thirteen years old"— half his age. "I look at the girl; I send every prejudice packing; I see her neither slovenly nor in rags, I find her a perfect beauty." Her extreme youth gave him no qualms. He considered her ripe for initiation.

He tried to examine her, but she shied away until he offered a higher price, which instantly made her as "docile as a lamb, and since her only fault was being dirty I wash her all over with my own hands." She let him do whatever he wished with her, except for the one thing he most wanted to do; for *that*, the price, according to her older sister, would be even higher. "I tell her we will haggle about it some other time; and thereupon she gives me every indication of her future consent to everything I could want."

After these preliminaries, he claimed he enjoyed his tumble, "though leaving her a virgin." Apparently her exquisite beauty offered enough satisfaction, and he had learned his lesson about sleeping with young girls from painful experience with the Quinsons. Casanova visited again and again, paying hundreds of francs for the privilege of viewing this perfectly lovely girl. He hired a German portrait artist to paint her naked, resting her arms and her bosom on a pillow and her legs and thighs drawn in such a way "that the eye could not wish to see more." At Casanova's urging, the artist titled the picture "O-Morphi," a pun on her name of Murphy, as Greek for "beauty."

The portrait, and the well-known likeness of Marie-Louise O'Murphy by François Boucher, had spectacular consequences.

Patu was so struck with the sensual image that he insisted on obtaining a copy. Realizing that he had a valuable property on his hands, the German artist transported another copy to Versailles, where he displayed it to Monsieur de Saint-Quentin, the Gentleman of the Bedchamber, who in turn presented it to the King, who became curious to know if the portrait of the "Greek girl" was a true likeness. If so, Louis XV "claimed the right to sentence the original to quench the fire that she had kindled in his heart." The two sisters were overjoyed at the prospect of going to Versailles, so Casanova reports, "and there to submit to the decrees of Providence" in the form of an all-powerful monarch who would shower them with benefits. On the basis of that slender, haphazard series of events, he gravitated toward that level of society where the basest behavior was the norm: the court of Louis XV.

——————

On arrival, they made their way through the maze of bureaucracy to Louis XV, who wanted assurances that "O-Morphi" who'd just appeared in his midst was in fact a virgin. He bestowed a royal kiss on her, and she burst out laughing, because, she explained to the puzzled ruler, he precisely resembled his portrait on a six-franc piece. He gazed at her and saw an image of love; she looked at him and beheld a simulacrum of money.

The corrupt fairy tale unfolded swiftly, to Casanova's pleasure. "The monarch burst out laughing and asked her if she would like to stay at Versailles; she answered that she must arrange it with her sister, and her sister told the King that nothing could make her happier. The King then left, locking them in. A quarter of an hour later Saint-Quentin came and let them out, put the younger sister in an apartment on the ground floor in the custody of a woman, and went off with the older sister to find the German, to whom he gave fifty louis for the portrait, but nothing to La Morphy. He only took her address, assuring her that she would hear from him. She received a thousand louis, which she showed me the next day. The honest German gave me twenty-five louis for my portrait and made me another by copying Patu's. He offered to paint for me, gratis, all the pretty girls whose portraits I might wish to have."

According to Casanova, the King called his newest mistress by the nickname the Venetian had given her, O-Morphi, and installed her in an apartment in a wing of Versailles known as the *Parc aux Cerfs*, "where His Majesty kept nothing short of a seraglio and which no one was allowed to enter except ladies presented at court." Some accounts claimed a vast entourage of women were ready to perform at the snap of the royal fingers, that the place was a vast brothel, with Madame de Pompadour acting as chief procuress, while other accounts said that this notorious seraglio consisted of merely a few guest rooms and nothing more. No matter the extent of her domain or her competition, Louise O'Murphy stood out, and held the King's attention.

The following year, 1753, she suffered a miscarriage, a source of grief for her and for the King, and then she gave birth to a daughter, Agathe-Louise de Saint-Antoine, in 1754. Casanova also mentions her bearing a son who met an unknown fate "for Louis XV would never hear anything about his bastards as long as Queen Marie"—Marie Leszczyńska, Polish, educated, and forbearing—"was alive."

After two years of the King's favor, O'Murphy ran afoul of the royal harem's social order when a malicious female courtier told her that she could make the King laugh "by asking him how he treated his old wife," Queen Marie. If she'd been a bit more perceptive, she would have realized the question was bound to offend; instead, she "asked the King the impertinent and insulting question, which so astonished the monarch that, rising and looking daggers at her, said, 'You miserable wretch, who got you to ask me that question?'" Although Louise O'Murphy told him the truth, the King never saw or spoke to her again.

All at once the King's former favorite young lover found herself expelled from the seraglio and married off to a young nobleman, or as Casanova put it, "the King gave her four hundred thousand francs, which she brought as a dowry to a staff officer"—as Jacques de Beaufranchet—"in Brittany." The couple had two children in swift succession before her husband died in battle. Louise O'Murphy never returned to the lost paradise of the King's favor.

Casanova had much to show for the encounter. He'd indirectly acted as a procurer for the King of France, quite an accomplishment for a Venetian adventurer, and believed he knew why. "Despite all the wit of the French, Paris is and will always be the city in which imposters"—himself, especially—"will succeed. When an imposture is discovered, everyone shrugs and laughs, and the imposter laughs even more, for he has already become rich," he declared. He believed he knew why: "This characteristic that makes the nation fall into a trap so easily comes from the supreme influence that fashion exercises over it."

Casanova navigated Paris with the daring of a born adventurer; all the while, his younger brother Francesco struggled to gain acceptance as an artist. Casanova accompanied Francesco on one occasion to present a picture, a battle piece, a popular genre at the time, to a nobleman who lived close by the Louvre.

The interview was devastating: "In comes a man dressed in black, sees the picture, stops in front of it for a moment, and says, addressing no one: 'It is bad.'" As if that were not humiliation enough, two more men came by to examine it and started laughing. "It is by some student," said one. Francesco was "sweating profusely" as the viewing hall filled with people. "The badness of the picture was the butt of all those who stood around it snickering and criticizing. My poor brother was almost expiring and kept thanking God that no one knew him."

Casanova was moved to laughter rather than compassion, or perhaps embarrassment, and quietly made his way to the next room, gesturing to his brother to follow. When they were alone, he tried to cheer Francesco by asserting that when the noble appeared, he would pronounce the painting a success, and the others would follow suit. Francesco listened, "but with great good sense he did not agree with me." They sent a servant to retrieve the painting, and ran down the stairs, and fled in a coach. At home, "my brother slashed his picture a good twenty times with his sword and instantly resolved to settle his affairs, leave Paris, and go elsewhere to study and master the art to which he had devoted himself."

The final disgrace occurred when Casanova was taking a frugal meal by himself at a hostelry operated by a couple named Condé near the Tuileries Garden and the Louvre. When he received the bill, he found the charges had been padded, doubled, in fact. He argued with the proprietress over the amount, but she refused to budge. In disgust, he paid in full, but not before he added in pen the word "*Labré*" to the signature "*femme Condé*" (wife of Condé) at the bottom of the page. The resulting phrase, Condé-Labré, or "*con délabré*" was deeply vulgar.

Casanova strode out of the hostelry, and was soon overtaken by a short man wielding an enormous sword, threatening to cut Casanova's throat—if he could reach it. In his fury Casanova called the insolent little man a dwarf. The bantam-sized tormentor declared that he was a chevalier and informed him, "You have insulted a respectable woman under my protection. Unsheathe."

Swordplay was as common in Paris as pigeons and chestnuts. Casanova assumed a pose of *en garde* before launching his *fleche*, or attack, "and, not waiting for him to guard his body, I wound him in the chest"— as if to obtain revenge for the outrageously padded bill, for the insults his brother's painting had sustained, and for the other obscure resentments against the social order lurking in his heart. "He jumps back and says that I have wounded him treacherously." The two traded accusations, Casanova insisting that his thrust "was legitimate, for he had his sword out before I did. If he did not guard his body it was his own fault." The Venetian could become, when wronged, a vicious street fighter; he had proven his mettle at home, and he proved it again now as he drove his tormentor away.

When he caught his breath, Casanova deemed it time to quit Paris, "where I had stayed for two years and where I enjoyed all the pleasures of life without any drawbacks, except perhaps that I was often short of money," in favor of the tranquil, refined city of Dresden, where his mother held court as an actress in exile.

Mid-August 1751 found the Casanova brothers on the road to Dresden—celebrated as Florence on the Elbe, resplendent with palaces, theaters, concert halls, gardens, and fountains inspired by Italian and French architecture. For young men on a grand tour of Europe in search of culture and sophistication, a visit to Dresden was de rigueur. For Casanova, Dresden was home to the "most brilliant court in Europe," even if it lacked the "amorous intriguing" he craved.

On arrival, "we saw our mother, who also greeted us most affectionately in her delight at seeing the first two fruits of her marriage, whom she could not hope to see again." They settled in quickly, with Francesco devoting himself to his studies in art, industriously copying battle pictures in local museums for the next four years, until he felt ready to face the critics in Paris once again.

Life in Dresden left Casanova bored and disengaged. He dabbled in playwriting, no doubt influenced by his mother. From February 6 to 10, 1752, the Royal Theater of Dresden housed Jean-Philippe Rameau's opera *Zoroastre*, whose libretto Casanova translated into Italian, modifying the French original by Louis de Cahusac. Notably, it starred Zanetta Farussi, but her son's memoir made no mention of his collaboration with his mother after years of separation.

A few months later, he enjoyed the fleeting satisfaction of seeing a "tragicomedy" of his performed "in which I had two characters playing the role of Harlequin." And he received approval, if not acclaim, for *La Moluccheide*, a lightweight parody of *La Thébaïde* (1664), an early tragedy by the French dramatist Racine about a son of Oedipus. The young Venetian man of letters was seemingly launched as a dramatist, yet the fierce ambition and cunning that he brought to his other pursuits was absent. Perhaps he felt unable to escape the shadow of his mother's reputation, or perhaps he felt burdened by the thought that a respectable literary vocation required long years of study and struggle such as his brother had endured for the sake of art. Or perhaps he was simply bored.

After months of limited sexual intimacy in Paris, he unleashed his libido in Dresden, "making the acquaintance of all the mercenary beauties," that is, prostitutes, whom he considered "superior to those of Italy and France in physical endowments, but very inferior in grace, in wit, and in the art of pleasing, which chiefly consists in appearing to be in love with the man who has found them attractive and pays them. In consequence they have the reputation of being cold." His acerbic assessment derived in part from his seventh—by his count—case of venereal disease, acquired from a Hungarian harlot he'd tossed in a dreary Dresden brothel. "I got rid of it," he wearily remarked, "by dieting for six weeks," ruefully adding, "I have never done anything in my life except to try to make myself ill when I had my health and try to make myself well when I had lost it." He would be condemned to repeat this cycle of libertinage and self-denial throughout his life, and over the years he had come to embrace his fate. Looking back in old age, he boasted of his "perfect health, which I wish I could ruin again; but age prevents me." And as for all those bouts of venereal disease that he had suffered over the years, the "French disease," as it was known to blame-shifting Italians, "does not shorten life when one knows how to cure it"—actually, neither he nor his contemporaries had any idea how to treat it, and resorted to ineffective procedures while the disease ran its course. "It merely leaves scars; but we are easily consoled for that when we consider that we gained them with pleasure." He likened himself to a soldier taking pleasure in old wounds, the wellsprings of fame, as he saw it. And he was correct; he would become famous and remain so, his name a byword for promiscuity and seduction and romance.

When he recovered from his latest bout of venereal disease, he journeyed south, to Vienna, halfway to Venice.

———————

"So here I am, in the capital of Austria for the first time, at the flourishing age of twenty-eight. I had a few possessions, but scarcely any money, so I had to go slowly until the return of a letter of exchange which I at once drew on Signor Bragadin." With funds, he drew on his contacts to introduce himself "to the celebrated Abate Metastasio"—a famous and learned Italian poet and librettist now resident in Vienna, and as such a possible inspiration and mentor—"whose acquaintance I was most eager to make."

After an hour's intense discussion with the great man, "I found him even more learned than his works proclaim him to be and with a modesty which at first I could not believe was natural; but I very quickly perceived that it was genuine when he recited something of his own and pointed out its beauties." When reciting verses he'd composed in honor of his late teacher, he cried, "touched by the sweetness of his own poetry," and even asking, rhetorically, "Is it possible to write better?"

It was certainly his right to think so, Casanova replied, asking if the lines had cost him much effort to produce. "He at once showed me four or five pages filled with erasures due to his trying to bring fourteen lines to perfection," an entire day's output. Metastasio explained that the lines that looked the most effortless were the hardest to devise. This lofty commiseration was highly enjoyable for Casanova, and flattering, as well. In fact, "everything in Vienna was splendid, there was much money and much luxury; but there was great hardship for those who were votaries of Venus"—in other words, libertines like himself. "Rascals" working for an official chastity commission "pitilessly persecuted all the pretty girls."

The Chastity Commission had begun with the Empress Maria Theresa, the mother of sixteen children, thirteen of whom survived beyond infancy. She was anti-Protestant, anti-Jewish, and ultraconservative, and in Casanova's estimation she lacked "the virtue of tolerance in the matter of illegitimate love between a man and a woman." Avarice, gluttony, even murder had a way of bringing about their own punishments, she believed, "but lust is what I cannot pardon." So ran her orthodoxy. "Rome is indulgent in the matter," she admitted, but "my Germans don't have the devil in their bodies like the Italians."

Yet for Casanova, "illegitimate love" was genuine. "Legitimate" love was anything but. It was a form of hypocrisy, a legal construct, wishful thinking. But the Viennese authorities believed otherwise, and the Chastity Commission brutally enforced its will. "At every hour of the day, any girl who is walking alone in the streets of Vienna, even to earn an honest living, is seized and hauled off to prison." No fewer than five hundred plainclothes spies followed such women, and waited for them when they left whatever house or place of business they visited. Once they had their quarry in their grip, they questioned her, and if not satisfied with her answers, took "whatever money or jewels she had" and imprisoned her. Witnessing one of these incidents, Casanova found himself the unexpected recipient of a gold watch, pressed on him by a girl just before these vigilantes spirited her away to jail. He returned it after she'd obtained her freedom.

To ward off persecution, the women of Vienna took to carrying rosaries wherever they went. "Then they could not be arrested out of hand, for they said they were going to church, and Maria Theresa would have had the Commissioner hanged." There were so many of these spies about, Casanova complained, that there was nowhere a man could take a piss without being disturbed. On one occasion, a "fellow in a round wig" surprised him in the middle of such an act, and threatened to arrest the Venetian if he did not complete his business somewhere else. Why? "Because to your left there is a woman at a window who can see you." He looked up; she hovered four stories above him, so distant she would have needed a spy glass to see "whether I was a Jew or Christian"—circumcised or not.

———•———

He would have quit Vienna in frustration if not for a chance meeting at an inn, the Sign of the Crawfish, with former gambling acquaintances from Venice. He persuaded them to introduce him to counts, dukes, and ambassadors, as well as "several Fräuleins." To gain entrée, "I was made a baron," he gleefully recalled. "It was in vain that I said I had no title; I was told that in such company I had to be *something* if I wanted to be received anywhere in Vienna." Inevitably, he agreed.

Immediately thereafter, a baroness let it be known that "she would be glad to receive my attentions." He called on her the next day, and she drew him into her privileged circle, including three or four ladies "quite unawed by the Chastity Commission" and so "devoted to love and so kindly disposed that they had no fear of sullying their nobility by accepting money." In other words, they were courtesans, their claim to titles as suspect as his baronetcy. (It was possible to buy a patent of nobility, or the right to a title, but it cost a fortune. He preferred to invent a convenient identity.) So that's how it was: "After discovering the privileges enjoyed by these young ladies, I saw that the Chastity Commission was a hindrance only to people who did not frequent good houses."

He lost himself in a whirl of gatherings and flirtations until he happened to find himself at a lavish picnic at the mammoth Schönbrunn Palace, on the outskirts of Vienna. "I did not stint myself in anything; but I returned to Vienna with such a case of indigestion that within twenty-four hours I was at the brink of the grave." From that moment on, "I used the dregs of intelligence I had left to save my life."

At his bedside were several of the acquaintances he'd made in Vienna, one of whom invited a physician, even though Casanova opposed the idea. The physician sent for a surgeon, and suddenly, "I was about to be bled, without my consent and against my will." No good could come of it. "Half dead, I do not know what inspiration made me open my eyes, whereupon I saw the man with the lancet about to pierce my vein." Despite his feeble protests, "the butcher was going to restore me to life despite myself, and I see my arm grasped."

He seized a pistol lying on his night table, "and I fired it at the man who had sworn to obey the doctor. The ball uncurled a lock of his hair, and that was quite enough to send away the surgeon, the physician, and everyone who was with me." Casanova's medical instincts had been correct, and he had saved himself from the doctors just as he saved his benefactor Bragadin's life from doctors years before in Venice. Only the chambermaid remained with Casanova, supplying drafts of water for the next four days, (and that was all she supplied), by which time he considered himself restored to "perfect health."

Stories of his medical ordeal circulated around Vienna. Two doctors told him that if he'd been bled, he would have died, and others advised that he was within his rights to resort to a pistol to prevent the procedure. He acquired a reputation as the "man who had defended himself against Death by firing a pistol at him." And yet, "I had to beware of falling ill, for no physician would have dared to visit me again."

When he recovered his strength, Casanova visited Prague, another center of art and culture, which for him meant an abundance of gamblers and dancers, and Bratislava, sprawling along the banks of the Danube about fifty miles east of Vienna, as the arrival of spring brought a resurgence of life to the Hapsburg empire. He concluded that the time had come to return to Venice, where he arrived on May 29, 1753, "delighted that I was back in my native country, which the greatest of prejudices endears to all men."

Chapter 7

Maria Eleonora

Everything seemed exactly as he had left it: "In the study where I slept and wrote I saw with pleasure my papers shrouded in dust, certain proof that no one had entered it for the past three years." Although Venice hadn't altered during his absence, he had ripened in exile, and returned more confident and cynical for having traveled through European capitals. He'd behaved like a cad, as Mimi and her mother would attest, and at other times like an adventurer, a wanderer, and a poet manqué. Although he'd tried his hand at a literary vocation, his real passions were gambling and women.

Two days later, on Ascension Day, marking Jesus' ascent to heaven, Venice staged its annual spectacle commemorating its union with the sea. Casanova expected to observe the day by accompanying the mammoth *Bucentaur*, or state galley, powered by two hundred rowers, "in which the Doge, according to custom, was going to marry the Adriatic." Just before joining the splendid event, a gondolier paused at his lodgings to give him a letter from a young nobleman, "a rich patrician," with "no right to summon me, but he counted on my good manners. I went at once."

At the nobleman's house, he received another letter, unsealed, from Teresa Fogliazzi, the object of a failed flirtation in Vienna, now urgently writing to claim her miniature portrait. "I am sure that is in your possession," she advised. "Since I do not receive thieves, everything in my house is safe." She instructed him to deliver it to the young nobleman who had diverted him from the celebration. Without delay Casanova gave it to the surprised young man.

The two bantered, one Venetian to another, and at the young nobleman's invitation, Casanova penned the lady a scathing reply: "The pleasure that Casanova feels in ridding himself of this portrait is far greater than that which he enjoyed when an unworthy caprice prompted him to the folly of putting it in his pocket."

———•———

Immediately afterward, a storm forced the postponement of the Wedding with the Sea. At loose ends, Casanova accompanied his patron Signor Bragadin on a short trip to Padua to escape the mayhem surrounding Ascension Day. "A truly amiable old man leaves boisterous pleasure to the young." Looking back over this apparently haphazard sequence of events, Casanova realized, "If I had left Padua ten seconds earlier or later, everything that has happened to me in my life would be different." The crucial factor, of course, was a woman.

On the outskirts of Venice, near Oriago, he encountered a cabriolet (a two-seater carriage) drawn by a pair of horses, bearing a "pretty woman" and a "man in a German uniform." In the next instant, a jolt sent the woman tumbling in the direction of a stream. Leaping from his own coach, Casanova caught her, "quickly pulling down her skirts, which had exposed all her secret wonders to my eyes." Bewildered, she thanked the tall young Venetian profusely, and even called her rescuer an "angel" several times. After apologies and expressions of gratitude, "the lady set off for Padua, and I continued my journey. I had scarcely reached Venice before I masked and went to the opera."

He prepared to head to the Lido, the sandbar where *Bucentaur* rode the waves. The sight prompted him to comment: "The least contrary wind could capsize the vessel and drown the Doge with the whole Serenissima Signoria, the Ambassadors, and the Nuncio of the Pope, founder and guarantor of the efficacy of this strange sacramental ceremony, which the Venetians rightly revere to the point of superstition."

Casanova paused at the Piazza San Marco to sip a *caffè* and survey the crowds, among them "a beautiful female masker" who stopped to give him "a playful blow on the shoulder with her fan." He didn't recognize her, and steadfastly sat finishing his *caffè* before rising to join Signor Bragadin in his gondola. He passed the same masker, stopping to inquire what she intended by striking him. "To punish you for not recognizing me after you saved my life yesterday." It was the woman who'd nearly tumbled into the stream beside her coach.

He invited her to join him in his gondola to watch the festivities, and she accepted, along with the same German officer who had accompanied her earlier. He had to assure himself they were not connected with some ambassador or other—if they had been, he would "have been in trouble with the State Inquisitors," who prevented communication with outsiders. As they proceeded in the gondola to *Bucentaur*, Casanova took "a few liberties under cover of her cloak," but she remained indifferent to his touch. After the ceremony, they glided safely on the swells back to Venice. The German, if that's what he was, invited Casanova to dine with them at an ancient inn known as the Wild Man. He accepted at once.

The moment he found himself alone with the masked woman, he blurted out his love—*love!*—for her, offered her his box at the opera, and proposed to accompany her throughout the fortnight of festivities following the Ascension observance, that is, if he wouldn't be wasting his time and attention. "So if you intend to be cruel to me, be so good as to tell me." She begged him to cease; his aggrieved "tone" was making her resent if not hate him.

He understood, "but I am afraid of being deceived."

"And for that reason you want to begin where people usually end," she shot back.

During supper at the Wild Man, with nothing settled, she unmasked, revealing her disarming beauty. But who was the German officer accompanying her—her husband, a relative, or even a procurer? In brief, "I wanted to know on what kind of adventure I had embarked."

Overcoming the awkwardness of this threesome, he took them both to the comic opera, the opera buffa, then to supper, and then, in his gondola, under cover of darkness, "the beauty granted me all the favors propriety permits a woman to grant when there is a third person to be considered." These preliminaries boded well in Venice as the beginning of a serious relationship. He learned the particulars from the German soldier who accompanied the lady; he was neither German nor a soldier, but a shrewd Venetian businessman named Pier Antonio Capretta, a captain in the service of Austria but in reality a supplier of beef cattle to the Venetian State, or at least an assistant to one of these wealthy men, and unfortunately estranged from his own prosperous father. And the lady was Maria Ottaviani, the wife of a broker of unspecified goods. All he asked of Casanova was a "necessary favor that will unite us in the closest friendship. Become my backer *without risking anything yourself.*" As security, he offered his entire supply of cattle, tied up in Trieste.

Casanova adamantly refused, at which point Capretta redoubled his efforts to convince him, to no avail. As the young man took his leave, he heard Capretta mutter that he and the lady would be looking for him that evening in the Piazza San Marco. Did he mean these words as an invitation or threat? "Disgusted with the man's designs on me," Casanova wrote, "I was also disgusted with mine on Signora Capretta. I thought I saw a plot; I thought I saw that I was being taken for an easy mark," so he made a point of avoiding the Piazza San Marco. He did visit the man's lodgings the following morning, and just before he left, Signor Capretta introduced his mother and sister to Giacomo Casanova.

His spirits surging, he fell in love with them both, the "ingenuous and respectable woman" as well as the "very young girl who strikes me as a prodigy." After half an hour alone with the girl, he considered himself her slave. Her name was Caterina Capretta, and in his *Histoire*, he referred to as "Signorina C. C." She "never went out except with her mother, who was pious and indulgent. She had read only the books in the library of her father, a serious man who possessed no novels." She had no visitors, and "she had not been told she was a miracle of nature." It seemed to him as they talked that "her soul was in chaos." When he finally left the house, he felt a wave of sadness come over him again. He would never see her again, yet he wished he could ask her father for her hand in marriage. "I thought her uniquely endowed to make me happy."

Meeting Pier Antonio Capretta in the street a couple of days later, Casanova was overjoyed to hear that "his sister did nothing but talk of me." Her brother had concluded that the two would be a good match, and she came with a dowry. Why not visit their residence for a *caffè* to discuss the matter? Inevitably, Casanova went, "despite the fact that I had promised myself not to go there again. *It is always easy to break one's word to one's self.*" He fell even more deeply in love with her on the next visit. When he declared that he envied the man whom Heaven had destined for her, her cheeks flushed scarlet. "No one had ever said as much to her before."

———•———

Doubts assailed him.

He gambled—"a great palliative for a man in love"—and won a "quick hundred *zecchini*." Marriage and money: both were so capricious, yet operated according to different rules. He could gamble many times; in marriage, he could try his luck but once.

Meditating on these complications as he traversed a narrow *calle*, or alleyway, he was accosted by an older man whom he recognized as Count Giuseppe Bonafede, confessing that he was in "dire want and reduced to despair by his obligation to support his numerous family." Casanova remembered him from their time in the fortress of Sant'Andrea about ten years earlier. The aristocrat begged for a single zecchino, enough, he said, to sustain him for nearly a week. Flush with his winnings, Casanova gave him ten zecchini— what a strange city was Venice, where a man of no means felt obliged to give money to a member of the nobility reduced to begging—at which the Count sobbed with shame and gratitude. Through tears, he mentioned his beautiful daughter, whom he could no longer afford to support, and who "would rather die than sacrifice her virtue to necessity," that is, sell herself.

Casanova promised to call on her.

He found her still living in her "almost bare" home, yet she'd retained her beauty and spirit. She appeared "transported with joy," as she embraced this phantom from her past. "She could not have welcomed an adored lover more fondly." With her invalid mother hidden away in a remote corner of the house, he generated "a storm of kisses, which were given and received under the merest guise of friendship." No matter that he'd left behind a woman in Paris who'd recently given birth to their child, or that he was negotiating the terms of marriage with another woman who lived in Venice; at the moment, only the Contessa held his interest.

She described her family's poverty, "her brothers roaming the streets in rags, her father who literally had nothing to feed them." It occurred to him that he couldn't have been the first to penetrate the circle of the Bonafade family; surely the Contessa had entertained a lover at one time or other. "A lover!" she cried. "What man would have the courage to be a lover in a house like this? Do you think me a woman to give myself for thirty *soldi*? There is no one in Venice who would set a higher price on me, seeing me in this wretched house. Besides, I do not feel I was born to be a prostitute."

He pressed twelve zecchini into her hand, a fraction of his recent winnings. "The amount astonished her; she had never had so much money." He'd correctly guessed her price, and won her heart at a discount.

The next day Pier Antonio Capretta declared that his mother had given his cloistered young sister, who'd never seen the inside of a theater, permission to attend the opera. Sidetracked by his conquest of the Contessa Bonafede, Casanova had overlooked the innocent young girl. He took a jaundiced view of her scheming brother, who had "conceived the pretty plan of selling her to me." He felt sorry for the mother, and he felt even sorrier for the girl who was being manipulated, "but"—and it was an important "but"—"I was not virtuous enough to refuse the invitation" any more than he'd been able to refuse the previous invitation to her home. He rationalized thus: "Since I loved her, I should be present to guard her against other snares." If he refused, her brother would recruit someone else, someone wholly unsuited to her, "and the idea was poison to my soul." For this reason, he made good on his promise to invite the Capretta family to join him in his opera box at the esteemed Teatro San Samuele, with its long-standing ties to his family.

On the day of the performance, he was so anxious to meet them that he forgot all about dinner. Caterina Capretta appeared, "ravishingly beautiful and elegantly masked," along with her insufferable brother. He directed them into his gondola. After a time, her brother announced he had to leave on an errand to see his mistress. Good riddance. On her own, Caterina Capretta, surprisingly, seemed "neither afraid nor reluctant." Since it was hot, he encouraged the child to unmask, and "she did so instantly." Casanova regarded her with equal measures of concupiscence and gallantry, as his "love became immense," his member swelling in his tight breeches. Alone with this delicate beauty, he was tongue-tied, staring at her face for fear of becoming mesmerized by her bosom. "Cut too low in front, her bodice let me see the buds of her breasts.... I had seen them only for an instant, and, terrified, I did not dare look at them again."

"Do speak to me," she implored. "You only look at me and say nothing." She went on artlessly to say that she felt "freer and safer" with him than she did with her brother. "Do you remember telling me that you envied the lot of the man who would marry me?" He did. "At the very same moment I was saying to myself that the girl who gets you will be the happiest girl in Venice." It seemed to Casanova that she spoke with such "angelic sincerity" that he wanted to kiss the lips that uttered those words. To be loved by this "angel incarnate" evoked the "sweetest joy." They would have to be married, "united forever," as he put it, except, "I could be your father." Nonsense, she replied. She was all of fourteen.

"And I am twenty-eight."

"So there you are! What man of your age has a daughter like me?"

———•———

That night, having disembarked from the gondola, they "ate ices, then went to the opera," where they were joined by Caterina's brother, who urged his little sister to kiss Casanova. She offered him her lips, but the thought of engaging in this intimate activity under scrutiny repelled Casanova. The girl assumed that he didn't find her attractive, and said so. He repeated his love for her, and printed a kiss on her mouth, as he put it. "She left my arms blushing crimson and as if stunned to have discovered my love in such a fashion." As she fumbled to put her mask back in place and collect herself, her brother congratulated the couple. She knew Casanova loved her, she said, but he didn't have to hurt her to prove it.

Days later Pier Antonio Capretta begged a "small favor" from Casanova. It seemed there was "some excellent Cyprus wine for sale, cheap," and he could obtain a cask, certain to resell at a nice profit, for a guarantee. Would Casanova be willing to provide it? "With pleasure," he replied, as Pier Antonio flourished the paper for signature.

Later that day, he reunited with Caterina for an excursion to La Giudecca, known for rustic restaurants and gardens. They found their way to the island's eastern end, "where a *zecchino* made me lord and master of the place for the whole day." They stowed their masks and outer clothes and went for a stroll. Casanova likened her to a "young greyhound released from days of tedious confinement in its master's room and given the freedom of the fields at last" as she darted around the garden, exhilarated, and reveling in her "untrammeled freedom." As he looked on, "She ran and ran until she was out of breath, and then laughed at the astonishment that kept me motionless and staring at her." She wiped her forehead, and challenged him to a race. He agreed, on condition that the loser must do whatever the victor commanded. The first one to touch the gate leading to the lagoon would be the winner. Of course, he could outrun her, but he planned to hold back to see what she would "order me to do."

He allowed her to reach the gate well ahead of him. For a penalty, she concealed her ring on her body, sentencing him to discover it. He must search with determination, for she would "think very little of me if I did not find it." How delightful. Seated on a carpet of grass, he explored her pockets, "the folds of her short bodice and her skirt, then her shoes," but his fingers found no ring. "I turn up her skirt, slowly and circumspectly, as high as her garters." Nothing. His hands slid down her skirt, and "since I am free to do anything, grope under her armpits." She laughed, and he felt the ring. To seize it, he unlaced her bodice. His fingertips came into contact with her breast, soft and warm, inviting and forbidden, but as he moved toward it, the ring fell so that he had retrieve it from her skirt. As he did, his hand shook.

"Why are you shaking?"

Because he was excited to find the ring, he explained, and challenged her to another race. This time he resorted to an "unfailing ruse. I left myself, crying, 'Oh, my God!' She turns, she thinks I have hurt myself, and she comes to me. But as soon as I see that I am one step ahead of her, I look at her. I laugh, I run to the gate, I touch it, and I cry victory." He was a twenty-eight-year-old satyr stalking a fourteen-year-old virgin.

"It's against the rules to win by a trick," she complained. But he didn't have kissing in mind, as she might have expected.

Instead: "I sentence you to change garters with me."

She was horrified. "You saw mine. They're old and ugly, they're worth nothing." She reluctantly handed over her "ugly garters," receiving to her amazement a beautiful pair in return. The ruse had been his roundabout way of offering her a love token, for the elaborate ones he wore he intended all along to present to her. She promised to wear them always.

Famished, they ate an omelet, and she asked him to put the garters on her "in perfect good faith, with no thought of evil and not a grain of coquetry. . . . Caterina pulled her skirt up to her thighs and finding that her stockings were too short for her to put the garters above the knee, but I at once gave her the dozen pairs of pearl-gray stockings that I had bought. In an ecstasy of gratitude, she sat on my lap, giving me the same sort of kisses she would have given her father when he made such a present." He fought against "the violence of my desires with a strength more than human."

"After strolling until nightfall," Casanova recalled, the mismatched couple quit Giudecca, and "went to the opera wearing our masks, for, the theater being small, we might have been recognized" by spies for Caterina's father. Casanova felt more urgent concern about her meddlesome brother, who might be shadowing them, too. He scanned the audience, eerily masked, men and women alike, but detected no sign of the brother. During the performance, when Caterina placed the libretto on the ledge of the box, a man snatched it away. Even though the culprit was masked, Casanova recognized Pier Antonio Capretta lurking in the next box with his mistress: the same woman whom Casanova had rescued as she tumbled from a carriage.

Against his better judgment, he joined Caterina at a post-performance supper at her brother's chosen casino. "I did not like it; but I could not avoid it except by a direct challenge; and I was in love." Unmasked at dinner, Casanova squirmed as Pier Antonio's mistress showered the young Caterina with praise, despite her envy of the girl's youth. Later that night Pier Antonio drunkenly threw his girlfriend on a sofa and pulled up her skirts to display her thighs to Casanova and to anyone else who cared to observe. "She slapped him in pretended punishment, but she was laughing." As for the brother, "his lewd behavior disgusted me," as he "displays his bestial condition," that is, exposed his erection to the group, "and adjusts the lady to himself, holding her astride him while she, still pretending that she was powerless in his hands, lets him perform." Casanova placed himself between Caterina and her brother "to hide the horror that she must have already seen in the mirror."

Afterword, Pier Antonio and his mistress tried to embrace Casanova and Caterina, who "modestly answered that she did not know what there had been for her to see," but he realized that "her beautiful soul was in the greatest perturbation" after having been tricked into observing just the sort of lascivious behavior from which Casanova had tried to shield her, even as he contemplated taking even greater liberties. He trembled with anger, as "the infamous scoundrel believed he had given me great proof of his friendship," when in reality he was "dishonoring his lady and debauching and prostituting his sister." The thought inflamed him "to the point of very nearly drenching the scene in blood. I do not know how I restrained myself from cutting his throat." By this time, the parties, exhausted, left the casino and stumbled to their separate homes.

The next day, Casanova called on Pier Antonio—the pig—to condemn his behavior at the casino. He would have nothing further to do with him, even if it meant severing relations with young Caterina. If her brother thought he could pimp her out to someone else, Casanova vowed to prevent him.

His declaration stunned Pier Antonio, who realized that he had wrongly assumed that the man who stood before him and his sister were carrying on a carnal relationship. He begged Casanova to forgive him, and hugged him "with tears in his eyes."

At that moment, his indulgent mother appeared with Caterina, the two of them oblivious to the strife between Casanova and Pier Antonio, to thank her suitor for the presents he'd given the girl. Summoning his most proper behavior he promised to speak with the girl's father about marriage "after I had secured a sufficient income to make her happy." As he bowed to kiss her hand, his tears began to flow, "which set hers flowing," while her brother looked on in stony silence. "The world is full of mothers of this stamp," Casanova commented to his readers with a sigh, "every one of them honest and endowed with all the virtues," and as a result of the trust they place in people they believed to be honest, they became victims.

Glancing over his shoulder, Casanova saw her brother sobbing with the rest of them, but "the scoundrel could command his tears."

Both the best and worst came of the situation. Pier Antonio produced his little sister for a reunion with Casanova in the casino. "Burning with love, I foresaw what must happen." They ordered a supper to be delivered later, and went upstairs to a private room, where they intended to spend seven hours. When they were alone, she unmasked and threw herself in his arms, saying that he'd "won her heart and soul during that terrible supper where I had been so considerate to her," as they exchanged kisses of ever increasing intensity.

They discussed her brother's drunken behavior; Casanova asked if she was afraid he would do the same thing to her. No, she maintained. "We will keep ourselves until we are married. Shall we not?" They amused themselves by discussing the bawdy couplet on the garters he gave her—"You who see my beauty's jewel every day / Tell it that love bids it be true"— which, he explained, meant that the "jewel" actually referred to her "little such-and-such," and that the garters, if they had eyes, could see it every day. Caterina blushed deeply. Now she wouldn't show the garters to anyone.

The two of them confided that they were both overcome with desire. "We are free," Caterina said, "and my father will be obliged to consent." He wished to ask for her hand in marriage first, but she demurred: "He will say I am too young."

As they bantered, Casanova burned with lust. "Let us marry before God, in his presence," he proposed. "We have no need of documents." The formality of a church service could wait. In the meantime, they should consider themselves truly married as of this moment. "Now come to my arms. We will complete our marriage in bed."

She threw herself across the bed fully clothed, but Casanova reminded her that "Love and Hymen went naked." Moments later, he held her in his arms with nothing between them, kissing her without pause, engulfing her, "regretting that my mouth must move less swiftly than my eyes." He told her that her beauty was divine, and transported him beyond the limits of mortality. She was, at that moment, the ultimate prize: a fourteen-year-old virgin who loved him and whom he desired beyond anything else. She was "white as alabaster, with black hair, and her puberty was apparent only in the down that, divided into little curls, formed a transparent fringe above the little entrance to the temple of love." Her laughter roused him from this reverie, as she pointed out that *he* remained fully clothed. "Never have I undressed more quickly," he wrote. "Then it was her turn blindly to obey the promptings of instinct."

"Great power of love!" she exclaimed. "I feel no shame. Would I have believed it ten days ago?" Before he replied, she added, "Please don't tickle me there, it's too sensitive."

"Dear heart, I am going to hurt you more than that."

"What a difference between you and my pillow," she murmured, by which she meant that "these last four or five nights I couldn't get to sleep unless I had a big pillow in my arms and kissed it over and over and imagined it was you. I only touched myself *there*, dear, just for a moment at the end and very lightly." The charged exchange reveals that Casanova was aware of the allure of the female orgasm, which he called *la jouissance*. "Then a pleasure for which there are no words left me motionless and as if dead."

So it was that Caterina became his "like a heroine, as every girl in love must do, for pleasure and the assuagement of desire make even pain delicious." On it went. "I spent two whole hours without ever separating from her. Her continual swoons made me immortal." Only the approaching night and growling stomachs interrupted their embraces and spasms and exclamations. They sent for the supper they'd ordered, and "ate gazing at each other" in pregnant silence. "We found our supreme happiness in the thought that it was we who created it and that we would renew it whenever we wished."

Their hostess materialized to ask if they were finished with dinner and ready for the opera. If only she could go—she'd heard it was "such a fine spectacle"—but she'd never been, explaining that it was "too expensive for people like us. My daughter is so curious about it that she would give— God forgive me!—her maidenhead to go just once." At that, he handed the astonished lady the key to his opera box, impressing on her that it cost two zecchini. Go with your daughter, he urged, "and tell her to keep her maidenhead for something better," giving her another two zecchini, and throwing in the use of the gondola. Casanova and his young love intended to stay in the room, he explained, "for we were married this morning."

A good-natured busybody, the hostess went to the bed where she espied "signs worthy of veneration," meaning blood from Caterina's ruptured hymen, whereupon she embraced and congratulated the girl. Turning to her daughter, the hostess said she hoped the same thing would happen to her, and the embarrassed child replied that she, too, would be a virgin at the altar of marriage. Neither the hostess nor her daughter realized, of course, that Casanova and Caterina, though in love, were still not man and wife. When the hostess and her daughter left for the opera, "we locked ourselves in and went back to bed" for four hours. When he saw her "ravaged by Venus, the supreme degree of pleasure seized on my senses," and the lovers collapsed in an exhausted heap, to be wakened hours later by the hostess knocking on their door to announce that she had returned with their gondola.

As the lovers hurriedly dressed, the hostess's blond daughter prepared coffee and stole glances at Casanova suggesting that she was far more experienced than her mother believed. When his gaze returned to Caterina, he saw that her eyes had "such dark circles that they looked as if they had been bruised. The poor child had sustained a combat that literally left her another person." Parting "by the light of early dawn" they rejoiced in the knowledge that they were truly married in their minds and hearts, if not in the eyes of the law. He promised himself to persuade his patron, Bragadin, "to obtain the girl's hand for me." That would have been the honorable thing to do, and if his plan worked, it would have set Casanova on a different course, the reformed gambler and libertine living in blessed union with his child bride, putting his difficulties behind him as he vaulted through a fortunate marriage into respectability and solvency. Before he could pursue that worthy goal, he tumbled into bed and slept until noon. When he rose, his resolve had drained away, and, in his words, "I spent the day gambling and losing."

Caterina's scheming brother turned up, asking for another enormous loan against a suspect transaction involving a note and ring. The ruse no longer fooled Casanova, who sadly realized that Pier Antonio was, in his indirect way, pimping for his sister. "How could I refuse the wretch what he asked of me?" He'd established a disastrous precedent regarding his intimate relations with Caterina, and without funds of his own, he felt powerless to resist being drawn deeper into her brother's debt. "And so Caterina Capretta, who should have brought me nothing but happiness, became the cause of my ruin."

In the ensuing weeks, Caterina and Casanova renewed their love on La Giudecca as the hostess's blond daughter continued to flirt ever more boldly, exposing her bosom "which on the excuse of the hot weather she exposed too lavishly," while he tried to extricate himself from his dealings with the covetous Pier Antonio. In time, Caterina became aware of this mischief. All the while, the couple awaited an audience with her father. In case he refused Casanova's request for her hand in marriage, "she begged me to do everything possible to make her pregnant." If he initially prevented them from marrying, the sight of her swelling belly would make him change his mind in a hurry. Casanova tutored her about the process of "becoming a mother," predicting that she was more likely to become pregnant "when we reached the sweet ecstasy at the same time." They toiled day and night "to arrive together at that life-endangering death that was to ensure our happiness."

At last the hour came when either Caterina or her brother was to meet Casanova with definitive word from her father. It was a Monday morning, Casanova nervously waiting, but no one appeared. He lingered for four hours until "on the stroke of Angelus"—6:00 p.m.—Caterina hurried toward him, "masked but alone." The answer she brought was not what they had wished. No approval was forthcoming from her father, who was outraged at her temerity. But nothing he said would stop them.

To console themselves, "We went to our garden, despite a very violent storm, which, our gondola having only one oar, terrified me. Caterina, unaware of the danger, frisked about, and the movement she imparted to the gondola put the gondolier in danger of falling into the water, which would have meant our death." Alarmed, the gondolier shouted at the couple to be still or risk drowning. "We arrived at last, and the gondolier smiled when I paid him four times the fare."

The next six hours passed "in a state of happiness." They removed their masks and pressed their lips close, and then their bodies. As he put it, "sleep was not our company." In the morning, they took their leave of their lair, their amiable hostess, and the garden to return to Venice.

Unable to forget Caterina Capretta, Casanova beseeched Signor Bragadin and his two close friends to grant him a private audience, during which he made his case that he was in love with the girl, and "determined to elope with her" if her father stubbornly refused to cooperate. "It will be necessary to provide me with an income on which I can live and to guarantee the ten thousand ducats the girl will bring me as her dowry." As was their custom, the old men, as mystical as ever, deferred to their Kabbalistic spirit, Paralis, whose pronouncements they slavishly followed. "I asked nothing better," Casanova commented because it was up to him to interpret the oracle's remarks for them. He constructed pyramids, invoking Freemasonry, and manufactured a decree: Signor Bragadin would negotiate with Caterina's father, who was rusticating. Upon his return, the three old men would meet with him on behalf of Caterina and Casanova.

He expected this latest development would cheer his love; instead, she and her mother were grief-stricken that Pier Antonio had been jailed for debt. Suppressing a smirk of satisfaction, Casanova gave them twenty zecchini to reduce his financial burden, cautioning them to give him two or three zecchini only at a time. This generosity bought him access to Caterina at night in her house for more blissful lovemaking, punctuated by anxiety over her father's return. Caterina warned that his father looked on her as a child, and wouldn't allow her to marry until she turned eighteen, and then only to a merchant, not a good-for-nothing adventurer and gambler. "I know my father, and I am afraid." In that case, Casanova said, they would elope.

When Signor Bragadin, his two close colleagues, and her father met, he declared his intention to send his daughter to a convent for at least four years. If, at the end of her time there, Giacomo Casanova had a "well-established position, he might grant me her hand." *Four years!*

Refused admittance to Caterina's house, where the door had been locked from inside, Casanova retreated to his apartment "neither dead nor alive." It no longer seemed possible to elope with the girl now that she was sequestered in a convent on the island of Murano. In desperation, he visited Pier Antonio in jail, who "tells me any number of lies, which I pretend to believe": he'll be sprung from prison in a matter of days, and then will pay Casanova the hundred zecchini owed to him, forgive him for the delay, and then he will make good on that note for two hundred zecchini, an obligation that Casanova had incautiously guaranteed. And what news of his beloved Caterina? "He knows nothing, and believes there is nothing new." Accustomed to flinging money around, Casanova flings two zecchini at the wretch and leaves, thinking about how he might communicate with his love.

Unable to eat or sleep, he haunted Bragadin's deserted palazzo. The aristocrat and his two inseparable friends had gone to Padua for a month or two to celebrate the Fair of St. Anthony. Alone and vulnerable, Casanova ventured forth only to play cards, and to lose. As his gambling debts mounted, he pawned everything he could lay his hands on, as "thoughts of suicide" preoccupied him. On June 13, St. Anthony's Feast Day, as he was shaving, the bell rang, and he admitted a courier, a woman, bearing a letter from Caterina, dated June 12. So great was his surprise, "I thought I should drop dead." With a trembling hand, he put down his razor to read her words: "I am boarding in this convent, and very well treated; and I am in perfect health, despite the anxiety of my mind. The Mother Superior has orders not to let me see anyone and not to allow me to correspond with anyone; but I am already sure that I can write to you despite her prohibition. I do not doubt your constancy, my dear husband, and I am sure that you do not doubt and will never doubt mine." After reading these words, it took Giacomo "four or five minutes" to recover. Now he had to be in touch with Caterina at all costs.

In his manuscript, Casanova obscured the convent's name, but it was likely Santa Maria degli Angeli, the Church of the Angels. The ancient edifice had housed a convent at least since 1188, and had been rebuilt not long before Caterina's arrival. It was a place apart, dedicated to religious observance and the protection of the daughters of wealthy Venetian families wanting to keep their bloodlines off limits to gamblers and adventurers seeking a shortcut to fortune. But Casanova's imagination transformed it into a high order of brothel, a place to encounter young women from some of the best and wealthiest families in Venice.

The woman who'd brought the letter explained that she served the nuns of the convent. She made the journey from the island of Murano to Venice each Wednesday to deliver letters. He wanted to know if she could read. Indeed she could; she couldn't perform her job of delivering letters unless she could read the addresses. "The nuns want to be sure—and they're right—that we won't give Peter a letter they write to Paul." Yet she assured him she was discreet. "If I didn't know how to hold my tongue I'd lose my employment." She informed Casanova that the young nun who gave her the letter was sly, and passed it to her without any other nun seeing it. Eager to play a role in the intrigue, she persuaded him that he could trust her with his reply; she wouldn't tell the nuns. Carrying a letter from one Christian to another wasn't a sin, was it? Even if it were, her confessor happened to be a deaf old monk. His secrets were safe with her. Her name was Laura.

He composed a four-page reply overflowing with protestations of love, offers to send funds, expressions of relief that she was safe and well, promises to write faithfully every Wednesday, and requests for "every detail of the life she was being forced to lead" as well as "all her ideas on the subject of breaking all the chains and destroying all the obstacles standing in the way of our reunion, for I belonged to her just as she told me that she belonged to me." Finally, she must "burn all my letters." He concealed a *zecchino* in the envelope, sealed it with wax, and handed it to the courier with an additional zecchino for her, eliciting tears of gratitude from the recipient, who'd likely been hoping for just this result.

Elated to have reestablished a line of communication with the young woman he still called his wife, Casanova ordered his valet to pack his trunk. Three hours later, he knocked on the door of Signor Bragadin's summer residence in Padua. The two rejoiced, and, joined by Bragadin's companions, sat down to dinner. How hungry he'd been! Later that evening, he gambled, and once again lost. "Fortune showed me she was not always on love's side." In that case, he resolved to assist her as best he could.

———•———

During that week in Padua, Casanova joined forces with the "celebrated swindler" Don Antonio Croce—the "Don" was ceremonial, disguising his low repute—to operate a private faro, or gambling, operation. This particular card game was all the rage at the French court, and the name "faro" was a corruption of "Pharaoh," whose image appeared on one of the cards in the deck. For seed money, Casanova approached Signor Bragadin, who quickly obtained funds from a "Jewish usurer" who advanced a thousand Venetian ducats "at five percent per month, payable at the end of the month, and with the interest deducted in advance," recalled Casanova, never forgetting a detail concerning love or money. When the gambling began, the money rolled in. A Swedish army officer and deserter by the name of Gillenspetz gambled away two thousand zecchini, and an English Jew named "Mendex" (probably Joshua Mendes, of London), lost another thousand zecchini. Two days later, the house won four thousand zecchini, and Casanova's scheme had paid off, demonstrating to him that it was more profitable to maintain a gambling establishment than to be a gambler. The lesson would not be lost on him.

His business completed, "I set off at full gallop at nightfall in very bad weather, but nothing could have held me back. I was to receive Caterina's letter in the morning." But, "six miles from Padua my horse fell on its side, so I was caught with my left leg under its belly." He feared that he'd broken his foot, but when the postilion dragged him from under the horse, he realized to his relief that he was uninjured; his steed, in contrast, had been hurt. He got into a violent argument with the postilion, who refused to turn over his horse, as Casanova believed correct. "I fire my pistol at him point-blank, at which he makes off and I pursue my journey." He reached Fusina, near Venice, "by the first light of dawn," braving this new onslaught in a four-oared boat to the Bragadin palazzo, arriving "safe and sound, though roughly handled by the rain and wind." At least he had his missive from Caterina, seven pages long, not all of them chaste and penitent.

In her letter, Caterina explained that despite her isolation and threats of excommunication if she violated the slightest rule, she'd befriended a playful twenty-two-year-old nun. She'd heard from still another nun that "as she was rich and generous, all the other nuns treated her with deference." Of greater interest, he read, "when they were alone, she gave her kisses of which I could rightly be jealous if she were of a different sex." That was worth pondering, as were her latest thoughts about eloping: it was entirely possible to spirit her away from the monastery, but she advised him to wait and remain faithful. With luck, "in five or six months she would be in a condition to scandalize and dishonor the convent" if she were ostentatiously pregnant.

Morality aside, becoming pregnant was to embark on an extremely danger-ous course. Women who became pregnant for the first time made out their will, for their days might be numbered. One in ten women died in child-birth, it is estimated; if a married woman became pregnant five times, she faced a fifty percent chance of dying in the throes of childbirth during those years. Young Caterina gave no sign of awareness of the risks she faced. Over-come with love for Casanova, she requested his portrait, concealed in a ring, for her to keep close by at all times. Both the secrecy and vanity of the proj-ect appealed to him. He engaged a "skillful Piedmontese"—from northern Italy—who "made a great deal of money in Venice" plying his trade. At the same time Casanova commissioned "an excellent jeweler who made the ring for me surpassingly well." The exterior displayed the image of a saint, with a tiny blue dot on a white enamel field. When the dot was depressed with a pin, the saint flipped up to reveal Casanova's likeness.

Whenever she was alone, she poked the ring with a pin to make it re-veal his portrait, which she kissed "a hundred times and did not leave off if someone came in, for she instantly made the cover drop over it." A nun of-fered her fifty zecchini for it, claiming the outer portrait resembled its own-er's namesake, Saint Catherine.

In late July, he received another letter via Laura. "A misfortune befell me," she wrote. "I am losing blood. I do not know how to stop the flow, and I have very little linen." She urgently needed quantities of linen. "If the hem-orrhage kills me the whole convent will know what I died of," she wrote. "But I think of you; and I tremble. What will you do in your grief. Ah, my dear! What a pity!"

Laura revealed Caterina had suffered a miscarriage. Frantic, Casa-nova and Laura took a gondola to the Ghetto, the Jewish quarter, where he bought "a Jew's whole stock of sheets and more than two hundred napkins" and tossed the lot into a sack. He proceeded to Murano, where Laura hast-ily concealed him in her house. She stuffed all the linen she could manage beneath her skirt, and went to the convent as he waited. Laura "returned an hour later and told me that, having lost much blood all night, [Caterina] was in bed and very weak, and that we must commend her to God, for if the hemorrhage did not stop she would succumb within twenty-four hours." She removed the soiled linen from her skirt, revealing a "little shapeless lump."

Casanova "very nearly dropped dead. It was sheer butchery." Laura later brought him a heart-rending note: "My dear, I have not the strength to write to you. I am still bleeding, and there is no remedy. God disposes; but my honor is safe. My only consolation is knowing you are here."

When he finished reading, "Laura terrified me by showing me ten or twelve napkins soaked in blood." There was nothing he could do. "I was really in despair. Seeing myself the murderer of this innocent girl, I did not feel I could survive her." He lay down on a cot, refusing to eat or to allow Laura's daughters to take off his clothes. They were nice-enough-looking girls, but "they filled me with loathing. I saw them as the instruments of my horrible incontinence, which had made me the executioner of an angel incarnate."

At dawn, he heard from Laura that his beloved had a faint pulse, was as pale as wax, and had eaten nothing. The stifling July heat aggravated her suffering. He decided to consult a physician, whom he would regard in this situation as an oracle. "I had good reason to laugh at all oracles," he confessed, but he needed to confide in one now.

As he waited for news of Caterina's condition, Laura's daughters tended to him by bringing him dinner, which he waved away, and consuming it themselves "with ravenous appetites." Meanwhile, the eldest daughter, "the showpiece," snubbed him. He spent hours monitoring reports from the faithful go-between, Laura, who "came at last and told me that the patient was still in the same state of starvation, that her extreme weakness had greatly surprised the physician, who did not know to what to attribute it."

A few hours later "I saw very well that if she could sleep she would recover, so I longed for morning. I gave Laura six *zecchini* and her daughters one apiece, and ate some fish for supper." With that, he went to bed.

In the morning, "Laura came in looking cheerful and told me that the patient had slept well and that she was going back to the convent to take her a dish of soup. However, it was too soon to cry victory, for she still needed to regain her strength and replace the blood she had lost. I now felt sure she would recover her health," and so she did.

Casanova lodged in Laura's house for another week until he left amid a deluge of tears—from Laura because he'd given her all the linen he'd bought, and from the girls because "they had not managed to persuade me to give them at least a kiss during the ten days I spent in their house."

In Venice, his life resumed its former patterns; he gambled and won, but it scarcely mattered. He managed a faro casino in partnership with a wealthy backer "who protected me against the frauds of certain tyrannical aristocrats in competition with whom a mere private citizen is always in the wrong in my charming country." He crossed paths with other lives en route to his own obscure destiny, lacking the one essential for happiness: "a real and satisfying love affair."

Instead, he received letters on Wednesdays from the girl he called his wife, and heard occasional bits of news about her from Laura, who told him that Caterina had become even more beautiful now that she had regained her health. He correctly interpreted this observation as an invitation to see her. He finally achieved the opportunity to espy his love during a "profession," that is, a ceremony in which a nun takes the veil of the most solemn vows. "I thought I should die with pleasure when I saw her four paces from me, staring at me in her surprise at seeing me there." She seemed taller to him, more "developed" after her ordeal. Among all the nuns at the ceremony, "I had eyes only for her, and I did not return to Venice until the gate was closed."

Her grateful letters inspired Casanova to travel between Venice and Murano, especially on feast days, when he worshipped at a church where he knew he would see her, taking care to safeguard his anonymity from "the plain citizens of Murano and their womenfolk." If word of his visits reached the ears of her father, Caterina would be moved to another, undisclosed convent forever. Among the nuns, his regular attendance at feast days aroused amusement and speculation. He must be grieving, said the old nuns as they saw him washing with holy water, while the younger nuns believed he suffered from melancholy as "a misanthrope who shunned the world at large."

The letter was white, and the seal the greenish hue of aventurine, a style of glass shimmering with gold flecks, fashioned on Murano. (For centuries, Murano had been a center of glassmaking, Venice having banished glassmakers for fear of fire caused by their equipment.) Such was the curious object that Casanova found casually dropped at his feet as he boarded his gondola after mass on All Saints' Day, November 1, 1753. Seated, he unsealed the envelope, and read, "A nun who has seen you in her church every feast day for the past two and half months wishes you to make her acquaintance." There followed instructions of Byzantine complexity concerning the protocol for an introduction to a nun, awaiting him, improbably, at a casino on Murano, or, if he wished, at a place of his choosing in Venice. "You will see her leave a gondola masked, provided you are on the quay alone, without a servant, masked, and holding a candle." This intrigue tinged with mysticism delighted him. He was to give his written reply to the same nun who dropped the letter at his feet; she would await him at the Church San Canziano, near the Rialto, the central bridge in Venice, "first altar on the right."

He considered the epistle "sheer madness," yet he couldn't resist the scheme described therein. What if the nun happened to be "beautiful, rich, and a flirt," acting without Caterina's knowledge? "I dismissed the suspicion precisely because it pleased me." His considered reply, written in the best French he could muster, "straddled the ditch," as he put it, between desire and propriety. Was she respectable? Should he fear a trap? Did she have the right person in mind? These were all worthy questions. And he had one requirement, that he learn *her* name, since she obviously knew his. "Very impatient in my turn," he concluded, "I will go tomorrow at the same hour to San Canziano to receive your answer." He received another letter, with even more convoluted questions and stipulations, and crafted another reply bristling with his concerns. "I thought the note a masterpiece of the spirit of intrigue," he said of his handiwork. "There was something lofty in this way of proceeding." He had yet to decipher what these dealings meant, but he had been pulled in too far to ignore them. What sort of woman was he dealing with—young and pretty, or "some old woman," in which case he was prepared to laugh at his folly. He would ask Caterina to elucidate, but thought the better of it, acknowledging that in his imagination he was already being unfaithful to her. "Then, too, I was surprised at the great freedom enjoyed by these holy virgins, who could so easily violate their rule of enclosure."

On his guard, following instructions from his anonymous correspondent, he met the Countess who was to act as his go-between, "a domineering woman, beginning to fade a little but still beautiful." She escorted him to another convent on Murano, San Giacomo di Galizia, where they saw the "celebrated" nun, Maria Eleonora Michiel, of a wealthy Venetian family, whose mother was related to the Bragadins; thus they were known to one another by reputation. A metal grate separated them, but when he pressed on a spring, four sections of it opened, and "any man of my stature could pass through it." As the three of them sat and talked, he "could examine this rare beauty of twenty-two or twenty-three at my ease." She could only be Caterina's special friend. Her habit hid many of her physical features—he guessed from her eyebrows that her hair was the color of burned sugar—but her hands, forearm, and elbow spoke eloquently of her beauty. He was certain that he would possess her "in a few days."

As he returned to Venice with the Countess, who was deep in thought, she remarked, "*Maria Eleonora Michiel is beautiful, but her mind is even more extraordinary.*"

"I have seen one, and I believe the other," he replied.

On reflection, "I saw that I was on the verge of becoming unfaithful to Caterina Capretta; but I did not feel restrained by any scruple."

What extraordinary secret lives these nuns led, he marveled; he could learn from their clandestine ways. They traveled, arranged assignations, and who knows what other secular activities, while paying lip service to the requirements of their convent. Paradoxically, it afforded women who'd taken the veil an advantage over their suitors and a refuge from the consequences of their behavior because they could disappear behind the convent's metal grating at will. Why women of wealthy families embraced a life of renunciation mystified him; but it wasn't their choice. Their families confined them to keep them from getting pregnant, diluting fortunes and bloodlines, and upsetting the established order. His go-between, the Countess, had a better idea of what went on behind the closed doors of a convent. Following oblique hints dropped by the Countess he became convinced that Maria Eleonora Michiel had a lover, "but resolved not to let it trouble me." And so he gave chase.

Here is Giacomo Casanova in pursuit of a cloistered woman who has gone to great lengths to invite him to call on her: he goes to Murano, anxiously sits in a waiting room, takes off his mask, dons his hat as he awaits an appearance by the "goddess." An hour passes, and then an entire day. He puts his mask back in place, and inquires whether she's been informed of his presence. Yes, she has been informed. He must wait. Like a schoolchild, he takes his seat again, "a little thoughtful, and a few minutes later I see a hideous lay sister, who says: "*Mother Maria Michiel is occupied the whole day.*"

"Such are the terrible moments to which a pursuer of women is exposed," he reminds his readers. "There is nothing more cruel. They degrade, they distress, they kill." The ordeal of waiting was humiliating, unnecessary. "She was mad, a wretched creature, shameless" in the way she callously wounded his *amour-propre*, "impudent . . . a raving maniac." He would feign indifference, never allow her to see the wounds she'd inflicted as he plotted preposterous revenge scenarios as he had when he was a boy. He'd convince her that her churlish behavior "only made me laugh." No more epistles, no attendance at mass on Murano; he wouldn't give her the satisfaction. "I wanted her to be certain that I scorned her." He wrote letters to her and, upon re-reading them, tore them to shreds; they made him look "weak"; they "would have made her laugh." He did his best to obliterate the memory of her face—that aspect of eternity.

After twelve days, he returned the letters she'd written to him, along with an irate reply. He supposed she was already "boasting" of her little game to her friends. One should retain a few illusions, he sniffed, but her behavior had shattered them. "Do not take it amiss if I give you this little lesson, after the only too substantial one that you apparently gave me only in mockery. Be certain that I will profit by it all the rest of my life." He sealed the letter, entrusted it to a Friulian messenger, and assumed the matter was closed until he encountered the same Friulian several days later, who said he'd delivered the letter to a "nun who was as beautiful as the morning star" and who'd questioned him about the sender. She'd written a reply and wanted an answer; it was that simple. The hapless messenger protested that he'd merely been trying to carry out his duty, in the course of which he "looked carefully at every masker of your height," and finally recognized Casanova by his buckles. Would he please reply to the nun's letter? It was worth money to the Friulian to bring a response back to Murano.

Casanova scrawled his reply: "I have received your letter. Farewell." He changed his buckles so as not to be recognized again. Then he set himself the task of reading Maria Eleonora Michiel's lengthy missive, which veered between apology, explanation, and accusation that his reply was "cruel, barbarous, unjust." She would die "unless you come to justify yourself immediately." She included the letters she'd written, the ones he'd tried to return in anger. He would be "the cause of my death" if he failed to return to Murano to see her; honor demanded it.

His artful reply addressed "the noblest of all women" whom he'd "most cruelly insulted." More in this maudlin vein followed. "I cannot live except in the hope of your forgiveness, and you will grant it to me when you reflect upon what made me commit my crime." How could she have inflicted such cruelty on him? "It was nothing short of a thunderbolt, *which did not kill me and did not leave me alive*," he said, invoking the climax of Molière's adaptation of Don Juan's scandalous career, when a bolt of lightning sends him to hell as divine retribution for a lifetime of misdeeds. "I felt duped, mocked," he wrote. With the illogic of love, he promised to be "at your feet an hour before noon." Before he appeared, would she please burn the letter he'd sent to her. "I will now lie down for three or four hours. My tears will flood my pillow."

By the time he finished writing, dawn was breaking.

Six hours later, he arrived at Santa Maria degli Angeli, and made his way to the waiting room. He fell to his knees when Maria Michiel materialized on the other side of the grating, and she told him with no little embarrassment to rise before they were seen. So they sat, and they looked at one another through the grating for "a quarter of an hour" before uttering a syllable. She extended her hand through the grating: "I bathed it with my tears and kissed it a hundred times. She said that our acquaintance having begun with such a fierce storm should make us hope for an eternal calm." Through innuendo-laden pleasantries, they negotiated to meet beyond the convent's walls, either in a casino or in Venice; she needed only two days' advance notice to make arrangements. Casanova couldn't resist boasting that he was in "easy circumstances" and "far from fearing to spend money I delight in it," especially because "all I have belongs to the object I adore." That was lovely to hear, she replied, because she, too, was "tolerably rich" and felt "I could refuse nothing to my lover" who was "completely her master." He recoiled at the mention of her lover.

"For six months I have lived in perfect celibacy," he confessed.

But he still loved Caterina, did he not?

He conceded that he couldn't think of her without love, "but I foresee that the seduction of your charms will make me forget her."

Maria Eleonora said that she understood: the poor child was torn from him, and he'd been "consumed with grief, shunning society" ever since. But if she—the woman on the other side of the grating—took her place, "no one, my dear friend, shall tear me from your heart," not even her own lover, who, she insisted, "will be delighted to see me in love and happy with a lover like you."

He sighed as he contemplated the magnanimity of this mysterious individual. "Heroism beyond my strength."

At the end of their long conversation, in which they came to know each other better, she briefly opened the grate with a press of the button so that he could kiss her, and as he left, "She followed me to the door with her amorous eyes."

————•————

Never had he been so much in love! "Joy and impatience absolutely prevented me from eating and sleeping for two whole days." To make his rapture more delicious still, "she was a vestal," that is, a nun pledged to chastity on pain of death. At the same time, she evoked memories of all the other "pretty women I had loved in the thirteen years I had been skirmishing on the fields of love" (a conservative estimate of his career in seduction), but never mind. He would make her his courtesan.

Adhering to the rules of clandestine love, Maria Eleonora gave him precise instructions for their next assignation; it would take place in the casino—in reality, a luxurious and private house of pleasure—where he would talk to no one, wear his mask, and follow directions. "You will go up the stairs opposite the street door and at the top of the stairs you will see by the light of a lantern, a green door, which will open to enter an apartment that you will find lighted. In the second room you will find me, and if I am not there, you will wait for me. I will not be more than a few minutes late. You may unmask, sit by the fire, and read. You will find books." On arrival, she would trade her nun's habit for "secular clothes" and "masking attire." Even the thought of her wearing a wig thrilled him, so long as he did not glimpse her without it.

Concerning her mysterious lover, she explained that he was not old, as Casanova had supposed, and he had been the first man to possess her. Two days before, she had read Casanova's letters to him, and now he was curious to meet their author, who, though Venetian, sounded so French in his love letters.

"That night, at the appointed hour," Casanova noted, he found his way to the casino, followed her instructions, and was rewarded with the sight of her "dressed in secular clothes of the utmost elegance," lit by flickering candles set in girandoles backed by mirrors. Wasting no time, he fell on his knees, and commenced what he called "classical amorous combat," only to be met by the expected resistance from her. They grappled, they argued, they cooed. "In this struggle, as sweet as it was painful to us both, we spent two hours. At the end of the combat, we congratulated ourselves on having carried off the victory," which, he implied, meant passionate investigation rather than actual lovemaking; in any event, he reveled in the sensual contest of wills.

About eleven that night, they feasted on eight dishes set on porcelain plates atop boxes of heated water to keep the food "always hot." They imbibed burgundy and champagne the color of a partridge's eye, that is, pink, and Giacomo began to suspect that his beloved's patron and protector must be French. She arranged the meal with so much savoir faire that, he calculated, "she had a lover who had taught her." Who was he?

He would have to wait to satisfy his curiosity, she told him, even as their conversation turned to France and to Madame de Pompadour, Louis XV's influential mistress. In passing, she mentioned the Abbé de Bernis, François-Joachim de Pierre de Bernis, the ambassador to Venice and a member of the Académie Française, the forty "immortels" charged with maintaining the integrity of the French language.

As Casanova suspected, the abbé was acquainted with the casino and with Maria Eleonora Michiel. He was polished, ingratiating, talented. Voltaire called him "the flower girl of Parnassus" out of envy mixed with grudging admiration, and perhaps the abbé was Maria Eleonora's sponsor.

By midnight, they succumbed to fatigue. Casanova suggested they spend the night together, fully clothed. As they prepared for bed, he discovered that Maria Eleonora's wig was, in fact, "the most beautiful head of hair." Inspired, he fell "more on her than beside her" as they resumed their combat, and she began to yield. As he undid the six ribbons fastening her dress, "I find myself the fortunate master of the most beautiful of bosoms." Even better, "she is obliged, after I have contemplated it, to let me devour it." She stopped his hands from roaming and allowed him no other liberties even as she slowly moved her mouth from his lips to his chest after he'd spent hours constantly swallowing "her saliva mixed with mine." He drifted off to sleep in her arms, and she in his, until the pealing of bells woke them, and she dressed in her confining corset and habit, and ran back to the convent.

Before leaving, she kissed him on his neck and said she would make him "completely happy" at their next meeting. "Full of unsatisfied desires, I put out the candles and slept deeply until noon."

Within hours, he was in possession of a letter delivered by the reliable Laura from his "wife," Caterina, in which she protested that "I am not jealous of what can divert your mind and help you bear our separation patiently." She claimed she saw him—through a conveniently placed chink in the convent wall—deep in conversation with "my dear friend" Mother Maria Eleonora Michiel. All she asked was for him to tell her *everything*, "the whole story of this remarkable occurrence." If it hadn't been for her, Caterina wrote, the miscarriage would have been discovered.

The letter made Casanova uneasy. Who else might have seen him with Maria Eleonora? He replied that she was mistaken; enchanting as her friend might be, there was no love between them.

On November 25, as he made his way by gondola to mass on Murano, he noticed that he was being followed. He disembarked, the man on his trail followed suit, and his suspicions grew. Casanova forced his antagonist into a corner, "putting the point of a knife to his throat," but at that moment, a passerby swung into view, and the pursuer escaped. From then on, Casanova decided to go to Murano only by night, carefully masked. When he mentioned the spy to Maria Eleonora at their next meeting, she talked of other things, much to his dismay, and delayed the consummation of their happiness yet again. More alarming still, her mysterious lover would visit the following day to take her to Venice: a most troubling development.

Under the circumstances, he resolved to give her a master class in seduction. He chose "the most elegant and hence the most expensive" casino, which he rented in San Moisè until Easter for a hundred zecchini, payable in advance. It featured five rooms and revolving dumbwaiters so that masters and servants never saw one another; mirrors; chandeliers; a white marble fireplace; and walls decorated with small squares depicting "amorous couples in a state of nature, whose voluptuous attitudes fired the imagination." He furnished it with the finest linens, slippers, and a delicate lace nightcap. There would be Burgundy, champagne . . . every kind of refinement . . . and, he told the servant, don't forget the sheets! He chastised the hapless cook for having forgotten the hard-boiled eggs, the anchovies, and salad dressing, at which the poor man "rolled up his eyes with a contrite look, accusing himself of having committed a great crime."

At the appointed hour, he went to greet his beloved Maria Eleonora. "The night was cold but magnificent, and without the least wind." A gondola with two rowers appeared, and a masked figure disembarked, but it seemed to be a man, and Casanova disappeared into the shadows, regretting that he didn't have his pistols on his person. The masked figure approached, extended a hand, and at that moment, "I recognize my angel, dressed as a man." They hurried across the Piazza San Marco to the casino, where they unmasked, and Maria Eleonora savored the details of all that he had prepared for the occasion, while he studied her with fascination and admiration. Mirrors lit by candles multiplied her portrait, scattering her image. He studied her attire: "a coat of short-napped rose velvet edged with an embroidery of gold spangles, a matching hand-embroidered waistcoat, than which nothing could be richer, black satin breeches, needle-lace ruffles, buckles set with brilliants," and other jewelry. She wore a *bauta* decorated with "black blond-lace." He searched her pockets and found a snuffbox, a phial, a toothpick case, opera glasses, scented handkerchiefs, and a pair of English flintlock pistols.

Overwhelmed with her charms, he melodramatically draped himself on a sofa, complaining that the mere sight of her sapped his confidence. "In a quarter of an hour I may no longer exist," he said.

"Are you mad?" she demanded. "Let us go to bed."

But first, more talk, followed by the supper, and hints from her about her protector, who took care of all her needs, yet left her heart feeling empty. "I think he is richer than you are," she speculated, "though this casino might make one conclude the opposite." By then, they were enjoying the ices and punch and oysters. He indulged in his favorite new game, passing a raw oyster directly from the mouth of one lover to another, savoring the warm, rubbery, slightly tangy texture, lubricated with saliva from different sources. Then he playfully dropped the oysters into the bodice of his beloved, and made an elaborate game of searching for it with his eager fingers and lips.

Finally, he coaxed Maria Eleonora to the bedroom. "I flung myself into her burning arms, on fire with love and giving her the most lively proofs of it for seven continuous hours that were interrupted only by as many quarters of an hour that were devoted to the most feeling talk." Seven hours! He elicited quantities of her "sighs, ecstasies, transports, and unfeigned sentiments" as he "taught her that the slightest constraint spoils the greatest of pleasures." When dawn approached, they hastily dressed, took coffee, and he escorted her to a gondola bound for the island of Murano.

Deeply satisfied, he went home to Venice, "where ten hours of sleep restored me to my normal state."

At large once again, he noticed a "poorly masked" spy tailing him, disembarking from a gondola that Casanova strongly suspected was in the service of the French Ambassador. "He was not in livery, and the gondola was plain, like all gondolas belonging to Venetians," he noted. The observation made him gleeful rather than concerned, "pleased that the Ambassador was my senior partner" in his lovemaking with Maria Eleonora. What excellent company he, the arriviste, the progeny of actors, had joined! From then on, the French Ambassador, François-Joachim de Pierre de Bernis, round-faced, jovial, connected at the highest levels of the French court, became a partner in their trysts. He was only now, approaching forty years of age,

François-Joachim de Pierre de Bernis,
French cardinal, statesman, and libertine

taking holy orders, and would later become a cardinal, but at the moment he gave no indication of being in any hurry to curtail his libertine ways.

No match for Casanova's intensity and expressiveness, he appeared content to stage-manage Maria Eleonora's affair from a distance, and to savor it vicariously. "One thing greatly troubles him," she confided, "he wants me to beg you not to expose me to the danger of a big belly." Aware of Caterina's miscarriage, she had no desire to suffer the same destiny. Casanova proceeded with caution, his trysting schedule interrupted by observances for the approaching Christmas season.

Awaiting his beloved's arrival at the next meeting, he came across a "small library in the boudoir" containing volumes devoted to "all that the wisest philosophers have written against religion and all that the most voluptuous pens have written on the subject which is the sole aim of love." These "seductive books, whose incendiary style drives the reader to seek the reality, which alone can quench the fire he feels running through his veins," excited his libido, as did "folios containing only lascivious engravings." Maria Eleonora appeared, dressed in her nun's habit, startling him. She arrived in time, he told her in mid-embrace, "to prevent a schoolboy masturbation."

She exchanged her habit for a plain muslin robe that he considered "the height of elegance." They had supper, they went to bed, and they made plans for the future. In this way they spent ten days together in the casino, their romance an open secret. "I had her four times and thereby convinced her that I lived only for her." And what of his neglected "wife" Caterina, who dwelled in the same monastery, and who'd recently survived a miscarriage? Casanova explained that his wild love for her "had grown calm." In Maria Eleonora's case, he could "never have her except with the greatest fear of losing her," which increased his ardor for her.

He paused to wonder about the role her silent partner, the Ambassador, played and decided that "her lover's tact and money had done it all, including muzzling the cook and the gondolier. Nevertheless, Casanova couldn't rid himself of the suspicion that the gondolier, or someone like him, "must certainly be a spy for the State Inquisitors," in which case he'd attracted their scrutiny, for the Inquisitors were everywhere, on the lookout for traitors, blasphemers, and other enemies of the Republic to arrest. The idea elevated the importance of his romance with Maria Eleonora. Better notorious than invisible.

It was late December 1753. He'd just arrived at the Palazzo Bragadin after his extended stay in the casino. He opened a letter from Maria Eleonora and read that during his soirees with her, de Bernis, her protector, had been present, "ensconced in a perfect hiding place from which he would not only see all that we did without himself being seen but also hear all we said." De Bernis had managed this feat by concealing himself in a "closet whose existence cannot be guessed." She promised to show it to Casanova, quickly adding that he should not take it amiss. "You pleased him, not only by everything you did but also by all the amusing things you said to me." Of course, the arrangement made her anxious, she was terrified about what Casanova would say about de Bernis, "but fortunately all you said could only be flattering to him. This is the complete confession of my treachery, which, as a sensible lover, you must forgive me." There was more . . .

. . . when she reunited with Casanova, on the last day of the year, "my friend will be at the casino." He would not make himself known. Instead, "you will not see him, and he will see everything." She cautioned to be careful in his choice of words; he could talk of literature, of travel, politics, every subject under the sun except faith. "The question remains whether you are willing to let a man see you during the moments when you surrender to the furies of love."

"Her letter surprised me greatly," Casanova admitted. On further thought, the idea appealed to his intellect. "I can never understand how a man can be ashamed of letting a friend see him at a moment when he is giving the greatest proofs of love to a very beautiful woman," he wrote. It mattered little if de Bernis happened to be a "strange man dominated by this strange taste." He now considered de Bernis (whom he'd never met) his friend, "and I love him." If she had no sense of shame about being observed, neither did he. Her friend was welcome to "share our pleasures" from the vantage point of his hiding place, if that's what suited his predilections. And if the sight of the two of them in ecstatic communion drove him into a frenzy, and forced him into the open, and onto his knees, "begging me to give you up to the violence of his amorous desires"—if that happened, "I will laugh and give you up to him."

He sent his letter, and spent the holiday week with his friends gambling at the Ridotto, losing four thousand, even five thousand zecchini, his "entire wealth" at the time, thinking only of Maria Eleonora with more longing than ever.

On a frigid day at the beginning of 1754, he returned to his trysting place at the casino, where his love waited, "dressed as a woman of fashion" in a sky-blue quilted dress. "Her shy and modestly smiling face seemed to be saying: 'This is the person you love.'" He was surprised to see that she wore rouge in the manner of the ladies of Versailles, "in a seemingly careless manner." This detail excited his interest, as if it were an aphrodisiac: "The rouge is not meant to look natural, it is put on to please the eyes, which see in it the tokens of an intoxication which promises them amorous transports and furies." She'd applied it not to please him, but her unseen lover. "He deserves to be cuckolded," Casanova remarked, "and we shall work at it all night. I have lived in celibacy for the past week, but I need to eat, for I have nothing in my stomach but a cup of chocolate and the white of six fresh eggs which I ate in a salad."

He lifted her off the ground, grasped her by the thighs, swung her around, sat on the carpet, and pulled her on top of him, "whereupon she had the kindness to finish the job with her beautiful hand, collecting the white of the first egg in the palm of it," his ejaculate.

"Five to go," she said, as she cleaned her hand with a "potpourri of aromatic herbs," and offered it to him to kiss.

When they sat down to supper, "She ate for two, but I ate for four." Later they devoured oysters Casanova-style, "exchanging them when we already had them in our mouths. She offered me hers on her tongue at the same time that I put mine between her lips; there is no more lascivious and voluptuous game between two lovers, it is even comic, but comedy does no harm." He reveled in exchanging sweet, viscous fluids. "What a sauce dressing an oyster that I suck from the mouth of the woman I love!" he exclaimed. "It is her saliva. The power of love cannot but increase when I crush it, when I swallow it."

As she readied herself for bed, Casanova opened a box resting nearby; it held condoms fashioned from linen or the intestine of an animal. Their presence was one more proof of Maria Eleonora's lavish spending. He pilfered the condoms, replacing them with a few stanzas of bawdy verse, and then lifted his head to see his love resplendent in a "dressing gown of India muslin embroidered with flowers in gold thread." He flung himself at her feet, pleading for release then and there, but "she ordered me to hold my fire until we were in bed." (This could only have made for great theater for her concealed person of importance to behold.)

"I do not want to be bothered with keeping your quintessence from falling on the carpet." To prevent the unwelcome occurrence, she opened the box, finding Casanova's doggerel instead of her precious condoms. Inspired by his little jest, she contributed a few lines of her own: "When an angel fucks me, I am at once sure that my only husband is the author of nature. But to make his lineage free from suspicion Love must instantly give me back my condoms." Once he complied, and presumably wore one, "I encourage my friend to fuck me without fear." Casanova returned the condoms while "giving a very natural imitation of surprise."

By now it was midnight, and they collapsed onto the sofa. "After imperiously putting my sultana in the state of nature and doing the same to myself, I laid her down and subjugated her in the classic manner, delighting in her swoons." He slid a pillow under her buttocks and moved her knees apart to "afford a most voluptuous vision to our hidden friend." Their "frolic" lasted an hour, after which she removed the condom and admired the glis-

A condom demonstration

"Straight Tree," among Casanova's favorite
works of erotic art, by Pietro Aretino

tening "quintessence" filling it, while realizing that she herself was "wet with
her own distillations."

They performed their ablutions, and then took their places "side by side
in front of a large upright mirror, each putting an arm around the other's
back." Admiring themselves as much as their invisible guest probably did,
they "engaged in every kind of combat, still standing," until Maria Eleonora
sank to the Persian carpet. "She would have looked like a corpse if the beating of her heart had not been visible," Casanova remarked, injecting a note of
ruthlessness into the proceedings. Even though she was exhausted, he "made
her do the 'straight tree,'" a gymnastic feat depicted in Pietro Aretino's scandalous and popular sixteenth-century series of illustrations, *I Modi*, "The
Ways." In his "Straight Tree," a startlingly erect nude male attempts intercourse with an upside-down nude female clasping a small wheel. "In that position I lifted her up to devour her chamber of love, which I could not reach
otherwise since I wanted to make it possible for her, in turn, to devour the
weapon that wounded her to death"—climax—"without taking her life."

Although they were so depleted he begged her for a "truce" in their combat, she demanded revenge. She insisted that they reverse roles and perform the "Straight Tree" again. She grasped him "by the hips" and lifted him up. Given his height, his legs and feet must have towered above her. As she prepared to devour him, she was horrified to see her breasts "splattered with my soul distilled in drops of blood." Unnerved, she let him tumble to the ground and collapsed on top of him. When they untangled themselves, he laughed off the drops of blood as "the yolk of the last egg, which is often red."

As he washed her breasts clean, he calmed her fear that swallowing his ejaculate could be harmful, and she slowly donned her habit and made him promise to write as soon as he returned to Venice. He departed before her, guessing that she spent the remaining time with her concealed friend in a celebration of libertinism.

On waking in Venice, Casanova returned to the artist who'd produced the miniature portrait for Caterina, this time to commission a larger image to conceal behind a medallion depicting a sacred picture for Maria Eleonora to wear around her neck. If matters went on like this, all the nuns of Santa Maria degli Angeli would have concealed images of a certain daring young Venetian! No sooner had he arranged for the portrait to be made than he opened a letter from his "wife" Caterina in which she revealed that she and Maria Eleonora had become lovers, to his delight. She'd stopped telling her confessor anything about herself, in contrast to the gossip that filled the convent and spilled over to the outer world.

From Maria Eleonora, Casanova heard that their impassioned performance at the casino had received enthusiastic reviews from their audience of one. "He is mad about you," she wrote, "and determined that you shall make his acquaintance." He would eat salads with egg whites to emulate Casanova. His only reservation was that Maria Eleonora made efforts "beyond the delicacy of my sex." (That "Straight Tree"!) To give her love concrete expression, she sent him a double portrait disguised as a snuffbox. On the outside, she was depicted a nun, standing; on the inside, she was naked on a black silk bed.

Now he faced juggling his affections for two nuns who were in love with him and intimate with one another. The situation was growing more complicated all the time, yet he thrived on the complications without hope of resolution. Casanova assured Caterina "that the fancy I had taken for her dear friend in no way detracted from the constancy of my passion for her."

———•———

Carnival approached. He would attend a ball given at the convent, "masked in such a way that my dear friends could not recognize me." As he explained to readers who might be incredulous at the thought of such an event, "During the Carnival in Venice nuns are allowed to have this innocent pleasure." The nuns observed "the festivities from behind their wide gratings," as if they were prisoners, and at the end of the occasion they left "well satisfied to have been present at one of the pleasures of the laity."

He dressed as Pierrot, the *commedia dell'arte* character, powdering his face with flour and wearing a floppy white outfit. The stylized ethereal Pierrot seems to be a clown, but perpetually mourning his lost love, the coquettish Columbina, who, according to convention, has betrayed him for the rakish Harlequin. "There is no costume better fitted to disguise a person, provided he is neither hunchback nor lame," he observed. The day was cold, he shivered in his flimsy costume. "One cannot be more lightly clad," he sighed, nor was he wearing a cloak as he rode by gondola to Murano, his only accessories consisting of a handkerchief, the keys to his casino, and his purse.

He entered the visiting room and took his place amid the festivities. "I see Punches, Scaramouches, Pantaloons, Harlequins, and behind the grating, following intently with their eyes, sat the nuns, some standing, others seated, both Caterina and Maria Eleonora among them." Casanova meandered through the crowd, pretending to be inebriated, as Pierrot would be, attracting curious stares. "I stop in front of a pretty girl disguised as a female Harlequin and rudely take her hand to make her dance a minuet with me." Everyone laughed as Casanova made a show of falling with every other step, and when they finished, he exhausted himself by dancing one strenuous *furlana* after another; following that display, he feigned rest and sleep, until a reveler dressed as Harlequin smacked him with a lath, a thin strip of wood associated with the character. When the Harlequin's mate followed suit, he lifted her over his shoulder, "hitting her on her behind" while he ran, terrifying her that if he stumbled, her underwear or thighs would be exposed to the excited crowd. The stunt continued until another *commedia dell'arte* character, Punch, tripped Casanova, who fell on his face. His temper flaring, he challenged his tormentor to a wrestling match, and "I made him bite the dust and I handled him so roughly that his coat came unbuttoned, whereupon he lost his hump and false belly." As applause erupted, he breathlessly escaped.

He hailed a gondola, and shut himself inside its small cabin to take refuge from the chill and to dry the sweat coating his hair. He gambled the night away at the Ridotto, then rode another gondola to Murano and its casino, where he strode into the bedroom, expecting to see Maria Eleonora, but the woman who turned to face him was young Caterina, his "wife, in her nun's habit." He felt as if he'd been struck by lightning. How could Maria Eleonora have betrayed him by sending Caterina, her rival and secret lover? "I alternately saw that I was tricked, deceived, trapped, scorned." And, he didn't have to add, found out.

The silent confrontation lasted half an hour. "I had to resolve on a course, for I could not think of spending the whole night there masked as I was and saying nothing." And, perverse thought, what if Maria Eleonora now hid herself in the concealed closet, observing the scene? On this assumption, he removed his white Pierrot mask to be welcomed into Caterina's arms. In a torrent of words, she explained that she had only just become intimate with Maria Eleonora, and the two of them had gone to the dance, where they happily watched Pierrot caper without realizing who it was: the lover they shared. "You are fortunate," she concluded, "and I wish you happiness. Mother Maria Eleonora is the only woman, after me, who is worthy of your affection, the only woman with whom I can be content to share it." She commanded: "Kiss me."

What choice did he have? "I should have been an ingrate and a barbarian if I had not then clasped to my breast with unfeigned signs of the most sincere affection the angel of goodness and beauty," although he considered that their mutual friend had played a "vile trick" on him. Later that night, the caretaker brought supper—egg white salad, he noted with a laugh. His hunger calmed, he reflected, "I have always held that there is no merit in being faithful to a person one truly loves." However noble or practical the sentiment sounded at first blush, it was entirely situational and self-serving. What else could a man caught between two nuns—of all things!—say in self-defense? Fortunately, the women, perhaps because of their intimate connection to one another, allowed his explanation to stand.

The midnight hour struck, and Casanova, having given up hope of seeing Maria Eleonora on this occasion, embraced Caterina. He still loved her, but he was at a loss as to how to describe his feelings for her. "I resumed my disguise to cover my head and shelter myself from a very strong whistling wind, and I hurried down the stairs after giving Caterina the key to the casino and telling her to return it to Maria Eleonora." But when he returned to the *traghetto*, or gondola stand, no watercraft stood ready to take him to the mainland. "According to Venetian police regulations, this can never happen, for at all hours each *traghetto* is required to have at least two gondolas ready for public service." He was still dressed in his flimsy Pierrot costume, exposed to a sharp wind from the west. His pockets were filled with gold he'd won at the Ridotto, posing another hazard. "I had reason to fear the robbers of Murano, very dangerous and determined cutthroats." If he encountered one, he had no weapon with which to defend himself. "I was to be pitied, and I was shaking with cold."

He subtracted a portion of the small fortune he carried with him to enlist the services of a local man to find him a gondola to take him to Venice before daybreak. Yet once aboard, he faced the danger of drowning in the lagoon off the island of San Michele, midway to Venice itself. He considered himself a "good swimmer," but doubted he could resist the powerful current. He directed the oarsmen to seek shelter on San Michele, but they refused. How typical of the obstinate gondoliers! As the wind increased, "the foaming waves were coming in over the side of the gondola, and my men, despite their strength, could not drive it forward." All at once, a "furious gust of wind" knocked the oarsman on the deck into the waves, "but he caught hold of the gondola and had no difficulty getting aboard." In that chaotic interval, he'd lost his oar and the gondola had been carried far off course. "The situation was desperate."

He barked more orders and flung a handful of coins at the gondoliers. They "instantly obeyed" this incentive and soon they were traversing a canal in northern Venice, the Rio dei Mendicanti. Casanova directed the gondoliers to the Palazzo Bragadin, where a bed and security awaited him. Trying to warm himself under blankets, he felt so wretched that sleep proved impossible.

Later that day, he received a visit from his protector, Signor Bragadin. Casanova was still suffering, "but that did not keep Signor Bragadin from laughing when he saw my Pierrot costume"—damp, soiled, and torn—"on the couch." The older man left Casanova to sweat out his fever with its delirium and chills. When the illness abated, he vowed to consume only healthy foods.

Chapter 8

Tonina

As his mind cleared he set about reading long, anguished letters from both Caterina and Maria Eleonora in which they tried to reconcile their reckless behavior with their love for one another, for him, and with their religious vocation. It was an impossible task, of course. Even while he assured the two of them of his love, as well as his own sense of inadequacy as a "weak and imperfect creature who cannot imitate you both," he confessed that he harbored a "curiosity that I dare not confide to paper; but you will satisfy it, I am sure, the first time we see each other." He was confident that they knew precisely the transgression he had in mind.

On February 4, 1754, he reunited with Maria Eleonora. She was attired in her habit, "our mutual love declaring us equally guilty" as they knelt before one another, eager to repent of any misunderstandings or hurt feelings they may have caused one another. Lost in kisses, they stumbled to a sofa, "where we remained inseparable until the time came for a long sigh that we could not have restrained even if we had been sure that it heralded our death." His cloak and rigid *bauta*, remained in place, props increasing the rapture of the reunion.

When they'd recovered, Maria Eleonora led him to the secret little room that had concealed their witness on previous occasions. It was a closet "where I saw everything necessary for a person to spend a few hours in it": a sofa bed, chair, desk, candles, and candlesticks. A mobile board next to the bed slid back to reveal "twenty holes" opening onto the room where Casanova and his beloved had become one. As they studied the setting for their orgies with the utmost seriousness, Maria Eleonora veered between jealousy and devotion, selflessness and selfishness. "If you marry her," she said, meaning Caterina, "you will have a divine wife. When I lose her, I shall be miserable; but your happiness will make it up to me." It was a mystery to her how he loved them both, just as it was a mystery how Caterina did not hate Maria Eleonora for luring his affections. As for her own intimacy with Caterina, Maria Eleonora dismissed it as nothing more than "sterile pleasures."

In truth-telling mode, she revealed the name of their unseen observer. He was the Abbé de Bernis, the French ambassador. As such, de Bernis could not be seen even briefly, even informally, with Casanova or any Venetian patrician. That would be a "grave crime" in the eyes of the Venetian Inquisition. For that very reason, even the most tenuous associations of Giacomo Casanova, residing at the Palazzo Bragadin with three patricians, placed him in a precarious position.

Maria Eleonora had assumed Casanova belonged to the aristocracy, an impression he did little to discourage, for it was a congenial role to play and went well with his gambling and apparent life of ease. Now that she had a better idea of his background, she wanted to introduce the two men by "name and title." Of course, the meeting would have an elaborate protocol: "Remember that he is aware that you must know he is my lover, but you must not show that you are aware that he knows of our mutual affection." The little deception appealed to Casanova's love of intrigue, but he remained keenly aware of the dangers inherent in the meeting. "If I were a patrician, the State Inquisitors would have come prying in good earnest," he said, "and the terrible consequences of that make me tremble."

In fact, the State Inquisitors were already circling. They were distinct from the ruling Council of Ten, an internal prosecutorial body established on September 20, 1539. The State Inquisitors functioned as the Supreme Court in political matters and matters concerning public security, especially surveillance. Their dreaded sentences could be issued only when consensus was reached in secret. Here and there Casanova had caught glimpses of figures he thought might be spies for the State Inquisitors; in Venice, where spying was common, that was a credible assumption. And what was de Bernis if not a spy of love?

For the moment, Casanova put aside these worries and wondered only when the supper would occur. The date was set for February 8. For the next two hours, he recorded, he and Maria Eleonora made love. The couple fell asleep, and their mouths were still "clinging together" when they awoke six hours later to make love once more before racing to dress for the new day.

As arranged, Maria Eleonora brought together Casanova, bowing deeply, and the ambassador, who, upon removing his mask, recalled that the two had met before, in Paris. At first, Casanova believed they were strangers, but then he recalled they had met briefly at a dinner. "From this moment," said de Bernis, "we can never forget each other. The mysteries that unite us are of a nature to make us intimate friends." The ensuing feast at the casino, with its splendid wine, oysters, and witticisms, went off with Gallic flair. Seriousness played no part. And when the conversation turned to the women, Maria Eleonora and Caterina, Casanova had the presence of mind to appear oblivious to the fact that de Bernis had been observing the combat from his little closet.

Casanova gathered that de Bernis planned to incorporate Caterina into their sport, but it was too late to back out. "Self-esteem, which is stronger than jealousy, will not allow a man who aspires to be accounted intelligent to show that he is jealous." Still, the thought of the wealthy, highborn de Bernis seducing little Caterina pained Casanova, his many betrayals of her notwithstanding. Such were his reflections on "weakness, jealousy, and shame." Caterina appeared and Maria Eleonora gave rein to their passion. Within minutes, he wrote, "the two fond friends begin giving each other caresses, which make me laugh, and which gradually arouse my interest. I am of a mind to excite and enjoy a spectacle with which I had long been familiar."

At that instant, Maria Eleonora produced a volume of provocative engravings by an artist known as Meursius, the nom de plume of Nicolas Chorier, a French lawyer depicting, in Casanova's words, "a fine series of amorous encounters between women." The book, *L'Académie des dames*, or *The School of Women*, told the story of a twenty-six-year-old married woman taking her young female cousin into her bed to initiate her into sexual gratification before the girl submitted to the rigors of married life.

Turning the pages, Casanova noticed Maria Eleonora casting a "malicious glance at my face," as she "asks me if I would like her to order a fire lighted in the room with the alcove." De Bernis watched from the shadows.

Caterina and Maria Eleonora made punch as they nonchalantly undressed one another, revealing their breasts. "Instantly intoxicated with the desire to compare and to judge everything," Casanova selected an illustration from the book "and in less than five minutes we are all in a state of nature and prey to pleasure and love. They set to work with the fury of two tigresses ready to devour one another. The sight of my two beauties in combat making me ardent, I am at a loss how to begin." Should he favor Caterina at first, or Maria Eleonora? Caterina was thinner, yet he judged her thighs and hips to be more commodious. "Her ornaments were brown, the other's blonde, and they were both equally skilled in combat, which was tiring them without the possibility of our reaching a conclusion."

He couldn't resist their charms a moment longer. "I fling myself on them, and, pretending to separate them, I put Maria Eleonora under me, but she escapes, throwing me onto Caterina, who receives me with open arms and makes me give up my soul in less than a minute, accompanying my death by her own, with neither of us ever thinking of taking any precautions." When they recovered, they attacked Maria Eleonora, whom he "held in subjection for a good hour." At the end of this bout, the group slept for two hours. At dawn, the three of them, "transported by continual furies, played havoc with everything visible and palpable which Nature had bestowed on us" until they found they'd "all become of the same sex in all the trios that we performed." When they finally parted, the lovers felt satisfied and even a bit humiliated, "but not surfeited." Giacomo Casanova, dilettante and dandy, had at last found his vocation: he would be the philosopher pimp, the emperor of Eros, the impresario of ecstasy.

In the morning he felt remorseful about having manipulated the two women, although they had manipulated him, as well. "I was certain that the Ambassador's absence had been arranged between them," he concluded, but would that now mean that de Bernis was entitled to the same privilege? If so, Casanova had no choice but to acquiesce in their plans. Another thought sent a frisson of horror down his spine. What if he'd gotten one of them pregnant? Or both? The consequences would be intolerable for all. For once, he felt overwhelmed by the circumstances he'd done so much to bring about. Rather than face the women, and de Bernis, he offered the flimsy excuse that he had to attend to his patron, Signor Bragadin, and in a foul mood gambled at the Ridotto, "where I lost my money three or four times over."

In the following weeks, the volatile arrangement among the libertines unraveled. At dinner one evening with de Bernis and Maria Eleonora,

Casanova worried aloud about the discretion of the gondoliers ferrying them from Venice to Murano, but more than that, he expressed the belief that their relationship was being tracked by the Inquisition, who could be counted on to employ it in a hostile fashion, and in danger of being betrayed by a nun who realized that Maria Eleonora and Caterina came and went from the convent with disreputable intent. The thought that they might soon be exposed was enough to send Maria Eleonora to bed and to prompt de Bernis to make elaborate excuses that he was now "going to work" on an elaborate diplomatic project "which will set all Europe talking." He advised Casanova to "speak out against anything that could expose you to calamities" that might turn out to be "fatal." He talked of scandalous relationships between nuns and laity that ended in tragedy. At least in his case neither of the women was pregnant, but de Bernis chastised Casanova: "You risked a terrible misfortune! She believed that it was easy to bring on an abortion by taking certain drugs, but I disabused her." After the scolding, de Bernis escorted Casanova back to Venice, where he "spent a most uneasy night." He lost all interest in his "wife" Caterina, his heart adrift on a sea of doubt.

De Bernis failed to realize that reason might make room for romance, but romance, more tyrannical, would never make room for reason. To demonstrate to Maria Eleonora that he retained deep feelings for her, Casanova arranged for a reunion in late May, the Friday after Ascension Day.

Fearing betrayal by gondoliers in the pay of the Inquisition, he employed his own boat and even dressed in the attire of a gondolier. "Stationed at the poop," he conveyed the little craft to the convent's quay, took on Maria Eleonora "concealed in the hood of her cloak," and wafted them to the casino, where he made certain to fasten the boat to a mooring with a chain and padlock "to secure it from thieves, who amuse themselves at night stealing as many boats as they can when they find them fastened only with rope."

Although he was "dripping with sweat," he recalled, "that did not prevent my angel from falling on my neck." They devoted two hours in the casino to making love; only then did they fortify themselves with supper. He was surprised to find that Maria Eleonora seemed more impassioned than ever. He intended to return her by stealth to the convent at three in the morning, but as they finished their repast, a violent storm and heavy rain blew in. "I said nothing," he wrote, "but it terrified me." He decided they had to leave immediately if she were to reach the convent in time. Once aboard the gondola, he guided them past an exposed point, where on a calm night one needed only ten minutes to reach the quay, but in the storm, the current pushed him backward, and he exhausted himself battling against it. To pause for even a minute would be to risk disaster. He spied a boat approaching, shouted for help, accompanied by offers of zecchini.

The rescue took place efficiently, and within minutes Casanova was able to guide his vessel safely to the quay.

Casanova and Maria Eleonora held more clandestine meetings during the next three months, but de Bernis, always aware of their activities, warned that he "could foresee nothing but misfortunes if we did not resolve to make an end."

As if to hasten his doom, Casanova befriended yet another foreigner, John Murray, an English diplomat "full of wit, learned, and a prodigious lover of the fair sex, Bacchus, good eating" and, to add his credentials—he was "keeping the celebrated Ancilla," the notorious courtesan who'd bewitched Casanova in Padua, Lyon, and Venice. Despite his proximity to Ancilla, he held back. She exhibited troubling symptoms; she was hoarse and complained of a "pain in her throat." In fact, she was in the late stages of syphilis, not that her malady cooled her lust in the slightest. Casanova wrote, "A quarter of an hour before she expired, her lover Murray, in my presence, yielded to her insistence and paid her the homage of a devoted lover." The sight of the two of them ravishing one another as Ancilla was dying impressed itself deeply on Casanova's memory; he called it "one of the most striking spectacles I have seen in all my life." As the lovers wrestled, he noticed that "her nose and half of her beautiful face" were diseased. The disfigurement was likely caused by ulcerations spreading from her esophagus to her pharynx and larynx until they attacked the mucous membranes of the mouth and nose, leaving her unable to speak or to eat. The juxtaposition of her great beauty and great suffering left him stupefied.

As the year progressed, his love for Maria Eleonora faded. De Bernis withdrew from Venice when Madame de Pompadour summoned him to France, much to the sorrow of Maria Eleonora, to whom he had been benefactor, lover, and inspiration. At the same time, in 1754, the Seven Years'

War broke out. Before its conclusion nine years later, it would involve most of the countries in Europe, as well as their colonies, and claim at least a million lives, perhaps many more.

La Serenissima, buffered by its navy, State Inquisitors, and cult of secrecy, went its own way. With de Bernis attending to the war and its demands, Casanova lost his casino, and Maria Eleonora became ill. Casanova wrote of seeing her at the convent grating on February 2, 1755, and perceiving that "her life was in danger. Her face displayed the signs of approaching death." In preparation, she transferred her diamonds, "scandalous books," money, and letters to him with orders to return them all to her if she recovered or to keep them if she died. He remained nearby on Murano to tend to her during her illness, returning briefly and with great sadness to Venice to conceal everything she'd given him in the Palazzo Bragadin. He then went to his furnished rooms on the island of Murano for the vigil over Maria Eleonora. His go-between, Laura, had thoughtfully included the services of her fifteen-year-old daughter, Tonina, who stayed overnight in the foyer.

Casanova being Casanova, it was not long before he struck up a flirtation with young Tonina, who was eager for his affection. Even though he gave her six lire a day for her trouble, he was careful to keep some distance between them, "for I should but too easily have yielded to my natural inclination for amusement, which would have dishonored my grief."

Descending the vortex of his sorrow, he wrote to Caterina, claiming that if Maria Eleonora died he'd follow her to the grave . . . but wait . . .

On second thought, if she died, he wished to run away with Caterina. The two of them would live off her wealth and his winnings at the Ridotto. He had about four thousand zecchini to his name, a good start.

When Caterina read the letter aloud to Maria Eleonora, still gravely ill, it seemed to induce "spasmodic twitchings," a high fever, and hours of raving in French, as luck would have it, so the other nuns could not understand it. If they had, they would have been scandalized. "The ominous effect of my letter made me desperate," Casanova intoned.

———•———

Carnival arrived and departed, and by the end of March the patient was out of danger and hoped to leave her sick room after Easter. Casanova vowed to remain ensconced in his Murano apartment until the day he saw her face at the grating. By his count, he passed forty-eight days "without ever leaving my room," barely eating or sleeping, with Tonina seated in an armchair by his bed, ministering to him "as if she had been my mother."

During the ordeal, he'd never given the girl a single kiss and never let her see him undress, and he had reason to feel proud of his mortification. He was annoyed only by the thought that no one, least of all Caterina, Maria Eleonora, or Tonina's mother, Laura, would have believed it was true. The crisis of Maria Eleonora's illness served to reveal the deep ties binding them, despite the corrosive effects of time, distance, and his other love affairs. As Maria Eleonora's health returned, his preoccupation with her diminished once again.

Casanova roused himself to leave his apartment on Murano for a brief trip to Venice. He returned soaking wet from a storm, at which point the flirtation with little Tonina became irresistible. As she dried him, her loose-fitting shift slid upward to reveal "a budding bosom whose power only a dead man would not feel." How could they proceed without driving one another to distraction? He proposed that they blindfold one another before she helped him undress, but as she moved to him, "I clasped her in my arms, and there was no more thought of playing blind man's buff." On the bed, he "covered her with kisses and swore that I would be hers until death," and then, as he put it, "I picked the beautiful flower, finding it, as always, better than any of those I had picked during fourteen years." When they made love a second time, he believed that he was more deeply in love with sweet young Tonina than he'd ever been with any woman.

At the same time, Tonina (or her mother) had been transporting letters between Casanova and Caterina, but she dismissed that complication, saying, "She is in there, and I am here. You are my master, and it rests only with you to be my master always." Her devotion persuaded him that "Tonina seemed to have become another person." How could he have overlooked her "rare qualities"? He'd been too distracted with Caterina, and then with Maria Eleonora, to give Tonina the attention she deserved. As she prepared an elaborate, Venetian-style dinner for the two of them, he considered her "at once my wife, my mistress, and my servant." So it was that Tonina became a minor but illuminating entry in the catalogue of Casanova conquests. She was simple and sweet, seemingly indifferent to his other loves. And she was unlettered, which suited his need for discretion, but how long would he, who was nothing if not literary, put up with her limitations? He claimed they spent twenty-two days in this blissful state until the end of April, when, as he promised himself, he saw Maria Eleonora at the grating again, and she was "greatly changed." He did his best to conceal the fact that he no longer loved her. "I was too much afraid that she would fall ill again if I deprived her of that hope."

Many of the thirty-five convents in Venice served as harems and schools for scandal. The nuns, confined against their will by their wealthy families to prevent them from getting married or pregnant, concealed sex manuals in their prayer books, and passed their idle hours pleasuring themselves with the *pastinaca muranese*, or crystal turnip, a dildo fashioned of Venetian glass manufactured on Murano and filled with warm water.

Flouting the rules, many members of religious orders engaged in trysts, not just Maria Eleonora and Caterina. Unwanted pregnancies and illegitimate children abounded, as did secret abortions and maternal deaths. Within their convents' walls, nuns with exposed breasts held balls and performances during which they received lavish gifts from their lovers and admirers. The abbess on occasion took a fee and turned a blind eye to the nuns' illicit activities. Foreigners from across Europe traveled to Venice expressly to see the convents and have sex with the nuns. A "nun" became slang for "prostitute." Male visitors with a taste for transvestitism donned habits to preserve their anonymity. Casanova heard a nun boasting of her ten lovers, and he reported that one hundred zecchini purchased the sexual favors of the abbess of the Convent of the Virgins.

This behavior was not a recent development in Venice. In the fifteenth century a priest named Giovanni Pietro Leon of Valcamonica maintained a harem of four hundred nuns in a convent on the island of Giudecca. He blackmailed nuns with their confessions or tempted them with gifts, setting the stage for more blackmail. He sold their embroidery to purchase luxuries for himself. In warm weather, he kept his favorite nuns close by, naked. If they became pregnant, and many did, he insisted on abortions. Ultimately, the nuns reported him to the authorities; he was tried, convicted, and beheaded.

Convent erotica, all written by men, became popular: *Venus in the Cloister or the Nun in Her Chemise*, and *The Carthusians' Porter* (1745), a tale of the sexual initiation of a young nun by an older sister. Denis Diderot, known for his massive, popular *Encyclopédie*, wrote *La Religieuse—The Nun*—in secret, and the work was published twelve years after his death, in 1796. This notorious novel was based on a true story of Marguerite Delamarre, forced by her parents to become a nun against her will. She spent thirty years as a prisoner in a convent, until the French Revolution. "I do not think a more terrifying satire of convents has ever been written," he said.

Nor was Casanova immune to intrigue and misfortune. The brother of his protector, Bragadin, died, leaving a fortune and prompting Bragadin at the advanced age of sixty-three to consider marrying his longtime mistress, with whom he'd had a son out of wedlock. The marriage would legitimize the son and save the Bragadin line from extinction. Casanova cast a cold eye on these financial machinations: "I was very much concerned for the life of my dear benefactor, whom the activity of marriage would have killed." To add to his worries, he began losing "very large sums" at gambling, including all of Maria Eleonora's diamonds. There was no more talk of elopement. He played on with small stakes against poor players, hoping his luck would turn.

And finally, he had a peculiar dinner with John Murray, the wanton Englishman, and Tonina. In the morning, Murray wrote, "I am irretrievably in love with your Tonina," and proceeded to lay out detailed plans to set her up in a household with servants, an income, all that she could need, on condition that he have unlimited access to her. "I give you eight days to answer me." Casanova needed just three to reply that Tonina might be pregnant, but that did not stop him from urging her to accept the Englishman's terms: "You will belong only to your new lover. Consider that you come into possession of a dowry that can bring you a very good marriage and that I am not in a position to make any such provision for you." When her mother, Laura, learned of the terms, she instantly agreed, and before Tonina knew it, she had a contract with the Englishman for two hundred Venetian ducats annually to become his official mistress. If she was pregnant, the Englishman would give Casanova the child; in fact, she could continue to give Casanova "proofs of her affection until her pregnancy was over." With negotiations concluded, young Tonina, in tears, declared that she would feel friendship for her Casanova but would love only Murray.

At that point, Tonina's little sister, Barberina, took her turn seducing him. Her chosen arena was a small enclosed garden with a fig tree, and she ostentatiously climbed a ladder to expose herself to him, "presenting me with a picture that the most consummate experience could not have imagined." She saw that she'd sent him "into ecstasies," and in no time they were planning their first night together. Casanova exulted once more. If only he had a fortune to set her up in a lavish household as the Englishman had with Tonina! He consoled himself that Barberina, unlike Tonina, was still a virgin. A day or two later, she could no longer claim that status, and Casanova boasted, "I was enjoying a fruit whose sweetness I had never so fully tasted in the past." He planned to rent a two-room apartment for them on the Fondamenta Nuove on the northern edge of Venice, facing Murano, where she could ripen like one of the figs she'd plucked in the garden.

But all the while, the spies of the Venetian Inquisition were watching him, and reporting on his activities in secret reports, or *riferte*. Before long he was forced to contend with what he called "the catastrophe."

———•———

The skein began to unravel when Casanova denounced the work of another Venetian, Pietro Chiari, a Jesuit turned playwright. Chiari wrote dozens of pieces in the genre known as *comédie larmoyante*, or tearful comedy, mixing farcical and tragic themes, ending in moral uplift. Casanova's literary vilification reached Chiari's ears, and insults between the two circulated around Venice. Chiari caricatured his tormentor in a novel, *La Commediante in Fortuna*, published in 1754. In the English-language version (1771), titled *Rosara, or the Adventures of an Actress, a Story from Real Life*, a passage refers to "Vanesio, of unknown, and, as it was reported, of illegitimate birth. He was a well-made man; of a brown complexion; his manners were stiff, and affected, but, he was very presuming, and bold." The question of Casanova's paternity had been whispered about in Venice from time to time; he didn't address it publicly, but the possibility that his birth father wasn't the failed actor Gaetano Casanova who'd died young, but some other, unknown figure could only have nagged at his sense of self and security.

Chiari portrayed Casanova (in the guise of Vanesio) in tones both acid and admiring, describing him as "one of those phenomena in the civil atmosphere, whose brightness we cannot account for: they have neither estate, nor office, nor talents to procure them that affluence." Anything foreign excited his interest: "he talked of nothing but London, and Paris, as if those two capitals comprehended the whole world. Always as trim as a Narcissus, always vain, and strutting like a peacock; always whirling about like a windmill, he made it his daily business to intrude himself into every company; to be the gallant of every lady; to adapt himself to every circumstance that furnished him with the means of making money, or of being fortunate in love." Despite his dynamism, he was two-faced, and a "friend to no one."

Words turned to threats when Casanova received an anonymous letter warning that he should fear being cudgeled, or worse. At that moment, he happened to meet Giovanni Battista Manuzzi, whom he realized was a "spy for the State Inquisition." Posing as a gem dealer, Manuzzi generously offered "diamonds on credit" upon condition that Casanova receive him in his apartment. Casanova's suspicions should have been aroused; instead, he received Manuzzi at home. "Looking at a number of books I had lying about, he paused over some manuscripts dealing with magic. Enjoying his astonishment, I showed him teaching the art of becoming acquainted with all the elemental spirits"—a feature of the Kabbalah, considered a suspicious compilation of mystical thought. Several days later, Manuzzi returned to Casanova's home not to deal in gems but in books. He claimed that "a collector whom he could not name was ready to give me a thousand *zecchini*"—a remarkable sum—"for my five books." There was only one condition: the collector wanted to see them beforehand to determine if they were genuine, and Manuzzi promised to return them the next day.

"I really set no value on them," Casanova recalled. "I entrusted them to him."

Manuzzi kept his word, and returned them promptly, but said that his collector had determined they were "forgeries." In fact, Manuzzi had delivered the damning documents to the Secretary for State Inquisitors, "who thus learned that I was an arch-magician." It was true that Casanova fancied himself a mystical interpreter of the Kabbalah, a pursuit he shared with Bragadin and his other two benefactors, often to manipulate them to do his bidding, but he was no devil worshipper, blasphemer (even when losing at cards), or subversive dedicated to the overthrow of the Republic. Quite the opposite: he considered himself religious and longed only to become part of the Venetian establishment. Nevertheless, Manuzzi's odious secret charges stuck. Word reached Casanova that certain patricians believed that he'd led Bragadin astray with the Kabbalah. "To all this they added that I frequented foreign embassies and that since I lived with three patricians it was certain that, knowing everything that was done in the Senate, I revealed it for large sums of money." To top it off, he was a Freemason, a byword for treason. When these matters came before the State Inquisition, Casanova declared, "it was the very thing to ruin me."

———•———

Over a period of seven months, Manuzzi compiled a dossier of secret *riferte* about Casanova designed to reveal their subject in the worst possible light. Manuzzi wrote on November 11, 1754, "Casanova habitually exaggerates; with his lies and deceptions, he lives off others. He has been the ruin of His Excellency Sir Zuanne Bragadin, having gotten much money from him on the pretext that the Angel of Light was coming. It is surprising how someone who has gained such prestige in the country would allow himself to be deceived by such an impostor."

Manuzzi learned that Casanova frequented the café Bottega delle Acque. Passing incognito among the patrons, Manuzzi overheard him loudly criticizing Pietro Chiara's creaky dramatic efforts. Five days later he filed another report. At the same time, Manuzzi made it his business to discover the identity of the author of several scurrilous satires circulating at the Bottega delle Acque. The culprit, of course: Giacomo Casanova. "In order to gain fame for his satires he distributes them among the noblemen mentioned above, thinking in this way to gain merit in their eyes, and they dismiss him as an impostor and a good for nothing." Manuzzi tried repeatedly to obtain a copy of at least one satire, according to his aggrieved *riferte* of November 30, but Casanova sent word that he needed to catch up on his sleep before he could comply, leaving his nemesis both frustrated and fascinated by this elusive subject.

As if these matters were not sufficient to damn Casanova, the impoverished aristocrat Contessina Lorenza Maddalena Bonafede returned to haunt him. Before she could induce him to declare himself as her official lover, he became distracted by Caterina and Maria Eleonora, the two nuns, among other women. His utter lack of interest did not deter the Contessina Bonafede from trying to ensnare him; he suspected that the urgent need for money for her and her family motivated her to pursue him. Even her father, Count Bonafede, faced the prospect of imminent eviction, and they all looked to Casanova as their financial savior. He extricated himself by giving them the money he had with him, but not before he accused her, and her father, of trying to entrap him. Drama ensued: "She denies it, she weeps, she falls on her knees. I do not look at her. I take my cloak, and I flee."

He avoided the Contessina for months, until, as he put it, "passion, hunger, and poverty addled her brains. She went mad to the point that one day at noon she went out naked, running about the Campo San Pietro"—the haunt of prostitutes—"and asking whomever she met and the men who arrested her to take her to my house." This outrageous incident became the talk of Venice. What had Giacomo Casanova done to drive her to such extremes? The chatter became "a great annoyance to me," as he rather heartlessly put it while the afflicted woman was confined to a hospital. The State Inquisition decided that "the young Contessina Bonafede had gone insane from the drugs and love philtres I had given her." To add to the spectacle, "in her fits of madness, she never failed to name me and heap curses on me." When released, she "went begging through the streets of Venice like all her brothers," except for one who'd found work as a bodyguard in Madrid. She died not long after in a mental hospital.

Friends advised Casanova to flee; the all-powerful Venetian Inquisition was investigating him. Among those warning him was Bragadin, who had been an agent of the Inquisition himself and spoke with authority. As Casanova knew, "the only people who can live happily in Venice are those whose existence is unknown to the formidable tribunal; but I made light of their advice." To heed it would make him uneasy, "and I detested uneasiness." There was much else to cause him anxiety. Losing steadily at gambling, he admitted, "I had pawned all my jewels . . . people were avoiding me." Eventually, "All these black, heavy clouds gathered above my head to strike me with a thunderbolt." It was only a matter of time before he was summoned to appear before the Inquisition's tribunal.

On March 22, 1755, Manuzzi resumed stalking his prey, who he claimed appeared to be involved in a conspiracy to cheat at cards—a major enterprise in gambling-mad Venice—and to associate with devotees of another blasphemous creed: "Don Gio Batta Zini of the parish of San Samuele, friend of Casanova, told me that as per revelations told him by Casanova himself of certain secrets he has with patrician noblemen of those who like to keep the cards in their hands, recommended that he not get involved because should any accident happen, they would all say that he cheated and all the fault would fall on him, that said Casanova is very much in the public eye here especially for cheating at cards." Also of concern, Giacomo Casanova had befriended the patrician Memmo brothers, and from his sources Manuzzi heard the damning phrase, "They are a bunch of Epicureans."

The outlandish philosophy that Casanova had embraced was an ancient system succinctly expressed by Philodemus of Gadara, born in Greece around 100 BC, in four concise parts:

> *Don't fear God;*
> *Don't worry about death;*
> *What is good is easy to get;*
> *What is terrible is easy to endure.*

That was blasphemous enough; Manuzzi considered it an even greater coup to persuade Casanova to reveal his complicity in Freemasonry. In his *riferte* of July 12, 1755, Manuzzi reported, "I requested a composition from Giacomo Casanova." Its three confidential pages concerned "intercourse in the direct and indirect way, mixing fables, sacred and profane writings, and the birth of Jesus Christ." Casanova proceeded to open his trunk to display the accoutrements of Freemasonry. "He showed me a white leather [object] that he had in this trunk in the shape of a small sash to be tied around the waist. I asked him what it was for and he answered that it is used when one goes in a certain place, where one is also to use certain tools, and a black suit. I asked him where the tools were and he answered that they are kept in the lodge because it is too dangerous to keep them at home. I remembered then that Casanova himself had told me in the past about a Sect of Masons, telling me about the honors and advantages to be had from being among its brethren." Casanova a Freemason? The account sounded alarms at the State Inquisition.

Something had to be done. "That nothing has happened to him so far while frequenting with such brazenness these patrician noblemen and pulling the wool over their eyes with such ideas is an enigma. If some of them spoke up, he would be in trouble." It was Manuzzi's ambition to call this disgraceful Freemason, confidence artist, and cardsharp to account.

Even worse, Casanova's malign influence metastasized beyond the confines of Venice. "For about the past seven years, rumors spread throughout the country that His Excellency Bragadin and he communicated with the spirits, [and] that having been warned by Bragadin that this issue had been submitted to this Grand Tribunal, in order not to be punished or exiled, he left Venice." Manuzzi elaborated: "He has many acquaintances with foreigners and with the most fortunate youth; dealings in the homes of many daughters, married women, and women of other kinds. He manages to entertain himself in many ways and always attempts some great coup to improve his fortunes, although he has no dearth of money to fulfill his every pleasure."

Only last Monday night, Manuzzi reported, one of his informers happened to be present at the Bottega delle Acque when "Casanova read a blasphemous verse composition in the Venetian dialect that he is working on right now." Manuzzi tried to obtain a copy of the manuscript, but Casanova refused. "The subject is very sensitive," Manuzzi warned, "because it shows what is necessary to do with women from [the time of] David's adultery, from which was born Solomon, all the way down to Jesus Christ." Manuzzi concluded, "I don't know what is more monstrous than his thoughts and conversation on the subject of religion, since Casanova holds that those who believe in Jesus Christ are feeble-minded. In trying to understand Casanova, one can see that disbelief, imposture, lewdness and voluptuousness combine in a manner inspiring horror." Days later, Manuzzi submitted supporting documents, including the blasphemous verses in the Venetian dialect. On the basis of this evidence, the Casanova case proceeded quickly.

In July 1755, that "fatal month," in Casanova's estimation, the Inquisition issued a warrant for his arrest, "alive or dead." This was a grave matter indeed, for "its slightest order is never promulgated except on pain of death to him who infringes it," he explained. At his wits' end, so he said, he turned to Maria Eleonora for a loan; she entrusted him with five hundred zecchini, which he again lost in the course of a night's gambling.

"At daybreak, needing to calm myself, I went to the Erberia," the Venetian herb and flower market near the Rialto bridge. All around him, other gamblers boasted of their winnings and strutted about with their latest lovers, as he lamented the passing of the old days, when Venetian women, rarely glimpsed, were the object of fascination and mystery. Now, "If a man goes there with a woman it is to reduce his friends to envy by showing off his luck; and if alone, he is prowling around in hopes, or trying to make someone jealous. The women are only there to be seen and ostentatiously embarrassed. They could hardly be trying to attract admiration in the state they are in—as though they have all agreed to appear looking like wrecks to give people something to talk about." And as for their beaux, "their careless manner and general nonchalance are calculated to convey boredom after the event and imply triumphant responsibility for their companions' disarray."

Walking on to his apartment, he was surprised to find the door ajar, the lock broken. He heard that the authorities had been there in force, on the pretext of searching for a trunk filled with salt, "which was strictly contraband." They'd left before he arrived. Closing the door after him, he fell into a brief, troubled sleep.

The next day, Casanova demanded help from his protector, Signor Bragadin, but the wise old man hesitated. Instead of seeking to redress the wrong he'd suffered, Bragadin advised, Casanova should think of "escaping to safety." The "trunk full of salt" the police sought was only a pretext. It was possible they'd missed Casanova on purpose to allow him to flee. In any case, he would be well advised to board Bragadin's gondola and travel by coach to Florence to await word about when it would be safe to return to Venice. "If you have no money, I will give you a hundred *zecchini* for a present." Casanova protested that he hadn't done anything to incur the Inquisition's wrath, and preferred to stay, at which point Bragadin urged his protégé to consult the oracle. Casanova refused to do even that much, insisting that fleeing the city would imply that he was guilty, and he absolutely was not! As a last resort, Bragadin urged his protégé to spend the night in an apartment in the palazzo, where he would be safe from arrest, but, Casanova wrote, "I am still ashamed that I refused him the favor." Bragadin took the prospect of arrest and its consequences far more seriously than Casanova.

Having done all he could, Bragadin remarked that it would be best if they "did not see each other again," and Casanova in turn "begged him not to make me sad." The severing of their link might have been a worse blow than anything the Inquisition would inflict. "I embraced him in tears, and I left." The somber occasion marked the last time they saw each other. Bragadin would die eleven years later.

That night, July 25, 1755, Casanova returned home, where he tried to sleep. The next thing he knew, it was morning, and a knock on the door startled him awake.

An official of the tribunal stood in the doorway and demanded to see his papers. "The word 'tribunal' petrified my soul," Casanova recalled, "leaving me only the physical ability to obey him." His desk was open, and the official together with several aides confiscated Casanova's manuscripts and letters. They were also looking for books about magic, "and then I saw it: the gem dealer Manuzzi had been the infamous spy who had accused me of having those books when he gained entrance to my house." The incriminating items were the *Key of Solomon*, a book of magic trading on Solomon's reputation as a sorcerer; the *Zohar*, a work, in Hebrew, considered a cornerstone of the Kabbalah; and *Picatrix*, a medieval study of devil worship; and other works about "conversing with demons of all classes." In the eyes of the tribunal, volumes such as these indicated that Casanova practiced forbidden arts. The thought crossed his mind that "those who knew I had those books thought I was a magician, and it rather pleased me." And the books on his night table were almost as damning. Ariosto, Horace, and other unbelievers, as well as "the little book of lubricious postures by Pietro Aretino that Manuzzi had also reported" told more incriminating tales about their owner.

Having gathered the evidence, the agent directed Casanova to dress, which he did, taking his time to select a crisp ruffled shirt, a lightweight silk cloak, and a stylish cap decorated with lace and a feather for the occasion. He would meet his fate in style.

As he entered the drawing room, he faced thirty constables—thirty! "It is strange that in London, where everyone is brave, only one man is used to arrest another, and that in my dear country, where people are cowards, thirty are sent." The official in charge ordered Casanova into a gondola, and took a seat next to him for the trip to the headquarters of the State Inquisition in a wing of the Doge's Palace. The contrast between the splendor of the palace, its artwork, jewels, and gold, and the Inquisition's rooms could not have been greater. He passed through a door, from light into gloom, descending into hell. Would he ever escape?

Chapter 9

I Piombi

Casanova spent four hours locked in a holding cell, his sleep interrupted every fifteen minutes by an urge to make water. It was very unlike him, but he filled one chamber pot after another, and he attributed the phenomenon to the "act of oppression" to which he'd been subjected. His "terrified mind" made him behave as though he were in a wine press, expelling fluids.

A bell rang, and a constable appeared, declaring that he had orders to place Casanova "under the Leads." He was forced into another gondola that took a roundabout route through the Grand Canal to the Quay of the Prisons. They climbed several flights of stairs to a bridge, later known as the Bridge of Sighs, connecting the Doge's Palace and the New Prison "over the canal called the Rio del Palazzo." They traversed a gallery and came face-to-face with the patrician Domenico Cavalli, the Secretary to the Inquisitors, who said, "*È quello; mettetelo in deposito*"—"That's him; put him away"—simple words marking the end of a life.

Casanova was delivered not to the New Prison, as he expected, but to the Leads, I Piombi, located directly beneath the lead roof of the Doge's Palace. Security was so tight that so far as he knew no one had ever escaped. Confinement there was akin to being buried alive.

He confronted more doors, locks, and galleries extending into an endless gloom relieved only by narrow shafts of light crisscrossing overhead. Motes of dust floated in and out of view, a sight creating an unbearable sense of isolation, as if he were about to glimpse the tomb where he would rest for eternity. "I entered a large, ugly, dirty, garret, twelve yards long by two wide, badly lighted by a high dormer." The jailer "opened a heavy door lined with iron, three and a half feet high and with a round hole eight inches in diameter in the center, and ordered me to enter just as I was looking attentively at an iron mechanism fastened to the strong wall with nails in the shape of a horseshoe." With a smile, the jailer explained, "When Their Eminences order someone strangled, he is made to sit on a stool with his back to this collar, and his head is placed so that the collar goes round half of his mask. The two ends of a skein of silk pass through this hole leading to a winch to which they are fastened. A man twists it until the patient has rendered up his soul to Our Lord, for his confessor never leaves him until he is dead."

Casanova stooped to enter, and a guard locked him in his cramped cell. Now it was his turn to be confined on the other side of a metal grating, not in a monastery, but in the most feared penal institution in Venice. A window, "crossed by six iron bars an inch thick that formed sixteen openings five inches square," would have admitted sufficient light, were it not for one of the "main roof timbers," eighteen inches thick, blotting out the sun. Under the low ceiling, he had to stoop at all times to keep from hitting his head. Groping in the near-darkness, Casanova found no bed, no chair, no table, no furniture at all "except for a bucket for the needs of nature" and a rude board fastened to the wall. "On it I put my beautiful floss-silk cloak, my fine coat that has started its life so badly, and my hat trimmed with Spanish point lace and a white feather," as if relinquishing his identity. Sinking into despair, he confessed, "I have ended up in a place where the false seemed true and reality seemed a bad dream." Not since his earliest boyhood had he known such deprivation, helplessness, and claustrophobia.

"The heat was extreme. In my astonishment, instinct led me to the grating, the only place where I could rest while leaning my elbows," he wrote. "Rats as big as rabbits were walking about. Those hideous animals, whose sight I loathed, came directly under my grating without showing the least sign of fear. I quickly drew the inner blind over the round hole in the center of the door, for a visit from them would freeze my blood." He spent the next eight hours with his arms crossed on the sill, "in the deepest reverie," paralyzed by fear, and contemplating the horror surrounding him. It was said that another prison, in the basement, exceeded even I Piombi for sheer misery, but Casanova made no mention of it. And it was said that prisoners in I Piombi could summon food and furniture from the outside to ease their stay, but Casanova did not avail himself of those small luxuries. The seven cells in I Piombi generally held political prisoners, disgraced members of the Council of Ten, or other notables awaiting trial. Yet Casanova hadn't been formally accused, which made his torment even worse, for he had nothing to defend himself against, no trial date, nor hope of discharge, only an endless Purgatory stretching before him. Why had he been arrested? Was it his collection of books on blasphemous subjects, his gambling debts, his varied indiscretions on Murano? Had he been betrayed by de Bernis, or even by Bragadin? Who had sent Manuzzi to plague him? In the Venetian police state of spies and secrecy, he had no way of knowing. Most remarkable of all, he was confined not to some remote fort on a distant island in the lagoon, but to the top floor of the eastern wing of the Palazzo Ducale, the Doge's Palace, the residence of the Doge himself, and the seat of the Republic's Senate, Council of Ten, and more than a dozen other institutional entities. Elegant, whimsical, and colorful works by Bellini, Tintoretto, Pisanello, and Titian adorned the palace's hallways and ceilings. Yet he was cut off from them, living in a world of darkness and vermin, reeking of human and animal waste, as if he were a thousand miles away. His physical distance from the opulence of Venice and the center of government was negligible, the psychological distance immeasurable.

In summer, the lead in the roof absorbed the heat and turned I Piombi into an oven, and in winter the lead absorbed the cold and turned it into an icebox; the extreme temperatures subjected the prisoners to pneumonia, dehydration, and unrelieved misery. If he didn't starve to death in his cell, or succumb to a lethal illness, he would go mad from the confinement and near-total darkness. No one checked on him, "not even to bring me a bed, a chair, or at least bread and water." He prayed that someone would appear before midnight, but when no one did, he recalled, "I succumbed to something very like madness, howling, stamping my feet, cursing, and accompanying all this useless noise that my strange situation drove me to make with loud cries. After half an hour of this exercise in fury, seeing no one come, with not the slightest sign that anyone heard my ravings, and shrouded in darkness, I closed the grating, fearing that the rats would jump in the cell. I threw myself on the floor after wrapping my hair in a handkerchief. Such pitiless desertion seemed to me unthinkable, even if I had been sentenced to death. My consideration of what I could have done to deserve treatment so cruel could continue no longer than a minute, for I found no cause for arresting me. As a great libertine, bold talker, a man who thought of nothing but enjoying life, I could not find myself guilty, but seeing that I was nevertheless treated as such, I spare my reader all that rage and indignation and despair made me say and think against the horrible despotism oppressing me." The only thing left to do was go mad and die, "yet my anger and the despair that preyed on me and the hard floor on which I lay did not keep me from falling asleep; my constitution needed sleep; and when a person is young and healthy his constitution can satisfy its need without giving it any thought."

The tolling of the midnight bell awakened him. "I could not believe that I had spent three hours insensible of any discomfort. Not changing my position but still lying as I was on my left side, I put out my right arm to get my handkerchief, which memory assured me I had placed there. As I groped along with my hand—God! what a surprise when I find another hand cold as ice! Terror electrified me from head to foot and every one of my hairs stood on end." After waiting a few minutes, he decided that "what I had touched was only a figment of my imagination; in this conviction I again stretch out my arm to the same spot and I find the same hand, which, frozen with horror and giving a piercing shriek, I grasp and drop, drawing back my arm."

Giving the matter some thought, "I decide that while I was asleep a corpse had been placed near me," perhaps a friend of his, "who had been strangled and laid beside me so that when I woke I should find an example of the fate that I must expect." Infuriated, he reached out to the corpse's hand, "I grasp it, and at the same moment get up, intending to pull the corpse toward me and so ascertain the fact in all its atrocity; but as I try to raise myself on my left elbow, the same cold that I am holding comes to life, draws away, and to my great surprise, I instantly realize that the hand in my right hand is none other than my left, which, numbed and stiffened, lost motion, feeling, and warmth."

He paused to reflect: "the incident, though comic, did not cheer me. On the contrary, it gave me cause for the darkest reflections." His numb hand had terrified and repelled him as a symbol of extinction and horror, of the depths to which he would sink if left unattended. Once it prickled to life, he reincorporated it into his body, and to acknowledge his connection to it and to the darkness it represented. His reason was compromised, his imagination bent on subjecting him either to false hopes or profound despair. He was trapped in the grotesque, nightmarish reality envisioned by the Venetian artist Giovanni Battista Piranesi, whose fantastic etchings of prisons, *Carceri d'invenzione*, portrayed a world turned on itself, a spiral staircase with no bottom, a lock with no combination, a riddle with no answer. This prison was as much a psychological trap as a physical one, the essence of claustrophobic Venice as an immense jail, with its spies and secrecy, masks and masquerades, extending across the lagoon to islands honeycombed with garrisons, monasteries, convents, and other forms of confinement that served as a way of life.

It was only a matter of time before he joined the other victims of I Piombi, forever broken in body and spirit. To retain his sanity, he turned to the consolations of philosophy as he had in his most trying and stressful moments in life. He sat motionless, lost in a reverie in which he led the people of Venice to "massacre the aristocrats." It was not enough to leave the executions to others, "It was I myself who should massacre them."

He spent hours trying to calm his anger. Finally, "the profound silence of the place, the Hell of living humanity, was broken by the squeak of the bolts in the vestibules of the corridors that had to be traversed to reach my cell. I saw the jailer in front of my grating asking me if I had had 'time to think about what I wanted to eat.'" Ignoring the mockery, Casanova ordered rice soup, boiled beef, a roast, bread, water, and wine. Later, the jailer, warning of an extended stay in I Piombi, gave Casanova paper and pencil to write a list of all that he needed: a bed, shirts, stockings, slippers, dressing gown, nightcaps, armchair, table, combs, mirrors, razors, handkerchiefs, his confiscated books, ink, pens, and paper. As it happened, books, ink, paper, mirror, and razors were all forbidden in I Piombi, and he would have to pay for dinner. Casanova offered one zecchino.

Hours later, around noon, the jailer returned accompanied by five constables, who brought dinner, the requested furniture, and one other essential item: "My table service consisted of an ivory spoon that he had bought with my money, knife and fork being forbidden as well all metal implements." And so his life in jail settled into a routine, occasionally punctuated by mirthless jests with his keepers. Casanova expressed appreciation for being confined by himself rather than with criminals, which drew the rejoinder: "What, Signore? Criminals? I should resent that very much. There are only respectable people here, who have to be sequestered from society for reasons that only Their Excellencies know. You have been put in a cell alone to increase your punishment, and you want me to convey your thanks for it?"

The Entrance to the Grand Canal, Venice, by Canaletto
(Giovanni Antonio Canal), c. 1730.

The *bauta* mask, an essential
feature of Carnival, concealed
the wearer's identity and encouraged misbehavior.

The *moretta,* a Venetian mask designed to mute women,
who gripped it with their teeth.

Girl Resting: Louise O'Murphy, the youthful mistress of Louis XV, in 1753. Portrait by François Boucher.

Departure of *Bucentaur*, the state barge of the Venice doges, for the Lido on Ascension Day, to perform the annual rite known as the "Marriage of the Sea."

A lady in a masquerade habit, also known as *The Fair Nun Unmask'd,*
by Henry Robert Morland, suggested the blurring of boundaries between
the sacred and profane of Casanova's era.

The Parlour of the San Zaccaria Convent, by Francesco Guardi, where nuns
entertained their well-heeled admirers, as if confined to a seraglio.

Carnival Scene, by Giandomenico Tiepolo.

Manon Balletti was the fiancée (1757–1760) of Giacomo Casanova, one of many women whom he loved and spurned.

Jeanne-Antoinette Poisson, Marquise de Pompadour, also known as "the Little Queen," was the official chief mistress of Louis XV and an influential presence in the royal court.

Catherine II "The Great" of Russia impressed Casanova with her
intellectual brilliance and steely resolve.

Casanova portrait by Anton Raphael Mengs, who admired
and sheltered the volatile Venetian.

"I did not know that," Casanova quietly replied.

In the days to come, he came to appreciate how solitude and isolation make for the "most wretched of mortals. He longs for Hell, if he believes in it, if only for companionship." He longed for the company of a murderer, maniac, or a man "stinking of disease"—even a bear. If only he could distract himself with a desk, and pen, ink, and paper. Instead, he had only the booming clock of San Marco to distract him and fleas borne by the ubiquitous rats. "A million fleas romping all over my body, avid for my blood and my skin, and piercing them with a voracity of which I had no conception" tortured him for hours on end, in the dark, alone, as "the accursed insects gave me convulsions, made my muscles contract spasmodically, and poisoned my blood."

When he exhausted his money buying his meals, the tribunal granted him an allowance of fifty soldi a day, but the intense heat had diminished his appetite, and he did not spend even that trifling amount on food. "It was the season of the pestilential dog days: the power of the sun's rays striking on the lead plates that covered the roof of my prison kept me as it were in a sweating room." He sat in his armchair, stark naked, perspiration oozing from every pore. Constipation gripped him for two weeks, and when he did force himself to evacuate his bowels, "I thought I should die from the pain of which I had no conception." The cause, hemorrhoids, tormented him for the rest of his life.

The extreme heat gave way to "violent chills" caused by fever. He took to his flimsy bed, assured by his jailer, Lorenzo, that the tribunal would magnanimously provide him with a physician and medication "all for nothing." Later, a doctor with "imposing physiognomy," Bellotto by name, appeared at his door, only to be rebuffed by the fever-racked prisoner. As he departed, he warned that Casanova was in danger of dying, and the prisoner for once agreed: "It was what I wanted."

Later that day, the physician returned, candlestick in hand, advising his patient to "banish grief" and take a "large quantity of lemonade" at frequent intervals. Casanova drank and dreamt of "mystical extravagances." In the morning, a surgeon came to bleed the patient, and brought cheering news: Casanova was to be moved to another part of I Piombi, where it would not be so hot. He refused to move, fearing a fresh onslaught of rats, but in any event he busied himself with barley water and a syringe. "Keep yourself amused with enemas," the surgeon advised.

"He made four visits and he pulled me through," Casanova gratefully noted. "My appetite came back. By the beginning of September I was in good health."

———•———

Still, the heat and fleas tormented him, and his jailer, Lorenzo, pinched donations intended for a priest to say masses in Casanova's name. "The least injustice Lorenzo could do me was to appropriate my money and say my masses for himself in some tavern."

Each night he fell asleep in the hope that the following day would bring deliverance from captivity, but he remained confined to his cell. He heard nothing from his protectors, although they must have known of his whereabouts; nor did he hear from his siblings; his mother; Maria Eleonora Michiel and Caterina Capretta; or the other women he'd loved. Except for the tolling of the bells in San Marco, and the alternation of heat and cold, the world beyond his cell had ceased to exist. He lived only in the desperate moment.

He consoled himself with the thought that he was, day by day, serving out a fixed sentence ending on October 1, 1755, when the three Inquisitors who'd sentenced him, Andrea Diedo, Antonio Condulmer, and Antonio da Mula, would be replaced. His conjecture proved erroneous. Without his being aware of it, he'd been found guilty and sentenced to five years' imprisonment for "atheism," an offense covering a multitude of sins. "The only business of the Venetian tribunal is to judge and to sentence; the guilty person is a machine that does not need to take any part in the business in order to cooperate; he is a nail that only needs to be hammered into a plank." October 1 passed without any announcement regarding his impending freedom. He suffered days of "rage and despair," convinced that he'd been given a life sentence, not that it would last very long. "Either they would kill me or I would succeed in it."

By Saturday, November 1, All Saints' Day, he began to contemplate a plan to escape from I Piombi, something no one had ever done successfully. Better to endure martyrdom than this misery. About this time, as Lorenzo and two other jailers were leaving his cell, the thick beam looming directly over their heads began to tremble, turning to the right, then resuming its original position. As Casanova puzzled over the meandering beam, he lost his balance. All at once he and the other men realized they were in the midst of a major earthquake. The shocks kept coming at briefly spaced intervals, as the jailers bolted, afraid for their lives, and to experience the wrath of God in the presence of their atheistic captive. Overwrought, Casanova imagined the Doge's Palace collapsing, freeing him from torment, depositing him "safe, sound, and free on the beautiful pavement of the Piazza San Marco." Much later, he realized he'd been seized by temporary madness.

The shock actually came from the Lisbon earthquake of 1755, a major disaster that snuffed out the lives of forty thousand of Lisbon's inhabitants and claimed many more lives throughout Portugal, Spain, and Morocco. Fires and tsunamis raged for days afterward. Nearly all of Lisbon was leveled by the tremors, including the city's palaces, royal archives containing records of voyages by Vasco da Gama, Magellan, and others, along with masterpieces by Titian and Rubens.

Across Europe the Lisbon earthquake shattered the belief in a benevolent deity. Catholics blamed Protestants, who in turn blamed their accusers. All wondered why the earthquake struck on All Saints' Day. Was this event God's judgment on a sinful society? Yet the Alfama, Lisbon's red-light district, had been spared. What sort of divine judgment was that? How could this cataclysm occur in the best of all possible worlds, as philosophers were fond of repeating? The devastation impressed Voltaire, who devoted his "Poème sur le désastre de Lisbonne" to the subject; Rousseau; and other Enlightenment philosophers, who tried to fashion a response to the implacable forces of nature.

Spared from extinction, alone in his cell, meditating on his wild plan to escape, Casanova remained safe, at least for the time being.

He reviewed the layout of the prison as he came to know it. Above, the lead plates three feet square covered the cells, three to the west, including his, and four to the east. On the other side, the cells were high enough to allow a prisoner to stand, would that he could, where the huge beam loomed overhead, and made him stoop at all times. Looking down, he realized that the floor happened to be directly above the Inquisitors' room, where people assembled at night, after the daily deliberations of the Council of Ten. "Having a perfect conception of the topography of the premises," he wrote, "the only way I could think of escaping with any chance of succeeding was to make a hole in the floor of my prison; but I needed instruments, a difficult matter in a place where all outside communication was forbidden." If he strangled his jailer and the constable, another constable further down the hallway would soon take his place. Nevertheless, "when a man takes it into his head to accomplish some project and pursues it to the exclusion of anything else, he must succeed in it despite all difficulties."

———•———

In mid-November he acquired a cell mate, "a handcuffed young man who was weeping. They locked him into my 'home' and went off without even a word." The new arrival was short, only five feet tall, and thus able to stand upright in the cell. Casanova learned he was Lorenzo Mazzetta, of Milan, who told a complicated tale involving a countess and a pregnancy. He did not realize the seriousness of his situation until Casanova informed him that he was in I Piombi, when "he began to weep hot tears." The distraught prisoner was brokenhearted, but he was young and alive; worn down by months in jail, Casanova knew that dead men were heavier than broken hearts. As the grieving young man awaited a bed and food, Casanova informed him that they would not be arriving any time soon, and offered to share his meal, but the young man couldn't swallow. Eventually, the new prisoner received his own pallet, and arrangements were made for meals, and the two of them received permission to walk the length of the garret.

He came across discarded notebooks, which he claimed for himself; they were records of long-forgotten criminal cases, accusations regarding confessors who had "abused their female penitents, schoolmasters convicted of pederasty, and guardians who had cheated their wards," and the like, stretching back for "two or three centuries," a catalogue of cunning, depravity, and mean-spiritedness that gave him a "few hours of pleasure to contemplate."

As he grew stronger on the walks, he contemplated his escape. The hour was approaching, or so he thought, but he would have to endure another eleven months of incarceration before risking his life to obtain freedom.

Casanova's tearful cell mate was transferred to another, more comfortable prison called I Quattro, where inmates could summon their jailers at will, and had the benefit of an oil lamp to illuminate their quarters. He was soon replaced. Casanova's new cell mate appeared to be about fifty years of age, "slightly stooped, gaunt, with a big mouth and long dirty teeth; he had small hazel eyes and long red lashes, a round black wig that stank of oil, and a coat of coarse grey cloth." He was a Friulian peasant's son named Squaldo

Nobili ("Carlo," in the prison records) who drove Casanova to the brink of madness. In his isolation, he concluded the world had forgotten him. Unable to trim his beard, he had grown a woolly bush, and looked like a bit of a maniac himself.

On January 1, 1756, his jailer Lorenzo arrived with gifts that brought tears to the prisoner's eyes: a dressing gown lined with fox fur, a silk coverlet, a bearskin bag to warm his legs in the bone-chilling cold, and enough zecchini to purchase "all the books I wanted." These exquisite presents had come from Signor Bragadin, at last taking notice of his disgraced protégé. Casanova immediately wrote his guardian in pencil: "I am grateful to the mercy of the tribunal and the virtue of Signor Bragadin." The rush of words seemed to derive from temporary insanity. "In the intensity of my gratitude I forgave my oppressors and almost abandoned my plan of escaping; so pliable is a man when misfortune degrades him." He heard from Lorenzo that Signor Bragadin had pleaded in tears, on his knees, before the three stern Inquisitors to beg them to allow him to send these gifts to Casanova, "if I was still among the living." So he was, just barely. Summoning his presence of mind, he wrote down "the titles of all the books I wanted."

Rejuvenated, he took to walking the length of the garret as before, coming across a "long bolt" on the floor. Feeling its heft, "I considered its possibilities as a weapon of attack and defense" and concealed it under his coat.

In the privacy of his cell, he rubbed the bolt against a piece of marble, frustrated by the difficulty of fashioning a deadly tool in darkness. "Having no oil with which to wet and soften the iron on which I wanted to put a point, I used nothing but my saliva and I toiled for two weeks filing down eight triangular facets," he wrote. "The result was an octagonal stiletto as well proportioned as one could have expected from a good cutler." The task dislocated his right shoulder. "The palm of my hand had become one great sore after the vessels broke; despite the pain I did not stop my work; I was determined to see it perfected."

If he were caught with the tool, the consequences would be devastating. He concealed it in the bottom of his armchair against the day of his escape. Now he had a tool to "make a hole in the floor under my bed." Through it, he could lower himself on a rope made of bedclothes fastened to his bed into the room where the tribunal met. Once there, he would conceal himself beneath a great table, clutching his weapon, and flee in the morning, at a moment when no one was looking. If he happened to encounter a constable, he'd kill him "by plunging my pike into his throat."

For now, it was essential to prevent the constables from sweeping the floor of his cell and discovering the hole, but they insisted on performing this menial task. To prevent them, Casanova feigned illness. He pricked a finger, bloodied a handkerchief, and convinced Lorenzo to summon a physician, who bled him and wrote a prescription as Casanova blamed his bloody condition on the dust caused by sweeping entering his lungs. "Lorenzo swore he thought he was rendering me a service and that he would never have any sweeping done again as long as he lived." Casanova laughed privately at the success of his ruse before succumbing to a new misery. "The overlong nights of winter distressed me. I had to spend nineteen mortal hours in absolute darkness; and on foggy days, which are not uncommon in Venice, the light that came through the window and the hole in the door was not enough for me to read my book by. Since I could not read I went back to thinking of my escape, and a mind always fixed on one idea can go mad."

In the midst of his madness, he came down with "a sort of measles," but he survived the illness, though it left him covered with itchy scabs. He obtained a prescription for an ointment to soothe his arms. Wishing to concoct the salve himself, he asked the jailer for matches to heat the ingredients, and by this time the trust between them had grown to the point that Lorenzo obliged without hesitation. Casanova planned to use the matches to light a lamp he had been constructing to banish the endless winter gloom. *Success!* "For me, there were no more nights." In his elation, he planned to "begin breaking the floor on the first Monday in Lent." But just before he could execute his escape plan, the door to his cell opened, and Lorenzo admitted "a very fat man," who took the place of "Carlo."

Casanova recognized the new arrival on sight. He was "the Jew Gabriel Schalon, celebrated for his ability to raise money for young men by ruinous deals; we knew each other, so we exchanged the usual greetings the occasion demanded." (Casanova places Schalon's arrival at the beginning of Lent 1756, but prison records indicate it actually occurred on December 19, 1755.) The introduction of the new cell mate confounded his carefully thought-out escape plan, and tapped a vein of anti-Semitism. "This Jew, who was brainless, talkative, and stupid except in his trade, began by congratulating me on my having been chosen above all others to share his company," complained Casanova, cursing his misfortune at being thrown together with this scoundrel. Schalon, for his part, considered Casanova a common criminal. "Strictly between ourselves," he blustered, "the State Inquisitors blundered when they had me arrested, and they must be wondering how to set their mistake right."

"They may give you a pension, for you are a man to be treated with consideration," Casanova sarcastically replied. Schalon boasted that he was so well connected that he might help his poor cell mate obtain his freedom. "The idiotic scoundrel thought he amounted to something!" Casanova groused, but there was no respite from this singularly irritating figure. "I had this stone around my neck for the next eight or nine weeks," he complained as Schalon acted "demanding, ignorant, superstitious, blustering, timid, sometimes giving in to tears and despair." He complained that his imprisonment was ruining his reputation, but, Casanova recalled, "I assured him that as far as his reputation went, he had nothing to fear, and he took my gibe as a compliment."

At night, the sleepless Schalon took to waking Casanova to keep him company. "Hateful man!" Casanova responded. "I believe your insomnia is a real torture, and I am sorry for you," but he warned that if Schalon woke him again, Casanova would strangle him. ("I do not believe I would really have strangled him," he later explained in an early account of his escape, "but I know that he tempted me to do so. A man in prison who sleeps peacefully is not imprisoned during his gentle sleep. . . . He must therefore look on anyone who wakes him as a brute who comes to deprive him of his liberty and to plunge him back to misery."

By day, Schalon demanded that the constables clean the place and thus risk exposing the escape hole Casanova had painstakingly fashioned. It required all of his ingenuity to keep the constables away by insisting the dust raised by sweeping would make him seriously ill.

The prospect of release from jail tantalized and tortured both prisoners. At one point, Schalon was convinced he was about to be sprung when a representative from the tribunal arrived. Casanova observed the door open, and Schalon leave, but instead of cheers or cries of thanks, Casanova heard "only sobs and cries" as Schalon returned to the cell. Then Casanova was summoned. He bowed to the representative in the darkness, and then remained still and silent. "The mute scene lasted about as long as that of my comrade." The official nodded slightly, perhaps half an inch, and withdrew. Casanova scuttled back to his cell and put on his fur coat. The cold was brutal. "The minister of the Tribunal must have had to employ all his strength to keep from laughing when he saw me, because my appearance, gallantly dressed, but disheveled and with a black beard of eight months, would make the most serious men laugh."

He sought solace, or at least diversion, in religion and began to pray for the means to escape. What saint would guide him to freedom? He settled on Saint Mark, "to whose protection I, as a Venetian, could lay some claim, so I addressed my prayers to him, but in vain." He next tried to propitiate Saint James, and then Saint Philip, "but I was wrong again." Finally, he settled on a local figure, Saint Anthony, who, "so they say in Padua, performs thirteen miracles a day; but no less in vain." In this way, he said, he became "accustomed to hoping in vain for protection from the saints." The only means he could trust was the weapon he'd slowly and painfully wrought.

When Schalon, his insufferable cell mate, was transferred to the grim cells of I Quattro, Casanova quietly returned to his work "with the greatest eagerness." His prayers had been answered, after all.

———————

He set about enlarging the hole in the floor leading to the Inquisition chamber, taking care to wrap in a napkin every fragment that he chipped loose, and dumping the lot "behind a pile of notebooks at the end of the garret," where no one would notice.

On the second day of his renewed labor, he encountered an impenetrable layer of marble chips cemented with lime below the floorboard. "I was appalled when I saw that my bolt was not biting into it; it was in vain that I bore down and pushed; my point slipped. It discouraged me completely." His mood recovered when he recalled a passage from the Roman historian Livy about Hannibal traversing the Alps by wearing down rocks with vinegar—"a thing I had considered incredible." Despite his doubts, he poured a bottle of strong vinegar on the marble layer, "and the next morning, whether as a result of the vinegar or of greater patience, I saw that I should succeed." The vinegar had dissolved the lime between the marble fragments, and he broke through that level and confronted another board, the last, he assumed. Now his hole was ten inches deep, and he continued his labors.

He had a fright on June 25, a day of celebration in Venice. "Stark naked, running with sweat, and lying flat on my stomach, I was working at the hole, in which, in order to see, I had set my lighted lamp," he wrote. "I was mortally terrified to hear the shrill grating of the bolt in the door to the first corridor. What a moment!" He blew out the lamp, left his pike in the hole, not forgetting to toss a napkin over it and to drag his pallet over the lot, falling on it "as if dead just as Lorenzo is opening my cell. One minute earlier, and he would have caught me in the act." This image of Casanova, glistening with sweat, prostrate on the floor, penetrating it with his tool as if it were the most recalcitrant lover he'd ever encountered, reveals the passion he brought to the task.

The noise was caused by Lorenzo bringing with him a new prisoner, Count Fenaroli of Brescia, fifty years old, a gambler, wealthy, well connected, and already known to Casanova. The two men embraced, crying at their shared misfortune even as they laughed at the circumstances of their unlikely reunion. To be incarcerated with a genuine Count rather than a swindler energized Casanova, who drew self-esteem from the company he kept, and helped to soothe the wounds his vanity had suffered in I Piombi. The remedy for the despair of prison life turned out to be bonhomie. If only they could gamble in these surroundings, he'd be halfway to happiness.

The two talked throughout the night—it was all too interesting to stop!—ignoring as best they could the fleas devouring them. The Count had his share of woe; he tearfully confessed his ardor for Signora Alessandri, so beautiful and talented, a singer and the mistress—actually, the wife—of a friend of his, and now that he was in jail, he missed her terribly. "The more a lover is in favor," Casanova observed, "the more miserable he becomes if he is torn from the arms of the woman he loves." Recovering a bit, the Count claimed everyone in Venice was trying to guess why Giacomo Casanova had been sent to jail. Some said it was for blasphemy, others said atheism, and still others because he had publicly criticized the comedies of Abate Chiari and even threatened to kill him.

"They were all fabrications," Casanova snorted. "I did not care enough about religion to be interested in founding a new one." His atheism was equally questionable, as he vacillated between faith and skepticism. As for Chiari's pathetic skits, if the State Inquisitors locked up everyone who hissed at them, the jails would overflow.

At dawn, Lorenzo returned with coffee and a generous dinner for the jovial Count, who raised an eyebrow at the timing of the repast. After an hour's vigorous perambulation, the Count insisted on having the dusty cell swept, and Casanova had no choice but to reveal his entire plan, the hole, the weapon, the napkin, everything. The Count was surprised, even "mortified" to learn of the outrageous scheme, but he encouraged Casanova to finish the job—if possible, on that very day. He even volunteered to hold the rope that would let Casanova down into the chamber below, and afterward pull it up. He himself had no interest in risking escape, but he congratulated Casanova on his skillful and daring plan.

On July 3, after only a week in jail, the Count received word that he would soon be freed. Casanova regretted losing his "precious companionship," and the two of them spent their last three hours together "vowing the tenderest friendship" before Lorenzo materialized to escort the Count to freedom.

———◆———

Alone, Casanova returned to shaping the hole and perfecting his plans for escape. He set the date for August 28, St. Augustine's Day. "I knew the Great Council met on that feast," and his escape route would be clear. But three days before that event, Lorenzo poked his head through the grating of the cell to announce that Casanova would be moving from "this vile cell to another, which is light," and from which he could see "half of Venice from its two windows." The ceiling would be "high enough to allow him to stand upright."

Casanova whimpered. "I felt that I was dying." The transfer meant the discovery of his plan. In a daze of disappointment, he abandoned his cell, noticing that one of the constables was carrying the armchair in which he'd hidden his weapon. "I wished I were also being followed by the fine hole I had made with such effort, and which I had to abandon, but it was impossible. My body moved on, but my soul remained behind."

He dutifully followed Lorenzo to his new cell, which afforded a panorama of Venice from the lagoon to the Lido, "but I was in no state to be consoled," now that his meticulous plans for escape had been ruined. He sank into his familiar armchair, combing his memory for the consolations of philosophy, "motionless as a statue," and convinced that his efforts had been for naught. "I had nothing to hope for, and the only relief left to me was not to think of the future." If only he'd set the day of his escape three days earlier, he would have been a free man. Instead, he tormented himself by imagining worse to come, the claustrophobic horror of confinement for the rest of his life. "The tribunal, master of garrets and the cellars of the great palace, might well have decreed Hell for anyone who had tried to run away from Purgatory."

Lorenzo interrupted his reverie, "frothing with rage, blaspheming God and all the saints," and demanding that Casanova return all the tools he'd used to make a hole in the floor of his former cell. The prisoner replied that he had no idea what Lorenzo was talking about. The jailer would show him! He ordered the *sbirri* to strip Casanova naked and search his body, and then his pallet, the cushion of his armchair, and even "the stinking chamber pot." After all that, nothing turned up.

Defiant, Casanova declared that if he had made a hole in the floor, he'd tell everyone that Lorenzo supplied the tools. Overhearing this, the *sbirri* roared with approval while Lorenzo shouted, stamped his feet, and banged his head against the wall as if insane. He ordered the men to drag Casanova's personal items into a stifling, narrow corridor with two sealed windows. Surveying his new lair, barely able to breathe, Casanova realized that the jailer hadn't found the weapon concealed in the armchair. "I adored Providence, and I saw that I could still count on making it the means of my escape."

——•——

After suffering for eight days in the intense heat, refusing spoiled food and threatening Lorenzo, he received a basket of lemons and a bottle of water: a gift from Signor Bragadin. Even the chicken accompanying these items looked edible, and to illuminate the scene, a constable opened the two windows. As a calmer mood prevailed, he dispatched Lorenzo to acquire works by the Italian art critic and playwright Marchese Maffei. The guard wondered why the prisoner wanted more books when he already had so many?

"I have read them all, and I need new ones." Lorenzo offered to exchange books in Casanova's collection with those of another prisoner. "They are novels, which I do not like."

These were "learned books, and if you think you are the only one with brains here, you are wrong," Lorenzo said. The prisoner agreed to the jailer's plan.

As the give-and-take got under way, Casanova, his fingernail sharpened to a point and daubed in the juice of black mulberries, wrote a concealed message in one volume. That drew a response from a Venetian patrician and monk named Marin Balbi, who indicated that he was prepared to embark on a clandestine correspondence concealed in the books they passed back and forth. Although Balbi cautioned that the two of them must conceal their messages, Casanova realized that Lorenzo would inspect the books and show any handwritten notes he found to "the first priest he came upon in the street." And so, "I at once decided that this Father Balbi must be a blockhead." Balbi boasted that he'd been sentenced for impregnating three virgins, each of whom bore a child baptized "under his own name" out of the "paternal love he felt for the poor innocents"—and because he was wealthy and their mothers were not. He advised his unseen correspondent, "There is no danger that my Superior will fall into the same fault, since his pious affection is shown only to his boy pupils." Balbi's posts also revealed that Lorenzo, their jailer, feared for his life if he was found to have provided Casanova with the tools to make the getaway. On the other hand, Signor Bragadin had promised Lorenzo a thousand zecchini to aid Casanova in his escape. Serving two masters placed the jailer in a precarious position.

In exchange for this intelligence, Balbi begged to hear more from Casanova, who fabricated a tale about a "big knife" that he'd concealed near the window close to his cell. Since Lorenzo hadn't gone looking for the knife, Casanova concluded the jailer must not have read the clandestine letters. Reassured, he recruited Father Balbi for his master plan to escape. "I began by asking him if he wanted his freedom and if he was prepared to risk everything to gain it by escaping with me." Father Balbi replied that indeed he was, but he attached a four-page list of obstacles to achieving that goal that "would have kept me occupied for the rest of my life if I had tried to circumvent them." Once the monk had gotten that off his chest, Casanova went ahead with his scheme.

As always, it was important to treat Lorenzo with care; the crafty jailer could aid or subvert their illicit enterprise. Casanova distracted him with giant bowls of gnocchi and melted butter and Parmesan cheese to celebrate the feast of St. Michael on September 29. It was a daring plan, and *sfacciato*—cheeky. Lorenzo agreed to bring a bowl to Father Balbi for the occasion, and Casanova placed it atop a large Bible concealing a bolt suitable for making a gaping hole. Carry the gnocchi carefully, Casanova warned the

jailer, "so that the butter will not spill out of the dish and run over the Bible."
Receiving the gnocchi, Bible, and bolt, Balbi blew his nose three times to
signal that all was in order, and took up the bolt, but after all that he'd removed only one brick from the wall by October 8.

Never mind, Casanova "had to do what I was doing or give up my whole
plan." When it came to a great enterprise, the thing was to execute it, not
talk about it. The same applied to Father Balbi, who returned to his labors,
and "removed thirty-six bricks from the wall." The escape was beginning to
take shape.

———•———

By October 16, as he was distracting himself by translating Horace's *Odes*—
poetic considerations dating from 23 BC of subjects as varied as love, nature, and the vanity of riches—Casanova heard a series of knocks from
the monk indicating that the excavation was nearly complete. "With a
companion," Giacomo estimated, "I felt sure that in three or four hours I
could make an opening in the great roof of the Doge's Palace," clamber on
to it somehow, and let himself down to the ground . . . just then his blood
froze when he heard his cell door open to admit Lorenzo, accompanying
the "beggarly scoundrel" destined to be Casanova's next cell mate. He was
a mess, filthy, bound hand and foot, scrawny, and wearing a "round black
wig." His name was Francesco Soradaci, and he posed a "fatal obstacle" to
the escape plan. He put on such an elaborate display of piety, praying and
searching for a crucifix or some other religious object on which to lavish his
devotion, that his behavior "made me think he took me for a Jew." Casanova
disabused him of that notion, at the cost of more time. He accompanied the
wretched man in all manner of Christian observance, even as he suspected
that his cell mate was a "monster" deserving of jail. Would these awful distractions never end?

Under cover of darkness, Casanova wrote to Father Balbi to resume
work; the moment of escape approached. The first three days of November were given over to a holiday in Venice during which State Inquisitors
and other prominent Venetians abandoned their palazzos for their villas
arrayed beside the Brenta, a bucolic waterway in the Veneto region, to the
south. With his masters away, Lorenzo was sure to get drunk. Once again,
Casanova took heart. "The greatest relief a man in misfortune can have is
the hope of soon escaping from it." To divine whether the hour had come

at last, Casanova consulted Ariosto's *Orlando furioso*, an epic poem in forty-six stanzas completed in 1532. "I worshiped his genius and I thought him far better suited than Vergil"—the traditional resource for divination—"to foretell my good fortune." Influenced by Kabbalistic training, and numerology, he scrutinized a stanza that mentioned a period between the end of October and the beginning of November. It seemed to him that the passage pinpointed midnight on October 31, and so he selected that moment for his departure.

Until then, he distracted his demented cell mate Soradaci by pretending to converse with the Holy Virgin, who admonished the cell mate to give up his perfidious ways and allow Casanova to go about his business. With all the gravity that he could muster, he predicted that the roof of the cell would open and an angel from heaven would descend to spirit them away, *if* Father Balbi vowed not to spy on Casanova. The dialogue persisted for hours, "and the comedy entertained me vastly, for I was sure the arrival of the angel would set the brute's miserable reason tottering."

The angel—Father Balbi—was scheduled to arrive in their midst at about two o'clock. When Casanova heard faint noises, he ordered his credulous cell mate, Soradaci, to fall to his knees. "He obeyed, looking at me like an idiot with unseeing eyes." Casanova prostrated himself, and pushed his cell mate to the floor. They remained supine until Balbi had completed his excavation and departed. As matters stood, Casanova calculated that they would escape on October 31. In the meantime, he fantasized about ways of ridding himself of Soradaci, strangling him, if possible, "as any other reasonable man more cruel than I would have done." As Casanova analyzed the situation, "his loyalty would last only as long as the frenzy of his fanaticism, which was bound to disappear as soon as he saw that the angel was a monk." As he stage-managed the escape, he was clearly taken with his own ability to manipulate his way to freedom, and, although he barely acknowledged it, the willingness of Lorenzo to allow the exodus from I Piombi to occur, a willingness purchased by Signor Bragadin on behalf of the young man who'd once saved his life. Other prisoners had died or gone mad in custody, but Casanova grew stronger and more resolute. The pleasure-loving gambler, would-be writer, social climber, and seducer displayed a fierce will to survive.

Before leaving, he cut off the beards of his fellow prisoners. Once he had trimmed his own whiskers, he climbed through the holes that he and Father Balbi had painstakingly dug. Creeping toward "an immense sloping roof covered with lead plates," he encountered yet another prisoner lurking in the darkness, who cautioned him against the perilous flight. "All I ask," Casanova declaimed, "is to go forward until I find freedom or death."

He set about boring a hole through the rotting timbers of the roof. "With each blow I made with my pike, everything it entered fell to pieces." It was all rotting away, a symbol of Venice's crumbling glory, vulnerable to the blows inflicted by a single individual. Having penetrated the roof to his satisfaction, he returned to his room, where he made a rope out of sheets and napkins, remembering to employ "weavers' knots, for a badly made knot could have come undone and whoever was hanging from the rope at that moment would have fallen to the ground." Then he went back to work on his escape route, planning to complete it by eight o'clock that evening, "Putting my head out of the hole, I was distressed to see the bright light of the crescent moon," which would cast too much light on the planned escape until it set after midnight. "On a splendid night, when everyone of any account would be strolling in the Piazza San Marco, I could not risk being seen walking about up there." They'd cast long shadows in the moonlight, the *sbirri* would take note, arrest them, and "ruin all my fine plans." But after the moon set, according to his calculations, they'd have seven hours of complete darkness to escape.

———·———

Retreating to Casanova's cell, the conspirators talked excitedly among themselves in anticipation of their getaway, with the exception of Father Balbi, who told him "ten times over that I had broken my word to him, since I had assured him in my letters that my plan was all laid and infallible, whereas it was nothing of the kind." If the monk had been aware of this uncertainty beforehand, he would *never* have cooperated!

With the escape at hand, they faced a host of practical concerns. The roof sloped at an angle so steep that they could not walk across it, or even stand. Their ropes would be of no help because they wouldn't be able to fasten them to the slippery roof. There was more: it would necessary for the first to abscond to let the others down to the ground by rope, as if lowering a bucket into a well. What would the solitary man left behind do? Whom would he betray to save his own skin? If they didn't kill themselves while trying to escape, they would likely be captured by *sbirri*, holiday or not. They had neither gondola nor boat at the ready. In their weakened condition they would have to swim for their lives, those among them who could swim, that is. And what if they lost their footing on the sloping leads, and fell? The shallow canal would not save their necks. If they were very fortunate, they might break their arms and legs, and once they were recaptured, find themselves back in prison under worse conditions and longer sentences. Casanova believed he prepared for such exigencies, but he preferred not to discuss his strategy with these untrustworthy companions.

In half an hour the moon would slip from view. At the moment a thick fog coated the roof with a slippery mist.

Soradaci sank to his knees, kissing his hands. "I am certain I will fall in the canal," he whimpered. "Leave me here and I will spend the whole night praying to St. Francis for you." Glad to be rid of him, Casanova granted the man his wish, and then turned to the monk, saying that the coward was unworthy of the honor of escaping with them, fully aware that Father Balbi was simply "another coward in whom I hoped to arouse some sense of honor."

Casanova turned his attention to composing a formal letter with pen, ink, and paper acquired illegally from Lorenzo, "who would have sold St. Mark himself for a scudo." In it, he set about memorializing his adventure, with the knowledge that he might be entering his final hours. The knowledge came over him that escaping from I Piombi amounted to the first— and very possibly, the last—significant event in his life.

Our Lords the State Inquisitors are bound to do everything to keep a culprit in prison by force but the culprit fortunate enough not to be on parole must also do everything he can to gain his freedom. Their right is founded upon justice; the culprit's upon nature. Just as they did not need his consent to lock him up, so he does not need theirs to flee.

Giacomo Casanova who writes this in the bitterness of his heart knows that he is liable to the misfortune of being caught before he leaves the State and returned to the hands of those whose sword he seeks to flee, and in that case he appeals on his knees to the humanity of his generous judges.

The note in his cell struck a more defiant tone: "Since you did not ask my permission to throw me in jail, I am not asking for yours to get out."

If he succeeded in escaping, Casanova instructed his jailers to bestow his belongings on the hapless Francesco Soradeci, whom he labeled a coward; indeed, "Casanova begs the magnanimous virtue of Their Excellencies not to deny the wretch the gift he has made him." With a final melodramatic flourish, he noted that he wrote "an hour before midnight without light" on October 31, 1756. He handed it to another prisoner, and "the idiot answered me that he hoped to see me again and return everything to me."

The moon slipped from view; the time had come to depart. Casanova secured himself to Father Balbi with ropes, donned a vest containing essentials, clamped his hat on his head, as did the recalcitrant monk, and so "we set forth to see what we might find" in the dark and fog, two hundred feet above terra firma. Casanova went first, followed by Father Balbi, while Soradaci returned the lead plate to its place.

On his hands and knees, Casanova slithered along the damp rooftop, guiding himself by the edges of the plates, and so, he writes, "I was able to help myself along to the top of the roof" as he dragged the monk, who kept four fingers of his right hand in Casanova's belt buckle so that Casanova felt "like a beast of burden at once carrying and drawing, and what is more climbing a slope wet from the fog." When the monk bleated that one of his bundles had come loose and fallen into the darkness, "my first response is the temptation to give him a good kick," but he resisted the impulse, recognizing that he needed the hapless monk to complete his escape.

They traversed sixteen plates or so and rested astride a metallic peak, surveying the fog-shrouded lagoon. Behind them stretched the island of San Maggiore, in front, the domes of St. Mark's, a prospect generally seen only by birds and spirits.

Catching his breath, Casanova put down his ropes and bundles, and instructed the monk to follow suit, but as he did, one of his bundles plummeted into the canal. A bad omen, the monk claimed.

Nonsense, said Casanova, a routine mishap; not even a superstitious person would consider it an augury. How fortunate that it fell where it did; if it had fallen into the courtyard, the guards would have discovered it, and "found some way to pay us a visit."

Every step invited catastrophe as he crossed a sea of wet panes. His time in jail had prepared him for the ordeal; had he escaped sooner he would

have been too soft and fearful to put himself to the test. Now he was ravenous for freedom.

Over the course of an hour he searched for places to drop their rope
and lower themselves to the ground, but without an obvious path he found
himself "in the greatest perplexity," yet he must advance, to be "bold but not
foolhardy." Contemplating his surroundings, he spied a dormer window in
the middle distance . . . he gingerly slid toward it—one slip, and he'd crash
to the ground—and by the time he reached it, as if by a miracle, the midnight bell from St. Mark's tolled, announcing the beginning of All Saints'
Day, and he recalled the enigmatic passage in *Orlando furioso* regarding the
end of October and the beginning of November that seemed to indicate
the proper moment to execute his plan. "The sound of the bell spoke to me,
told me to act, and promised me victory."

Grasping his bolt, he smashed the window and the wooden frame. His
hand bled from a superficial wound caused by the jagged edge of a broken pane as he removed the grating and returned to the monk, "desperate,
furious, and in an atrocious humor" at having been abandoned for two
hours. Casanova shushed him, and the two crawled back to the smashed
dormer.

Panicked, the monk endeavored to persuade Casanova to lower him
into the open space and rejoin him at the time of his choosing. Again, Casanova summoned his self-control in the face of this cowardice, but then
decided, *why not?* He looped a rope around the monk's chest and slowly
lowered him, feet first, to the floor of a loft.

Casanova estimated that the distance from his position on the rooftop
to the floor amounted to "ten times the length of my arm"—too far to risk
jumping, he might break his leg, or worse. At that moment, he stumbled
across a ladder used for repairs, fastened his rope to a rung, and struggled
mightily to push the ladder through the dormer window and into the opening below. That expedient might have worked, but it meant leaving the ladder exposed after his descent, signaling the *sbirri* of his whereabouts.

Instead, he positioned himself in the gutter and pushed the ladder toward the dormer while trying to maintain his footing, or risk tumbling
headlong to the canal below. If only he'd kept the monk close to help with
maneuvering the cumbersome ladder! Alone, he pushed, he pulled, he
dragged . . . at one point, he lost his footing and "my body dropped off into
space as far as my chest, till it hung from my two elbows."

As he pressed against the gutter to regain his balance, a vicious cramp "practically paralyzed me in every limb." After it relented, he clambered into the dormer, dragging the ladder after him, hurling his rope and bundles after him, and fell into the waiting arms of Father Balbi, who pulled in the ladder, safe from the *sbirri*, and greeted Casanova in triumph. "Arm in arm, we make the round of the dark place we were in, which might have been thirty feet long and ten wide."

They stowed their equipment, and at that moment Casanova succumbed to an "utter exhaustion of body and mind" and fell "so irresistibly asleep that I thought I was yielding to death." He and his feckless companion remained unconscious for three and a half hours until he was awakened by the monk's piercing cries. Even though it'd been a day or perhaps two since he'd eaten, Casanova felt invigorated from his rest and the realization they were not in a prison anymore but in a loft. "There must be a perfectly simple way of getting out of it." Yet he still found himself confined, trapped by the Doge's Palace and by all Venice, a prison of the body and spirit.

They forced their way past several doorways with the bolt, descended a "short, narrow stone stairway," passed through a glazed door, and found themselves in the Cancelleria ducal, an archive for storing decrees. He peered through a window; it would let him to the courtyard beside St. Mark's—"God forefend!" Instead, he searched for money—"God knows with what pleasure I would have appropriating it . . . by right of conquest." There was nothing to be had.

He cut through the door, a half hour of banging and cracking the wood, frightening the monk, who feared that it would summon a swarm of *sbirri*—"I knew the danger, but I had to risk it"—until he completed a hole bristling "all around with points jagged enough to tear our clothes and lacerate our skins." He placed a stool under it, the monk climbed onto it, and Casanova pushed him "out into a dense darkness." Repositioning the stool to suit his height, he entered the hole, lacerating himself, with no one to help ease him through, until the monk grasped him and pulled him through "without mercy" as he silently bore the pain inflicted by the wooden splinters.

Their pace accelerated as they passed through a doorway "as big as a city gate" leading to the Royal Stairs, or Scala dei Giganti, where, on the highest landing, the Doges are crowned. The doorway was locked. No bolt or knife could pierce it or pry it open. Casanova sank to the floor, telling the monk they've done all that they can, and it's up to "God or Fortune to do the rest."

Perhaps the palace sweepers will come, and they can make their escape, but on All Saints' Day, they're not likely to be at work.

They might die of hunger. The monk shouted at Casanova. *Madman! Liar!*

The clock struck seven in the morning. If they were to complete their escape, they must exchange their clothes. Father Balbi, in Casanova's opinion, looked like a "peasant," but at least he wasn't bleeding or in rags, and his leather breeches were intact. But Casanova had been "torn and scratched from head to foot," covered with blood. He stanched the wounds on his knees with his silk stockings. He tried to disguise his dire state by putting on clothes he's been carrying with him—white stockings, a shirt trimmed with lace. He draped his cloak over the monk's shoulders—it looked so out of place it seems as if he'd stolen it—and as for Casanova, he looked as though he left a ball and gone to a brothel, where he'd been "roughed up." At least he sported a fine *cappello* on his head, topped with a plume . . . this is Venice, after all, and he is Giacomo Casanova.

He rashly opened the window, attracting the attention of several slackers in the courtyard below who dispatched an attendant with a key to release the two of them without realizing they were escaped prisoners. The sound of approaching footsteps filled Casanova with anxiety. "In the greatest perturbation I get up, I look through a crack in the great door, I see a man alone"—his name is Andreoli—"wearing a black wig and no hat, calmly carrying the keys in both hands." Casanova stationed himself by the door, prepared to race down the stairs the moment the man opened the lock, willing to cut his throat if necessary.

The door swung wide and the man froze at the sight of the two trespassers. Casanova and Father Balbi charged past him (at an inquiry, Andreoli testified that Casanova collided with him and knocked him out cold) and rushed down the Royal Stairs as the monk insisted, "Let us go to the church!"

No! Casanova declared. "The churches in Venice do not enjoy the slightest immunity as asylums for any wrongdoer." The immunity he sought lies "beyond the boundaries of *La Serenissima*." He had escaped in spirit, "and I had to get my body there." His time in jail had been a rite of passage confirming his direst fears—that he is a wretched, unloved outsider with no hope—and his fondest imaginings—that he can master circumstances and emerge as the hero of his own story.

Casanova and Balbi strode past Sansovino's towering, virile statue of Neptune and approached the royal entrance, the Porta della Carta, looking neither to the left nor to the right. The pair crossed the Piazzetta, reached the quay, and entered the first gondola they saw, loudly ordering the gondolier to take them to Fusina, a village across the lagoon, a bit of misdirection. Casanova summoned a second gondolier to join them. And then: "I drop nonchalantly down in the bench, and the gondola at once leaves the quay." He and his bedraggled companion, "wrapped in my cloak," looked like a pair of "charlatans."

After fifteen months and five days in prison, he was free.

Their gondola rounded the Customs House at the southern end of Venice, and they headed into the Guidecca Canal, whereupon Casanova directed the gondoliers to take them to the port of Mestre, on the mainland, not Fusina; the alteration triggers an argument among them all, settled when one of the gondoliers announce, "We shall be in Mestre in three quarters of an hour, for we have the current and the wind is in our favor."

Casanova turned and looked down "the splendid canal; and seeing not a single boat and admiring the most beautiful day one could hope for, the

Casanova escaping from I Piombi, Venice, October 31, 1756

first rays of a magnificent sun just rising above the horizon, the two young gondoliers rowing at top speed, and thinking at the same time of the cruel night I had spent, of the place where I had been the day before, and of all the coincidences that had been favorable to me, feeling took possession of my soul, which rose up to a merciful God, setting the springs of my gratitude in motion, touching me with extraordinary power and so profoundly that my tears suddenly found fullest vent to relieve my heart, which was choking from an excess of joy." He cried "like a child forced to go to school."

——————

With more than a little irony, Casanova notes that "my charming companion thought it his duty to calm my tears, of whose noble source he was unaware." When they arrived at Mestre, on the mainland, Father Balbi vanished. "I look about, I ask where he is, nobody knows." Finally, "it occurs to me to stick my head into a coffeehouse, and there I see him, standing at the counter drinking chocolate and talking with the waitress." No one would have guessed that he'd just completed the most astonishing jailbreak in Venetian history. The monk gestured to Casanova to join him in a cup of chocolate. "I must pay," Casanova observed, "for he has no money." Gripping Father Balbi's arm so hard that it might break, he plunked a few coins on the counter and dragged the monk to a waiting carriage, where they confronted "a citizen of Mestre named Balbo Tomasi, a good man but one who has the reputation of being a spy for the tribunal of the Inquisitors."

"You there, Signore!" he shouted. "I am delighted to see you. So you have just escaped. How did you manage it?"

No, Casanova said softly, he'd been freed. Tomasi didn't believe him, and the fugitive realized that Tomasi might arrest him, "merely by winking at the first *sbirro*, of which Mestre was full." Casanova grasped him by the collar, gripped his pike, and prepared to run him through, at which point Tomasi ran off, occasionally turning to wish Casanova a good journey, until he disappeared from view. He doubted that Tomasi had any "evil intentions," but no matter. "My situation was dreadful. I was alone, and at open war with all the forces of the Republic." And he was still harnessed to the monk.

The two walked for hours, starving, exhausted. He tried to explain their predicament to the monk: "I am sure that we are now being searched for everywhere and our descriptions have been circulated so accurately that we should be arrested at any inn that we dare enter together. . . . So farewell."

"You promised we would never separate."

In frustration, Casanova took up a shovel and warned the monk, "I am going to bury you alive in this hole." If he chose to run away, Casanova would not give chase. The monk threw himself at his companion, and the two embraced, drawn together and pulled apart by their exploit. Casanova impulsively gave all his money, down to the last soldo, to the monk, who agreed to go his own way, but only when Casanova promised that they would reunite at an inn at the northern border of the Venetian State. Having accomplished the most delicate escape of all, he felt certain "that I should succeed in getting out of the State."

Casanova spied a distant village, and within it, a red house, and decided to spend the night there, even though it belonged to the Capitano della Campagna, "the chief of the *sbirri*"—the Inquisition's zealous police. Although logic dictated that he should avoid the place, an invisible force led him on. "I admit that in all my life I never took so daring a step"—in many ways. This was a time of transition, mental and geographical. He'd traded a world of accusation and dread and guilt over nameless crimes for the possibility of regeneration.

Entering the red house, Casanova paused to ask a child for his father; instead, the little boy ran to his mother, pretty and pregnant, who informed him that her husband had left on horseback days before with all his men. As if some demon had gotten ahold of him, he pretended familiarity with him, and requested a bed for the night, to which she agreed, offering supper, as well. She promised that her husband, the Capitano della Campagna, would greet him on his return home, but at the moment he was searching for two prisoners who'd escaped from I Piombi. "One is a patrician, and the other is a person named Casanova." Unfazed Casanova said he needed to go to bed at once.

"What is the matter with your knees?" asked the boy. Casanova explained that he'd taken a tumble while hunting on the mountain, and the boy assured him that his mother would tend to him. She, too, trusted in his story, oblivious to his torn white stockings, taffeta coat, and lack of a horse, treating him, he thought, "like a mother and always addressing me as 'son' while she was dressing my wounds." In another time and place, he would have expressed his gratitude with displays of physical affection, but this was not the moment, even after his months in prison. Allowing her to tend to his wounds, he fell asleep and woke around seven o'clock the following morning. When he realized his perilous circumstances, he dressed as quickly as he could and strode from the house, not pausing to look at the two *sbirri* hovering near the door, reflecting that he'd experienced only courtesy, hearty food, and much needed rest mingled "with a feeling of horror that made me tremble, for I saw that I had most imprudently exposed myself to the most obvious of dangers." He marched for five hours across the undulating countryside before daring to rest when he saw a little church. It was All Souls' Day, and the faithful were going to mass, and so would he, but when he entered the church, he confronted Signor Marcantonio Grimani, the nephew of the State Inquisitor, together with his wife, both of whom stared at him in bewilderment.

After mass, Signor Grimani demanded to know what possessed Casanova to attend mass at this church, and incidentally, where was his companion? As brazen as ever, he explained he'd paid the monk to go his own way, and now was headed for the border. "If Your Excellency would be so kind as to give me some assistance, I could manage better." He hadn't a soldo to his name. Grimani wouldn't give him any money, but he did want to know how Casanova had managed to escape from jail.

The subject of these inquiries excused himself as politely as he could, and resumed walking from one home to another, presuming briefly on the hospitality of the owners before he moved on, his arduous journey a recapitulation of his life on the fly until he came to a house he believed belonged to a friend, a "broker on the Exchange," who refused him anything at all. Incensed, Casanova shook the broker and threatened to stab him until he received gold pieces worth six zecchini—and ten times more, if he wanted it. "No, I am going, and I advise you to let me go quietly, or I will come back and set your house on fire."

That night he wolfed down a wretched dinner and slept on straw. In the morning he purchased a donkey, a tattered redingote, and boots, and rode in the chilly air toward Brento, about one hundred miles northwest of Venice, where he happened upon a figure in a green redingote and a hat with the brim turned down: Father Balbi, awaiting him at the inn Casanova had specified when the two parted. The monk evinced surprise; he hadn't expected wily Giacomo to keep his promise. Exhausted, he spent the next day at the inn, in bed, writing twenty letters addressed to Venice, in which he explained the trials he'd endured "to obtain six *zecchini*" from a broker who was indebted to him. At the same time, "the monk wrote impertinent letters to Father Barbarigo, his Superior; and to his patrician brothers; and love letters to the servant girls who had caused his ruin."

He left the next day, still yoked to Father Balbi; wherever they went the monk made clumsy advances at the servant girls. "Since he had neither the figure nor the face to make them kind and submissive, they received his approaches by giving him hearty slaps, which he received with exemplary patience." Casanova took modest pleasure in observing this sad behavior.

They reached the relative safety of Munich by mid-November, and soon after he deposited the hapless monk in the embrace of a receptive church. In fact, he was "delighted to get rid of him in such an honorable way." On his own once again, Father Balbi considered abandoning the priesthood, reasoning that if he were no longer a monk, the Tribunal in Venice would not consider him guilty. Venice saw things differently. He was recaptured and sent to a local jail, and ultimately returned to I Piombi—so Casanova later heard—for two years.

Rid of Father Balbi at last, Casanova sought refuge in Strassburg, Austria, two hundred miles northeast of Venice, rested at an inn for several days, and completed the final leg of his journey by coach to Paris, five hundred miles to the west.

———————

He arrived in Paris on January 5, 1757, a Wednesday. His friend Balletti, the dancer, took him to the family home in the rue Petit-Lion-Saint-Saveur. Casanova embraced Balletti's father and mother, "whom I found treating me just as they had done when I left in 1752." What's more, Balletti's seventeen-year-old sister, Manon, seemed "very pretty," especially in the eyes of a man who'd been imprisoned for more than a year.

But first, he attended to business, renting a room nearby and leaving that same day to call on his influential friend the Abbé de Bernis, with whom he spent so many libertine hours on the island of Murano. Formerly the French Ambassador to Venice, de Bernis was soon to become Secretary of State for Foreign Affairs, and Casanova "had good reason to hope that he would put me on the road to fortune."

Casanova learned that de Bernis had gone to Versailles, a short distance from Paris, and set off after him in a coach known as a "chamber pot." On arrival, Casanova discovered that his friend had already returned to Paris in the company of the Spanish Ambassador to Venice, and felt he had "no choice but to do likewise." But when he reached the gate, "I see a great crowd running in all directions in the utmost confusion, and I hear people crying right and left:

'*The king has been assassinated. His Majesty has just been killed.*'"

The Swing (1767), by Jean-Honoré Fragonard

Book Two

PARIS AND BEYOND

Chapter 10

Madame d'Urfé

On January 5, 1757, snow fell on the Palace of Versailles as man and beast shivered. Louis XV, who had ruled France for more than four decades, and whose popularity was rapidly declining, stayed indoors for most of the day. Accounts of the King's movements mention his calling on his daughter, Madame Victoire, who was suffering from influenza. At six in the evening, his coaches assembled to return him to his residence at Trianon. As the King walked along the Marble Courtyard, illuminated by torch-bearing sentries, a grizzled figure, later identified as Robert-François Damiens, slipped past the guards and stabbed the King between the fourth and fifth ribs with a small knife. Conspicuous in his hat, the assassin was quickly arrested.

Although bleeding, Louis XV remained calm, wondering if the blade had been coated with poison. "Somebody hit me," he said, bewildered. An onlooker pointed to the man in the hat as the culprit. "I am wounded, arrest that man, but don't hurt him," said the King, before making his way to his bedroom. Assuming death was imminent, Louis summoned his confessor and fainted. The Queen whom he'd neglected during his years of infidelity to her rushed to his side, and when he revived he asked her forgiveness. He vowed that if he lived, he would confess more fully. And he announced: "I completely and entirely forgive my assassin."

Louis survived the stabbing because, as Voltaire explained in his *Histoire du parlement du Paris*, the blade "struck the King through a very thick overcoat & all his clothes, in a way that the wound was fortunately scarcely more significant than *un coup d'épingle*"—a pinprick. The extent of the wound hardly mattered; Damiens had attacked the very heart of France.

A rumor spread that the King had been assassinated. "My terrified coachman thinks only of going on; but my carriage is stopped," Casanova re-

Robert-François Damiens, the would-be
assassin of Louis XV

called of that chaotic moment. "I am ordered out of it and put in the guard-house, where in three or four minutes I see more than a score of people arrested, all just as astonished and guilty as I am. . . . Since I do not believe in witchcraft I thought I was dreaming. There we were, looking at each other and not daring to speak . . . and every one of us, though innocent, was afraid."

Casanova hired another "chamber pot" for the return trip to Paris, but the roads were so crowded that the journey took three hours, during which time scores of couriers galloped past, "shouting the news to the four winds." From these couriers, he heard that the King had been bled, that the wound wasn't mortal, in fact, it was so superficial that "His Majesty could even go to Trianon if he wished."

On arrival in Paris, Casanova tried to dispel rumors that the King had been assassinated, to the tremendous relief of his friends the Ballettis, with whom he was staying, and "the whole neighborhood." He imagined they could sleep well because of the reassuring news he'd brought. On second thought, he realized the French harbored the same ambivalent relationship toward the monarchy that he'd noticed on his previous, more carefree visit. "In those days the French imagined that they loved their King," he observed. "Today"—that is, after the bloodthirsty French Revolution, when he is writing his memoirs—"we have come to know them somewhat better."

No matter, he was back "in the great city of Paris, and since I can no longer count on my own country, obliged to make my fortune there." He must avoid "dubious company" and, above all, avoid "the reputation of being a man not fit to be trusted with important business." There would be no more outrageous escapades; in their place, he "decided to practice a systematic reserve in both word and deed that would lead to my being considered even more fit for affairs of consequence than I had any reason to suppose I was." In other words, he would impersonate a worthy man. And he needed to look the part, "for I had neither suits nor shirts," when he presented himself to the Abbé de Bernis, soon to be a government minister.

At their meeting, de Bernis revealed that he'd read of the miraculous escape from I Piombi in letters written by their shared lover, Maria Eleonora Michiel, who longed to see the two of them again. Deprived of their company and affection, she wrote that "her life had become a burden to her." Nor was her confidante Caterina Capretta content with *her* new husband. How strange to think they preferred the confines of the monastery on Murano and its clandestine libertinism to the more settled circumstances of their current lives.

Perusing the letters from Maria Eleonora, Casanova saw at once that she had gotten many details of his escape wrong, and he promised to write an accurate account for de Bernis, and to give him permission to show it to those who could help Casanova in Paris. (Indeed, he would tell the story of his escape to anyone who wished to listen, so long as they pledged two hours to hear him out.) Coming to his friend's aid, de Bernis interceded with the Venetian Ambassador to France, the patrician Niccolò Erizzo, who declared he would neither pursue nor receive Casanova, "not wanting to compromise himself with the State Inquisitors." The minister added a piece of crucial advice: "Try to think up some project profitable to the royal exchequer, avoiding anything complicated."

Casanova expressed gratitude for the suggestion, but he remained "at a loss to find a way to increase the King's revenues." Under the erratic Louis XV, France had blundered into an awkward alliance with Austria in the Seven Years' War against Prussia. At the same time, France and England were fighting each other in the French and Indian War—an undeclared, bitter contest for colonies in North America. These conflicts had drained the French coffers and, combined with chronic famines, set the stage for the French Revolution. Amid these dismal circumstances, Madame de Pompadour was said to have turned to her King and prophesied, "*Après nous le déluge.*"

The only remedy that occurred to Casanova was to levy new taxes on the already overburdened populace—an impossibility. After several false starts, he found himself in the presence of the newly appointed Comptroller-General, Jean de Boulogne, Count of Nogent, again under the auspices of de Bernis, who had primed the bureaucrat to regard Monsieur Casanova as a financier of note. At that, Casanova "nearly burst out laughing." The Comptroller-General in turn introduced the gentleman from Venice to Joseph Pâris Duverney, who'd made a fortune selling supplies to French troops, and who'd helped rescue France from a previous financial crisis. Now he intended to fund an academy to train urgently needed French officers, the École militaire, on the Champs-de-Mars. The institution had opened its doors just six years earlier, and he needed twenty million francs to sustain it. "The thing is to find them without burdening the State or embarrassing the royal treasury," he explained. Casanova mastered the first rule of finance, always to maintain a serious expression and manner, and started thinking.

In Venice, merchants made money, as did brothels. He had no desire to become a tradesman, nor did he aspire to function as a pimp—not after all he'd endured. The way he and other Venetians made their zecchini was by gambling. *Gambling!* "I have a plan in mind that could yield the King the return on a hundred millions," he announced.

"And how much would such a yield cost the king?"

"Only the cost of collecting it," he replied. The French nation would supply the revenue, not through taxes, difficult if not impossible to collect, but *voluntarily.*

Having heard enough, Duverny invited the Venetian to dinner the next day. To prime himself for the event, Casanova promenaded around the Tuileries Garden, "reflecting on the fantastic piece of luck that Fortune seemed to be offering me. I am told that twenty millions are needed, I boast that I can furnish a hundred millions without having any idea how to do it."

———•———

At the grand dinner, Casanova met the leading financiers in France, to whom he bowed as elegantly as he could. After dining, Monsieur Duverney invited Casanova to join the men in the drawing room to discuss the finances of France. They presented Casanova with a plan that they assumed was precisely the same as his, a lottery. Why hadn't they adopted it, he asked. Would the King "not allow his subjects to gamble?"

The King had no objections to his subjects gambling, but, they all wondered, "How is the money to be raised?" And once raised, how would it be retained?

Casanova improvised his answer: the royal treasury would advertise that it would pay out—he named a figure off the top of his head—"a hundred millions." The sum would be sure to attract many players. And to the skeptical faces he explained, "The thing is to dazzle."

What if the King lost the money at the very first drawing? In that case, "the success of the lottery is assured," Casanova explained. "It is a misfortune to be desired." And he proceeded to give his audience a short lesson in the emerging mathematical concept of probability: "I will prove to you before all the mathematicians in Europe that, granted God is neutral, it is impossible that the King will not profit by this lottery." The way to keep the lottery honest and reputable, he explained, was "a scheduled drawing each month, for then the public is sure the backer can lose." The publicity resulting from that outcome would attract players, enrich the lottery, and underline the crown's credibility. "Were not all the insurance companies wealthy?" The lottery under consideration would follow similar mathematical principles, and the King would realize an annual profit of about twenty percent. The exact amount could not be guaranteed, it would fluctuate according to the laws of probability, but it wasn't the result of luck, he explained, or gambling. They would rely on the immutable laws of probability.

Next, Casanova addressed the Council of the École militaire. The plan was simple enough: a rotating cage known as a "Wheel of Fortune" held ninety sequentially numbered tokens. After players placed bets on the outcome, a facilitator selected five winning tokens from the Wheel of Fortune. Players could bet on a single number, a pair, or a trio of numbers. The odds of winning grew longer, and the payoff greater, with every increase in the number of tokens. (Later variations took the risks and rewards to dizzying heights.)

Over the course of two meetings, Casanova energetically defended his plan. Among those he seduced, intellectually speaking, were Jean d'Alembert, the *philosophe*, mathematician, and coeditor of the influential *Encyclopédie*; and an Italian émigré who'd made himself essential to the enterprise: Giovanni Antonio de Calzabigi, a diplomat. "Your fortune is made," he told Casanova after one of the sessions. "We have been moving heaven and earth for two years to get this project accepted, and we have never had anything for our pains but stupid objections, which you demolished last week." He proposed that the two of them join forces, along with his brother, who had devised a lottery format that strongly resembled Casanova's. The ambassador's brother was Ranieri de Calzabigi, a librettist born in Livorno, known for his collaborations with the composer Cristoph Willibald Gluck of the Paris Opéra. "He is ill," Giovanni said of his brother the librettist, "but his mind is perfectly active. We will call on him." And when they did, Casanova beheld a grotesque figure covered with scabs, "but that did not keep him from eating with appetite, writing, conversing, and performing all the functions of a man with health." He did not appear in public because, in addition to the disfiguring scabs, "he had constantly to scratch some part of his body, which in Paris is an abomination."

Casanova humored the librettist, and they went to work. "I found that he was very intelligent," he recalled, "a great arithmetician, thoroughly acquainted with theoretical and practical finance, familiar with the commerce of all nations, versed in history, a wit, a worshiper of the fair sex, and a poet." In fact, his brother "was inferior to him in every respect." Casanova was persuaded to join forces with them "without letting them know that I needed their help."

That night at dinner at Silva's, he was uncharacteristically silent, thinking of business, despite a distracting array of women present, including his friend's attractive young sister. He could only marvel at how he, a Venetian adventurer, fugitive, blasphemer, and charlatan, had seized a place among France's intelligentsia. "Two hours before dawn the next day I set off for Versailles, where Minister de Bernis received me banteringly, saying that he would wager that, but for him, I should never have discovered I was an expert in finance."

At the Palace, Casanova made his way to the power behind the throne, Madame de Pompadour—"Reinette," as she was called, or Little Queen— still the King's principal mistress in name but no longer in fact. During the years of Casanova's absence, she'd deftly consolidated her position at court, where she owed her influence both to the King and to the political situation. As Casanova paid his respects to Madame de Pompadour, she remarked that she considered his escape from jail "most interesting." And she ventured to jest about the Venetian State Inquisitors, who were "greatly to be feared." Casanova responded with a strained smile, as she expressed the hope that he was "thinking of settling among us." Indeed he was, but he required patronage, and had "learned that in this country it is accorded only to talent," a source of discouragement that Madame Pompadour suavely did her best to alleviate.

Later that night, when he returned home, he studied tables "of the entire lottery." They proved that so long as only five numbers out of six were drawn, it was "scientifically certain" that the lottery could not lose.

In the morning, at the École militaire, Casanova vigorously defended his plan, citing the precedent of insurance companies, "all of them rich and flourishing," who "laugh at Fortune and at the weak minds that fear her." Nothing could offer a better assurance of the outcome than the immutable laws of probability, and to clinch the deal, Duverney reminded the Council that they could abolish the lottery if they wished. All those present signed an agreement, and Casanova found himself the recipient of a generous share of the proceeds: an income of four thousand francs every year and the management of six sales offices.

The Hôtel de la Loterie in the rue Montmartre housed the principal lottery office. To bolster his income, he sold five of his six offices for two thousand francs each, netting another fortune before a single ticket had been offered to the public, and installed the sixth on rue Saint-Denis. He personally supervised this luxurious bureau, on occasion selling tickets himself. He had once thought to supervise a gambling establishment in Venice; now he had something in his grasp that was incomparably finer, a royal lottery. "Within twenty-four hours I had bills out to the effect that all winning tickets signed by me would be paid at my office in the rue Saint-Denis twenty-four hours after the drawing. The result was that everyone came to my office for tickets. My profit consisted in the six percent on receipts."

The first drawing was scheduled for April 18, 1758, and after settling all the winnings, "the lottery made a profit of six hundred thousand francs on

Gamblers in the Ridotto, Johann Heinrich Tischbein the Elder

the total receipts, which amounted to two millions. Paris alone contributed four hundred thousand francs." The lottery was a grand success, reflecting glory on Casanova, the Calzabigi brothers, and the other backers. The publicity accorded the winners only served to increase ticket sales in the future. "The rage being on, we expected the receipts at the next drawing would be twice as large." To many Parisians, Casanova personified the lottery. "In all the great houses to which I went and in theater lobbies, as soon as people saw me they gave me money, asking me to stake for them as I chose and to give them the tickets, for they knew nothing about it. I carried tickets for large and small amounts in my pockets, from which I let people choose, and I returned home with my pockets full of money." He went about town in a handsome carriage that imparted a "reputation and unlimited credit. Paris was, and still is, a city where people judge everything by appearances; there is not a country in the world where it is easier to make an impression."

Casanova's lottery generated a frenzy; Parisians rushed to purchase tickets. There were five drawings in 1758, and from then on, drawings took place once every month. As the French government groaned under the weight of mounting debt the lottery was later transferred from the École militaire to the crown, and renamed the Loterie royal de France. Drawings occurred twice a month, and the lottery proved far more stable than the regime it helped to sustain.

By this time, Casanova had welcomed his younger brother Francesco, the painter, now thirty-one. The two hadn't seen each other for six years, and held a cordial reunion. Casanova grandly offered to use his newly acquired influence to win admission for his brother to the French Academy, but Francesco replied that he didn't need Giacomo's influence. He had overcome his early setbacks and won renown. To prove his point, he exhibited one of his battle scenes at the Louvre, and he won admittance on his own together with twelve thousand francs for the picture. So Giacomo wasn't the only Casanova to make an impression in Paris. "After his reception my brother became famous, and in twenty-six years he earned nearly a million; however, extravagance and two bad marriages ruined him."

Giacomo Casanova, in contrast, evaded the snares of matrimony. Secure as his jittery temperament ever permitted him to become, he embarked on flirtations with the women of Paris, in particular, "Mademoiselle de la M-re," who has never been identified, and who proposed marriage to him by letter. "Do you understand that I cannot be happy unless I marry you or forget you?" she implored, and gave him four days to think matters over. She was striking, she loved him, she possessed a fortune, but, he decided, "I knew myself too well not to foresee that in a settled way of life I should become unhappy and hence my wife would be unhappy, too. My vacillation in coming to a decision . . . convinced me that I was not in love with her," yet he lacked the resolve to reject her plea and incur her wrath. And so he dithered.

Events overtook him, especially the impending execution of Damiens, who'd stabbed the King. All Paris was in mourning, as if Louis XV had died, although he was barely injured.

Crowds assembled to watch Damiens's punishment at the Place de Grève (now the Place de l' Hôtel de Ville). Not to be left out of the excitement, Casanova offered his acquaintances access to a "large window" from which they could view the "horrible spectacle." All that remained was to find one quickly, which he did, "a good window one flight up between two staircases for three louis," facing the scaffold.

A more delicate task involved formulating a reply for Mademoiselle de la M-re. Yes, he would marry her, and so would a hundred other men, but he needed time "to take a house, furnish it, and put myself in a position to be considered worthy to marry a girl of your position." He was ashamed to admit that, at the moment, he looked like an unkempt adventurer.

On March 28, the day of the execution, he hired a carriage to convey Mademoiselle de la M-re and several friends to the window he'd rented for the gruesome event. While his special friend sat in his lap, three other women "crowded in front of the window, leaning forward with their elbows to allow us to see" Damiens's agony. How could such bestial behavior occur in Paris, the epitome of civilization? That, according to Casanova, was the paradox of the French. No matter that Damiens had barely injured the King, "the populace at his execution called him a monster spewed up from Hell to assassinate 'the best' of kings," he noted, "yet it was the same populace that massacred the whole royal family, all the noblemen of France, and all those who gave the nation the fair character that made it esteemed, loved, and even taken as a model by all other nations."

On the appointed day, Damiens, judged guilty of "regicide" and wearing only a long chemise, was conveyed in a cart to the Place de Grève, where a scaffold awaited. "The citizens of near and far provinces, even foreigners, came for the festival," an observer recalled. "The windows, roofs, streets, were packed" with curious people who "strained for a closer look at the torture."

They saw the executioners secure Damiens and tear large pieces of flesh from his body. They then poured molten lead and sulfur into the suppurating wounds. When the sulfur was ignited, "the flame was so poor that only the top skin of the hand was burnt, and that only slightly." The acrid smell of burning flesh and sulfur wafted through the air. "Then the executioner, his sleeves rolled up, took the steel pincers, which had been especially made for the occasion, and which were about a foot and a half long, and pulled first at the calf of the right leg, then at the thigh, and from there at the two fleshy parts of the right arm; then at the breasts."

As the procedure advanced, "The clerk of the court went up to the patient several times and asked him if he had anything to say. He said he had not; at each torment, he cried out, as the damned in Hell are supposed to cry out, 'Pardon, my God! Pardon, my Lord.' Despite all this pain, he raised his head from time to time and looked at himself boldly. The cords had been tied so tightly by the men who pulled the ends that they caused him indescribable pain." Damiens summoned the strength to kiss a crucifix as the horses wrenched his limbs from his body, but the beasts gave out

The public torture and execution of Damiens, Place de Grève, Paris,
March 28, 1757

before they'd completed their task. The ropes were changed, the procedure repeated until his arms were pulled out of their sockets and broken
at the joints.

During the ordeal, Damiens cried, "My God, have pity on me! Jesus,
help me!" as a priest attempted to console him.

The executioner requested permission to sever the prisoner's legs. A observer recalled that the executioner and an assistant "each drew out a knife
from his pocket and cut the body at the thighs instead of severing the legs
at the joints; the four horses gave a tug and carried off the two thighs after
them." When it was over, the Place de Grève reverberated with applause.

Damiens was dead, but his mouth trembled as if he were talking or
praying as the executioners moved his body to a stake surrounded with logs
and dry straw. An executioner set the tinder ablaze, and the flames reduced
the body to ashes. The burning continued until eleven that night, charring
the surrounding grass. Afterward, the would-be assassin's torment inspired
no remorse. Damiens was referred to as *le monstre, le détestable assassin*, and
le parricide, as if he'd succeeded in his crime scheme rather than suffering,
in the words of one observer, the Duke de Croy, "the greatest tortures that a
human being has ever been called upon to endure."

Casanova still entertained his literary ambitions, having published a poem in a literary journal, *Mercure de France*, dedicated to "Camilla"— Giacoma Antonia Veronese, an actress, whom he'd met seven years earlier at Fontainebleau. When he reencountered her in Paris, he "fastened" on to her to gain entry to her salon near the Barrière Blanche, a customs checkpoint on the right bank of the Seine, where she lived with her wealthy young primary lover, Nicolas Rouault, the Count of Égreville. There Casanova went in search of Camilla. It did not suffice to be in love or to make love, one must be seen to be in love. Camilla doled out favors to a roster of admirers including the Count of La Tour d'Auvergne, "a nobleman of ancient lineage who adored her and who, not being rich enough to have her entirely to himself, had to be content with the share in her that she granted him."

Awaiting Camilla's favors, Casanova pursued a fifteen-year-old servant girl, "simple, ingenuous, without a grain of ambition," by the name of Babet, "enjoying her artless remarks with which she enchanted the entire company." His chance to have Babet to himself arrived when he found himself in a hackney coach—four wheels, two horses, very tight space—with Count La Tour d'Auvergne and the girl, who sat in Casanova's lap. "Wasting no time, since the coachman was driving fast, I take her hand, squeeze it, she squeezes mine, I gratefully raise it to my lips, covering it with silent kisses," but as he began to devour her, the Count interrupted:

"I am obliged to you, my dear friend, for a piece of your country's politeness of which I thought I was no longer worthy; I hope it is not a mistake."

Casanova froze on hearing these "horrifying words." The Count was upbraiding him in the most dignified way possible, made all the more painful when he dissolved into laughter that drew a quizzical look from Babet. Undone, Casanova "felt an utter fool" before disembarking from the carriage at his apartment, with the Count's peals of laughter ringing in his ears. Half an hour later, Casanova saw the humor of the situation and started to laugh himself, "for I saw that I must be the butt of many jokes."

Sensing Casanova's vulnerability, La Tour relentlessly taunted him, mincing like a girl when the two saw each other. He dared Casanova to appear at the salon to face Babet. Despite the prospect of severe humiliation, Casanova complied, and heard little Babet call him a "dirty swine." The confrontation led to an unexpected outcome: "For unfathomable reasons the episode turned me against her and attached me to La Tour d'Auvergne."

Perhaps the incident was not so unfathomable after all: servant girls came and went, but nobility was rare and to be prized, that is, until d'Auvergne vexed him again, this time over a sum of money. On a Monday, the "charming Count" suddenly needed a hundred louis that he promised to repay on Saturday. Casanova offered ten or twelve louis, the entire contents of his purse.

"The collector of the lottery must have over a thousand," the Count insisted.

"Of course," Giacomo replied, "but my cash box is sacred." A government agent collected the entire contents each week. The Count promised to replace the money on his "word of honor" before the collector arrived. Intimidated, Casanova went to his lottery office in the rue Saint-Denis, gathered a hundred louis, and gave it to the Count, who considered it his due. Saturday arrived, but the Count did not appear, and the following day, Casanova resorted to pawning his ring to replenish the cash box in time for the government agent to collect it on Monday. The Count La Tour d'Auvergne materialized later that week to apologize for failing to keep his promise and vowed to return the money by next Saturday. Casanova waved his hand at the Count to make light of the Count's promise—at which point, Casanova "saw the gallant nobleman turn as pale as a corpse." He'd insulted the honor of a French nobleman, "and the wrong can only be undone by the blood of one of us."

La Tour expertly staged the dénouement. By arrangement, the two men strolled toward the *Étoile*, the striking intersection of twelve avenues in Paris. When no one else was looking, the Count passed a roll of hundred louis to Casanova "with the greatest courtesy," and then stepped back four paces to unsheathe. One thrust from each man's sword should do it, the Count declared. Casanova lunged at the Count, convinced he'd wounded his antagonist in the chest. The Count lowered his sword, "put his hand to his chest, and, showing it to me stained with blood, said that he was satisfied." As the Count applied a handkerchief to his wound, Casanova spoke calming words. Had he defeated the Count, or had the Count, by blood sacrifice, conquered him?

No one knew of the duel. A week later, they were dining at Camilla's as if nothing had happened, and not long after that, Casanova found himself ministering to La Tour's debilitating case of sciatica with a mixture of poultices, incantations, and quasi-Masonic ritual. He then wrapped the

Count's thigh in three napkins, and advised him to remain motionless for twenty-four hours, after which he would be cured. Casanova considered his remedy shameless charlatanism, but the Count recovered. In gratitude, La Tour offered to introduce Casanova—healer, mystic, and lottery wizard— to his aunt, who was "dying" to meet him. This was a coveted invitation, for she was the Marquise d'Urfé. "I did not know her, but the name Urfé impressed me at once."

La Tour's aunt happened to be one of the richest women in France— and one of the most eccentric.

It was as if his quackery had led him to a new Bragadin, only this time his wealthy patron belonged to the French aristocracy. Jeanne Camus de Pontcarré had married Jeanne de la Rochefoucauld, the Marquis d'Urfé, to attain her noble rank. In her early fifties, she hosted a salon renowned for its exploration of the occult. Her regular guests included François-Joachim de Pierre de Bernis, the corpulent, scheming ambassador to Venice whom Casanova knew so well; Madame Bontemps, a socially adept fortune-teller to Madame de Pompadour; and the Conte Alessandro di Cagliostro, a sinister hypnotist and skilled counterfeiter who on one occasion forged a letter from Casanova.

In his insistent, unctuous way, Casanova told La Tour that he'd happily go to his friend's house at any time, so long as there were only three of them. "She has twelve people to dinner every day," La Tour d'Auvergne replied, "and you will eat at her house in the best of Parisian society." That, Casanova explained, was exactly what he didn't want, "for I loathe the reputation of magician," by which he meant a quack healer, a fraud and charlatan, despite his therapeutic gift, especially among the wealthy, but his friend was having none of it: "What you have done for me convinces me that you could have a brilliant and lucrative career." Casanova considered his treatment for sciatica nothing more than a "prank," and any healing that had occurred was strictly imaginary or inspired by the power of suggestion. The last thing he wanted was the reputation as one of Madame d'Urfé's cranks. "I absolutely declined to make a spectacle of myself."

Ultimately, he obtained a private audience with the lady, "who received me most courteously with all the easy grace of the old court in the days of the Regency," by which he meant a relatively informal period of court life, or so he imagined it, before the ascension of Louis XV to the throne. Throughout the pleasant, superficial conversation, "she was studying me as closely as I was studying her. Each of us was trying to trap the other into admissions." It seemed obvious that his hostess "could not wait to parade her lore" and, after La Tour left, she launched into a discussion of "chemistry, alchemy, magic, and all the things with which she was infatuated." He nonchalantly brought up the subject of alchemy—a long philosophical, mystical, and scientific tradition best known for the effort to transmute metals into gold—to which she responded with a "gracious smile" suggesting to Casanova that she "already possessed what was called the philosopher's stone" to perform alchemy, and more than that, "she was versed in all the great operations." She displayed her manuscripts about magic and mysticism to demonstrate the extent of her interest in the occult. She seduced him with a manuscript showing how to manufacture the "universal medicine," suitable for curing all illnesses. Her laboratory, on inspection, "really astonished me," for it contained a powder capable of transmuting all metals into gold in a minute's time. They discussed incantations and potions and symbols for hours, each testing the depth of the other's knowledge of the occult.

She impressed him when she discussed a "precious manuscript" that she kept under lock and key in an ivory casket, containing alchemical lore annotated with commentary by ancient scholars and philosophers from both Europe and Asia, men who, she brightly insisted, "were not dead." In another cask she kept a substance that Casanova called *patina del Pinto*, which she took to be silver, but was probably platinum, often confused with silver. (The name platinum derives from the Spanish word *platina* or "little silver.") She bolstered her alchemical bona fides when she confided that she'd been given the substance by the English inventor Charles Wood, who'd discovered platinum in 1741, and brought it to London in 1743, the same year he'd given it to her. "She showed me the same platinum in four different vessels, three of which contained it intact in sulfuric nitric, and hydrochloric acid, in the fourth, in which she had used *aqua regia*"—nitric acid mixed with hydrochloric acid. There was so much more in her laboratory; they talked of other chemicals, of spells and symbols, of the attributes of the invisible world.

Casanova realized he'd met his match in Madame d'Urfé the moment the conversation turned to the secret society known as the Brothers of the Rosy Cross—specifically, the oath, which could be "exchanged between men without indecency, but a woman like Madame d'Urfé must hesitate to give it to a man whom she was seeing for the first time." It became apparent that their descriptions of rituals were substitutes for more intimate transactions. When La Tour returned to his aunt's home that night, he found the two of them deep in conversation.

——·——

In the days to come, Casanova joined Madame d'Urfé's privileged circle, and met an array of characters—a physician "who bored me extremely," a monk (also a tedious fellow), and the ninety-year-old Chevalier d'Arzigny, who reminisced about the court of Louis XIV. His cheeks rouged, his coat adorned with antique pompoms, professing endless affection for his mistress while keeping company with other, younger girls, the old chevalier was a man after Casanova's heart. "This amiable though decrepit and shaky old man had such sweetness of character and such unusual manners that I believed everything he said." His grooming was marred only by his teeth, which "gave off an extremely strong smell, which Madame Urfé did not mind, but which I found intolerable."

Casanova saw a reflection of himself in another notorious participant, the Comte de Saint-Germain—a "scholar, linguist, musician, and chemist, good-looking, and a perfect ladies' man." What's more, he claimed to be three hundred years old and capable of melting diamonds. The Comte de Saint-Germain wormed his way into the good graces of Madame de Pompadour, who in turn prevailed on Louis XV—"a martyr to boredom," in Casanova's aperçu—to construct a laboratory to manufacture dyes at a cost of a hundred thousand francs, including lavish living quarters for the Comte in the grand Château de Chambord.

Once Casanova took his place among these charlatans, even Madame Urfé "believed that I was a genuine adept in the guise of a man of no consequence." He skillfully played on her longings for transcendence, no matter how far-fetched. When she expressed frustration at not being able to converse with spirits, he explained that he communicated by means of pen and ink. "I can even let you question him yourself by telling you his name," he offered: Paralis, the guiding spirit of his three elderly protectors in Venice. Deploying his Kabbalistic techniques, he converted her written queries into numbers, arranged them into a pyramid, and manipulated her into decoding the answer by converting the numbers into letters, at first consonants, later vowels, to arrive at "a perfectly clear answer, which surprises her."

Having worked his calculating magic on the woman, he left, "taking with me her soul, her heart, her mind, and all her remaining common sense."

He took to boasting that he was Madame d'Urfé's "only friend." As such, all her relatives were bound to treat him respectfully, and he dined with Madame "nearly every day." The servants "considered me her husband," even though he was young enough to be her son. He encouraged her to believe that he was rich and "had taken a post in the École militaire lottery only as a mask." He persuaded her that he possessed the philosopher's stone and could transmute metals into gold, and "converse with all the elemental spirits." Infatuated, "she believed that I had the power to turn the world upside down and determine the fortunes of France for good or evil." And Casanova saw no reason to contradict her.

Invoking her lack of standing as a woman in the spirit world, she proposed that Casanova would certainly know how to "make her soul pass into the body of a male child born from a philosophical union between an immortal and a woman, or between a man and female being of divine nature." It was anyone's guess what form that "philosophical union" might take. He lent his support "to the lady's crazy notions," which was not quite the same as deceiving her. He took to "drifting with the tide" of this lady with a great income from her investments and estates. Yet he was disappointed to discover that "Madame d'Urfé was a miser." She scrimped on herself and followed the advice of a broker; in this way "she had greatly augmented her portfolio." For all her success in investing, she told Casanova that she'd "give all she had to become a man," and, failing that, she was relying on him to carry out this "operation." He insisted he could never do such a thing, "because I would have to take her life."

"I know that," she told him. "I even know the kind of death to which I must submit, and I am ready." She had a mystical poison in mind: surely Casanova with his Kabbalistic connections could locate it in Paris. Further discussion revealed that she herself possessed the poison; all she needed for the concoction was semen "drawn from an immortal creature," for instance, Giacomo Casanova. She told him not to indulge in any "mistaken pity you may feel for my old carcass."

Casanova excused himself and went for a breath of air on the quay, where he passed a "quarter of an hour reflecting on her idiocies." He returned to her presence with eyes dampened, but his heart hardened, as he encouraged Madame to believe that he'd been weeping. And then he turned his back on his mark at the moment of conquest. Casanova would have his readers believe that he abandoned Madame d'Urfé at this moment but the prospect of success with her frightened him more than failure. He might find himself married to one of the richest women in France, but he'd be ensnared as surely as he'd been in I Piombi, living out his days as a reclusive alchemist confined to her laboratory, ruled by the folly of an eccentric woman intent on harvesting his semen for her "operations."

Casanova turned his attention to "the great scarcity of money" in the deteriorating French economy. The challenges went far beyond this symptom. The imploding French aristocracy, the endless Austro-Hungarian war, and a series of frigid winters had combined to deplete the treasury. Nonetheless, he was convinced that a monetary solution could be found by selling royal securities to brokers in Holland. He went about claiming that he'd been assigned to a clandestine mission to bolster the French economy. In the process, he schemed to increase his personal wealth. Passport in hand, he bid farewell to his friends in Paris, with the exception of Madame d'Urfé, "with whom I was to spend the whole of the next day." He'd put aside his misgivings about her alchemical "idiocies," but not for the sake of her bizarre appeal for his seed. Instead, he arranged to sell shares at her request in Holland rather than on the Paris Exchange "because there was no money there." In his absence, he authorized his clerk to sign lottery tickets at the office in his stead.

On October 15, 1758, he began the journey north.

At The Hague, he called on Tobias Boas, the most prominent member of the most prominent Jewish banking family in The Hague. Boas functioned as a kind of financial diplomat with excellent connections to the House of Orange, the most important dynastic order in Holland, and he interceded on behalf of Jews across Europe. Casanova considered this influential figure simply "the Jew Boas," but to his surprise, the banker extended hospitality toward the Venetian adventurer: "On leaving the Embassy I took a carriage to the house of the Banker Boas, whom I found at table with all his ugly and numerous family," Casanova noted. "He asked me why, since it was Christmas Eve, I was not going to rock the Infant Jesus to sleep; I answered that I had come to celebrate the Feast of the Maccabees"—that is, Hanukkah—"with him. He and his whole family applauded my answer, and he begged me to accept a room in his house." Briefly disarmed, Casanova accepted the offer, and "sent word to my valet to come to the house with my luggage, and when I took leave of Boas after supper I asked him to find me some good piece of business by which I could make eighteen or twenty thousand florins during the short time I intended to stay in Holland." Boas offered to consider the matter overnight.

In the morning he surprised Casanova by taking him to his study, giving him three thousand florins, and expressing confidence that he could easily make twenty thousand a week. No, Casanova said, he'd been joking, but Boas persisted, outlining a step-by-step strategy to buy ducats cheap from the Dutch Mint and sell high. Casanova admitted that he hadn't the resources to buy the ducats in the first place.

"Judging from the proposal you made to me yesterday," said the banker, "I thought you were a millionaire." Instead, Boas had one of his sons make the transaction, humbling Casanova in the process.

Later, his French contact cautioned Casanova not to discuss business with Jews, "the most honest of whom was only the least dishonest." Despite the assurances he gave to non-Jewish bankers, Casanova continued to do business with Boas, to learn the basics of Dutch finance from him, and to conduct several transactions with him on behalf of Madame d'Urfé, on whose behalf he arrived in Amsterdam on December 7.

———•———

In the wealthy capital city, he completed his financial transactions as his former whoring partner de Bernis tracked every move, and found his way to a banker whom he called Monsieur D. O.—a pseudonym for the Scottish banking family of Thomas and Zachary Hope. Of greater interest was Zachary's fourteen-year-old daughter, Lucia. "She was a beauty except that her teeth were not good. She was heir to all the wealth of her amiable father, who adored her. With her white complexion, her black hair, which she wore unpowdered, and her eloquent, very large black eyes, she made a great impression on me." She spoke French, played the harpsichord, and "was passionately fond of reading."

On New Year's Day 1759, he found himself alone with young Lucia and her neglected teeth in the splendidly furnished Hope household. After she finished playing the harpsichord, she inquired if Casanova was planning to attend a concert. No, he replied, because he was with her. She could hardly go alone. "I would be very happy to escort you, but I dare not hope as much," he said.

"You would be doing me a great favor, and I am certain that if you make the offer to my father he will not refuse you." If he did, he'd be "guilty of rudeness." Casanova remained skeptical of her offer. "I see that you do not know Dutch customs," she replied. "In this country unmarried girls enjoy a decent freedom; they lose it only when they marry. Go to him," she commanded, "go to him."

An hour later, her father having given his permission, she appeared before Casanova, radiant and ready to assist at the concert. "I could only have wished she used a little hair powder," he said of his pert, fourteen-year-old companion. "But [Lucia] was proud of her hair color, which made her complexion look even whiter. A transparent black fichu"—kerchief—"covered her bosom, which it revealed as just beginning to develop." Swelling with emotion, he begged to kiss her hand. Instead, she kissed him, as she would in her father's presence. So it was that Casanova received lessons in love from a fourteen-year-old Dutch virgin.

At the concert, Casanova was beguiled by throngs of attractive young girls. The orchestra performed a symphony, and then the singer, "highly praised under the name Trenti," took her place next to the harpsichordist. Teresa Imer! He vividly recalled her from their encounter eighteen years before in Venice, when "Old Senator Malipiero had given me a caning when he caught me in some childish naughtiness with her," and later, in 1753, he reckoned, "we had made love once or twice, not as children but as real lovers" before he was confined to I Piombi. Since then, Teresa had performed across Europe.

When Teresa, in the midst of passing her silver plate, recognized Casanova she "was very much surprised." As he placed a small roll of money on her plate, his attention came to rest on a little girl who followed Teresa. When the tot kissed his hand, "I was extremely surprised when I saw that the child had precisely my features." She stood still, staring at him, as he gallantly offered her bonbons, along with the box containing them. It was fashioned of tortoiseshell, but even if it had been solid gold he would have given it to her.

Laughing, Lucia said the child precisely resembled him. Casanova shrugged off the remark, yet he'd been shaken.

That night, as he consumed a plate of oysters, "Teresa and the girl appeared in my room. I rose to give her the ecstatic embrace that the occasion demanded." The girl appeared to faint, and he revived her with a few drops of cool water. The three of them proceeded to have supper and the adults regaled one another with stories of their years apart until seven o'clock the next morning. Not surprisingly, her misadventures, infidelities, and failed theatrical projects had landed her deeply in debt. Her husband, she claimed, had committed suicide "during a fit of madness brought on by intestinal pains; he had opened his abdomen with a razor and had died tearing out his entrails," and she'd fled to Holland to avoid prison. The debts of which she spoke were real, but the grotesque death of her husband more likely the product of her theatrical imagination.

As they talked, the lovers tried to rekindle their passion. Eventually Teresa declared that the girl, named Sophie, was Casanova's daughter, and produced a baptismal certificate. But was she? Casanova recalled that he and Teresa had been lovers in Venice "at the beginning of the Fair of the Ascension in 1753," in early May. Yet at that moment Casanova had been swept up in his affairs with Caterina Capretta and Maria Eleonora Michiel, and made no mention of Teresa. Sophie was born eight months later in Bayreuth, and had just turned six. Casanova pronounced himself persuaded by the unlikely story. What's more, "since I was in a position to provide her with the best education I was ready to take care of her."

If he thought his magnanimous gesture would win a ready-made family, he was mistaken. Teresa resisted the idea of giving up her daughter, calling Sophie "her jewel." If Casanova adopted the girl, he would "tear her soul from her body." As a substitute, he could assume responsibility for her twelve-year-old son, who lived in Rotterdam with a man "who will never give him to me unless I pay all I owe him." They agreed to meet again at The Hague, where he would pay to free the boy and claim possession of him. "The transports of her gratitude and joy were extensive," he remarked, "but they did not have the power to reawaken my old fondness, or rather, the old hankering I had for her, for I had never loved her passionately." For a quarter of an hour or more she hugged and caressed him, "but in vain." The fire in Casanova's loins had been extinguished in the Dutch winter. He "returned her caresses without ever giving her the proof that she sought that they came from the source to which Sophie owed her birth." Defeated, Teresa "melted into tears" and left with Sophie in tow, reminding Casanova that they would meet again.

He concluded his business negotiations, calculating that he'd bring Madame d'Urfé a better than expected return, which would persuade her of his honesty.

Amid a wondrous Dutch snowfall, he returned to the Hope house, where Lucia boldly teased him in her father's presence about spending the night at an inn with Teresa Trenti. With relief Casanova heeded the call from his hosts to put on ice skates and ventured onto the frozen Amstel River. "Since I am a complete novice at the sport, the reader can imagine that, having fallen abruptly on the hard ice at least twenty times, I thought I would end by breaking my back," but he survived to enjoy a midday dinner. However, "when we got up from table I felt as if I were paralyzed in every limb." Lucia gave him a jar of ointment to ease his aches and pains. "I realized the whole skating party had been got up only to make me a laughing-stock, and I saw nothing wrong in that." His unusually magnanimous mood was inspired by the hope that "so much submission and obligingness on my part" would endear him to Lucia.

When he awoke next morning, "I thought I was done for." His tailbone "seemed to be in a thousand pieces." An invitation from Lucia to give her a goodbye kiss before he left Holland finally roused him from bed. He found her "in a merry mood, with a complexion of lilies and roses," flirtatiously mocking him.

"I am certain that you would not have come if I hadn't used the word 'kiss,'" she said before surrendering to his "eager lips," which whetted his appetite for more. "Glimpsing the pink buds of her young breasts, I was about to lay hold of them, but as soon as she saw it she stopped laughing and defended herself."

He told Lucia he'd return to Amsterdam someday "in love only with her." She gave him such a sweet kiss goodbye that he "felt certain that she would grant me everything on my return. I left very much in love . . ."

Chapter 11

Miss Wynne

On arrival at The Hague, Casanova received a dinner invitation from his former lover, prospective mate, and would-be antagonist Teresa Trenti. "I found this most unusual woman on the fifth floor of a dilapidated house with her daughter and her son," newly arrived from Rotterdam, possibly with help from Casanova. In the middle of the room there was a table covered with a black cloth on which stood two candles. Because The Hague is a court city, I was richly dressed. The woman, clad in black with her two children, made me think of Medea." (In Euripides' tragedy, Medea murders her two offspring.) At least the appearance of the children dispelled his qualms. "Nothing could be prettier than the two young creatures. I fondly embraced the boy, calling him my son. His mother told him from that moment on he was to consider me his father." More evidence that Casanova paid for the privilege.

The two received one another into their lives politely, as Casanova reserved his attentions for little Sophie, whom he lifted onto his lap and covered with kisses. "For all her silence she enjoyed seeing that she interested me more than her brother had." She wore a light petticoat, he noticed, as his lips devoured "every part of her pretty body, delighted to be the man to whom the little girl owed existence." Sophie patiently submitted to his affectionate embrace, as she reminded herself that her real father was dead, and this strange man could be her "fond friend," as Casanova suggested, after which they gave one another "a good hug."

At dinner, Casanova assessed his "son," whom he planned to take along despite the boy's character flaws. "I discovered he was false, secretive, always on his guard, always preparing his answers in advance, and never giving answers from his heart." The boy covered his guile with a show of manners, which prompted Casanova to lecture him on the importance of sincerity.

When his mother, rushing to his defense, explained that she had taught the child such reserve, "I told her to her face that it was abominable, and that I could not imagine how a father could have any fondness for—let alone a predilection—for a son who never spoke out." He offered more advice: "The thing is to disclose your soul . . . and to reveal to me even things that might make you blush." Casanova arrived at the conclusion that his "newly-adopted son's soul was not so attractive as his person." Worse, he proved "incapable of friendship."

Casanova had an ulterior motive for subjecting Teresa's son to scrutiny; he planned to present him to Madame d'Urfé as the embodiment of her mystical longings for fulfillment. "The more I made his birth a mystery," he thought, "the more her Genius would lead her to invent wild fantasies."

Watching this give-and-take between Casanova and her brother, little Sophie started to cry. "*Why are you crying?*" asked her mother. "*It's stupid.*"

Sophie burst into laughter and kissed her mother. Casanova, observing intently, took the girl's affectionate gesture to be false, her tears real.

On January 8, 1759, Casanova returned to Paris, where he made straight for his patron, de Bernis.

"How long have you been in Paris?" asked the portly minister.

"No time at all. I just alighted from my post-chaise," or horse-drawn carriage. De Bernis directed Casanova to go to Versailles *immediately* to give the news of his financial success in Holland to the Comptroller-General. "You have performed miracles. Go and be adored."

De Bernis's urgency amused Casanova. "One does not go to Versailles at noon, but this was the way Ministers talked when they were in Paris. It was as if Versailles were at the other end of the street." Instead, he paid a call on Madame d'Urfé, who, on first seeing Casanova, declared that her Genius—her mystical guide—had foretold their reunion "that very day." She appeared to be overwhelmed by his financial success, and apologized for setting his fee so low, but he gallantly dismissed her concerns. He brought even better news, actually a bigger scam, for he now considered her his mark, whom he enticed with Teresa's son. Just mentioning the boy caused Madame d'Urfé to "tremble with joy." She immediately made plans to educate him in a prestigious Parisian boarding school.

He went next to the Comédie Italienne, the French version of the *com-*

media dell'arte, where he encountered a woman he called Madame XCV, the Greek-born Lady Anna Wynne. Six years earlier, he'd fallen in love with her eldest daughter, then sixteen years old, earning banishment by her mother. Casanova would have been more devoted, but "being then in love with Maria Eleonora Michiel and Caterina Capretta, I easily forgot her," that is, until this evening.

The young woman recognized Casanova, and pointed him out to her mother, who summoned him to their box with a flick of her fan. He received an affectionate welcome, especially from the daughter, who looked to him like a "goddess." He promised to call on the family after he visited Versailles the next day. There he boasted to the ministers, "I have an infallible plan for increasing the King's revenues by *twenty millions* without causing any complaint among those who will provide them."

"Execute it," a minister replied, and "the King himself will give you a pension of hundred thousand francs and a patent of nobility if you will become a French citizen." He would have a secure fortune and permanent standing at a stroke. Madame de Pompadour herself offered her good wishes, commiserating with him that he wasn't appreciated "down there" by Venice and its Inquisitors, but he'd soon be rewarded in Paris. As if to illustrate her point, a visiting Venetian patrician and poet, Tommaso Giuseppe Farsetti, glanced in his direction and inquired condescendingly if his post at the lottery paid well.

As Casanova renewed his contacts in Paris, he summoned the courage to call on Lady Anna Wynne, now installed at the Hôtel de Hollande in the rue Saint-André-des-Arts, approximately equidistant from Saint-Germain-des-Prés and the Seine. Despite appearances, Lady Wynne's origins were as suspect as Casanova's. She'd been born out of wedlock to an English father, Sir Richard Wynne, a baronet, and a Venetian mother who had struggled throughout her life to secure a place in society, as did Casanova, who annoyed her to no end. "He is attired resplendently," she admitted. "He has two beautiful diamond rings, two tasteful pocket watches, snuffboxes set in gold, and always plenty of lace. He has gained admittance, I don't know how, to the best Parisian society." In sum, this Casanova was "quite full of himself and stupidly pompous. In a word, he is unbearable. Except when he speaks of his escape, which he recounts admirably."

Casanova acknowledged that Lady Anna "did not like me, but she re-

ceived me very cordially. In Paris, and rich, I seemed another person to her."
And her alluring daughter retained her fascination: "It was difficult to be
near her and not fall in love with her," even if she appeared "cold without
being impolite." Yet he'd run out of patience with the girl's difficult ways.
"Unless it receives a certain amount of food, a libertine's love very quickly
becomes cold."

————•————

When he returned to Madame Urfé's, she wore a large magnet around her
neck, explaining that "it would draw lightning down on her and thus she
would go to the sun." The whole time, she clasped Casanova's "supposed
son" in her arms, and with a laugh he admonished the boy to treat Madame
as his queen. The boy revealed that Madame had directed him to sleep with
her. These developments furthered Casanova's plot; in fact, he "thought it
sublime." The boy in her bed "might be the person to assure her rebirth," as
she had been wishing, but, he advised, "she would spoil everything if she did
not wait until he reached puberty." Off the lad went to boarding school at
her expense.

To enjoy his newfound wealth, Casanova inspected several estates,
choosing Cracovie en Bel Air, situated in a tranquil Parisian suburb known
as Little Poland. The retreat featured two gardens, three apartments, a stable for twenty horses, baths, cellar, and "a large kitchen with all the necessary
pots and pans" all for rent at a hundred louis a year, including an excellent
female cook, Madame Saint-Jean, whom he called "The Pearl" for her value.
Within a week's time, the wandering adventurer had hired a coachman, two
carriages, five horses, a groom, and two liveried footmen. Venturing out,
he discovered that he could arrive almost anywhere in Paris within fifteen
minutes of leaving his suburban home, especially with his swift horses.
"One of the greatest pleasures in Paris is driving fast," he remarked.

When Madame d'Urfé visited his new residence, she cheerfully assumed that Casanova had acquired the estate *for her*, a misconception he let
stand. When Madame informed him that his "supposed son" belonged to a
secret Rosicrucian order, that he'd come into this world through a mystical
operation, and that one day "he would die without ceasing to live," Casanova
nodded solemnly in agreement, and she left the house "supremely content."

On another occasion the unlikely couple visited the philosopher Jean-
Jacques Rousseau living in straitened circumstances in Montmorency,

north of Paris. "We did not find what is called a pleasant man," Casanova lamented. Rousseau's maid-turned-girlfriend-turned-wife, Marie Thérèse Levassuer, displayed no interest in socializing, and "scarcely looked at us." Disillusioned by the encounter, "We went back to Paris laughing at the philosopher's eccentricity."

In pursuit of other women, he attended a masked public ball at the Opéra, but for once he was out of costume. "Not being masked," he recalled, "I was attacked by a female black domino who, telling me in falsetto many things about myself that were true, made me curious to know who it was." He enticed her to remove her mask; it was Giustiniana Wynne, hiding from her family and enjoying herself thoroughly.

Casanova tried to rekindle the flame for her, as he put it, even as they discussed her engagement to Alexandre Jean Joseph Le Riche de La Poupelinière, the wealthy sixty-six-year-old *fermier général*, or tax collector, for the King. He was a generous patron of music who maintained a private orchestra led by the composer Jean-Philippe Rameau. La Poupelinière had been touched by scandal ever since he banished his wife; yet, when he became seriously ill, she returned to care for him until she died from cancer. He lived on, acquiring mistresses who stubbornly refused to quit his large house on the rue de Richelieu.

It was Farsetti, Casanova's condescending Venetian rival, who introduced Miss Wynne to the aging Monsieur de La Poupelinière, who took an instant liking to her, and with her mother pulling strings, Miss Wynne became engaged to one of the wealthiest men in France. Although he guaranteed her a dowry of a million francs, she vowed never to consent to the marriage, saying she didn't want to make herself miserable "with a man whom I dislike." She had her other suitors to consider, and, in addition, she'd gotten herself into a serious predicament.

After paying several visits to the young Miss Wynne, who was often in bed when he arrived, Casanova received a letter delivered by her footman to his rented estate, Cracovie en Bel Air. It contained shocking news: "Here it is, dear Casanova: I am pregnant, and I shall kill myself if I am found out." In the next breath, she pledged "My whole being, and everything I possess, will be yours if you help me. I will be so grateful." If she could only rid herself of "the burden that dishonors me" Monsieur de La Poupelinière would provide for her. At no time did she reveal who the child's father might be. Instead, she implored Casanova to find her a doctor who could "lift me out of my misery," even "if necessary by force." She didn't fear pain, she wrote, and she'd pay the surgeon by selling her diamonds. She considered Casanova her "guardian angel," perhaps the first time anyone had conceived of him in quite that way, and she urged him to ask the "theater girls"—surely he knew the type—for a solution to her problem. She let out a heartfelt wail: "Oh God, if you only knew what I am going through!" She redoubled her plea. "I am in despair. I put myself in your hands. You must procure me an abortion."

"It is a crime," he reminded her.

"I know," she replied, "but it is no worse than killing one's self. Either [I will have an] abortion, or I will take poison." She had the toxin at the ready. "So, my only friend, you have become the arbiter of my destiny," she said as she dissolved into tears.

Casanova explained that abortion was life-threatening. "I will never take the risk of becoming your murderer, but I will never abandon you." As a middle way between abortion and suicide, he would provide a special drug, an opiate, on condition that she maintain secrecy, "for it is a matter of breaking the severest laws. It is an infringement punishable by death." He proposed to begin by bleeding her with the assistance of a midwife.

At that moment, he made an "outrageous" mistake—interjecting the Italian word *madornale* in his French memoirs. Instead of taking Miss Wynne to a proper midwife, he asked a madam named La Montigny for advice. She directed him to the Marais, where dwelled Reine Demay, an unkempt, disreputable woman in her thirties. He made an appointment for Miss Wynne without delay. "With a laugh she"—the midwife—"tells her without beating around the bush that she will be very easy to abort and she will accommodate her for only fifty louis," half to be paid now, half after the "miscarriage." Fifty louis! A considerable sum, even for Miss Wynne.

To recover from the ordeal, Casanova invited Miss Wynne to his suburban estate. "I thought the moment of my happiness was at hand."

———•———

On arrival, he commanded Pearl, his cook, to light a fire and prepare an omelet accompanied by champagne. The couple snuggled in front of the fire, with Miss Wynne offering no resistance to his advances until "she sees . . . I am about to reach the summit of triumph."

She would not let him finish. He pulled her to the bed "with gentle force," but she resisted. With a show of indignation, he proclaimed, "The mere idea of violence revolts me," as he began to plead his cause. Still frustrated, he sank to his knees, begging for forgiveness, until their lips met, and they held each other. He visited her the following morning and many mornings thereafter, restraining his yearning to the point that she taunted him for not loving her enough.

Entering her sixth month, Miss Wynne took to her bed, filled with demands. "She made me miserable," Casanova grumbled. Since she believed he no longer loved her, she cajoled him into examining her hips and belly. "I played the role of midwife, displaying a complete indifference to her charms," he explained, "but I was at the end of my rope." When she talked of poison now, he remained mute. At the end of his tether, he sought the advice of Madame d'Urfé about a "sure way to bring on an abortion." She recommended Paracelsus's aroph, infallible and easy to administer. Look at the manuscript, she advised, which "called for preparing an unguent of which the ingredients were powdered saffron, myrrh," and honey. "The woman who hoped to empty her womb was to put a dose of this opiate on the end of a cylinder of the proper size and insert it into her vagina in such a way . . . as to stimulate the channel leading to the closed door of the little house that sheltered the little enemy whose departure we sought. This procedure, repeated three or four times a day for six or seven days, so weakened the little door that it finally opened, and the fetus tumbled out."

When he visited Miss Wynne again, "in bed as usual and depressed because the opiate I had prescribed was having no effect," he extolled Paracelsus's aroph as an "infallible topical remedy for weakening the ring of the womb." In a burst of inspiration, he added that the aroph "had to be mixed with sperm that had not lost its natural heat for a single instant." In fact, "it is necessary for the sperm to touch the ring immediately upon coming out." In the absence of a lover, he explained, she required a "friend who would live in the house with her, and whom no one could suspect, to administer the amorous remedy to her three or four times a day." Casanova was surprised that he'd "rattled off this nonsense with all the earmarks of truth yet completely on the spur of the moment."

Miss Wynne accused Casanova of cruelty; he'd never loved her, not now, not *ever*, and with that she burst into tears. Moved, Casanova fell on his knees before her, and she began to cooperate with his plan. He prepared the aroph, bribed the servants, especially the English chambermaid, Magdelaine, to cooperate with his scheme. It emerged that she, too, had a secret lover, the kitchen boy, who had to be brought into their confidence.

At the appointed time for the procedure, Miss Wynne concealed herself in a garret with the assistance of her chambermaid. That night, Casanova appeared, shutting the door behind him, and barricading it. By the light of a single candle, "we undress very fast, entirely dispensing with the preliminaries that always precede our performance when love leads up to it." They played their roles as surgeon and patient to perfection, Miss Wynne lying on her back, spreading her thighs, raising her knees, arching her body, as Casanova, holding a candle in one hand, applied the aroph to the orifice with the other. He added his sperm to the mixture. "The astonishing thing is that we neither laughed no felt any desire to laugh, so engrossed were we in our roles."

When the act was completed, "the timid Miss Wynne blew out the candle, but two minutes later she had to let me light it again." Although he was convinced they had executed the procedure perfectly, she wasn't at all sure. "I obligingly said that I did not mind repeating the performance," and so he entered her again. "The second time the application of the remedy took a quarter of an hour, and she assured me that it had been perfect. I was certain of it." Perhaps they should sleep? But they had no need. Instead, Miss Wynne yielded to him again, and then, "Another preparation, another combat to the most successful conclusion, which was followed by a long sleep."

In the morning, she returned to her room, and Casanova slipped out through a hidden door revealed to him by the kitchen boy whom he'd bribed. And when he paid a call on Miss Wynne at noon, "she outdid herself in thanks, which really exhausted my patience."

———•———

The effort to induce an abortion having failed, Miss Wynne intended to flee to avoid marriage to La Poupelinière, and begged Casanova to help her. He pretended to sympathize, but in reality he had no intention of being found guilty of abducting her or, for that matter, "uniting our destinies by marriage." The thought of marriage to anyone, even an attractive, wealthy young woman, was anathema. Better a convict than a spouse. No jail could hold him for long, but the married state with its financial obligations, children, and restrictions was inescapable.

In search of a way out, he turned to a confidante who arranged for Henriette Marguerite de Mérinville, the abbess of the Prieuré de Notre-Dame de la Conception, to hide the unfortunate unwed mother in a convent in Conflans, near Paris. Not even her family would know of her whereabouts. After giving birth, she would go to confession, and receive a "formal certificate" from the abbess to present to her mother, who, the abbess predicted, would be happy to see her, and, seeing that she'd run off to avoid marriage, cease to press her daughter on that matter.

He brought the welcome news to Miss Wynne in her garret at ten o'clock at night. "I put out the candle, and we spent the night like real lovers without any further thought of aroph."

Miss Wynne entered the convent on April 6. A month later, she gave birth to her child, said by Casanova to be a "fine baby boy." Possibly he was placed in an orphanage, his name and fate unknown. Lady Anna Wynne, Monsieur de La Poupelinière, and various family retainers streamed to the convent, where Miss Wynne greeted them while concealed behind a grille in the visitors' area. La Poupelinière declared that he was still ready to marry Miss Wynne, but the thought of joining his seraglio was unbearable to her, and she resisted his suit.

As the weeks passed, she went for walks, she lost weight, and she appeared at the convent grille to tempt La Poupelinière on his occasional visits. In time, the scandal surrounding the events died down, and she left the convent to rejoin her family.

In July, the Wynnes, including Giustiniana, moved from Paris to London, and returned to Italy in 1760; she was twenty-three years old. The following year, she married Philip Joseph, Count Orsini-Rosenberg, the wealthy, elderly Austrian Ambassador to Venice. The couple had no issue. In her later years, she turned to writing, and when Casanova came across her book, *Du sejour des comtes du Nord à Venise* ("Visits of Northern Counts to Venice"), he wrote to the author to praise her "easy and unpretentious style," for which he received a curt note of thanks from the woman who'd once promised him everything.

———•———

Disengaged at last from the Wynnes, Casanova resumed his libertine's existence. "The style in which I lived in Little Poland made it famous. Everyone talked about the excellent table I kept. I had fowl fed on rice in a dark room. They were as white as snow, with an exquisite flavor." In addition, "I matched well-chosen guests with exquisite suppers, as my company saw that my pleasure depended on the pleasure I provided for them." While in this effusive mood, "Ladies of distinction, all of them versed in love, came during the morning to walk in my garden with unseasoned young gallants who did not dare open their mouths, and whom I pretended not to see." Those who caught his eye found themselves the recipients of fresh eggs and butter from his pantry. He professed to be "delighted with this life," yet he needed at least one hundred thousand francs a year to maintain it, and at the rate he was spending money, he'd soon be broke.

He sought escape from his dilemma in a new venture inspired by a man "sent by Heaven to provide me with an income above even my hopes. He talked to me of the extravagant profits made by silk manufactories." This individual claimed "there was a vast fortune to be made" by pricing the locally produced wares at about a third of their Chinese competition to "make a profit of a hundred percent." With this proposition, "he definitely captured my interest." Casanova's source had a point; fashionable Europeans at the time were enthralled by chinoiserie, Chinese designs applied to bolts of fabric, especially silk. If he could make them cheaper, his chinoiserie would find an enthusiastic market in Paris. "I congratulated myself that I would become rich in a manner that would recommend me to the State." He performed his due diligence, having "thoroughly investigated receipts and expenditures and engaged or made sure of trustworthy persons"; carried samples in his pockets to impress his friends; and rented workspace, cost be damned.

He hired twenty pretty women between the ages of eighteen and twenty-five to decorate the silk. He took an interest in one—never named—and gave her lodgings. "The example of the first one was enough to make them all demand a house and furniture as soon as they saw that they had aroused desires in me." His flings lasted only three or four days, but he went on paying their expenses long afterward. His problems worsened when a financial backer absconded with the assets and proceeded to sue Casanova. The final blow fell when the Seven Years' War halted sales. "I had four hundred pieces of painted fabrics in my storehouse," he complained, "and there was no likelihood of selling them before the peace."

The debacle forced him to consider his circumstances. "The life I was leading was that of a happy man, but I was not happy." He felt as if he were impersonating himself, trying without succeeding to become the libertine he imagined himself to be. Although he'd won and lost more wealth and status in Paris—*Paris!*—than he'd ever enjoyed in Venice, he remained distracted and ill at ease. "I amused myself," he said, "and the pleasure I took in spending money lavishly kept me from thinking of the future."

The longer his exile from Venice, the more Venetian he became. He whiled away his evenings with a succession of barely remembered women while carrying on a complicated relationship with his primary mistress, Manon Balletti. After reencountering Casanova, Manon had broken off her engagement to her music tutor, Clement, and began writing in secret to her new love, only to find herself thrust into an emotional whirl, revealed in a series of letters, forty-one in all, composed in a mixture of French and Italian.

In April 1757, she'd written to Casanova, "I wish no other thing more than to see your love for me last forever, [but] will it? I know you will rebel against my doubt. But finally, my friend, isn't it up to you to stop loving me, or to love me forever?" Casanova remained maddeningly indifferent to her. "There were times when I figured that perhaps you might love me back and that you gave me no sign of your love because circumstances did not allow you." She had her faults, but she urged him to look at her soul and decide. He turned the pages, considered her words, and did nothing.

In May, she wrote of her mother's frantic efforts to find her a suitable husband. Fortunately, this matchmaker was taking her time, "thank God!" Manon remained fixated on Casanova. "Love me, my dear Casanova, love only me, and make me happy!" She warned Casanova that if he put off seeing her, "I will go to sleep without supper, I will not write at all." Not only that, but she'd been struck with a "pain in my eyes."

She intensified her attack in subsequent letters. "I am writing to you, sir, to tell you how furious I am with you, to tell you how I'm convinced I am of your scant love for me." How was it possible for him to show her so little regard and "so little love?" Her feelings of sadness and grief were overwhelming. "God, am I angry with you, and even more with myself!" He was "the most ungrateful of men."

Casanova still couldn't bring himself to marry her, even though he loved her. "She kept saying I was deceiving her," he lamented, acknowledging that she spoke the truth.

Throwing the matter into sharp relief, Manon's mother, Silvia, died of consumption "in her [Manon's] arms and mine," in Casanova's words. "Ten minutes before she expired, she commended her daughter to my care." He did the only thing he, a libertine, could do: "I promised from my soul that I would make her my wife, but Destiny"—his exit from the hasty commitment—"was against it."

———•———

Casanova sold his interest in the Chinese silk painting enterprise to an investor. He received his share of the proceeds, but a robbery entangled him in financial squabbles. He fired all the girls he'd employed, and he retained an advocate who assured him he had nothing to worry about.

At eight in the morning of August 23, 1759, while driving in his carriage, Casanova was arrested by the chief constable, who escorted him to For-l'Évêque, a state prison for debtors and actors. "As soon as I got there the record clerk told me that if I paid fifty thousand francs or gave security, I could go home at once; but having neither the money nor the security ready I remained in prison." Demanding writing materials, he penned urgent letters to Madame d'Urfé, his brother, and all the friends whose addresses he could recall to ask for help. Manon Balletti, his neglected mistress, sent a pair of her earrings as security; a friend sent her advocate; his brother did not answer. And Madame d'Urfé wrote to say that she expected him for dinner. "I thought she had gone mad." He proclaimed himself "extremely annoyed" to be detained over a business fraud in which he'd considered himself the victim rather than the perpetrator. Aside from the "discomfort of prison," his embarrassing situation "could not but hurt my reputation all over Paris." A rumor that he was to be hanged cheered his enemies.

At that moment, a jailer freed him and confided that "a lady was waiting for me at the door in her carriage." His savior was Madame d'Urfé, who greeted him "with great dignity." (In his memoirs, he writes that he spent only "a few disagreeable hours" in prison; in reality, his incarceration lasted two days.) She advised him to "go walking in the Tuileries and the Palais-Royal at once, to convince the public that the rumor of my imprisonment was false. I took her advice." During his promenade, he observed "all my acquaintances were astonished to see me." He returned the earrings to a tearful Manon, and dined with Madame d'Urfé, who joked that he'd planned his arrest simply to start people talking about him. Her quip contained a grain of truth: whether in anger or admiration, he adored hearing the sound of his name. Afterward, he returned to Manon Balletti, "who was delighted to have seized the opportunity to give me a proof of her affection." After they made love, "Her joy knew no bounds when I told her I was going to give up my manufactory, for she thought my working girls were the reason why I could not make up my mind to marry her." Manon was neither the first nor the last to believe she would become Casanova's wife.

He decided the commercial life was not for him "My soul was in torment every time I had to curry favor, spend my money on advocates, and waste my hours, which I thought only well used in procuring me pleasure." What he needed, he told himself, was a "regular income sufficient to give me complete peace of mind." And so he decided to "abandon everything." He would return to Holland to "renew my financial resources," as he put it, then return to Paris, invest the money wisely, and marry Manon Balletti. "I informed her of my plan, and she could not wait to see it executed." Perhaps he even believed this fantasy himself, but his deeds told a different story. In his frenzy to purge, he gave up his estate in Little Poland and withdrew from the lottery and the École militaire, his principal anchors in Paris. "I resigned my paltry position of collector of the lottery," he explained, and turned over his office to his clerk, who made himself a small fortune from the windfall. "I sold my horses, my carriages, and all my furniture," and still more painful, "I left Manon in tears," clinging to his promise to return. With these swift strokes he undid nearly everything he'd accomplished since arriving in Paris.

On December 1, 1759, he set off in a post chaise with a hundred thousand francs on his person. In his pocket he carried an inflammatory work by the French philosopher Helvétius, De l'esprit ("On Mind"), sure to raise eyebrows among those who saw it. In Amsterdam he halfheartedly pursued his plan to make enough money to wed Manon, who complained mightily in his absence. "How can one stay more than three months with people who stink of cheese, smokers, tea-drinkers," she wrote, imagining him adrift in an alien environment "without chairs, nor bed, and evil at best! Oh, my dear friend, come back already." Poignantly, she concluded, "I am your wife who loves you tenderly."

He soon learned that was not necessarily the case. A bolt from the blue struck, "and nearly killed me."

The letter from Manon Balletti, in Paris, was dated February 7 (1760). "Be reasonable and receive the news I send you calmly," she began. She enclosed his letters, two hundred in all, as well as his portrait. "Return my portrait to me, and if you still have my letters, burn them," she commanded. He was to think of her no more, and she would do everything in her power to forget him. The reason was simple: she would soon marry Jacques François Blondel, fifty-five, an architect and member of the Académie royale d'architecture. In conclusion, she advised, "You will greatly oblige me if, when you return to Paris, you will pretend not to know me."

He contemplated his portrait with pain and sorrow. "My countenance, which had been cheerful before, now seems threatening and angry." Although he'd never demonstrated an abiding affection for Manon, her abrupt rejection pitched him into emotional chaos. He began to write a reply to her, tore it up, and started again, but could not adequately express himself on paper. He had a bowl of soup for supper and went to bed. Unable to summon sleep, he formed a wild plan: he'd go to Paris "and kill this Blondel whom I did not know and who had dared to marry a girl who belonged to me." He seethed endlessly, ignoring his own compulsive infidelities. Confined to his room, he wrote and discarded more letters. "My empty stomach sent vapors to my head which prostrated me; when I recovered, I raved, talking to myself in fits of rage that lacerated my soul." He was to attend an important Freemasons meeting at The Hague with "all the notable Freemasons of Holland," but was unable to make himself go. Instead, he ruminated about Manon, who, it seemed, had presented his last hope for happiness, the last time he would find a place in a Venetian family that would accept him, and where he felt at home. Their unrealized romance hinted at darker passions lurking beneath the era's diaphanous surface.

The Scottish banker, Hope, dispatched his daughter to tend to Casanova. Her calming presence helped to restore his equilibrium, as she fed him bowls of broth and chocolate to restore his well-being. "She was a treasure willing to be mine," he noted of her lust for intimacy, "which I could not give her." With her help, "I began to think that I did not hate Manon but felt contempt for her; analyzing this new feeling gave me hope and courage." As the Hope girl read through his correspondence, she found herself falling in love with Casanova through words he'd written to another woman. "These accursed letters will be the death of me," he muttered, and asked her to help burn them.

"Give them to me instead; they shall never leave my hands."

She took an interest in Casanova's romantic inventory, especially O-Morphi, and he complied. How much easier it was to talk about love than to be in love. "The portrait of Maria Eleonora Michiel as a nun and then stark naked made her laugh." Later, when he desired her, she let him kiss her "rose and lily face." Soon enough, he made contact with her "alabaster bosom." They began to feel they were born for each other. So Casanova discovered that the best cure for a broken heart was a new love. He spent two more days with her, reading the twelfth-century love letters of Abelard and Héloïse, as his fingers probed for the secret between her legs until she rearranged herself "to expose it to view." He looked carefully. There it was, a mark on her labia minora, "no bigger than a millet seed." He knelt and brought his mouth close to the glistening membrane. "She let me kiss it until I almost lost my breath." They spent "two hours in amorous toying without ever coming to the great act, which she was right to refuse me." At some point she told Casanova it was time to discuss marriage. Of course, he could no more marry this girl than he could Manon. He turned the conversation to the Kabbalah. She beseeched him to instruct her. The Kabbalah would be their bond. In the morning he brought her books about alchemy and mysticism that "were sure to entertain her." Having completed his task, he excused himself. He was off to Germany on business, he said mysteriously. He promised to see her again by year's end, and of course he never did.

"Such is the whole story of my second stay in Holland, where I accomplished nothing to better my fortune," but when he looked back, "I conclude that love made up for everything."

At the end of March, Casanova arrived in Stuttgart, where he joined actors, dancers, theater people from Venice in search of work and diversion from the chilly climate. Lodged at The Bear, he fell in with three personable officers—terrible judgment on his part—who prodded him to gamble until he'd lost all his money. The officers took him to a brothel, forced him to drink doctored wine, and stole his possessions. Casanova had no excuse for his recklessness, only his own stupidity. "My head was spinning so fast that they had to send for a sedan chair to take me back to my inn. As he undresses me my valet says I have neither my watches nor a gold snuffbox." In this tableau the supine Casanova personified the Libertine, the Adventurer, and the Gambler, the emblems of the age.

The three officers called on him promptly at nine the next morning to collect their debts. "Gentlemen," he announced, "I have lost an amount that I cannot pay, and that I should certainly not have lost were it not for the poison you made me swallow in your Hungarian wine." A shouting match erupted. Casanova gave his antagonists a choice: they could settle the matter in court, or they could "take it out on my body in all honor and in complete secrecy, one at a time and sword in hand." Rather than beat him, they preferred that he paid them—in full—and then they would kill him.

He resolved to go to court, plead his case, and defeat the three officers through fair and legal means. Three days later, he was summoned to give a deposition to a notary. "I spent two hours with the man, who wrote down in German all that I told him in Latin." He was told to sign, but he refused on the grounds that he couldn't understand the German text of his deposition.

In the morning, an officer politely informed him in French that he was under arrest in his room at the inn. A sentry had been posted at his door, and he was required to yield his sword, which he surrendered with the greatest reluctance. "It was steel, worth fifty louis, and had been a present to me from Madame d'Urfé." His friend Binetti advised him that if he wanted to regain his freedom, he should sacrifice every bit of his gold and diamonds to his "pretended creditors," yet he couldn't bring himself to give up his rings, watches, cases, portraits, and other precious items, all of which came to about forty thousand francs, in his estimation.

An advocate taking his case explained that witnesses would be found to testify that he was a suspicious "professional gambler" who'd lured the three officers to the gambling den, and while he was away defending himself against these charges, "officers of the court will come here and empty your two trunks, your strongbox, and your pockets, everything will be listed, and everything will come up for auction the same day," and if the proceeds didn't cover his debts, he'd be enrolled as a "common soldier in the troops of His Most Serene Highness," a destiny that "petrified" Casanova. He felt that "all the fluids in my body were seeking an outlet": the same reaction he'd suffered on arrival at I Piombi in Venice.

Before he was incarcerated Casanova wrote to the police magistrate, promising to sell all his possessions to satisfy his creditors in exchange for his freedom. The negotiations over the timing of the sale bought him a few days to maneuver. He summoned three Venetian allies—named Balletti, Binetti, and La Toscani—and revealed his "decision to escape without losing any of my belongings." Binetti endorsed the plan, telling Casanova that once he reached Binetti's house, the open countryside would lead him to freedom. La Toscani promised to supervise his trunks, and Balletti offered his wife's assistance. The idea of escaping with all his possessions except for his carriage struck Casanova as difficult, "but not so difficult as escaping from I Piombi." Soon La Toscani was busy hiding two of his suits under her skirt. Three other women visiting him on successive days also walked away with his possessions concealed beneath their clothing. His escape was planned for the next Sunday, a few days before his thirty-fifth birthday, April 2, 1760. It seemed to him that throughout his life momentous events occurred around that anniversary.

That night, "I put a wig-block in a nightcap on the bolster and propped up the covers in such a way that anyone would be deceived." As conspirators distracted the sentry guarding the room by drinking with him, Casanova waited for darkness, armed with a hunting knife and two pistols. After dark, he crept out of his room, tiptoed down the stairs, and passed through an open door "without meeting anyone." It was shortly before midnight. He ran to Binetti's house, where his wife opened the door and quickly guided him to a window through which he would escape. "Balletti's wife was there to help let me down, and her husband was in mud up to his knees to catch me." The women put a rope around his chest under his arms, held tight to the two ends, and "gradually let them out in time with my very smooth, easy, and completely safe descent. Never was any man better served." He savored the thrill of another escape, symbolically eluding the constraints of morality and mortality.

On the ground, he ran through the mire, sinking to his knees, scaling hedges, until he reached the high road, where a carriage arranged by Balletti awaited him.

"After supping well and sleeping even better," he recalled, he wrote identical letters to the three officers who'd been the cause of his misery, challenging one and all to a duel. He vowed to wait three days for them to appear, "hoping to kill all of them and thus become famous throughout

Europe"—as if the Continent took notice of his misadventures. This was another instance of the grandiose fantasies that occasionally came over him. If he couldn't attain status through respectability perhaps he could do so through notoriety.

The days passed, the officers failed to appear, but "the innkeeper's daughters made the time pass as pleasantly as I could wish."

On the fourth day, Casanova received an urgent warning to flee to Switzerland to avoid being murdered by henchmen hired by his three antagonists, who had been infuriated by the decoy he'd arranged before his escape. Arriving in Zurich, he lodged comfortably at a renowned inn, The Sword. "Alone after supper in the wealthiest city in Switzerland," he reminisced, "I give myself up to reflections on my present situation and my past life. I recall the good and the bad that has befallen me, and I examine my conduct." He'd done nothing but abuse "all the favors Fortune had accomplished for me. . . . I shudder and decide to stop being Fortune's plaything." As a stay against chaos, he would invest his money "to secure a permanent income subject to no fluctuation." Lulled to sleep by this comforting thought, he dreamed of enjoying his freedom in the countryside until he suddenly awoke at dawn, restless and angry. "I get up, I dress, and get out, not caring where I am going."

He trudged along ruts worn into a nameless road, refusing to ask for directions from the peasants he encountered. Six hours later, he stood on a plain surrounded by four soaring mountains. He wandered toward a distant church, "and I feel glad that I am in a Catholic canton." At the conclusion of mass, the Benedictine monks offer an impromptu tour of the "extremely rich ornaments, chasubles covered with large pearls, and sacred vessels covered with diamonds and other precious stones." Lacking German, he conversed in Latin with the abbot, who insisted that Jesus had personally consecrated the church and "shows me on the surface of the marble five concavities that the fingers of Jesus Christ had left in it." The abbot, "delighted by the obedient attention with which I listened to this nonsense, asked me where I was lodging."

"Nowhere." Casanova had made the journey to Zurich on foot.

The abbot raised his hands to thank God for bringing this sinful stranger to the church—"to tell the truth, I have always looked like a great sinner," Casanova interjected—and invited him to dine with the monks. At the repast, he learned that he'd arrived at Our Lady of Einsiedeln, revered for its Black Madonna, darkened by centuries of candle smoke. Within this refuge from past sins and present dangers, "I breathed again."

Amid the thin mountain air and the susurrus of monks, he contemplated a return to the monastic life he'd known as a young man. The abbot advised Casanova to deliberate for two weeks before deciding. During that interval, he familiarized himself with the monastery's library, esteemed for its collection of incunabula—books printed before 1500. He noted "Bibles, commentators, the Fathers, several legists"—authorities on Roman law— "and Hoffman's great dictionary" in four volumes, dating from 1668. Experiencing a reawakening of his scholarly impulses, he could happily have remained amid these massive volumes, free from the turmoil of the libertine's life. "It was then that I first felt a desire to become a monk, but I did not tell him so." Instead, he made a "general confession of all my manifold sins." There was a lot to discuss. "In less than three hours I told him a quantity of stories that were scandalous enough but devoid of literary grace since I had to use the style of the penitent." The abbot dispatched the new arrival to a chamber to devote the day to prayer, although Casanova had a different idea: "To be happy I thought I needed only a library."

To keep occupied, he studied German for three hours each morning, with little to show for his efforts. To his amusement, his instructor "solemnly termed all monks the vilest scum of the human race." He said the monks of Our Lady of Einsiedeln in particular were nothing more than "a gang of eighty lazy, ignorant, vicious hypocrites, real swine," and the abbot himself a "clown."

———◆———

After two weeks of indoctrination, on April 23, Casanova happened to gaze out the window early one morning to see a woman attired in a riding habit—*en Amazon*, as he put it—a brunette, with a lily complexion, rose cheeks, and a blue satin bonnet from which dangled a devastating silver tassel. When she caught sight of her admirer in the monastery, she turned in his direction, cried out, and then, shocked at herself, burst out laughing.

"Defend yourselves, mortals, against such an encounter, if you have the strength," Casanova warns in his memoirs.

He threw himself on his bed to regain his composure. He heard the "Amazon" was coming to the monastery with two female companions for supper prior to performing her devotions the following morning at six. He hit upon the idea of borrowing a waiter's green apron with which he'd serve the ladies at their table. It would be a most delightful diversion. He adopted just the look of "baseness and false modesty demanded by the part I am to play." Later, at the ladies' table, he nimbly carved a succulent capon rubbed with coarse salt. Noticing his skill, the Amazon asked if he's been in service for long. Only a few weeks, he replied, adding, "You are too kind." At that moment she noticed the "magnificent lace" around his cuff, unusual for a servant. The gift of an Irish nobleman, he modestly replied.

Early the next morning as he served her again, his "eyes breakfasted on her alabaster breast." When she bid him fetch her boots, he begged her to allow him to lace them. She regarded him with disdain and departed. In his frustration, he found his way to "some young and mercenary beauty"—two of them, in fact—and enjoyed a "sufficiently amusing time" with them until midnight, paying for the privilege.

He did see the Amazon one last time as she prepared to depart, having learned her name: Baroness Marie Anne Louise Roll von Emmenholtz. Recently married. As he watched from his window, she climbed into her carriage in the rain, removing her blue satin bonnet adorned with the tassel and saluted him with a gracious smile.

To be considered worthy of the Baroness and others of her class, he took to calling himself the Chevalier de Seingalt. He had already impersonated a baron, much to his enjoyment, and this new title had a more adventurous ring to it. A "chevalier" was an archaic name for a knight; the title also applied to a high rank in various French orders of merit, usually conferred by a monarch. The name Giacomo Casanova sounded common, but the patrician Chevalier de Seingalt hinted at secret assignations, espionage, and wealth beyond measure. The longer Casanova maintained the pretense, the more letters and manuscripts he signed with this title, the more persuaded he became of his manufactured identity. With it, he repeatedly crossed the line between fantasy and fraud.

By the end of April, the Chevalier de Seingalt left Zurich for Lucerne and Bern, Switzerland, where he lodged at a snug, comfortable inn, La Couronne, and continued to pursue the Baroness. At the same time, his patroness in Paris, Madame d'Urfé, sent a letter introducing him to the Marquis de Chavigny, the long-serving French Ambassador in Venice. Casanova had naturally heard all about him, and could "scarcely wait to make his acquaintance." The two got along famously, with Casanova at his most unctuous and charming, until the Marquis startled him by saying that two ladies had told him he wasn't the Chevalier de Seingalt after all, he was a waiter who'd served them when they were on their way to make their devotion. Of course the story couldn't be true, could it?

It was both true and not true, Casanova explained. He'd disguised himself as a waiter to court a woman, who, needless to say, had already been promised to another. Disguises and masks came naturally to him. He was always playing a role to suit his fancy or further his ambitions.

Casanova's romantic intrigue delighted the Marquis, and the two maintained their friendship while Casanova lived in a small rented castle and wooed the Baroness. One night, he nearly achieved his goal, but at great cost. After supper with his inamorata and several other guests, he announced that he was retiring to his room to write. Before he did, he set out in search of her. "I grope my way around half the house. I go to the open door." At that moment, "I feel a grip. The hand she puts over my mouth tells me I must not speak. We let ourselves fall on the wide couch, and I instantly attain the height of my desires." The summer night was brief; he had only two more hours with her. "I used them to give repeated proofs of the fire which was devouring me to the divine woman I was sure I held in my arms. I thought that her decision not to wait for me in her bed had been supremely farsighted, since the sound of our kisses might have wakened her husband. Her furies, which seemed to exceed mine, raised my soul to heaven, and I felt certain that of all my conquests this was the first in which I could rightly take pride."

The first inkling that things had gone wrong occurred the next morning, when he encountered the Baroness, who blurted out, "I did not go to sleep until four o'clock, after waiting for you in vain. What mishap kept you from coming?"

"Horror-struck," as he put it, he realized that he'd bedded another woman, whom he called Madame F., instead of the Baroness! It was more than a faux pas; it was an insult to the social order. "I felt I was dying. To keep from falling I leaned my head against a tree." Perhaps the Baroness was trying to deny their meeting, which would be her right, but he could not imagine a woman of such fine sensibility capable of such base behavior. By now he knew the brutal truth; Madame F. had duped him, and how she'd managed it he could not tell. How could the "infallible tribunal of all my senses" have failed? "Touch alone should have sufficed." He cursed Love,

Nature, and his own weakness, and sentenced himself to death—after he tore apart the woman who'd duped him.

"Somber and speechless," he retired to his room to read a letter from the "happy who had made me the most wretched of men." Her words were even more wounding than he'd imagined:

"For ten years I have had a slight indisposition that I have never been able to cure," wrote Madame F. "You did enough last night to contract it; I advise you to take remedies at once. I warn you, so that will be careful not to transmit it to your beauty, who in her ignorance might give it to her husband, and to others." Each phrase twisted the knife. "If you need a doctor, impress discretion on him," she advised, "for it is known . . . that I suffer from this little ailment, and people might say you got it from me." As her malevolence sank in, he contemplated the misery of treating his eighth case of venereal disease. There would be no love affair with the Baroness, and no revenge on the false-hearted Madame F.

He had only himself to blame. "I spent a cruel night, which has always been a most unusual thing for a man of my temperament," he recalled. And when he rang for his housekeeper in the morning, "she said I looked like a corpse" as she served him breakfast. "No sooner had I drunk my chocolate than I vomited it up." If he hadn't known his servant had prepared it for him, he would have thought Madame F. was trying to poison him. "A minute later I vomited all that I had eaten for supper and, with great effort, a bitter, green viscous phlegm."

Exhausted, he slept for seven hours and, having composed himself, received a visit from a "surgeon for treatment."

———•———

As he recovered, he fashioned his revenge on Madame F. He replied to her letter, telling her that she was badly mistaken: "Know, monster from hell, that I did not leave my room, so you spent two hours with God knows whom." He added that if he'd read her letter in her presence, "I would certainly have pursued you and killed you with my own hands." Having vented his spleen on paper, "I sent it to the wretch who had made me wretched." An hour later, he sent another screed to announce that his valet had recently discharged "symptoms of the pox," and, said Casanova, his valet admitted that he'd "received this fine gift" from her. Apparently she'd mistaken the valet for Casanova. In closing, he congratulated her on having enjoyed in her imagination a pleasure that she "would certainly never have obtained in reality."

She wrote back a few brief lines to insist that she hadn't fallen for any of Casanova's lies.

Undaunted, Casanova dispatched his servant to threaten Madame F. with legal action. She'd knowingly infected the blameless valet, who needed money for a cure. Under pressure from Casanova, the offending woman eventually capitulated, writing back: "I am in despair that I have harmed an innocent person, and I willingly pay the penalty." She included twenty-five louis for the valet's treatment, and a plea to keep the matter in "the strictest silence." If Casanova did not comply, she wrote, "you must fear my vengeance."

Casanova replied with a vengeance of his own: "Learn, wicked woman, that the world is not entirely peopled by monsters who set traps for the honor of those who hold honor dear," and having discharged that volley, he repaid the money she'd sent with the valet. Casanova expected that his servant would return after having delivered the message, which he did after an anxious delay.

But the next morning, Casanova "saw the first symptoms of my wretched disease." Fortunately, within a few days, "I saw that it amounted to very little," and a week later he considered himself cured.

Through it all, he entertained his sweet-natured, innocent housekeeper with stories, often blunted for her sake, of his misadventures. As the days passed, they switched from the formal *vous* ("you") to the casual *tu*, a sign of their growing rapport. "She listened with the utmost interest when I recounted my vicissitudes in love." When she detected he was concealing something, she "urged me to tell her everything plainly," and so he obliged. When he recounted finding the "millet seed" mark on the labia minora of the Scottish banker's daughter, the housekeeper collapsed with laughter and fell into his arms. "In her spasms of laughter she could offer me very little resistance." His adventures with other women acted as an aphrodisiac on the housekeeper. There was almost as much pleasure in "overfaithful descriptions" of intimate acts as in performing them.

Still unable to have intercourse because of his highly contagious pox, Casanova and his housekeeper caressed one another until they happily reached their mutual "crisis." They looked at each other, and the housekeeper, no longer completely innocent, told him, "My dear friend, we love each other, and if we are not careful, we shall not long confine ourselves to mere trifling."

———·•———

By the time he reached Lausanne, Casanova craved intellectual stimulus as much as erotic provocation. In this Protestant stronghold, a refuge for French Huguenots, he deployed his letters of recommendation from Madame d'Urfé to meet eminent scientists and philosophers, some of whom he recalled from his student days in Padua, when they had lectured there. Among the most prominent was Albrecht van Haller, the Swiss physician and botanist, classicist, and poet, whose best-known verse, "The Alps" ("Though Nature spread with stones the barren land, The plough yet tames your soil, and harvests grow"), was far removed from Casanova's Venetian sensibilities. Haller's access to Voltaire, who lived nearby, mattered greatly to Casanova. Voltaire was, as everyone knew, the nom de plume of François-Marie Arouet, the author of innumerable books and pamphlets. In Casanova's mind, the two men were of equal stature, a delusional but telling opinion. In reality, his literary reputation was negligible, whereas Voltaire—wit, playwright, polemicist, *philosophe*, and historian—ranked among the leading figures of the Enlightenment. "When I told him that I was eagerly looking forward to making the acquaintance of the famous Voltaire, he replied without a trace of bitterness that I was justified in wanting to make his acquaintance, but a number of people had found him, despite the laws of physics, 'greater at a distance than close at hand.'"

Realizing that Haller could arrange an invitation to Voltaire, Casanova's opinion of the Swiss doctor shot up, and he impressed Casanova by having been married three times—and widowed twice. "The stout Swiss was a learned man of the highest order, but in the most unostentatious way possible."

In the morning, during the coach ride from Lausanne to Geneva, he engaged in a spirited debate with a Calvinist pastor, whose rational, robust embrace of his faith amazed the Venetian, who, despite everything, clung tightly to Catholicism. "There were no mysteries for him, everything was reason," marveled Casanova, of whom the opposite was often true. "I never encountered a priest to whom Christianity came as easily as it did to this worthy man." Still, when the two debated papal infallibility, and Casanova began "quoting the gospels, I struck him dumb." After all, he had trained as a priest.

Their unlikely camaraderie deepened when the pastor mentioned his twenty-year-old niece. "She is a theologian and pretty."

"God keep me from arguing with her," said Casanova, finding his tongue.

"She will force you to argue, and you will be very glad of it, I promise you."

In the evening, as Casanova arrived at his inn, Á la balance (The Scales), he glanced at a window, and saw the words *You will forget Henriette, too.* She'd scratched them into the glass pane a dozen years earlier. Seeing them now, "I felt my hair stand on end." He was haunted by the memory of their passion, the most idyllic he'd ever known, and by her sudden disappearance from his life. Her prediction, of course, did not hold true; he would *never* forget her. "Noble and fond Henriette whom I had so greatly loved, where are you?" He yearned to rush to Henriette's side, if only he knew where to find her.

Instead, he was distracted by the prospect of coming face-to-face with Voltaire. Would some of the great man's moral stature rub off on Casanova?

Chapter 12

The Black-Eyed Nun

This is the happiest moment of my life," Casanova exclaimed, or so he would have Voltaire believe. "At last I see my master; it is twenty years, Monsieur, since I became your pupil."

"Honor me with another twenty, and then promise to bring my wages," Voltaire, now sixty-six, replied, in the same jaunty spirit.

"I give you my word, and only death—not I—will break my word."

Shortly before Casanova appeared, Voltaire had published *Candide, or Optimism*, a satire on the resolutely cheerful philosophy of Gottfried Wilhelm Leibniz and, by extension, the self-serving, hypocritical ethos of the French ruling class. He lived on an estate near Geneva called Les Délices with Louise Denis, née Mignot, who was his housekeeper, niece, and, more recently, his lover. With a Voltairean wink, he proclaimed himself the "innkeeper of Europe." His latest guest was Giacomo Casanova.

At their initial meeting, the two tested each other's knowledge of language, literature, and philosophy by discussing the eminent minds of the era—Isaac Newton and Bernard Fontenelle, among others.

"Do not French terms of expression make your language more beautiful?" Voltaire artfully inquired of his tall, anxious visitor. (This, of course, was Casanova's recollection of their encounter.)

"They make it more intolerable," replied the young challenger, "just as French stuffed with Italian expressions would be, even if it were written by you."

"You are right," said Voltaire. "One must write purely." A new thrust: "To what branch of literature have you devoted yourself?"

None, Casanova parried, to conceal his scant literary output. "I read as much as I can, and I indulge myself in studying humanity by traveling."

That is one approach, Voltaire conceded, "but the book is too big. The easier method is to read history."

François-Marie Arouet Voltaire and his
companion Marie-Louise Mignot Denis

"History lies," Casanova retorted. "One is not certain of the facts; it is boring; and studying the world on the fly amuses me."

They crossed swords over poetry both ancient and modern—Casanova in his intellectual element, for once—with Voltaire delighting him by reciting from memory two passages from Ariosto's *Orlando furioso*, "never skipping a line, never pronouncing a word except in accordance with strict prosody; he pointed out their beauties to me, with reflections that only a truly great man could make."

Casanova listened without breathing, without blinking, trying in vain to catch the great man in a mistake—just one!—but there was none, only his observation that flawless Voltaire was "insatiable for praise." And all the while Madame Denis, a literary figure in her own right, looked on approvingly and challenged Casanova to recite from memory thirty-six stanzas of the epic poem. He complied, speaking "as if they were prose" rather than emphatically declaiming the verse, "animating them by voice, eyes, and the varying intonation necessary to express feeling." He held his emotions in check until "tears burst from my eyes so impetuously and abundantly that everyone present shed tears, too." Voltaire ran to embrace Casanova, who kept his distance as he wept his way to the end of his recitation, and at the conclusion, "somberly received the congratulations of the entire company."

Voltaire's declared, "To draw tears, one must weep one's self; but to weep, one must feel, and then the tears come from the soul." Vowing to recite the same stanzas the next day, also weeping, Voltaire insisted that his talented guest stay "for at least a week." The two bickered good-naturedly, and compromised at three days.

———•———

During this interval, Voltaire drew out Casanova on the subject of the Venetian government, "knowing I must bear a grudge." Both men had been imprisoned by their respective governments, yet Casanova argued that Venice nevertheless allowed abundant freedom, a judgment tinged with intense nostalgia. Casanova explained that Venetians were as free as possible "under an aristocratic government. The freedom we have is not as great as the English enjoy, but we are content. My imprisonment, for example, was an outright act of despotism," yet "I considered that they had been right to imprison me without the usual formalities." It was the Venetian way.

"At that rate," Voltaire sneered, "no one is free in Venice."

"Possibly," Casanova countered, but "to be free, it is enough to believe that one is so." Voltaire wouldn't grant that much, and pointed out that Venetian patricians holding government posts couldn't travel without first obtaining permission. (The situation was even worse than Voltaire described; Venetian diplomats and ministers were forbidden to meet with foreigners at all.) Casanova defended the idea, which was second nature to him, because it allowed Venetians to maintain their power.

Later, Voltaire displayed his garden as he chattered on about Homer, Dante, and Petrarch, often betraying a lack of judgment and precision to Casanova's way of thinking. Worse, the panjandrum indulged in tiresome bouts of "raillery, ill-humored jests, and sarcasm," laughing at his own jokes, praising his own opinions. As they wandered through Voltaire's house, past towers of correspondence, Casanova gained an idea of the life of an eminent man of letters. Could it be his someday, as well? Voltaire evidently enjoyed an immense income that enabled him to live as extravagantly as he did, but what was the source? "Those who said and say that he became rich only by cheating the booksellers are mistaken," Casanova remarked. "On the contrary, the booksellers cheated him badly" with the exception of the Cramer brothers, Voltaire's Genevan publishers.

The extended visit with Voltaire set Casanova's mind on fire. He harbored a "grudge against him for ten years," criticizing everything the "great man" wrote or spoke. If only Voltaire hadn't indulged in that damned "raillery" on the third day, the Venetian would had thought him "sublime in every respect." Instead, he intended to inform Voltaire "how many faults there are in his books."

At the beginning of August 1760, Casanova quit Geneva for northern resorts catering to the titled, the avaricious, the restless, and the snobbish. His itinerary included Aix-les-Bains, southwest of Geneva, and Grenoble, where he leased a country house, and continued to feud unnecessarily but quite enjoyably with Voltaire by letter. In the vicinity of Aix, he spied a nun resembling Maria Eleonora Michiel, whom he hadn't seen for more than five years. "I walk toward her, she quickly lowers her veil, and she takes another path, obviously to avoid me." He followed, assuming that she's fled her convent, "desperate, perhaps mad," and had come to Aix to take its therapeutic waters. He asked others about her, but elicited no useful information. Scheming to arrange a rendezvous with her, he seized a ladder, and leaned it against a wall below her window by moonlight. Believing he heard Maria Eleonora herself clearly enunciate, "Come and fear nothing," he sprang into action.

"I climb up, I enter, and I clasp her in my arms, covering her face with kisses. I ask her in Venetian why she has no candle, and I beg her to satisfy my impatience at once," but when she spoke, it was not with the voice of a Venetian, and not the voice of his beloved. He apologized profusely to the woman, whoever she was, probably French, for his indiscretion. After a pause, she told him her tale of woe: pregnant, caught between the confines of a convent and whim of her lover, a French hunchback. "How could you fall in love with him?" Casanova demanded. She explained that she hadn't been in love; she pitied him. "He wanted to kill himself. I was afraid." No, he hadn't forced himself on her, he'd pleaded tearfully to have her until she finally yielded. She hadn't been afraid of becoming pregnant "since I have always believed that for a girl to become pregnant she had to do it with a man at least three times." ("Unlucky ignorance!" Casanova declared.) Yet, without her understanding why, she did become pregnant, with nowhere to turn. Having confided her story, she dissolved into sobs.

Casanova promised to visit her again the next day, and then he descended the ladder. He went straight to his bed, "all in all very glad that I had been wrong in my idea that the nun might be my dear Maria Eleonora." Nevertheless, he desired to know this new, strange nun much better than he did. Yet when he visited the nun again, he decided her face was "such a perfect likeness that I cannot think I am deceived." When she opened her eyes to gaze at him, and he saw they were black, not blue like Maria Eleonora's, he realized he'd been deceived again. Nevertheless, "I fall madly in love with her, and I take her in my arms." As he covered her with kisses, she sneezed so forcefully that she couldn't respond in kind. As she hurriedly put on her veil, she expressed her fear of her abbess and excommunication if she allowed a man even to see her. Casanova administered a sternutative, or sneezing powder, and departed, "fearing that the effort of sneezing might bring on her delivery."

Try as he might to rid his mind of her, he realized he'd fallen in love with "this new, black-eye Maria Eleonora Michiel." He wouldn't permit her to return to the convent in her condition. He ascribed this bizarre turn of romantic events to a "command from God. God had willed that I should take her for Maria Eleonora." Indeed, all the events of his life could be attributed to God, "yet the rabble of philosophers have always accused me of atheism."

When he next saw the black-eyed nun, he learned that the sternutative powder he'd administered—but only in small quantities!—had brought on labor, and she'd given birth. "I had only one violent pain," she told him with relief. The baby was quickly taken from her and "put on the wheel," a turntable in the wall of the lying-in hospital, together with a note saying the child had yet to be baptized. With a turn of the wheel, unwanted newborns became foundlings, available to anyone who happened by.

She ascribed her recovery from the ordeal to Casanova's affection. "Tell me if you are a man or an angel, for I fear to sin by worshiping you," she sighed. Yet the intensity of her devotion troubled him to the point where "I thought she would go mad with gratitude." Although he promised to see her the next day, "I could not wait to be out of this perilous situation" despite the sympathy he felt for the black-eyed nun who had been so naive and trusting. He calculated that she wouldn't remain his long-term lover because "she had repented too sorely to run the same risk with another man." Yet the next day, when she complained that her lactating breasts were painful, he offered to examine her. He caressed her breasts, and moved his hand as low as he dared, begging her pardon, and bestowing on her a "tender kiss" when he departed, calling her "dear daughter" to put her at ease, as he became the latest man to abuse her.

He returned to her bedside after a night of gambling, and, buoyed by his winnings, continued to court her. "She was twenty-one years of age, and I thirty-five. My affection for her was much stronger than a father's." She received him undressed in her bed, and he mentioned that if he saw her wearing her habit the next day, the sight would trouble him. "Then you will find me undressed in bed," she assured him. He requested permission to pay his respects from time to time, even at the risk of excommunication. And when he revealed the details of his romance with Maria Eleonora Michiel, he was stunned to learn that the two nuns shared the same name. Shaken by the coincidence, Casanova and the black-eyed nun remained silent for long minutes. When he resumed, displayed a portrait of the original Maria Eleonora. "It is *my* portrait," her successor judged, "except for the eyes and eyebrows. It is my habit! It is wonderful."

With each revelation, Casanova coaxed the black-eyed nun nearer to consummation. Next, he set about urging her to allow him to imbibe milk from her still engorged breasts. "What madness!" she exclaimed. "I believe you are drinking your poor daughter's milk."

"It is sweet, my dear friend," he replied, "and the little I have swallowed is balm to my soul. You cannot be sorry you have granted me this pleasure, for nothing is more innocent." To encourage her lust, he displayed a nude portrait of her predecessor; the image inspired raptures as she kissed it. She revealed her hair, sinful as that might be. "I really believed I was seeing Maria Eleonora Michiel with black hair," he marveled. When he compared her to the portrait, "the living object triumphed over the painted image." Rather, almost triumphed.

"I love you so much that I am sorry you are not a woman," the black-eyed nun sighed. Casanova rebuffed the notion; if he were a woman, he wouldn't love her as much as he did as a man.

He invited her to sit up so that he might "suck the last sweet drops of your milk." As he imbibed this forbidden nectar, she proclaimed that she had never known a purer joy than he had given her "by clinging to her breasts." They kissed until they were exhausted, but she refused to grant him additional favors. He exercised his self-restraint, and, stimulated but unsatisfied, returned to his lodgings at two o'clock in the morning, in love with his black-eyed nun.

On his return, she wore a corset adorned with pink ribbons—a gift from a peasant woman, as she explained, not from an admirer. Plumping and fussing, the black-eyed nun pointed out the comfort and size of the bed, the "fine sheets," and the loose-fitting shift she wore. "I shall sleep the better tonight, provided I can defend myself against these seductive dreams that set my soul on fire last night," she said with a coquettish trill.

Casanova sighed. He wished to act but feared "giving her pain."

"Too much pleasure," she corrected him. But his pleasure was innocent, hers altogether sinful, he ventured. After more banter, she invited him to unlace her corset. He plied the black-eyed nun with glasses of claret as she pulled off her cap, shook out her hair, removed her corset, "and, drawing her arms out of her shift, displayed herself to my amorous eyes." As she made room for him in the bed, he understood that "it was time for me to reason no more and that love demanded I should seize the moment. I flung myself beside her rather than on her, and, clasping her in my arms, I pressed my lips to hers . . ." as he commenced making love to her. The result was a master class in seduction. Her cheeks flushed scarlet in her sleep, or, as Casanova gently expressed it, "The poppies of Morpheus made her face radiant." She murmured in her slumber. "Undressing, and holding her close, I consummated the sweet crime in her and with her; but before the climax she opened her eyes. 'Oh, God,' she cried in a dying voice, 'so it is true!'" In a world of passion and indulgence, rapture was all.

Between bouts of gambling Casanova returned to his black-eyed nun. With nude portraits of her as their aphrodisiac, she took him into her arms, "but I told her to wait a moment." He had a little package she would value highly, a "little jacket of very fine, transparent skin, eight inches long and closed at one end, and which by way of a pouch strong at its open end had a narrow pink ribbon." As she examined the condom with nervous laughter, he explained that he'd used a jacket just like it with her Venetian counterpart, Maria Eleonora Michiel.

At first, she seemed reassured. "I will put it on you myself," she declared, "and you cannot imagine how glad I am." Studying his phallus, sheathed but alert, she concluded that "despite the fineness and transparency of the skin, the little fellow pleases me less well in costume." In fact, "this covering degrades him, or degrades me—one or the other."

Yes, yes, Casanova agreed, "we will philosophize later." He wanted only to take her into his arms.

She proclaimed that the "shameless artisans who make these pouches" deserved punishment. They "should be excommunicated a hundred times over" and subjected to fines and corporal punishment. At that moment, he thrust into her, desperate for relief, climaxing prematurely.

"You couldn't wait another minute?" she gasped when she realized what had occurred. Having expended himself, he assured her that no harm had been done. "No great harm done?" she cried. "He is dead! You laugh!"

He pleaded that "in a minute you will see the little fellow revived, and so full of life that next time he will not die so easily." He gently removed the condom and offered the black-eyed nun a replacement, which she placed on him as soon as his member could sustain it. He coaxed her into another round of lovemaking, and then he staggered back to his lodging, and the black-eyed nun returned to her convent.

When he reached Genoa, the city reminded him so poignantly of Venice that he felt the weight of his exile—until he found two women to distract him. There was the playful, flirtatious Rosalie, with whom he believed himself in love, and Veronica Alizeri, an impoverished aristocrat who set him "on fire" even as she rebuffed his advances.

He pressed his suit publicly when he performed in a theatrical production with Veronica of Voltaire's popular *l'Écossaise, ou Le Caffé*, which Casanova had translated from French into Italian as a way of maintaining his connection with the controversial literary celebrity.

Voltaire had composed this five-act satire in eight days in 1760, hiding behind a pseudonym, as he often did, be it priest, rabbi, or philosopher. In this case, he posed as "Mr. Hume" of the Church of Edinburgh and the brother of David Hume, the philosopher, and fooling no one, especially because the satire's target happened to be Élie Catherine Fréron, who'd made a career out of attacking *philosophes* such as Voltaire and launched a short-lived movement known as the Counter-Enlightenment. In *l'Écossaise*, Fréron, best known to the reading public as the editor of *l'Année littéraire*, or *The Literary Year*, appears as the pompous chief of *L'Âne littéraire*, or *The Literary Ass*. The play had met with success in both France and England, with Voltaire enjoying every bit of scandal it stirred up.

Casanova sent his translation to the great man, "together with a very polite letter in which I asked him to excuse me for having made bold to turn his beautiful French prose into Italian." Voltaire disdained this tribute, and the dismissal left Casanova "so irritated and offended" that he reaffirmed his intention to become "that great man's enemy."

Against this background of literary thrust and parry, rehearsals for the Genoese production of *l'Écossaise* proceeded smoothly. A week before the performance, bills appeared in Genoa to annouce: "We shall give *l'Écossaise* by Monsieur de Voltaire, translated by an unknown hand, and we shall perform it without a prompter."

Casanova rated their performance an "unqualified success," filling a large theater—not with common folk, he noted, but with "noblest and wealthiest in that great city." He received requests for five additional performances and another play from his pen. Instead, he devoted himself to the pursuit of Rosalie, even though he learned to his mortification that she was carrying on with another man, who might have gotten her pregnant. By now Casanova wanted no part of her. In the end, Rosalie married a Genoese merchant, and Casanova turned his attention to Veronica and her sister, Annetta.

"You set me on fire," he declared.

"Oh, calm yourself, please! Tomorrow evening I won't set you on fire. Please, please let me alone." He pulled Veronica down on the sofa, groping for her most sensitive areas through her clothing . . . until she fled.

That night he went to bed frustrated and "extremely ill-pleased with myself." The next day, in his distraught state, he walked for two hours to try to regain his composure. At a village tavern he consumed an omelet before he realized that he lacked the strength to return to Genoa on foot. With night coming on quickly, he settled for a horse and guide, with six miles to travel. "Rain was my companion all the way to Genoa, where I arrived at eight o'clock soaking wet, dying of cold and fatigue, and with the whole upper part of my thighs chafed raw by the rough saddle, which had torn my satin breeches."

He returned to his lodging, exhausted, soaked to the bone, to find a letter of apology from Veronica, but she failed to appear in the flesh. In her absence, he had supper with her younger sister Annetta, "observing with pleasure that she drank only water, but ate more than I did. My passion for her sister kept me from thinking of her." He plied her with wine, and the conversation turned to her sister. "Do you think she is right to make me suffer?" he asked.

No, Annetta responded, "but if you love her you ought to forgive her."

So he kept his distance from the girl, "for I feared I should find her too com-pliant." He asked her to fetch a jar of "unscented pomade" to soothe the wounds caused by the "accursed saddle on which I rode for six miles." She could examine him on the bed, have a closer look, touch his delicate places. "I can wager that, short-sighted as she was, she had never seen it so well be-fore, and that she must have enjoyed it." In time, her fingers strayed beyond the sore spots, until he could no longer endure the treatment and begged her to stop, which she did, wondering what she'd done wrong.

Catching his breath, he asked Annetta to spend an hour or two with him, and after changing into her shift, she complied "on condition that you will think no more of my sister." Casanova swore, and then he took her.

"In the morning," Casanova was surprised to see that "the victim had not stained the altar with blood." She wasn't a virgin, after all. "It has often happened to me," he said of this discovery, but, he cautioned his readers, "no legitimate conclusions can be drawn from either a flow of blood or the lack of it. A girl can be convicted of having a lover only if he has made her preg-nant." He drifted off to sleep, and when he awoke, he found both sisters at his bedside, with "not the least sign of a misunderstanding between them." He naturally took advantage of the sitation. As they romped in bed, Veron-ica replaced the covers whenever they fell away, and Annetta "displayed all her treasures to me."

An energetic rapping on the door startled them out of their erotic stu-por. It was his servant, announcing that a felucca was waiting to carry him away. "Furious at the interruption," Casanova staggered to the door, or-dered the servant to pay the captain, and instructed him to return the fol-lowing morning. By the time the felucca did return, the wind was blowing the wrong way, and the voyage was delayed yet again. Casanova remained with the sisters for another night, until the captain finally pronounced the weather fit for sailing. As he departed aboard the felucca, he reflected on the paradox of his desires; he was happier in pursuit of an unattainable goal than in its midst.

He traveled south through Livorno, Pisa, and Florence, where he took an apartment with a view of the Arno River.

He hired a carriage and a lackey dressed in the blue and red livery of the Bragadin dynasty. He introduced himself not as Giacomo Casanova, but as the Chevalier de Seingalt. ("I did not want to impose on anyone, but I wanted to make an impression.") In his new incarnation, he visited a banker to establish credit, attended the theater, and took a box at the opera situated so that he could see the performers, among them the *prima virtuosa*, Teresa Lanti, formerly the celebrated "castrato" Bellino, still singing after all this time, still "beautiful, fresh, and . . . just as young as when I had left her." They were maturing in tandem, two ships traveling toward their destinations at the same speed, and seeming not to advance.

"At the end of her aria she goes offstage, and she is scarcely in the wings before she turns and signals me with her fan to come and speak to her." His heart's beating relentlessly, as he recalled having neglected to reply to her last letter, thirteen years ago. "I approach her, and we remain mute. I take her hand, and I put it against my chest so she can feel my heart, which seems to try to leap out." He informed her that he was not married, but her husband, a very well-dressed handsome young man, introduced himself. Even after he learned that he was rich and has nothing else to do except lavish attention on Teresa, Casanova confessed that "I feel my old fire rekindled, and I think I am not sorry to have found her married."

He materialized on her doorstep at seven o'clock the following morning. "We embrace like two fond friends, or like lovers enjoying the happiness of a moment for which they have longed." Tears of joy flowed, and wiping their eyes, they burst out laughing at Teresa's young husband, gaping at the two of them in astonishment. She rescued the moment by addressing Casanova as "father," even though he was only two years older than she.

He explained to Teresa's youthful husband, "She is my daughter, she is my sister, an angel without sex, she is a living treasure, and she is your wife."

Turning to Teresa, he apologized for not replying to her letter of long ago, but she explained she "knows everything" about his exploits: the nun who became his lover, his escape from I Piombi, and his adventures in Paris and Holland. To reassure her husband, Teresa twined herself around him, but the sight of the two of them embracing annoyed Casanova, who felt his old passion for her stirring in his loins. The awkward moment passed, and the trio sat down to breakfast.

The moment Teresa's husband left, the lovers fell into one another's arms, Teresa wishing to embrace Casanova a hundred times on this day "and afterward leave it at that." They managed to "satisfy some of our fire," but Teresa maintained that she loved her husband, and never wanted to deceive him, so she told Casanova that they must forget what they'd done. He vowed to keep their ancient affair a secret. Teresa agreed, saying that she prefered harmless falsehoods to damaging truths. For instance, she claimed to be twenty-four years old, but as they knew, said Casanova, she was actually thirty-two. "You mean thirty-one," she corrected.

As he was about to fling himself at her neck like a vampire, her husband returned, followed by a beautiful chambermaid (Casanova wouldn't help but notice her bearing "three cups of chocolate on a silver-gilt tray.") Chocolate was all the rage; everyone drank it, Louis XV drank it, and so did his mistress. Casanova declared himself "passionately fond of chocolate." So they all drank, Teresa's husband peering over the rim of his cup at his unusual guest. At length, Casanova decided he could excuse Teresa for "having fallen in love with his pretty face, for I knew the power of a beautiful countenance only too well; but I disapproved of her having made him her husband, for a husband acquires sovereign rights."

Teresa had one more surprise in store for Casanova. Conversing with her days later, "suddenly a figure appears who absorbs and bewilders all the faculties of my soul. A youth of perhaps fifteen or sixteen, but with the sort of maturity an Italian can attain at that age." As the lad bows and enters, Teresa introduced him as her brother. Casanova maintained his composure, but he was "flabbergasted," for "this supposed brother of Teresa's was the image of me, except that he was not as dark; I instantly see that he is my son. Nature had never been more indiscreet."

Amid awkward glances and stifled coughs, Casanova studied the youth, who could only be his, and realized he must have gotten Teresa pregnant years before, and she had hidden this singular fact from him. He took pleasure in the "youth's fine bearing and the intelligence he showed as he discoursed in the Neapolitan dialect." He was a musician, Teresa announced, a talented harpsichordist. Casanova spontaneously arose, approached the youth, and embraced him. The name of his handsome lost son, he learned, was Cesarino.

"He is the happy fruit of our love," she explained, adding that the boy was raised by a duke, believing Teresa to be his older sister. "My heart bleeds because I cannot tell him I am his mother; for I think he would love me all the more." Casanova entirely credited Teresa's story about the boy's origins. Perhaps it was too good to be true, but the circumstances answered his need for a son while relieving him of responsibility for his care. He inquired if young Cesarino had the makings of another Casanova, that is, his first love affair? "I do not think so," Teresa answered, "but I think my chambermaid is in love with him."

"Give him to me," his presumed father commanded, "and I will teach him the way of the world."

Later that day Cesarino returned to entertain the guests with spirited Neapolitan songs that "made us laugh heartily" as he accompanied himself on the harpsichord. Teresa glanced from Cesarino to Casanova and back, occasionally hugging her young husband. To be happy in this world, she declared, "one must be in love."

"So I spent that day," Casanova recalled, "which was one of the most blissful of my whole life."

———•———

From Florence, Casanova advanced to Rome, with an agenda; he wanted badly to return to Venice, but needed a papal dispensation to avoid confinement in I Piombi again. The visit occasioned an uneasy reunion with his brother Giovanni, an artist, whom he hadn't seen for a decade and "who must then have been thirty years of age and was in Rome studying under the famous [Anton Raphael] Mengs"—a somber neoclassical painter who'd fled from Dresden to Rome during the Seven Years' War.

The Casanova brothers embraced and talked for an hour or so, "he giving me an a brief account of the little happenings of his life and I of the great ones of mine." Such was Giacomo's view of their reputations; in reality, Giovanni was the better known Casanova, the up-and-coming artist and younger brother of an elusive adventurer and social climber.

Casanova next met Cardinal Alessandro Albani, the Vatican Librarian, blind and babbling incoherently. When he realized the lanky Venetian standing before him was the notorious Casanova who had escaped from I Piombi, "He rudely says that he is amazed that I have the effrontery to come to Rome, where at the least request from the State Inquisitors a Papal ordinance would oblige me to leave." Irritated, Casanova shot back, "It would be the State Inquisitors who could be accused of effrontery if they dared to ask for me, since they would be unable to state for what crime they have deprived me of my freedom." This "tart reply silenced the Cardinal." At least his brother's friend "the indefatigable painter Mengs, who was truly great in his art, but no less an eccentric in society" treated Giacomo Casanova with civility. Casanova in return considered him "the greatest and most pains-taking painter of this century," not that his art rubbed off on Giovanni, "for my brother never did anything to deserve the name of his pupil." (Casanova was clearly consumed by sibling rivalry.)

Nevertheless, Giovanni obtained an introduction for Giacomo to Silvio Passionei, a "most unusual Cardinal, an enemy of the Jesuits, a man of intel-ligence, and graced with a rare knowledge of literature." If anyone could put him on the road to redemption in Venice, it would be he. Casanova soon found himself in the Cardinal's presence.

"He received me in a great room in which he was busily writing; a minute later he put down his pen. He could not give me permission to sit, for there were no chairs." The two bantered about the Holy Father, Clement XIII, whom the Cardinal called a "fool" out loud. "How my soul rejoiced!" Casanova remarked on hearing this spiteful remark. The Pope (Carlo della Torre di Rezzonico) was caught in a controversy concerning the Jesuits and the leading *philosophes* of the Enlightenment. Bowing to pressure from the Jesuits, he listed Diderot and d'Alembert's *Encyclopédia* and the works of Diderot on the *Index Librorum Prohibitorum*, or *List of Prohibited Books*. The Cardinal, to name but one of his adversaries, em-phatically disagreed with the Jesuit position, and so called the Pope a fool at every opportunity. It was just the kind of controversy in which Casa-nova delighted.

When they met again the following day, the Cardinal asked Casanova to recite the well-known story of his escape from I Piombi, "of which he had heard wonders." He knew the general outline, but he wanted to hear the de-tails from Casanova's lips.

"Shall I sit on the floor?" Casanova asked, with a hint of impudence. The Cardinal rang for a lackey, who brought Casanova a stool, but "a seat without arms or a back makes me angry."

Disgruntled, "I tell my story badly, and in a quarter of an hour" instead of the two or three hours he usually devoted to the tale.

The Cardinal agreed with Casanova's glum assessment of his perfor-mance that day: "I write better than you speak." However, his performance, though inadequate, earned an audience with the Pope.

"You may go to kiss the Holy Father's foot tomorrow at ten o'clock."

Before the audience, Casanova made a gift of a rare book to the Cardi-

nal, whom he considered a man of intelligence, even if "haughty" and "vain."
This was no ordinary tome. It was the *Pandects*, or digest, of Roman jurists,
a code of laws dating from the sixth century, when it was compiled under
the direction of the Emperor Justinian. Casanova had once received it as a
gift himself, but claimed to have no use for it. The *Pandects* filled a set of
fifty volumes, "well bound and in a state of preservation." He assumed that
Cardinal Passionei, as the Vatican's chief librarian, would esteem this exceptional gift. In return, he received the text of a funeral oration given by
the Cardinal years before, in 1736.

And then it was time to be ushered into the presence of Clement XIII
at Monte Cavallo, the Pope's summer residence on the Quirinal, one of the
seven hills of Rome. "I had scarcely entered and kissed the holy cross depicted on his holy slipper before, laying one hand on my left shoulder, he
said that he remembered the time I left his reception at Padua as soon as
he began chanting the Rosary." (Clement XIII had been Bishop of Padua
from 1743 to 1758, when he was elected to the papacy.) Casanova blushed to
admit it, and declared, "I have come to prostrate myself at your feet to receive absolution," which he received without delay, along with permission to
ask a favor of the Holy Father.

Casanova had his request ready: "Your Holiness's intercession, so that
I can freely return to Venice." Clement XIII said he would discuss the request with the authorities, including the Ambassador to Venice. Overrul-
ing the Venetian Inquisition was a serious matter, but with his gift of the
Pandects Casanova demonstrated his familiarity with an unusual and scholarly work designed to erase the memory of the blasphemous and subversive texts that had originally attracted the attention of the Inquisition. He
bantered with the Holy Father about Cardinal Passionei's quirks until "the
Pope laughed so hard that he was seized by a fit of coughing, and, after spitting, he laughed again." The moment was pure Casanova, capable of charming courtesans and the Pope as the occasion arose. After the audience, he
heard that his gift of the *Pandects* had won the approval of the Cardinal,
who considered it "rare and valuable and in better condition than the one in
the Vatican." In fact, he insisted on paying for it because he wanted it for his
own library. Drawing himself up, Casanova explained to an intermediary
that he had no intention of selling it. "Tell the Cardinal that I will be honored if he will accept it as a present."

"He will send it back to you."

"And I will send him back his funeral oration. I will not take presents from someone who refuses to accept them."

Ultimately, the Cardinal returned the *Pandects* to Casanova, who reciprocated by returning the funeral oration to the Cardinal.

He exchanged the clergy for the pleasures to be enjoyed with the family of the painter Anton Raphael Mengs, whom he'd met through Giovanni. He learned that Mengs's sister, a talented miniature portraitist in her own right, homely but sprightly, had been rebuffed by Giovanni, whom she considered "the most ungrateful of men: to have treated her so scornfully." Casanova knew exactly what she meant; Giovanni had treated him the same way.

Mengs's wife, Margherita Teresia Geltrude, "was pretty, virtuous, very scrupulous in performing all the duties of a wife and mother, and very submissive to her husband, whom she could not have loved because he was not lovable," according to Casanova, who found his host "stubborn and cruel," drunk at home, and sober in public. "His wife had the patience to serve as his model for all the nudes he had occasion to paint," and she did, Casanova

Anton Raphael Mengs, self-portrait, c. 1778

guessed, out of concern that her husband would just as soon replace her with another model.

————•————

He received a summons to present himself to the Secretary of the Council of Ten, perhaps the most powerful person in the Venetian government, but Casanova hesitated, maintaining he would do so only if he had a papal "letter of recommendation." Without it, "I will never expose myself to the risk of being shut up in a place from which the invisible hand of God released me by a series of miracles," that is, if he so much as showed himself to the Secretary, he risked a second confinement in I Piombi, with little chance of escaping.

To discharge his obligation to the Pope, he went down on bended knee and begged to present his *Pandects* to the Vatican Library. In return, the Pope promised a "token of our singular affection." But what would it be?

Before his departure from Rome, he received the Order of the Golden Spur from Clement for achievements in science and art. "Such a glittering medal is very useful to a man on the road," Casanova noted. "It is an ornament, a substantial decoration that elicits the respect of fools," and in a world full of fools, "there's nothing like a medal to whip them into shape and leave them confused, ecstatic, and humbled." The honor came with a diploma "sealed with the Papal seal" making him a "Doctor of Civil and Canon Law." Ignoring convention, he draped the cross around his neck "on a broad poppy-red ribbon," and considered having it set with diamonds and rubies. In fact, the Order had become so devalued that "only charlatans wear it," but Casanova took comfort in reminding himself that "Popes gave it to Ambassadors, even though they give it to their valets."

So many people wore "fanciful devices," he reflected, "hunters, academicians, musicians, bigots, lovers"—why not he? And as for the varied ornaments worn by women, "Let us love them and not seek to penetrate their mysteries," especially since the object in question more often than not "turns out to be some bauble or grotesque that they wear only to get themselves looked at and to arouse curiosity." People have become so prickly that "you can no longer ask a man from what country he comes." And it was better not to ask a nobleman "what his arms are, for if he doesn't know the jargon of heraldry you will embarrass him." For that matter, don't compliment a gentleman on his hair—he might be wearing a wig—and don't compliment a woman on her teeth—they might be false. Don't ask a woman her name, either; in France, Countesses and Marquises receive so many when they're baptized that they can't remember them all. The "height of bad manners" was to ask someone what religion they practiced. "In short, if one wants to be liked, the safest thing is to ask nobody anything."

The next morning, "after breakfasting well and fondly embracing my brother," he set off for Naples, arriving "when the whole city was in a state of alarm because the fatal volcano was threatening to explode."

——•——

The eruption of Mount Vesuvius, thirteen miles west of Naples, commenced on December 23, 1760, and continued until January 5, 1761. The volcano had been venting at infrequent intervals since AD 79, most recently in in 1737; those inclined to superstition took the latest disturbance as a sign that God meant to destroy Naples. But these concerns failed to trouble Casanova as he skirted the ash and smoke and arrived in the city after an absence of eighteen years.

There was much he wanted to see in Naples—palaces and gardens and opera houses, distant relatives and local gentry, who welcomed him even during the volcano's eruption. Among the most hospitable was the Duke of Matalona, who gave Casanova access to his opera box, located on the third tier of the lavish Teatro di San Carlo, as well as to the box of his mistress. A strange gesture, it seemed, but the Duke explained that he loved his wife; he kept a mistress only "for form's sake." It was rumored that the Duke was "impotent with all the women on earth."

"I take it you are not joking," Casanova responded, "but I find it hard to believe. Can a man have a mistress he does not love?"

The Duke insisted he loved his pretty, seventeen-year-old mistress, who, among her many attributes, spoke French. When Casanova met her, he found her to be charming, indeed, striking, as the Duke reminded him that he loved her as a father loves a daughter, and no more. "I reply that is incredible."

The curtain rose on *Attilio Regolo* by Metastasio, the stage name of Pietro Antonio Domenico Trapassi, a poet and acknowledged master of *opera seria* libretti. The performance of this "serious opera" lasted five hours, during which the audience merrily bantered. Casanova encountered the Duke's enchanting young mistress, Leonilda. Later, the three of them gambled in seclusion, for the activity was prohibited in Naples. Casanova seemed determined to lose a considerable amount of money to the Duke, who gave his new Venetian friend as much time as he needed to pay his debt. To make further amends, he invited Casanova to join him in feast of an "an enormous dish of macaroni and ten or twelve dishes of various sorts of shellfish." Early the next morning, the Duke arranged for Casanova to meet King Ferdinand IV of Naples on the occasion of his tenth birthday. "I kissed the King's hand," he recalled, "which was swollen with chilblains," an affliction from which the young king would suffer throughout his life.

Throughout these activities, Casanova stole glances at Leonilda, who captivated him by flashing her breast and thigh. She took breakfast in a room decorated with Chinese lovemaking positions, to which both she and the Duke appeared oblivious, but on examining them, Casanova was "shocked; however, I concealed it." The Duke expected the erotica would arouse Casanova, but saw no sign, even when he felt with his hand. But when Casanova pressed Leonilda's hand to his lips, "the Duke withdraws his wet hand, exclaiming, laughing, and getting up to fetch a towel. Leonilda has done nothing, but she succumbs to uncontrollable laughter, as do I and the Duke." The erotic sport left Casanova glowing with happiness rather than humiliated. "All three of us transgressed certain limits," he marveled, "though we managed to remain within certain others." The group ended the scene with a warm communal hug, with Leonilda's lips pressed tightly to Casanova's, as he gave way to the "intoxication of the love that fetters the mind." So besotted with her was he that he asked the Duke to "relinquish her" so that he could marry her right away. The Duke suggested that Casanova speak to the young lady himself, which, after another losing bout of gambling, he finally did, in her box at the opera, where, during the course of four hours he told her that the love she inspired within him "could tolerate neither rivals nor delay nor the slightest possibility of future inconstancy," and with that he proposed to her, offering a generous dowry. In reality, he was no more capable of becoming Leonilda's devoted husband than he was of flying to the moon.

His luck at gambling turned, and after a feverish night, he broke the bank. Confidence and solvency restored, he saw Leonilda that morning, but made no mention of the marriage. Instead, "we spent the rest of the day looking at the wonders of nature in the environs of Naples," and when he

met his beloved again to negotiate the terms of marriage, "she found me amorous only in words," although, true to form, he "again swore that it rested
entirely with her to leave Naples with me, bound by marriage to my destiny until death." Skeptical and smiling, the Duke inquired if Casanova still
wanted to marry the girl after spending the morning alone with her. "More
than ever," he responded.

He entered in a two-hour discussion with the Duke concerning Leonilda's annuity, jewelry, and wardrobe, all of which Casanova would pay to the
Duke, who would secure it with a mortgage on a country house, and eventually turn over to Leonilda's mother. "You can be certain that you will be
the first man whom my dear Leonilda will clasp to her bosom," the Duke
stated. All that remained was for her mother to sign the documents and a
priest to marry the couple. Leonilda fainted in the Duke's arms, as he called
her his "dear daughter" and kissed her over and over. When she revived, "we
all three dried our tears."

Casanova now considered himself a married man, and as such ceased
gambling. All that remained was for him to meet his bride's mother. He expected her to be elderly but was surprised to hear that she was no more than
thirty-seven or thirty-eight years of age. That evening, he came upon the
Duke standing between mother and daughter. "I look first at the mother,
who, the instant I appear, gives a piercing cry and sinks to the sofa. I stare
at her."

———————◆———————

She was Lucrezia Castelli. "I sit down; I understand it all; my hair stands
on end, and I sink into the gloomiest silence." The Duke and his protégée
Leonilda realized in an instant that Casanova and Donna Lucrezia had a
history, "but beyond that they could not go." He calculated that their time
together, coupled with Leonilda's age, meant that his beloved could be his
daughter, even if Lucrezia's doting husband had no idea.

Lucrezia pulled Casanova into an adjoining room and told him point-
blank that Leonilda *was* his daughter. "I am sure of it." Even her husband
knew about her origins and "made no protest." She offered to show Casanova the child's baptismal certificate so he could see for himself. What's
more, as a child she had been called "Giacomina," after her father. As to
the marriage now before them it horrified her, yet she could not oppose it
openly. "What do you think?" she asked. "Do you really have the courage to

marry her? You hesitate. Have you consummated the marriage before contracting it?"

No, no, no, he insisted. And besides, "she has none of my features."

"That is true. She looks like me."

There followed an awkward scene in which Lucrezia explained to her daughter that the name she was once called, Giacomina, derived from the man who stood before her, her father *and* fiancé. "Go and kiss him as a daughter," Lucrezia ordered, "and if he has been your lover, forget your crime."

Bursting into tears, she cried, "*I have never loved him except as a daughter.*"

The Duke and Casanova looked on, mute as marble statues. They remained together for two or three more hours, until they bid adieu to one another at midnight. Later, he reflected on the taboo he'd nearly broken. "If a father takes possession of his daughter by virtue of paternal authority, he exercises a tyranny that nature must abhor," which he recognized as the "eternal subject of Greek tragedies."

"I went to bed, but I could not sleep. The sudden transition I had to make from carnal to fatherly love caused all my moral and physical faculties the deepest distress." He decided to leave Naples the following day, but the Duke cautioned that his departure would be viewed with displeasure. Couldn't Casanova consider his entire marriage scheme a little joke? "I advise you to renew your affair with Donna Lucrezia," the Duke said. "You must have found her as she was eighteen years ago; she cannot possibly have been better." Casanova considered; the Duke's advice had a certain logic, but in love, as he put it, one piece of merchandise cannot substitute for another.

Leonilda, by way of contrast, seemed the picture of gaiety, hugging his neck and calling him "Dear Papa." At the same time, as soon as her mother, Lucrezia, called him "dear friend," the years melted away, and she stood before him, unmarked by time. They reminisced about their first night together, and he offered to marry her as he should have many years earlier. Hours later, Lucrezia came to his bed. "We surrendered ourselves to the one true author of nature, to love." Casanova had found a new family, with a wife and daughter. "I was the happiest of mortals in those days."

Lucrezia told Casanova that if he truly loved her, he had only to buy the estate where she would live with him without demanding that he marry her, unless she became pregnant. He imagined the idyll of their lives to-

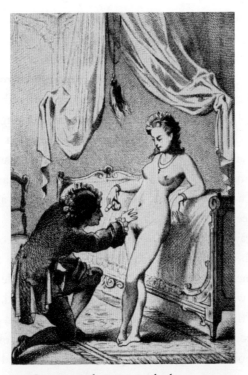

Casanova admiring a naked woman,
engraving by Chauvet

gether. Yet there were problems. Although rich, "I would have had to adopt a prudent course of conduct that was absolutely foreign to my nature," and as a libertine, he "loathed the idea of settling down anywhere." The most he could offer Lucrezia was a promise to refrain from seducing Leonilda, or, as he gently expressed it, "trouble her innocence"—if she really was innocent. How could the Duke, who kept her as his mistress, have left her intact?

"The Duke is impotent," Lucrezia told him, confirming the rumor. "Now you understand all."

At that moment, Leonilda burst in, laughing and kissing them both. Lucrezia responded by undressing Casanova, tossing his clothes out of reach, and inviting "innocent" Leonilda to join them in bed. "Your father," she explained meaning Casanova, "will confine his attention to your mother." Leonilda shimmied out of her clothing, saying that as her father, Casanova was at liberty to view "all his handiwork," and so he did. Lucrezia situated herself between Casanova and the girl who might have been his daughter, but "it was only upon her [Lucrezia] that I extinguished the fire."

Leonilda looked on in wonder. "So this is what you did when you en-
gendered me eighteen years ago?"

Sensing that Lucrezia would soon climax, Casanova believed it his "duty
to withdraw" to spare her embarrassment, but, "moved to pity, Leonilda
sends her mother's little soul on its flight [to orgasm] with one hand, and
with the other puts a white handkerchief under her gushing father."

After they climaxed, Lucrezia gratefully covered her daughter with
kisses before twirling the other way and remarking to Casanova that the
girl remained "unstained." Laughing, Leonilda directed Casanova's attention
once more to Lucrezia. And so, "The combat began again and did not end
until we fell asleep."

When the rays of the morning sun awakened them, "Leonilda, as naked
as my hand, obediently goes to the curtain, showing me the beauties of
which, when one is in love, one never has seen enough." He smothered the
girl with kisses when she returned to the warmth of the bed, "but as soon as
she sees me on the edge of the precipice she slips away and gives me to her
mother, who receives me with open arms and imperiously orders me not to
spare her." It took an exceedingly long time in his depleted state, but ultimately he summoned the strength to comply.

———•———

Later that day, Casanova reaffirmed his intention to travel to Rome to enjoy
the last week of Carnival, and if he encountered an orgy there, so much the
better. Nor had he forgotten his vital scheme to coax a pardon from Clement XIII to allow him to return to Venice.

He departed in a stagecoach bound for Rome along one of the most
dangerous stretches of highway in Italy, where robbers and steep trails menaced travelers by night and day. He ignored all these hazards, preferring to
obey the dictates of his unconscious to recapture his lost life in Venice and
the love of his phantom mother: the original Casanova and still the thief of
his heart.

Chapter 13

Hedwig and Helena

With Carnival running from January 26, 1761, until February 3, Casanova hurried to Rome. Naples and its women receded from his consciousness as if it had all been a dream. Awaiting him now were his brother Giovanni and Mengs.

On arrival he rented an opulent horse-drawn landau to drive in fine style along the broad and straight Via del Corso from the Piazza Venezia to the Piazza del Popolo, presenting a *bella figura* in the midst of the Carnival crowd. "They go masked or unmasked as they choose; they wear all sorts of masking costumes, on foot and on horseback; they throw candy to the people, they hand out satires, pasquinades, pamphlets. The lordliest people in Rome mingle with the humblest, there is general confusion, and the Barbary horses race down the middle of the Corso between the landaus, filled with spectators, which are drawn up to the left and right. Toward nightfall the whole crowd makes off to fill the theaters for operas, plays, pantomimes, and rope-dancing exhibitions, in all of which performers have to be men or castrati."

Returning to his lodgings at Mengs's home, he was accosted by a young nobleman whom he recognized: Lord Tallow, James Daniel O'Bryan—actually Viscount Tallow until recently, and now the new Earl of Lismore. How the Chevalier de Seingalt adored these titles! They'd met in Paris, and Casanova remembered him as handsome, fair, full of wit, and, most important, "unbridled in his pursuit of all the vices." He followed his esteemed friend to supper, where he met the other guests, among them "seven or eight girls, each prettier than the one before; three or four castrati, all fit to play women's parts to perfection in Roman theaters," and, most scandalously, "five or six *abati*, husbands to all wives and wives to all husbands." The *abati* boasted of their profligacy and dared the girls "to be more shameless than they." Yet the girls were not prostitutes, as the *abati* assumed; they were amateurs, lovers of the arts, husband hunters, and "dabblers in libertine philosophy." Appraising this dissolute company, Casanova, for all his experience, considered himself a mere apprentice.

The next thing he knew, he was "at supper, where we were twenty-four," emptying a hundred or so bottles with the other guests. At the end, the guests rose from the table, with the exception of Casanova, too intoxicated to stand. "It was then that the great orgy began," and it contained at least *three* sexes: female, male, and castrati, or transgender. "It is impossible to describe all the excesses I saw," he marveled, before describing things he'd never before witnessed:

> A castrato and a girl offered to undress in the next room, stipulating that they would keep their heads covered and lie in bed on their backs. They defied anyone to go see them and be able to decide which was male and which was female. Bets were laid, and they went. We all entered, and no one ventured to decide. We were allowed only to look. I offered to wager his Lordship [the Earl of Lismore] a hundred *scudi* against fifty that I would say which was the female. The probabilities were equal, and His Lordship accepted. I won, but there was no question of his paying me. This first act of the orgy ended with the prostitution of the two naked bodies. They defied all the men in the company to sodomize them, and everyone set to work with the exception of myself . . . and no one succeeded; but afterward we were treated to the spectacle of five or six copulations, in which the *abati* shone by alternating between the active and passive roles. I alone was respected.

All at once the Earl of Lismore, stark naked, attacked Casanova's friend, a young French poet named Poinsinet, who tried without success to keep his clothes on. Next, the Earl offered his watch to the first person who gave him or the hapless poet an erection.

> The hope of winning the watch put the girls, the *abati*, and the castrati on their mettle. Everyone wanted to be first; it was decided to write each name on a slip of paper and draw them. This was the most interesting part of the drama for me, who, during the whole

incredible performance, never felt the slightest sensation, except that I laughed, chiefly at the distress exhibited by Poinsinet, who was reduced to being afraid of having an erection, since the drunken Earl swore that if he made him lose the watch he would have him pitilessly sodomized in the presence of all the actors. The scene, and the drama, ended when there was no one left with any hope of winning the watch.

The depraved display appalled Casanova. It was one thing to go to bed with a mother and daughter, but this display of cruelty belonged in a category by itself. "What I gained from this hellish debauch is a better knowledge of myself. I risked my life. I had only my sword, and I would certainly have used it if His Lordship, in his Bacchic frenzy, had taken it into his head to force me to behave like the others." Having reached this point, he glimpsed the emptiness and absurdity of extreme libertinism. He tiptoed toward the exit, promising to return, which he had no intention of doing.

Once outside the stinking rooms, I thought I was restored to life. All sorts of foul things littered the floor of the abominable stage. Nevertheless, I went to bed well satisfied to have witnessed a spectacle whose like I had never seen before and which I never saw equaled later.

The next time Casanova encountered the Earl of Lismore, the young man behaved as though nothing out of the ordinary had occurred.

In Rome, Casanova met the celebrated castrato Giovanni Osti. "He was the favorite of Cardinal Borghese, with whom he was invited to sup alone every evening," and everyone knew what that meant. To encounter Osti on the street, "one saw at once that he was not a whole man, but on stage, dressed as a woman, he was a firebrand." Watching the castrato perform, Casanova tried to fathom how "the little monster bewitched everyone in the audience." It began with his costume: "Tightly laced in a very well-fitting corset, he had the figure of a nymph, and few women could show a firmer and more enticing bosom than his. The illusion he created was such that it was impossible to resist. One looked, the spell worked, and one either fell in love or became the most stolid of all Germans. . . . When he swept his gaze over the boxes his black eyes revolved so tenderly and modestly that they ravished the soul." Some spectators loved him as a man, others loved the illusion of a woman. In that way he struck Casanova as quintessentially Roman. "Yet Rome, the Holy City, which thus drives the whole human race to become pederasts, refuses to admit it, as she refuses to admit the existence of an illusion which she does everything possible to foster in the minds of the audiences." A highly placed priest, probably homosexual, agreed with Casanova on this point.

Shouldn't the Pope put a stop to it? Casanova was bewildered.

Of course not, said the priest. "One could not have a beautiful actress to supper alone without causing a scandal; but one can have a castrato to supper," adding, "It is true that afterward one goes to bed with him, but no one is supposed to know that, and if it becomes known one can swear that there was no wrongdoing, for after all he is a man." Casanova allowed himself to agree, but he later placed the blame for the phenomenon on papal edicts banishing women from the stage in Rome. Here was a Pope "who believed that dancing was damnation and permitted gambling." A few years later, his successor would do the reverse, as if one decision made more sense than the other.

There was another papal decision that mattered greatly to Casanova: his exile. At the end of Carnival, he visited the Holy Father yet again.

————•————

"He kept me waiting for a good hour, talking of Venice and Padua, and when I again commended myself to his good offices in the matter of a pardon to permit me to return to Venice, he told me to commend myself to God," Casanova said of his papal audience. So there would be no pardon, no end to his exile. At least he had credit at various banks, a servant or two when he needed them, a fine rented landau, and a few ephemeral literary efforts. That was all. Like the wrestler Antaeus, mythic giant who weakened when his feet could not touch the ground, Casanova was slowly losing his sense of self on his travels, and he required contact with the Venetian lagoon to regain it.

In late February, Casanova arrived in Modena, where the authorities immediately menaced him. Baffled, he made inquiries and discovered that his reputation as the man who'd escaped from I Piombi had preceded him. The chief of police, or *Bargello*, wanted to interview him. "What an outrage!" Casanova exclaimed. "What deliberate subversion of morality and even of the good of the State!" He left early the following morning, but not before a cutthroat offered to blow the *Bargello's* brains out for a fee of fifty *zecchini*. "I thank you," Casanova responded, "and I beg you to let him die his natural death," as he tossed the would-be assassin a *scudo* for his trouble.

He proceeded to Parma the next day and registered at an inn as the Chevalier de Seingalt, "for once a man of honor takes a name to which no one else can lay claim, it is his duty to keep it." After only a week, he was en route to Turin once more, under the welcome protection of the Abate Gama. The air was crisp and invigorating; the distant alps beckoned. The Ligurian Sea lay a hundred miles to the south.

———————

By May, Casanova, menaced by the Turin authorities, bolted. He carried with him a letter from the Abate who recommended him as an observer to a congress in Augsburg, Bavaria, to discuss the end of the Seven Years' War. The credential imparted a patina of legitimacy to his journey. Perhaps he intended to go to the congress, but first, he desired a reunion with his former love Maria Eleonora Michiel, "for whom I sighed every time I remembered her." He found her at a convent near Chambéry, France, about one hundred and thirty miles west of Turin, where she met him at the grating, as they had met before, in other convents.

She resisted his embraces, fearing that spies were watching, urging him to forget their shared past, and to spare himself the torture of unfulfilled desire, but he refused to leave. She seemed "more beautiful than ever." She was "made for love." How could she live "in continual abstinence?" (How could anyone?) She confided that "when one cannot have the reality, one plays at it." In her case, she had found a substitute, a young girl in whose "innocent passion" she took comfort, or, as she phrased it, "sufficient to quench the flame that would kill me if I did not diminish its intensity with make-believe." Casanova, skeptical, questioned her. She said her confessor, a "wise old man," tolerated this scandalous arrangement, and she sent him away without exchanging so much as a kiss. Casanova claimed—and he was probably letting fantasy get the better of him—that he persuaded the girl to fellate him through the grating: "She was moved to eat me, and she may have hoped to swallow me; but the excessive pleasure she aroused in my soul melted my heart. She did not leave me until she was convinced of my exhaustion. I sat down, and in gratitude pressed my lips to the sweet mouth that had sucked the quintessence of my soul and heart."

He felt no guilt, only a sense of relief and accomplishment.

He departed for Lyon in the morning, and immediately made plans to return to Paris. He dispatched his unreliable servant, Costa, to carry a note to Madame d'Urfé, still wealthy, mystical, and besotted with Casanova, to announce his imminent arrival. "Costa was quite handsome but spoke French very badly and was rather stupid, so that I was sure that Madame d'Urfé would take him for some extraordinary being."

On reading the note, Madame d'Urfé muttered incantations in a mirror, burned incense, and walked around the room three times to prepare for Casanova's arrival.

———·———

Paris in June came as a relief to Casanova after his sojourn in Italy. "For all its imperfections," Paris remained "so attractive that no city in the world can dispute its right to be considered the city of cities." He went straightaway to mistress of mistresses, Madame d'Urfé, with the urgency of a lover, and to his delight she received him "with open arms." Although she was more than twenty years older than Casanova, he loved Madame d'Urfé in his way.

Beyond the renewal of their warm affection for one another, Casanova came to Paris with a plan for an "operation by which she was to be reborn as a man." It promised to be a mystical quest that would engage all her resources, and he knew she would pay him handsomely for the pleasure.

One afternoon, Madame d'Urfé invited Casanova to ride with her to the Bois de Boulogne, the rambling park and gardens on the western perimeter of Paris. Arriving at an estate on the northern edge, Madame reminisced about a mystical experience she'd had there eighteen years earlier. She'd fallen asleep, and on waking she witnessed one of her Kabbalistic creatures "ascend to Heaven," but not before he left her pregnant with a daughter, "whom he took from me ten years later, doubtless to punish me for having so far forgotten myself." One never knew whether to laugh or cry when listening to Madame recount incidents in her life. "Are you perfectly certain that Monsieur d'Urfé is not her father?" Casanova inquired, reasonably enough.

"Monsieur d'Urfé never had intercourse with me again after he saw me lying naked beside the divine Anael," she replied, referring to a Kabbalistic angel. And in time this angel also abandoned her. Casanova ventured that these experiences had prepared her for the even larger transformation he had in mind.

Casanova sought relief from the demands of Madame d'Urfé in the company of the wife of his brother Francesco, who constantly complained that "he was incapable of fulfilling the functions of a man toward a woman."

In that case, why did she, a woman of the world, marry him?

She invented reasons for his lack of performance to spare herself humiliation, for she was in love with him. "He looks such a Hercules," she offered. Casanova advised that her only options were to take a lover or to have the marriage annulled. But she *loved* her impotent husband, "for the wretch treats me so well that my love for him has only grown." Casanova considered demonstrating for her benefit exactly what was missing in her marriage to Francesco, but he considered it "out of the question," and so reassured himself that despite all else that he had done, he still maintained some sense of propriety. And he didn't want his brother's wife carrying his child, come to think of it. He was a libertine, not a fool. Still, he couldn't resist kissing his indulgent sister-in-law "in a way that showed her I was not my brother" before bidding her good night.

Casanova looked up lovers and other prospects that he recalled from previous visits to Paris, more from curiosity about their fate than from lust. Some were now widowed, others had moved from Paris to the provinces, or were lost; so much had changed during his absence. "Women, intrigues, and principles changed there as quickly as fashions," he mused.

He spent four wretched weeks in Munich, and "during that period I lost all my money, I pawned more than forty thousand francs' worth of jewels, which I never redeemed, and finally, worst of all, I lost my health." He excoriated himself for his "folly," his "fatal Genius," and his "incredible ineptitude" at allowing himself to be fleeced at faro, a circumstance that "reduced me to intolerable anxiety."

Amid the frenzy of gambling, he pursued a dancer named Renaud, who

stole whatever possessions he hadn't already gambled away. Worse, "she infected me with a disease that was devouring her," even though she appeared
perfectly fresh and healthy. When he suspected he'd contracted a venereal
disease from her, Renaud—a "serpent dispatched from Hell"—persuaded
him to refrain from seeing a surgeon while they were together in Munich
for fear that her reputation would be ruined. Even though he "added fresh
virulence to the poison she had instilled" into his system each day, he submitted to her wishes.

He tore himself away to seek treatment from an eminent Augsburg
physician, Salomon Ambrosius Kephalides, who placed Casanova on a
strict diet, prescribed baths, and administered "mercury massages." After six
grim weeks of this treatment, the patient felt worse than ever, having become "terrifyingly thin," with two painful tumors in his groin. Afraid for his
life, he sought out another physician, Francesco Antonio Algardi of Bologna, who placed him on a regimen of "ninety pills," taken with diluted milk
and barley water. After enduring ten weeks of this martyrdom, he began to
recover his health, although he remained rail-thin until late that year.

By September, his spirits rebounded. "Forgetting all my past sufferings,"
he remarked, "I went back to amusing myself," by which he meant, chiefly,
indulging his suddenly "gluttonous appetite" for food for three solid weeks,
"in order to restore my person to its original corpulence."

———•———

He left Augsburg in mid-December, bound for Paris, where he arrived on
the last day of the year. He'd promised Madame d'Urfé to sup with her on
the first day of 1762 in a furnished apartment that she'd provided for him
on the rue du Bac, in the 7th Arrondissement, and decorated, she informed
him, with "magnificent tapestries" depicting the Great Work of Alchemy—
transforming base metals into gold.

After moving into the apartment, he devoted the next three weeks to
his "promise to accomplish her rebirth as a man." It is entirely possible, indeed, likely that the mismatched couple spent their time at the rue du Bac
in bed, indulging their appetites on the pretext of preparing themselves for
a magical quest involving impregnating a virgin, who would give birth to a
reincarnation of Madame d'Urfé. "In her insane exaltation, she considered
the possibility of the operation a self-evident truth, and she was on fire with
impatience to see the virgin who was to be its chosen vessel." Casanova tried

to discourage Madame d'Urfé by pointing out that "she would have to die, and I counted on the natural love of life drawing the thing out," but she insisted he fetch a virgin immediately.

In need of an "unscrupulous hussy," he turned to a former traveling companion young enough to pretend to be a virgin. On January 25, 1762, he left Paris for Prague. There he found Maria Corticelli, a ballet dancer known as La Corticelli. When he arrived, "La Corticelli threw herself at my neck, laughing as always." She'd always been a lot madcap, but she had matured. She had blossomed into a "very attractive girl." And then he took her.

Afterward, he wrote to Madame d'Urfé that he was returning to Paris with a young virgin from a family as old and distinguished as Madame's, the Lascaris. They should meet at a country house to "perform certain cabalistic ceremonies." Madame d'Urfé knew the ideal place for their operation, an ancient castle outside Paris. Within its walls, she expected to be "reborn from the off-spring of this favored virgin." To put his plan into action, Casanova would have to moderate Madame d'Urfé's expectations while "instructing my young scatterbrain," La Corticelli, to play the role of a virgin princess. He accomplished this task mainly by threatening to send the girl back to obscurity if she didn't obey his every word, but if she cooperated, she'd earn a fortune. Looking back on the scheme, Casanova "was sorely to repent of my persistence." To his mind, he was embarking on "the greatest mistake I have made in all my life!"

The spectacle commenced with the arrival of Casanova and La Corticelli at the castle of Pont-Carré: four crenelated towers surrounded by a moat. The drawbridges had been lowered, and all the servants of the household stood in readiness, "like a general prepared to surrender the place to us." The scene unfolded like a fairy tale come to life: "The dear lady, who was insane only because she had an excess of intelligence, gave the pretended princess a reception so flattering that she would have been astounded if I had not forewarned her." The girl and Madame d'Urfé embraced tenderly and recited their genealogies.

Swarms of "venomous" gnats "produced extremely painful swellings on our faces." Casanova would have preferred to cut and run, but they'd agreed to spend a week at the castle, with the day of the operation fixed for the 14th day of April. On that day, Casanova wrote, "Madame d'Urfé brought me the virgin Lascaris." "She undressed her, perfumed her, draped her in a magnificent veil," and then awaited the "operation that was to result in her being reborn nine months later." What exactly occurred during the operation was left to the reader's imagination. He invoked the moon, always a powerful influence in séances, the highly useful oracle whom he claimed to consult, and it amounted to a beguiling deception. In reality, Madame d'Urfé was too old to be a socially acceptable paramour, but as he repeatedly lamented, he lately felt his virility slipping away, and the dowager would scarcely have noticed or cared. If so, the two of them were lovers under cover of the Kabbalah, the true nature of the "operation."

At the same time, La Corticelli inaugurated a romance with a youth attending to these rites, much to Casanova's displeasure. "I had twice surprised her in her room with the youth, who was interested in her only as a young adolescent is interested in all girls." His solution was to move the proceedings several days' journey away, to Aix-la-Chapelle, where he lodged at an inn, and not very happily. It pained Casanova to hear La Corticelli complain bitterly about losing her "pretty boy," who had supplanted the Venetian adventurer in her heart. Casanova tried to discipline her for her own good, as he explained, and to keep her from "behaving like a prostitute," even though he had placed her in this situation. Even more humiliating was the idea of losing out to youthful rivals.

He dreaded that the girl would betray her lowly origins. "I begged her to dance like a young lady of station and not like a ballet girl." She defied him, raising his hackles. "Vengeance never ceases to burn in my heart until it has been satisfied," he vowed. And when Madame d'Urfé gave the girl a pair of diamond earrings and a ring worth sixty thousand francs, he confiscated the jewelry at the first opportunity and gambled it away. Afterward, he began to lose interest in La Corticelli, who, he now claimed, retained only a "slight hold" on his heart as he went in search of a new object of his affections.

Madame d'Urfé continued to make her alchemical demands. Over breakfast, he found her "inconsolable." According to her lunar calculations, "at exactly three minutes past four o'clock I was to accomplish the mysterious creation of the child from whom she was to be reborn." At that moment, he was supposed to impregnate La Corticelli, impersonating Lascaris, who suddenly refused to go along, "writhing on her bed, feigning convulsions that would make it impossible for me to accomplish the task of fecundation." Keeping his wits about him, Casanova "affected a hypocritical grief" as he realized he could use this incident to distance himself from La Corticelli, with whom he'd grown thoroughly disenchanted.

To ease Madame d'Urfé's distress, he "lavished consolations" on her in the form of prescriptions from his imaginary oracle, directing him to search for a "predestined girl whose purity was under the protection of the higher Geniuses." Casanova labored to make this chicanery sound convincing, and "the mad Madame d'Urfé" pronounced herself "perfectly content with the oracle's promises."

La Corticelli tried to regain the upper hand by claiming that he'd gotten her pregnant. "Greatly surprised, I stared at her without saying a word, but I was considering how best to get rid of the impudent wretch" whom he had recently loved to distraction. Just then her mother added a clarification; La Corticelli was indeed pregnant, but by a count in Prague, not Casanova. Freed from one sort of bondage, he returned to "my poor infatuated Madame d'Urfé," convincing her through devious alchemical reasoning that young Lascaris had been defiled by an evil genius of the spirit realm, and as a consequence had become pregnant "with a gnome." To rectify matters, Casanova directed Madame d'Urfé to "write to the moon," a Kabbalistic exercise that "filled her with joy."

He moved the scene of the séances once again, this time to Burtscheid, in western Germany, away from creditors, and declared that the exact date of the "operation" depended on the phase of the moon. At the proper moment, "I had arranged to have a large bath filled with perfumes pleasing to the luminary of the night." A scene of zany mystical communion between the two unfolded:

When we had burned the aromatics and sprinkled the perfumes appropriate to the worship of Selenis [the moon], and recited the mystic prayers, we undressed completely, and, holding my letter concealed in my left hand, with my right I escorted her to the edge of the bath, in which was an alabaster cup filled with spirits of juniper, which I ignited, meanwhile uttering cabalistic words that I didn't understand and which she repeated after me, handing me the letter addressed to Selenis. I burned the letter in the juniper flames on which the full moon was shining, and the credulous Madame d'Urfé assured me that she had seen the characters she had written ascending along the luminary's rays. After that we got into the bath, and the letter which I held concealed in my hand, written in silver on glazed green paper, appeared on the surface of the water ten minutes later. As soon as Madame d'Urfé saw it she took it up reverently and left the bath with me.

After they'd dressed, she read that the much hoped for "hypostasis," or accumulation of bodily fluids needed to attain immortality, would be postponed until the following year, 1763, in Marseille. As Madame d'Urfé swallowed her disappointment, Casanova savored his reprieve and, on returning to Aix-la-Chapelle, amused himself with several flirtations.

In Geneva, Casanova pursued Helena and her twenty-year-old cousin Hedwig (as he called Anne Marie May), the niece of a Swiss Protestant pastor. As Casanova had been told, Hedwig seemed more concerned with matters of theology and philosophy than with amorous pursuits.

Nevertheless, as he strolled with the cousins along Lake Geneva, "we arrived at the edge of a superb basin of water with a flight of marble stairs down which one went to bathe." Before they dipped their feet in the chilly water, he offered to remove their shoes and stockings, and they readily agreed. Of course, to bathe, they must remove their dresses as well, which they did, and when they emerged from the water, holding their dresses, "it was my part to dry them with all the handkerchiefs I had. This agreeable office allowed me to see and touch in perfect freedom." Hedwig, the young philosopher, took exception, but Helena yielded "in a manner so tender and languishing that I had to use all my will to keep from going further." As he helped them on with their shoes and stockings, he rhapsodized about "having seen the secret beauties of the two most beautiful girls in Geneva." Accompanying them to a garden house "full of pot-pourri jars, charming engravings," and best of all, a couch, he dared to "expose to their gaze the principal effective cause of humanity," that is, his erect manhood. He began to feign a climax, when all at once "an abundant emission of liquid threw them into the greatest astonishment."

The two girls laughed and squealed as Casanova, pleased with himself, entreated Hedwig, that is, "*beautiful* Hedwig," to sit on his lap.

"I have never done it with a man," she protested.

"Nor have I," Helena added.

Not a problem! He invited them to sit close to him and while they cir-
cled him with their arms, "I explored their charms with my hands," while he
"let them amuse themselves by touching me as they pleased until I finally
wet their hands with a second emission," which they "curiously examined on
their fingers."

In the meantime Voltaire expected Casanova at his estate, Ferney, to
resume their argument, but the libertine "stupidly made up my mind not
to go there," and frittered away his time in philosophical debates with
Hedwig, the youthful theologian, and in escapades with Helena. He hid
in a closet that reeked of ham and cheese, and was infested with nausea-
inducing rats, until Helena arrived. Permitted to escape the prison of the
closet—he'd remained confined there long enough to relive the misery of I
Piombi—he was led by Helena's hand, "as soft as satin," to the bed, where
both cousins joined him. "Our destinies must be one and the same," Helena
proclaimed, and Casanova responded by saying that he loved them both
equally. What else *could* he say? He undressed and jumped into the middle
of the bed.

"Come quickly to my sides," he said, "and you will see if I love you as
you deserve to be loved." Hedwig disrobed as Casanova spouted praise until
"at last Venus appears in the state of nature," trying in vain to cover her
breasts and "secret charms," but "aghast at all that she cannot hide." He rapidly donned a "protective covering"—a sturdy, British sheepskin condom—
and "made Hedwig a woman." In his estimation, "the moment of pain was
nothing in comparison with the pleasure."

Helena, six years younger than her cousin, also experienced his "painful
rupturing" but "uttered only sighs of happiness." He decided that she was
even more "voluptuous than her cousin" and capable of multiple orgasms.
"I admired this amazing capacity," he enthused as he envied the intensity of
her pleasure, for "she passed from life to death fourteen times while I was
accomplishing a single operation." *Fourteen climaxes!* At dawn, he returned
to his lodging and slept until noon.

Afterward, he received a communiqué from Madame d'Urfé, in residence at her estate near Lyon. The occasion of the third attempt at regeneration was approaching, she reminded him, and she would be enchanted to
see him. Of course, "I went without losing a moment."

On February 10, 1763, the Treaty of Paris marked the end of hostilities between Britain and France. France agreed to surrender its possessions east of the Mississippi River to Britain, to the relief of British colonists in the New World. The war had nearly bankrupted France, and it prompted Britain to raise taxes, disrupting its transoceanic empire. Days later, another treaty, this one between Austria and Prussia, led to the restoration of a reduced state of Saxony.

With hostilities ended, Casanova flew to Teresa Lanti—formerly Bellino—whom he described as "my old passion." (For the time being, he forgot all about Madame d'Urfe's invitation.) When he came upon Teresa in bed, appropriately enough, he claimed to be overcome with deep feeling. She explained that she had parted ways with her husband months before, but she still looked after their son, Cesarino, staying at a boardinghouse nearby, but available to Casanova. "She said that she was happy, and that gossip had attributed a lover to her, but it was not true, and that I could come to see her in perfect freedom at any time."

As they compared their recent adventures, Casanova found himself falling in love with Teresa all over again; she was still as "beautiful and fresh" in his eyes as she'd been years before when they'd first met at Ancona and everything about her, even her gender, was mysterious. Now the mystery had been replaced by experience. If she still pleased him, she said, they could "live together until death."

They could talk about this subject next time, Casanova retorted; at the moment, he needed to "prove my love to her on this instant." And so he took her there and then. Afterward, he reproached her for being cold, but Teresa swore that she was thrilled "to have found me full of fire"—even if she didn't share his passion at that moment. As he left, Casanova felt his love for Teresa to be as strong as ever—even while he indulged in yet another diversion.

He was living out the libertine's philosophy, but not everyone rejoiced in his good fortune. The trouble began when he accepted a pinch of snuff from an acquaintance whom he called "Countess Rinaldi"—the name was invented—who was the wife of "Count Rinaldi," a gambler and adventurer like Casanova, but it was not the mild sternutative he expected. The powder caused nosebleeds thought to remedy headaches. But he didn't have a headache! Not to worry, the Countess said, it would provoke only a little bleeding and would have a therapeutic effect. "We instantly fell to sneezing together five or six times in succession." Soon their noses bled so copiously they had to resort to large silver bowls to catch the bright red droplets, twenty or thirty in all from each of them. She laughed, and so did he, although he knew not why. "Our mingled blood will bring an eternal friendship between us," she confided. What *was* this powder called? She wouldn't say. Would she give him some? She shook her head.

When they parted, he went to an apothecary for further inquiries, but she knew nothing about the mysterious sneezing powder. Perhaps it was euphorbia, an herb with some of these properties, but the substance Casanova described was more powerful.

He began to learn more about the plot when he received word that a Capuchin friar urgently needed to speak to him. Puzzled, he allowed the Capuchin into his room, and shut the door. "Beware of disdaining my words," the friar warned, "for you might pay for your scorn with your life." The friar presented himself as the instrument of Casanova's guardian angel. "God in his goodness will not abandon you."

"Speak, I beg you," said Casanova, barely able to contain his patience.

The friar instructed him to go to a nearby house, ascend to the third floor, ring the doorbell, ask for a woman, and press one or two zecchini into her palm. When she locked the door, he was to request a "little bottle and everything that goes with it." When Casanova did as told, the old woman laughed and said she knew he was in love. It was his own fault that he wasn't successful, but she would give him the methods to get his wish.

"At these words I saw I was dealing with a witch." He wasn't there to talk about love; he wanted a certain bottle "and everything that went with it." She twisted her face and trembled. He flourished a knife to keep her seated, and offered to pay twice her price for the items. When he asked her who he was, she astonished him by reciting his name, and he gave her even more money, at which point she cried from gratitude. She wouldn't have killed him, she said; she would have cast a spell over him, to make him miserable and in love. To demonstrate, she led him to a closet, and "in utter astonishment I see a thousand things it is beyond common sense to explain. Vials, stones, metals, minerals, small nails, spikes, tongs, furnaces, coals, misshapen statues, and I know not what." Amid the clutter she pointed to the bottle containing his blood mixed with that of the Countess. A devilish brew! He was bathed in sweat. The witch explained that she was prepared to apply the unguent to him.

To demonstrate, she opened a long coffinlike box containing a grotesque wax statue, "stark naked," with his name on it and his features, crudely fashioned, carved into its face. There was a ribbon around the statue's neck with a replica of the cross he wore. The bizarre sight reminded him of a "monstrous Priapus," and, succumbing to "hysterical laughter," he collapsed into a chair. The witch told him he was a fool to laugh; if she'd applied the blood in the bottle and cast a spell and burned his wax effigy, woe unto him! Experienced in the ways of witches—a benign sorceress had saved his life as a child, and now this witch wanted to wrest control of his soul—he handed over twelve zecchini to halt her incantations. The tactic worked. The witch melted the effigy in the fireplace and tossed the blood out the window.

When it was over, the witch kissed his hand, told him he was as good as an angel, and begged his forgiveness, and of course his promise of secrecy. To his amazement, she offered to make the Countess fall "madly in love" with him, on condition that he pay another twelve zecchini. Having the upper hand at last, he declined, and urged her to renounce her "accursed trade" before she was burned at the stake.

He spent an enjoyable carnival in Milan, filled with numerous pursuits. His rendezvous with Madame d'Urfé, awaiting him in Marseille, would take place around Eastertide, so he departed from Milan on March 20, 1763, bound for Genoa, where he heard that a mysterious visitor wished to see him.

Chapter 14

Marcolina

It was a young priest; stranger still, he was Casanova's nearly forgotten brother, Gaetano, whom he'd "always despised." Yet there he was.

He endured Gaetano's "stupid embraces" and stood back to look at the wretch: "dirty, disgusting, and in rags." The young man's only assets were his "pretty face, fine hair, good complexion," and his youth, for he was twenty-nine—nearly ten years younger than his brother.

"You have become a vagabond," Casanova said. "Why did you leave Venice, and what do you want of me?"

"I beg you not to drive me to despair," Gaetano countered, "for really I am capable of killing myself."

Casanova was having none of it, and told his forlorn brother to return to Venice and live off his sermons. But it was not that simple, Gaetano explained; he wasn't alone. "A gang of thieves?" Casanova ventured.

No! "It is a girl." He'd abducted her from her father's house.

Casanova demanded to see the girl in question, so they went to the shabby inn where Gaetano was lodging, trudged up the creaky stairs to the fourth floor, entered a "wretched den," and there she stood: pretty, tall, dark, "appetizing, with a certain haughty pride." The moment Giacomo Casanova saw his brother's luscious Venetian mistress, he wanted her, and she wanted him. He could feel the heat rising from her body. This woman needed passionate sex to set her right, and his little brother was not the man to do it. *What was she doing with a priest?* She wanted only to be rid of Gaetano, who'd infuriated her with false promises: "He made me believe that the world beyond Venice was a paradise; I wanted to see it, and I left my home; I found that one is nowhere as well off as in our country." Not surprisingly, Gaetano had been scheming to seduce her. If his older brother had a sliver of compassion, he would arrange to return her to Venice immediately.

"I listened to his whole tirade standing and in real astonishment," Casanova recalled. It was tragic, but the sight of his young brother holding his head in his hands while she blustered contained a "touch of comedy." They could have been enacting a scene from the latest *commedia dell'arte*. Not only that, but the girl's typically Venetian nature—"her frankness, her just indignation, her revulsion of feeling, her courage"—along with her obvious sexual hunger and pungent Venetian dialect—awakened intense longing both for his lost home and for her body. Now that she'd made her plea, he couldn't abandon her. He promised to return her to Venice "accompanied by a decent woman" in the weekly coach from Genoa. That should have been the end of the matter, but it turned out she had a child, reluctant as she was to admit it. In extremis, she gave Gaetano "a backhanded slap with the utmost vigor." Rather than retaliate, he quietly "turned to the window, raising his eyes to heaven, and burst into tears."

Moved, Casanova spoke to the girl. "You are quite a little devil, my beautiful Signorina. The man you are mistreating is unhappy because you made him fall in love with you." His words had the opposite of their intended effect. That wasn't the first slap she'd given him, she boasted.

Gaetano roused himself and excommunicated the girl, "for I am a priest." She threatened to give Gaetano more of the same, but Casanova intervened, told her to collect her things, and come with him. Twenty zecchini purchased his brother's grudging cooperation and silence. As Casanova had learned, every woman had her price, and this one came cheap. Her name, he learned, was Marcolina. She couldn't have been more than seventeen years old, and she quickly transferred her affection to Giacomo Casanova, who offered the prospect of escape from her wretched existence with Gaetano. Soon she was saying she wanted to marry the dashing and confident adventurer standing before her. *Marry?* Impossible, Casanova snapped, he was already married: a convenient lie making him all the more desirable in her eyes. All at once, he pressed her for physical favors, "using only the gentleness that any woman finds harder to resist than force," but she ran away, locking a door after her. When he caught her in bed, fondling another woman, who was his servant, he treated the matter with levity, as an unusual but revealing quirk. No matter. She would make a fine mistress.

His brother, meanwhile, refused to relinquish Marcolina. "She can't bear you," Casanova remarked.

"She loves me," Gaetano bleated.

"She slaps you."

But that was only because she loved Gaetano, or so he tried to persuade himself. If Casanova had tried to spirit her away, "she would have beaten you half to death" and then gone to the police. No, Casanova had a better idea. He would find a new posting for his brother in France "under some bishop." He hurled invectives at his brother, he was a "proud fool," an "ignorant hypocrite" who profaned his calling and lacked talent of any sort.

In that case, Gaetano replied, he was off to Paris, where he would find their brother Francesco, the well-known and successful artist, "who has a kinder heart than yours" and would shelter him.

Excellent, Casanova said. He would send the young man to France by sea.

"The sea makes me sick," Gaetano complained.

"Then you shall vomit."

Having settled the matter, he turned his attention to Marcolina.

CASANOVA: I love you, and if you do not consent to become my mistress it will kill me.

MARCOLINA: Never, for if I fell in love with you, when you left me, it would kill me, too.

CASANOVA: I will never leave you.

MARCOLINA: Very well, take me to France, and there we will begin sleeping together.

Her insistence that the servant whose favors she'd enjoyed come along with him added to his anticipation. "Having acquired the right to witness their sport, I had no objection." The only loser in the transaction was his unfortunate brother, who still yearned for Marcolina, twenty zecchini notwithstanding, and whom she taunted with coquettish glances from behind her *zendale*, a large Venetian scarf of black silk. Not only that, said Casanova, "the cruel creature clung so closely to my arm that we appeared to be on the best of terms." Despite appearances, Marcolina refused to grant his brother "the slightest favor" as he trailed them to Marseille, where Madame d'Urfé waited to complete the third and final operation of her regeneration.

———•———

Casanova settled into his lodgings in Marseille, Aux Treize Cantons, and greeted Madame d'Urfé after his long absence. Despite his numerous love affairs, she had more of a hold over him than he cared to admit. Old, wealthy beyond imagining, and besotted with him, she was all he desired, and all he wished to flee.

He played along as Madame displayed seven packages each containing seven pounds of "metal governed by a planet, and seven precious stones governed by the same planet, each weighing seven carats: diamond, ruby, emerald, sapphire, chrysolite, topaz, and opal." With these objects in hand, she explained, they were ready to "perform the consecration," that is, engage in ritualized sex for three hours a day for a week.

Casanova had no intention of spending tedious sessions in bed with Madame, and announced that his oracle told him that "for seven days in succession I must go to the country to sleep, practice perfect abstinence from every mortal woman, and worship the moon with the proper ceremonies every night in the open air to prepare to regenerate her myself." Madame d'Urfé expressed gratitude to Casanova for his adherence to the protocol "to ensure the successful outcome of the operation."

She was eager to get down to the business of her regeneration, but Casanova delayed, invoking the mystical figures who supposedly controlled her destiny. He gave her the name "Seramis" for purposes of the rite and explained that the "Word," or semen, to regenerate her would arrive from Casanova himself via the Milky Way. He proceeded to explain how this would occur: two days after they completed their "ceremonies of consecration," and purified themselves in a bath, he would "inoculate Seramis" in sexual congress. Yet even as he spoke he felt no ardor for the task. "I began considering how best to avoid cutting a poor figure," he recalled. "The Marquise was beautiful but old. I might find myself a nullity. At *thirty-eight* years of age," he emphasized, "I was beginning to see that I was often subject to that disastrous misfortune."

His aphrodisiac would be Marcolina, "transformed into a bath attendant." In this guise, she would "instantly procure me the generative power that I needed." He desperately needed her help with this, his most elaborate seduction to date, and she blindly agreed. To disguise her as a page assisting him, he ordered a suit of livery consisting of a waist-length jacket of green velvet and matching breeches, green stockings, green shoes, even a green net for her black hair. The costume enhanced rather than concealed her femininity. He instructed Marcolina to present herself to the Marquise in this costume, and to pose as a mute. "She was beginning to speak broken French, but so badly that I told her never to open her mouth," he complained. At a prearranged signal, she was to give Madame a note.

"Will you have the courage to do that?" he asked. Of course she would. And so the *folie à deux* became a *folie à troix*.

At the appointed time, she would undress the Marquise completely, and then she would massage the lady from the tip of her toes to the top of her thighs, "and no farther." Casanova would simultaneously remove every stitch of his clothing and "embrace the Marquise closely" while Marcolina looked on. After the star-crossed couple completed the act, "You will wash her amorous parts with your delicate hands and then dry them. You will do the same to me, and I will embrace her closely a second time." And then a third, "until the end of the skirmish," after which Marcolina would cleanse and dry Casanova and the Marquise one last time. The thought of Casanova embracing another woman made Marcolina wince, but when told that the Marquise was nearly sixty, the girl said, "I am sorry for you, my dear Giacometto."

When the group had completed their propitiations to the planets, Casanova had the imaginary oracle "declare that Seramis was to be regenerated" according to a confluence of the planets in the "planetary system of magicians" and in the equally imaginary system of Ptolemy—"so the reader, if he knows anything about magic, will see that I had to perform the operation on Madame d'Urfé from half past two o'clock to five minutes before six."

As the hour neared, he concealed Marcolina in a cupboard in his room, giving her the name "Undine" for purposes of this exercise, and put on a magic dressing gown. He warned Madame d'Urfé to prepare herself for the operation and reminded her they were following orders from the oracle. He would have pitied the deluded Marquise, but "she moved me too strongly to laughter." And when she told him that tomorrow he would become her husband and father, she moved him to concern.

On April 26, 1763, having refrained from intimacy with Marcolina to preserve his energy for the task at hand, he was confronted with Madame d'Urfé in a lace cap, a blond mantle covering her bosom "which forty years earlier had been of a beauty unequaled in France," and a heavy application of rouge suggesting a prostitute, an aristocrat, or both. His gaze fastened on the fortune in diamonds and emeralds with which she had covered herself. As he tried to kneel to kiss her hands, she reached out to embrace the man she expected to become her mystical husband.

At the appointed hour, half past two, "Undine" in her green velvet livery appeared from her hiding place, knelt, and presented "Seramis" with the note Casanova had prepared. *"What is written under water can only be read under water."* Declaring that she understood what the note meant, "Seramis"— that is, Madame d'Urfé—descended into her bath, dipped the paper into the water, and read the writing thus revealed: *"I am dumb but I am not deaf. I have come out of the Rhône to bathe you, the Oromasis has begun."* Obeying the note, she sat on the bed as Marcolina took off her clothes and washed her feet. Casanova invoked the King of the Salamanders—salamanders playing a significant role in the occult—to witness the union. In a flash, "I consummate the marriage to Seramis while admiring the beauties of Marcolina." As he expected, he needed the girl's assistance; without her, "the operation would have failed" because Madame d'Urfé, while "affectionate, amorous, clean," left him cold. After completing the act, he bid Marcolina— that is, "Undine"—to "embrace the bride" and to wash the tops of her thighs and then do the same with Casanova.

Madame d'Urfé wanted more. Casanova commenced "the second assault, which would be the most strenuous," he recalled. "I work for half an hour, groaning and sweating and tiring Seramis without being able to reach the final point and feeling ashamed to cheat her; she wiped from my brow the sweat from my hair mixed with pomade and powder." Marcolina's soothing caresses had no effect. After an hour of strenuous effort, "I finally determined to make an end, after imitating all the usual signs that appear at that sweet moment," and so he declared his undeserved victory, his fake orgasm. "Even Marcolina was deceived."

His guile won him a third invitation. When Marcolina "instantly became Lesbian" with the Marquise, he felt himself come alive but unable to ejaculate. "Undine" became undone by the failure, and "Seramis" by now only wanted him to finish, but he couldn't maintain his erection. "I decided to cheat again by an agony accompanied by convulsions that ended in motionlessness." He eventually pretended to wake from his stupor. In a postcoital trance, the three of them bathed and dressed, and Madame d'Urfé, generous as always, put one of her necklaces around "Undine's" neck.

Had the operation worked? The Marquise's urgent question "terrified" Casanova, who struggled to inform her that the Word was now "in her soul." Next February, "she would give birth to herself with her sex changed." For now, she must rest in bed for one hundred and seven hours. She was overjoyed. Would Casanova join her? Unfortunately, he could not, explaining that he had to retrieve the paraphernalia he'd employed to propitiate the moon. After he excused himself from her presence, "I made infinitely merry with Marcolina until half past seven o'clock." After spending fourteen hours in bed with her, he decided that she was the equal of the most passionate, intense lovers he'd ever experienced, including Maria Eleonora and Henriette. But afterward, he told her she would soon return to Venice with all the money he'd been giving her, her new velvet suit, and there she would find herself a rich husband. And then they made love one more time, much to her surprise at his athleticism. Hadn't he anointed Madame d'Urfé twice? No, he explained, just once.

"Do you always need to have a young girl before your eyes when you want to be loving with her?" Marcolina inquired. Of course not, he explained. On this occasion he'd promised her a child. "So you have undertaken to make her pregnant!" she exclaimed. "Let me laugh, please." Did she truly believe she was pregnant?

Surely she did, said Casanova, for she believed "that I gave her the seed."

"*Oh, what a joke!*"

Casanova was convinced that completing his great "operation" would satisfy Madame d'Urfé, but within days she insisted that she felt symptoms of pregnancy and that he must marry her. "You will be the guardian of my child, who will be your son; by so doing, you will help me keep possession of my entire fortune and have control of what I will inherit from my brother." But if he neglected her come February, when she would give birth to the male version of herself, she foresaw a calamitous outcome: "I shall be declared a bastard, and I shall be forced to lose an income of eighty thousand livres, of which you can keep me in possession." And one other concern: she was so in love with young "Undine" that she wished to "sleep with her in fourteen or fifteen years"—in her incarnation as a man. "The softness of her skin is incredible. Her saliva is sweet." Had Casanova slept with her, too?

He fumbled for an adequate reply. The truth would have "made her miserable," because "only chimeras could satisfy her."

At that impasse, saucy Marcolina caught the eye of a Venetian merchant who owned wine warehouses in Marseille. At first, Casanova felt relieved and flattered that she had attracted a match of this caliber, and he showered her with money and clothing—a dowry of sorts—and when he stepped back he saw that she had "become a great beauty and had acquired the manners of good society." It was apparent that "she had set the worthy merchant on fire." But on second thought, he was reluctant to part with his prize. They fought. They reconciled. They fought again. And there were others, some new, some old, who briefly reappeared to tantalize him and to remind him of what once was or what might have been. Despite these conflicting romantic impulses, he insisted, "It was one of the best moments in my life." On reflection, "I saw myself as the author of the whole delightful comedy, very satisfied to find that on balance I did more good than evil in this world." As if to confirm his good cheer, Henriette, the lover whom he valued above all others, reappeared, in a rather mysterious fashion.

One day in May, when he was riding with Marcolina to Avignon, their carriage broke down. They could not proceed until a cartwright repaired the damage. They took refuge in a grand domicile. On their best behavior, they were served lemonade, and they later called on the lady of the house, who, having injured her ankle, lay in bed in an alcove shadowed by "curtains of crimson taffeta." In the dim light, "it was impossible to see her well enough to know if she was ugly or beautiful, young or getting on in years."

Casanova introduced his Marcolina to the lady, a Countess. To his surprise, the two conversed in the Venetian dialect, the older woman explaining that she'd often talked with Venetians. He still didn't know whose house it was, and didn't dare to ask. Marcolina and the Countess got on so well that they decided to spend the night together, which he took as a sign of "fond friendship," and nothing more. When he saw Marcolina in the morning, he asked her over coffee how she and the unseen Countess had passed the night, and was shocked by her reply: "We indulged in all the wantonness in which you know two women who love each other indulge when they are in bed together."

"Faithless wretch, you prefer a woman to me."

No, Marcolina replied, "It was a passing fancy," and to redeem herself in his eyes described their lovemaking. First, the Countess put her soft tongue between Marcolina's lips, and Marcolina responded in kind. When they went to bed after supper, "I managed to tickle her you know where, and she did the same to me." One thing led to another, and "I made her happy." She flourished her hand. "Look. This proves how pleased she was," she chirped as she displayed a "ring set with four stones of the first water of two or three carats each." (The "stones" were likely diamonds, and the greater a diamond's clarity, approaching that of water, the higher its value. A diamond of the first water signified the highest quality.) He estimated the jewelry could fetch two hundred louis—a very respectable night's work. He was so pleased that he lavished kisses on Marcolina and "forgave her everything." He had only one question: Why hadn't the Countess wanted to see him?

Marcolina said, "I think she felt ashamed to let herself be seen by my lover."

When they reached Avignon in the newly repaired carriage, Marcolina surprised "dear Giacometto" with a letter, courtesy of the anonymous Countess. His heart was "pounding" as he read the salutation, "To the most honorable man I have known in this world." He unfolded the letter to behold a blank sheet of paper with a single word at the bottom: "Henriette."

It was her style, her laconic manner. *Henriette!* When they parted years before, she'd scratched a message on a windowpane predicting that he'd forget about her, but he still thought of her with longing every day of his life. Casanova, the very opposite of laconic, proclaimed that he loved her with the same ardor. He was *devasté, ravagé, disastrato* . . . "You saw me, and you did not want me to see you? Perhaps you thought your charms might have lost the power with which they chained my soul sixteen years ago," he exclaimed. "Cruel Henriette! Unjust Henriette! . . . Adorable and generous Henriette!" He rambled on as if possessed, pleading with the image of her burned into his mind and heart, trying to understand her unnecessary absence. "You are a widow, Henriette. You are rich. Let me imagine that you are happy. Perhaps you only toyed with Marcolina to let me know that you are happy." Marcolina was stunned by the outburst. He'd frightened her, she said, "You went pale, you spent a quarter of an hour like an idiot." His "trance" ended only when the innkeeper stopped by his table to offer his compliments and to ask how his guests had enjoyed the meal.

With calm restored, Marcolina revealed that the Countess—Henriette— had advised that if she wanted to be happy, "I must never leave you." Yet she knew that Casanova planned to send her home to Venice while he traveled to England.

As their journey continued, Marcolina again went to bed with her "wife," as Casanova remained "the spectator of a scene that was always new though I had witnessed it so many times." When the two women were done, they

A scene from the German edition of Casanova's memoir

attacked him "violently," and he spent "almost the whole night abetting the furies of two bacchantes" who refused to quit until he could no longer become aroused, or "become a nullity offering no hope of resurrection." In the morning, the girls were still in bed, fast asleep, "wrapped around each other like two eels."

Later in May, Casanova arrived in Lyon with Marcolina on his arm. They took rooms at the splendid Hôtel du Parc; he went directly to a house belonging to Madame d'Urfé in the spacious Place Bellecour, in the center of the city. He found her as before, nattering about Paralis and her mystical ceremonies. Playing along, he consulted the oracle to advise about her lying-in and the best way to avoid a descent into poverty after her rebirth as a man. Trying to extricate himself from this sticky situation, he said the oracle had decreed that she marry a gentleman chosen by Casanova to preserve her immense inheritance.

He rushed back to Marcolina, who brought disturbing news. A certain Giacomo Passano, with whom Casanova had a brief, bitter history, had gotten wind of the "operation" involving Madame d'Urfé, seen it for the elaborate scheme it was, and claimed that Casanova had attempted to poison him. This lunatic Passano wanted the world to know that Casanova was "the greatest scoundrel on earth" who was "ruining Madame d'Urfé by blasphemous lies." Passano had made it his business to accuse Casanova of being a "sorcerer, a counterfeiter, a thief, a spy, a coin clipper, a traitor, a cardsharper, an issuer of false bills of exchange, a forger of handwriting, and in short the worst of men . . ."

. . . leaving Casanova no choice but to hire a lawyer to defend himself. Passano aimed to have him sentenced to death. As if that weren't bad enough, he'd persuaded Casanova's brother Gaetano to testify against him. But Casanova also learned that payment of a thousand louis would cancel these charges. He needed no time to think matters through. He refused to yield to extortion, to the fury of his accusers.

When he visited his brother Francesco, the artist, who did he find there but Gaetano! "I consider you a monster," Casanova told him plainly. Francesco, almost as talkative as Casanova, recited a litany of indignities that Gaetano had inflicted: "In the three or four weeks that he has been here he has turned our house topsy-turvy. He's eaten all the food . . . distracted the servants . . . made the place all but unlivable . . . in short, our brother is an intolerable individual." How fortunate that Casanova had appeared, "for I hope that between us we will tell him tomorrow and no later to mind his own fucking business."

Casanova nodded. "Nothing could be easier." Send his rags to a furnished room and obtain a police order banning him from your household! He would give his brother money just to go away.

Gaetano complained bitterly, accusing Casanova of "despotism."

"Thank God, you monster, that instead of giving you a beating I give you money. You tried to get me hanged."

All the while, Marcolina bustled about Lyon, shopping for clothes, and meeting women with whom she exchanged the "petticoat password"—a signal of mutual recognition among lesbians. In this way she remained true to herself and followed her whims. At the same time, Casanova had been planning to flee to England, far from Marcolina and Madame d'Urfé. Marcolina begged him to take her along, but he planned to go alone once he summoned the willpower to abandon her bed.

He confided to several prominent Venetians that he proposed to visit London "in the expectation of making my fortune by a project I had in mind." He required only the approval of the English Secretary of State. The project was a lottery similar to the successful enterprise he'd introduced in Paris, but two lotteries were already operating in England, both controversial. He believed his version would meet with more favor. The Venetians were quick to remind him of "the crime I had committed" and his status as persona non grata in his homeland. How could he hope to succeed in London?

What a relief when Marcolina returned from shopping to distract him. The moment they were alone, "I flung myself over the bed in my dressing gown, refusing to listen to all the very reasonable things Marcolina was saying to me." She begged him to stay. Why was he so intent on leaving her? "Consider that it is not I who am leaving you, but you who are sending me away." (At that moment, Casanova's servant was readying his carriage "for a long journey"—without her.) He consoled her with enough gems and Venetian ducats to guarantee her a comfortable income if properly invested. The prospect of riches made her giddy. "Marcolina was crying while she laughed and laughing while she cried." He couldn't articulate a precise reason for ending this love affair—it wasn't her roving eye, for Marcolina's flirtations with other women only excited him more—but he believed he "must let her go to make room for the others whom heaven had destined for me." Having made his decision, "We supped gloomily, and, despite love, the night we spent was not gay." She could not comprehend his obstinate behavior. "She said it over and over again, how could I be my own executioner; and she was right, for I did not understand it, either," a worry that led to some larger reflections about his mounting sense of disillusionment. "In the course of my life I have done countless things I did not want to do, and each time I was driven to it by some occult power that I took it into my head not to resist." And so he found himself always in search of the perfect love, always unable to find it or sustain it, and predisposed to reenact his mother's bewildering abandonment of him.

He "embraced Marcolina for the last time" and mounted his horse. "Then I left at full gallop, hoping to kill the horse and perish with it; but death never comes to the wretch who longs for it." Days later, he chartered a boat and "crossed the Channel in two and a half hours with the strongest of winds." He could only guess what trials awaited him on arrival.

Chapter 15

La Charpillon

The white cliffs of Dover emerged from the mist like an apparition. Concealed within the shadows were smugglers who lived on the beach; their presence kept customs inspectors on high alert. A self-proclaimed Venetian adventurer such as Casanova, traveling with gems and foreign currency, was certain to attract the interest of both robbers and customs officials. Their inquiries struck him as "extremely tedious, impertinent, indiscreet, and even indecent, but I had to put up with it and conceal my feelings." Ashore, he savored a fresh palette of sensations. "The island called England is a different color from that which one sees on the surface of the Continent. The sea is extraordinary, for being part of the Atlantic Ocean, it is subject to the ebb and flow of the tides"—a novelty to those familiar only with the Mediterranean. "The water of the Thames has a different flavor from that of all the rivers on earth. Horned animals, fish, and everything one eats has a different taste from what we eat, the horses are of a species of their own even in their shape, and men have a character not found elsewhere and common to the whole nation, which makes themselves superior to all others." From a distance, he admired the "great cleanliness, the substantial fare, the beauty of the countryside and of the great roads." Even the postal carriages excited his admiration, "always at a trot, never at a gallop," the sole irritant being the customs officers to which he had to submit "to see if I had any contraband articles."

He reached London on June 14, 1763, free of Madame d'Urfé's grasp and hoping to repeat his success with the lottery. London offered both dignified public places, such as Pall Mall, and grotesque private behavior limned by William Hogarth. It was as though he'd progressed from *Les liaisons dangeureuses*, the scandalous eighteenth-century French novel of seduction and humiliation to the *The Beggar's Opera*, John Gay's Italianate satire of corruption. It was the city of Samuel Johnson and his devoted biographer, James Boswell, a libertine and angst-ridden Catholic convert recently arrived from Scotland; Boswell was visiting Johnson the day Casanova arrived in London. By night, Boswell acquainted himself with the demimonde. During the course of his seventy-eight years, Casanova recorded eleven bouts of venereal disease; Boswell recorded nineteen before he died at fifty-four.

Despite the sense of alienation Casanova felt in London, he found his way into the Venetian expatriate community in no time. On June 19, days after his arrival, he called on Teresa Imer. In Italy, he'd known her by her stage name, Teresa Trenti, and had endured a troubled romance with this daughter of a Venetian impresario. The two had a child, Sophie, whom he'd briefly dandled on his knee and subsequently neglected. (Teresa's mother claimed that the Marquis de Montperny actually fathered the child.)

Amid the brittle, tarnished elegance of London, Teresa had reinvented herself, acquired an English lover, John Fermor—make that *Reverend* John Fermor—and assumed the name Madame Cornelys. Posing as a well-to-do widow, she rented a mansion known as Carlisle House in Soho Square, and

Tavern scene from *The Rake's Progress*, by William Hogarth, 1735

it was here that Casanova appeared by invitation. He alighted from his carriage, expecting to greet her at once, only to be told by a manservant to meet her at another house. "I find nothing strange in this. She might have reasons for it." He is shown to his room in the next house, and learns that he's been assigned two valets and a servant. He listens to an "excessively fat" Frenchwoman, Madame Raucour, enlighten him about "Mrs. Cornelys"— her "splendid position, her extensive enterprises, her immense credit, the magnificent mansion she had built, the thirty-three servants she kept, two secretaries, six horses, country house, and I know not what." As for Mrs. Cornelys herself, she was "busy with her lawyer," owing to a "great lawsuit."

He made his way to the Prince of Orange, a coffeehouse opposite Haymarket Theatre, popular with artists, writers, opera singers, and, as Casanova winkingly judged them, "the dregs of all the unscrupulous Italians in London." He sat down by himself, ordered a lemonade, and struck up a conversation with Vincenzo Martinelli, a sixty-one-year-old Italian expatriate writer whom Casanova knew by reputation. Martinelli was correcting proofs of an annotated edition of *The Decameron* to be sold to subscribers later that year. Introducing himself as Seingalt, Casanova offered to add his name to the list of subscribers. Martinelli handed him a receipt and a warning: the Prince of Orange happened to be the "most disreputable coffeehouse in London."

But you go there, Casanova remarked. Only because my purse is empty, Martinelli shot back, invoking a popular verse from Juvenal. "The rogues have no way of getting their teeth into me," even after five years. He busied himself with his literary labors, including a three-volume history of England, the first to be written in Italian, and other worthy endeavors. "I am single, I earn enough to live in a furnished room and take my dinner in a tavern. I have a dozen shirts and this coat, and I am in good health." Such productive austerity impressed Casanova, who asked for advice about his own stay in England, absorbing the recommendation to rent an entire furnished house in which he could be the lord and master, "domiciled like an Englishman and responsible only to the laws." Martinelli obviously had no idea what his new companion was like, but Casanova asked for more details, at which point Martinelli flourished a copy of *The Advertiser*, among the most popular of London's fifty-three dailies.

In its pages, Casanova found a listing for a house "in a broad street called Pall Mall"—a former playing field for a lawn game similar to croquet, and later a fashionable address. He inspected the premises with Martinelli and was impressed. "Everything was scrupulously clean—porcelain, mirrors, bedpulls; it was perfection." The rent came to twenty guineas a week, he paid four weeks in advance, and received a receipt in the name of the Chevalier de Seingalt. "I never used any other name in London." Others took many days to find lodgings in London, he said, whereas he required only two, and made himself a fast friend along the way, Martinelli, whose companionship compensated for the profound "shock" he'd experienced at being kept waiting by Teresa, who proved cool and distant when she did see him, more interested in talking with her daughter, Sophie. During the meal they shared, she explained how she raised money by giving lavish suppers and balls, twelve of them a year, at two guineas a head, for hundreds of people at a time.

Casanova envied Teresa's apparent triumph. She'd transformed Carlisle House into an illustrious venue for musical and social events. She gave him a tour of the great room she used for her balls and suppers, "four hundred people all seated at a single horse-shoe-shaped table. I was easily persuaded that there was not a bigger room in London." At various times Johann Christian Bach and the German composer Carl Friedrich Abel performed there. Of a recital he attended at Madame Cornelys's establishment, the writer Laurence Sterne marveled at "the best assembly and the best concert I ever had the honour to be at." The acclamation cost considerable money. It was bruited about that her annual income came to twenty-four thousand pounds, an amount making her the highest-paid woman in all England. In reality, her finances were precarious; she ran up huge debts, and she was locked in a costly legal battle to which she alluded in conversation with Casanova, even as she invited him to purchase admission to one of her dinners. She couldn't offer him a ticket, those were for nobility only, and when he arrived, she advised, he should stay near her. Summoning all his self-control, Casanova replied: "I am most grateful to you."

Although their dinner lasted until two o'clock in the morning, Teresa—Mrs. Cornelys—displayed "no curiosity" concerning Casanova's affairs or plans for London. "I amused myself by telling her nothing about them." She offered neither "her services nor her credit," despite her supposedly extravagant income. He went to bed "annoyed but not angry," telling himself that he was "glad to have discovered her bad character."

On a subsequent visit to the Cornelyses' establishment, he studied Sophie, who he believed might be his daughter. "I saw a beautiful soul, and I silently pitied her for having to live under the domination of her mother, who was a fool." He marveled at her skill with the harpsichord, the guitar, and voice. Dancing a minuet with Casanova became the occasion for a rapprochement between father and daughter; Teresa encouraged the child to allow Casanova to take her onto his lap, embrace her, and shower her with kisses, "which she returned with all the affection I could wish."

———•———

In the days ahead, he familiarized himself with his surroundings, beginning with "all my bankers," as if they were his cronies, which he soon discovered they were not, and frequented taverns "in order to acquaint myself with English ways." He hired an English cook who spoke French; he moved the cook's entire family into Casanova's lodgings in Pall Mall. And Casanova familiarized himself with the best bagnios to be found in London, fancy brothels "where a rich man goes to bathe, sup, and sleep with a choice prostitute." Cost: six guineas, but available for four, although, as he noted, "economy spoils pleasure."

He tried his hand at gambling—whist, actually, four players, fifty-two cards—for "small stakes," paying out his losses in gold rather than in banknotes. The transaction earned him a reproof from one of the game's organizers, Lady Harrington (Caroline Stanhope). "Here in England paying in gold is a little unmannerly, though pardonable in a foreigner, who cannot know our customs; but try not to let it happen again."

During a visit to Court at the invitation of the Count of Guerchy, the French Ambassador, Casanova came face-to-face with George III, "who spoke to me, but in a voice so low that I could reply only by bowing." Although the devout and anxious British monarch had little to say, his queen, Sophia Charlotte, learning that a Venetian stood before her, burbled about the entertaining ambassadors of that country, especially Signor Zuan Querini. "He told me that I am a little devil," she gleefully confided.

"He meant, Madam, that Your Majesty has the wit of an angel," Casanova offered.

From his initial encounters in London, Casanova decided that the English were even more prone to democratic rebellion than the French, "and the great test of wise government is to keep it dormant, for if it wakes it is a torrent that no dam can withstand."

His fears about the English tendency to anarchy became a reality when he visited the Drury Lane Theatre to see the celebrated actor-manager David Garrick. When Garrick announced from the stage that the company would perform a play different from the announced offering, the "groundlings in the pit" rioted. Garrick tried to quiet them, but "the raging mob shouted, 'Every man for himself!'" He fled the stage for safety. More seriously still, Casanova saw "the King, the Queen, and everyone else leave their boxes . . . and abandon the theater to the rage of an angry populace" tearing the theater to bits. Such behavior—this was the era of the notorious Drury Lane riots—provoked worry about the prospects of the English monarchy. The King and Queen, he noted, rarely appeared in public. The bloody tide of revolution was rising.

As if in sympathy with the monarchs' predicament, Casanova retreated to his house on Pall Mall each night for dinner, where he feasted on "very delicate French ragouts" prepared by his cook, but "what pained me was that I was alone." Neither his flight from I Piombi, fast fading in popular memory, nor his counterfeit title carried weight in London society. "I had neither a pretty mistress nor a friend, and in London one can invite a gentleman to dine at a tavern, where he pays his share, but not to dinner at one's own table." To those who inquired why he kept to himself, he feebly explained that taverns didn't serve soup, fooling no one.

How to conquer the loneliness of London? His newfound friend Martinelli escorted Casanova to the British Museum for instant edification, and later "instructed me in the customs of the country I was visiting, to which I must conform if I wanted to live well there," which meant, chiefly, avoiding debt. Mrs. Cornelys, for instance, feared leaving her house "except on Sundays, on which days debtors could not be arrested." But arrested she was, as her son later informed Casanova, bearing the inevitable plea for assistance from one whom she'd spurned only a few weeks earlier. "Get me out of here at once, my kind friend," read her note. "Prevent my ruin and that of my innocent family." He refused to help, adding that he'd be ashamed to ask any of his friends to come to her aid. He handed his reply to her downcast son, and sent the boy away.

———•———

He distracted himself by roaming the lush expanses of Vauxhall Pleasure Gardens—less than half the price of admission of its rival, Ranelagh House!—"but the pleasures to be had there were great. Good food, music, strolls in dark walks where the bacchantes were to be found, and strolls in lantern-hung walks where one saw the most famous beauties in London, from the highest rank to the lowest, side by side." All that could be had for a shilling, there on the South Bank of the Thames. London did have its charms, after all, but "amid so many pleasures I was bored because I did not have a dear mistress in my bed and at my table," and he'd already been in London five weeks! "How was I to find in London the girl exactly to my taste and of a character like that of the women I had so greatly loved?" If he'd seen one attractive woman in London he'd seen fifty, but "not one among them had completely won me over." What to do?

He asked the caretaker to post the following note:

> Third-floor or fourth-floor furnished apartment to be let cheaply to
> a young lady alone and her own mistress who speaks English and
> French and who will receive no visitors either by day or night.

Reading this notice, the elderly caretaker, "who had sown her wild oats," laughed so hard "that I thought she would die of coughing." Did she laugh because no one would respond? On the contrary, said the caretaker, the girls will come around to see what it's about.

At first, the notice drew little attention, but on July 5, not one but two newspapers commented on it. (Could these notices have been the handiwork of his literary friend Martinelli?) Relying on a translation, Casanova read that the girl who answered it "would use it only to sleep in" and "might even refuse to receive the landlord if he took it into his head to pay her a visit." He regarded the public criticism as constructive, "well-argued," and helpful in preparing him for any eventuality, and "that is why the English newspapers are engaging; they chatter about everything that happens in London and they have the art of making trifles interesting." For once, Casanova, unusually sensitive to slights, took pleasure in the "humorous parodies" that appeared in newspapers all over town. He cited one that advertised an apartment for a "pretty lady who was leaving her husband because he objected to her cuckholding him on the day after her wedding." The others, "all of them indecent," afforded him equal amusement at his own expense.

Martinelli warned Casanova to take extreme care with any woman who approached him. And many did. He interviewed old women trying to pass themselves off as young, "hussies, trollops, saucy wenches," and then finally a promising candidate appeared, twenty-two years of age, perhaps twenty-four, tall, "simply dressed," and "beautiful in every way, with black hair and a pale complexion." She curtsied, he rose to greet her, offered her a chair and refreshments, invited her to be seated, and the game began.

Her name was Pauline, and she claimed to be the daughter of a Portuguese Count, although she spoke excellent Italian. They came to terms regarding rent and use of the rooms in his home, and he instructed "all my household to treat the young lady with all possible deference and courtesy." But after she left, his maid warned, "beware of a trap." Mistress Pauline "came here pale, and she left red as fire." There *is* something mysterious about Pauline; next to nothing is known about her, not even her full name. He might have embellished, if not invented, this love affair, yet he brought the quirky specificity to it that animates his other amours.

Casanova says he fell in love with Pauline soon after he began visiting her, but his plans seemed to go awry when young Sophie unexpectedly appeared, tearfully calling him "father" and condemning her mother, Mrs. Cornelys. To save face, Casanova insisted that he was not her father, that she was "the legitimate daughter of Pompeati, the dancer, who killed himself in Vienna and who, when you were born, was living with her." As Pauline listened "spellbound" to this convenient lie, he tried to cheer the child by pressing "four fifty-pound bank notes" in her hand as a present for her mother. By the time Sophie departed, Pauline was laughing, calling Casanova her "husband," and declaring that she couldn't remember when she'd had a more pleasant dinner. *Husband!*

Casanova coldly informed her that "marriage is a sacrament that I detest."

"Why?"

"Because it is the tomb of love."

"Not always," she said.

———————

Before long Casanova was arranging for Sophie to join him and the mysterious Pauline in musical entertainments. "Sophie sang Italian, French, and English airs." If only they'd had a harpsichord! "She sang English duets with Pauline, which gave me the greatest pleasure." After they had raised their voices in song, Casanova nearly seduced young Sophie, who "hid under the covers when she saw me appear." He threw himself down on the bed beside her, tickled her, and cover her little face with kisses. "I took advantage of my paternal rights to see exactly how she was built everywhere and to applaud everything she had, immature as it was. She was very small, but ravishingly built." Pauline looked on approvingly, "but she was wrong" to do so. If he had been left alone with Sophie, "she would have had in one way or another to quench the fire that her miniature charms had kindled in her papa."

At the same time, he remained in constant attendance on Pauline, whom he loved more with every passing day "precisely because we tried to make our love die of starvation." If they'd gone on this way much longer, this love would have killed him, he believed, because he was losing weight and sleep. Pauline believed that his declining strength had more to do with his confinement than with emotional deprivation. When he did go out for a ride on horseback at her urging, he fell from his mount and dislocated his right ankle. The recovery would take a week in bed at home. During his convalescence, she distracted him by reading aloud passionate stanzas from *Orlando furioso*, his favorite epic, and discussion of its many overwrought double entendres blended into foreplay between the two incipient lovers. As the copy of the book tumbled to the floor, "Pauline came into my arms; at first we gathered our forces in profound silence. Our ardors mingled, and her moans were my assurance that her desires were more intense than those I felt and that her needs were greater than mine." At the last instant, he yielded to the "unavoidable duty of safeguarding her honor," which meant withdrawing after penetrating her, and ejaculating into a handkerchief. Breathless, he looked upon her with "respect and gratitude."

As their love deepened and intensified, he decided he wouldn't leave his house so long as Pauline stayed in London. "I shut my door to everyone." His sprained ankle healed of its own accord. He commissioned an artist recommended by Martinelli—most likely Jeremiah Meyer—to paint a miniature portrait of Pauline. After three weeks of intimacy, "we could no longer find the slightest difference between us" as they indulged in an "unending succession of enjoyments." The idyll lasted until two letters for Pauline arrived from Lisbon, bidding her to return as soon as possible to her family, her property, and to complete an arranged marriage to a Count. She explained to Casanova that she had no choice in the matter, and she wanted Casanova to promise that he would never come to that city unless she invited him. Despite her plea, the idea of visiting Lisbon remained in his thoughts for the next several years, and he may have made one or more clandestine visits to the city in the course of his wanderings. For now, he "dissolved in tears and clasped her in his arms."

He accompanied her when she set out for Calais on August 10. The departure put him in mind of his separation from Henriette fifteen years earlier, "which had lacerated my soul." By now his pattern of seduction and abandonment was so predictable that it could be called the Casanova syndrome.

After Pauline sailed for Lisbon, he glumly returned to the Pall Mall residence she had once enlivened. There, "I shut myself up in my house, thinking of how I was to go about forgetting Pauline." When his elderly maid suggested he try his luck with another advertisement for feminine companionship, he was dismayed, infuriated, and finally amused.

———•———

The next time he saw Mrs. Cornelys, she proved as difficult as ever, and her daughter, Sophie, suffering from a "continual fever, extremely thin, and looking at me with eyes that told me she was dying of grief." He urged that she be sent to a boarding school for two years. Mrs. Cornelys confessed that she couldn't afford the tuition, and Casanova offered to pay the schoolmaster directly, to the relief of mother and daughter.

He obtained a glimpse of that most idiosyncratic institution, the English boarding school, when he accompanied Sophie, now recovered from her illness, and whom he called "my daughter," to her new educational establishment, where they were greeted graciously by a "Catholic noblewoman, who, despite her sixty years, still looked fresh and displayed the wit and manners of good society." Casanova being Casanova, he took a special interest in the sixteen or so girls at the seminary—five or six were "angels incarnate," and two or three "were so ugly they frightened me." They were "playing innocently together" when Sophie arrived, and when she was introduced to them, "they all hastened to give her the fondest caresses," all the more appreciated because she was shorter than the others.

Touring the school, in September, he eagerly spoke to the girls, his eyes roving everywhere. "I was in ecstasies. Their short dresses, with an English-style whale-bone corset, that left their bosoms entirely bare, put my soul in a stupor." It is difficult to imagine him in a more distracting or unsettling environment than this Catholic girls school, and he left—for the time being.

———•———

The next phase of his life in London began innocently enough, when he bumped into an acquaintance, who invited him to dinner, where he met a young lady who said that she remembered him, although he did not remember her. He'd known her under the name Augspurgher, she said, but now she went by the name Charpillon. (She was Marie Ann Geneviève Augspurgher.) With prompting, he did remember the young woman after all. "We are living in Denmark Street, Soho," she informed him, as her mother and several aunts—all accomplices—looked on. "It was on that fatal day at the beginning of September 1763 that I began to die."

He soon fell for La Charpillon—seventeen or eighteen years old, Swiss, an accomplished flirt, and exquisitely beautiful. "Her hair was of a beautiful chestnut color and of astonishing length and luxuriance; her blue eyes had a languor natural to their shade and all the brilliance of a woman of Andalusia; her skin, which had the tints of the rose, was of dazzling fairness, and her tall figure was almost as finely modeled as that of Pauline. Her breasts, perhaps, were rather small, but of a perfect mould; she had white, plump, tiny hands together with the prettiest feet and that proud and graceful carriage which gives charm to the most ordinary woman." He was surprised that the memory of Pauline did not interfere with La Charpillon's allure; as soon as he slept with her, he told himself, he would cease to "find her marvelous."

She invited him to tea. He declined, claiming another engagement. She then appeared at the tea to which he'd gone, much to his irritation. "You think you can make anyone you choose fall in love with you, and then propose to play the tyrant? The scheme is monstrous, and it is a pity you do not let men see more plainly the kind of woman you are," he told her.

La Charpillon and her female relatives—aunts, mother, and grandmother, all of whom lived with her—made a practice of separating naive gentlemen from their fortunes, and the tall Venetian adventurer became their next mark. An acquaintance, the libertine Henry Herbert, Earl of Pembroke, warned that "she is a scheming wench who will do everything she can to trap you." He would have bedded her himself, had she not hoodwinked him into giving her twenty guineas, with which she made off. (For

Casanova, money was a way to obtain sex, while for La Charpillon, sex was the way to obtain money.) When he encountered her again, she taunted him for having fallen for her little joke, and promised not to run away the next time he gave her money. "That is possible," said Lord Pembroke, "for I will not pay you in advance." Casanova's visit to her Soho lodgings confirmed his suspicions; in addition to her scheming relatives, three professional cardsharps were in attendance: a breed he knew well. Still he was undeterred. "Toward midnight I went home, bored and in love with La Charpillon."

Casanova wooed her with gifts, to which she responded with a mixture of manipulation and double entendres. "The present that you had sent me is so pretty that I can't begin to express how much it pleases me and what a fuss I made of it," she replied. "I wish I could make you so sweet and patient that your blood will turn into a veritable clarified syrup." Despite her words, she refused to yield to his desires.

Humiliated and seeking distraction, he visited Sophie and her beguiling schoolmates at the boarding school almost every day, bringing trinkets and "small articles of attire that delighted them." Less than three weeks later, "I congratulated myself that I had forgotten La Charpillon and had replaced her with innocent affections," even if Sophie's schoolmates "pleased me a little too much."

He considered himself free of La Charpillon's attraction until he happened to encounter "the coquette's favorite aunt," who beseeched him to visit. Without thinking, he donned his redingote and was knocking on her door, only to be told to return in half an hour. Infuriated by the delay, he pushed his way inside, and there "I see La Charpillon stark naked in the tub." The moment she caught sight of her uninvited guest, she cried out. Casanova found the sight of her irresistible; he had to have her, no matter how low he sank. At that moment, the aunt returned, and invited him to step into the parlor. It was time to do business. He tossed a banknote in her direction, and left, refusing to accept that his love was a prostitute, a public woman, and an expensive one at that. "I felt certain I would never again set foot in the house of those women."

Inevitably, he encountered her during a stroll at Vauxhall, and when he spoke to her, she replied "with an appearance of sincerity, which very nearly deceived me, that she wanted to be mine entirely," but first, to earn her trust, he must visit her every day. So far, he'd given her a hundred guineas without a single kiss to show for it. "She herself boasts of having tricked you," an acquaintance warned. Even now she and her relatives were "considering how to get you into their toils again, and they will succeed if you are not very careful."

Casanova half jokingly offered another hundred guineas to spend the night with La Charpillon, if that's what it would take—an offer that brought her to his room the next day, "not gay but serious," demanding an explanation. Did he think he had the right to insult her? Did he think she was a prostitute? Casanova apologized, and she issued an invitation: "You can come to our house, but keep your despicable money," she ordered. "Conquer my love as an honest, straightforward lover, not as a brute, for you must believe it now, I love you." He estimated that he spent four hundred guineas on her during the next two weeks. When her mother finally agreed to allow her daughter to spend part of the night with him, she asked for another hundred guineas—in advance.

That night, she dressed in a tight negligee, teased him, and refused to disrobe. "I thought her behavior was meant to be a joke," but he was wrong, "I am duped, a fool," and she—La Charpillon—was "the vilest of whores." His love, as he recalled, turned to rage. "I lay hold of her as if she were a bolt of goods, but I can accomplish nothing." He ripped open her negligee, his hands turned to claws as he grasped her neck. "I felt a strong temptation to strangle her."

They struggled for three hours in an embrace of fury. At three o'clock in the morning, "feeling my head on fire," he made himself get dressed and walked home attended by a night watchman in an era before streetlamps. At dawn, he took a cup of chocolate, but he was too upset to keep it down. A fever overcame him, and he stayed in bed, convinced that he'd cured himself of his "insane love." What's more, "Shame had made me loathe myself."

After four days, he began opening his mail and read a series of letters written by La Charpillon's mother informing him that her daughter was in bed, running a fever, and covered with bruises "from the blows I had given her, which obliged her to sue me in court." In the next letter, she changed course, saying that she was sorry to hear that he, too, was ill and admitting that, as her daughter confessed, "I might have reason to complain." And in the third letter, La Charpillon herself wrote that she was surprised he hadn't strangled her, and if he had, she wouldn't have resisted. In conclusion, she wished to deliver a message "by word of mouth." She did not come herself, as she implied; instead, she sent the friend who'd warned Casanova to stay away from La Charpillon. At the same time he attempted to claim her one-hundred-guinea fee; Casanova refused and sent him away.

The go-between came back with a special chair, not uncommon at this time, equipped with springs that seized a person's arms and legs, spreading them as far apart as possible, or, as Casanova put it, "in the same position in which an obstetrician would put a woman whose labor he wanted to make easy."

"Get La Charpillon to sit here," the go-between said, "and your business is done."

Casanova would have none of it. The "crime" of confining someone to this chair "could have cost me my life in the view of English judges," and he couldn't imagine subjecting La Charpillon to this "formidable contrivance, which would have made her die of fear." But he considered displaying it to her—for effect.

———•———

Two weeks later, La Charpillon herself, conveyed in a sedan chair, appeared at Casanova's house, where he received her coldly. Of course, she had a plan: "The scheming wench rises and shows me the whole surface of her body marked here and here and there with bruises still livid despite their age. Coward that I was, why didn't I turn my eyes away? Because she was beautiful." As he studied her, and her bruises, he felt as though he were "tasting poison and even gulping it down."

She dressed herself again, and said she'd come to ask his forgiveness, which he gave, and worse, convinced himself that on this occasion, she'd come "not to deceive me but to persuade me that she loved me. She was even willing to live with him under the same roof, and he agreed, on condition that he "sealed the bargain with her mother." He knew how wrong-headed his actions were, "but a man in love cannot see his mistakes until he is no longer in love."

When he conveyed his plan to La Charpillon's mother—a house in Chelsea and fifty guineas a month for her daughter to spend as she wished—the older woman insisted that he still owed her the hundred guineas he should have given her when they spent their violent night together. In swift succession, he rented a house in Chelsea, choosing from the scores available, and moved the girl's possessions into the house. Only then did he pay the disputed hundred guineas. When they went to bed together that night, she readily granted him some favors "but as soon as I want to proceed to the heart of the matter I am disappointed to encounter difficulties." She alleged her menstrual cycle prevented it, but he didn't "consider that condition repellent enough to keep me from proving my love to her." Yielding nothing to Casanova, she burbled sweetly until he fell asleep. In the morning, he realized he'd been deceived yet again. Resolved to avoid physical force, he began "calling her all the names she deserved." She laughed at him. He slapped her face. He kicked her out of bed. By the time the caretaker responded to the noise, blood was streaming from her nose. She staunched the flow of blood, dressed, and departed from the house in the sedan chair.

After long reflection, he pronounced himself "unworthy to live" and ordered La Charpillon's possessions returned to her house. Alone, he felt "overwhelmed by melancholy," took to his bed, and immersed himself in lacerating reflections on his grievous mistakes.

His friend the go-between returned to warn him that his life was in danger. La Charpillon and her mother were determined to accuse him of the most serious crimes. Just when it seemed his affair with La Charpillon had ended for good, he received word that her mother wished to return the hundred guineas and make peace over dinner. He unwisely accepted the invitation. When he arrived, he found La Charpillon calmly sewing, her head wrapped in a bandage, which she loosened to reveal her face bruised and swollen, disfigured where he'd slapped her. From time to time she dabbed at her tears.

He visited every night for the next week as a form of penance, until her latest wounds had healed. In his guilt, he forgot rather than forgave the "misdeeds" that had provoked his anger, and fell deeply in love with her again. He sent gifts with notes of apology. The loathsome cardsharps disappeared from the household, and after supper one evening she invited him to spend the night in her room, with her mother's blessing. Once again, he pressed himself against her, certain that this time she would yield, but instead she cried. Would she change her mind when they were in bed together? She shook her head. After fifteen minutes, he rose and put on his cloak. "I left that accursed house."

He could not forgive her, even when she appeared at his house, declaring herself prepared at last to cooperate with his desires, and insisting that her love now matched his. "The passage from irritated love to black anger is short and swift, while the passage from anger to love is long, slow, and difficult." He could be angry briefly, but indignant indefinitely, or until "forgetfulness intervened." In this case, La Charpillon knew he'd refuse her offer. After a visit lasting eight hours, "the young monster" quietly took her leave, expressing the hope that he would come back to her, as she phrased it, as soon as he came back to himself. When she finally departed, he regained enough presence of mind to sip broth. His memory retrieved a line from *Orlando furioso*, that touchstone of his imagination: "*Che non è in somma amor se non insania*"—love is nothing but madness.

Still he could not forget La Charpillon. Strolling with her on a fine autumn day in Richmond, west of London, known for its gardens, he criticized her constant lies, "her base character, and her infamous behavior." Convulsing with rage, he called her *putain*—whore—and reeled off the names of men with whom she'd slept.

"She was well-versed in her trade . . . she let me talk, holding my arm and smiling, but asking me to speak softly, for I might be heard," Casanova recalled; he didn't care what she said, he wanted to be heard. At lunch, she tried to soothe him with "wanton words and gestures." Anyone who overheard them would think she was deeply in love. She led him into a maze in the middle of the garden, where she exposed herself and used all her wiles to seduce him, finally awakening his desire, convincing him that now she would belong to him completely. After fiery kisses, she pushed him away—again!

Infuriated beyond reason, he flourished a "knife with a pointed blade" and place the tip against her throat. "I threaten to kill her if she moves." She calmly told him that he'd be arrested immediately. He came to his senses and realized he'd been "within a hair's breadth of my ruin." He got to his feet and walked away, but "she took my arm as if nothing had happened." How could a seventeen-year-old girl have had such presence of mind? Only if she had experienced these ordeals many times and learned to manage them, or even to revel in them.

Returning to London, he told himself that he must rid himself of the girl. Irate letters flew back and forth in the penny post. Succumbing again to this destructive passion, even as he recognized the folly of it, he set out for her house, in Demark Street, Soho, with pistols stuffed in his pockets.

When he arrived, she was having her usual Saturday evening appointment with her male hairdresser. He waited until eleven at night, but still the hairdresser remained. Unable to restrain himself any longer, he opened the door to the parlor, and there he found La Charpillon and her hairdresser stretched out on the sofa, copulating. Catching sight of the intruder, "the wench gives a cry [and] her fancy man breaks away from her." Casanova beat the hairdresser with a cane as La Charpillon cowered at the edge of the couch, afraid of being struck with the same instrument. The maids, aunts, and mother tried to break up the melee. Cursing them all, his "righteous wrath descends on the furniture," as he destroyed the glass and china gifts he'd given them, and then smashed all the chairs. If they all didn't stop shouting at that instant, he'd "break their heads open."

La Charpillon ran into the street in the dead of night, and he trembled with fear for her safety. He went in search of her with two household maids, but the "unfortunate girl" had disappeared. "How weak and stupid is a man in love!"

He ordered the maids to resume their search at dawn, promised to pay for all the furniture he'd smashed, and went home to sleep for six hours, "broken by hideous phantasms and agonizing dreams." At eight in the morning, he learned from one of the maids that La Charpillon, after taking refuge overnight in a shop in Soho, had returned home "in a pitiable condition" and went to bed. The maid was worried, because the girl was having her period . . .

. . . Not so! said Casanova, who'd seen her *in flagrante* with the hairdresser hours before.

"That makes no difference," the maid said, further demoralizing Casanova.

———•———

He returned to Denmark Street in the afternoon to find that La Charpillon's aunt and two friends had barred the door. The girl was "delirious from a burning fever." Hearing his voice, she cried out, "There is my murderer, there is Seingalt. He wants to kill me. Save me!" In despair, he slunk home, drank himself into a stupor, vomited bile, and tried to sleep.

The following morning found him raging at La Charpillon's door once again. A doctor warned that the girl's life was in danger. The fright Casanova had given her had caused her menses to stop, said the aunt. "You should have pretended not to see anything," she advised.

"*God damn it!*" Casanova fumed. "You Swiss filth!" He hurled a ten-pound note at her and ran off.

After three days, he returned to La Charpillon's household, where her mother sobbed that the poor child was on her deathbed. Clergy fluttered about the house like dusty moths, whispering that there was nothing left to do but "trust in God." One predicted La Charpillon's demise within an hour. Overwhelmed with guilt, he burst into tears. He stumbled home, resolved to take his own life. In his room, he placed his watches, rings, snuffboxes, purse, and portfolio in a strongbox on his desk. He wrote a letter saying that all his possessions were "the property of Signor Bragadin," his longtime patron. He locked the strongbox, placed the key in his pocket along with his "good pistols," and went out, "firmly intending to drown myself at the Tower of London." He proceeded to a shop where he purchased "as many lead balls as my pockets could hold," deciding that his suicidal plans were the best, indeed, the only course of action. "If I remained alive I should be in hell every time La Charpillon arose in my memory." Not only that, he considered himself guilty for bringing a premature end to her life, "which Nature had created for love." He savored his doom. "I walked slowly because of the immense weight I was carrying in my pockets, which assured me that I should die at the bottom of the river before my body could rise to the surface."

He set out across Westminster Bridge, where he encountered Sir Wellbore Agar, a "rich and amiable young Englishman who enjoyed life by catering to his passions." The ne'er-do-well twenty-eight-year-old son of a member of Parliament, Sir Wellbore accosted Casanova, who swerved to avoid him, but the young fellow nabbed him by the lapels.

"What is the matter with you, my dear friend?"

"Nothing is the matter," Casanova said. Noticing the pistols in Casanova's pockets, Sir Wellbore assumed his friend was on his way to a duel, and insisted on observing. Casanova explained that he was just out for a walk. In that case, said Sir Wellbore, he would invite two girls to join them, and the four of them would dine at Cannon Coffee House in Cockspur Street. Casanova again tried to excuse himself, saying he hadn't eaten "for more than three days."

That did it! Sir Wellbore concluded that his Venetian friend suffered from an intestinal infection, cholera morbus, "which can make you lose your mind." Lacking the strength to overcome his friend's insistence, Casanova decided he might as well play along; he would kill himself a few hours later. In the meantime, the lead balls he carried were growing heavy, exhausting him.

Casanova and his friend agreed to meet at the Cannon, where he could rest. Once there, he emptied his pockets, and gradually recognized that the young Englishman had become his wholly unexpected salvation. "We are our own masters only up to a certain point."

The two girls arrived—Casanova called them "young light-o'-loves"—brimming with cheer. One English, the other French, "they were made for joy." They thought him a *cacochyme*, a doddering valetudinarian. A flicker of self-esteem inspired him to "play a role resembling the man I ought to be." Although he hadn't eaten or slept for three days, he responded to the girls. And when they recognized his name, they brightened, and so did he. Unlike his previous assertions to the contrary, "I had a reputation, and I saw they were filled with respect." He was still Casanova!

Hungry though he was, the food made him gag. "The dinner being in the English style," he recalled, "I was absolutely unable to swallow a bit of roast beef or a little pudding," but he did enjoy oysters and decent wine. His friend Sir Wellbore suggested that the English girl dance naked, "and she consented, provided that we could find some blind musicians, and that we would undress too." Blind musicians were located, everyone stripped naked, including Casanova, who, unable to stand, watched as the music began to play and his young friend danced with the two girls. Why hadn't he ever tried dancing naked himself? When the music ended, Sir Wellbore "paid them both homage, going from one to the other," until he could no longer perform. The French girl examined Casanova for signs of life, and, "finding me powerless, said that it was all over with me." But at least he was alive.

Casanova marveled, "Could I have guessed that morning that, instead of drowning myself, I should find myself at so charming a party?" He decided he wouldn't commit suicide until the following day, and maybe not even then, as his friend marched him around London from one gambling establishment to another, until they arrived at Ranelagh House, the pleasure garden, where Casanova became fascinated by a woman who resembled La Charpillon, although he supposed that she must be dead or on her deathbed by this time. When the woman turned to look at Casanova, he realized she bore only a passing resemblance to La Charpillon, as he tried to quell the "violent palpitations of his heart." When Sir Wellbore went off to amuse himself for an hour or so, Casanova thought he might go mad at any moment, but by the time his amiable friend returned, Casanova was laughing, and exulted, "I owe you my life."

The two of them went back to Casanova's house. They ate, they slept, and when he awoke the next day at noon, he confided to his friend the whole horrible story of his plan, "which would have ended with my death if I had not happened to meet him halfway across Westminster Bridge."

And then, to his astonishment, he read a note from a friend relating that La Charpillon, "far from being on her deathbed, has gone to Ranelagh," which he'd visited only the day before. He'd seen her there, on the arm of her next victim! Casanova plotted his revenge on La Charpillon, her mother, and aunts. He "resolved to have them arrested" for the debts they owed him. The next day, Casanova gave a statement in court under oath. He arranged for the arrest, and to make certain the constable collared the right people, accompanied him to Denmark Street, where he "pointed out the mother and two aunts," hurrying away before La Charpillon caught sight of him. If she'd thrown herself at him at that moment, gazing imploringly as she caressed him, his vindictive resolve would have evaporated. Instead, the constable arrested the women, and Casanova relished "the pleasure of vengeance" at a safe distance. No one would bail out these unfortunates. He recalled their detention as lasting weeks, but it might have been only a matter of days.

———•———

Two weeks later, Sir Wellbore visited Casanova's home, bearing money from, of all people, La Charpillon.

Casanova immediately suspected a plot. "Does she know I owe you my life?" he asked. And how did his esteemed friend meet her? Sir Wellbore explained that La Charpillon came to him, to tell him that Casanova was a "monster of ingratitude." Once she loved him, but now she loathed him.

Putting his reservations aside, Casanova received the two hundred and fifty guineas La Charpillon owed him and renounced his claims on her "in writing." With that, he thought the entire matter with the girl and her family was ended.

———•———

As he was leaving a party in Soho Square in late November 1763, he faced six men armed with pistols, prepared to take him into custody. The arrest was all the more surprising because it was early Sunday morning, "that sacred day." The men announced they would conduct him immediately to Newgate Prison. Casanova loudly insisted he was entitled to know with what crime he'd been charged; even passers-by drawn by the disturbance added their voices, saying he was right. No matter, he and his servant soon found themselves confined to a "large room" with "nothing but some benches and large tables." The judge appeared five hours later, at seven in the morning as Casanova was reflecting "on my swift passage from the most brilliant assembly in London to the infamous company in which I found myself."

When the time came to hear his case, Casanova made an entrance befitting an aristocrat. "A sedan chair was called to carry me, for, dressed as I was, the mob would have thrown me into the gutter had I gone on foot." In another room, he recalled, "fifty or sixty persons . . . at once fix their eyes on the barbarian who dares to show himself clad in such offensive finery."

The magistrate that morning was most unusual. "The poor man was blind. He had a black bandage two inches wide that went around his head and covered his eyes. Since he could not see, it made no difference to him if they were covered." Casanova heard that the blind magistrate was fair-minded and just, "a man of intelligence, kind-hearted, and the author of several novels." This could only mean "the man was Mr. Fielding."

Casanova's supposition was partly correct. The blind magistrate was not Henry Fielding, London's acclaimed Chief Magistrate and the author of the novels *Joseph Andrews* and *Tom Jones*. He had died ten years earlier, in 1754, at only forty-seven years of age. *This* magistrate was his half brother and successor, Sir John Fielding, blinded in an accident years before and known as the "Blind Beak" for his ability to recognize the voices of thousands of criminals. Both Fielding brothers enjoyed reputations for exceptional fair-mindedness, and in the person of Sir John Fielding, justice was indeed blind.

When he heard the words uttered, "Casanova, Italian," the accused made his way to the bar and said, "*Eccomi, Signore.*" Here I am, My Lord. He proceeded to converse with this "honest magistrate" in Italian, and "wrote it down word for word the same day." And so, "I am happy to give my reader the following faithful and literal translation."

It did not begin well. "Signor di Casanova, Venetian, you are sentenced to the prisons of His Majesty the King of Great Britain for the rest of your natural life," said Sir John Fielding.

Sir John Fielding, English magistrate
known as the "Blind Beak" of Bow Street

"I am curious, Sir, to know for what crime I am sentenced. Will you be so good as to inform me of it?"

Sir John Fielding told Casanova that he was accused "of having attempted to scar a girl's face." Two witnesses supported the charge. She had called upon the law to safeguard her, and he was being sentenced to prison for that reason.

"Sir, it is a calumny," Casanova said. "I can swear to you that I have never thought of such a base act." Why, he'd never given the girl—"Miss Charpillon"—"anything but tokens of affection."

"Then it is not true that you intended to disfigure her?"

"It is false."

"In that case, I congratulate you. You shall dine in your own house"— but first—"two householders must vouch to us that you will never commit this crime."

Casanova gave the names of all the house owners or renters he could recall at that moment, and waited for at least two to respond. Hours later, no one had appeared, and the magistrate left for dinner. "Suddenly I hear the most unpleasant news." He was being taken to Newgate, the oldest prison in London, dating from the twelfth century, "to which only the lowest and most miserable criminals are sent." The detested La Charpillon had paid the constable to convey Casanova to Newgate as soon as possible, he learned, "Hence, it was in my power to remain where I was by giving him money." Ten guineas to keep safe until nightfall.

As a connoisseur of prisons from which some part of him was forever escaping, he was curious to visit the notorious jail, and arranged a tour. He found himself amid jeering prisoners and scowling guards as if he were about to start a life sentence. Half an hour later, word arrived that his sureties were waiting in court to vouch for him. And then: "Once more I am before the man with the bandaged eyes."

To his relief, there stood John Pagus, of Church Street, Casanova's tailor, and Lewis Chateauneu of Marylebone Lane, Casanova's vintner. Both men "greet me and congratulate themselves on being able to do me this small service." In the distance stood La Charpillon with her lawyer. His security came to a modest forty guineas. If the blind magistrate could have seen the girl, Casanova joked, the security would have amounted to ten thousand guineas. As the parties negotiated court costs, three or four more Englishmen arrived to vouch for Casanova, his sense of gloom and injustice by now dispelled. "They all begged me to forgive the English laws, which were too often hard upon foreigners."

Exhausted, he went straight to bed. Casanova the charmer, fraud, and swindler had been outsmarted and humiliated by a Swiss girl less than half his age.

———•———

Casanova couldn't restrain himself from indulging in one last prank at her expense when he came upon London's Parrot Yard. "Seeing a pretty one in a brand-new cage, I asked what language it spoke, and I was told that, being very young, it spoke none." He paid ten guineas for the bird, and "decided to put it near my bed and constantly say to it in French: 'Miss Charpillon is more of a whore than her mother.'" Within two weeks, "the obedient parrot learned the few words so well that it repeated them from morning till night."

On hearing the trained bird, a friend said that it could fetch upward of fifty guineas. "I at once adopted his happy idea." Casanova was more interested in hearing the parrot call La Charpillon a whore than in selling the creature, but if she produced two witnesses to testify that he'd taught the bird to defame her, he would be in serious legal trouble once again.

He dispatched the bird to the London Exchange with his servant and awaited a response; onlookers made offers, but none reached fifty guineas. He refused to sell the parrot: "I had fallen in love with my avenger." Even La Charpillon, when word of the talking bird reached her ears, found the stunt amusing, so Casanova claimed, but her mother and aunts, as vindictive and litigious as ever, consulted "several advocates on the subject," who advised that "there were no laws to punish a calumny" uttered by a parrot. The parrot's squawk attracted the notice of the *St. James Chronicle*, which speculated on the owner's identity. Eventually Casanova sold the parrot for fifty guineas to Lord Grosvenor, who happened to be one of La Charpillon's occasional clients, and the chattering bird was heard from no more. The tormented relationship between Casanova and La Charpillon was finished, and when he crossed paths with her "at promenades and theaters," he claimed that he couldn't remember who she was, "so indifferent had I become to her."

Not long afterward, Casanova received a letter "in bad Italian" from a young man who identified himself as his "godson Daturi," apparently born out of wedlock. Daturi was now in prison for debt, and urgently in need of funds. Casanova visited the lad, twenty years old, who produced his baptismal certificate, containing his name, that of Casanova, the boy's mother, and the parish in Venice where he was born, but, as he studied the document, Casanova claims, "I remember nothing." After hearing the boy reminisce about his mother, he decides that Daturi "was perhaps my own son." Who was he? A performer, he'd come to London with a troupe as a *pagliaccio*, or clown, lost his job, and fallen ten pounds in debt, for which he'd been jailed. Casanova paid the obligation, arranged for Daturi's release, and agreed to give him two shillings a day on which to live. The unlikely way he'd encountered his son—if Daturi really was his son—and his daughter—if Sophie really was his daughter—mattered little to Casanova.

Just when he had arranged the next phase of his life, he received a stern letter from the banker who'd loaned him five hundred pounds, Mr. Lee, who claimed that Casanova had given forged documents as a guarantee. If Casanova didn't replace the funds immediately, Mr. Lee would have him arrested.

Casanova threw himself on his bed, bathed in a cold sweat. There was no one in London or Venice to send funds. "I saw the gallows before me." Casanova went to see Gershon Treves, a Jewish banker from Venice, to obtain funds. No result. In desperation, he sold his linens, and fled with Daturi to Dover, where a packet was about to sail. He paid the six-guinea fare, and endured a six-hour crossing battling March gales.

Chapter 16

Zaïre

The ship arrived in Calais, where Casanova was afflicted by a fever he attributed to his venereal disease. After a crisis lasting three or four days, he felt "restored to life."

He looked back with remorse at this period of his life. He'd missed the boom in London's banking and publishing industries, written nothing beyond a tawdry personal advertisement, and ruined his credit. His servant had abandoned him. Love had proved cruel and elusive. Supremely vain, he admitted that "I looked frightful, had lost flesh, my skin was yellow and all covered with pustules." For the moment, "I had no idea where to go." Yet he was lucky to be alive. And Daturi, his presumed son, remained at his side to look after him. Who could say how many other children of his thronged the streets of Paris or the alleys of Venice?

Still searching for an antidote for his "venereal poison," he traveled to Wesel, Germany, and sought out a sympathetic physician, Heinrich Wilhelm Peipers. Weakened from the journey, Casanova arrived in a sedan chair, holding a handkerchief over his disfigured face, ashamed to show himself to the physician's mother or sister. (In Venice, he could have concealed his face beneath a mask, but not here.) No sooner had Casanova begun the toxic and ineffectual treatment than he heard that Madame de Pompadour, the mainspring of the French court, had died on April 15, 1764. The old order was passing, and with it the reckless assumptions of his libertine life.

Committed to a course of treatment at Wesel, he complained that he'd been condemned to a "murderous rest" necessary for the treatment's success, he believed, but "the boredom would kill me." Daturi provided distraction from the tedium. "He could scarcely write," Casanova noted with disappointment, "and he had been taught nothing but rope dancing and the art of pyrotechnics." True, "he was courageous" but "a little too fond of wine," and concerning women, "he had no more than the usual inclination," which was disappointing to Casanova, who affirmed that he'd known "a number of men who owed their success to women"—and, he might have added, their misfortune.

He found respite in the town of Wolfenbüttel in lower Saxony, "for it is there that the third-finest library in Europe exists." The Herzog August Bibliotek was esteemed for its collection of thousands of manuscripts and incunabula. "I wanted very much to examine it at my leisure." Here Casanova could indulge his love of language, of ancient knowledge, and his still hazy aspirations of literary accomplishment.

He felt entirely at home from the moment the "learned librarian" told him that a man would be put at Casanova's disposition to "fetch me all the books I asked for," including "the manuscripts that are the chief treasure of that celebrated library." He spent a week amid the volumes, "without ever leaving except to go to my room." He made a close study of Homeric epics and conceived the idea of translating these works into Italian. Alexander Pope had done it to great acclaim and profit in England—why not he? Ten years later, Casanova began issuing excerpts of his labors.

During the Wolfenbüttel interlude, he recalled, "I lived in the most perfect peace, never thinking of the past or future, my work preventing me from knowing that the present existed." He had occasionally experienced this tranquillity in his anxious life, never for long, and now it came as a revelation, an escape from the bonds of mortality. He indulged in uncharacteristically benign reflections. "To be a true sage in this world I should have needed only a concatenation of very small circumstances, for virtue always had more charms for me than vice," except, he added as an afterthought, "in the exuberance of my heart."

In September, he left Germany for Russia, out of reach of the English bankers and moneylenders to whom he was indebted. To distance himself further from his tainted reputation, he applied for a passport not as Giacomo Casanova or the Chevalier de Seingalt, but as Count Farussi, the name of his once famous mother. On December 21, "Count Farussi" crossed the border at Riga, having bid farewell to Daturi, to arrive at the new Russian capital, St. Petersburg, founded in 1703.

His first impression of this strange and unsettling place was of peasants stealing whatever they could from travelers' carriages. He found lodgings in Ingria, a district whose inhabitants spoke Finnish—"which has nothing in common with other languages"—rather than Russian—not that he knew Russian, either. At least some people he encountered spoke German, "which I understood with difficulty but in which I expressed myself as I do today." Adding to the strangeness of it all, his arrival coincided with the winter solstice, so he went about his business in the dark and cold. "I can assure my reader that the longest night in that latitude lasts eighteen hours and three quarters." Settling in amid the gathering darkness, he familiarized himself with his lodging's admirable and wholly necessary stove, twelve feet high and six feet wide. "Only in Russia is the art of building stoves known," he exuded, "as the art of making cisterns or wells is known only in Venice." Everything was cheap—lodging, food, heat—which reassured him, as he moved a chest of drawers into the house "and a large table at which I could write and on which I could put my books and papers."

In St. Petersburg, he discovered, Italians were appreciated as they never were in London. He was more than one thousand five hundred miles from Venice, and no one concerned themselves with his background, reputation, or his escape from I Piombi. His lack of reputation was both liberating and daunting as he plotted to present himself before the young German-born Empress, Yekaterina Alexeyevn, now known as Catherine the II, and, later, as Catherine the Great.

Having come to power two years earlier, Catherine was just beginning her turbulent thirty-four-year reign over Russia. Her husband, Peter III, had died after only six months on the throne, and some held that his wife was involved in a conspiracy to assassinate him so that she could succeed him, while others believed that Peter had been the victim of a coup d'état and died in a struggle with his guard. Casanova, for his part, believed that Grigory Teplov, "fond of handsome youths," had been responsible for strangling Peter III, and later became part of Catherine's cabinet. In any case, she received considerable help from her lover Grigory Orlov, with whom she had two illegitimate children, and whom she appointed Count and General-in-Chief, among other titles. Orlov served as her chief counselor until his numerous infidelities angered her; when she heard that he'd seduced a thirteen-year-old girl, Catherine replaced Orlov with an attractive young aristocrat. To win back the Empress's affections, Orlov presented her with a huge diamond mined in India, later known as the Orlov Diamond, but by that time she'd moved on to the dashing young military officer Grigory Potemkin, and Orlov was consigned to exile.

Catherine could be elusive, but she was no recluse. She constantly placed herself on display. Casanova caught sight of her on February 22, 1765, from a respectful distance at a masked ball at the Winter Palace, Catherine's official residence. She was shadowed by her lover and confidant, Orlov, as she passed unrecognized through the crowd, bumping into—or spying on—her subjects. On another occasion, Casanova saw her wandering among "people conversing in Russian," which meant that "she exposed herself to unpleasantness, but she had the rare satisfaction of hearing some truths." Casanova was struck by her "affability and smiling sweetness," and "although she was not beautiful, whoever examined her had reason to be pleased, finding her tall, well built, gentle, easy of access, and above all never perturbed." He followed the Empress to mass, where the Bishop received her as she kissed his ring, and the prelate, "decorated with a beard two feet long," bent his head to kiss her hand. At no time during the mass did she reveal any sign of devotion, at least to Casanova's watchful eye. So it was with music. After she attended an opera, he overheard her say that she was "bored listening to it. Music is a beautiful thing, but I do not see how one can love it passionately, unless one has nothing important to do and think about." That, according to Casanova, was how she always spoke. Despite her cold-bloodedness, he hoped to win her favor, and a fortune, by making himself useful. To this end he circulated letters of introduction among the expatriate community, and did whatever he could to make himself known. As always, he was trying to be a somebody to counteract his fear of being a nobody.

———·———

In the course of his socializing he encountered an extroverted young officer named Stepan Zinoviev, who offered to assemble a seraglio of "as many girls as I could want" in exchange for one hundred rubles. In other words, he would pimp for Casanova, who readily agreed. What better way to learn about a nation?

At a "peasant's hut," Zinoviev made arrangements with the girl's father, who eagerly cooperated. With a glance, the girl in question assented, but Zinoviev admonished Casanova to confirm that the girl was a virgin "since in signing the agreement I must state that I had bought her for my service as such." After a moment's hesitation, "I sat down and, taking her between my thighs, I explored her with my hand and found that she was intact." Zinoviev then gave the hundred rubles to her happy father, who passed them to the daughter, who in turn presented them to her mother.

Casanova called the girl Zaïre, after the heroine of a tragedy written many years before by Voltaire, about a Christian slave—a very beguiling Christian slave. Casanova left the hut with his prized serf, who wore only a coarse shift. He sequestered her in his home, with its impressive stove, and taught her how to dress in the French manner, "simply and neatly." Knowing no Russian, he taught her Italian, which she spoke haltingly, but well enough to make herself understood. "She began to love me, then to be jealous," he recalled, and "once she came very near to killing me." Zaïre was nearly thirteen years old.

When Casanova left St. Petersburg for Moscow in May 1765, she had become "so pretty" in his eyes that he took her along, in part to have someone with whom he could converse. "The pleasure I took in hearing her talk to me in Venetian was inconceivable." They went to the sauna together, surrounded by thirty or forty others, men and women, all naked, "who, looking at no one, supposed that no one looked at them." Amazingly, "no one looked at Zaïre," but he found her mesmerizing. "Her breasts were not yet developed. Nowhere did she show the indubitable imprint of puberty. Snow white as she was, her black hair made her even more brilliant." Yet he had to contend with her ferocious jealousy, "a daily burden," and her absolute faith in the fortune-telling cards that she read each day. If not for those stumbling blocks, "I should never have left her."

There were distractions. At a gathering of Russian officers, he encountered a young lieutenant by the name of Pytor Lunin, as "blond and pretty as a girl," and rumored to have been Teplov's lover. "He lavished such pretty attentions on me," Casanova recalled, "that I really thought he was a girl in men's clothing." But when he told Lunin of his suspicions, the young man "immediately displayed" his sex to Casanova, and groped the Venetian. Convinced that Casanova had responded, Lunin "put himself and me in a position to make himself and me happy."

Casanova would have responded, had not one of the women present, most likely a courtesan, "angry that a youth should infringe on her rights," chased away the pretty boy. Casanova laughed, and told the courtesan to mind her own business. Taking his words as a declaration of interest, Lunin reappeared and "displayed all his treasures," as he and the woman cursed each other. When she stormed away, "the young Russian and I gave each other tokens of the fondest friendship, and we swore that it should be eternal." Afterward, he spent the night gambling.

When Casanova returned to his lodgings an hour before dawn, "I enter my room, and by the purest chance I avoid a bottle that Zaïre has thrown at my head and that would have killed me, if it had struck me on the temple. It grazed my face. I see her throw herself down in a fury and beat her head on the floor; I run to her, I seize her, I ask her what is the matter with her, and, convinced that she has gone mad, I think of calling for help. She calms her frenzy, but, bursts into tears and calling me 'murderer' and 'traitor.'" And the basis for her accusations? "She points to a square of twenty-five cards, in which she makes me read in symbols the whole of the debauch that had kept me out all night. She shows me the wench, the bed, the encounters, and even my sins against nature." There was no persuading Zaïre that his evening had actually consisted of a homoerotic flirtation followed by gambling. Out of patience, "I threw her accursed abracadabra into the fire, and looking at her with eyes in which she could see both my anger and the pity I felt for her, and telling her in so many words that she'd nearly killed me, I declare that we must part for ever." Exhausted, he tumbled into bed, and Zaïre followed, and he fell asleep despite her efforts to arouse him and "assure me of her repentance."

In the morning, as he dressed, his thoughts were consumed with "how best to get rid of a girl who, one day or another, might very well kill me in her jealous rages." But how could he do that when she kneeled before him and pleaded for forgiveness? He took her into his arms, and "gave her unmistakable tokens of the return of my affection on condition, which she swore to fulfill, that she would not consult the cards again as long as she lived with me." Who was the slave, and who the master? In time he taught her to behave by taking her to visit her family, "where I always left a ruble," and beating her "two or three times when she had tried to keep me from going out."

At the same time, he suffered from "an intolerable pain in the rectum, which returned every day," and made him feel "melancholy and wretched." He'd first experienced this affliction during his imprisonment in I Piombi, and now it returned with a vengeance. He submitted to the excruciatingly painful treatments of an octogenarian physician, who probed his rectum, and located a large cavity filled with "acrid lymph." He inserted a probe into the anus, withdrew it, and examined it with a surgeon to determine the extent of the cavity, which was "two inches away from the sphincter." Casanova could undergo surgery, which would relieve the pain but increase the risk of infection. It was preferable, the physician advised, "to be patient," forgo surgery, and to drink the "excellent water of the Neva," which had the "facility of purifying the body by forcing out the noxious humors."

Beyond the purifying waters of the Neva, St. Petersburg baffled Casanova, who considered the city a work of misguided genius—imported Italian genius, as it happened, in the person of Catherine's architect Francesco Bartolomeo Rastrelli—wrought of stone in unforgiving terrain. When Casanova arrived, in 1765, "it was still in its infancy. Everything seemed to me ruins built on purpose. The streets were paved in the certainty that they would be repaved six months later." Rastrelli's masterpiece, the Winter Palace, struck Casanova as "barbarous" and impractical, and, like the entire city, a collection of contradictions.

To educate himself about Russia, and to prepare for an eventual meeting with the Empress, Casanova traveled to the royal residences surrounding St. Petersburg: Tsarskoye-Selo; Peterhof, the so-called Russian Versailles; Oranienbaum; and Kronstadt. "One should see everything when one goes anywhere," he cheerfully recommended. As he toured, he wrote "on several subjects" to qualify for the Russian civil service, and he believed that the Empress saw his efforts, "but my efforts were useless." With a sigh, he realized he was going about this the wrong way: "In Russia only men who are expressly sent for are regarded. Those who go there by their own choice are not esteemed." By late summer, he was getting nowhere and decided the time had come to leave Russia. Friends encouraged him to stay until he had accomplished his goal, which seemed out of reach until he was advised by one of them, Count Panin, to go for a morning walk in the splendid Summer Garden, on the left bank of the Neva, where he was likely to encounter the Empress, who might speak to him.

As he did, he saw her, the sovereign, accompanied by Orlov, Count Panin, and "two ladies." Casanova stood aside to allow Catherine to pass, and as she passed, she smiled, and asked if he were interested in the melodramatic statues dotting the path. Indeed he was, he replied—presumably in German, her native tongue. "I hope," she said to him, "that you have not found everything you have seen in our country as absurd as these statues," whereupon Casanova, polymath, flirt, and supplicant, "entertained her for more than an hour about everything I had found remarkable in St. Petersburg." When he finished, Catherine remarked that she'd never seen him at the Sunday court concerts, which were open to the public. He replied that he'd been there once, but, unfortunately, he was not "fond of music." She nodded and said she knew someone else with "the same misfortune," meaning herself.

In the days to come, Casanova heard that Catherine had asked about him twice, and he should avail himself of opportunities to meet her again, so that she might think of employment for him, "though I did myself not know for what employment I might be fitted in a country that . . . I did not like." Nevertheless, he returned to the Summer Garden each morning.

On their second meeting in the garden, Catherine and Casanova fell into a discussion on the differences between the Gregorian Calendar, introduced by Pope Gregory in 1582, and Julian Calendar, dating to the era of Julius Caesar in 46 BC. Knowing of Catherine's interest in exposing Russia to the Enlightenment, he urged the adoption of the Gregorian Calendar. "All the Protestants conformed to it, and England did so, too, fourteen years ago, excising the last eleven days of February," adding, "Europe is astonished that the old style remains in force here." He rashly speculated that Peter the Great would have made the change during his reign if the alteration hadn't meant conforming with Russia's rival, England.

Catherine carefully responded that "the great Peter was not a learned man." But Casanova considered Peter a "true and sublime genius," nonetheless. In place of learning, Peter had "delicate tact that led him to judge rightly of all he saw."

At their third meeting, Catherine and Casanova resumed their discussion of calendars. Of particular concern to the Empress was the vexing question of when to celebrate Easter, a point she debated with enthusiasm and erudition. "She had the pleasure of seeing me surprised and leaving me in my surprise," Casanova reported. "I felt certain that she had studied the subject on purpose to dazzle me, or that she had conferred with some astronomer."

More meetings in the Summer Garden followed as the adventurer and the Empress displayed their knowledge of the intricacies of the Gregorian calendar. It seemed he was making progress until the subject turned without warning to timekeeping in Venice, where the days began half an hour after sunset, much to her bafflement. "What will not habit do!" Catherine exclaimed. "It seems easier to you. Whereas I should find it very difficult." With this remark, Casanova realized he had no hope of advising the Empress about the Russian calendar.

Their conversation turned to gambling in Venice, Casanova's primary interest. If he could establish a lottery in Russia similar to the one he'd inaugurated in Paris with such *éclat*, it would benefit the Empress—and offer a chance of making a fortune for himself in Russia. Catherine revealed that she'd been encouraged to permit gambling, "but on condition that the amount risked should never be less than a ruble, in order to keep the poor from playing." Unlike the elite gamblers of the Venetian Ridotto, Russian peasants would ruin themselves in such schemes, and she would not permit it. Casanova had seen enough Russian superstition and fatalism to recognize that the Empress's point was based on "profound wisdom." He made a "very low bow." The game was over. In defeat, he admired her prowess and power. "This was the last conversation I had with that great lady, who was able to reign for thirty-five years without ever making a crucial mistake and without ever departing from moderation."

Without a purpose, he realized it was time to leave Russia. He indulged in one last night with Zaïre, and in the morning he falsely promised to return to her. By the time he was ready to depart, she realized she'd never see him again and was already considering his replacement. At the last minute, Zinoviev, who'd introduced Casanova to Zaïre, offered to arrange for her to travel with him. The idea was tempting. "I loved her," he reflected, "and it would have been I who became her slave." The wisest course of action would be to return young Zaïre to her family in the manner he'd originally taken her from them. He brought the girl to her father's hut, where "I saw her whole family on their knees before me, addressing me in terms that are due only to the divinity. But Zaïre looked very much out of place in the hovel, for what they called a bed was only a big straw mattress on which the whole family slept together." He bid adieu, and that was the end of the matter.

By October 1765, Casanova found himself in Warsaw, his resources nearly exhausted, when his tenacity and literary curiosity asserted themselves. "Not having enough money to frequent the gamesters, or to obtain the tender acquaintance of some girl of the French or Italian theater, I took a fancy to the library of Monsieur Zaluski, the Bishop of Kiowa, and especially to him, personally." The Bishop's manuscript collection provided an idyllic refuge for Casanova. "I spent almost every morning there, and it was from him that I received authentic documents concerning all the intrigues and secret plots whose purpose was to overthrow the old system of Poland, of which that prelate was one of the principal supporters." Zaluski was later exiled to Siberia for his role in the affair, but for the moment, Casanova led a "very regular" life of healing and recovery amid the shelter of the library. But he lacked funds. "Carriages, lodging, two servants, and the necessity of being always well-dressed kept me in straits," he complained, "and I did not want to confide in anyone." It was crucial to maintain his *bella figura*. "I was right. A man in need who asks help from a rich man loses his esteem if he obtains it, and wins scorn if he refuses it."

He came to the attention of the new Polish King, Stanislaw August Poniatowski, memorialized as the last Polish monarch. A decade earlier, this outgoing King had been the shy, uncertain lover of Catherine the Great, in St. Petersburg. She was twenty-six at the time, he was three years her junior, spoke several languages, and romantically inexperienced, especially in comparison to the precocious and poised Catherine. "She was only just recovered from the birth of her first child," he later wrote. "She was at that age when any woman endowed with beauty is ordinarily at her loveliest." Her "dazzlingly fair complexion, very long black eyebrows, Grecian nose, [and] mouth that seemed to invite kisses" overwhelmed him. Poniatowski "forgot there was a Siberia" on the night Catherine appeared before him "in a little white satin gown, without other ornament than a light trimming of lace mingled with pink ribbons" and efficiently seduced him. "Although I was only twenty-three years old," he boasted, "I was able to offer her what no one else had." But scandal drove Poniatowski into exile, and he spent the rest of his days pining for Catherine, swooning at the memory of her ardor while he tried to adapt to the challenges of ruling Poland.

Casanova found this king to his liking, cheerful, personable, and, literate. He was "very well read and knew all the classics as no King ever knew them. At times he brought up anecdotes of ancient Roman writers, citing manuscript scholars." Casanova was, for once, nearly speechless, "replying only in monosyllables when politeness demanded it." He forced himself to remain silent during a silly discussion of Horace, and his self-control was rewarded the next day when, as he was leaving mass, King Stanislaw August offered his hand to kiss, and simultaneously slipped into Casanova's hand a "carelessly made packet, telling me to thank Horace and to say nothing about it to anyone." The packet contained two hundred gold ducats, sufficient to settle his debts. From then on, he paid his respects to the King every day, as did the world. "Foreigners came there from every corner of Europe for no other reason than to see the fortunate mortal who had become a king," yet "his eagerness to show himself was extreme. I saw him become uneasy when he knew there were some strangers in Warsaw whom he had not yet seen. No one needed to be presented to him," Casanova noted, "and when he saw people he did not know he was the first to speak to them."

———— · ————

Casanova was always aware that he'd "never been able to keep from being a trifle superstitious." In late January 1766 his premonitions culminated in a garish nightmare in which he saw himself "dining in good company," when "one of the guests threw a bottle at my face, covering it in blood." He ran his sword through his attacker, and fled in his carriage.

Casanova disregarded the dream until he found himself dining several weeks later with Prince Charles of Kurland, and "halfway through the dinner a bottle of champagne burst without anyone touching it, and a splinter, striking my forehead, cut a vein, from which blood quickly flowed over my face, my coat, and the table"—almost as events had occurred in the dream. He received medical attention, and the party continued, but over the next several days he wondered what the dream and ensuing incident portended.

At the time, he recalled, "the life I was leading was exemplary; no love affair, no gaming; I worked for the King, hoping to become his secretary." He paid court to the royal family. He attended a performance of a comedy in Polish with the King in the royal box ("This novelty interested everyone, but it was a matter of indifference to me, for I did not understand a word of Polish."), and flirted with an Italian dancer named Teresa Casacci. Her lover was the young and handsome Count Branicki—Xavier Branicki, Podstoli, or honorary butler, to the Crown, Chevalier of the White Eagle, and so on—who was also the occasional lover of another dancer, La Binetti.

When Branicki caught Casanova embracing La Casacci, a confrontation became inevitable. "I am not in the mood to put up with rivals," Branicki snorted. "Fuck off."

"That is a trifle strong," Casanova replied, glacing at the hilt of his sword as several officers looked on. Taking three steps outside the theater box, Casanova heard himself honored, as he put it, "with the title of 'Venetian coward.'" He spun on his heel and told Branicki that a Venetian coward "could kill a Polish bravo"—Italian for "thug." He expected that Branicki would chase after him, and the two would unsheathe, but nothing happened. He was relieved, because Branicki and his minions might well have murdered him on the spot. Even so, something had to be done. Three officers had witnessed the confrontation, and Casanova considered himself "dishonored" and so "needed full satisfaction." He would "tell the King the whole story and leave it to His Majesty to force Branicki to beg my pardon," but the King failed to appear.

Alone that night in his lodgings, Casanova decided he must either "kill Branicki or force him to kill me." If they dueled, all would be well. If Branicki refused to duel, Casanova would have no choice but to murder his antagonist, even it meant "risking losing my head on the scaffold afterward." Resolved to act, Casanova seized a pen and paper:

March 5, 1766, at 5 o'clock in the morning.

Monseigneur, yesterday evening at the theater Your Excellency wantonly insulted me, having neither a right nor a reason to behave in that fashion. That being so, I conclude you hate me, Monseigneur, and that hence you would be glad to remove me from the number of the living. I can and will satisfy Your Excellency.

Half an hour later, Casanova received his reply:

Monsieur, I accept your proposal; but you will have the goodness to tell me at what hour I shall see you. I am, Monsieur, entirely your very humble and very obedient servant, Branicki, Podstoli to the Crown of Poland.

"Delighted," Casanova replied. He would appear at Branicki's apartment at six in the morning of the following day. Further correspondence between them concerned details of the duel and the length of the swords they would use: thirty-two inches, the distance between life and death.

To Casanova's alarm, Branicki appeared in the flesh to insist that the duel take place *that very day*—March 5—or not at all.

"I cannot do it today," Casanova stalled. "It is Wednesday, the day of the post; I must finish something to send to the King."

Send it *after* we have fought, Branicki ordered. "You will not be left for dead, believe me, and in any case, if you succumb, the King will forgive you. A man who is dead is beyond the reach of any reproach."

In that case, Casanova would have to draw up his will before the duel.

"Now it is a will!" Branicki roared. "You will make your will fifty years from now."

They bickered over the timing of the duel until Casanova relented; they would fight the duel later that day. Branicki then asked, "What is this about the length of your sword? I want to fight with pistols." Casanova had given Branicki the choice of weapons. "Will you grant me this pleasure?"

"I like your way of putting it," Casanova replied, aware of the drama inherent in the moment. He agreed to grant Branicki the "barbarous pleasure" of pistols and outlined the "precise conditions" of their duel: "You will come with two pistols, which you will have loaded in my presence, and I shall be allowed to choose mine. But if we miss each other, we shall fight with swords until the first blood, and no longer, if that is what you want, for I feel ready to go on until death."

"Excellent," Branicki declared "You are a man one can like." And so they reached an understanding on the brink of battle. Branicki wanted Casanova's word of honor that he would keep all matters pertaining to the duel secret, to avoid arrest.

"How could you think I would take that risk?" Casanova asked.

"Then it is all settled."

Casanova prepared his packet and instructed his emissary to take it to the King if Casanova died in the duel, or to return it that night in the event he survived.

At dinner, he ate well, finished a bottle of "excellent Burgundy wine," and noted the "witnesses to my good appetite and my unusual gaiety." At quarter to three, he collected himself and from his fourth-floor window calmly observed Branicki's coach appear, pulled by six horses, preceded by two grooms, two hussars (cavalry), and two aides-de-camp, and followed by four menservants, not to mention a Lieutenant-General and a chasseur (soldier). As he prepared to go downstairs, Casanova turned to his two servants and instructed them not to follow him. But wait, Branicki advised that Casanova would need them, and he replied that if he had as many servants as Branicki, he would bring them; otherwise, he would place himself in Branicki's hands, confident that Branicki would take care of him, if necessary. Branicki went so far as to pledge to take care of Casanova before taking care of himself.

Casanova entered in the fine carriage, and it drove off with its combatants to a secret destination.

"Do you expect, Monseigneur, to spend the spring and summer in Warsaw?" Casanova inquired as they went.

"I expected it yesterday, but you may keep me from doing it," said Branicki.

"I hope I shall not interfere with any of your plans."

Within half an hour, they arrived at a "beautiful garden" in the suburbs of Warsaw: a landscape of life and death. They emerged from the carriage and walked toward a bare arbor with a small stone table. "The chasseur puts on the table two pistols a foot and a half long, takes from his pocket a bag of powder, then a pair of scales. He unscrews the pistols, weighs the powder and the balls, then loads them, screws them to the mark, and crosses them."

The Lieutenant-General pointed out that dueling is illegal in this place. "Then why have I been brought here?" Casanova asked. The Lieutenant-General told him to bring the matter before the King, who would no doubt take Casanova's side.

Branicki glared at Casanova. They were there "to fight, not to discuss."

Casanova realized he must go along with these grim rites. "Branicki urges me to choose. I throw off my fur, and I take up the first pistol that comes to hand." He felt the pistol's heft and the dark gunmetal; he embraced the lethal metal mechanism with his fingers. Branicki snatched the other pistol and guaranteed "on his honor" that the pistol Casanova held was "perfect." Casanova replied that he would "test it on his head."

"At this terrible reply he turns pale, throws his sword to one of his pages, and shows me his bared chest. . . . I show him my chest, too, and I fall back five or six paces." Casanova removed his hat with his left hand, asked

Branicki "to do me the honor of firing at me first," and then replaced his hat. Branicki wasted a precious few seconds "hiding his head behind the butt of his pistol," presumably to take aim, "but the situation did not demand that I wait upon his every convenience."

The two fired at each other in the same instant.

"When I saw him fall, I quickly put my left hand in my pocket, which I felt was wounded, and, throwing down my pistol, I ran to him," only to confront the points of three swords aimed at him by three of Branicki's assistants, "who would instantly have made mincemeat of me where I had dropped to my knees beside him," if Branicki had not shouted "in a voice of thunder":

"*Villains, respect this gentleman.*"

The potential assassins withdrew at their master's command, and Casanova and the Lieutenant-General helped Branicki to his feet. Bent over in pain, he walked to a nearby inn, glancing occasionally at Casanova, and wondering at the source of the blood streaming over Casanova's breeches and white stockings. Who wounded whom, and where? At the inn, Branicki "throws himself into a big armchair, he stretches out, his clothes are unbuttoned, his shirt is raised as far as his stomach, and he sees that he is wounded to the death. My ball had entered his abdomen at the seventh true rib on the right and had gone under the last false rib on the left. The two holes were ten inches apart. The sight was alarming; it seemed that the intestines had been pierced and that he was a dead man."

Branicki looked straight at Casanova. "You have killed me, and now get away, for you will lose your head on the scaffold. . . . If you have no money, take my purse."

A feeble toss. The purse fell to the floor. Casanova had no need of it. He replaced it in Branicki's pocket. He expressed the wish that Branicki's wound was anything but mortal. In despair over the harm he'd wrought, "I kiss his forehead," and then, "I leave the inn."

Everyone else had gone to "fetch a doctor, a surgeon, priests, relatives, friends." He was alone, without a sword, lost in a "countryside covered with snow, wounded, and not knowing the way back to Warsaw." Perhaps he wouldn't outlive Branicki. He spied a sleigh pulled by two horses, and cried, "Warsaw!" The peasant holding the reins pulls to a stop. A weakened Casanova "lies down in the sleigh, and to keep me from being splashed he covers me with the mat. He drives at a fast canter." He encountered Branicki's friend Bisinski "riding at a full gallop, with his bare saber in his hand." Had Bisinski paid attention to the peasant's sleigh, he would have seen Casanova's head and sliced it in two.

Spared, Casanova sought sanctuary on arrival in Warsaw at a Franciscan monastery. He rang at the door, a monk opened it, saw Casanova "covered in blood," and, assuming the stranger to be a fugitive from the law, attempted to shut it tight, but Casanova kicked him in the belly and knocked him down on his back, his legs in the air like an upended beetle as he shouted for help. When other monks arrived, Casanova made threatening gestures and demanded sanctuary. They led him to a room that resembled a dungeon, where he asked for his servants, who promptly appeared. He sent for a surgeon. Two local officials arrived, along with two princes, who "began reviling the monks who lodged me like a galley slave. They excused themselves by saying that I had gotten inside by mistreating the porter; which made the princes laugh, but not me, for I was suffering from my wound. They at once gave me two fine rooms."

He examined the injury: "Branicki's ball had entered my hand through the metacarpus under the index finger, and, after breaking my first phalanx, had lodged there; its force had been weakened by the metal button of my waistcoat and by my abdomen, which it had slightly wounded near the navel. The ball had to be extracted from my hand, which was causing me great discomfort." The surgeon, Gendron, cut on the opposite side, "which made my wound twice as long." Meanwhile, Casanova recounted the duel with Branicki, while "concealing the agony that the unskillful surgeon caused me when he inserted the pincers to take hold of the ball. Such is the power of vanity over the human mind."

Another onlooker, Prince Lubomirski, evoked the mayhem that erupted after word of the duel spread. "It is rumored that Branicki is dead, and his Uhlans"—light cavalry—"are looking for you on horseback, galloping everywhere to avenge their colonel by butchering you. A good thing you are here!" As he spoke, a Grand Marshal ordered two hundred mounted soldiers to surround the monastery, "on the pretext of making sure you do not escape; but really to prevent that frenzied mob from forcing their way into the monastery to butcher you."

More news on Branicki reached Casanova. His antagonist wasn't dead, after all, yet still in great danger. If the ball fired by Casanova pierced Branicki's intestines, he would die. If not, he'd live. They would know on the morrow. The King had gone to see him. Meanwhile, the General present at the duel said that what saved Casanova's life was his threat to wound Branicki in the head. "Having tried to protect his head, he put himself in an awkward position, and he missed you. If not for that, he would have pierced your heart, for he fires at the sharp edge of a knife and cuts the bullet in two."

Casanova disagreed. If he'd killed Branicki, "I should have been butchered on the spot if he had not said three words that stopped his friends, who already had their sabers raised over me." If any good came of the affair, it was a note written by the compassionate Polish King: "I have not forgotten Casanova. You can assure him of his pardon, even if Branicki should die."

After reading the message, Casanova "printed a respectful kiss on the note, and I showed it to the noble company, who expressed their admiration for a man truly worthy of his crown."

———————◆———————

Crowds assembled to show support for Casanova, or so he thought. Actually, they demonstrated against the political faction Branicki represented. Noblemen and noblewomen offered money to Casanova, who, by his count, refused four thousand ducats, "and I prided myself on it." (He later regretted this vainglorious gesture.) He did accept a gift of dinner for four each day, courtesy of Prince Adam Czartoryski, but did not partake on the advice of his surgeon, "who was no genius."

His condition worsened The wound in his abdomen suppurated, and on the fourth day, "my badly swollen arm and the blackening of my wound, which threatened to turn gangrenous, made the surgeons decide . . . that my hand must be amputated." He learned this news not from the surgeons themselves, but from the pages of the *Court Gazette*, and it came as a relief to know that his name was before the public again, and on the lips of courtiers, circumstances be damned. Long ago, in Paris, he learned how scandal can spread and enhance his reputation. Better to be notorious than obscure. Moreover, he did not believe he suffered from gangrene, a loss of blood supply causing the death of tissue. So he laughed at the broadsheet, he laughed at those who offered condolences, and he laughed at Count Clary of the Imperial Court, who tried to persuade him to undergo the amputation.

Three surgeons examined him, the number necessary to arrive at a consensus. One removed the bandages and drain, examined the wound and the swelling. The other two confered in Polish, to Casanova's frustration, and "then the three of them tell me they will cut off my hand at nightfall." Despite their verdict, "they are all in high spirits, they tell me I have nothing to fear, and that it will assure my recovery." He responded as only Casanova could. "I am the lord and master of my hand, and I will never allow them to perform this absurd amputation."

The surgeons warned Casanova that the gangrene was spreading; by tomorrow they would have to amputate his arm. He still saw no sign of gangrenous necrosis and dismissed them. He then wrote to the King, denouncing the surgeons as "ignoramuses and butchers." Everyone at court read his savage letter; everyone was insulted. "It was impossible that the three best surgeons in Warsaw should be deceived in so simple a manner," said Prince Lubomirski. They are not deceived, Casanova replied, "but they think they can deceive me . . . to flatter Count Branicki, who is very ill, and who perhaps needs this comfort in order to recover."

That night, *four* surgeons unwrapped his bandages and examined the wound in his arm, swollen to twice its normal size. The drain was removed. He saw pus, but said nothing. The surgeons declared the arm infected and said they must remove it in the morning. "Tired of arguing, I tell them to come with the necessary instruments, and that I will submit to their operation"—as life-threatening as the original wound, if not more so. "They go off very well pleased," but in the morning Casanova gave orders that they were not to enter his room. Instead, he inveigled a French physician to examine the wound, and he agreed with Casanova: no gangrene. Even better, the *médecin* conferred with the four Polish surgeons, and persuaded them to forgo the operation. "On Easter Sunday, I went to mass with my arm in a sling, though I did not wholly recover the use of it until eighteen months later."

He emerged from seclusion into robust health. "Those who condemned me found themselves obliged to praise me." The surgeons who'd advocated amputation "had to admit that they were all either completely ignorant or extremely imprudent." Casanova had cheated death once again. His life resembled a Mobius strip of quasi-tragic episodes sliding into farce before plunging into fresh uncertainty.

Three days later, he arrived at the mansion where Count Branicki had been staying. "I thought I owed him a visit." A bond had formed between the two adversaries, and the Count had sent a lackey each day to inquire after Casanova's health. Branicki had even troubled to return Casanova's sword, discarded "on the field of battle."

Casanova entered Branicki's room. The Count wore a "dressing gown of some gold-glazed stuff." Pillows adorned with rose-colored ribbons supported him: the image of wounded noble decadence. "Pale as a corpse," Branicki removed his nightcap at the sight of Casanova, who bowed, a sling cradling his wounded arm.

"I have come, Monseigneur, to ask you to pardon me," Casanova began. "You have honored me far more than you offended me, and I ask your protection in the future against your friends."

Branicki declared himself the enemy of "all those who will not respect you." And as for his being safe from Branicki, Casanova could rest assured that he enjoyed the esteem and protection of the King. "Be seated, and in the future let us be good friends. A cup of chocolate for Monsieur! So, you are cured?

"Completely, except for the joint, the use of which I shall not recover for a year."

"You put up a good fight against the surgeons," Branicki said, "and you were right to tell someone that the fools thought they would be pleasing me by leaving you with only one hand."

At least *your* wound is healing, said Casanova to his Polish frenemy.

Their chivalrous sparring persisted until they had exhausted the possibilities for one-upmanship. As Casanova put it, "After a number of cheerful and interesting remarks, I took leave the hero." And lived to fight another day.

———•———

Accounts of his duel appeared in gazettes throughout Europe. Everyone wanted to see the notorious Casanova, who put himself on display in drawing rooms, dining rooms, gardens, and courtyards. "I spent two weeks going to dinners and suppers to which I was invited, and at all of which I was summoned to tell the story of the duel in the greatest detail," often before an audience of luminaries, including the King of Poland, "always pretending not to listen to me"—except when His Majesty asked an interesting question: If Casanova had received an insult in his native Venice from a patrician, would he have challenged his antagonist to a duel? No, Casanova explained, for a Venetian patrician would not have bothered to respond. "But if the same Venetian dared to insult me in a foreign country, he would have to account to me for it."

The King's question concealed a threat, and Casanova soon received an unsigned letter stating that the "King no longer wishes to see me at court because he had learned that I had been hanged in effigy in Paris." Although he'd fled Paris seven years earlier, rumors that he'd stolen funds from the École militaire lottery—the lottery that he'd helped to launch, and which was still thriving in Paris—as well as a ridiculous story that he'd "practiced the base trade of actor in Italy, wandering from province to province with troupes of strolling players" circulated throughout the distant capital. He could only sigh in resignation. "It is very easy to make these allegations, and very difficult to refute them." He put them down to the envy that infested courts, "where hatred is ever at work."

To add to his sense of oppression, he received an order from the Polish King, who previously had given him money, extended hospitality, and taken his side against Count Branicki in the duel, to leave Warsaw within eight days. *Eight days!* "In a towering rage I write the King a long letter. I show him that my honor demanded"—*insisted!*—"that I disobey his order." Casanova resorted to sarcasm, a dangerous tactic when addressing a monarch: "My creditors, Sire, will forgive me when they learn that I have left Poland without paying them only because Your Majesty compels me to leave it."

By way of reply, he received a thousand ducats and a warning that he was in greater need of preserving his life than paying his debts. Going about at night, the King explained, exposed Casanova to "obvious dangers." Casanova admitted that "five or six people sent me challenges that I had not even answered." They might attack at any time, and the King, with sarcasm of his own, said that he no longer wanted to worry about Casanova's safety. He should consider the order to leave Poland not a disgrace but rather an expression of the King's concern for his life.

Casanova paid his debts, two hundred ducats in all, and in mid-July 1766 departed for Dresden, Germany, where his mother, Zanetta, and other family members lived.

Chapter 17

Doña Ignacia

W as it my good or my evil Genius who bestowed her on me?" Casanova mused. "I could not know." She was twenty. Her family name was Maton, but he never bothered to find out her given name. She spoke French. She said she'd had two lovers, one who had seduced and abandoned her, the other a poor but honest lieutenant who'd rejoined his regiment. At present, she had no lover. What could be simpler? He supposed there was one chance in a hundred that she would accept his proposal to travel with him, but she did, even though he calculated that she'd cost him "a great deal of money."

Having installed himself in an apartment in Dresden, he went to see his mother, Zanetta, now a retired actress and courtesan of fifty-nine living modestly on a pension "in the country." He recalled that she was "overjoyed to see me with my arm in a sling, which made a dramatic picture. Then I saw my brother Giovanni"—the director of the Academy of Fine Arts in Dresden—"and his Roman wife Teresa Roland." He saw his sister, Maddalena, married to Peter August, a Saxon court musician. All greeted him with a combination of enthusiasm and curiosity befitting his adventures. "Everyone made much of me, and I had to tell the story of my duel everywhere." In fact, "I was glad to tell it, for I was proud of it."

On his first night in Dresden, he invited Maton to share his bed, and so "the nuptials were celebrated, and we rose the next morning the best friends in the world." He spent the day buying her gifts, "dress, shifts, stockings, petticoats, bonnets, shoes—everything, in short, for she had nothing." When visiting friends who wished to meet her, he explained that she was merely his housekeeper, not his wife, and kept her out of sight, away from society; she was forbidden to receive visitors on her own, and he rebuffed a Count who tried to steal her away. At first, he believed he'd succeeded in driving away his rival, but in the days to come, he gathered evidence that Maton and the Count were conspiring to deceive Casanova.

When not with Maton, he visited Zanetta. Although Casanova in his memoirs strove to project an impression of civility and affection between mother and child, he was merely respectful, as if toward a distant cousin. She had been so absent for so long, so oblivious to his welfare, and so pre-occupied with her lovers and her once thriving career that Casanova the libertine lacked a template for love. He had availed himself of countless substitutes, including his latest amour, Maton, but abandoned every one as he had once been abandoned. In the several million words that make up Casanova's memoir, a mere handful concern Zanetta, never with the candor and feeling that he brought to evoking the other women in his life.

When Casanova confirmed that Maton and the Count had cuckolded him, he fell out of love with her as swiftly as he had fallen in love. He came down with a "bad headache, to which I was not usually subject." He was bled as his mother kept him company: a suitable tableau for a wronged lover. He felt worse the next day, and medicated himself. "That night when I went to bed, I found myself attacked by a love token whose symptoms were very ugly. I knew enough about it not to be mistaken." Maton had pre-sented him with his eleventh round of venereal disease. How could he have been so careless? "I spend the night very angry with the trollop, I rise at day-break, I go into her room, I draw the curtains, she wakes. I sit down on her bed, I throw off the sheet, and I pull from under her a towel folded double, the sight of which disgusts me. . . . I examine all that I had examined before, and I see a hideous pesthouse. She tearfully confesses that she has had the malady for six months; but that she believed she had not infected me with it because she had always taken great care to keep clean and to wash herself each time she expected that I would make love to her."

"'Wash yourself, you wretch!'" Casanova roared. "Look at what you have done to me. You have robbed me of my one treasure, my health. But no one must know it, for it is my own fault, and I am ashamed of it." He sent her to a nearby, inexpensive inn. She cried, he gave her money. When she kneeled to pray, he turned his back on her "without being troubled by the slightest act of pity, for what she had done, and what she was engaged in doing, showed me that she was a little monster who would perhaps . . . have cost me my life." Already, "the glands in my groin were swollen and hard." To those who inquired about his pretty young companion, he referred to her as a "servant whom I had dismissed, and in whom I took no more interest."

A week later, his brother Giovanni disclosed that Giacomo's rival, the Count, sought the care of a physician for the same malady, as did "four or five other young men," all "reduced to a very bad state by my housekeeper." Appalled, Casanova believed that Maton's victims should suffer in silence. "They must be very stupid" to announce their private problems, for "they deserve the disease she has given them." And so did he, by that reasoning. To have contracted his eleventh case of venereal disease while visiting his family was upsetting, and to hear that the trollop he'd brought with him had opened her legs for half the town was humiliating. He felt frail and prey to the infirmities of advancing age. Where had the pleasures of libertinism fled?

Casanova submitted to the wretched cure once again, and considered himself healthy by the middle of August. Come September, he was gorging on roasted larks to replace the weight he'd lost.

———•———

Later that month he arrived in Spa, a popular gambling resort located between Aix and Liège, where he resumed his alliance with the gambler "Don" Croce, accompanied by his "wife"—actually his mistress—who was seventeen, pregnant, and devastatingly attractive to Casanova. Her name was Charlotte Lamotte, and she kept him in "constant distraction." As Casanova socialized with the mismatched couple and gambled successfully at Spa, he stared at Charlotte, sighed, and fell under her silent spell. "I thought I could aspire to no more than her friendship, and I feared that it would diminish if she came to know that I loved her and that I was even jealous of the scoundrel who had seduced her."

In the September weeks that followed, Croce gambled and lost on a daily basis until he had "emptied his purse of its last copper." When he had nothing left to his name, he spoke confidentially to Casanova: "My dear friend, one of two things: I must either kill myself here and now, or leave as I am." And so he left, but not before he placed his young "wife," Charlotte, in Casanova's care, "for you adore her and you do justice to her merits." Take her to Paris, Croce advised, as he gave Casanova several louis. "I commend Charlotte to your care; she would be happy if I had never known her."

When Casanova related the story to Charlotte, "she remained motionless and thoughtful, with her beautiful eyes cast down, then she wiped away two tears, and, looking at me sadly and tenderly, said that if she could count on me she was far from considering herself unfortunate." Casanova swore that he'd never leave her, unless it was to restore her to Croce, and she, in turn, vowed "the obedience of a good daughter." They lingered at Spa for four days, keeping to themselves. Casanova treated her with paternal regard only, to his way of thinking. In reality, that meant holding her in his arms "for hours, kissing her beautiful eyes and demanding no other recompense for my affection; I enjoyed seeing that my restraint filled her with gratitude."

They made for Luxembourg, where they engaged a manservant, and left for Paris. With a lascivious wink, Casanova remarked, "On the journey my dear daughter always insisted on going to bed with her new father and putting him to sleep in her arms." She wished the two of them would continue this way for the rest of their lives, but he knew "things would be different after her confinement, and I indulged myself in sweet imaginings of that time."

By that time, they had arrived at the Hôtel de Montmorency in Paris, So much had changed since he had abandoned the city in 1763. Wherever he looked, "My old acquaintances had different houses and different fortunes, I found the rich become poor, the poor rich, brand-new courtesans, the ones I had known gone to cut a figure in the provinces, where everything that comes from Paris is welcomed and acclaimed." New buildings abounded, as did new streets "so strange in their architecture that I lost my way in them. Paris seemed to me to have become a labyrinth." He got lost walking from the Church of Saint-Eustache to the rue Saint-Honoré on his way to the Louvre. All these "vast round buildings with unsymmetrical exits, and little streets wider than long—it was the height of French architectural folly, which, to the innovating genius of the nation, seemed a masterpiece." All around him, "new rules, new actors, and new actresses; everything had become more expensive."

In his disoriented state, he erroneously convinced himself that Madame d'Urfé had died. He was relieved to find his former confidante Madame du Rumain in good health, but vexed by so many family problems that she believed that Casanova had returned to Paris "opportunely to rid her of them by my cabala"—magic and alchemy. He made gestures in this direction, for "it was the least I could do for a woman of her character" to demonstrate that he was still the Casanova she recalled. Meanwhile, his brother Francesco, the artist, had moved to the rue des Amandiers; both he and his wife appeared happy to see Casanova again; Francesco remained impotent, yet she loved him. They implored their wandering brother to stay with them.

———•———

Charlotte, had developed a "prodigiously big belly," and by October 7, he arranged to send her to a midwife, Lamarre, on the rue Faubourg Saint-Denis. As their carriage emerged onto the rue de Montmorency, they were compelled to halt for a quarter of an hour to allow a funeral procession "of some rich person" to pass. Charlotte dabbed her eyes with her handkerchief and rested her pretty head on his shoulder, confessing that she felt that encountering a funeral procession when she was about to give birth was a "very bad omen." Charlotte had reason to be scared. About ten percent of deliveries resulted in the death of the mother at that time.

"Omens are nothing but vanities that can become real only with the help of superstition," Casanova cooed, as he tried to soothe her.

Once he had installed her in the midwife's house, he moved from the hotel to his brother's home, "but as long as Charlotte lived I returned there only to sleep." He stayed with her every day from nine in the morning until midnight.

"On October 13, Charlotte was attacked by a high fever that never left her. On the 17th in my presence she gave birth to a boy with no difficulty, and the next morning, the midwife, at Charlotte's express order, took him to the church to be baptized." Afterward, she instructed the midwife to take the infant, Jacques Charles, to the Foundling Hospital with his baptismal certificate tucked into his linen. "I tried in vain to persuade her to leave the child in my care," Casanova recalled, but Charlotte insisted that his father, Croce, could retrieve the baby from the orphanage in which he would be placed.

Casanova returned to Charlotte's bedside, where he remained day and night. At four in the morning of October 26, "She gave me her last farewell," he remembered, "and before letting go of my hand she raised it to her lips in the presence of the priest who had confessed her at midnight." An hour later, she died of fever in Casanova's presence, despite the efforts of a physician. (Nearing the end of his own life when he committed this account to paper, Casanova shed tears one last time to honor the "memory of that charming creature, victim of love and of a man who still lives and who seemed bound to make people unhappy only in obedience to his cruel destiny.")

After she was gone, he sat beside the bed "on which lay what had been Charlotte, now a corpse." The midwife tried to persuade him to leave; he waved her away. At noon, Francesco and his wife appeared. "Seeing the spectacle and my tears, they could not hold back theirs." After they departed, Casanova remained in the room "until Charlotte had been carried away to be buried." He received her death certificate in silence.

Who else would? He had become the mourner of last resort.

More sorrowful news came his way, this time in letters from Venice. Signor Matteo Bragadin, his great helper, protector, and recourse in time of need, had died. Coming right after Charlotte's death, Casanova had no more tears left to shed. Here was a man "who for twenty-two years had been as a father to me, living himself with the greatest economy and going into debt to support me." Under the Venetian laws of inheritance, he could leave nothing to Casanova, who had once saved his life. "His furniture, his library were to be sold to his creditors in part. His two friends, also mine, were poor. I could count only upon their hearts." Twenty-four hours before he died, he sent Casanova one last monetary gift, his last, all he had to bequeath in a world of isolation, silence, and sorrow. They would never see one another again, except, perhaps, as insubstantial shades in the afterlife.

"Overwhelmed as I was, I defied Fortune to give me a blow that I could feel." Fortune obliged on November 4, when he attended a concert with a ticket bestowed by an acquaintance. Halfway through the performance he heard his name, turned, and saw a young man speaking "scornfully" about him. It was the Marquis de Lisle, a nephew of the Marquise d'Urfé. The Marquis de Lisle was telling his companions that Casanova had cost him a fortune. The adventurer had stolen it from his aunt, and so she was unable to leave it to him.

Casanova reacted furiously, probably because the Marquis spoke the truth. "If you were outdoors, I would teach you how to talk by kicking you in the behind." With that, he rose and stormed out of the concert as the Marquis, enraged, was restrained by his two companions. A couple of days later, a representative of the French crown visited him. "He hands me a paper. I read it. I see that it is signed 'Louis.'" It was a dreaded *lettre de cachet*, a letter of expulsion. "The monarch, in the letter he wrote me, ordered me to leave Paris within twenty-four hours and his kingdom within three weeks." There was no reason given, and it seemed to Casanova that the Marquise d'Urfé's spiteful nephew had obtained his revenge.

Madame du Rumain offered to travel to Versailles to plead Casanova's case, but he refused. He would go, he knew not where or why, but he would go. He received a passport from the Minister of Foreign Affairs. It was for Spain, so he would go to Spain, even though he did not know the language.

At six in the evening, by the light of the moon, with a chill descending, he embraced his brother Francesco and his sister-in-law, not knowing if he would see them again. "I left on the 20th, all alone, without a servant, sad because of Charlotte's death, but calm, with a hundred louis in my purse and a bill of exchange for eight thousand francs," he noted. "I enjoyed perfect health, and I thought I was armed with new principles." He would need them, because he'd arrived at a certain age "which Fortune commonly scorns and for which women care little."

He traveled all night, and by seven in the morning he arrived in Orléans, eighty miles south of Paris, and took his bearings. He journeyed south across the Pyrenees, separating the Iberian Peninsula from the rest of Europe, "riding a mule and with another [mule] carrying my trunks." The trail was icy and dangerous, the air sharp and clear. "I thought these mountains much more imposing than the Alps."

At year's end he arrived safely in Pamplona, Spain, to commence the last segment of the journey. For the first twenty leagues, he remained alert and agile, "for the road was as good as in France," but afterward he found no road at all, not even a bad road, only "uneven stony climbs and descents, where one nowhere saw the least sign to indicate that carriages passed there." He endured wretched inns, fit for "muleteers who lodge with their mules." He fetched his own wood, built his own fire, and cooked his own supper. This wasn't the Spain of myth, of night air heavily scented with the perfume of orange blossoms. Every stony mile he traveled bore him away from the Enlightenment into darkness. There was worse to come in Agreda. "It is called a city. It is a prodigy of ugliness and gloom." He wanted no part of it, and subsided into stoic resignation.

He was compelled to sacrifice another luxury he'd taken for granted in France: privacy. His room at an inn bolted from the outside only, so he could not lock himself safely inside at bedtime. The innkeeper informed him that the Inquisition, Spanish edition, insisted on the unlocked door to see "what foreigners might be doing at night in their rooms."

"What can your accursed Holy Inquisition be curious to know?" he demanded of the innkeeper.

"Everything. To see if you eat meat on a fast day. To see if there are several people of both sexes in the room, if the women sleep alone or with men, and to learn if the women who sleep with men are their legitimate wives," and to be able to imprison them if they weren't. He was not in Paris anymore. When a priest ordered him to kneel and pray on the street, he was bound to obey. Foreign snuff was forbidden; a clerk tossed the contents of Casanova's snuffbox in the mud to make the point. Spanish snuff proved hard to come by, and he had to endure three or four weeks without it. Wearing breeches without codpieces led to imprisonment; even the tailors who fashioned them were punished. "What pleases mankind everywhere is forbidden," he philosophized.

Only language engaged him, and it was through Spanish that "little by little" he gained exposure to the Iberian mystique. "Guadalajara, Alcalá, and Madrid"—such names sounded magical to his ears. He made a study of Arab influences on the Spanish language. "Arabic must be the oldest of all languages," he theorized, since it brimmed with *a*, "the easiest of all vowels, because it is the most natural" and among the most beautiful in the world, "sonorous, energetic, majestic . . . capable of the harmony of the most sublime poetry." In the next breath, he admired the women of Spain. "In the public walks, in churches, at the theaters, they speak with their eyes to those whom they wish to speak, possessing the seductive language to perfection." Any man who understood was "sure to be successful" in his romantic quest.

In Madrid, he agonized over presenting his credentials to the Venetian Ambassador, although the Ambassador could do him no harm. He presented himself to Gasparo Soderini, the Secretary of the Embassy, who was baffled by Casanova's unannounced appearance. The Secretary urged Casanova to write to the Ambassador, "and you may be given a hearing." At the embassy, he was confronted by the son of Giovanni Battista Manuzzi, "who had served the state Inquisitors as a spy in order to get me imprisoned under the Leads [I Piombi], the same man who had cleverly obtained from me the books of magic I had and which were apparently the incriminating evidence that, without any other legal proceedings, had brought on me the terrible punishment to which I had been subjected." Casanova kept this information to himself, and cajoled him into confirming rumors of the younger Manuzzi's homosexual activities.

Next, he called on the neoclassical painter Anton Raphael Mengs, whom he'd last seen in Rome seven years earlier, when his brother Giovanni was studying with him. Now Mengs enjoyed an appointment "in the service of His Catholic Majesty at an excellent salary." With his wife and children still in Rome, he lived as he wished in Spain and "talked with his Majesty whenever he pleased."

As he made a place for himself in Madrid, Casanova attended masked balls and plays. "The Spanish theater was full of absurdities, but it did not displease me." Even here the Spanish Inquisition intruded, for the boxes opened in front so that others could see if the occupants were putting their hands "to evil use" during the performances. Laughing, Casanova remarked that the "Italians and French do not soil their minds with such suspicions."

Strict adherence to religion appeared to permeate every aspect of Spanish life. "There is not a courtesan who, being with her lover and yielding to amorous desire, decides to perform the act without first having placed a handkerchief over the crucifix and turned the pictures of saints to the wall." And if her lover laughed at such measures, she would denounce him as an atheist to the authorities. Despite these prohibitions—or was it because?—"Profligacy runs riot in Madrid," Casanova observed. For example, at masked balls as a foreigner he could "obtain the company of a woman or girl much more easily than a Spaniard from Madrid," and that "four thousand girls who have no lover are at home crying" because they were forbidden to attend the balls alone. Almost any mother or father would gladly permit him to escort their daughter to a masked ball, so long as he provided her a costume, mask, gloves, a carriage to fetch her, and promised "to bring her back home." If the girl's parents refused, she "cries, falls ill, and goes to bed, cursing and swearing at their tyranny and calling God to witness that she has never seen you in her life." This "novel discourse," Casanova decided, had "the stamp of truth," and for the first time in a long while, he felt his libido stirring as he anticipated "some rare adventure" in which he would decide to whom he would toss his handkerchief.

Not long after, at a ball, he saw couples dancing the fandago, twirling, gyrating, pulsating, and taunting, and he was captivated. "I had never seen anything wilder or more interesting. . . . Each couple danced face to face, never taking more than three steps, striking the castanets, which are held in the fingers and accompany the music with attitudes more lascivious than ever seen." It was so sensuous and daring that "no woman could refuse anything to a man with whom she had danced the fandango."

Casanova worried that the Inquisition had banned the dance that "set the soul on fire," but Count d'Aranda, a well-traveled Spanish diplomat turned reform-minded minister, overrode the Inquisition to permit the fandango. Armed with this knowledge, Casanova located an actor who spent three days showing his Venetian student "the motions of the dance." Casanova learned so well that even Spaniards said that no one in Madrid danced the fandango better—at least, that's what he wished they were saying.

What he required now was a skillful partner, and found her one day as she was coming out of confession. She seemed fine-looking, "with an air of contrition" as she knelt on the floor, Spanish-style. He followed her home, watched her go upstairs, then mounted the stairs and rang the doorbell, preparing himself to be dismissed. The door opened. She stood with her family beside her. "Speaking Spanish very badly but well enough to be un-

Fandango dancers in Portugal, 1797

derstood, with my hat in my hand, and a serious and respectful manner," Casanova said he'd come "by chance to ask her father for permission to take his daughter to the ball, assuring him that I was a man of honor and that I would bring her back to him at the end of the evening." The father was baffled, but the daughter expressed a desire to go with this stranger. As the two negotiated, Casanova went home to await the outcome.

The next day he received word that the girl would be allowed to accompany him so long as her mother kept vigil in her carriage throughout the evening.

On the following night, his "devout beauty" ready at last, "her face prettily flushed," awaited him in the carriage with her mother. He eagerly joined them. Shortly after arriving at the ball, the girl revealed her name: Doña Ignacia.

———•———

"I enter the ballroom with the beautiful Doña Ignacia, we take several turns around it, everywhere meeting the gaze of soldiers with fixed bayonets who were walking slowly about, ready to apprehend anyone who should disturb the peace by quarreling." They danced minuets and contradances, and went to supper as Doña Ignacia remained nearly silent to discourage him from taking liberties with her. When it was finally time to dance the fandango, he stepped in with his partner, who danced ably and was more than a little surprised "to find herself so well accompanied in it by a foreigner." In no time, the "seductive dance" had "set us both on fire." Exhilarated, Casanova tells her that he was ready to die on the spot if he couldn't find a way to make her happy. "I was a man to run all risks," he declared, "ready for anything." She promised her reply in writing, and then it was time to return to her coach, where her mother awaited them. He took her hands to kiss them; she gripped his hands to keep him from going too far and proceeded to talk about the ball with her mother, not releasing Casanova's perilous hands until the carriage arrived at her doorstep. She asked him to remain seated, thanked him, and returned home with her mother.

The next day, January 18, 1768, he received a letter from Doña Ignacia in which she explained that Don Francisco de Ramos, her fiancé, would call on him. When he did, Don Francisco explained that he was "certain that I could have conceived only a fatherly fondness for her." In that light, would Casanova kindly lend Don Francisco a hundred doblones—four hundred pesos—so that he could marry his sweetheart before Carnival; life was very expensive in Madrid for a newlywed couple.

After explaining that he lacked a hundred doblones, Casanova studied his rival, who looked about twenty-two years old, "ugly and misshapen." He felt his ardor for Doña Ignacia cool. Still, he wanted someone. "There was an intolerable void in my heart; I needed, as I had needed several times before, a charming passion," some lovely thing neither too easy nor too difficult to obtain—and free of venereal infection!

Toward the end of Carnival, he was surprised to receive a visit from Doña Ignacia's father, a hidalgo—that is, minor nobility—and a cobbler. He brought boots and the compliments of his daughter, still marveling at the ball she'd attended with Casanova and impressed by the respect he'd shown her. Why hadn't he called on her again? Casanova explained that he hadn't dared to return "because I was afraid I might injure her reputation." Insisting that her standing was above reproach, her father said that he would be honored if Casanova would visit his house again.

When Casanova arrived at Doña Ignacia's house, he discovered her father at work, mending old shoes ("I laughed at myself having to accord 'Don' to a cobbler"), and Doña Ignacia, rosary in hand, sitting cross-legged on the floor—"a vestige of the Moorish manner of old Spain." She offered profuse thanks for his taking her to the ball. In this spirit, Casanova replied that he would be honored to escort her to another ball; in fact there was one that evening. The moment he was left alone with her, he confessed that he adored her, but if she kept him waiting, she would never see him again. She reminded him that it was her duty to "preserve my innocence for the man who will be my husband."

Casanova replied, "You must yield to my ardor without resisting me in the slightest, and be sure that I will respect your innocence." He launched an attack on her, as he phrased it, against which she "vigorously" defended herself. He assured that "she will find me submissive and respectful throughout the night, but not tender and loving, which would be far better." She responded that it was her duty to resist, "despite herself." Casanova sensed an advantage embedded in her reply; now it was a matter of "conquering duty" felt by this "pious Spanish woman."

If so, he said, "it follows your duty is a burden to you; it is your mortal enemy," and in that case, "why yield it the victory?" Better to trample on it!

Impossible, she replied.

He asked her to close her eyes, and he attacked her in "the weak place," and she repelled him, "but not roughly." She admitted that he could seduce her, if he chose, but that if he loved her, he should "spare her that shame." Seizing his advantage, Casanova encouraged her to allow him to do whatever he wanted, and he convinced himself that she loved him, "without your troubling yourself to tell me so." Love alone should be their arbiter, rather than embarrassment or duty.

As they sparred, "my bold hands gained the advantage, she let me guide them where I would, and my pleasure came to a fruition that she did nothing to disavow." He considered himself "perfectly satisfied" afterward, and accompanied his new love to the ball. He later showered Doña Ignacia with gifts, not forgetting her watchful mother, waiting in the carriage, where she received two bottles of *ratafia*, a fruity liqueur, the better to help her sleep while the lovers romped. And as for Don Francisco de Ramos, Doña Ignacia's young lover, who was becoming suspicious that Casanova and the girl had become intimate—he was easily bought off with gold coins. One doblón de ocho, and he started calling Casanova his "father," his "good angel" worthy of "eternal gratitude," as he labored under the false assumption that Casanova was bit by bit giving the young man the dowry necessary to wed Doña Ignacia after Lent.

By now, Casanova was "convinced that she had resolved to give herself to me." She performed the fandango so voluptuously that she "could not have promised me everything more eloquently in words . . .

"What a dance! It burns, it inflames, it carries away . . ."

Spaniards advised him that the fandango was merely a harmless pasttime, without particular meaning, and the Duke of Aranda encouraged the balls as innocent distractions and charity events, but Casanova was not persuaded by this rationale. The fandango was seduction itself.

In preparation for yet another ball, he wished to transform Doña Ignacia's female "tall cousin" into a man. "After laying out all her male attire before her, I made her begin by taking off her slippers and stockings, putting on white stockings and the shoes that fitted her best. I sat down before her, telling her that she would sin mortally if she suspected my intentions were less than decent, for, since I could be her father, it was impossible that I should have anything like that. She replied that she was a good Christian, but not a fool." Undeterred, "I pulled on her stockings myself, then put on the garters, saying I should never have believed that she had such a well-shaped leg or such white skin, and she laughed." He handed her his breeches. She drew them up and buttoned them to her waist. Next, he handed her his shirt, and turned away; when he looked at her again, he saw that she had a "beautiful, firm bosom." But she still looked like a woman.

He sat before her, "unbuttoned her breeches to gather together the shirt and put the bunch of material where she had nothing and where, as a man, she ought to have something." He looked, he touched her gingerly, and then, "I put on her domino, her hood, and her mask, and I exhibited her." All were impressed. Doña Ignacia offered compliments. "She could not but be taken for a man by the most knowing." Women were as malleable as his needs and fantasies.

Now it was Doña Ignacia's turn to undergo a transformation. When they were alone, she surrendered to Casanova's vision. "I saw that she was born for love; I kept her for a good hour." He took the measure of this creation of his, and found his handiwork to his liking.

Off they went to the ball at sunset. They expected to dance the fandango, but the crowd was so large there was nowhere to perform. Supper was served at ten, and they walked around as two orchestras played until midnight struck, beginning the six weeks of Lent, during which orgies were forbidden—but not for everyone. Casanova escorted Doña Ignacia to his room "for a couple of hours in perfect freedom. It was obvious that she had the same desire." When he went to fetch coffee, he encountered Don Francisco, her neglected young fiancé, who asked to join them. Bending to local customs, "I had to conceal my fury. I told him I was his to command and that I was sure his unexpected visit would give Doña Ignacia the greatest pleasure." In fact, when she saw Don Francisco she called him an "indiscreet boor for having dared to inconvenience me at such an hour." Even Casanova leapt to the lad's defense. "I tried to calm Doña Ignacia by telling her that it was quite natural that Don Francisco should be at the coffeehouse at that hour on the last night of Carnival, that he had seen us only by chance, and that it was I who had invited him to come upstairs, thinking that it would please her. After drinking coffee Don Francisco thought it his part to take his leave. I told him I hoped to see him sometimes during Lent; but Doña Ignacia would grant him only a slight bow."

After he departed, Doña Ignacia told Casanova she regretted having been deprived of an hour alone with him. "Take me home," she ordered Casanova, "and if you love me come to see me during Lent." He assured her that as long as he remained in Madrid, "she should be the only object of my attentions."

Just when matters seemed settled, Casanova was approached by a Spanish official, an *alcalde*, warning that "forbidden weapons" had been found beneath a mat in the corner of his room. That, along with other suspicions, meant he was in danger of being arrested and sentenced to a *presidio* in North Africa where convicts were condemned to hard labor. "Do not make light of my warning," the official said. "Put yourself in a place of safety." Casanova did have several pistols and a carbine—a rifle with a short barrel—concealed in his room. He retrieved the weapons, wrapped them in a cloak, and ran to the house of Mengs, the court painter, where he believed he'd be safe, "for it belonged to the King."

Mengs, "an honest, ambitious, proud man, but suspicious and on his guard with respect to anything that could compromise him," gave Casanova asylum for one night only. Casanova insisted that he was "guilty of nothing" but keeping weapons in his room. In that case, Mengs replied, Casanova shouldn't have removed them; he should have known that "every man in his own room was free by natural right to keep firearms, if he chose." Casanova explained that he sought asylum with Mengs simply to avoid spending an unpleasant night in jail, but he agreed that he should have left the pistols and carbine under the mat in his room.

"And you should have stayed there yourself," Mengs snarled. "I didn't know you frightened so easily."

As the two argued, Casanova's landlord informed him that the *alcalde* had entered the apartment, searched everywhere, and found nothing, nevertheless, he sent Casanova's page to jail on the assumption that he'd warned his master. Yet Casanova also had his doubts about this page, a "rascal" who was probably "the informer and the spy, for after all he was the only person who knew where my weapons were hidden."

Mengs stormed off to bed, but in the morning he lavished attention on Casanova, ordering a valet to provide shorts, stockings, underdrawers, collars, handkerchiefs, and scents. His housekeeper served chocolate; his cook offered to prepare a meal. Casanova, on edge, accepted only a cup of chocolate and a handkerchief. As he stood in Mengs's room bidding his host goodbye, an officer arrived to escort him of his "own free will" to a more luxurious prison than the *presidio*, the guardhouse at Buen Retiro, better known as a royal palace, now abandoned, and park. And he would have to turn over his weapons immediately.

"Monsieur Mengs can give you my weapons, which have traveled with me for eleven years and which I carry to defend myself from murderers." He asked permission to write four notes before leaving. Permission denied. "I shall remember Spain when I am back in Europe and come upon decent people, my equals, who may feel tempted to journey there," Casanova sniffed. He embraced Mengs, "who looked mortified," climbed into his carriage along with his weapons, and proceeded to the Palace of Buen Retiro to stay in one of its apartments. He was led into a "huge room on the ground floor," where his senses were assaulted by a "very trying stench." Looking around, he saw twenty-five or thirty other prisoners, beds, and benches. He asked a soldier for paper, pen, and ink, giving him coins to buy it; the soldier palmed the coins with a laugh and disappeared.

To his surprise, he spotted his page standing nearby as well as Count Marazzani—Antonio Luigi Marazzani, a priest turned adventurer, and no more a count than Casanova. Marazzani feared that he and Casanova would be confined to some awful fortress for three or four years. It was either that or Africa. Casanova's best hope for deliverance, Marazzani advised, was the Venetian Ambassador, but the idea made Casanova swallow "bitter saliva," for the Ambassador was Alvise Sebastiano Mocenigo, a patrician who would be of little help. And his own patron, Bragadin, was dead. Who would save him now?

"I sat down on a bed, which I left three hours later, seeing myself covered with lice, the mere sight of which is enough to turn the stomach of an Italian or a Frenchman, but not a Spaniard, who laughs at these little annoyances." But he was not a Spaniard, and their proximity kept him motionless and silent, "devouring all the bilious humor that was circulating and poisoning my fluids." One can't help but gain the impression that he relished his ordeal, and already imagined how best to describe it. Marazzani offered to bribe a soldier to provide a decent meal for the two of them, but Casanova angrily replied that he did not want to eat, and he refused to pay a soldier for anything until the one who'd promised to buy him pen and paper returned his money. Hours later, Mengs's servants delivered an ample repast to assuage his hunger pangs, and afterward he negotiated to receive the pen, ink, and paper he ardently desired to write letters to those who could help him. Soldiers, officers, and other prisoners interrupted him at every turn as he worked. "One came to snuff my candle, and put it out. I imagined I was in the galleys and bore it without complaining." He worked amid the stink and cacophony of prison. "Despite all these damned souls I finished my letters and sealed them. There was no art in my letters. They breathed the venom circulating in my soul." For example, he wrote to the Count d'Aranda ("the strongest of my four letters") to say that if murderers came for him, he would die believing that the Count himself had ordered the deed. "Either release me at once, or order your executioners to dispatch me quickly, for if they take it into their heads to send me to a presidio, I will kill myself first by my own hand."

When Manuzzi read the letters, he advised their author that "the proper tone for obtaining what one asked for was mildness" rather than petulance or ire.

That night, the beds were all filled, "the floor was soaked with urine," and no one would provide him with straw for a pallet. He passed the long hours sitting on a backless bench.

In the morning, Doña Ignacia and her father the cobbler visited. Don Diego believed that Casanova had been jailed by mistake and would soon be freed. He pressed a roll of money into Casanova's hand, but the prisoner, fearing "the thieves by whom I was surrounded," returned it to Don Diego, who wept.

Later, an official subjected the prisoner to formal questioning, but Casanova refused to respond in Spanish because of his lack of mastery in the language. Even the slightest misunderstanding could worsen his predicament. Instead, he wrote a statement:

I am Giacomo Casanova, a subject of the Republic of Venice, a man of letters, moderately rich; I am traveling for my pleasure; I am known to the Ambassador of my country, to the Count d'Aranda . . . I have not broken the least of His Catholic Majesty's laws, and nevertheless I find myself being murdered, and confined with criminals and thieves by ministers who would deserve to be treated far more harshly than I. . . .

My weapons have traveled with me for eleven years, I carry them only to defend myself against highway robbers, and at the Puerta de Alcalá they were seen in my carriages and they were not confiscated; which shows that their confiscation now is only a pretext to murder me.

After the document was translated into Spanish, "The official rises, looks at me with eyes venomous with anger, and says, '*Válgame Dios*, you will repent of having written this document.'"

Manuzzi informed Casanova that the Count d'Aranda agreed that he had been mistreated, "but one does not write such letters."

On hearing the Count's verdict, Casanova decided "my troubles are over." As for the tone of his letters, "everyone has his style. I became angry and maddened because I had been treated like a dog." He had no bed, the floor was an open sewer reeking of urine, and he would spend a second night sitting on a bench. "Do you think it possible that I do not want to eat the hearts of all my executioners? If I do not leave this inferno tomorrow I will kill myself or go mad."

Manuzzi sympathized and advised Casanova to pay for a bed for the third night, but, horrified by the prospect of bloodsucking lice, and afraid of having his watch, snuffbox, and coins stolen while he slept, he refused. Instead, "I spent a terrible night dozing on the same bench, constantly starting to wake when, losing my balance, I was on the verge of falling into the stinking filth on the floor." Manuzzi returned at eight the following morning, "terrified" by the sight of Casanova's face, bringing hot chocolate to fortify this wrongly imprisoned Venetian. Shortly afterward, three officers arrived. Casanova repeated the story of the soldier who had palmed his coin, and the officer ordered it replaced immediately. Casanova accepted the coin "with a laugh" and was gratified to hear the officer declare that the soldier who'd confiscated it should be flogged in Casanova's presence.

Later, in the guardroom, he observed the flogging of the soldier who'd stolen his coin. Justice had been served. He rested briefly on a clean bed provided for him, and "Manuzzi, before leaving me, embraced me again and again." Casanova was convinced the man was his "true friend."

At three in the afternoon, an official in a black cloak returned the pistols and carbine to Casanova. Thirty constables escorted him to his lodgings and removed the seal. He inspected the premises; all was in order, and he was free—but not before he had words with the *official*. "Let us forget everything," he began, "but admit that, if I had not known how to write, you would have sent me to the galleys."

———•———

Having washed and changed into fresh clothing, he was off to see Mengs, whom he found "in gala dress," congratulating Casanova on his deliverance. At the same time, he received official notification that the Venetian Ambassador who'd long avoided Casanova was now free to provide introductions without having to fear displeasing the State Inquisitors. To Casanova, this authorization meant that the curse of banishment from Venice was nearly lifted. Mengs grandly informed Casanova that he could now make his fortune in Spain, "provided that I behave myself." Casanova took a carriage to the Ambassador's "for after sixty hours of continual torture I could not stand." When he arrived the Ambassador was nowhere to be found, so he went home "to enjoy ten hours of the deepest sleep." In the morning, Manuzzi brought news that Casanova had been invited to court at Aranjuez, thirty miles south of Madrid, which served as the residence of King Carlos III during the months of April and May.

At court, the Venetian Ambassador appeared, fawned over Casanova, and "heaped praise on the painter Mengs" for providing asylum. Casanova entertained those present with a "detailed account of all that I had suffered at Buen Retiro." His letters had been circulated, read, and analyzed. The Ambassador termed them "ferocious." Don Rodrigo de Campomanes, the director of the Royal Historical Society and a particular new favorite of Casanova, who considered him both intelligent and actively opposed to the "prejudices and abuses" accompanying religion in Spain—how unexpected was this point of view!—said the letters "were just what was needed to make the reader see that I was in the right."

Reinvigorated, he commenced work on a study of "the colonies, treating them from the point of view of the natural sciences and of philosophy." Word of his intellectual prowess circulated throughout the Spanish court and among the intelligentsia, and he received encouragement to apply for support for projects to the Spanish government. He frequented salons, and he called on Doña Ignacia, "but since I could never be alone with her I was bored." He proposed stealing away to the countryside, but with Holy Week approaching, she reminded her suitor, "God died for us, we must not think of criminal pleasures but of doing penance. After Easter we could think of our love." Casanova had no choice but to accede to her wishes: "Such is the character of almost all the pious beauties in Spain."

Two weeks before Easter, as he sat in Mengs's carriage, he was stricken. "The fever, which came on with chills such as it is impossible to conceive, made me shake so much that my head struck the roof of the carriage. My teeth were chattering. I could not utter a word." Alarmed, Mengs ordered Casanova to bed, where a "violent sweat . . . expelled from my body at least twenty pints of water," soaking two mattresses, a straw pallet, and spilling onto the floor. The fever abated after forty-eight hours, but he remained bedridden for a week.

On the day before Easter, he felt strong enough to journey to the Venetian Ambassador—not without difficulty. A pustule, or blister, had formed near the fistula that had tormented him in Russia. Overnight, the pustule swelled, and on Easter Sunday, the holiest day of the year, he was unable to go to mass. The pustule had become "an abscess the size of a melon, terrifying all who beheld it," yet it caused him no pain, and remained soft. He confidently instructed a surgeon to open and drain it. The surgeon made a six-inch incision, and copious amounts of liquid drained from the wound. Four days later, Casanova considered it healed, although he still felt weak, and while still in bed received a letter from Mengs, who said that he'd been visited by a priest, who noted that Casanova had not taken the sacrament at Easter. Mengs feared he had "granted hospitality" to a heretic, and Casanova ran the risk of excommunication. To preserve his reputation, Mengs told Casanova to move out.

Infuriated, Casanova immediately dressed, went to confession, received the sacrament, and obtained a certificate from the monk. He then wrote to Mengs sarcastically suggesting that he "deserved the insult he had placed on me by turning me out of his house since I had been stupid enough to do him the honor of going there." As a Christian "who had just done his Easter duty," he supposed he should forgive Mengs, not that it would be easy.

Casanova complained of this ill treatment to the Venetian Ambassador, who reminded him that "Mengs was esteemed for nothing but his talent, for in other respects all Madrid knew that he was full of absurdities." Casanova took this theme much further: the man was "a drunkard, lascivious, bad-tempered, jealous, and avaricious." He beat his children "even at the risk of crippling them," and "more than once" Casanova had snatched away the eldest son lest Mengs "tear him to pieces with his teeth."

Despite his infuriating behavior, Mengs possessed a profound understanding of painting, according to Casanova. "Nothing that comes from the hands or minds of men is perfect in this world except a mathematical calculation," Mengs said, a sentiment that prompted Casanova to embrace him. Mengs would "go down in posterity as a philosopher, a great stoic, learned, and endowed with all the virtues," thanks in part to a biography assembled by his admirer. Casanova dismissed the volume as a "tissue of lies."

Pressing his suit, he spent so much time with Don Diego and Doña Ignacia that he virtually lived at their modest home. "In the large room in which he worked at repairing shoes and boots with an apprentice, he had his bed, in which he slept with his wife. In the adjoining room, which was smaller, I saw Doña Ignacia's bed, a stool on which to kneel before a great crucifix, a picture four feet high representing St. Ignatius of Loyola." Her "very ugly" younger sister occupied a smaller bedroom, and the kitchen contained a narrow cot for the cook. Despite his proximity to Doña Ignacia, she "remained completely unresponsive to the amorous pleas that I made to her."

She wrestled with her romantic ambitions and frustrations. "I do not know if I am pretty," she explained, "but I am courted; I must either resist or be damned; and there are men whom it is impossible to resist." As God was her witness, she had visited a girl during Holy Week who had smallpox in the hope that she would catch it and "become ugly" with scars. Her dire strategy failed to work, but her confessor, alarmed, told her that such actions indicated that she was unworthy of the beauty with which the Creator had endowed her. He told her to apply rouge to her cheeks to heighten her beauty and thus her discomfort.

As Casanova absorbed her story, especially her fear of dying in a state of mortal sin, he concluded that a "devout girl . . . feels a hundred times more pleasure than a girl without prejudices." He speculated wildly on "the womb's appetite," so strong that "if the woman does not give it the food it demands through the channel she alone controls, it often becomes furious and so gains an ascendancy over her which no strength can resist. It threatens her with death, it makes her a nymphomaniac." What's more, "the womb is an animal so self-willed, so irrational, so untamable that a wise woman, far from opposing its whims, should defer to them." He further speculated, "This ferocious organ is susceptible to a degree of management;

it is not malicious except when a fanatical woman irritates it; to one such it gives convulsions; another it drives mad; another it turns into a mirror or a monster of piety." The thought tormented him so much that he couldn't sleep, and he had to think of his health. He had no choice but to move out of her house, but if Casanova left, she would be the "unhappiest girl in all Madrid." She lowered her eyes and shed tears. If he stayed, and refused him, she would make *him* unhappy.

"Tell me what I must do. Am I to go or to stay? Choose."

"Stay," she whispered. That didn't mean they would become lovers. She'd promised God that she "would not succumb again." If he stayed, they would become so accustomed to one another that within a matter of days they would regard one another as brother and sister. Casanova agreed to "deceive" himself on that score. Privately, he felt "cheated of what she would have granted me if she had not been under the domination of a misunderstood religion" so he must forget her, "for even if I had the luck to enjoy her again one day, taking her by surprise at some moment when my words of caresses had troubled her soul, Sunday would come, and new promises to her confessor would send her back to me sullen and intractable."

Don Diego, aware of the tantalizing ambiguity of the situation, could think of nothing fitting to say and announced instead that he was off to *los toros*—the bullfights. Casanova had never seen a bullfight, and all at once it was arranged that Casanova, Doña Ignacia, her cousin (with whom Casanova suddenly declared he was in love, to taunt Doña Ignacia), and Don Diego went to "the scene of the magnificent and cruel festival that is the delight of the nation."

Casanova's party took their places, the women in front, "as was only right." He sat on a higher bench, directly behind the Duchess of Villadarias, with whom he had recently conducted a brief flirtation, and whose head now occupied the narrow space between his knees. With Doña Ignacia seated beside her, the Duchess asked Casanova if the young woman was his mistress or his wife, and he replied that she was a "beauty" for whom he longed in vain. The Duchess laughed, and invited Casanova to call on her the following afternoon at four. The prospect filled him with anxiety. "What terrified me was that she said she would be alone. It indicated a formal assignation."

Before he could reply, "A bull comes out of a small door in a fury, and swiftly enters the arena, then stops and looks to the right and left, as if to discover who will be challenging it. It sees a man on horseback who gallops toward it with a long lance in his hand; the bull runs to meet him, and the *picador* gives a thrust of his lance, avoiding it; the angered bull pursues him, and if it has not plunged one of its horns into the horse's belly at the first encounter it does so at the second or fourth, and often at each of them, so that the horse runs about the arena spilling out and dragging its entrails, covering the ground with the blood that spurts from its wounds, until it falls dead." Casanova considered the fight-to-the-death contest "an atrocity" that "makes the foreigner shudder." Whatever the outcome, "the spectacle struck me as gloomy and terrifying."

Afterward, "Our supper was a sad occasion, for, being in a bad humor, I could find nothing amusing to say." Disturbing his reverie, Doña Ignacia asked if he meant to keep his assignation with the Duchess, and he absent-mindedly explained that "it would be bad manners on my part not to go." After supper, when he attempted to kiss her, she asked again: would he go to see the Duchess the next day? No, he wouldn't, "if you promise me that you will not go to confession on Sunday"—implying that she should put aside her religious scruples and make love with him.

They were both "in the most decisive posture," as Casanova coyly put it, and he was "enjoying the palpitation of her amorous heart." He gently asked if she was thinking of repenting on Sunday of the voluptuous sin she was about to commit with him. Yes, she would "certainly confess it." And if she did, would she continue to love Casanova? In his mind, it was so simple, all she needed to do was sin, confess, and sin again. That's what he did, and so did countless others. She must choose: either stop going to confession for as long as he remained in Madrid, or allow him to withdraw from her in grief and disappointment. "While preaching her this terrible sermon, I tenderly clasped her in my arms, giving her every kind of caress." Once more he asked her to refrain from going to confession on Sunday. At that moment, her father arrived, and the lovers promptly "returned to a decent position." Don Diego greeted Casanova and retired, whereupon Casanova doused the candles and spent half an hour spying on Doña Ignacia as she sat in an armchair, dejected.

In the morning, when he went down to breakfast, he heard from Don Diego that his daughter was suffering a headache so intense that she hadn't gone to mass and lay in bed "in a state of collapse." For three hours Casanova sat beside her, trying to change her mind. "She kept her eyes closed through it all, never answering me, only sighing when I said something very touching to her." The contest of wills continued throughout the day. "The pain she caused me was incredible; I thought I could not bear it, for I loved her"—and, he noted, "I had no diversion in Madrid to make up for this abstinence."

As matters stood, "I did not think that it was God with whom I was vying, but with her confessor." That was it! He had a solution to the impasse.

———•———

The following day, she was to take Communion, the Blessed Sacrament; above all, she had to remain pure, her conscience untroubled. He surreptitiously observed her going to confession, as unpleasant as that was. "The confession bored me, revolted me, for it never ended; what could she be saying to him?" He stayed through three masses until at last she rose, eyes lowered, and she "had the look of a saint." He assumed that "the monster, true to his calling, refused her absolution." In that case, "I am lost."

He struggled home, locked his door, got into bed, and slept until one o'clock. Eventually he descended for dinner, where he was intrigued to see Doña Ignacia "wearing a black bodice with silk ribbons at every seam. In all Europe there is not a more seductive garment when the woman has a beautiful bosom and a narrow waist." He concluded that she had made her mind to join him, after all. She asked if he still loved her—*of course!*—and she wanted him to take her back to see *los toros* in action. He threw on his best coat, and the two of them walked briskly to the bullfight, too impatient to take a carriage. They watched the fight from a large box, one slaughter after another to propitiate the gods and satisfy man's hunger for gore. When the spectacle ended, she asked him to escort her to the Prado museum in the city center "where we find all the most fashionable people of both sexes in Madrid. Holding my arm, she seemed proud to display herself as mine, and she filled me with joy" as they strolled past the paintings of the Spanish Royal Collection.

At home that night, her father pulled Casanova aside to say that he was prepared to give his blessing to the union with his daughter so long as Casanova could demonstrate that he belonged to the nobility. As a hidalgo, or nobleman's son, Don Diego could give his daughter in marriage only to another nobleman. Casanova responded that as a Venetian, his claim to Doña Ignacia was based on love rather than on birth. "I adore you," he told her. "I have reason to believe that you will make me entirely happy here and now."

Now it was time to achieve a physical intimacy to match their emotional and spiritual affinity. He swept Doña Ignacia into his arms and conducted her to his bed, "where she remained with me, free from any scruples, until the first rays of dawn." Perhaps he had liberated her from the hypocrisy of religion; or perhaps he had led her deeper into doubt and damnation; it didn't matter. He loved her more than ever.

———•———

At that moment, a new Venetian Ambassador to Spain arrived. Alvise Sebastiano Mocenigo departed for a new posting at Versailles, and his nephew, Zuan Querini, a patrician, presented his credentials at the court of Carlos III. It was essential for Casanova to maintain good relations with the Ambassador, and fortunately the two got along well. "I was convinced that in a few days I should be able to count on him even more than on Signor Mocenigo." In an expectant frame of mind, Casanova paid a visit to both Ambassadors, who were sharing the embassy for the moment, but no one was at home. Worse, Casanova unwisely started babbling about Manuzzi—he was homosexual . . . his titles were fake . . . what a scandal. The gossip got back to Manuzzi, who was predictably furious—to think that he had once considered this traitor Casanova a friend! He advised Casanova to leave Madrid within a week.

He wrote Manuzzi a letter of abject apology: "I am willing to leave it in your power to have me murdered; but I will not leave Madrid except when I choose." The letter had no effect. He distracted himself with Doña Ignacia, and later, at a bullfight, "where by chance I found a place in a box next to Manuzzi and the two Ambassadors." He bowed in their direction, but received no flicker of recognition.

Manuzzi had made sure that Casanova was out of favor at court and everywhere else that mattered. Casanova made a final appeal to the Count d'Aranda, who asked in bewilderment, "What have you done to your Ambassador?" Cringing, Casanova ran through the litany of his missteps regarding Manuzzi and his proclivities. "You did wrong," the Count reacted, "but what's done is done." Mocenigo, the outgoing Ambassador, departed, and the incoming Ambassador still refused to welcome Casanova. There was nothing left to do. He'd run out of money. "Carriage, table, theater, and all the other little expenditures necessary to maintain life had brought me to the end of my resources, though Doña Ignacia did not know it."

He sold his gold-inlaid snuffbox and his repeating (that is, chiming) watch. He bade farewell to Doña Ignacia. "Nothing is more bitter than separation when love has lost none of its strength. The pain seems infinitely greater than the pleasure."

Observing the lovers, "Don Diego did not cry, he congratulated us on the tenderness of our hearts."

Two weeks later, Casanova found himself adrift in Zaragoza, in the kingdom of Aragón, in northeastern Spain, noting the hypocrisies of the clergy and attending bullfights, which he considered superior to the mortal contests in Madrid.

Wherever he went, he remained in the thrall of his Spanish lover. "I was shown courtesans; but, with the image of Doña Ignacia pursuing me everywhere, it was impossible for me to find any woman worthy of love." But how long would that conviction last?

Chapter 18

Nina

He caught a glimpse of a magnificent woman outside a bullfight arena at Zaragoza, a courtesan by the name of Nina Bergonza, the daughter of a charlatan who hawked "healing oil" in Venice. "The famous Nina," Casanova learned, has been kept by Ambrosio Funes de Villalpando, Count of Ricla and Captain-General of Catalonia, who was frantically in love with her. "She indulges in some folly every day that costs him a great deal of money." Anyone endowed with a scintilla of common sense would have avoided her, but Casanova was "extremely curious to make the acquaintance of such a woman." He tossed a compliment her way, "which she unabashedly returned," resting her hand, weighted down with rings and beautiful bracelets, on his. Would he come to breakfast with her the following day? Or course, "I do not fail to keep the appointment."

He found her living in a large rented house, "well-furnished though without taste, and open to the air of the countryside, with gardens in front and behind." She was scolding a manservant about the lace he was wearing, paused to ask Casanova for forgiveness, and returned to quarreling with the manservant, cutting the lace to pieces with a "great pair of scissors," whereupon her companion cried that everyone would call her mad. "Be still, pimp," she shot back, startling Casanova. Apparently the two of them talked that way to one another all the time. She slapped her companion with the back of her hand. He withdrew, "calling her a whore." She gradually calmed down, sent for chocolate, and invited her Venetian guest to join her. As they sipped, she told Casanova not to be alarmed; the other man was Ricla's spy. "I treat him badly on purpose so that he will write him everything."

Casanova believed Nina mad. "In all my life I had never seen or imagined that such a woman could exist." Nevertheless, he continued to associate with her. "She told me any number of stories of fucking, in which she was the principal figure" during the course of her twenty-two years. And then she introduced her latest stud. As Casanova looked on, Nina stripped and "made use of the man, inviting me, if I wanted to amuse myself, to come and see how he went about it." Casanova participated with reluctance, "for I was in a state of impotence," and angry at seeing a beautiful woman "surrender herself to a man whose only merit was that of a donkey." She exhausted the other man, then washed herself and forced wine down his gullet until he vomited his supper. "Shrieking with laughter," Nina ran into another room, Casanova following close behind, "for the stench was making me nauseous." Sitting beside him, naked, she remarked that her "donkey" did not enjoy the paces she'd put him through, but so what? "I make him work. If he loved me, I would die rather than satisfy him, for I loathe him." She used him for pleasure as she would "use a dildo."

Stunned by her coarseness, Casanova determined that Nina possessed the "pure truth of a depraved nature." That night, "though at my age I was no longer a novice in anything, I went to bed astonished at the woman's licentiousness." She'd confessed to him "what no woman had ever confessed to anyone." In the days to come, he heard of her malice regarding her protector, Count Ricla: "I'd love to ruin him; but he is so rich it is impossible."

Appalled, Casanova considered Nina "beautiful as an angel, black as a devil, an atrocious whore born to punish every man who had the misfortune to fall in love with her." A guard seconded his opinion. "You run a great risk by going every night to call on La Nina," he warned. Casanova replied that he would not stop calling on his dear friend Nina unless she told him to, or the Count intervened. "He would never do that," the guard responded, "for he would consider it humiliating." To illustrate his point, the guard recited a litany of former admirers of Nina whom the Count had ruined or jailed.

Two days later, on November 15, 1768, as he left a soiree at Nina's house, Casanova was set upon by two men. "I give a great leap back, I unsheathe my sword, shouting 'Murder!' and thrusting it into the nearest body, after which I jump out of the arcade into the middle of the street. . . . At the same time I hear the report of a gun or pistol, I run, I fall, I rise without troubling to pick up my hat, and, still running and holding my naked sword in my hand, not knowing if I am wounded, I arrive at my inn breathless." Although the blade of his sword was smeared with blood, the bullets had missed him, "but I find two unmistakable holes in my greatcoat, below the armpit."

At seven in the morning, a knock on his door. A police officer had arrived to escort him to the star-shaped Citadel, or Ciutadella. Positioned on the eastern side of Barcelona, it was considered the largest fortress in Europe. He was taken to a room on the second floor. Bare floors. No furniture. No grating in the windows. To his surprise, a soldier brought "an excellent bed with a coverlet of crimson damask" to warm him in the November chill. Alone in his large cell, he wondered why the Citadel was so "mild"? And what about the two men who tried to shoot him? "Should I write to Nina?" he asked himself. "Is one allowed to write here?"

Dinner arrived, not the expected inedible prison fare, but "choice" helpings. He bribed a soldier to provide a table and chair, and, on request, "as much paper and as many pencils as I wanted" (but not pen and ink), candles and a candlestick. He had an ambitious plan; he commenced writing *Confutazione della Storia del Governo Veneto d'Amelot de la Houssaie*, a sprawling rebuttal of de la Houssaie's history of Venice. Ever since its appearance nearly seventy years before, de la Houssaie's history had enraged readers and no one ever attempted a rebuttal, until now. Casanova, portraying himself as a loyal Venetian, hoped to work his way back into the good graces of the Inquisition, win a pardon, and return to Venice. The longer his exile, the greater his devotion to Venice.

After four days, he was relocated to the Torre de San Juan, the Tower, reserved for hardened criminals. In a downpour, soldiers laboriously transferred Casanova's personal effects to a circular cell, "a sort of cellar paved in stone," with slits high on the wall to admit a bit of light and air. He found himself in solitary confinement, with meals brought to him once a day, and a sentinel posted near his door. Yet the meals in the Tower contained "food enough for six." He offered the surfeit of dishes and the "excellent wine" accompanying the meal to the grateful guards. How strange. Who was paying for these items? Were the authorities charging him? Was Nina responsible for the bounty? Count Ricla?

With nothing else to do but write, he began his *Confutazione*. In a span of forty-two days, he set forth his argument, marking blank spaces to be filled later with quotations from de la Houssaie's history. He intended to write a pamphlet, but he expanded it into three volumes (compared with de la Houssaie's eight), to be published the following year, in 1769.

"On December 28," he wrote, "exactly six weeks after the day I was imprisoned, the officer on duty entered my cell and told me to dress and go with him."

"Am I to be released?"

"I know nothing about it. I shall deliver you to an official of the Government, who is in the guardhouse." There, Casanova received his trunk, the keys to it, the papers contained within it, and his three passports. Later, he received his "naked sword," wiped clean of blood, and his greatcoat, and the hat he had lost during his attempt to escape the would-be assassins. As he left, he noticed a placard announcing an opera to be performed that evening, and he looked forward with pleasure to seeing the performance. Afterward, he would travel to Madrid, or to France, he did not know which.

"That, my dear reader, is the whole of the strange story of what befell me in Barcelona." On the last day of the year, he left for France, and freedom.

But only four days later, on January 3, 1769, he was the target of another assassination attempt. Three cutthroats were waiting to murder him as he crossed over the Pyrenees into France. He rose early that morning, his last full day in Spain, and his coachman vowed to reach the border and safety by midnight. "We made eleven leagues in seven hours," Casanova recalled, "it was ten o'clock when we arrived at a good inn in a considerable village in France, where we had nothing more to fear." He credited the coachman with saving his life, and he was flooded with relief. "I breathed again, finding myself in France after so many misfortunes had assailed me in Spain; I seemed to be reborn, and I felt rejuvenated."

He found his way to Nîmes, in southern France, about two hundred and forty miles from Barcelona, and while lodging at Le Cheval Blanc, the preeminent hotel in the city, he struck up a short-lived friendship with a well-known naturalist, Jean-François Séguierand, whom he might have met through mutual acquaintances. The two spent several days together, a respite Casanova appreciated. "In the wonders of his collection, he showed me the immensity of nature." Then it was time for Carnival, where the crowds, wearing masks and costumes, tossed confetti, flour, and eggs with joyful abandon. He moved on to Aix, where he befriended Count Gotzkowski, and where, "Assemblies, suppers, balls, and very pretty girls made me spend the whole of Carnival and part of Lent in Aix, always with Gotzkowski," as the two of them indulged in "parties of pleasure." He reveled in the Provençal gaiety even as he shivered under blasts of the Mistral, which blew hardest at this time of year. "Returning to Aix in an open chaise against a very strong north wind and without an overcoat, I arrived chilled to the bone."

After wrestling in vain for two hours with a young prostitute, having made the unpleasant discovery that "the age for exploits of that sort was long behind me," he returned to his inn. He went to bed that night "with a very severe pain in my right side," slept for six hours, and awoke feeling "as ill as possible." He diagnosed himself with pleurisy (an inflammation of the lung), and sent for a physician, who bled him. "A violent cough began to torment me; the next morning I was splitting blood." A week later he was so weak that he received last rites. But after ten days, the "skillful old physician" who'd been caring for Casanova assured everyone that the patient would recover, even as he coughed up blood for another eight days. He recuperated for three more weeks. Convalescence proved more of a trial than the illness, "for a sick person suffers but is not bored."

A mysterious woman waited on him day and night during his recovery. "She was not old; but she was not of a figure to make me think of amusing myself." He had no idea who she was, and when he recovered sufficiently to thank her and to pay her, she informed him that his physician had brought her, but when Casanova asked the physician about the woman, "he replied that she had deceived me, for he did not know her." Casanova came to believe that the vanished love of his youth, Henriette, had anonymously provided the medical care, balancing her goodwill against Manuzzi's malice. He expected to find her "at some gathering in Aix," but his hopes for a reunion went unfulfilled. "Several times I heard her name spoken in different connections," but he took care not to question those who referred to her.

By Easter, when he felt strong enough to retrieve his mail, he read a letter from his brother telling him that the scoundrel Manuzzi had hired the "three cutthroats" to assassinate Giacomo Casanova, and had even announced that the deed had been accomplished, carelessly revealing himself as the malefactor, not that it mattered. "When I came upon him in Rome two years later and tried to convince him of his baseness, he denied everything," Casanova said.

With reports of his death greatly exaggerated, he traveled to bucolic Éguilles, not far from Aix, where he ingratiated himself with the Marquis d'Éguilles and his younger brother the Marquis d'Argens. Casanova judged the elder Marquis "very voluptuous, a perfect gentleman, amusing, amiable, a determined Epicurean, and married to an actress named Cochois who had proved worthy of it. As a wife, she considered it her duty to be her husband's first servant." And he was "deeply learned, thoroughly versed in Greek and Hebrew, endowed by nature with a most excellent memory, and hence full of erudition," all characteristics to which Casanova aspired. The Marquis presented the wandering Venetian with a complete set of his works, twenty-four volumes of letters, essays, novels, and fictitious memoirs, "which no one reads any longer." The sole omission was a volume of memoirs, printed in his youth, which he regretted having issued. "Why?" Casanova asked. "Because with the mania of wanting to write the truth, I made myself eternally ridiculous. If the urge ever comes to you, resist it as you would a temptation; for I can assure you that you will repent." As a gentleman, Casanova would be obliged to write the truth, and "not to spare yourself in all the sins you have committed, while, as a sound philosopher, you must bring out all your good actions." Even if he did all that, he would not be believed; he would make enemies with such writing, and betray confidences. And if he withheld actual names, "they will be guessed." In conclusion, he urged Casanova never to think of writing his autobiography.

In time, the Marquis's warning, turned on its head, would serve as the basis for Casanova's twelve-volume memoirs, which would generate abundant scandal and controversy, and provide him with lasting renown, but for now, "I promised him I would never be guilty of that folly." Seven years later, when he embarked on the project, he thought back on that moment.

"I write in the hope that my history will never be published; I flatter myself that in my last illness, grown wise at last, I will have all my notebooks burned in my presence." If he never got around to undertaking that purge, he prayed that the reader would understand that "writing my memoirs was the only remedy I thought I could employ to keep from going mad or dying of chagrin. . . . By keeping myself busy writing ten or twelve hours a day, I have prevented black melancholy from killing me or driving me mad." He'd become a writing machine, sublimating his desire into prose.

———————

Unable to quell his longing for Henriette, he traced her to Aix. He inquired after her; she was not at home, but to his surprise he saw the woman who had tended to him during his illness; she confirmed that her mistress, Henriette, had assigned her to his care. She added, "I am amazed that you did not see Madame in Aix." So Henriette was there!

"Has she changed?" Casanova asked. "Has she aged?"

"She has put on weight," the woman admitted, but otherwise Henriette looked the same as she had a decade earlier. "To see her, you would think she was a woman of thirty." She left, and Casanova found himself alone, "astonished to the point of confusion." Henriette represented the only perfect love he'd ever known, and in her absence his imagination embellished her memory until she represented all the love denied him as a child, and afterward. She was the most elusive woman in his life, and therefore the most loved.

A letter from Henriette arrived the next day; she reminded him that twenty years had passed since their cherished idyll, and "We have both aged." She held out faint hope of a reunion. "Will you believe that though I still love you, I am very glad that you did not recognize me? It is not that I have become ugly, but putting on flesh has given me a different countenance." In this way she encouraged him to look elsewhere for a lover while the two of them maintained their connection and their memories. "I am a widow, happy, and well enough off to tell you that if you should be short of money with the bankers you will find it in Henriette's purse." She was glad to have provided a nurse who could help him through his illness, and she hoped to "maintain a correspondence." She was "curious to know what you did after your escape from I Piombi." At the same time, Henriette admonished him to stay away, at least until some future date, and in parting, she had one more question, filled with mischief: whatever became of the charming girl he'd snatched from his brother Gaetano, Marcolina?

Waking from the auto-hypnosis of romance, Casanova saw for himself that "Henriette had grown wise; the force of temperament had diminished in her as it had in me. She was happy"—or portrayed herself that way—"I was not." He couldn't return to Aix mooning after her. People would talk, and he would become a "burden" to her. He had matured into a man of ambitions and grievances, as his fortunes shrank the wealth of his experiences had grown, he needed to find a way to spin the dross of memory into gold. He wrote back to her of his many vicissitudes, and the two of them exchanged letters for years, nearly all of them lost.

From Marseille, he journeyed to Antibes, Nice, across the Alps by way of the Colle di Tenda to Turin, where two acquaintances awaited him. "They both found me aged, but after all I could only be relatively so at my then age of forty-four years." He spoke about his plan to publish his confutation of de la Houssaie's history of Venice, the one he'd written in prison in Barcelona, and before long friends were subscribing to the edition. The Comte de la Pérouse offered "twenty-five Piedmontese gold pistoles for fifty copies," and within a week, Casanova had collected two thousand Piedmontese lire. So there was money in writing, after all.

He set out for Lugano, in southern Switzerland, in search of a printing press. There he introduced himself to Giovan-Agnelli Battista, an abate and printer, with whom he contracted to pay for twelve hundred copies of four octavo sheets to be printed each week. (An octavo consisted of one large sheet folded into eight leaves, yielding sixteen pages.) The abate reserved the "right of censorship" over the work, but the two men assumed they were of like mind. In Lugano he spent his days correcting the proofs and his nights adding additional material to be set in type the next morning.

Words consumed his life. He spent the entire first month in his room, working constantly, leaving only for mass. Not even the appearance of an old flame, now married and with a son, distracted him, in part because, as she told him, he no longer had the glow of youth that had once attracted her, and that proved sufficient to make him "renounce any idea that I might have had of resuming an amorous relationship with her."

"So much the better," he told himself. "A love affair would have absorbed the better part of my time." When he desperately needed a woman, he paid a pimp to obtain the pleasure.

By October 1769, the printing of the *Confutazione* was complete in three volumes. He relished the prospect of exposing de la Houssaie's "lies and blunders"—which had gone unchallenged—"to all Europe." He returned to Turin to await the reaction of the Venetian authorities, confident that the work would win their favor and a pardon after fourteen years of exile. "It seemed to me I could no longer live anywhere else," he reflected, but the State Inquisitors were unmoved. "They made me wait five more years." And so he was confined to a prison from which there was no escape: the world outside Venice.

By March 1770, in Livorno, he was still awaiting word on his *Confutazione*; on he went to Parma, Pisa, and Siena, in search of a meaningful assignment or mischievous caper. Nothing held his attention for long. Even when he joined forces with a Venetian actor, Angelo Bentivoglio, and two willing women, "I was not in the mood for amusement." His love of women, the chief joy and excitement in his life, had diminished, if only because he could no longer perform as he had as a young man. "The older I grew," he philosophized, "the more attracted I was to women's intelligence. It became the medium which my blunted senses needed." His situation came down to this: "I had about two hundred *zecchini*, and I was forty-five years old; I still loved the fair sex, though with much less ardor, much more experience, and less courage for daring enterprises"—farewell Straight Tree!—"for, looking more like a father than a lover, I believed I no longer had rights or justifiable claims."

An air of melancholy regret hung over subsequent adventures; there were no new worlds to conquer, only the same world, over and over. Without love what would he live for?

In the summer of 1770, as famine decimated Czechoslovakia and bubonic plague erupted in Russia, Casanova sojourned in Naples, undisturbed. At dinner one day, "I see Donna Lucrezia herself enter my room with her face the picture of joy and run into my arms." He stepped back to behold her. "The enchanting woman was exactly my age, but she looked at least ten years younger." Of course he wanted to know about their daughter, Leonilda (assuming she was their daughter). Donna Lucrezia, at the moment, was single, while Leonilda was married, but, said her mother, talked constantly of Casanova. Soon he came face-to-face with her, now three inches taller than when he last saw her, "and, at the age of twenty-five, become a perfect beauty." She was with her husband but ran to Casanova with open arms. After greeting her, he kissed her husband on either cheek, as was the custom, "and I was surprised by a third kiss, which he offers to my lips, and which I returned with a sign that sufficed to tell us that we were brothers"—Freemasons, freethinkers, in other words.

Casanova, Donna Lucrezia, and Leonilda vividly recalled their sensual experimentation ten years earlier. When Donna Lucrezia saw her daughter and Casanova embracing tightly, she warned them to exercise restraint. "Her words, followed by her departure, had the very opposite effect." They became "determined to consummate the so-called crime" of incest. They moved closer until "an almost involuntary movement forced us to consummate it so completely that we could not have done more if we had been acting according to a premeditated plan conceived by the free exercise of reason." Afterward, they remained wonderfully still, "astonished . . . to feel neither guilty nor tormented by remorse." Instead, they slowly dressed, as Leonilda called him "husband" instead of "father," and he called her "wife." Even Donna Lucrezia when she appeared was "edified to find us become so calm." They realized they had to keep their relations a secret, and Donna Lucrezia told herself that her daughter and Casanova had indulged in "inconsequential toying."

To Casanova's relief, his activities with Leonilda did not offend her husband, who welcomed him into their home and to their table. "Having dined on nothing but soup, I ate like an ogre," which pleased his hosts. At the same time, he contemplated making Donna Lucrezia pregnant to compensate for the lost opportunities of ten years ago.

His Neapolitan idyll extended through the first week of September. He had come to regard the city as his "Temple of Fortune," but he feared he'd grown too old for its pleasures. If he dared to return to Naples later in his life, "I should die of starvation." Although the idea of sin and punishment were still alien to him, he suffered acutely from the prospect of old age, senility, impotence, and extinction. He had done nothing to deserve these afflictions, and there was nothing he could do to avoid them.

———•———

On September 11, he rode out of Naples bound for Rome, where he reconciled with Mengs, recently returned from Madrid. Still banished from Venice, Casanova intended to devote the next six months not to women, but to his literary ambitions, a more respectable activity for a man of his age and station. Outwardly, he was more cautious than he had been during his Neapolitan adventures, aware that others were watching, and eager to give proof of his ability in the intellectual arena amid the peerless libraries of Rome—and Casanova loved libraries almost as much as he loved women, and was no less obsessive in his devotion.

Starved for print, he satisfied his hunger at the Biblioteca Casanatense, established by Cardinal Girolamo Casanate in 1701, based in the Dominican convent of Santa Maria sopra Minerva. Casanova lusted after libraries no less than women, and the Casanatense, among his favorites, housed twenty thousand volumes, including Greek and Hebrew manuscripts, in a vast cloister. Later, he lost himself amid the shelves of the Library of the Collegio Romano, administered by the Jesuits, and the Biblioteca Apostolica Vaticana—the Vatican Library, one of the oldest and largest collections in the world. A friend introduced him to a librarian, who in turn alerted his assistants to Giacomo Casanova. "From then on I found I could not only go to the library at any day and at any hour but could also take home whatever books I needed, only writing the title of one book on a sheet of paper that I left upon the table at which I was working." When it grew too dark to read, he obtained candles, "and the courtesy I was shown even extended to my being given the key to a small door by which I could enter the library at all hours, very often without being seen." The Jesuits in attendance proved uniformly courteous to him "and, if I may say so, the only courteous ones," perhaps because the order was under threat in Spain and Portugal and in Rome itself.

In his spare hours in his pleasant apartment he carried on a discreet flirtation with his landlady's daughter, sixteen or seventeen years old, "who, despite her rather too dark complexion, would have been very pretty if she had not been deprived of one eye." Her name was Margherita, and she went about with a "false eye, which being made of a different color

The Collegio Romano

from the other and also larger, made her face repulsive." Casanova had no feelings for her, but he considered the girl an easy mark, especially after he took her to an "English oculist" who fitted her with a porcelain eye that "could not have looked better." Cost: only six *zecchini*. His attentiveness caused her to believe he'd fallen deeply in love, and her mother held her suspicions about his motives in check. For his part, he had only three thousand *zecchini* to his name, so he would make love to his one-eyed mistress on the cheap.

The intensifying rapport between Casanova and the young girl alarmed her mother, who notified him that "there can be no doubt that your meetings are immoral." Indignant, he offered to vacate the premises the following day to put her "conscience at rest." She would lose the modest rent he'd been paying her. Only if Margherita resumed her playful visits to his room would he reconsider. In fact, he insisted on her visiting at that moment. "She is asleep," said her mother.

"Wake her," Casanova directed.

Three minutes later, in came Margherita, "without her false eye, which she had not had time to put in, at which I burst out laughing." Looking disdainfully at her, Casanova relented: "I will stay, but you must continue to come to my room alone." From then, the two of them carried on despite driving her mother, father, and another lodger to distraction. Unable to restrain herself after hearing whoops and shouts emanating from his room for an hour, Margherita's mother barged in, "expecting to catch us in the act." Instead, "she sees me with Margherita's cap on my head, and Margherita with a pair of mustaches that I had painted with ink. She could not help laughing, too."

"Well," Casanova asked, "do you think us great criminals?"

Margherita was so pleased that Casanova "could not keep from doing her the justice she deserved; she spent an hour in my bed without laughing, then left, proud of her victory."

Soon after, Casanova won an introduction to Margherita's girlfriend Buonaccorsi, "whose attractions were much greater than hers." And he met a tailor named Marcuccio who'd claimed the virginity of both young women. Marcuccio was a sensitive, playful, and extremely well-endowed youth to whom both girls remained attracted. Before long, the four of them were "performing amorous exploits."

In time Casanova learned that the young man actually loved a *third* woman who'd been confined to a convent since the age of ten. Marcuccio had seen her only a handful of times, always briefly, when he had gone to the grating to visit his sister, who was in the same convent: the *Istituto di Santa Caterina de' Fumari*, where the girls learned manual trades and lived in fear of an impoverished existence beyond its confines. According to the rules of the convent, the only way Marcuccio could have his beloved was to marry her, but he could barely afford to live alone, never mind support a wife and family.

Casanova accompanied his lovesick friend to the convent, located in a "solitary and deserted square," and when he arrived he shrank before the oppressive edifice, with its "cruel gratings" and apertures "so small that one could not put one hand in except at the risk of scraping the skin from the wrist to the knuckles." Nearly all the girls confined here by their families were pretty; in fact, that was the reason they were here, lest they become pregnant; homely women were believed to have little or no risk of attracting attention.

When his beloved materialized, Marcuccio explained, she usually lit a candle to cast a flicker of light, but on this occasion, because an outsider—Casanova—was present, the lovers conversed in darkness as he eavesdropped. "The voice of my young friend's sister went to my soul; I concluded that it must be by the voice that the blind fall in love, and that their love would become as strong as that which had its origins in sight." Casanova could be a prodigy in matters of the heart, especially when it was not his own.

Meanwhile, the prospects for Marcuccio's romance looked very poor indeed. An elderly nun told Casanova that in all her years at the *Istituto*, only four girls had wed, all to men whom they met *after* they left. Anyone seeking to marry one of the girls must be a "desperate fool," she said.

Casanova had heard enough: "Whoever established this house must be in hell." He put together a petition for the nuns to sign to ask the Pope to allow them to receive visitors under the same "honorable and discreet conditions in force in all the establishments in which women were cloistered," and sent it to his old friend Cardinal de Bernis, now in Rome. To his surprise, the petition, signed by the nuns and their supervisors, met with a favorable reception. Pope Clement XIV put the convent's administration on trial for misused funds, reduced the number of "recluses" to fifty, and ordered that every girl there who reached the age of twenty-five without having married receive a sizable dowry. A sense of humanity circulated within the *Istituto*'s confines. Under the new regime, girls began leaving to get married—three in the first six weeks alone—including Marcuccio's own sister. In reality, she was Teresa Fidati; to preserve her anonymity in his memoir, he called her Armellina.

Before long, Casanova was courting her. Darkness, gratings, garments that all but swallowed up their occupants—all of these deterrents to romance only served to spur him on. The first time he kissed her hands, she "blushed scarlet" because "no man had ever touched her hands, and she was amazed when she saw the sensuous delight with which I covered them with kisses. I went home in love with Armellina . . . and not at all disheartened by the difficulties I would encounter in my efforts to obtain her." All the while, Marcuccio was "in an ecstacy of bliss" and made plans to marry his beloved, and he expected that Casanova would marry Armellina.

He saw her throughout the autumn. On New Year's Day, 1771, he gave her a winter coat to ward off the chill, and coffee and sugar to appease the Superioress, "who was infinitely obliged to me." By this time, "Armellina's sweetness made me fall hopelessly in love with her." Frustrated by kissing only her hands, "I begged her to put her mouth to the grating; she blushed, she looked down, and she would not." He compensated for the love denied him by Armellina with vigorous Margherita, who awaited him at the inn where he stayed, always ready to hop into bed with him. "My fond caresses gave her reason to conclude that I had not been guilty of any infidelity."

———•———

As his painfully constrained courtship of Armellina advanced, he persuaded her to accompany him in a carriage to see an opera at the capacious Teatro Aliberti, near the Piazza di Spagna. She was still inexperienced—that would have to change—and her naiveté a source of wonder. "I was in despair when I saw Armellina's face lose all its cheerfulness when I asked her if she knew the difference between a girl and a man."

Later, he dined at an inn with the innocent Armellina and her sister Emilia. There he ordered a delicacy new to the girls: oysters, direct from Venice. And he wanted them opened in the girls' presence, a hundred of the glistening bivalves, "filling four large dishes." He'd tried and failed to kiss Armellina, and for that matter Emilia, and now their astonishment at the sight of the oysters would have entertained him if he hadn't been "desperate with love." Unable to satisfy his desire for Armellina, "we sat down at table, where I taught the two girls to eat oysters by setting them an example. They were swimming in their liquid. Armellina, after swallowing five or six of them, said to Emilia that anything so delicious must be a sin." Between mouthfuls of the chewy flesh, Armellina exclaimed, "If this isn't a sin of gluttony, I'd like to know what gluttony means."

This declaration made Casanova's soul rejoice, but what about his body? "My love which was dying of starvation envied the luck of my mouth." As his love waited, the three of them ate fifty oysters and emptied two bottles of champagne, "which aroused laugher in the two girls who had to commit the indecency of belching." If only he could devour Armellina with kisses instead of his eyes! He forbade water at the table, "counting somewhat on Bacchus" to dissolve Armellina's resistance. "I ordered up lemons, a bottle of rum, sugar, a big bowl, and hot water, and after having the other fifty oysters put on the table, I dismissed the water. I made a large quantity of punch, which I enlivened by pouring a bottle of champagne into it." Casanova and the two girls consumed five or six oysters each, and washed them down with the alcoholic punch, and, noticing that they were "carried away by so charming a beverage, I took it into my head to ask Emilia to put an oyster into my mouth with her own lips." Considering his proposition, she suggested that he try it first with Armellina. "If you have the courage," Armellina told her sister, "I will have it, too."

"What courage does it take?" Emilia inquired. "It's a child's game. There's no harm in it."

"I thought I could count on victory." Casanova put the shell to Emilia's mouth, and instructed her to suck in the liquid while keeping the oyster between her lips. Tipsy, she laughed and complied, and then he "took the oyster by pressing my lips to hers with the greatest decency." Armellina applauded, saying that she didn't think that Emilia had it in her to do it, "and she imitated her to perfection." Having won their trust, "I taught each of them to insert the oyster and the liquid into the other's mouth as I did by simultaneously inserting the full length of the tongue." And so they sucked one another's extended tongues along with the oysters, "laughing heartily afterward at the pleasure afforded by the game" even as they agreed that "nothing could be more innocent."

They consumed all the oysters and emptied glass after glass of punch, the three of them seated in a row, their backs to the fire, Casanova ensconced in the middle. "Never was intoxication gayer or more justified or more complete." Warmed by the fire, he removed his jacket and they carefully unlaced their fur-lined dresses. He advised them that a water closet was close by, available for their needs, and they visited it together, holding hands. They returned bursting with laughter, unable to stand upright. Casanova then rose and visited the water closet himself, and, on his return, gazed drunkenly at "the beauty of their bosoms." They mustn't leave until they had finished all the punch, he advised, and, shrieking with laughter, they agreed it would be a shame to leave *any*, so they finished it, as he stared at their legs, revealed by their open skirts and short petticoats.

When an oyster slipped from the shell into Emilia's bosom, she moved to retrieve it, but Casanova claimed it first. He then unlaced her dress and proceeded to "gather it with my lips from the depth to which it had been dropped" as an unsmiling Armellina looked on. He invited her to sit in his lap and dropped another oyster into her bosom, eliciting a flicker of jealousy from Emilia. "Armellina was delighted by the mishap, though she refused to give any sign of it."

"I want my oyster," Casanova told her.

"Take it," said Armellina.

He unlaced her bodice and worked his way down her breasts, "hard as marble," in search of the oyster. He found it, retrieved it, and swallowed it as he held one of her breasts, demanding to suck the liquid spilled from the oyster shell, whereupon "I seized the rosebud with avid lips . . . inspired by the imaginary milk that I sucked for a good two or three minutes." He recovered slightly from reverie as she asked if he enjoyed imitating "the babe at the breast."

"Yes, for it is an innocent game."

Armellina thought otherwise, and hoped that he would refrain from mentioning it to their Superioress. "We must retrieve no more oysters."

For her part, Emilia said a splash of holy water would suffice to wash away their sins. Additionally, they hadn't actually *kissed* one another.

By the time they left, it was three o'clock in the morning, and he escorted his companions to their convent, left them at the gate, and went home, where "the one who satisfied me was Margherita, who would have scratched my eyes out if I had not repeatedly convinced her of my perfect fidelity." When she inquired as to where he had been, he responded that he'd been "detained playing cards," and she had no choice but to believe him.

Several days after, he heard from Armellina that her confessor had laughed when she told him that she had "eaten oysters by taking them from a man's lips with hers. He had told her that it was no more than a piece of nastiness."

At their next meeting, in similar circumstances, he lubricated his two companions with champagne, as before, and proposed a game of blind man's buff. Immediately, "we all blindfolded one another, and the great game began, and, standing in front of me, they let me measure them several times, falling on me and laughing each time I measured them too far up." He removed his blindfold and observed them, drunk, laughing, and aroused, continued until "nature, overcome with pleasure, deprived me of the strength to go on." By the time the others removed their blindfolds, he had "restored myself to a state of decency."

From playing blind man's buff he found it natural to escort Armellina, whom he was certain was a virgin, and Emilia, whom he was certain was not, from their convent to a ball in a distant quarter of Rome, where they would have no fear of being recognized for the vestals they were. Balls had become not merely a passion but madness "of all the girls in Rome," said Casanova, after the new Pope, Clement XIV, Giovanni Vincenzo Antonio Ganganelli, had ended the ban put in place by his predecessor. "He saw no reason to prevent his subjects from hopping about," and outlawed gambling instead. And so they went to the ball, Casanova more in love with Armellina than ever, yet he could not win her heart. "Will you refuse to be my love?" he plaintively inquired.

Emilia, in contrast, seemed ripe for the taking. He passed hours with her on a couch, insisting on "obtaining the final favor. The girl would never consent to it." Yet she remained unvaryingly sweet. "She never granted me what I persisted in demanding, yet she never appeared to refuse it to me." He staggered home in the early hours of the morning, "laughing at all the reproaches with which Margherita assailed me." He hoped that some other man might fall in love with Margherita, and so be rid of her.

When Emilia finally left the convent to marry, Armellina acquired a replacement, Camilia di Sanctis, or Scholastica, who would "thenceforth be Armellina's inseparable companion." Before long Scholastica was telling Armellina and Casanova, "You love each other, and it's perfectly clear: I prevent you from giving each other token of it. I am not a child. I am your friend."

Casanova corrected Scholastica: yes, he loved Armellina . . . but . . . she . . . did . . . not . . . love . . . *him*. The confession encouraged Scholastica, and before long he was kissing the new arrival playfully and passionately.

As the three revelers—Armellina, Scholastica, and Casanova—attended more balls—the women dressing as men, and dancing with men dressed as women—Scholastica lobbied to establish intimacy between Casanova and Armellina, but to no avail. After one more futile attempt, he overheard the two of them kissing, and he took a closer look. "Scholastica, more than gay from the punch, was covering Armellina's bosom with kisses, while Armellina, at last become cheerful, did as much to her ardent friend in my presence." Swept up in the deliciously libertine moment, Casanova found himself "becoming a babe at the breast" of Scholastica, the sight of which inspired Armellina, who was not a little competitive, to allow him the same favor with her, "and Scholastica triumphed when she saw for the first time the use to which I put Armellina's hands," presumably to stroke him to climax, but not before "Armellina demanded that Scholastica serve me in the same way." To his pleasure and relief, "she did everything" until he convulsed with his explosion.

Upon post-orgasmic reflection, "it was too hard to decide which of the two was more beautiful; but Armellina had the advantage of being loved, Scholastica's advantage was the beauty of her face." Wasn't Armellina the beauty, and Scholastica the enthusasitic companion? It scarcely mattered as he dallied with the two of them, reminding himself that they were both virgins. "I ended by doing everything that a skilled practitioner can do with the charming object whom he deprives of the final pleasure." In his practiced hands, "Scholastica succumbed, voluptuously overcome and convinced that I had only failed to fulfill her desires from respect and delicacy." Armellina congratulated the two of them as Scholastica begged her dear friend's pardon. He escorted the young women to their convent and stumbled home to bed, "unable to decide whether I had won or lost the game I had played...."

It went on like this for weeks, until he attended the opera with Scholastica on Shrove Tuesday, just before the beginning of Lent, when she at last "yielded" to his affections. For Casanova, this event marked the end, not the beginning, of their affair. He encouraged Armellina to marry a sincere, well-heeled Florentine suitor although he was racked with conflicting emotions about parting with her in order to gain his freedom; the former was exquisite torture, the latter dreary relief. The Florentine provided a generous dowry, "which he deposited in the Spirito Sancto Bank" (the principal public bank in Rome), married Armellina shortly after Easter, and moved with her to England, where they lived, so Casanova heard, quite happily.

———•———

"I left Rome at the beginning of June 1771," Casanova wrote, "all alone in my carriage, with four post horses, well outfitted, in good health, and fully resolved to adopt a manner of life entirely different from the one I had so far pursued. Tired of the pleasures I had enjoyed for thirty years, yet glad that I had them, I had not thought of renouncing them altogether but of confining myself in the future to entering into them lightly, forbidding myself any serious entanglements. In pursuit of this plan, I was going to devote myself entirely to study Homer's *Iliad*, which since I had left London had delighted me for an hour or two each day in the original language, had made me want to translate it into Italian stanzas" or ottava rima—a heroic or mock heroic form popularized by Boccaccio. The idea was not entirely original, for he had been given a recently published translation of the epic in Italian. Nevertheless, "It seemed to me that its Italian translators had falsified it," with the exception of a version by Antonio Maria Salvini, but that was "so dry that no one could read him." Casanova also knew the stately stanzas rendered into English by Alexander Pope, as well as the lucrative business deal that gave rise to Pope's translation. Between 1710 and 1715, Pope received two hundred guineas per volume—there were six in all—sold by subscription, and as a result he became both wealthy and esteemed. Samuel Johnson pronounced the translation "a performance which no age or nation could hope to equal," but Casanova expressed reservations about Pope's handiwork: "In his notes he could have said much more."

More than literary ambition impelled Casanova to seek refuge there as he made his way to Florence; he wanted a home for his declining years. "I thought I had grown old. Forty-six years seemed to me a great age. There were times when I found the pleasures of love less intense, less seductive than I had imagined them before the act, for the previous eight years my potency had been diminishing little by little. I found that a long bout was not followed by the soundest sleep, and that my appetite at table, which before then love had sharpened, became less when I was in love." There was more. He no longer fell in love "at first sight" as he once had. "I had to talk. Rivals were preferred to me, I was made to feel that it was already a favor if I was secretly allowed to share with another man; but I could no longer expect that sacrifices would be made for me." Most infuriating of all, when he made a play for the object of affection of "some young blockhead," her lover considered Casanova no threat. Then came the day when he overheard someone say of him, "He's getting on in years." He had no choice but to admit the truth of this observation, although it took a toll on his *amour-propre*. He found himself alone so often now he contemplated a "dignified retirement" in reduced circumstances.

When he reached Florence, he would dress in black to declare that he was far from wealthy and had no interest in socializing. He'd outlived his ambitions, and seen all of the world that he wanted to see—its palaces, prisons, soldiers, gamblers, courtesans, assassins, monks, nuns, and even a few literary men. He'd romanced every lady and fucked every whore he dared—consequences be damned. "My vices have never burdened anyone but myself, except in cases in which I seduced; but seduction was never characteristic of me, for I have never seduced except unconsciously, being seduced myself." In comparison, "the professional seducer is an abominable creature, inevitably the enemy of the object on which he had designs. He is a true criminal."

Chapter 19

The Minx

Arriving in Florence in mid-July, attired in black and wearing his sword, Casanova went to the Pitti Palace, a behemoth consisting of nearly a thousand rooms, and presented himself to Grand Duke Leopold of Tuscany to ask for asylum. He explained to the twenty-four-year-old Duke the archaic reasons preventing his return to Venice and offered assurances that "for the necessaries of life I needed no one, and that I intended to spend my time in study." He made no mention of gambling, whoring, dueling, or other excesses. By coincidence, Leopold was busying himself "compiling an anthology of Greek epigrams" to be published the following year, so there they stood, two members of the fraternity of letters. Leopold said that so long as Casanova's conduct passed muster, he would be safe in Florence. Determined to avoid the snares of the world, especially women, Casanova lodged in two rooms "in the house of a townsman who had an ugly wife and no nieces."

He maintained his studious lifestyle for one . . . two . . . three weeks until, at the request of an old friend, Count Stratico, recovering from a broken leg, he became the companion of the count's eighteen-year-old pupil, Cavaliere Morosini. The Count expressed the wish that Casanova would accompany the young man at all times, so that "he should not be left alone where he might encounter evil and dangerous company." It so happened that such company attracted the young Cavaliere, and Casanova soon found that his behavior "played havoc with my determination to live quietly," adding, rather disingenuously, "goodheartedness forced me to take part in the young man's debauches." Casanova recognized the absurdity of his attempting to take this "frenzied libertine" in hand, yet he kept the lad out of serious trouble. It took a libertine to protect a libertine.

In the span of two months, Casanova estimated, he saved Morosini's life at least twenty times, "but my sense of decency forced me not to abandon him." Even worse, he insisted that Casanova drink as much as he did and keep pace "in the work of the flesh, either with the same girl or with another," and he even paid for all these indulgences. Under the circumstances, Casanova could find no excuse to avoid these debauches, not even when a woman they shared assumed that Casanova was Morosini's father and berated the old man for not bringing up his son more strictly.

———•———

He arrived in Bologna on December 30, pleased to find that "there is not a city in Italy in which one can live with greater freedom, where living is not expensive, and where one can procure all the pleasures of life at little cost." The city struck him as beautiful, especially the arcades lining the streets. The scene was so appealing, so Venetian. He'd heard the Bolognese rabble, the *birichini*, were "even worse" than Neapolitan ruffians, the *lazzaroni*, "but the citizens in general are decent people." The University of Bologna was the oldest in Europe, and the city maintained an elevated intellectual level; not only that, but "printing is cheap there, and though the Inquisition exists, it is easy to deceive it."

A week later, he came across two satirical pamphlets written by male academics concerning the effect of the uterus on a woman's brain. One pamphlet said that the uterus made women behave as they did; the other pamphlet strenuously disagreed. Outraged, "I took it into my head to print a diatribe against the two pamphlets. I wrote it in three days; I sent it to Signor Dandolo in Venice to have five hundred copies of it printed for me immediately." As soon as he received them, he gave them to a bookseller in Bologna, "and at the expense of the two witty young doctors I made some thirty *zecchini*." This was a novelty for Casanova, earning money from his writing, and he enjoyed the sensation. He called his screed "Goat's Wool," a phrase borrowed from Horace, indicating strife or nitpicking. "I made fun of the authors"—anonymously, of course—"and I treated the subject lightly but by no means superficially."

The result, bristling with scholarly jokes, won him friends in Bologna, who in turn located "two fine rooms" for him to rent, complete with pastry chef and servant, for less than ten zecchini a month. To amuse himself, he wrote another "comic dialogue," printed it the next day, deposited it with a bookseller, and within days the sheets had sold out. Success! "Any writer who attacks a proud man by comic-satiric compositions is almost sure to triumph." In a modest way, he had arrived in Bologna, not as a social climber and libertine, but as a writer.

———•———

In September 1772, a Venetian patrician, Pietro Antonio Zaguri, offered to expedite his return to Venice. Galvanized, Casanova wrote to this august personage of his sincere wish for a pardon. Exile had taken its toll and humbled him. Zaguri recommended that Casanova quit Bologna for Trieste, a hundred miles to the east of Venice across the Adriatic Sea. Trieste belonged to Austria, but stood apart, a heterogenous center of the arts and commerce with a significant Jewish population. In Trieste, Casanova would await his pardon from the State Inquisitors, and at the same time, as a way of earning their favor and trust, perform certain assignments on their behalf, in other words, spy for the same entity that had spied on him years before. Of course, he was under no obligation to spy for the Inquisition, but it was his surest route home.

Following the promptings of a "secret voice," Casanova decided to travel via Ancona, lying to the south, which meant making the final leg of this journey over the Adriatic. The roundabout itinerary defied logic, he admitted, but in his experience "I have more often had cause to congratulate myself on having laughed at my reason than on having obeyed it."

As he approached the hamlet of Senigallia in his coach, close to Ancona, his coachman asked if he would share his carriage with a Jew who was going the same way. "I coldly reply that I want no one, least of all a Jew." On second thought, he overcame the "reasonable repugnance," recalled the coachman, and agreed, even though it meant leaving earlier to accommodate his traveling companion's need to complete his journey before the beginning of the Sabbath at sunset on Friday. The next day, on the road, the Jew, Mordecai, asked why Casanova disliked his kind. "Because your religion makes it your duty to be our enemies," he shot back. "You think it your duty to cheat us. . . . You hate us." The vehemence of Casanova's reply exceeded his conventional anti-Semitism.

"You are mistaken," the traveler told the Venetian. "Come to our assembly this evening, and you will hear us praying together for all Christians, beginning with our master the Pope." Casanova burst out laughing

at the idea. Jews prayed for Christians only because they ruled the countries in which Jews lived, and he startled his companion by quoting "in Hebrew passages from the Old Testament in which they were commanded to
seize every opportunity to do all the harm they could to non-Jews, whom
they constantly cursed in their prayers." After a long silence, Casanova unexpectedly invited the man to dine with him, but Mordecai refused on the
grounds that his religion restricted him to the food he carried with him;
instead, he invited Casanova to lodge in *his* house, where "he would feed
me more delicately, more substantially, and more cheaply than at the inn,
all by myself in a fine room facing the sea." He'd never lodged a Christian before, he said, but he was willing to make an exception in Casanova's
case.

"So I put up at the Jew's, thinking it very strange."

The next day, he went to the synagogue with Mordecai, "who, having
become my landlord, seemed to me another man, and the more so because I had seen his family and his house, where I found everything very
clean." After attending the "short ceremony," Casanova strolled along the
Loggia dei Mercanti in Ancona, which he'd last visited nearly thirty years
earlier. He still felt young, "but what a contrast when I took the measure
of my moral and physical existence in those days of my youth and compared them with the present!" He'd been happy then, and over time he
had become melancholy, "for the whole beautiful prospect of a happier future no longer stretched before my eyes." He had wasted his time in idle
pursuits, "which meant that I'd wasted my life." Yet on returning to Mordecai's house, he was cheered to find a dozen or so people at table, including his host's mother, ninety years old and still in good health, several
family friends, and Mordecai's daughter Leah, who commandeered Casanova's attention. "I said many things to her to make her laugh; but she did
not even look at me."

He studied Leah closely. She was between eighteen and twenty, with a
"firm bosom as white as alabaster." She was assigned to cleaning his linen,
which might take time, she advised. He replied that "it was in her power to
keep me in her house as long as she pleased," but she appeared to pay no
attention to his small talk. He tried again, critiquing the chocolate she offered. He preferred it "whipped and foamy," provocatively enough, and she
offered to prepare it herself. "In that case," he said, "I will give you twice the
quantity, and we will drink it." The invitation did not please her.

During an elaborate "meat dinner, prepared entirely in the Jewish fashion," Casanova observed that Leah became "enlivened by the good wine," and he appreciated the fastidious attention paid to the preparation of meals in Mordecai's household.

As Leah watched him intently, her eyes set him on fire; she must let him kiss her. "No kissing, and no touching," said Leah, who was dependent on the dictates of her father. He did not answer her, "and finding the Jewish pastries and compotes excellent at dessert, we drank some Cyprus Muscat." Late at night, when Leah was asleep, he tipped the housekeeper to talk about the girl, but the housekeeper had only good things to say about her. Leah always worked. There were no suitors. "It was just the sort of thing she would have said if Leah had paid her."

He continued to hover. "Her breasts drove me to despair, and I thought it impossible that she should not be aware of their power. "Do you know that the sight of your bosom gives me extreme pleasure?" he asked. If so, she said, she was glad, for she had no reason to reproach herself.

"The minx!"

He attempted to give her a heart fashioned of gold and "pierced by an arrow and covered with little diamonds," but she refused to accept the present. A girl who intended to give nothing must accept nothing. What to do? Resort to force? He rejected the idea. Instead, he called off his suit. They continued to eat together. He offered her shellfish, which she naturally refused, but when the housekeeper departed, Leah devoured it, saying that it was the first time in her life that she had "enjoyed the pleasure."

After admiring her bosom once again, he offered to show her "pictures of the most beautiful bosoms in the universe." Although she claimed the sight wouldn't interest her, he displayed a "picture of a woman lying on her back stark naked and masturbating, but I cover it up to the navel with a handkerchief, and I show it to her." When he revealed the entire picture, Leah seemed neither shocked nor impressed. That's what all girls did secretly, she told him, before they married. And so did she "every time I feel like it. Then I go to sleep." Her sincerity drove him to distraction, he said; in that case, she countered, he must be very weak. And then she asked to see another miniature.

This time, he displayed a book of artwork by his preferred pornographer, Pietro Aretino. *Straight Tree!* She calmly examined the entire collection, declaring them "natural," and adding that a "decent girl mustn't look long at these things, for you can imagine that they arouse a strong emotion." Casanova felt it, too, and he directed her attention to the bulge in his breeches. Leah smiled, rose, and went to the window with the book, and resolutely turned her back on her would-be seducer, who endeavored to calm himself "like a schoolboy." He believed he was getting close to his goal; one more day, at most. She asked him for explanations of the illustrations, but refused his offer of "demonstrations that would have given life to the explanation, which was only for the eyes, and which perhaps I needed more than she did." She voiced impulses that drove him to distraction, especially because she prevented contact yet sounded so knowledgeable, brimming with "the most voluptuous truths" in her account of the "internal and external movements" of sexual intimacy. It seemed impossible that her impressions were based on hearsay alone; she must have had direct experience to be so exact. Yet she "swore" that she knew nothing of it from personal experience; for that knowledge, she would have to marry. What, asked Casanova, if the husband chosen by her father turned out to be "poorly equipped by Nature," or, still worse, "one of those ill-constituted cacochymics" whose vital essence was depleted, drained, *exhausted*. What if they were able to "do their conjugal duty only once a week?"

Leah was confused. Weren't all men "able to be amorous every day, as they must eat, drink, and sleep every day?"

"On the contrary, my dear Leah, men who are amorous every day are very scarce."

Failing to get his way, Casanova considered himself "cruelly exasperated," all the more because "there was no decent place in Ancona where a gentleman could have his pleasure by paying for it." Worse, he felt himself falling in love with Leah, despite her resistance, and tried to persuade himself that her flaws were actually strengths. She was "all true, unstained by hypocrisy." He would never prevail in this contest and made plans to leave Ancona.

Before his departure he rose late one night to go to the water closet, located on the ground floor. He went downstairs barefoot (the house was always very clean) in the dark, and on his return to his bedroom he saw a light shining through a crack in the door of a room that he believed was unoccupied. It couldn't be Leah, for her room was on the other side of the house. He peered through the crack to see Leah lying naked on the bed, "practicing postures with a young man in the same state." They whispered, and "every four or five minutes presented me with a new tableau." Casanova was not upset by the sight; in fact, "the pleasure somewhat soothed my fury," even as he observed her imitating the postures she'd learned from Aretino's explicit pictures. They even tried Straight Tree: "Leah unashamedly played the Lesbian, and he devoured her jewel, and, not seeing her spit at the end of the act, I was sure she had imbibed the nectar of my fortunate rival." They climaxed with their hands rather than intercourse.

As soon as he recovered, the young man looked at his watch and said he had to be going, ignoring her protests and reproaches. The young lover tiptoed out of the house, believing himself unobserved, and Casanova went back to bed, by this time he felt "indignant" and "debased." Leah "seemed to me nothing but a wanton who hated me." But in the morning, when she brought him his chocolate, as usual, he forced himself to appear cheerful as he revealed to her the scene that he'd witnessed the night before, "dwelling on Straight Tree and on the excellent food, which, like a true Lesbian, she had taken into her stomach." Seemingly determined to hurt Casanova, she said she did not love him, and she defied him to reveal her secret. And then she left. Alone, Casanova realized he could demand nothing of her, and she owed him nothing. It was time to leave this house and its disappointments.

He found a boat bound for Fiume, close to his destination, Trieste, paid Mordecai for the expenses, and sat down to an unpleasant farewell meal. Leah taunted him by remarking that he had enjoyed for free a spectacle that she knew he would have paid gold to see; if he weren't about to leave, and could pay, she'd arrange for him to see it again. Damnable creature! He threatened to strike her with a wine bottle and would have gone through with this "shameful crime" had not her expression of "defiant assurance" stilled his hand. Still gripping the bottle in his fist, he uncertainly poured himself a glass, then stalked off to his room to pack. To his surprise, she appeared to help him, but he roughly escorted her from his room, and locked the door. Alone, he reflected on how he had every right to loathe her, but then again, she had every right to loathe him. "I have never been in a more violent state."

Sailors came to transfer his belongings, and he sailed for Fiume.

A violent storm sprang up, "pitching and tossing so cruelly that my stomach was upset, and I began to vomit." At midnight, the captain decided the only safe course was to return to Ancona, where they disembarked only three hours after leaving. Normally, arrivals were quarantined, but the officer on guard recognized Casanova and allowed him to go ashore. Destiny had conspired to bring him to Ancona in the first place, and now destiny conspired to keep him here. Before he knew it, he was back at Mordecai's house, despite vowing that he would never see Leah again. He was spared the sight of her that night, hearing that she was lying in bed, severely ill, but in the morning she was at his door as usual, asking if he wanted his chocolate. No, he growled, only coffee, adding that she had "the soul of a monster," and he feared she would poison him.

"Experience had taught me that girls of Leah's sort were not uncommon," he reflected! "I had known her like in Spa, in Geneva, in London, and even in Venice, but this Jewess was the worst of them all." At dinner, he talked only to Mordecai, never to Leah, and refused the wine she served. As the foul weather persisted, he returned to his room, began writing, and fell asleep. When he awoke, Leah was lying beside him, on top of the coverlet. Still upset, he asked her to leave; he needed to sleep; instead, she harangued him for a good hour: after admitting she was wrong, she said that he should forgive her, a weak girl of eighteen, on the basis of his greater age and experience. Her actions only demonstrated that she lacked the ability to control herself. She would have given Casanova what he wanted, but she found herself in love with the man he'd seen: a "Christian . . . beggar and a libertine who did not love her and whom she paid" for sex. Furthermore, she'd never allowed him to deflower her, it had been six months since she'd seen him, and she'd only summoned him because Casanova had "set her soul on fire" with his engravings and his wines. Now it was up to him to "restore peace to her soul" before he left.

He pretended to be convinced by her clever arguments. Yes, he had "wronged her by showing her lascivious pictures," how unfortunate that Nature had endowed her with an overpowering libido, and so on, but that was not enough for her; she wanted Casanova to understand that she loved him and had "confined him to trifles to make my love stronger by conquering my esteem." How far would this minx go to make amends? He could hardly wait to "overwhelm her with humiliation." He remembered the sight of her in the Straight Tree position, and he still wanted her.

Later that night, she crept into his room to retrieve a bar of chocolate to make his morning drink, "in the most lascivious undress," but she did not even bother to notice that he was awake, observing her. She was "as false and artful as ever," and he congratulated himself on resisting her wiles. In the morning she arrived with two cups, one for him and one for her, to assuage his "fear of being poisoned." Still, he remained "resolved to humiliate her by indifference."

He escaped the confines of the house in search of "amorous pleasures" to buy, but none was to be found, and so he returned to his room, bolted the door, and, as he dreaded, listened to Leah knock and plead to enter. He unbolted the door, got into bed, "resolved to resist all her artifices," and watched her enter. "Well, what have you to say to me?" he asked. She came to his bedside, let her petticoat fall, and then her shift, and lay beside him. "Sure of her triumph, she does not hesitate, she says nothing, she clasps me to her bosom, she bestrides me, she deluges me with kisses, and in short in a single instant she deprives me of all my faculties, except the one I do not want to have for her." Before he knew it, he was devouring her breasts, "and she brings me to the point of death on the surface of the tomb, in which to my astonishment she convinces me that she could not bury me except by unlocking it." The morbid metonymy deployed by Casanova is deeply unsettling; sex with Leah was not *similar* to death, it *was* death, and love a fatal illness. *In flagrante*, he forgave her everything, even if her goal was to humiliate him; he told her that his enjoyment far exceeded any pleasure she might have taken in her revenge.

That was emphatically *not* the case, Leah whispered. "I am here to give you the greatest proof of my love and to make you my true conqueror." She continued, "Break this barrier that I have preserved intact until now . . . and if the sacrifice I make you allows you still to doubt the sincerity of my affection, it will be you who become the most wicked of men." And so he entered her. "On Leah's beautiful face I saw the extraordinary symptom of a delicious pain, and in her first ecstasy I felt her whole person trembling with the excess of pleasure that flooded it." He was determined to delay his own climax as long as possible, and he "kept Leah inseparable from me until three hours after midnight, and I aroused all her gratitude by making her receive my melting soul in the palm of her beautiful hand." When she saw him "dead" a few moments later, she said it was only justice. "We parted content, in love, and sure of each other." He slept until noon, and when she reappeared in his room, she "carried away the sheet on which the maid would have seen signs of our criminal connection."

During Casanova's final meal with the family, he suspected that Mordecai knew all along about his daughter's nocturnal activities, but did not mind, since, according to Jewish law, the child would be Jewish. Despite this undercurrent of mistrust, Casanova entertained the notion of staying with the family for another month. "What blessings on the storm that had kept me from going to Fiume!" he exulted. "We went to bed together every night, even on those on which Jewish law excommunicates the woman who indulges in love," that is, during menstruation.

Finally, on November 14, 1772, he left Leah and Ancona, and arrived in Trieste the next day.

———•———

He took to Trieste as if it were Venice itself. Every important personage he met, every official, every society hostess congratulated him on his virtual return to Venice, and some treated him as if he was already a Venetian in good standing, that his rehabilitation was a fait accompli. At times, he forgot himself and assumed that he'd return to Venice anyday. (In reality he would spend another two years in exile.) But his daily life was no longer an unpleasant banishment, more of a prolonged posting abroad. He'd evolved over the years from a fugitive to an unofficial roving ambassador. This fling with respectability was the latest Casanova persona, as consciously constructed and as lovingly tended as Casanova the libertine, confidence artist, gambler, or seducer; it was less outrageous a pose than the Chevalier de Seingalt but a pose nonetheless, a new character based on old prototypes. Shielded by this veneer of propriety, he cringed in respectable horror at the reports of street violence in Paris, where the social fabric was being torn asunder, and his nostalgia for monarchy and all its pleasures grew keener than ever.

He devoted a week to "putting together the notes I had collected in Warsaw on everything that had happened in Poland." The country had since been divided among its neighbors. Working with his customary intensity, he completed three volumes about the decline and fall of Poland until a business dispute with the printer, Valerio de Valeri, halted the project, and succeeding volumes mentioned by Casanova—"whoever comes into possession of my papers may publish them if he pleases"—were never printed, not that he cared anymore.

In his analysis, Russian hegemony had fractured and destroyed Poland, where he had spent a long, ultimately fruitless sojourn, and, he'd warned, Europe would "regard Poland as no more than the depository of White, Red, and Black Russia and of the Kingdom of Prussia, and that sooner or later the successors of the sovereigns would relieve the depository Republic of the burden of the deposit." As it happened, the sovereigns dismemembered Poland themselves. Casanova referred to the First Partition of Poland (1772), when Austria, Prussia, and Russia dissolved what was known as the Polish-Lithuanian state; within three years it was no more. In the distintegration of Poland, Casanova saw a painful example for Venice, also entering the throes of disaggregation. "Ambition, revenge, and stupidity were the ruin of Poland, but most of all stupidity."

He perceived a similar folly afflicting France. Reflecting later on the French Revolution, he would write, "Every king who has been dethroned must have been stupid," he opined, "for no nation on earth has a king except by force. For this reason a stupid king must have an intelligent prime minister and make him very powerful. The King of France perished because of his stupidity," and as he looked ahead, "France will perish because of the stupidity of that ferocious, mad, ignorant nation, blinded by its very intelligence and always fanatical. The disease that now reigns in France would be curable in any other country, but it will lead France to the tomb." He added, "The French *émigrés* may inspire pity in some, but not in me." If only France and other monarchies under siege marshaled their resources to oppose the forces threatening them, they might survive. "A headless body can endure only for a time, for reason lies in the brain."

—————————•—————————

After ten days, he emerged from his literary cocoon in Trieste to meet the Venetian Consul, Marco de'Monti, "a man full of intelligence and experience, very amiable in company, making very amusing remarks, very eloquent, graceful in narrative" and in satire. "Since I had something of the same gift myself," Casanova recalled, "we were instantly on good terms, becoming rivals in the art of anecdote. Though he had not the advantage of me by thirty years, I was a not unworthy match for him." Of greater importance, the Consul lobbied on Casanova's behalf to obtain the all-important pardon. As a result of his association with the Consul, Casanova believed he could "no longer be regarded as an exile. I was treated as a man whom the Venetian government itself could not demand, for, having left my country only to escape from an illegal imprisonment, the Government, none of whose laws I had broken, could not consider me guilty." At least, that was how he interpreted his situation after nearly twenty years in exile.

In this Serbo-Croatian-German-Venetian city of Trieste, "I began to enjoy life . . . as I needed to if I was to stay there for any considerable length of time and in accordance with the economy that I must practice, for my only certain income was fifteen *zecchini* a month." This discipline meant he "never played cards, and at dinner time I went every day to take pot luck at the houses of those who invited me." He counted among his patrons of his impecunious phase the Venetian and French consuls. And when it came to his hunger for intimacy, or, as he phrased it, "the pleasure of love," having learned from experience, he found his way to "young girls of no consequence, thus spending very little and running no risk to my health." During Carnival, when he fell for the daughter of a ranking member of the Trieste elite, he mustered only a "fatherly fondness for her"—she was thirty years younger—and a "sense of shame that was something entirely new in my character." (Not *entirely* new, but infrequent.) As a result, "I never asked anything of her that went beyond the limits" of the boundary between affection and love.

———•———

Throughout the early months of 1773, he cautiously offered his services to the Inquisition, whose members would see that he was doing the work of Venice in exile, and he felt himself stepping out of the shadows of disrepute into the sunlight of respectability. "I wrote to the secretary of the Tribunal that I considered myself fortunate to have succeeded in giving the Tribunal a proof of my eagerness to be useful to my country and worthy to be granted the favor of being allowed to return to it when their Excellencies should decide that I finally deserved it." He did not receive a pardon, but he did collect "an honorarium of a hundred silver ducati" from the tribunal together with a far-fetched assignment: "Resolve the great problem of the Armenians"—an ancient Christian group who maintained allegiance to the Pope and commercial ties to Venice.

The "Armenian Church," comprising members of this splinter group, had established a monastery on the island of San Lazzaro degli Armeni, in the Venetian lagoon west of the Lido, where their community prospered until the abbot excommunicated four monks, who sought asylum in Vienna. These monks had made a highly profitable business of printing books for Armenian monasteries. "It was a matter of ousting Venice from her place in this branch of commerce and giving it to Austria," Casanova commented. Later, "the State Inquisitors justifiably wanted to make them return to Venice," but not for religious reasons. Money was at stake. Getting the income for Venice was as difficult a task for Casanova as could be imagined. Even the Consul had backed away from the business "because he thought it impossible, and he predicted that if I undertook it I should waste my time." Nevertheless, Casanova, fascinated by all things literary, took it upon himself to become acquainted with some Armenians.

After a week's study, he told the Armenians that "honor demanded" that they resume their former obedience to their abbot. That way they might "free themselves from their excommunication" and return to Venice. His proposal met with a favorable response, but first the monks wanted their capital returned—four hundred thousand ducats belonging to the Monastery of San Lazzaro. And they had other conditions, mostly minor disciplinary matters. "I wrote everything down. I gave the Consul my memorandum, which he sent to the Tribunal." And then Casanova waited for a reply. The financial part of the negotiation was acceptable, he heard, but the disciplinary matters became a sticking point. "When I read this counterproposal, which was in direct contradiction to what I had written, for the parties were completely at odds, I determined to abandon the business"—but not entirely. To extricate himself from the complicated matter, which involved Trieste, Venice, and Austria, and to present himself as advancing the interests of the tribunal, he remained in close contact with the Consul, and eventually was awarded another honorarium of a hundred silver ducats, as well as ten *zecchini* a month "to encourage me to deserve well of the Tribunal."

He believed the pardon was fast approaching—but still it failed to materialize. His lot had improved, no question, and he was pleased to "find myself in the pay of the same Tribunal that had deprived me of my freedom and whose power I had defied; on the contrary, I felt that I was the victor, and my honor demanded that I make myself useful to it." He found himself in an extraordinary, paradoxical position vis-à-vis the Inquisition, part capitulation and part revenge on the enigmatic, all-powerful mechanism that had tormented him.

———•———

In Venice, the Council of Ten (actually seventeen members, including the Doge himself), reconvened, with three new arrivals. Said Casanova, "My protectors—that is, the Procurator Morosini, Senator Zaguri, and my loving friend Dandolo—wrote to me that if they did not succeed in obtaining my pardon during the twelve months during which they were to sit, they must give up hope of ever attaining it in their lifetimes."

Casanova returned to Trieste on the first day of 1774, "thoroughly resolved to serve the Tribunal well and thus deserve to obtain from its justice the pardon for which I longed after nineteen years of traveling all over Europe." Surely the Inquisitors would find him a modest sinecure for his solitary dotage in his native land. He pointed out that he was being productive. The first volume of his history of Poland had recently gone to press. Next, he would return to his Italian translation of the *Iliad* in rhyming stanzas.

The Council, "the men of business, the ladies, and all the members of the Casino of the city," saw him again, "with the greatest show of pleasure." What a relief! Their reception augured well. "I spent Carnival there in the utmost gaiety, enjoying perfect health." It was only natural for him to commence a romance with a *commedia dell'arte* actress Irene Rinaldi, whom he'd encountered years before. Despite the passage of time, she still struck him as "pretty," but when he presented himself to her, she introduced her husband and their nine-year-old daughter. They negotiated a tenuous relationship based on his occasional participation in the game of faro, which she ran privately, for gambling was illegal in Trieste, but, when he attended the soirees, he found himself surrounded by a "company of cox combs, young merchants, all in love with her."

During the games, he noticed that La Rinaldi was a subtle and skillful cheat. "It was a trifle, but I did not want Irene to suppose me a dupe." The next day he congratulated her on her sleight of hand. At first, she feigned surprise, and then she offered to repay him whatever he had lost. Casanova had lost all interest in *her*, but kept her young daughter in mind; perhaps in several years, he could begin an intrigue with the girl, and if not, there was always another woman, and another after her. . . .

Chapter 20

Francesca

Casanova returned to *La Serenissima* on September 10, 1774, in reduced circumstances. He was no longer the excitable thirty-year-old fugitive capable of outmaneuvering his antagonists; he appeared brittle and stooped, his gray complexion marked with lines and scars from the difficult years of exile. Despite everything, he rejoiced. "My return to Venice after nineteen years was the most pleasant moment of my life."

He appeared before the Secretary of the Tribunal, who informed him that he had received a pardon on the basis of his impassioned refutation of *Confutazione della Storia del Governo Veneto d'Amelot de la Houssaie*, which he'd written as a prisoner in the Citadel five years before.

He found modest lodgings in the Calle delle Case Nove, a comedown from his halcyon days in the Bragadin palazzo. The three Inquisitors who'd signed his pardon—Francesco Grimani, Francesco Sagredo, and Paolo Bembo—invited him to dinner to hear the story of his famous escape from I Piombi. He was now recognized by the powers that be, but he was still not one of them—and never would be. Socializing with three Inquisitors did not mean he'd escaped their scrutiny; the Inquisitition would watch him nearly to the end of his life. Ultimately, there was no unconditional pardon for him.

For the moment, relief outweighed resentment, but he found that his newfound respectability threatened to consign him to obscurity. He'd made a name for himself as a libertine, fugitive, and gambler, not as a writer or philosopher. To redress this imbalance, he decided to preserve the most outrageous episodes of his life for posterity. He would write a brief narrative of his duel with Count Branicki and an account of his escape from I Piombi, but those episodes barely suggested the totality of his experiences, so many of them forbidden. His life resisted encapsulation in a familiar genre.

He had no amanuensis scratching away on his behalf; when he died, the whole of his experience, the good, the bad, and the outrageous, would perish with him unless he memorialized it himself. Still, it would be several years before he committed himself to this daunting undertaking.

His other diversions had fallen by the wayside. The Ridotto, Venice's state-run gambling hall, where he had refreshed his fortunes in years gone by, had closed permanently in 1774 by order of the reformer Giorgio Pisani, and along with it went the demimonde of vice on which Casanova thrived. "All Venice has succumbed to a morbid depression," lamented one inhabitant. "Usurers look as sour as lemons, shopkeepers can't sell a thing, artisans of masks are starving." Other trappings of his youth in Venice had vanished, as well. His generous and credulous patroness, Madame d'Urfé, died in 1775 at the age of seventy, poisoned, so he believed, by her alchemical formulas. Zanetta Farussi—actress, singer, mother of two respected painters, and, incidentally, of the notorious Giacomo Casanova—died in Dresden on November 29, 1776, at the age of sixty-nine.

———◆———

Diminished by these losses, he commenced a relationship with a seamstress by the name of Francesca Buschini. Because of the girl's youth, Francesca's mother opposed any romantic liaison.

Unconcerned, he set up house with Francesca and her entire family, including her mother, but not in an opulent palazzo on a canal or in an impressive house or apartment; conserving his limited resources, they found lodgings in a dreary alley called Barberia de le Tole. Francesca maintained the cramped home they shared, far from the grand residences on the canal favored by the noble families of Venice. (Even Casanova needed a place to rest his *bauta* and call home.) He enjoyed putting his young mistress on display, drawing satisfaction from passers-by in the wanton streets of Venice. She was affectionate, slatternly, needy, far removed from the lustful nuns and grand dames whose favors he'd once sought. His long-term relationship with her reveals a different Casanova, stripped of the glittering artificiality and pretense of Venetian society. "Real love is the love that sometimes arises after sensual pleasure: if it does, it is immortal; the other kind inevitably goes stale, for it lies in mere fantasy," he observed. In this case, the lack of formal structure helped to preserve their relationship. With Francesca, he found an "immortal" but not necessarily passionate bond that persisted long after their physical proximity ended.

He devoted twin bequests of ten zecchini from Dandolo and Barbaro, his former protectors, to providing servants for the household, and at times Francesca's mother, brother, and younger sister saw fit to visit. Amid these constraints, he was neither celebrated nor happy. How could freedom be so dreary? Only respectability could be worse. The promise of Venice, which had been denied him for nearly two decades, no longer existed, if it ever had.

From time to time he informed for the same Inquisition that had once confined him to I Piombi—there was no escaping this organization. During his absence, the Inquisition had become vastly more powerful, as the authorities became concerned about the tide of revolution threatening to sweep across Venice. The Inquisition's spies were everywhere, and they were chosen, or coerced, into reporting on those in the same milieu. Intellectuals informed on intellectuals, impoverished aristocrats incriminated wealthy aristocrats, Jews implicated other Jews, and libertines (including Casanova) kept tabs on other libertines, and to report on their fondness for "dangerous" writers such as Rousseau, Voltaire, and other proponents of freedom.

Casanova obliged with a report, dated November 26, 1781, warning of a corner of the Grand Canal near the Calle del Ridotto where an informal Painters' Academy gathered by night to draw naked male and female models—hardly shocking in a city known for excess. He warned that some of the artists were as young as twelve or thirteen, and others weren't artists at all, but "nosy" amateurs. The thought of Casanova, of all people, attempting to safeguard public morality suggests how desperate he was for something to report, and how hypocritical the aging libertine had become. In this era of growing paranoia, visiting foreigners were watched more closely than ever, and the nobility were strictly forbidden to have anything to do with them. The aristocracy were especially scrutinized because they were responsible for governing Venice. Against this background, Casanova wrote a secret report against Gian Carlo Grimani:

> To the Most Illustrious Excellency Lord Secretary of the State Inquisition:
>
> I believe it my most essential duty to notify Your Excellencies that the nobleman Gian Carlo Grimani of the late excellent nobleman Michele [Grimani] presumes himself not bound to the ordinary provisions

*concerning visits of foreign diplomats. . . . He considers himself so entitled
to enjoy this privilege with impunity that in the public square, if it so
happens, he speaks without a care with the Minister of Russia, although
so far as I know about irrelevant matters.*

Casanova's malicious gossip had its intended effect. On May 3, Gian
Carlo Grimani was "summoned by the Secretary and cautiously reminded
to abstain from frequenting foreigners and affiliates." If he hadn't been a
nobleman, a *Grimani*, it would have gone much worse for him. In the same
vein, Casanova's published anti-democratic pamphlets served as a loyalty
oath to the increasingly mistrustful Inquisition. For a time, his strategy afforded him protection from the authorities, whose spies were everywhere.

In 1782, having abandoned his ambition of living by his pen, he obtained
a sinecure as secretary of Signor Marquis Spinola. In reality, he was now a
humble clerk with a low salary. He remained perpetually short of money.

For the previous two years, he'd been publishing monthly numbers of as-
sorted correspondence, satires, and broadsides under the title *Opuscoli miscellanei*, or *Miscellaneous Works*. The first installment featured a love affair
between two noblewomen of the Quattrocento—the fifteenth century, in
the spirit of Aretino—written as an epistolary account. Subsequent numbers included a history of the calendar, a chronicle of civil disturbance
in Poland, and an attack on Voltaire—*Scrutinio del libro Éloges de M. de
Voltaire*—calculated to appeal to the prejudices of the Inquisition, which
had no use for a satirist stoking the fires of revolution. Voltaire having died
in 1778 in Paris, Casanova had the last, rather petty word in their long-
running dispute.

The final issue of the *Opuscoli* offered a critique of the American Revolution. This seemingly distant uprising, a continent away, became the talk
of Venice, and prompted ideas of reform for the Republic, which was more
than a thousand years old and showing its age. Even Casanova, a fervent
royalist, was aware that reform would benefit Venice, but he was vigorously
opposed to the idea of revolution; he favored violent suppression of the
American revolutionaries—mutineers, in fact. So did many other Venetians. "May the storm pass without consequence," said the Venetian ambassador in Paris in 1781. Above all, he did not want the American upheaval to

contaminate European countries, especially *La Serenissima*. Casanova detested the ideals and driving forces of the American Revolution; he could not admit the possibility of a successful democracy, and in print he urged King George to act forcefully to preserve the established order.

He denounced democracy as "the worst of all governments. . . . Simple democracy only serves to generate turmoil and to fuel hatred among those those who consider themselves best suited to fill the seat of power. . . . Simple democratic government cannot self-sustain, and in history, I find it only in wretched, vagabond nations." And "satirical writings" only made matters worse. They "always target the wealthy." As a result, "aristocracies must always forbid them under strictest penalty because magistrates don't have enough power to prevent the insults . . . from diminishing their authority." He'd twisted his arguments so far that he undercut his own earlier literary efforts. His ideas had become dated and out of step. Instead of American "rebels," Venetians began to refer to the "New American Republic" and the United States of America. Even Venice acknowledged that the world was changing. But Casanova refused to go along.

In May 1782, in the splendid Grimani palazzo, Casanova's temper flared during an argument with a certain Carletti, who believed he was owed money by Casanova's employer, Spinola. There was some truth to the claim. Casanova had reluctantly agreed to chase the funds for Carletti, and Grimani had arranged for Carletti to pay Casanova a fee for his trouble. The role of debt collector scarcely pleased the proud Casanova, but the prospect of payment had its appeal. Once Spinola agreed in principle to repay the funds, Casanova went to collect his fee from Carletti, who refused to pay Casanova until Spinola repaid at least some part of the debt.

At the Grimani palazzo, Casanova accused Carletti of reneging on their agreement, and Carletti directed a stream of abuse at Casanova. Grimani at first stood by silently, and then spoke up to chastise Casanova. Feeling wronged and betrayed by both men, Casanova responded with a blistering satire, *Nè amori, nè donne*—*Not for Love or Women*—that recounted the classical tale of Hercules cleaning the Augean stables. In this guise, it passed the censor's office, and Casanova received the license required to print it. On closer inspection, Venetian readers realized that its grotesque characters referred to actual people. Most shocking of all, the satire discussed in thinly veiled terms a love affair between Casanova's mother, Zanetta Farussi, and the patrician Alvise Grimani. Many recognized Casanova's savage portrayal of Grimani, if not his outlandish claim about his paternity. In *La Serenissima*, where ancestry was everything, and society—marriage, property, inheritance—revolved around conserving the fortunes of the nobility, often at great cost, Casanova had taken aim at the heart of the Venetian establishment.

The satire undid the work of nineteen years to achieve a pardon, and the nine years Casanova had maintained himself in Venice. The Grimanis were still among the most influential families in Venice, and Casanova was advised to leave immediately. He belatedly realized the damage he'd done and dashed off apologies to those whom he'd offended, but it was too late. He beseeched his brother Francesco, pursuing his distinguished career as a painter in Paris, for help, but none was forthcoming. He turned to his brother Giovanni in Dresden, again with no result. Casanova abandoned Francesca and Venice on January 17, 1783.

Looking back on the fiasco, he recognized that he'd "turned the entire aristocracy into enemies." Until this time, "everyone assumed I would obtain a position consonant with my skills, and necessary to my sustenance. Everyone except for me, that is." He'd had to content himself with his lowly secretary's job. "Any appointment that I might have obtained through a tribunal, whose influence has no limits, would have appeared as a reward." Instead, "All the efforts I made over the course of nine years were in vain," he lamented. "Either I am not made for Venice, I told myself, or Venice is not made for me."

He relocated to Augsburg, and hoped to go on to Paris, the scene of his early success, but the spirit of adventure no longer animated him. He wrote to a friend, "I am 58. I cannot just walk away from Venice. Winter is coming"—he meant that in several ways—"and if I think of going back to being an adventurer, I laugh at myself in the mirror." It was the laughter of Pierrot, tinged with regret, melancholy, and self-pity.

He briefly returned to Venice on June 16 to claim his belongings, his clothes, and, most important, his books, but he did not dare to return to the house he'd shared with Franceca, or even to set foot in his former haunts, lest the Inquistion's spies arrest him. Francesca bewailed his absence—he was so near, yet so far from her. She thought they would be together forever, but now he'd deserted her as he had so many other young women who'd dreamed of marrying him. Yet again he reenacted the central trauma of his life: abandonment.

He wrote to her several days later, after he'd slipped away, to make amends. On June 27, 1783, she responded with an emotional plea: "I am grateful to you and will be until I die because I have no one else in the world but you and only in you I put my hope and trust on my part I always do what you tell me because by doing what you tell me I will never fail." She knew with whom he had dinner, she claimed, and where he spent his nights. At the same time, she implored Casanova to disregard the rumors about her supposed suitor, a certain Bolis. She'd seen him from time to time because his parents lived across the street, but that was all. "I swear to you my dear friend that I have never spoken to him, that many times when he saw me at the window he greeted me and I always avoided him." On further thought, she might have "nodded at him once or twice because next to him at the window was his sister who greets me once in a while when we run into each other. You were still in Venice when this madman was here, but it's been eight or nine months since then." His behavior was impossible. "For your information, everyone who knows him here in Venice says he is crazy." In sum, "you should know that I am deeply hurt at the thought that perhaps you believed the lies of that imposter."

At least Francesca had paid the rent, as Casanova had anxiously asked. "Let me inform you right away that we did on the fifth of the month." Still, she lived on a meager budget. She even restricted the size of the pages on which she wrote to him, because the post office charged more for a larger, heavier letter. She did mention running into "His Excellency Bernardo Memo" as she was going to mass on Sunday with her sister. "He immediately asked me if you are fine and where you are now, and he was very surprised that when I told him you had been in Venice twenty days ago but that you had not wanted to get off the boat and you had only come to say farewell and I told him that right now I don't know where you are heading."

During their brief reunion, Casanova had remained aboard his gondola to avoid arrest, and when his craft drew close to their house in the Barberia de le Tole, which lacked access to water, he sent for her as he lurked under the black felze—the shuttered awning in the center of the gondola. It was the last time he saw her, or Venice.

Casanova boarded a ferry bound for Mestre, on the mainland, and went on to Bassano, Trento, Innsbruck, Frankfurt, Köln, and Spa.

In his absence, Francesca cheered herself by telling everyone that she was still living with Casanova in the Barberia de le Tole, and boasted that he paid the rent. She remained in Casanova's thrall as he wrote of wandering across the Austro-Hungarian Empire and the hardship he'd endured in Vienna during the winter of 1783–84, when extreme cold brought misery to northern Europe. She knew he was fearless, but, she confessed, "I am afraid of everything because I am a fool. I am even afraid of sheep." Did he remember the day he led her into a herd of sheep and she started to cry with fright as he laughed and made fun of her? Now she had only memories of their brief time together, and she felt happy only when she received letters from him "because when I read them it's like seeing you."

While she lived on the edge of desperation, she heard that he'd been celebrating Carnival! "You went to four masked balls where there were two hundred ladies and you danced the minuet and contradances to the great astonishment of Ambassador Foscarini"—the Venetian envoy in Vienna— "who tells everyone that you are seventy when you are not yet sixty." She'd heard about the sumptuous dinners he attended at the Ambassador's, the food that was served. "You always talk about food, and I always need money," she ruefully observed. By the way, should one of his brothers come to Venice, he was more than welcome to stay at Casanova's house "because the chickens are always in the attic, so there are no chicken doppings, and as far as the dogs are concerned, we will find a solution because they don't really make any mess." She reassured Casanova that with a few minor exceptions, everything in his house was exactly as he had left it.

In Vienna, Casanova talked his way into a position as a secretary to the Venetian ambassador, Sebastian Foscarini. And he reencountered someone he'd known in Venice. Both were outsider Venetians who created enduring personas, Casanova the son of actors styling himself as the Chevalier de Seingalt, and Emanuele Conegliano, the son of a Jewish tanner, who became a thoroughly dissolute priest and the librettist known as Lorenzo Da Ponte. The relationship between Casanova and Da Ponte was a fractious one. They were gambling cronies, drinking companions, and libertines. They were also rivals; Casanova's failure to repay a loan—very typical behavior for him—rankled Da Ponte, who took such matters seriously. Like other men, Da Ponte harbored reservations about the Venetian: "This singular man never liked to be in the wrong."

Da Ponte had become the leading librettist for composer Wolfgang

Amadeus Mozart, for whom in 1786 he adapted a popular play by Pierre Beaumarchais, *Le Mariage de Figaro*, into an Italian libretto. Soon after, Mozart and Da Ponte began discussing another libretto, also in Italian, for a new opera, *Don Giovanni*. Operas recounting the legend of Don Juan had been a popular genre for half a century, but Mozart's version was destined to become a masterwork that captured, condemned, and celebrated the age, its passions, and its excesses. And here before Da Ponte and Mozart stood Giacomo Casanova, a fellow Freemason and every bit as flamboyant as their fictional protagonist. Even better, he was eager to add incidents to the libretto.

The manuscript shows contributions in the hands of all three—Mozart, Da Ponte, and Casanova, who held *women* responsible for Don Giovanni's deeds: "The blame lies entirely with the female sex for bewitching his mind and enslaving his heart. Oh, seducing sex! Source of pain!"

Casanova attended the premiere of the work, formally titled *Il dissoluto punito, ossia il Don Giovanni* ("The Rake Punished, or Don Giovanni"), on October 29, 1787, at the Teatro di Praga. The production was received with jubilation. The final scene, in which Don Giovanni, Casanova's surrogate,

Lorenzo Da Ponte (1749–1838), the
Venetian opera librettist and poet

is consumed by the fires of hell, created a sensation. Da Ponte, who also attended the premiere, savored the acclaim, while Casanova privately took exception to the climactic scene. To his way of thinking, Don Giovanni, the archetypal libertine, had done nothing to deserve punishment, and the idea of going to hell for eternity for chasing women struck him as utterly wrong-headed. Surely that wouldn't be his fate!

———•———

By this time, Casanova had received an appointment as librarian to Count Josef Karl Emmanuel von Waldstein. The Waldsteins were among the most prominent and wealthy dynasties in Bohemia, and this was a highly desirable assignment. Spending his declining years in a large, well-appointed library was almost as appealing as spending the rest of his days in a luxurious brothel. He took up residence at the Castle of Dux (later known as Duchov) in Bohemia, sixty miles from Prague and six hundred miles from Venice. He spent most of the last fourteen years of his life here, subsisting on a modest pension of a thousand florins a year.

It was here that he oversaw an archive of forty thousand volumes, and devoted his time to literary endeavors. He assembled his reminiscences of his flight from the I Piombi three decades earlier into a dramatic account, *Ma fuite* "My Escape." The story became better and more satisfying with each retelling; he was nothing if not an escape artist amid all others obeying fate. The year after it was published, a German literary periodical commented on the interest the book had aroused. "The subject in itself is captivating; all prisoners awake our compassion, particularly when confined to a harsh prison and possibly innocent." Casanova was identified as the "brother of the celebrated painter." The faintly condescending description came as no surprise to the author of *Ma Fuite*, who was still trying to make a name for himself to equal or surpass that of his better-known siblings.

During May, June, and July 1788, he returned to Prague for the printing and publishing of the book. When the volumes appeared, Casanova became known to the public as an escape artist, not a literary figure. "Some thin-skinned ladies," he sniffed, "took great offense at the book."

He turned his attention to the *Icosameron*—the title is a play on Boccaccio's *Decameron*—a five-volume, free-flowing compendium of philosophical and theological arguments. He dedicated the effort to Count Waldstein, a shrewd gesture, and claimed it was a translation from an English original. In reality, Casanova had written it himself and persuaded a literary journal to print it.

Although Dux served as an essential sanctuary during his later years, he came to consider himself a virtual prisoner there, unappreciated by the lesser beings surrounding him. "In order to be agreeable with all of my neighbors, it suffices only that I do not reason with them, and nothing is easier than that." Alone, he brooded on the past, now irretrievably lost, but still vivid in his mind. "Age has calmed my passions by rendering them powerless," he allowed, "but my heart has not grown old, and my memory has kept all the freshness of youth."

He persisted in corresponding with Francesca Buschini, although he might have regretted it when he read her replies, in which she trotted out the gossip she'd heard about him, especially the case of a "young girl who merits all your solicitation and your love. She and her family of six adore you and give you every attention; she costs you all you have, so you cannot send me even a sou." According to the rumors reaching Francesca, this girl, Anna-Dorothea Kleer, the daughter of the castle's porter, became pregnant in 1786, and Casanova was accused of having seduced her. Of course! That was just like him! In fact, another man was responsible. Nevertheless, Francesca took revenge on Casanova by selling all the books he'd left behind: the fruit of a lifetime of collecting and reading. She claimed her mother "absolutely insisted" on this drastic step because Casanova had caused her daughter's ruin. "I am in a desperate situation, abandoned by all, almost on the streets, almost homeless," Francesca wailed. By this time Casanova was saying he would never return to Venice; they would never dine together, never live together. The separation was more than she could bear. "Where are the theaters, the comedies that we once saw together?" she plaintively inquired.

Where are all my books? he wondered.

———•———

Wherever he looked, Casanova saw ruin. On July 15, 1789, the Bastille, home to only seven prisoners but a powerful symbol of French authority, was stormed. On December 5, 1790, the politician and former lawyer Maximilien de Robespierre announced the ideals of *Liberté, Egalité, Fraternité* to guide the revolution; a few years later, the Reign of Terror took hold, and beheadings at the guillotine, the "national razor," became common as the revolutionary hysteria spread. Reflecting on this excess, Casanova experienced revulsion at the "raging, ferocious, uncontrollable people who flock together to hang, cut off heads, and murder those who, not being of the people, dare to speak their minds."

At least one of Casanova's acquaintances was sacrificed. Marie Louise of Savoy, Princesse de Lamballe, was married to the heir of the richest fortune in France and loyal to Marie Antoinette, the wife of Louis XVI and Queen of France and Navarre. Their bond inspired salacious gossip; popular pornographic pamphlets portrayed Marie Louise as the Queen's lover. In August 1792, Madame de Lamballe was imprisoned and told to swear an oath to Liberty and Equality and to an abhorrence of the King and Queen. She refused. The judges ordered her to be released, which was another way of condemning her to death. She was swept up in a wave of mob violence later called the September Massacres of 1792. As she appeared in the street, a drunken drummer in the National Guard by the name of Charlat struck her head, wounding her above the eyes. She stumbled forward, and a mob bludgeoned her to death. A butcher's assistant by the name of Grison

Death of the Princesse de Lamballe by the prison door, Paris, September 3, 1792

hacked off her head. Gabriel Mamin, a violent drunkard, claimed to have ripped out her heart. The mob dragged the Princess's naked body through the streets of Paris as crowds jeered. Then they mounted the Princess's head on a pike and went off in search of Marie Antoinette, determined to make her kiss the severed head of her supposed former lover.

The Queen was playing backgammon with the King at the Temple, the royal prison where they had been held captive since August 10. Now the disembodied head of her dear friend appeared outside the dining room windows. "Though bloody," said one observer, "it was not disfigured; her blond hair, still curling, floated around the pike." Officers closed the shutters and kept the royal couple away from the windows. When Louis inquired what was going on, one of the officers said, "They are trying to show you the head of Madame de Lamballe."

Later, her severed head was brought to a young maker of death masks in Strasbourg. In her memoirs, the woman describes a horrific scene in which she was forced to take a wax cast from the features of the dead Princess. She almost met the same fate as her celebrated subject. When the Reign of Terror took hold, the maker of the wax cast herself was ordered to the "national razor." Her head was shaved in preparation for the event, but at the last minute, friends intervened, and her life was spared. She went on to fashion famous death masks of Jean-Paul Marat and Robespierre. Years later, in London, she opened an exhibition hall. This was the origin of Madame Tussaud's wax museum, begun in the desperation and blood of the French Revolution.

———•———

Contemplating reports of these violent, bloody scenes, Casanova redoubled his determination to support the French monarchy. By October 1792, he discussed with Count Waldstein and others a plan to spirit the royal family out of France, involving specially trained horses capable of covering great distances swiftly. The King and Queen would use counterfeit passports and travel under assumed names. The plan reached the ears of the King himself, but, according to Casanova, he wouldn't agree to it, "saying that if he fled at least thirty-thousand people loyal to him would be sacrificed." Even the most recent massacres did nothing to change his mind. As the violent death of the King came to seem more likely with each passing week, Casanova unburdened himself in a letter he wrote to a friend.

A king of France, wishing to force tigers to love him, opens their cage, thinking they will turn to sheep. He pays this mistake with his head and drags his kingdom with him to ruin.

Six major powers forge an alliance to prevent this tide from inundating all of earth. Taking advantage of their flaws, the tide invades everything.

The little powers imagine that the best way to save themselves from the fury of this tide and wildfires is to stay calm. The incendiaries become fierce and indomitable, before their deceivers tell them they are the sole masters of France and prove this truth to them through anarchy. Enter one Robespierre to convince the misguided that he alone had been the master of everything all along. The reign of this monster lasts for eighteen months.

How he despised Robespierre—a "bloodthirsty monster," he called him, after Robespierre called for the beheading of the King. Thirty-six years earlier, Casanova had witnessed the torture and execution of a would-be assassin of Louis XV. Now, at ten o'clock on the morning of January 21, 1793, Louis XVI fell victim to the guillotine erected in the Place de la

Execution of Louis XVI, January 21, 1793

Révolution—formerly the Place Louis XV and later Place de la Concorde.
"I die innocent of all the crimes," he said, "I pardon those who have occasioned my death, and I pray to God that the blood you are going to shed
may never be visited on France." With that, he was undressed against his
will, bound to the scaffold, and the blade came down—not through his
neck, but through the back of his head and his jaw. When it was over, the
bloody head was displayed to the crowd.

"The monarchy of France, transformed into a headless democratic republic, is only conceivable as ephemera," Casanova wrote. "I believe that
having understood this reality, Robespierre also recognized the need to per-
petuate it by way of continuous sacrifice. . . . Robespierre must have thought
he was reasoning well. If it is possible to strong-arm entire nations, he must
have said to himself, into Christianity by means of an auto-da-fe, it might
be possible . . . to force a kingdom to turn into a republic by way of purging
it of anything that breathes of aristocracy." Appalled by these developments,
he still aspired to join the ranks of the aristocracy that had always excluded
him, imprisoned him, and tried to kill him even as he sought freedom and
liberation.

He drafted a one-hundred-and-twenty-page essay fulminating against
Robespierre and the tyranny he'd encouraged:

> *The violence of this executive directorate suggests it does not worry at all*
> *about ensuring the happiness of France. . . . Its only purpose is to make*
> *itself happy, to support itself, and for this reason to keep peace at arm's*
> *length as much as possible, because with peace will come its inevitable fall.*
> *For this reason it plunged the nation back in the revolutionary regime,*
> *and terror is at the order of the day.*

Casanova's lottery, however, outlasted the bloodshed and mayhem.
When the Bastille fell in 1789, the lottery did not miss a beat. When Louis
XVI was beheaded, the drawings continued. When Marie Antoinette followed the King to the guillotine in October of that year, the lottery paid off
with the mathematical precision Casanova had predicted decades earlier.

—————•—————

At about this time, Casanova found a new champion in Charles Joseph, Seventh Prince de Ligne, an Austrian blessed with an ebullient temperament—

Goethe once called him "the most joyous man in Europe"—wedded to an energetic intellect. After an extensive military career, the Prince wrote more than forty volumes while pursuing a libertine's diverse love life and tending to his opulent estates. If Casanova had been born an aristocrat with a fortune at his disposal, he might have been the Prince de Ligne.

The two were kindred spirits. The Prince noted that the former adventurer "made me happy with his imagination, as lively as it had been at twenty, his enthusiasm for me personally, and his useful and agreeable information. But"—and this was a significant exception—"it must not be supposed that in this tranquil haven, opened to him by the benevolence of Count Waldstein to save him from the storms of life, there were no storms of their own making." On the contrary, "Not a day went by without a quarrel in the house about his coffee, his milk, his macaroni, as to which he was very exacting." So much irritated Casanova: the cook forgot to prepare his polenta; the carriage driver was inept; dogs barked throughout the night; unexpected guests arrived; the ear-splitting hunting horn shattered his concentration; the vicar tried to convert him; and the Count himself overlooked him (or so it seemed to Casanova), or lent out a book from the library without first consulting him. Visitors snickered at his low, graceful bows and his "plumed hat and his suit of gold silk with his black velvet waistcoat, and his paste diamond buckles on his silk stockings."

Such colorful, passé behavior amused the mischievous Count Waldstein, who challenged Casanova to a mock duel by silently presenting a pair of pistols. Missing the humor entirely, Casanova wept, embraced him, crying out, "Shall I kill my benefactor?"

Having made a fool of himself, Casanova fled the castle, but not before composing an overwrought letter of farewell to Count Waldstein, who burst into laughter on reading it and confidently and accurately predicted that Casanova would return.

———•———

In his travels across Germany, Casanova, armed with letters of introduction supplied by the Prince de Ligne, often perplexed those whom he met. Was he a fussbudget librarian, or perhaps a chamberlain, or something else—a spy or nobleman traveling incognito? He was received in fine style by the Duke of Weimar, but when Casanova learned that the Duke championed Goethe and had gone so far as to ennoble him, the Venetian became resentful. How dare Goethe steal the literary renown that properly belonged to him!

On his return to Dux, Casanova expected Count Waldstein to pay the debts incurred during his travels. Fortunately, the Count agreed. Explaining this indulgence, the Prince de Ligne declared, "Casanova has a mind without equal, from which each word is extraordinary and each thought a book." And Waldstein, for his part, considered Casanova's instability a mark of genius. Reunited with his admiring patrons, he related his recent vicissitudes—all of them self-inflicted—"to which his sensitive pride gave the name humiliation. 'I am proud,' he said, 'because I am nothing.'"

His modesty concealed a fierce determination to set down the particulars of his life. Finally, he began to write, day after day, twelve or eighteen hours a day, week after week, month after month, year after year. He never wrote anything else as revelatory as this outpouring of experience, and for length, detail, and disreputableness, Casanova's literary feat remains unequaled. At times he relied on accounts he'd written years before, close to the events he described; at other times he relied on his extraordinary memory. One volume became two, two became three, and eventually he reached six volumes with more than half his life still to memorialize and to scandalize for the sake of posterity. He placed himself at the center of his universe, looking outward in all directions. In his self-absorption, it was as if no other memoirist ever existed, with the irritating exception of Voltaire. Otherwise, Casanova created the world as he wrote, *his* world.

The creation of this memoir became his reason for being, but occasionally he broke away to take note of the world going on around him. Every part of his mind was on fire. On July 27, 1792, he wrote to a new acquaintance, Jean-Ferdinand Opiz, a Jesuit turned lawyer, librarian, and tax official with whom he'd been engaging in heated debates about mathematics and astronomy, criticizing the work of Johannes Kepler, Tycho Brahe, and even Isaac Newton. "I demonstrate that light has neither body nor spirit; I demonstrate it comes in an instant from its respective star," he boasted until he had remade the universe to suit himself. He wanted Opiz to publish his "scientific" speculation, but Opiz, recognizing how difficult Casanova could be, categorically refused: "No offer of yours could make me a bookseller."

He dismissed potential criticism of his outrageous memoirs, which had grown to twelve volumes. "I am a detestable man," he explained to Opiz, "but I do not care about having it known, and I do not aspire to the honor or the detestation of posterity." To his way of thinking, his memoirs were bursting with "excellent moral instructions. But to what good, if the charming descriptions of my offenses excite readers more to action than to repentance?" He did not write to inspire a new generation of libertines but to memorialize his own activities, whether they were admirable or shameful. And then there was the question of discretion. Although he had concealed the names of many of the men and women he portrayed, readers could easily guess their true identities. "Their transgressions are unknown to the world, [and] my indiscretion would injure them, they would cry out against my perfidy, even though every word in my *Histoire* is true."

The more he and Opiz corresponded with one another, the more they argued. By February 2, 1794, with rancor overwhelming their friendship, Casanova wrote to Opiz, "You have become my enemy."

As they quarreled, Venice crumbled.

———————

A decade earlier, in October 1784, Napoleon Bonaparte had arrived in Paris. He was fifteen years old and wore his hair in a pigtail. He was accompanied by the principal of the provincial military school he'd been attending, where he'd won a reputation as a gifted but exceptionally pugnacious student. He was unperturbed by the harsh weather that winter as he made his way to the École militaire at 21 Place Joffre in the 7th Arrondissement. His new school was surpassingly elegant. The classrooms were decorated with blue wallpaper accented with gold fleur-de-lys. There was ample heat from a stove, Alençon linen on his bed, and a pewter jug in his wash basin. His blue uniform incorporated a silver braid, red collar, and white cuffs. Meals included three desserts. All this luxury came at considerable expense. A cadet's annual tuition came to 4,282 livres—more than forty thousand dollars. Much of that beneficence came from the continuing success of the lottery established by Casanova shortly after his arrival in Paris, in 1757, and it had become essential to the operation of the École militaire. So it was that Casanova's brilliant notion financed Napoleon's military training—with profound consequences for Venice.

Eleven years later, General Napoleon Bonaparte, not yet twenty-seven, was engaged in defending Paris and the French revolutionary government against royalist troops backed by England. He succeeded: advancement beckoned. Days after marrying his love, Joséphine de

Beauharnais, Napoleon departed on an Italian campaign, ostensibly to protect France but in reality to extend the French Empire. Leading a ragtag militia, he defeated the much larger armies of Austria. An amalgam of European monarchies, the First Coalition, opposed his forces. Undeterred, he conquered northern Italy and was rewarded with the command of the French army in Italy.

Determined to tighten his grip on northern Italy despite the shortcomings of his underpaid, understaffed army, he approached the stronghold of Venice with a measured strategy that belied his absolute contempt for the Republic. To forestall an outright invasion, Venice agreed to permit French troops in territory controlled by the Republic at a cost of five million francs. The Republic vainly hoped to remain neutral, taking sides with neither France nor Austria. During this waiting period, Napoleon's reputation as a heroic conqueror soared; peasants who'd hated their landlords looked on him as an emancipator, and the French idea of liberty took hold. Popular uprisings convulsed Bergamo and Brescia; at the same time, counterrevolutionary sentiment coalesced, supported by the clergy. (The revolution had

Ludovico Manin, the last Doge of the
Republic of Venice, by Bernardino Castelli

forbidden religious practices.) The French, meanwhile, agitated against Venetian interests.

Matters came to a head on April 20, 1797, when Venetian troops fired on a French ship, *Libérateur d'Italie*, as she sailed into the Venetian lagoon. This clash gave Napoleon the perfect excuse to act. "French blood has flowed in Venice," he declared. To forestall outright war, the Venetian government decided to release political prisoners and to negotiate with France. The population was split between those who supported the government and those who favored the revolutionaries. The prospect of anarchy loomed.

By May 12, as the Great Council of Venetian noblemen convened, Ludovico Manin, the 118th Doge of Venice, addressed a half-empty chamber. "Sir Panic," as he was known behind his back, advocated surrender of the fleet, abdication, and the abolition of their time-honored status as nobility. Five hundred and ninety-eight members ruled in favor of the desperate measures, seven against, and fourteen abstained. When the vote was concluded, the nobility fled, and the *Libro d'Oro*, the Golden Book of the Nobility, was burned. The last Doge remained preternaturally calm throughout the ordeal. When it was over, he removed his ceremonial cap and gave it to his valet, saying, "I shall not be needing it again." He retreated behind the walls of his palazzo and for the rest of his days refused to answer the door, even for friends. Thanks to Napoleon the Republic of Venice had ceased to exist.

Napoleon refused to inspect his trophy. In his stead, he sent his wife Joséphine on a five-day visit during which she toured St. Mark's, the Palace of the Doges, renamed the National Palace, and acknowledged introductions as "the wife of our liberator, Bonaparte." Wearing an unadorned white dress, green stole, and bonnet, she was conveyed in a sedan chair from one brief stop to the next. "She is neither pretty nor young," an Italian journal noted, "but she is very sweet and attractive and courteous."

When she returned to the mainland, the French resumed looting the city, snatching gold and silver, even from churches. Napoleon ordered the Doge's magnificent ceremonial galley, *Bucentaur*, burned to the waterline to symbolize the conquest of Venice. The four bronze horses above St. Mark's Basilica, icons of Venice, were dispatched to Paris. The last three prisoners held in I Piombi, where Casanova had languished for more than a year, were released. The Ghetto was opened. The death penalty was abolished.

On January 18, 1798, Venice became an Austrian province, heavily taxed and censored, its currency German, its spirit broken, and its days and nights of gambling and pleasure seeking gone. Those all-night parties and orgies, endless Carnivals, and bare-breasted nuns of Casanova's day faded into lore as the Republic adjusted to the new order.

———◆———

The swift fall of *La Serenissima* astonished Casanova. It seemed that history had been marking time for the first fifty years of his life, when he was in constant motion. Now events exploded while he was tethered to Dux. "We will laugh at the mention of the tragic buffoonery that preceded the fall of your Republic," he wrote to his Venetian friend Zaguri on December 4, 1797. "*Voilà*, you are free. What would you have said of an oracle had he told you seven years ago that you would have uttered these words? You will become free when you have lost your freedom. . . . Let us laugh at the stupidity and the buffoonery that in seven years overturned Europe, because if we don't, the tears of this cruel destiny will kill us."

Casanova did not exaggerate. His friend Da Ponte, the librettist, returned to Venice on November 7, 1798, after an absence of twenty years, seeking to recruit opera singers. In St. Mark's Square he saw just seven peo-

Casanova at age 62

ple rather than the boisterous crowds he remembered. The coffeehouses he'd frequented, and where Casanova had once flirted, gossiped, and plotted, were all but abandoned. New taxes imposed by the implacable Austrians had doubled the price of coffee, tobacco, salt, and other staples. Political discussions were outlawed. Those caught violating the new censorship faced jail and a beating. As he beheld this decline, Da Ponte became "more sad than a son who cries at the death of his mother." The Venice of tourists, courtesans, adventurers, and gamblers had receded as the remnants of the Venetian nobility descended into poverty.

As he approached his seventieth year, Casanova's vitality drained. His hair turned gray, and his bravado vied with uncertainty. He suffered from painful gout. Tiring of the world, its struggles, ambitions, and even women, he devoted thirteen hours a day to writing his memoirs.

Amid the isolation of Dux he occasionally fantasized about taking matters concerning his mortality into his own hands. In an essay completed on December 13, 1793, "Short Reflection of a Philosopher Who Finds Himself Thinking of Procuring His Own Death," he reflected on his "too long life." He mused: "Life is a burden to me. What is the metaphysical being who prevents me from slaying myself? It is Nature. What is the other being that enjoins me to lighten the burdens of that life, which brings me only feeble pleasures and heavy pains? It is Reason." At this low point, his constant companion at Dux, a lithe and spirited greyhound, suddenly died. He took solace in a successor given to him.

In 1794, Casanova returned to the orbit of Charles-Joseph, Seventh Prince de Ligne. The Prince comprehended the enormously complex Giacomo Casanova in his totality, as both "the knight and the Wandering Jew," in the Prince's words; an amalgam of lust, perversity, and genius.

The Prince presented a portrait of an eccentric, irascible, brilliant Casanova in his advancing years:

> He would have been a very fine looking man if he were not so ugly. He was built like Hercules with a bronzed tinge; keen eyes full of intelligence, but emitting at all times so much irascibility, uneasiness, and spite as to give himself an air of ferocity. You could sooner make him angry than gay. He laughed little, but he made others laugh; and

Charles Joseph, Prince de Ligne
(1735–1814), Belgian writer and diplomat

he had a way of saying things, between that of a numbskull and a Figaro, that was very diverting. There was nothing he did not know, and he prided himself on knowing the rules of dancing, the French language, taste, society, and *savoir vivre*. He was a fountain of knowledge; but he quoted Homer and Horace till you were sick of them. He had feeling and gratitude; but if you displeased him he was malignant, peevish, and detestable; a million ducats could not undo the smallest jest made at his expense. . . .

He was superstitious in every possible way. Fortunately, he had honor and delicacy, and if he said, "I have promised God," or "God wills it," there was nothing on earth that he was not capable of doing.

⸻

Casanova's goal now was to win a reputation as a writer or prophetic *philosophe* on a par with Voltaire and Rousseau. Although fluent in French, he stood apart from the examples of French literary expression all around him. "A strange nation," he observed, "that ceases to feel its affliction as soon as poems or songs make it laugh! In my day the authors of epigrams and songs that attacked the government and the Ministers were put in the Bastille; but that did not prevent the wits from continuing to amuse their particular circles ... with their particular jests." His approach to writing, in contrast, was observational, down to the last zecchino, a style that would, a century later, be seen as realistic, but in an era of allegory and artifice, his memory for dialogue, incident, appearance, and financial transactions stood apart.

"Fretting and distressing himself," recalled the Prince de Ligne, Casanova lamented the vanished glory of his "superb Venice, which had so long resisted all Asia and Europe." He became cranky, devoid of his former swagger and élan. In January 1792, while Count Waldstein was away, he became embroiled in a spat with one of the servants, who "tore my portrait out of one of my books, scrawled my name on it ... and stuck it on the door of the privy." Outraged by the lack of respect, Casanova hired an advocate, wrote out a complaint, arranged for it to be translated into German, but then thought the better of it and wrote a second complaint, this one in Latin, which he kept on file at Dux.

Amid the turmoil, he received a visit from Da Ponte, who happened to be traveling from Prague to Dresden when he "remembered that Giacomo Casanova owed me several hundred florins." The itinerant librettist showed up at the castle to collect the money he believed his Venetian compatriot owed him, "but soon observing that his purse was emptier than mine, I could not put him to the mortification of asking for something he would have been unable to give."

Rather than repay the loan, Casanova decided to accompany Da Ponte on a short journey by carriage to the city of Teplitz, but they met with an accident along the way. Casanova sold the horse and carriage at a loss, and "kept two zecchini for himself," claiming he needed the funds to return safely to Dux. In lieu of repaying Da Ponte, "I will give you three pieces of advice that will be worth much more than all the treasures of the world." The first piece of advice was to avoid Paris and go to London, but when in London "never set foot inside the Caffè degli Italiani." The third and final bit of advice: "Never sign your name!"

His life had been an extended improvisation as he tried unsuccessfully to claim what he—or his imagination insisted—was his rightful place in the Venetian aristocracy. In the ultimate act of self-invention, he arduously

Histoire

de Jacques Casanova de Seingalt venitien

ecrite par lui même à Dux

en Boheme *Nequicquam sapit qui sibi non sapit*

~~Chi~~ ~~~~

Chapitre Ier

L'an 1428 D. Jacobe Casanova né à Saragosse capitale de l'Aragon, fils naturel de D. Francisco enleva du
couvent D^a Anna Palafox le lendemain du jour qu'elle
avoit fait ses vœux. Il étoit secretaire du roi D. Alphonse;
Il se sauva avec elle à Rome où après une année de prison, le pape Martin III donna à D. Anna la dispense
de ses vœux, et la benediction nuptiale à la recomandation
de D. Jouan Casanova maitre du sacré palais oncle
de D. Jacobe. Tous les issus de ce mariage moururent en
bas âge exepté D. Jouan qui epousa en 1475 Eléonore
Albini dont il eut un fils nommé Marc-antoine.

L'an 1481 D. Jouan dut quiter Rome pour avoir tué
un officier du roi de Naples. Il se sauva à Come avec sa
femme, et son fils; puis il alla chercher fortune. Il mourut en voyage avec Christophe Colombo l'an 1493.

Marc-antoine devint bon poète dans le goût de Martial,
et fut secretaire du cardinal Pompée Colonna. La satire
contre Jules de Medicis que nous lisons dans ses poésies, l'
ayant obligé de quiter Rome, il retourna à Come, où il épousa
Abondia Rezzonica.

Le même Jules de Medicis devenu pape Clement VII lui
pardonna, et le fit retourner à Rome avec ~~sa~~ femme, où après
qu'elle fut prise, et pillée par les imperiaux l'an 1526, il mourut
de la peste. Sans cela il seroit mort de misere, car les soldats

began to assemble all these sketches into the final draft of his life: his memoirs. It seemed an impossible task, unsuited to his mercurial temperament, yet he accomplished it brilliantly.

With eremitical discipline, he devoted his last years to writing about his adventures, surveying a lifetime of debauchery with equanimity and candor. "I always willingly acknowledge my own self as the principal cause of every good and of every evil which may befall me; therefore I have always found myself capable of being my own pupil, and ready to love my teacher." In writing this exhaustive, exuberant memoir, he at last found the release he had sought throughout his tumultuous life, not through action, cunning, or deception, but though recollection and truth telling. In revealing all, he achieved a measure of redemption. "Worthy or not, my life is my subject, and my subject is my life." He distracted himself by seducing an aristocrat here, a young prioress there, and other women of distinction; otherwise, he wrote. "I write in order not to be bored; and I am delighted, I congratulate myself, that I enjoy doing it; if I wrote nonsense, I do not care, it is enough for me to know I am being amused."

Too frail to live with his former verve, he allowed death to overtake him amid the hope that his literary outpouring would one day bring him the attention he sought. He had dared to write about activities that were forbidden; he exposed them to the glare of his analysis and wit and as a result had more to say about the private life of the Enlightenment than anyone else. His incessant curiosity allowed him to explore behavior and modes of thought that would otherwise have been lost, as if he were the sole survivor of a protracted orgy.

Doubt overcame him. "I might have done well not to bind myself irresponsibly, though at my present age my independence is a sort of slavery. If I had married a woman intelligent enough to guide me (to rule me) without my feeling that I was ruled, I should have taken good care of my money, I should have had children, and I should not be, as I now am, alone in the world and possessing nothing." He grudgingly admitted in old age that he was "happy in his memories," and what memories they were. His reminiscences recalled Boccaccio's merrily fornicating characters, even as they anticipated the delicate psychological analysis of Marcel Proust's autobiographical deliberations. At other times, Casanova reveled in the idea that he was laying bare his ebullient secret self for the voyeuristic entertainment of others. Let others spend their late years in the shadows of penance; Casanova was determined to play the libertine for as long as he lived.

Casanova's *Histoire de ma vie* would not be published in its entirety until decades after his death. Its nearly four thousand pages, written in his own hand, amounted to a vast retrospective of his life and times. The combination of artifice and ruthless introspection impart a fierce intelligence to his masterwork, as he managed the trick of looking at himself and the people in his life from several perspectives, adoring and mocking them, noting their foibles even as he wished to emulate them. People come tumbling out of his handwritten pages with novelistic vitality. In its intricate blend of splendor, delusion, heroism, venality, his memoir is truly the story of his life as it was lived and felt, a comedy, cautionary tale, and historical record of an evanescent time and place rapidly disappearing as he wrote about it, a Jeroboam of champagne from a lost world of privilege and decadence.

Casanova suffered a severe bladder infection in February 1798, a legacy of the venereal diseases he had experienced since he was a young man. He wrote to friends to announce his illness—it was serious, he did not expect to survive—and they wrote back to offer support, medical advice, prayers for his recovery, soup, visits, whatever he desired. He became withdrawn and fastidious as he patiently waited for the end.

"I am but the shadow of the once-brilliant Casanova," he whispered. He took refuge in writing a whimsical, poignant fantasy, *The Fifteen Minute Dream*, in which he imagines meeting God, minute by minute. By the last minute, God makes peace between science and faith. "The essential is to be just," God tells Casanova, "and let everyone think as they will."

Casanova's physical condition deteriorated. He was tormented by hunger, thirst, hemorrhoids, and an inflamed prostate. His body was swollen with edema.

As the conclusion approached, said the Prince de Ligne, "He regretted very little in life, and ended it nobly toward God and Man. He received the sacraments with grand gestures and many phrases and said: "Great God, and you, witnesses of my death, I have lived as a philosopher, and I die as a Christian."

In his final days, he dashed off a brief sketch of his life for twenty-one-year-old Cecile von Roggendorf, the orphaned daughter of a count. He had become fond of her, but he was forced to turn over the task of communicating with her to a nephew. "I can no longer read nor write," he dictated, "and I could not give you any news of my life if my nephew were not here. Farewell." His nephew added: "My poor uncle is dying; he wanted to sign, but has no more strength."

On June 4, 1798, while confined to a chair at Dux, writhing in pain, Casanova drew his last breath.

He was buried in the local churchyard at Dux, Santa Barbara. The precise location of his grave is not known. A tablet placed on the exterior of the church reads:

JAKOB CASANOVA

VENEDIG 1725 DUX 1798

Casanova was dead, but his literary afterlife was just beginning. Carlo Angiolini, who was married to Casanova's niece, carried the manuscript of the memoirs with him to Dresden. Upon his death in 1808, Angiolini's daughter Camilla came into possession of it. In need of money, her family sold it to the publisher Friedrich Arnold Brockhaus. The first volume, in a German translation, appeared in 1822, causing consternation and fascination among readers and critics.

Inspired by the success of the German edition, the French publisher Tournachon, lacking access to the original manuscript, published a French version of the Brockhaus text, heavily censored. In response, Brockhaus brought out a second edition from 1826 to 1838, this one in French, which distorted Casanova's religious and political views and censored his sexual content. From 1838 until 1960, all editions of Casanova's memoirs were based on these unreliable versions, and a popular English-language version also drew on these inaccurate precedecessors.

Casanova's immense manuscript languished in the Leipzig offices of Brockhaus, surviving a direct hit from an Allied bomb in 1943. A concerned member of the Brockhaus family then bicycled it to a bank vault for safekeeping. In June 1945, the manuscript of *Histoire de ma vie* was liberated

MÉMOIRES

DE

J. CASANOVA

DE SEINGALT

ÉCRITS PAR LUI-MÈME.

Ne quidquam sapit qui sibi non sapit.

ÉDITION ORIGINALE.

TOME DOUZIÈME.

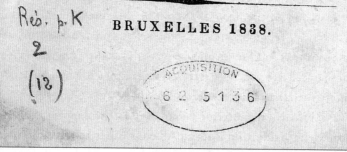

BRUXELLES 1838.

Title page of Casanova's twelve-volume memoirs

by Allied forces. The manuscript was conveyed in an American military truck to Wiesbaden, Germany. In 1960, the first unexpurgated version of the manuscript was published in French, one hundred and sixty-two years after Casanova's death. At last the world could read his memoirs and come to know Casanova in his own words. Six years later, a complete English version appeared. "Autobiography is only to be trusted when it reveals something disgraceful," wrote George Orwell. "Any life when viewed from the inside is simply a series of defeats." By that measure, Casanova's all-encompassing memoirs proved entirely successful.

In 2010, the Bibliothèque nationale de France purchased this manuscript, for over nine million dollars, the institution's most expensive acquisition to date, and brought it to Casanova's adopted home, Paris, organized an exhibition devoted to it, and at last provided a fitting home. The entire manuscript became available to the public.

Through Casanova's provocative writings, and his capacious knowledge of the human condition—exalted, fallen, noble, and ludicrous—he still seduces us today. And we continue to take the measure of this multifaceted individual, whose life posed the eternal question: What is love?

WORKS BY
GIACOMO CASANOVA

1752   *Zoroastro: Tragedia tradotta dal Francese, da rappresentarsi nel Regio Elettoral Teatro di Dresda, dalla compagnia de' comici italiani in attuale servizio di Sua Maestà nel carnevale dell'anno MDCCLII.* Dresden.

1753   *La Moluccheide, o Sia i gemelli rivali.* Dresden.

1769   *Confutazione della Storia del Governo Veneto d'Amelot de la Houssaie.* Lugano.

1772   *Lana caprina: Epistola di un licantropo.* Bologna.

1774   *Istoria delle turbolenze della Polonia.* Gorizia.

1775–78   *Dell'Iliade di Omero tradotta in ottava rima.* Venice.

1779   *Scrutinio del libro Eloges de M. de Voltaire par différents auteurs.* Venice.

1780   *Opuscoli miscellanei* (containing *Il duello* and *Lettere della nobil donna Silvia Belegno alla nobil donzella Laura Gussoni*). Venice.

1780–81   *Le messager de Thalie.* Venice.

1782   *Di aneddoti viniziani militari ed amorosi del secolo decimoquarto sotto i dogadi di Giovanni Gradenigo e di Giovanni Dolfin.* Venice.

1783   *Né amori né donne, ovvero La stalla ripulita.* Venice.

1785   Six articles in the *Osservatore triestino*, untitled and unsigned, published between January 22 and February 26.

     Exposition raisonée du différent qui subsiste entre les deux républiques de Venise et d'Holland. An Italian translation appeared in the same year, *Esposizione ragionata della contestazione, che sussiste tra le due Repubbliche di Venezia, e di Olanda.*

     Lettre à Messieurs Jean et Etienne L. Another work on the same subject, directed to Jean and Etienne Luzac, editors of the *Gazette de Leyde*, who had supported the Dutch position in the controversy.

Also appeared in Italian as *Lettera ai signori Giovanni e Stefano Luzac,* and in Dutch as *Brief van eenen Venetiaan aan de Heeren J. en E. L.*

Supplément à l'exposition raisonée. A continuation of his earlier work on the same subject.

1786   *Soliloque d'un penseur.* Prague.

1787   *Icosaméron, ou Histoire d'Édouard et d'Élisabeth qui passèrent quatre-vingts un ans chez les Mégamicres, habitants aborigènes du Protocosme dans l'intérieur de nôtre globe.* Prague.

1787–8   *Histoire de ma fuite des prisons de la République de Venise qu'on appelle les Plombs.* Leipzig.

1790   *Solution du probléme deliaque.* Dresden.

1790   *Corollaire à la duplication de l'hexaèdre.* Dresden.

1790   *Démonstration géometrique de la duplication du cube.* Dresden.

1797   *A Léonard Snetlage, docteur en droit de l'Université de Goettingue, Jacques Casanova, docteur en droit de l'Universitè de Padou.* Dresden.

1822–29   First edition of the *Histoire de ma vie,* in an adapted German translation in 12 volumes, as *Aus den Memoiren des Venetianers Jacob Casanova de Seingalt, oder sein Leben, wie er es zu Dux in Böhmen niederschrieb.* The first full edition of the original French manuscript was published in 1960 by Brockhaus (Wiesbaden) and Plon (Paris).

NOTES

Giacomo Casanova cut a wide swath through the eighteenth century, beginning in Venice and extending across the length and breadth of Europe, from Corfu to Russia, London to Prague, and especially Paris, the epicenter of passion and revolution. Few if any writers or adventurers have documented themselves and their exploits as thoroughly as Casanova, and he has left a rich store of reflections and records in the formless form of his memoirs. The reader generally knows where Casanova was at a given moment, what he was up to, and even what he was thinking; in many cases he provides several answers. Two major new editions of his original manuscript have recently appeared in French: the authoritative Pléiade edition in three volumes (Gallimard) and the no less thoroughly annotated Laffont edition, also in three volumes. Those wishing to get closer to Casanova's text can study a facsimile of the manuscript online at the website of the Bibliothèque Nationale de France, http://expositions.bnf.fr/casanova/livres/HMV/index.htm, and at the associated Gallica website, http://gallica.bnf.fr/ark:/12148/btv1b6000810t/f11.

I returned to the urtexts for a more accurate rendering. Why? Casanova wrote in an idiosyncratic Venetian-inflected French, and often his wit and irony were lost in translation. I have tried to suggest in English the essence of Casanova's French literary voice, often amused, but rarely mocking, conversational yet highly literary, and simultaneously vulgar and brilliant. One need only consult other memoirs of the era to appreciate how much further Casanova went in recording the world around him, and the skill he demonstrated in bringing an immense cast of characters to life. This trove of memoirs is supplanted by Casanova's auxiliary writings, especially *Ma Fuite*, his account of his escape from I Piombi, and numerous other works by him.

Venetian customs have long attracted the attention of historians and social commentators. Among the more vivid accounts are Pompeo Molmenti's *Venice, Its Individual Growth from the Earliest Beginnings to the Fall of the Republic* and two works by John Julius Norwich, *A History of Venice* and *A Traveller's Companion to Venice*. See also Peter Ackroyd's *Venice: Pure City* for a more contemporary perspective.

Preface

For a detailed discussion of the Venetian calendar, both secular and ecclesiastical, Carnival, and other date-keeping matters, see Eleanor Selfridge-Field, *Song and Season*, 29–133.

xvii *Patricians meeting with ambassadors:* For more on the significance and unusual customs concerning ambassadors and ambassadorial conduct in Venice, see Andrea Zannini, "Economic and Social Aspects of the Crisis of Venetian Diplomacy in the Seventeenth and Eighteenth Centuries," in *Politics and Diplomacy in Early Modern Italy.*

xvii *"I thought him a blockhead"*: Giacomo Casanova, *Histoire de ma vie jusqu'a l'an 1797,* Tome I, lxxiv (Pléiade edition).

Chapter 1: Zanetta

For Casanova quotations in Chapter 1, see Giacomo Casanova, *Histoire,* I, 18–63.

3 *The daughter of a cobbler: Histoire,* liv–lv.

3 *That winter was reportedly the coldest in five hundred years:* Stephanie Pain, "1709: The Year That Europe Froze."

3 *Carlo Goldoni:* Carlo Goldoni, *Memoirs,* 180–81; Childs, *Casanova,* 17. For more on Goldoni and artistic life in Venice, see Andrieux, Maurice, *Daily Life in Ancient Venice,* translated by Mary Fitton.

6 *"beautiful and very talented . . . taste perfect ear, and execution"*: Goldoni, *Memoirs,* 180–81.

11 *Dr. Gozzi was all of twenty-six:* Childs, *Casanova,* 30.

Chapter 2: Angela

24 *"Not wishing to occupy himself with affairs of state at his age"*: For Casanova quotations in Chapter 2, see Casanova, *Histoire,* I, 63–146.

38 *"These girls of Venice are lighter than a feather"*: Philippe Monnier, *Venice in the Eighteenth Century,* 58.

38 *their provocative, high-heeled, jewel-studded wooden clogs:* Andrieux, *Daily Life in Venice at the Time of Casanova,* 136.

38 *"Much, much too convenient"*: Ibid., 137.

38 *Goldoni satirized this fawning admiration:* Ibid., 139.

38 *sfrontata on her nose:* Ibid., 141.

40 *every Venetian woman of fashion went out with a cavaliere servente, or cicisbeo:* Monnier, *Venice in the Eighteenth Century,* 70; Norwich, *A History of Venice,* 594.

40 *In a family with three or four sons, the designated heir married:* Alexander Cowan, *Marriage, Manners and Mobility in Early Modern Venice,* 151–52.

40 *The prostitutes of Venice, numerous, anonymous, and generally tolerated:* Giovanni Dolcetti, *Le Bische e il Giuoco d'Azzardo a Venezia 1172–1807,* passim.

41 *"Prostitutes are there in plenty":* Andrieux, *Daily Life in Venice at the Time of Casanova,* 155.

41 *Their pimps,* mangiamarroni, *or "chestnut eaters":* Ibid.

41 *Jean-Jacques Rousseau:* Ibid., 156.

41 On the Venetian preoccupation with impotence: See Daniela Hacke, *Women, Sex and Marriage in Early Modern Venice,* 152–74.

41 *the convents of Venice often functioned as genteel brothels:* Charles de Brosses, *Selections from the Letters of de Brosses,* 30.

50 the *Razzetta* episode: Childs, *Casanova,* 34.

51 *they were* barnabotti: Norwich, *A History of Venice,* 596; Pompeo Molmenti, *Venice,* 30.

53 *twenty-eight days of quarantine:* Molmenti, *Venice,* 35.

Chapter 3: Bellino

60 *"I find myself obliged":* For Casanova quotations in Chapter 3, see Casanova, *Histoire,* I, 244–94.

61 *"I swear, I curse":* Ibid., II, 3–60.

Chapter 4: Zelmi

81 *Casanova faced limited prospects even if he were to marry:* For more about marriage in Venice, see Cowan, *Marriage, Manners, and Mobility in Early Modern Venice,* 5–6.

81 *Libro d'Oro, or Golden Book:* de Brosses, *Selections from the Letters of de Brosses,* 31.

Chapter 5: Henriette

97 *"There was gaming, lovemaking, and much amusing practical joking":* For Casanova quotations in Chapter 5, see Casanova, *Histoire,* I, 466–555.

101 *"I admired a wit in her which was entirely new to me:* Casanova, *Histoire,* I, 510.

101 *Some have proposed Jeanne Marie d'Albert de Saint-Hippolyte:* see Willard Trask, *Casanova,* 305, notes.

Chapter 6: Mimi

114 *"kind of despair that also has a certain sweetness"*: For Casanova quotations in Chapter 6, see Casanova, *Histoire*, I, 555–687.

118 *the most controversial alliance of them all, the Freemasons*: Steven C. Bullock, *Revolutionary Brotherhood: Freemasonry and the Transformation of American Social Order, 1730–1840*; Richard William Weisberger, "Speculative Freemasonry and the Enlightenment: A Study of the Craft in London, Paris, Prague, and Vienna."

119 *As Freemasonry flourished*: Weisberger, "Speculative Freemasonry and the Enlightenment: A Study of the Craft in London, Paris, Prague, and Vienna; Manly P. Hall, *The Lost Keys of Freemasonry*.

139 *Dresden—celebrated as Florence on the Elbe*: Bruce Redford, *Venice and the Grand Tour.*

141 *The Chastity Commission*: Dorothy McGuignan, *The Hapsburgs*, 234–37.

Chapter 7: Maria Eleonora

144 *"In the room where I slept and wrote"*: For Casanova quotations in Chapter 7, see Casanova, *Histoire*, I, 687–816.

144 *accompanying the mammoth* Bucentaur: Molmenti, *Venice*, 214.

158 *Santa Maria degli Angeli, the Church of the Angels*: Casanova, *History of My Life*, XII, 241, notes.

161 *"A misfortune befell me"*: Ibid., IV, 4–94.

169 *Abbé de Bernis*: Childs, *Casanova*, 79.

Chapter 8: Tonina

182 *"weak and imperfect creature who cannot imitate you both"*: For Casanova quotations in Chapter 8, see Casanova, *Histoire*, I, 822–901.

183 *The State Inquisitors functioned as the Supreme Court in political matters*: For an analysis of the operation of the Inquisition with respect to Casanova, see Rinaldo Fulin, *Giacomo Casanova e gli Inquisitori di Stato*, passim.

190 *pastinaca muranese*: Karen Newman, *Cultural Capitals: Early Modern London and Paris*, 143.

190 *Within their convents' walls*: Molmenti, *Venice*, 224.

190 *Giovanni Pietro Leon of Valcamonica*: Ibid.

192 *"Vanesio, of unknown, and, as it was reported, of illegitimate birth*: Piero Chiara, *Rosara; Or the Adventure of a Actress: A Story from Real Life*, III, 125–27.

194 *"In order to gain fame for his satires he distributes them"*: Giovanni Comisso, *Agenti segreti di Venezia, 1707–1797,* 67.

196 *"I requested a composition from Giacomo Casanova"*: Ibid., 71.

196 *"For about the past seven years:* Ibid., 73.

197 *"Casanova read a blasphemous verse"*: Fulin, *Giacomo Casanova e gli Inquisitori di Stato,* V, iii.

197 *blasphemous verses in the Venetian dialect:* Comisso, *Agenti segreti di Venezia,* 64–73.

198 *And as for their beaux:* Andrieux, *Daily Life in Venice at the Time of Casanova,* 144.

Chapter 9: I Piombi

200 *"act of oppression"*: For Casanova quotations in Chapter 9, see Casanova, *Histoire,* I, 902–1015.

206 *the three Inquisitors who'd sentenced him:* Ibid., 345, notes.

208 *I Quattro:* Ibid., 346, notes.

210 *Casanova places Schalon's arrival at the beginning of Lent 1756:* Ibid., 347, notes.

Chapter 10: Madame d'Urfé

235 *"My terrified coachman thinks only of going on"*: For Casanova quotations in Chapter 10, see Casanova, *Histoire,* I, 1015–Vol. II, 106.

239 *a lottery:* Stephen M. Stigler, "Casanova, 'Bonaparte,' and the loterie de France," *Journal de la société française de statisque,* 5–34.

239 *Next, Casanova addressed the Council of the École militaire:* Robert Kruckeberg, "The Loterie de l'École Militaire: Making the Lottery Noble and Patriotic," 85–94.

241 *The first drawing was scheduled for April 18, 1758:* Childs, *Casanova,* 91.

244 *On the appointed day, Damiens, judged guilty of "regicide"*: Iwan Bloch, *Marquis de Sade: His Life and Works,* 68–69.

250 *another notorious participant, the Comte de Saint-Germain:* Childs, *Casanova,* 95–96.

Chapter 11: Miss Wynne

257 *"I found this most unusual woman on the fifth floor of a dilapidated house"*: For Casanova quotations in Chapter 11, see Casanova, *Histoire,* II, 107–385.

259 *"He is attired resplendently"*: Giustiniana Wynne's letter about Casanova: Giuseppe Bignami, "Casanova tra Genova e Venezia. Comprimari, testimonianze e due ritratti." In *La Casana*.

261 *Alexandre Jean Joseph Le Riche de La Poupelinière*: Bruno Brunelli, *Casanova Loved Her*, 86–121. Brunelli employs a variant spelling of the name. See also Childs, *Casanova*, 104–6.

266 *He hired twenty pretty women*: Childs, *Casanova*, 109.

267 *his primary mistress, Manon Balletti*: Ibid., 1–79.

267 *In April 1757, she'd written to Casanova*: Aldo Ravá, ed., *Lettere di donne a Giacomo Casanova*, 5–31.

270 *"Be reasonable and receive the news I send you calmly"*: Casanova, *History of My Life*, VI, 30ff.

276 *He did see the Amazon one last time*: Childs, *Casanova*, 122.

Chapter 12: The Black-Eyed Nun

282 *"This is the happiest moment of my life"*: For Casanova quotations in Chapter 12, see Casanova, *Histoire*, VII, 326.

288 *"I shall sleep the better"*: Casanova, *History of My Life*, VII, 4–234.

299 Attilio Regolo: Ibid., 326, notes.

Chapter 13: Hedwig and Helena

305 *"They go masked or unmasked"*: For Casanova quotations in Chapter 13, see Casanova, *Histoire*, II, 631–943.

Chapter 14: Marcolina

321 *"always despised"*: For Casanova quotations in Chapter 14, see Casanova, *Histoire*, II, 832.

Chapter 15: La Charpillon

333 *"extremely tedious"*: For Casanova quotations in Chapter 15, see Casanova, *Histoire*, III, 6–200.

335 *Vincenzo Martinelli*: Childs, *Casanova*, 183.

337 *bagnios*: Childs, *Casanova*, 182.

340 *Pauline*: Childs explores her possible identity, ibid., 187–90.

343 For more on La Charpillon, see: Ravà, *Lettre di donne a Casanova*, 110–12; Alain Buisine, *Casanova, L'Européen*, 239–50; Childs, *Casanova*, 190–95.

351 *He decided he wouldn't commit suicide*: For Casanova's ruminations on suicide: *Dialoghi sul suicidio*.

353 *"Mr. Fielding"*: Ian Kelly, *Casanova: Actor, Lover, Priest, Spy* 263.

355 *"'Miss Charpillon is more of a whore than her mother'"*: Childs, *Casanova*, 194.

357 *"I saw the gallows before me"*: Casanova, *History of My Life*, X, 32.

Chapter 16: Zaïre

358 *"restored to life"*: For Casanova quotations in Chapter 16, see Casanova, *Histoire*, III, 201–347.

369 For Casanova's duel with Count Branicki: Casanova, *The Duel*, and Kelly, *Casanova*, 293.

Chapter 17: Doña Ignacia

378 *"Was it my good or my evil Genius who bestowed her on me?"*: For Casanova quotations in Chapter 17, see Casanova, *Histoire*, III, 356–540.

Chapter 18: Nina

404 *"The famous Nina"*: For Casanova quotations in Chapter 18, see Casanova, *Histoire*, III, 547–811.

406 *de la Houssaie's history of Venice*: Trask, XI, 345.

Chapter 19: The Minx

425 *Pitti Palace*: Casanova, *History of My Life*, XII, 249, notes.

425 *"for the necessaries of life I needed no one"*: For Casanova quotations in Chapter 19, see Casanova, *Histoire*, III, 812–918.

Chapter 20: Francesca

440 *"My return to Venice after nineteen years"*: For Casanova's relationship with Francesca Buschini and excerpts from her letters, see Francesca Buschini, *Lettere a Casanova: trentatré lettere di Francesca Buschini, l'ultima amante veneziana*.

442 *Casanova obliged with a report, dated November 26, 1781*: Comisso, *Agenti Segreti Veneziani nel '700*, 255. Comisso dates the report Nov. 26 but the original at the AVV is not dated (Busta 565, Casanova #39).

443 *critique of the American Revolution*: Casanova, *Opuscoli miscellanei*, August 1780.

447 *Casanova talked his way into a position as a secretary to the Venetian ambassador, Sebastian Foscarini*: Childs, *Casanova*, 284.

447 *The relationship between Casanova and Da Ponte*: For informed speculation about the collaboration between Casanova and Da Ponte, see Ibid., 287.

455 *"made me happy with his imagination"*: Charles Joseph Ligne, *The Prince de Ligne. His Memoirs, Letters, and Miscellaneous Papers*, II, 169.

459 *Ludovico Manin, the 118th Doge of Venice*: Norwich, *A History of Venice*, 604.

463 *Amid the turmoil, he received a visit from Da Ponte*: Ibid., 287.

SELECT BIBLIOGRAPHY

Archives Consulted

Venice
Archivio di Stato di Venezia
Biblioteca Fondazione Querini Stampalia
Ca' Rezzonico

Paris
Bibliothèque Nationale de France

Duchcov Château, Czech Republic
Museum Archive

Harvard University, Cambridge, Massachusetts
Houghton Library

Randolph-Macon College, Ashland, Virginia
J. Rives Childs Casanova Collection

Manuscripts

Bibliothèque Nationale de France, Paris
Histoire de ma vie de Jacques Casanova de Seingalt venitien.

Biblioteca della Fondazione Querini-Stampalia, Venice
Casanova, Giacomo. *Lettera autografata al nobiluomo Querini*, October 13, 1778.
Casanova, Giacomo. *Lettera autografata al nobiluomo Querini*, October 25, 1778.

Archivio di Stato di Venezia
Barbaro, Marco. *Arbori dei Patrizi Veneti integrati da Angelo Maria Tasca*. Registro IV, Grimani.

Avogaria di Comun. *Libri d'oro dei matrimoni con notizie dei figli.* Registro VII, 124 T.

Inquisitori di Stato. *Riferte dei confidenti.* Busta 612, 565. *Riferte di Gian Battista Manuzzi*; Giacomo Casanova aka Antonio Pratolini.

Inquisitori di Stato, Annotazioni. Busta 534. Annotazioni 21 August 1755 and 12 September 1755.

Periodicals

Bignami, Giuseppe. "Casanova tra Genova e Venezia. Comprimari, testimonianze e due ritratti." In *La Casana*, vol. 3, pp. 25–37. Genova: Gruppo Carige, 2008.

Bracco, Roberto. "Donna nel Teatro di Carlo Goldoni." In *La Donna*, a. III, no. 52 (Feb. 1907).

Brunelli, Bruno. "La cultura della donna Veneziana nel 700." In *Archivio Veneto*, series 5, vol. 12, pp. 40–64.

Childs, James Rives, ed. *Casanova Gleanings.* Nice, France: 1958–80.

Craig, Cynthia C, and Clorinda Donato. "Casanova at the Bicentenary: Familiar Questions, New Directions." *Eighteenth-Century Studies*, vol. 33, no. 4 (in *The Culture of Risk and Pleasure*, Summer 2000), pp. 579–86.

Gozzi, Gaetano. "Padri, figli e matrimoni clandestini (metà sec. XVI—metà sec. XVIII)." In *La Cultura*, vol. 14, 1976, pp. 169–213.

Johnston, Bruce. "Napoleon to Be Put on Trial 200 Years After the Capture of Venice." *The Telegraph*, January 10, 2003.

Kruckeberg, Robert. "The Loterie de l'Ecole Militaire: Making the Lottery Noble and Patriotic." In *Proceedings of the Western Society for French History*, vol. 37 (2009), pp. 85–94.

Lattes, Laura. "Una letterata veneziana del sec. XVIII: Elisabetta Caminer Turra." In *Nuovo Archivio Veneto*, vol. 27, 1914.

Lucca, Valeria de. "Negotiating Space." In *The Oxford Handbook of Opera*, ed. Helen M. Greenwald, Oxford, 2014.

Luciani, Gèrard. "Venise au XVIII siècle; une capitale de l'insolite." In *Cahiers du CERLI*, no. 6, 1983, pp. 153–69.

Marco, Guy A. "Repartee: Casanova Bibliotecarius: Some Addenda." *The Journal of Library History*, vol. 2, no. 3 (July 1967), pp. 250–52.

Marenduzzo, Antonio. "I cicisbei del settecento." In *Storia d'Italia*, a. 8, vol. 2, 1905, pp. 271–82.

Musatti, Eugenio. "Una veneziana del 700." In *Nuovo Archivio Veneto*, series 3, vol. 37, 1919, pp. 200–8.

Nettl, Paul and Theodore Baker. "Casanova and Music." *The Musical Quarterly*, vol. 15, no. 2. (April, 1929), pp. 212–32.

Occioni-Bonaffons, Giuseppe. "Di un epistolario femminile inedito nella Quiriniana di Venezia." In *Atti del R. istituto veneto di scienze, lettere ed arti*, tomo 6, series 6, 1888, pp. 845–65.

Pain, Stephanie. "1709: The Year That Europe Froze." *New Scientist*, February 7, 2009.

Pelzel, Thomas. "Winckelmann, Mengs and Casanova: A Reappraisal of a Famous Eighteenth-century Forgery." *The Art Bulletin*, vol. 54, no. 3 (Sept. 1972), pp. 300–15.

Perrottet, Tony. "When Casanova Met Mozart." *Smithsonian.com*, March 21, 2012.

———. "Who Was Casanova?" *Smithsonian Magazine*, April 2002.

Rees, Gillian. "The Italian Comedy in London, 1726–1727: Zanetta Casanova." *L'Intermediaire des Casanovistes*, Genève Annèe, vol. 13 (1996), pp. 25–32.

Robilant, Andrea di. "Love in Venice." *The New Yorker*, Aug. 18 and 25, 2003.

Stigler, Stephen M. "Casanova, 'Bonaparte,' and the loterie de France." *Journal de la société française de statisque*, tome 144, no. 1–2 (2003), pp. 5–34.

Stocchiero, Sebastiano. "La redazione di un giornale settecentesco." In *Nuovo Archivio Veneto*, series 3, vol. 40, 1920, pp. 173–78.

Symons, Arthur. "Casanova at Dux: an Unpublished Chapter of History." *The North American Review*, vol. 175, no. 550 (Sept. 1902), pp. 329–46.

Thomas, Chantal, and Noah Guynn. "The Role of Female Homosexuality in Casanova's Memoirs." *Yale French Studies*, no. 94, *Libertinage and Modernity* (1998), pp. 179–83.

Wolff, Larry. "'Depraved Inclinations'": Libertines and Children in Casanova's Venice." *Eighteenth-Century Studies*, vol. 38, no. 3 (Spring 2005), pp. 417–40.

Books

AA. VV. *Casanova, la passion de la liberté*. Parigi: Coédition Bibliothèque Nationale de France/Seuil, 2011.

———. *Il mondo di Giacomo Casanova; un veneziano in Europa*. G. Romanelli, ed. Catalogue of Ca' Rezzonico. Venezia: Marsilio, 1998.

Abbate, Carolyn; Parker, Roger. *A History of Opera*. New York: W. W. Norton, 2012.

Abirached, Robert. *Casanova o la dissipazione*. Palermo: Sellerio, 1977.

Ackroyd, Peter. *Venice: Pure City*. London: Chatto & Windus, 2009.

Andrieux, Maurice. *Daily Life in Venice at the Time of Casanova*, trans. Mary Fitton. New York: Praeger, 1972.

Aretino, Pietro. *The Secret Life of Nuns*, trans. Andrew Brown. London: Hesperus, 2004.

Bacchelli, Riccardo, and Pietro Longhi. *Teatro e immagini del Settecento italiano.* Torino: ERI, 1954.

Baccolo, Luigi. *Casanova e i suoi amici.* Milano: Sugar, 1972.

——. *Vita di Casanova.* Milano: Rusconi, 1979.

Baratto, Mario, and Jean-Pierre Vincent. *Sur Goldoni.* Paris: L'Arche, 1971.

Barbier, George. *Casanova: décors et costumes.* Paris: L. Vogel; New York: F. K. Ferenz, 1921.

Bartolini, Elio. *Casanova: Dalla felicità alla morte 1774–1798.* Milano: Mondadori, 1994.

Barzaghi, Antonio. *Donne o Cortigiane? La prostituzione a Venezia documenti di constume dal XVI al XVIII secolo.* Verona: Bertani, 1980.

Barzini, Luigi. *The Italians.* New York: Atheneum, 1965.

Baschet, Armand. *Les archives de Venise. Histoire de la chancellerie secrète. Le Sénat, le cabinet des ministres, le Conseil des dix et les inquisiteurs d'état dans leurs rapports avec la France, d'après des recherches faites aux sources originales, pour servir à l'étude de l'histoire de la politique et de la diplomatie, par Armand Baschet.* Paris: H. Plon, 1870.

——. *Les depeches des ambassadeurs venitiens en France pendant le 16.e le 17.e18.e siecle: Rapport a M. le Ministre de l'Instruction publique.* Paris: s.n., 1877.

Bell, David A. *The First Total War: Napoleon, Europe and the Birth of Warfare as We Know It.* Boston: Houghton Mifflin, 2007.

Berengo, Marino. *Giornali veneziani del 700.* Milano: Feltrinelli, 1962.

——. *La societá Veneta alla fine del 700.* Firenze: Sansoni, 1956.

Bergeret de Grancourt, Pierre-Jacques-Onésyme. *Voyage d'Italie 1773–1774.* Paris: Editions Michel de Romilly, 1948.

Bernard, Paul P. *From the Enlightenment to the Police State: The Public Life of Johann Anton Pergen.* Chicago: University of Chicago Press, 1991.

Bingham, Denis. *A Selection from the Letters and Despatches of the First Napoleon. With Explanatory Notes.* London: Chapman and Hall Limited, 1884.

Bleackley, Horace. *Casanova in England.* London: John Lane, 1923.

Bloch, Iwan. *Marquis de Sade: His Life and Works.* New York: Castle, 1948.

Boatto, Alberto. *Casanova e Venezia.* Bari: Laterza, 2002.

Boccardi, Virgilio. *Casanova la fine del mio mondo.* Treviso: Canova, 1998.

——. *Casanova. La Venezia segreta.* Venezia: Filippi editore, 2000.

Bolt, Rodney. *The Librettist of Venice.* New York: Bloomsbury, 2006.

Bonora, Ettore. *Letterati memorialisti e viaggiatori del Settecento.* Napoli: Riccardo Ricciardi, 1951.

Bourrienne, Louis Antoine Fauvelet de. *Memoirs of Napoleon*. Vol 1. Boston: Dana Estes & Co., 1885.

Brosses, Charles de. *Lettres familières sur l'Italie, publiées d'après les manuscrits avec une introduction et des notes par Yvonne Bezard*. 2 vols. Paris: Firmin-Didot et Cie, 1931.

———. *Selections from the Letters of de Brosses*. trans. Lord Ronald Sutherland Gower. London: Kegan Paul, Trench, Trubner, & Co., 1897.

Brown, Horatio. *Studies in the History of Venice*. New York: B. Franklin, 1973.

———. *Venice: an Historical Sketch of the Republic*. London: Rivington, Percival & Co., 1893.

Brunelli, Bruno. *Casanova Loved Her*. New York: Horace Liveright, 1929.

———. *Vita Di Giacomo Casanova dopo le sue memorie (1774–1798)*, Furio Luccichenti, ed. Roma: 1997.

Buck, Mitchell S. *The Life of Casanova from 1774 to 1798*. New York: N. L. Brown, 1924.

Buisine, Alain. *Casanova, L'Européen*. Paris: Tallandier, 2001.

Bullock, Steven C. *Revolutionary Brotherhood: Freemasonry and the Transformation of American Social Order, 1730–1840*. Chapel Hill: University of North Carolina Press, 1996.

Burnet, Gilbert. *Voyage de Suisse, D'Italie, et de quelques endroits d'Allemagne & de France, fait és années 1685, & 1686*. Rotterdam: Abraham Acher, 1688.

Buschini, Francesca. *Lettere a Casanova: trentatré lettere di Francesca Buschini, l'ultima amante veneziana*. Elio Bartolini, ed. Udine: Casamassima, 1986.

Caglioti, Giuseppe. *Casanova e la scienza*. Bergamo: Moretti & Vitali, 1998.

Cahusac, Louis de. *Zoroastro: traduzione dal francese ed adattamento di Giacomo Casanova. A cura di Furio Luccichenti con una nota di F. Luccichenti*. Vernier: L'Intermédiaire des Casanovistes, 2010.

Castelot, André. *Napoleon*, trans. Guy Daniels. New York: Harper & Row, 1971.

Cheke, Marcus. *The Cardinal de Bernis*. New York: W. W. Norton, 1959.

Chiara, Piero. *Il vero Casanova*. Milano: Mursia Editore, 1977.

———. *La Commediante in Fortuna*. Roma: Edizioni di Storia e Letteratura, 2012.

———. *Rosara: Or the Adventure of an Actress: A Story from Real Life, Translated from the Italian of Pietro Chiari*. Vol. 3, pp. 125–27. London: R. Baldwin and S. Bladon, 1771.

Childs, James Rives. *Casanova*. Milano: AREA, 1962.

———. *Casanova: A Biography Based on New Documents*. London: George Allen & Unwin, 1961.

———. *Casanova: A New Perspective*. New York: Paragon House, 1988.

———. *Casanoviana: An Annotated World Bibliography*. Vienna: Nebehay, 1956.

Chrisman-Campbell, Kimberly. *Fashion Victims: Dress at the Court of Louis XVI and Marie Antoinette*. New Haven: Yale University Press, 2015.

Colburn, Glen. *The English: Enabling and Disabling Fictions*. Newcastle: Cambridge Scholars Publishing, 2008.

Comisso, Giovanni. *Agenti segreti di Venezia, 1707–1797*. Milano: Bompiani, 1945.

Compigny des Bordes, A. *Casanova et la marquise d'Urfé; la plus curieuse aventure galante du XVIIIe siècle*. Paris: E. Champion, 1922.

Cowan, Alexander. *Marriage, Manners, and Mobility in Early Modern Venice*. Burlington, VT: Ashgate, 2007.

Craig, Cynthia C. "Utopia and Body: Gender and Androgyny in Casanova's Icosameron." In *Gendered Contexts New Perspectives in Italian Cultural Studies*, Edited by Laura Benedetti, Julia L. Hairston, and Silvia M. Ross. New York: Peter Lang P, 1996.

Croce, Benedetto. *Personaggi casanoviani in aneddoti e profili settecenteschi*. Palermo: Sandron, 1914.

Cronin, Vincent. *Napoleon Bonaparte: An Intimate Biography*. New York: William Morrow, 1972.

Curiel, Carlon et al. *Patrizi e avventurieri, dame e ballerine in cento lettere inedite o poco note*. Milano: Corbaccio, 1930.

Dahoui, Serge. *Le Cardinal de Bernis: ou, le royaté de charme*. Aubenas: Lienhart, 1972.

Damerini, Gino. *Amor di Venezia*. Bologna: Zanichelli, 1920.

———. *Casanova a Venezia*. Torino: ILTE, 1957.

———. *La vita avventurosa di Caterina Dolfin Tron*. Milano: Mondadpri, 1929.

———. *La vita privata e la vita sociale*. In *Storia della civiltá Veneziana*, vol. 3, part 2. Firenze: Sansoni Editore, 1979.

Da Mosto, Andrea. *I Dogi di Venezia nella Vita Pubblica e Privata*. Firenze: Giunti Editore, 1977.

D'Ancona, Alessandro. *Casanova a Venezia*. Firenze: Sansoni, 1974.

———. *Casanoviana*. Roma: Crescenzi Allendorf, 1992.

Da Ponte, Lorenzo. *Lettere di Lorenzo Da Ponte a Giacomo Casanova, 1791–1795*. Vittorio Veneto: Dario De Bastiani, 1988.

———. *Memoirs of Lorenzo Da Ponte*, trans. Elizabeth Abbott. New York: New York Review of Books, 2000.

———. *Memorie*. Milano: Garzanti, 1976.

Darnton, Robert. *The Forbidden Best-Sellers of Pre-Revolutionary France*. New York: W. W. Norton, 1995.

David, Hans T., and Arthur Mendel, *The Bach Reader: A Life of Johann Sebastian Bach in Letters and Documents*. New York: W. W. Norton, 1966.

Davis, James. *A Venetian Family and Its Fortune, 1500–1900: The Donà and the Conservation of Their Wealth.* Philadelphia: American Philosophical Society, 1975.

Dazzi, Manlio. *Testimonianze sulla societá Veneziana al tempo di Goldoni.* Venezia; Roma: Istituto per la collaborazione culturale, 1960.

De Fournoux, Amable. *Napoleon et Venise.* Paris: Éditions de Fallois, 2002.

Del Negro, Piero. *Il mito Americano nella Venezia del '700.* Padova: Liviana Editrice, 1986.

Delon, Michel. *Le principe de délicatesse: Libertinage et mélancholie au XVIIIe siècle.* Paris: Éditions Albin Michel, 2011.

Delon, Michel, ed. *Dictionnaire européen des Lumières.* Paris: Presses Universitaires de France, 1997.

Desnos, Robert. *De L'érotisme: considéré dans ses manifestations écrites et du point de vue de l'esprit moderne.* Paris: Éditions Cercle des Arts, 1953.

Diderot, Denis. *The Nun,* trans. Russell Goulbourne. Oxford: Oxford University Press, 2005.

Dipiero, Thomas, and Pat Gill, eds. *Illicit Sex: Identity Politics in Early Modern Culture.* Athens: University of Georgia Press, 1997.

Di Trocchio, Federico, and Romano Forle. *Casanova e le ostetriche.* Torino: Centro scientifico, 2000.

Dolcetti, Giovanni. *Le Bische e il Giuoco d'Azzardo a Venezia 1172–1807.* Venezia: Libreria Manuzio, 1903.

Ellis, Havelock. *Casanova: An Appreciation.* Boston: John W. Luce, 1929.

Farquhar, Michael. *A Treasury of Royal Scandals.* New York: Penguin, 2001.

Fattorello, Francesco. *Il giornalismo Italiano.* Udine: Casa Editrice Idea, 1941.

———. *Il giornalismo veneto nel settecento.* Udine: Istituto delle Edizioni Accademiche, 1933.

Ferraro, Joanne M. *Nefarious Crimes, Contested Justice: Illicit Sex and Infanticide in the Republic of Venice.* Baltimore: Johns Hopkins University Press, 2008.

Ferri, Pietro. *Biblioteca femminile Italiana.* Padova: Dalla Tipografia Crescini, 1842.

FitzLyon, April. *The libertine librettist; A Biography of Mozart's Librettist Lorenzo da Ponte.* New York: Abelard-Schuman, 1957.

Flem, Lydia. *Casanova: L'uomo che amava le donne, davvero.* Roma: Fazi, 2006.

Foscarini, Marco. *Della letteraturea della nobiltá veneziana. Un ragionamento.* Venezia: Alvisopoli, 1826.

Fraction, Matt, and Gabriel Bà. *Casanova Luxuria.* New York: Marvel Worldwide, 2010.

———. *Casanova Avaritia.* New York: Marvel Worldwide, 2011.

Fraction, Matt, and Fábio Moon. *Casanova Gula.* New York: Marvel Worldwide, 2011.

Fraser, Antonia. *Marie Antoinette: The Journey.* New York: Doubleday, 2001.

Fulin, Rinaldo. *Giacomo Casanova e gli Inquisitori di Stato.* Venezia: Tipografia G. Antonelli, 1877.

Furnberg, Louis. *Mozart e Casanova.* Palermo: Sellerio, 1993.

Galanti, Ferdinando. *Carlo Goldoni e Venezia nel secolo XVIII.* Padova: Fratelli Salmin, 1882.

Gamba, Bartolomeo. *Alcuni ritratti di donne illustri.* Venezia: Tipografia di Alvisopoli, 1826.

Georgelin, Jean. *Venise au siècle des lumières.* Parisa: École des hautes études en sciences sociales, 1978.

Geron, Gastone. *Carlo Goldoni cronista mondano; costume e moda nel Settecento a Venezia.* Venezia: Filippi, 1972.

Goldoni, Carlo. *Memoirs,* trans. John Black. Boston: Osgood, 1877.

González, Kathleen Ann. *Seductive Venice: In Casanova's Footsteps.* San Francisco, CA: Ca' Specchio, 2012.

Gozzi, Carlo. *Memorie Inutili.* Bari: Laterza, 1910.

Grosley, Pierre-Jean. *Mémoires sur les campagnes d'Italie de 1745 et 1746.* Amsterdam: Chez Marc Michel Rey, 1777.

Hacke, Daniela. *Women, Sex and Marriage in Early Modern Venice.* Burlington, VT: Ashgate, 2004.

Hall, Manly P. *The Lost Keys of Freemasonry.* New York: Jeremy P. Tarcher/Penguin, 2006.

Harmegnies, Evelyne. *Giacomo Casanova ou L'Europe d'un libertin.* Bruxelles: Presse Interuniversitaires Europennes, c. 1995.

Hesse, Herman. *La conversione di Casanova.* Milano: Guanda, 1989.

Hinckley, John, trans. *An accurate account of the fall of the republic of Venice, and of the circumstances attending that event: in which the French system of undermining and revolutionizing states is exposed: and the true character of Buonaparte faithfully pourtrayed.* London: Printed for J. Hatchard by J. Hales, 1804.

Ilges, Franz Walther. *Casanova in Köln; die Kölner Erlebnisse des Abenteurers auf Grund neuer quellen und Urkunden.* Köln: P. Gehly, 1926.

Johnson, James H. *Venice Incognito.* Los Angeles: University of California Press, 2011.

Joly, Jacques. *Le Désir et l'Utopie, études sur le théâtre d'Alfieri et de Goldoni.* Clermont-Ferrand: Université de Clermont-Ferrand, 1978.

Kelly, Ian. *Casanova: Actor, Lover, Priest, Spy.* New York: Jeremy P. Tarcher/Penguin 2008.

Kronhausen, Eberhard. *Pornography and the Law: The Psychology of Erotic Realism and Pornography.* New York: Ballantine, 1959.

Laclos, Pierre Choderlos de. *Les Liaisons dangeureuses*, trans. Douglas Parmée. Oxford: Oxford University Press, 1995.

Lalande, Joseph Jérome Le Francais de. *Voyage en Italie contenant l'histoire & les anecdotes les plus singulieres de l'Italie, & sa description: les usages, le gouvernement, le commeree, la littérature, les arts, l'histoire naturelle, & les antiquités; avec des jugemens sur les ouvrages de peinture, sculpture, sculpture & architecture, & les plans de toutes les grandes villes d'Italie.* Paris: Veuve Desaint, 1786.

Lamberg, Maximilian Joseph, Graf von. *Casanova und Graf Lamberg. Unveroffentlichte Briefe des Grafen Max Lamberg an Casanova aus dem Schlossarchiv in Dux.* Herausgegeben von Gustav Gugitz. Wien; Leipzig; Olten: Bernina-Verlag, 1935.

Leeflang, Marco, Marie-François Luna, and Antonio Trampus, eds. *Lettres de Francesca Buschini à G. Casanova*, 1996.

Le Gras, Joseph. *Casanova: Adventurer and Lover*, trans. A. Francis Steuart. London: Dodd, Mead, 1923.

Lettere di donna Giacomo Casanova, raccolte e commentate da Aldo Ravá. Milano: Fratelli Treves, 1912.

Ligne, Charles Joseph, Prince de. *Aneddoti e ritratti.* Palermo: Sellerio, 1979.

———. *Letters and Memoirs of the Prince de Ligne*, trans. Leigh Ashton. London: G. Routledge, 1927.

———. *Letters and reflections of the Austrian field-marshal Prince de Ligne: containing anecdotes hitherto unpublished of Joseph II, Catherine II, Frederick the Great, Rousseau, Voltaire, and others: with interesting remarks on the Turks.* Ed. Baroness de Stäel-Holstein; trans. D. Boileau. Philadelphia: Bradford & Innskeep, 1809.

———. *Mémoires.* Ed. du centenaire, par Eugene Gilbert. Paris: E. Champion, 1914.

———. *Mémoires et lettres du Prince de Ligne.* Nouvelle édition. Paris: Les éditions G. Crè & Cie, 1923.

———. *Oeuvres III.* Bruxelles: Éditions Complexe, 2006.

———. *The Prince de Ligne. His Memoirs, Letters, and Miscellaneous Papers.* Vol 2, trans. Katharine Prescott Wormeley. Boston: Hardy, Pratt & Company, 1899.

Limojon de Saint Didier, Alessandre-Toussaint. *The City and Republick of Venice.* London: Char. Brome, 1699.

Lindemann, Mary. *Liaisons Dangereuses: Sex, Law, and Diplomacy in the Age of Frederick the Great.* Baltimore: Johns Hopkins University Press, 2006.

Lopez, Claude-Anne. *Mon Cher Papa: Franklin and the Ladies of Paris.* New Haven: Yale University Press, 1990.

Loth, David Goldsmith. *The Erotic in Literature: A Historical Survey of Pornography as Delightful as It Is Indiscreet.* New York: J. Messner, 1961.

Luciani, Gèrard. "Carlo Gozzi: 1720–1806, l'homme et l'oeuvre." Diss., Dijon, 1974. Lille: Atelier Reproduction des thèses. Paris: Diffusion H. Champion, 1977.

Luna, Marie-Françoise. "Genèse de L'Histoire de Ma Vie de G. Casanova: étude des manuscrits." In *Sortir de la Revolution: Casanova, Stael, Constant, Chateaubriand*, pp. 75–100. Saint-Denis: Presse Universitaire de Vincennes, 1994.

Mainardi, Angelo. *Casanova l'Ultimo Mistero.* Roma: Tre Editori, 2010.

Malamani, Vittorio. *Frammenti di vita veneziana.* Roma: Bontempelli, 1893.

———. *Isabella Teotochi Albrizzi i suoi amici, il suo tempo.* Torino: Locatelli, 1882.

———. *Rosalba Carriera.* Bergamo: Istituto Italiano d'Arti Grafiche, 1910.

———. *Una giornalista veneziana del secolo XVIII.* Venezi: Visentini, 1891.

Manin, Lodovico. *Al servizio dell' Amatissima Patria.* Venezia: Marsilio Editori, 1997.

———. *Io. l'Ultimo Doge di Venezia.* Venezia: Canal & Stamperia Editrice, 1997.

Mansel, Philip. *The Prince of Europe: The Life of Charles-Joseph De Ligne, 1735–1814.* London: Weidenfeld & Nicolson, 2003.

Marceau, Félicien. *Casanova, ou l'anti-Don Juan.* Paris: Gallimard, 1985.

Marcello, Benedetto. *Il teatro alla moda.* Roma: Castelvecchi, 1993.

Marcuse, Ludwig. *Obscene: The History of an Indignation.* London: MacGibbon & Kee, 1965.

Markham, Felix. *Napoleon.* New York: New American Library, 1964.

Marr, Bernhard. *Corrispondenza tra bernhard Marr e Aldo Ravá (1910–1922).* Furio Luccichenti, ed. Roma: Furio Luccichenti, 2010.

Marsan, Jacques, Furio Luccichenti, Helmuth Wazlawick, and Luigi Bellavita. *Sui passi di Casanova a Venezia.* Venezia: Idealibri, 1993.

Masters, John. *Casanova.* New York: Bernard Geis, 1969.

Maynial, Edouard. *Casanova et son temps*, 2nd. ed. Paris: Mercure de France, 1910.

Mazzotti, Stefano. *Mémoires de Casanova.* Belgique: Éditions Delcourt, 2013.

McGuignan, Dorothy. *The Hapsburgs.* London: W. H. Allen, 1966.

Memoirs and Letters of Cardinal de Bernis, trans. Katharine Prescott Wormeley. 2 vols. Boston: Hardy, Pratt & Company, 1902.

Mentzel, Peter. *A Traveller's History of Venice.* Northampton, MA: Interlink, 2007.

Molteni, Giuseppe. *Tra il minuetto e la ghigliottina.* Milano: Baldini & Castoldi, 1945.

Montgomery, James Stuart. *The Incredible Casanova: The Magnificent Follies of a Peerless Adventurer, Amorist and Charlatan.* Garden City, NY: Doubleday, 1950.

Meucci, Carlo. *Casanova finanziere.* Milano: Mondadori, 1932.

Mioni, Maria. *Una letterata veneziana del secolo XVIII.* Venezia: Pellizzato, 1908.

Misson, Maximilien. *Nouveau voyage d'Italie.* La Haye: Henri Van Bulderen, 1702.

Mitford, Nancy. *Madame de Pompadour.* New York: New York Review of Books, 2001.

Molmenti, Pompeo. *Carteggi casanoviani, vol. I. Lettere di G. Casanova e di altri a lui.* Palermo: Sandron, 1916.

———. *Carteggi casanoviani, vol. II. Lettere del patrizio Zaguri a G. Casano.* Palermo: Sandron, 1918.

———. *Epistolari veneziani del secolo XVIII.* Palermo: Sandron, 1914.

———. *Venice, Its Individual Growth from the Earliest Beginnings to the Fall of the Republic,* trans. Horatio F. Brown. Chicago: A. C. McClurg, 1906–08.

"Mon cher Casanova—": lettres du comte Maximilien Lamberg et de Pietro Zaguri, praticien de Venise, à Giacomo Casanova. Paris: Homore Champion éditeur, 2008.

Monnier, Philippe. *Venice in the Eighteenth Century.* London: Chatto & Windus, 1910.

Montecuccoli degli Erri, Federico. *Cammei Casanoviani: personaggi ed eventi legati a Giacomo Casanova visti e narrati in base a documenti inediti.* Genève: L'intermédiaire des casanovistes, 2006.

Montesquieu, Charles de Secondat, Baron de. *Oeuvres complètes de Montesquieu: avec les variantes des premières éditions, un choix des meilleurs commentaires et des notes nouvelles / par Édouard Laboulaye.* Paris: Garnier frères, 1875–79.

Musatti, Eugenio. *La donna in Venezia.* Padova: A Draghi, 1891.

Musatti, Cesare, Alba Errera, and Angelo Padoa. *Isabella Teotochi Albrizzi e la prima vaccinazione in Venezia.* Venezia: Tipografia dell'Ancora, 1886.

Newman, Karen. *Cultural Capitals: Early Modern London and Paris.*

Nicolle, David. *Medieval Warfare Source Book.* London: Arms & Armour, 1995–1996.

Nissati, G. *Aneddoti storici veneziani.* Venezia: Tip. società m. s. compositori tipografi, S. Marco, 1897.

Norwich, John Julius. *A History of Venice.* New York: Alfred A. Knopf, 1982.

———, ed. *A Traveller's Companion to Venice.* New York: Interlink, 2002.

Orsenigo, Vittorio ed. *A Giacomo Casanova. Lettere d'amore di Manon Balletti-Elisa von der Recke.* Milano: Archinto, 1997.

Ortolani, Giuseppe. *Voci e visioni del Settecento veneziano.* Bologna: Nicola Zanichelli, 1926.

Pace, Antonio ed. "Benjamin Franklin and Italy." *Memoirs of the American Philosophical Society,* vol. 47. Philadelphia: American Philosophical Society, 1958.

Palmer, Robert Roswell. *The Age of the Democratic Revolution: A Political History of Europe and America, 1760–1800*. Princeton: Princeton University Press, 1959–1964.

———. "The French Idea of American Independence on the Eve of the French Revolution." Diss., Ithaca: Cornell University, 1934.

Parks, Tim. *A Season with Verona*. New York: Arcade, 2002.

Piranesi, Giovanni Battista. *Carceri d'invenzione*. Bergamo: Galleria Ceribelli: Lubrina Editore, 2007.

Pizzamiglio, Gilberto, ed. *Giacomo Casanova tra Venezia e l'Europa*. Firenze: Leo S. Olschki, 2001.

Plant, Margaret. *Venice: Fragile City, 1797–1997*. New Haven: Yale University Press, 2002.

Poncins, Léon de. *Freemasonry and the Vatican: A Struggle for Recognition*, trans. Timothy Tindal-Robertson. London: Britons Publishing, 1968.

Pollio, Joseph. *Casanova de Seingalt et la révolution française*. Paris: Impreimerie de la Cour D'Appel, 1914.

Prévost, Marie-Laure, and Chantal Thomas. *Casanova: la passion de la liberté*. Paris, Seuil: Bibliothèque nationale de France, 2011.

Ravà, Aldo, ed. *Lettere di donne a G. Casanova*. Milano: Fratelli Treves, 1912.

Ravel, Emilio. *L'uomo che inventò se stesso*. Milano: La Lepre Edizioni. 2010.

Ravoux-Rallo, Elisabeth. *La Femme au temps de Casanova*. Paris: Stock, 1984.

Redford, Bruce. *Venice and the Grand Tour*. New Haven: Yale University Press, 1996.

Renier-Michiel, Giustina. "Giovedì Grasso." In *Origine delle Feste Veneziane*, Vol. 2, p. 44. Milano: Gli Editori degli Annali Universali della Scienza e dell'Industria, 1829.

Rival, Ned. *Casanova: La vie a Plaisir*. Paris: Plon, 1977.

Robilant, Andrea Di. *Lucia*. New York: Alfred A. Knopf, 2008.

———. *A Venetian Affair*. New York: Alfred A. Knopf, 2003.

Roggendorff, Cécile von, Gräfin. *La dernière amie de Jacques Casanova: Lettres de Cécile Roggendorff, 1797–1798*. Paris: J. Fort, Librairie de la société casanovienne, 1926.

Romanin, Samuele. *Storia Documentata di Venezia*, Vols. 1, 3. Venezia: Pietro Naratovich tipografo editore, 1853.

Rousseau, Jean-Jacques. *Confessions*. In *Oeuvres Completes*, Vol. 1. Paris: Gallimard, 1959.

Rovere, Maxime. *Casanova*. Paris: Gallimard, 2011.

Samaran, Charles. *Jacques Casanova, Vénitien, une vie d'aventurier au XVIII siècle*. Paris: Calmann-Lévy, 1914.

Sbriziolo, Lia. *Le confraternite veneziane di devozione: saggio bibliografico e premesse storiografiche.* In *Quaderni della rivista di storia della chiesa in Italia, 1.* Roma: Herder, 1968.

Schnitzler, Arthur. *Casanova's Return to Venice,* trans. Ilsa Barea. London: Pushkin Press, 2013.

Selfridge-Field, Eleanor. *Song and Season: Science, Culture, and Theatrical Time in Early Modern Venice.* Stanford: Stanford University Press, 2007.

Selvatico, Riccardo. *Cento note per Casanova a Venezia 1753–1756.* Vicenza: Neri Pozza, 1997.

Sharp, Samuel. *Letters from Italy, describing the customs and manners of that country, in the year 1765 and 1766 to which is annexed an Admonition to Gentlemen who pass the Alps, in their tour through Italy.* London: Printed by R. Cave; and sold by W. Nicol. T. Becket and P. A. de Hondt, and T. Cadell, 1767.

Sharratt, Michael. *Galileo: Decisive Innovator.* Cambridge: Cambridge University Press, 1994.

Sollers, Philippe. *Casanova l'admirable.* Paris: Plon, 1998.

———. *Dictionnaire amoureux de Venise.* Paris: Plon, 2004.

Solomon, Maynard. *Mozart: A Life.* New York: HarperCollins, 1995.

Starobinski, Jean. "Le Rococo." In *La Mode en France 1715–1815, de Louis XV à Napoléon Ier.* Paris: La Bibliothèque des Arts, 1990.

Summers, Judith. *Casanova's Women.* London: Bloomsbury, 2006.

Tassini, Giuseppe. *Cenni storici e leggi circa il libertinaggio in Venezia dal secolo decimoquarto alla caduta della repubblica.* Venezia: Filippi Editore, 1968.

Tentori, Cristoforo. *Il matrimonio riflezioni filosofiche.* Venezia: s.n. 1795.

Thomas, Chantal. *Casanova: un voyage libertin.* Paris: Éditions Denoël, 1985

Thompson, J. M, trans. and ed. *Letters of Napoleon.* Oxford: Basil Blackwell, 1934.

Thomson, Katherine. *The Masonic Thread in Mozart.* London: Lawrence & Wishart, 1977.

Tichý, Vítèzslav. *Casanova v Čechách.* Duchcov: Kapucín, 1995.

Torcellan, Gianfranco. *Una figura della Venezia settecentesca: Andrea Memmo: Ricerche sulla crisi dell'aristocrazia veneziana.* Venezia; Roma: Istituto per la collaborzione culturale, 1963.

Vailland, Roger. *Éloge du cardinal de Bernis.* Paris: Fasquelle, 1956.

Vassalli, Sebastiano. *Dux: Casanova in Boemia.* Torino: Einaudi, 2002.

Vaussard, Maurice. *La vie quotidienne en Italie au XVIIIe siécle.* Paris: Hachette, 1959.

Vincent, Jean-Didier. *Casanova il contagio del piacere.* Venezia: Canal & Stamperia Editrice, 1998.

Vittoria, Eugenio. *Giacomo Casanova e gli inquisitori di stato.* Venezia: EVI, 1973.

Voyages d'Italie et de Hollande par l'Abbé Cover. Paris: Chez la Veuve Duchesne, Libraire, rue Saint Jacques, au Temple du Goût, 1775.

Weisberger, Richard William. "Speculative Freemasonry and the Enlightenment: A Study of the Craft in London, Paris, Prague, and Vienna." In *East European Monographs,* no. 367. Boulder: East European Monographs, New York: Distributed by Columbia University Press, 1993.

Young, Arthur. *Travels During the Years 1787, 1788 and 1789.* 2 vols. Dublin: Printed for R. Cross [etc.], 1793.

———. *Voyages en Italie et en Espagne pendant les années 1787 et 1789.* Paris: Guillaumin et C.ie, Libraires, 1860.

Zannini, Andrea. "Economic and Social Aspects of the Crisis of Venetian Diplomacy in the Seventeenth and Eighteenth Centuries." In *Politics and Diplomacy in Early Modern Italy.* New York: Cambridge University Press, 2000.

Zweig, Stefan. *Casanova: A Study in Self-Portraiture,* trans. Eden and Cedar Paul. London: Pushkin Press, 1998.

Works by Casanova

Casanova, Giacomo. *Confutazione della Storia del Governo Veneto d'Amelot de la Houssaie.* Amsterdam: 1769.

———. *Considerazioni Politico-filosofiche Sull'Antica Aristocrazia Romana esempio a tutte le nazioni che vogliono mantenersi libere: ad uso del popolo Inglese di Politropo Pantaxeno Selvaggio.* In *Opuscoli Miscellanei.* Modesto Fenzo. Venice: April 1780.

———. *Correspondance avec J. F. Opiz,* 2 vols. Leipzig: Kurt Wolff Verlag, 1913.

———. *Dialoghi sul suicidio.* Roma: Aracne, 2005.

———. *The Duel,* trans. James Marcus. Brooklyn, NY: Melville House, 2011.

———. *Epistolario, 1759–1798.* Piero Chiara, ed. Longanesi, 1969.

———. *Essai de critique sur les moeurs, sur les sciences, et sur les arts / texte inédit de Jacques-Jérôme Casanova.* Transcrit et présenté par Gérard Lahouati; avec la collaboration d'Helmut Watzlawick. Pau: Publications de l'Université de Pau, 2001.

———. *Examen des Etudes de la nature et de Paul et Virginie Bernardin de Saint-Pierre: un 'inédit', écrit en 1788–1789, á Dux / par Jacques Casanova de Seingalt; présenté par Marco Leeflang et Tom Vitelli.* Utrecht: Leeflang et Vitelli, 1985.

Casanova, Giacomo (attr). *Exposition raisonnée du différent, qui subsiste entre les deux republiques de Venise et D'Hollande.* Venise: 1785.

Casanova, Giacomo. *Histoire de ma fuite des prisons de la République de Venise qu'on appelle les Plombs.* Paris: Éditions Bossard, 1922.

————. *Histoire de ma fuite des prisons de la République de Venise qu'on appelle les Plombs*. Paris: Éditions Allia, 2010.

Casanova, [Giacomo]. *Histoire de ma vie jusqu'a l'an 1797*. Tome 1–3. Paris: Bibliothehèque de la Pléiade. Gallimard, 2013.

————. *Histoire de ma vie: suivie de textes inédits*. Jacques Casanova de Seingalt; édition présentée et établie par Francis Lacassin. Paris: R. Laffont, circa 1993. 3 v.

Casanova, Giacomo. *History of My Life*, trans. Willard R. Trask. 12 vols. Baltimore: Johns Hopkins University Press, 1966–1971.

————. *History of My Life*, trans. Willard Trask. Abridged. New York: Everyman's Library, 2006.

————. Casanova's "*Icosameron*," or, The story of Edward and Elizabeth: who spent eighty-one years in the land of the Megamicres, original inhabitants of Protocosmos in the interior of our globe, translated and abridged from the original French by Rachel Zurek: New York, N.Y.: Jenna Press: distributed by Talman Co., circa 1986.

————. *Il duello*. Elio Bartolini, ed. Milano: Adelphi, 1979.

————. *Istoria delle turbolenze della Polonia*. Giacinto Spagnoletti, ed. Napoli: Guida, 1974.

————. *Lana Caprina: Lettre d'un lycanthrope*. Paris: Librarie de la Sociéteé Casanovienne. 1926.

————. *Lettere della nobil donna Silvia Belegno alla nobil donzella Laura Gussoni*. Torino: Fògola, 1975.

————. *Lettres écrites au sieur Faulkircher*. Italian & French Casanova, Giacomo, 1725–1798. *Lettere a un maggiordomo*, trans. Carlo Martini. Pordenone: Studio Tesi, 1985.

————. *The Memoirs of Jacques Casanova de Seingalt*, trans. Arthur Machen. New York: A. & C. Boni, 1932.

————. *The Story of My Escape*, trans. Andrew K. Lawston. No publisher, 2014

Casanova, Jacques. *Nè amori, nè donne ovvero La stalla ripulita*. Venice: Modesto Fenzo, 1782.

————. *Opuscoli miscellanei, gennajo 1779*. Venezia: Presso Modesto Fenzo, 1780.

————. *Opuscoli miscellanei*. August 1780. Venezia: Presso Modesto Fenzo, 1780.

Casanova, Giacomo. *Scrutinio del libro Éloges de M. de Voltaire par differens auteurs*. Venezia: Presso Modesto Fenzo, 1779.

————. *Soliloque d'un penseur. Correspondance inédite 1773–1783*. Paris: J. Fort, 1926.

————. *Supplimento alla Esposizione ragionata della controversia, che sussiste tra la repubblica di Venezia, e quella d'Olanda*. [Venezia: Storti], 1785.

————. *Casanova, uno storico alla ventura: istoria delle turbolenze della Polonia*. G. Bozzolato. Padova: Marsilio Editori, 1974.

ACKNOWLEDGMENTS

My longtime literary agent, Suzanne Gluck of William Morris Endeavor, proved indispensable in making this book a reality from the moment I mentioned the idea to her. My sincere thanks also to her assistants, Clio Seraphim and Eve Attermann in New York, for their persistence, patience, and resourcefulness, and also to Tracy Fisher. In Los Angeles, I must acknowledge the encouragement of Alicia Gordon and Erin Conroy, and, in London, to Simon Trewin and Raffaella De Angelis, foreign rights agent.

At Simon & Schuster, I've had the good fortune to work with the astute Bob Bender, who contributed so much to keeping this complex book on track. From start to finish, it's been a pleasure to work with Bob and his colleague, Johanna Li. They were always there when the book needed their involvement; what more can one say? Lisa Healy and the copyediting department scrutinized this manuscript with great sensitivity and care. Alison Forner designed a compelling jacket. And I am grateful for the backing of Jonathan Karp, the president and publisher.

Libraries, museums, and archives where I conducted research on Casanova and related subjects were most generous with access, and their staffs were always at the ready to enlighten and further the cause of Casanova. Perhaps this situation was foreordained because Casanova always loved libraries and spent the last and most productive years of his life as a librarian himself as he wrote his famous memoirs in French. In 2010, the Bibliothèque National de France obtained nearly four thousand pages of Casanova's manuscripts, including the complete text of his celebrated *Histoire de ma vie*. As soon as I heard about this acquisition, I was on a plane to Paris and the BnF to examine these documents, which preserve a vanished time and way of life in almost Proustian detail. My sincere thanks to Bruno Racine, Président de la BnF and to Marie-Laure Prévost, *conservateur en chef au département des manuscrits*, for making my research there so rewarding. Also in Paris I wish to thank Véronique Timset for her generous help with research.

In and around New York, many individuals cheerfully assisted over the years with this book. They include Sara Bergreen, my daughter; Clémence Bouloque; Claudine Bouloque; my excellent friend Daniel Dolgin; Lewis Drummond for computer support; the wonderfully enterprising Paul Friedman at the New York Public Library; Hugh Fremantle, for his well-chosen words of advice; Loraine

Gardner and Beyond the Horizon Travel, who sent me wherever I needed to go and brought me back in one piece; my knowledgeable and imaginative photo researcher Toby Greenberg; Gail Jacobs; Sarah Herrington; Julian Perricone; Venetian expert and architect Caterina Roiatti; Susan Shapiro; Abigail Smith for Internet expertise; Mike Smith for additional computer support; Hillel Swiller, MD, of the Mount Sinai School of Medicine, whose seminar on Casasnova offered many provocative insights; Warren Wechsler; and Dr. Ruth Westheimer.

Libraries in New York where I conducted research include Butler Library at Columbia University and the New York Society Library, where I am privileged to serve as a trustee.

Other libraries where I conducted research on Casanova and related subjects include Widener Library and Houghton Library at Harvard University, as well as the McGraw-Page library at Randolph-Macon College, where Mary Virginia Currie assisted, and Trinity College Library in Hartford, where Richard Ring advised. Stephen Stigler, Distinguished Professor of Statistics at the University of Chicago and President of the International Statistical Institute, provided a helpful introduction to Casanova's use of statistics and probability in devising the French Loterie.

I must mention Anna Basoli, my brilliant researcher and translator, who pursued Casanova in New York and especially in Venice, where she tracked down original letters of Casanova at the Querini Stampalia Foundation, the Ca' Rezzonico, and the Archivi Di Stato Di Venezia. There the chief archivist, Dottoressa Michela dal Borgo, expedited access to manuscripts and original documents. Anna Bellavitis of the Université de Rouen in France, provided precious contacts and advice concerning research at the Archivi Di Stato Di Venezia. On the trail of Casanova in Venice, I also conducted research on the "Secret itineraries of the Ducal Palace" and at I Piombi, where Casanova was imprisoned. To stand in the dark, claustrophobic cell where he was confined was among the more memorable aspects of my research for this book. Also providing much-appreciated help in Venice were Dottoressa Paola Benussi and Dottoressa Monica Del Rio. On the island of Murano, Don Rino, the ninety-two-year-old monsignor in charge of Santa Maria degli Angeli, threw open the church doors beyond visiting hours for purposes of researching Casanova. I also acknowledge Anna Bigai for her expertise concerning Venetian landmarks.

At the Duchcov Chateau in northern Bohemia, Czech Republic, I reviewed Casanova's papers and memorabilia. It was here that Casanova worked as a librarian for the Waldstein family and wrote his memoirs and where the chair in which he died is preserved. My deepest thanks also to the inspiring Jacqueline Philomeno, who accompanied me on my Casanova travels to Prague, Venice, and Padua and helped with the research as well.

At the UCLA Center for 17th & 18th Century Studies in Los Angeles, California, I was fortunate to attend "Casanova: Libertine Legend," in early 2016 and to encounter legions of far-flung *Casanovistas* whose work I knew mainly from printed sources. They included Raphaëlle Brin, Université Paris–Sorbonne; Clorinda Donato, California State University, Long Beach; Jean-Christophe Igalens, Université Paris–Sorbonne; Mladen Kozul, University of Montana; Robert Kruckeberg, Troy University; Pierre Saint-Amand, Brown University; Malina Stefanovska, University of California, Los Angeles; Chantal Thomas, Centre national de la recherche scientifique; Christopher B. White; and Kathleen Gonzalez.

A final word: my mother, Adele Gabel Bergreen, enjoyed hearing about this book during the years I was working on it and kept waiting for the finished product—but, it was not completed in time for her to read it. She was a constant reader until the end and would have enjoyed the colorful drama of Casanova's life.

ILLUSTRATION CREDITS

354 Private Collection / Bridgeman Images

387 Photo © Tallandier / Bridgeman Images

415 Digital image courtesy of the Getty's Open Content Program

448 Private Collection / Bridgeman Images

451 © RMN-Grand Palais / Art Resource, NY

453 Erich Lessing / Art Resource, NY

458 Gianni Dagli Orti / The Art Archive at Art Resource, NY

460 © BnF, Dist. RMN-Grand Palais / Art Resource, NY

462 Photo © PVDE / Bridgeman Images

464 Bibliothèque Nationale de France

468 Bibliothèque Nationale de France

INDEX

Page numbers in *italics* refer to illustrations.